NO MORE SILENCE

NO MORE SILENCE

An Oral History
of the Assassination
of President Kennedy

LARRY A. SNEED

University of North Texas Press
Denton, Texas

Permissions:
University of North Texas Press
P.O. Box 311336
Denton, TX 76203-1336

The paper used in this book meets the minimum requirements of the
American National Standard for Permanence of Paper for Printed Library Materials,
z39.48.1984. Binding materials have been chosen for durability.

ISBN 1-57441-148-9

To Travis, Shane, and Barbara

and

the people of Dallas

CONTENTS

THE INVESTIGATION

THE OSWALD TRANSFER AND AFTERMATH

ACKNOWLEDGEMENTS

When I first became involved in researching the assassination of President Kennedy, I was told by a fellow researcher: "Don't expect encouragement in your research from much of anybody. Most are either so absorbed in their own research, or will be hypercritical of yours." In many respects, what he said proved to be true. One must be prepared to face ridicule, sarcasm, and sometimes worse, especially when dealing with a topic which frequently attracts UFO buffs among others.

On the other hand, though, during my fifteen year involvement with the assassination, a number of fellow researchers have been of great assistance in sharing information and providing materials for my collection on the subject. Among those whom I would like to thank include: Steve Barber, Warren Graham, Max Holland, Harry Irwin, Dave Perry, Gary Shaw, Richard Trask, Paul Weller, and Bob Porter and Gary Mack of the Sixth Floor Museum in Dallas.

I would especially like to thank Mark Oakes for the friendship developed over the past several years. Our many phone calls, meetings in Dallas, and his access to witnesses and documents has helped me keep abreast of the latest developments in Dallas. I have appreciated his continued encouragement in this project.

Indispensable to any researcher on the subject have been Andy and Linda Winiarczyk of the Last Hurrah Bookshop in Williamsport, Pennsylvania, and the President's Box Book Shop in Washington, D.C. Their biannual catalogs have been a treasure trove of material on the various assassinations and covert activities of the intelligence agencies.

Various periodicals and newsletters have also been of great assistance. Jerry Rose's *The Third and Fourth Decade*, R.B. Cutler's *The Grassy Knoll Gazette*, *Dateline Dallas* and its successor *The Assassination Chronicles*, CTKA's *Probe*, and Walt Brown's *Deep Politics Quarterly*, just to name a few, have been useful tools in keeping up with current research. *Dallas: 1963* from Great Britain, and *Probable Cause* from Australia have also provided insights from across the oceans.

Thanks, too, to a fellow colleague in education, Vance Barnwell, for convincing me to borrow his video camera on my first trip to Dallas, which ultimately led to the accumulation of over sixty hours of video-taped interviews, and to Roy Adcox of Wolf Camera in Suwanee, Georgia, for his assistance in preparing slides and photographs for the book which were taken from the 1972 Dallas Police Annual, lent by former Dallas policeman D.V. Harkness.

My appreciation, too, to the faculty and students of Parkview High School in Lilburn, Georgia, especially Drs. Robert Clark and John Hall, for their encouragement and promotion of *No More Silence*. And to friends Gary Petmecky, Rob Loveridge, and Norman Thomas for computer assistance, as well as to my editor and publisher, Darwin Payne.

Most of all, though, to the people of Dallas, and especially to all those who welcomed me into their homes, shared their memories, and ultimately became friends. Without their help, this could not have been written. Among those who deserve special mention for inviting me to stay in their homes and making me feel like part of their families are: James and Taimi Leavelle, Ed and Sue Smith, and John and Denise Beisiegel. Being on a tight budget each summer, their kindness has been much appreciated. Also to those who have helped in arranging interviews and taking me out to lunches, thanks to James Leavelle, Jim Ewell and the cooperation of Sheriff Bowles and the Dallas County Sheriff's Department, J.W. Courson, James and Clara Altgens, D.V. and Ellie Harkness, L.C. and Myrt Graves, Paul and Moselle Bentley, Jack and Jean Faulkner, Stavis and Nita Ellis, Austin Cook of Austin's Barbeque in Oak Cliff, W.R. Westbrook, Bill Alexander, and to "Butch" and Maxine Burroughs for allowing me access to the Texas Theater.

To those who have either loaned or given me photographs for use in this book, my heartfelt gratitude, and especially to J.W. Courson, Cora Dean Courson, Stavis and Nita Ellis, and Harry D. Holmes for personal memorabilia which I will always treasure.

Throughout the ten-year sojourn to and from Dallas, the foremost concern of most of those interviewed was that their stories be reported accurately and unaltered. It is with a sense of appreciation, obligation, and responsibility that I have attempted to achieve those wishes.

LARRY A. SNEED

INTRODUCTION

Like most everyone who is old enough to remember the tragic events of November 22, 1963, I recall in vivid detail what I was doing when I heard the startling news from Dallas about the shooting at the Kennedy motorcade. I was at the local Sears store during my lunch hour from high school looking at some of the newly displayed Christmas items when I overheard one of the employees mention that the President was dead. Being naive at the time, I thought that she was referring to the president of Sears. Not concerned, I walked back in the cold dampness toward school a few blocks away when I again overheard a pedestrian mention the same thing. Curious, but unsuspecting, I said to myself, "Why are these people so concerned about the death of the president of Sears? Who knows who he is, anyway?" It was only when I reached school and saw the stunned reaction of others that I learned of the magnitude of the tragedy.

Like countless millions of others throughout the world, I spent the next three days in front of the television witnessing the details of that weekend, including the shocking murder of Lee Harvey Oswald before 61 million Americans. Having read several books on the Lincoln assassination at the time, I knew that this latest tragedy would be as momentous, if not more so, because of the added element of the massive media coverage. As a result, I didn't want to miss anything.

But in the ensuing years, my life was absorbed in graduating from high school, attending college, finding a job, getting married, and later building a home, so the assassination remained only a passing interest to me until 1982. I had read the Warren Report and several other books about the assassination at that time, then was convinced by a friend to read the best seller *Best Evidence* by David Lifton in the fall of that year. From that point, I became absorbed with the subject, purchased all the available books I could find and entered into a semi-monastic period of research. Since I had completed by that time two graduate degrees and had always wanted to do extensive research on what I thought would be a manageable topic, the assassination seemed ideal: three murders in one city over a two-day period. How complicated could this be? After all, this wasn't like researching the Second World War or some other massive endeavor which seemed beyond my scope of complete understanding. Little did I realize the complexities involved as I entered the labyrinth of the assassination.

It didn't take long to realize that the subject was much more complicated than anticipated. Did a conspiracy exist in the assassination of President Kennedy or did Oswald act alone, as was claimed by the Warren Commission in 1964? Numerous theories were in abundance since at that time the House Select Committee on Assassinations had completed its hearings and published its multi-volume findings along with its Report in 1979. This newly released information naturally led to a flurry of books accompanied by further complexities on the subject. Undaunted, I was convinced that a thorough reading of the material, combined with an open mind, would lead me to a resolution as to whether a conspiracy existed or not, and if so, who was involved and why. However, despite some excellent writing by a number of authors who postulated a plethora of scenarios in Dallas in November 1963, it was frustrating because obviously all of them could not be correct. If a conspiracy existed, what group was the culprit: the CIA, the FBI, organized crime, the military, pro-Castro Cubans, anti-Castro Cubans, White segregationists, the Dallas police, or was it a combination of groups?

By the summer of 1987, I had become thoroughly perplexed that the answer had not become obvious to me beyond a reasonable doubt. I had noticed that the majority of research had been based either on previous research or on theories formulated by the authors and that a minority of the books utilized personal interviews of those who were closely intertwined with the events of that weekend. Furthermore, in the books that did contain references to interviews, were the participants quoted accurately or were their words contorted to fit some author's preconceived theory?

It was at that point, that I decided to try to locate some of those participants and learn for myself what they might have to say. Fortunately this was the year before the 25th anniversary of the assassination and several years before Oliver Stone's "JFK" when interest in the assassination seemed to reach levels approaching a crescendo.

The most obvious question was how to locate eyewitnesses, policemen, deputy sheriffs and other government officials in Dallas. I doubted that many, if any, would be located in the phone book but it seemed a logical point of origin. After finding a Dallas phone book in the local library, I was amazed that several of the more prominent names were listed. As a result, I then sent initial letters of introduction accompanied by letters of recommendation from my principal to those located and was pleasantly surprised by the response, especially since I was led to believe in my readings that one could expect a cold reception in Dallas and that people did not want to talk about the assassination, either because they were afraid or had something to hide. As I was to learn over the next eight years, however, nothing could have been further from the truth, at least from those that I encountered.

During the course of my research, there seemed to be an absence of biographical information regarding some of the key players in the scenario of the assassination, and especially among the lesser known figures. Their names might be mentioned in a footnote but little else. I was intrigued by who these "players of the game" were and sought to learn more about their backgrounds, many of whom, especially among the law enforcement personnel, were portrayed in numerous books and manuscripts as being either sinister or shadowy figures. I wanted to judge for myself the credibility of those primary sources without having to rely on the subjective opinions of others which permeated much of the material on the assassination.

After planning my first trip to Dallas, a fellow teacher encouraged me to borrow his video camera to tape the interviews. Realizing the importance of preparation, I also brought an audio cassette recorder as a backup sound system to the camera, a 35mm camera for still shots, and reference books to have signed by those I encountered. For the interviews themselves, a question-answer format was prepared which was designed to elicit responses regarding their backgrounds prior to the assassination, the chronology of events of their activities during the weekend of November 22-24, 1963, their views regarding conspiracy theories, and what had transpired in their lives since the assassination. To earn the trust and confidence of those interviewed, the interviews were to be conducted in an informal manner and in a relaxed setting.

With all preparations complete, I arrived in Dallas in June 1987 with reservations finalized at one of the motel chains east of the city. That summer I had ten or twelve interviews confirmed through the introductory letters. As I was to learn, though, one of the difficult chores was to arrange convenient times for the interviews and to become thoroughly familiar with the map of Dallas and the surrounding area. It reminded me of a military tactical situation.

After a number of introductory phone calls and schedulings, my first interview was with former deputy sheriff Luke Mooney, the man credited with locating the shell casings on the sixth floor of the Texas School Book Depository shortly after the assassination. Being naturally apprehensive as to my reception, I couldn't have been received more cordially. Mooney was the vice-president of Superior Products, a cosmetic company in the northern suburb of Farmer's Branch. I learned much from that initial interview. As I quickly ascertained, my questioning was more argumentative than I intended though Mooney was very accommodating. After the question-answer session, I was given a tour of the factory, treated to lunch, and led through Dealey Plaza retracing the steps that he had taken just after the shooting. It was certainly more than I could have ever anticipated. The hospitality during that initial encounter prepared me for the cooperation and friendliness that I was to receive on most occasions throughout the remainder of that trip as well as the subsequent seven trips.

The first two days I scheduled three interviews per day. However, I quickly learned that it would be impossible to complete that many per day due to the exhaustion factor. Slowing down to one or two a day thus allowed me to more leisurely complete my task and enjoy the process.

In addition I wanted to visit all the sites pertinent to the assassination, take pictures, and absorb the atmosphere. I found that there was no substitute for being in the presence of the locales of the assassination: the streets of Dallas and spending time at the Texas School Book Depository, Dealey Plaza, the Tippit death scene, the Texas Theater, Oswald's boarding house, the police basement where Oswald was shot by Jack Ruby, Ruby's apartment, Parkland Hospital and many others. At the risk of sounding trite, spending time alone in those settings, combined with getting to know those who were personally involved in the events, gives one a special feel for what really happened that tragic weekend over thirty years ago.

When I first began this project, I had no ax to grind or theory to promote. I was willing to talk with anyone who was receptive toward being interviewed. Not only did I want to personally record their stories, but it was hoped that certain "problem areas" of the assassination highlighted by conspiracy writers could be clarified or resolved. Many of these issues were presented to those interviewed, especially to the Dallas policemen, of whom much criticism has been leveled over the years.

Not surprisingly I found that those least interested in the assassination were those same Dallas policemen. Being the butt of sarcasm and ridicule, some were reluctant to talk, reasoning that whatever they might say would be twisted or altered to fit some writer's theory of conspiracy. In short, they were tired of having their words turned around and comments being taken out of context. Fortunately, that first year the interviews I had with former Dallas policemen James Leavelle, Paul Bentley, L.C. Graves, and Elmo Cunningham went extremely well and paved the way for future interviews with other policemen, several of whom had not been interviewed either by the Warren Commission or other researchers. They had stories to tell but for various reasons had either not been contacted or were unwilling to be interviewed prior to 1987.

I was particularly interested in talking with the Dallas policemen since they had generally either been ignored by assassination writers or because they were extremely selective with whom they talked. As I was to learn, this reluctance to defend themselves has made many of them easy targets for accusations, innuendoes, and in some cases outright libel. When they were convinced that I was sincere and had no hidden agenda were they willing to speak with me. Surprisingly, very few expressed serious concern about speaking on camera, though a few were reluctant to have their words published, apparently not wanting to become involved in all the controversy that it might entail with most of the assassination writers who, in their opinions, are concerned with little other than self-aggrandizement and the profit motive. They did not want their names associated with "mystery writers."

I originally did not intent to write a book. Instead, I merely was interested in making a series of video taped interviews which I could use in my classroom. When I reviewed the tapes after the first trip, I was sufficiently impressed with the quality of the interviews to justify another trip. And thus the process of preparation repeated itself the following summer.

Interestingly, though, I did not realize the full measure of quality of the tapes until I began to transcribe them and to see the interview in printed form. It then became apparent that what I had were insights into the events that I had not seen previously published and were of such significance that I entertained the idea of writing a book myself. However, I did not want it to be another work based on personal opinions or theories as were so many of the previously published books. Instead, I decided to let the subject of the interview speak for himself or herself and allow the reader to evaluate for themselves the merit of each story and its significance to the assassination. In short, it would be an oral history of the John F. Kennedy assassination. Amazingly, no one else had attempted or at least completed such a project.

I decided that a chapter would be devoted to each of those interviewed. The advantage of this decision was that the entire interview would be included thus eliminating the taking out of context and manipulation of language which has been attributed to various theorists and assassination buffs bent on "proving" their theories. This format would also allow the reader to better understand the background of the person prior to the assassination as well as to what happened to them after the event. From that point, my objective was clear: to interview as many people involved in as many of the events that weekend as possible and from as many perspectives as was feasible. This would include the mechanics of the motorcade, the assassination itself, the Tippit shooting, Oswald's arrest at the Texas Theater, the investigation, the murder of Oswald, and other related events. With no hidden agenda or theory to prove, this allowed me to pursue anyone who was willing to be interviewed without concern as to whether they would fit into any preconceived notions.

The obvious problem with any oral history written years after the event is the reliability of memory, and in some cases contamination of memory over the years from having been exposed to books, magazines, or television programs relating to the subject. I learned that it was not realistic to expect the subjects to be exact on times from an event over thirty years past, especially since none of the persons interviewed relied upon notes of any sort; it was strictly from memory. For that reason, the general reader as well as the assassination purists will hopefully understand the merit and overall gist of each story and should not be led astray by criticism of minute details long since forgotten by the participants.

Controversy has arisen in recent years as to the credibility of certain eyewitnesses in Dealey Plaza: Beverly Oliver has claimed to be the famed Babushka Lady who was taking home movies at the time of the assassination; Ed Hoffmann, the deaf mute who claimed to witness a gunman behind the picket fence while he was parked alongside the Stemmons Freeway; and Gordon Arnold, who claimed to be on the grassy knoll also taking home movies of the motorcade, though his presence is not revealed in the known photographs or film taken at the time. The legitimacy of each of these three has been questioned by a number of assassination researchers. In addition, there is the story of Jean Hill, whose presence at the scene was well documented by numerous photographs as well as film, but her reliability has been questioned since her observations, according to some researchers, have grown dramatically in recent years. Is what she now says about seeing a muzzle flash and a puff of smoke behind the picket fence on the grassy knoll what she really saw or has it been contrived since 1963?

The reader will discover that similar discrepancies are present in this work and that they are not peculiar to just eyewitnesses. At least three of the Dallas policemen relate different versions as to who first interrogated Oswald after he was arrested and brought to police headquarters at City Hall. Not that it is of extreme importance, but it does reveal either what the ravages of time can do to the human mind or that even policemen are not immune from embellishing the facts.

I also found it most interesting that, contrary to popular assumption, animosities existed between a number of the law enforcement personnel in Dallas. In fact, some loathed one another. Usually when seeking an interview with a policeman or deputy sheriff mentioning others in their profession as a reference that I had previously interviewed would help in securing the interview. But in one instance, it backfired. I learned, after dropping the name of one deputy sheriff as a reference, that he was despised by the other. Only after assuring him that I was not taking sides in their mutual antagonism and with the aid of James Leavelle was I granted the interview.

There were times while in Dallas that incidental comments revealed a lighter side to the research, especially if one was well versed in the minutiae of the assassination. Occasionally I would hear stories told to me that I knew could not be factual, though I'm sure that those tellling the stories assumed they were. While in a book store one day, a young woman in her 20's told me that her father had seen Jack Ruby standing in front of Greene's Department Store on Main Street in downtown Dallas as the motorcade passed. This, despite the fact that several eyewitnesses placed him at the *Dallas Morning News* just before and after the assassination. On another occasion, following an interview with a former Dallas policeman at the Frank Crowley Courts Building, a young man helped me with all my paraphernalia to my van in the parking lot. During the course of the casual conversation that ensued he said, "Did you know that my mother ran a beauty shop over in Oak Cliff on the day of the assassination?" When I replied, no, he went on to say, "Yes, and right after the assassination Oswald came in and got a haircut!" I'm sure that he honestly believed the story, but it obviously could not have been true. Even if it could have been fit into the time frame of Oswald's activities after the shooting, photographs of Oswald in police custody reveal that he needed the back of his neck shaved, something that would have been taken care of if he had just received a haircut. Seemingly, everyone has a story relating to the assassination in Dallas. In many cases it is caveat emptor for the researcher trying to learn more about the subject.

At times, when the occasion arose, I sought to clarify certain problems areas myself. One morning while crossing the street with fellow researcher Mark Oakes at the intersection of Main and

Houston Streets in Dealey Plaza, a loud backfire noise went off which sounded much like a gunshot. Looking at Mark I asked, "Where did that noise originate?" After pondering a moment, he said that he couldn't tell. I responded, "Well, Mark, I'm not sure either but it sounded like it came from over there," pointing to the old Terminal Annex Building south of the Texas School Book Depository. The point being that earwitness testimony can be highly unreliable in trying to determine the origin of shots.

During the first trip to Dallas in 1987, I drove over the Houston Viaduct into Oak Cliff to see Oswald's boarding house on North Beckley. After talking to the owner, I decided to walk the distance from the house to the site at Tenth and Patton where Officer J.D. Tippit was killed roughly nine-tenths of a mile away. Critics of the Warren Commission have claimed that it was impossible for him to have walked the distance in the twelve minutes allotted, which was the time that the Commission claimed that Oswald left the house with his pistol and the time that Tippit was killed. Having my camcorder with me and set to the timer, I was able to walk the distance in eleven minutes and forty-five seconds. Granted the timing was close, but I had several factors which would have slowed my progress as compared to Oswald: I was carrying the camcorder; I was fifteen years older and two inches shorter than Oswald; it was 95 degrees as compared to 66 in 1963, and I had on a rather uncomfortable pair of shoes that day. For those reasons, at least in that so-called "problem area," it is my belief that Oswald could have walked the distance in the allotted time.

Speaking of time frames, most critics have claimed that immediately after the shooting Oswald could not have raced down four flights of stairs at the Book Depository and then be confronted by Motorcycle Officer Baker within ninety seconds on the second floor. There just wasn't enough time! However, fellow researcher and friend, Warren Graham, who had access to the sixth floor prior to the Sixth Floor Museum's creation, conducted an experiment in the early 1980's. Graham went through all the supposed motions of Oswald by walking rapidly at a right angle across the sixth floor (remember books were stacked in 1963) and simulating the hiding of the rifle for several seconds near the stairway. Graham then went quickly down the stairs past the second floor lunchroom to the first floor, out the door, and onto the street. The total time elapsed: 51 seconds! Could Oswald have made it within ninety seconds from the sixth floor to the second floor lunchroom after the shooting? According to Graham's experiment: yes. Granted, these are just two examples, but it does reveal that little can be taken for granted in this subject area. From my own experience, I learned that there is no substitute for being on location and talking with the people personally who were involved in one way or another with the events pertaining to the assassination.

What follows are the stories in their entirety as they were related to me. I have made no changes in context or meaning, nor have I attempted to insert my own opinions into the narratives. One of my goals has been to allow the people to speak for themselves. The only alterations are in sentence structure and grammar to make the narratives more readable.

Each subject was given the opportunity to critically review their original transcript and the completed narrative, and to make any necessary corrections or additions. Though few alterations were made, I have complied when requested by deleting certain detrimental comments about others as well as stories told to me in confidence which in no way altered the story of the assassination or its investigation.

As each chapter unfolds, so, too, does the story of the assassination and related events. The narratives are arranged in a chronological fashion with the sequence based on the most important aspect of each story beginning with an overview of the situation in Dallas in 1963 and continuing through the trial of Jack Ruby.

Specifically, the initial chapters of Jim Ewell and Hugh Aynesworth are featured to present the reader with not only eyewitness accounts, but also a general overview of the political climate in Dallas in November 1963. With the eyewitnesses, the reader will follow the narratives of those who witnessed the assassination at approximately the same time. For the sake of organization, they are arranged in alphabetical order.

From the eyewitnesses, *No More Silence* looks at the assassination from the perspectives of the motorcycle policemen in the motorcade as well as those law-enforcement personnel who were in Dealey Plaza at the time.

The attention is then focused on the investigation at the Texas School Book Depository Building, the capture of Oswald at the Texas Theater and follow-up investigations of Oswald's background, family and acquaintances. What follows is the transfer of Oswald, his murder, the background of his assailant, Jack Ruby, and finally the trial of Jack Ruby.

In converting the information from the transcripts to the narratives, occasional reorganization was necessary since the interviews sometimes meandered from one subject to another. As a result, transitional sentences were inserted to facilitate continuity. Nothing was changed to alter any substance from the original transcripts.

For me, the most rewarding aspect of this project has not been just the interviewing process and the honor of meeting those who were interviewed. More so, is the warm reception afforded me and the ongoing friendships which have developed over the years. I was flattered recently when one of the Dallas policeman told me, "We never discussed the subject much until you came to Dallas and talked to many of us. Only then did we begin to talk more about the assassination. As a result, we have kept more in touch with each other because of the interest you have rekindled with us." If nothing else, I hope that my efforts have encouraged the belief among the participants in Dallas that there are researchers who are truly interested in learning what they saw and heard and not just in the dissemination of theories and speculations by innovative or creative writers.

Though I would like to think that most of the mysteries of the assassination would be clarified in this work, I realize that, in some cases, additional questions will be raised and fuel will be added to the debate surrounding the assassination. In any case, you are about to read the stories of ordinary people who were placed under the extraordinary circumstances of one of the greatest tragedies of American history. Here are the stories of those participants as they would want their stories told. Open your mind and listen to what they have to say.

LARRY A. SNEED
Lawrenceville, Georgia

NO MORE SILENCE

EYEWITNESSES

Jim Ewell

Hugh Aynesworth

James Altgens

Charles Brehm

Ruth Dean

Ruth Hendrix

Clemon Earl Johnson

Roy E. Lewis

T.E. Moore

Bill Newman

Malcolm Summers

James Tague

Otis Williams

JIM EWELL
News Reporter

"If any one of us had gotten in to where we could break 'the story of the century,' and that was the conspiracy behind the assassination of Kennedy, no lap dog reporter would have been sitting out there waiting for the story to break..."

After delivering his hometown newspaper as a boy in West Texas, Jim Ewell became interested in a career in journalism. After attending Hardin-Simmons College, Ewell began as a cub reporter for the *Abilene Reporter News*. Specializing in crime reporting and interested in police work, he became a part time crime beat reporter for the *Dallas Times Herald* in 1953, and by 1963 had become a full-time day side crime beat reporter for *The Dallas Morning News*. In that capacity, Ewell observed the capture of Lee Harvey Oswald at the Texas Theater and wrote extensively about the events of that tragic week end.

The Dallas Morning News was a Republican newspaper in a sea of Democrats across the Southwest, and though Dallas was a conservative city, it was probably an exaggeration that Dallas was that ultra-conservative. I never felt that we were so far politically to the right that it would intoxicate our thinking as sane people. I don't think that was the case. If nothing else, there were some incidents that played into the mind-set that Dallas was this ultra-right stronghold such as the little incident involving Adlai Stevenson when he came to Dallas and was bumped on the head with a small sign. The police were never convinced that that was an actual attempt by that woman to strike Mr. Stevenson. The story we heard was that she was bumped from behind as she was trying to get up in his face with the picket which resulted in his being conked on the forehead. Well, the press made quite a bit of that. They thought it was an insult. Then there was the spitting incident involving Lyndon Baines Johnson when he was Vice-President as he and Lady Bird were crossing the street between two main hotels.

But on the morning of the Kennedys' arrival, *The Dallas Morning News* printed the "Welcome Mr. Kennedy" full page statement. It created a great deal of controversy because the ad alleged that Kennedy was a traitor. I think this all fell back on his betrayal, to their thinking, of the pull back of American forces from the Bay of Pigs actions in Cuba that might have toppled Fidel Castro. There was also the idea that he was leaning toward the communists since the ad alleged that he was a communist sympathizer.

Kennedy was in Texas to try to shore up factions between the party leaders of the Texas Democrats. *The News*, as I recall, assigned about nine reporters to different areas of Kennedy's appearance in the city. I was assigned to watch his arrival at Dallas Love Field.

That morning, when I arrived at the airport, there was a large turnout of school kids and rank and file people. There had been a light rain, and as we waited for Air Force One to arrive coming over from Fort Worth, it seemed that when he was spotted the crowd stirred when Air Force One approached Love Field, the clouds parted, the light rain quit, and the sun broke out, making it a gorgeous morning. I thought it was most fitting that all this occurred for the arrival of Kennedy.

Jackie, dressed in her pink suit and hat, which we all remember, was given a large bouquet of red roses. The crowd was absolutely charmed by the President and the First Lady. He was so taken aback, I think, by the reception he got that that's when he broke away from the Secret Service and went to the fence line and went down the row. I was watching all of that, having a pass to be inside the gate as a member of the press. Once the arrival and the greetings were over, the motorcade got started on the appointed route that would take them to downtown Dallas. Now that was the end of my assignment because all I could tell the rewrite people was what I've already described here. I thought it was a very, very warm reception! They had to be impressed.

So I routinely got back in my vehicle and, instead of trying to follow the route of the motorcade down Lemmon Avenue and approaching the east side of downtown, I took the route back on the Stemmons Expressway. My intention was to go back to the pressroom at police headquarters since that was the quickest way for me to get around.

Had everything gone routinely I would have simply called in my notes to a rewrite unless they would have wanted a separate story about what I had seen at the airport. That wasn't likely because there were bigger and better things to come ahead in the Kennedys' visit in Dallas. But the setting was absolutely very cordial. In fact, I think the Kennedys were still swept up in this warmth in the motorcade through downtown Dallas. Now that's the real irony of it! At the west end of downtown Dallas was the sniper waiting for the Kennedy motorcade. They were just a jump from getting back on Stemmons. That's where I met the Kennedy motorcade.

After the shooting, I ran into the motorcade, but it was stretched out, speeding, and I knew immediately that something was wrong, although I had no radio communications at the time to tell me what had taken place. I could see the Secret Service agent hanging on the turtleback. My first thought was that a pedestrian crossing Stemmons had been hit by one of the cars in the motorcade because that was five lanes each way, and pedestrians were crossing that ten lane freeway to get on the side closest to the motorcade. I could not believe that people were risking their lives to cross the freeway in front of my traffic and the northbound traffic. That was the only thing that I could think of that had happened.

When I first saw the motorcade, it must have been halfway between the Triple Underpass and the Trade Mart, somewhere beyond Continental. The speed was what attracted me. First I saw the lead car with Police Chief Jess Curry, then I saw the Kennedys, the Presidential limousine, and then I remember there were three buses carrying the White House Press Corps. All of this was strung out! As I came under the Triple Underpass, coming off Stemmons up Commerce, there was an explosion of ant hills, so to speak, with people still running in every direction. This was within minutes of the assassination. There was a swarm of people mainly over on the Elm Street side going down toward the Triple Underpass.

I turned on my car radio, and I remember that KLIF, the lead spot-news radio station in those days, owned by Gordon McLendon, had a female telephone clerk in the Dallas Police Dispatching Office saying that shots had been fired at the Kennedy motorcade. So I just went up Commerce Street and then went down into the basement of police headquarters where two days later Oswald was murdered by Jack Ruby. As I got out of my car, parking it there in the press lot, Sergeant Jerry Hill, who at one time was a former *Dallas Times Herald* crime beat reporter, came running out, and I said, "Jerry, what the hell's going on?"

And his exact words were, "Some son of a bitch just shot Kennedy!" He then ran around and jumped into a black and white squad car; there was a uniform officer behind the wheel already, so I just ran over there and got in the back seat. This officer drove us back from east to west through downtown on the most circuitous route I can recall, and we were back there at the School Book Depository probably in less than two minutes.

When we arrived the police had their squad cars across the intersection in kind of a circular position. There were officers still standing behind and in front of the squad cars training their shotguns up to the windows of the School Book Depository. We found ourselves standing right out in the middle of the intersection of Houston and Elm. I'm going to say this was probably inside of fifteen minutes from the time that I had seen the swarm of people near the Triple Underpass and heard on the radio that shots had been fired. It happened that quickly!

I had been a newspaper reporter for about fifteen years, and I thought that I was a seasoned professional. But now that the weight of this was coming down on me, I was beginning to get woozy. I felt light headed. But I do remember standing there with the police not knowing if they still had somebody trapped upstairs, or if there was going to be an outbreak of gunfire if they exposed somebody. And again, we didn't know how badly hurt Kennedy was, at least I didn't. Meanwhile Jerry Hill worked his way up to the sixth floor, leaned out an open window, and he had what was thought to be Oswald's little fried chicken lunch. It was in a little pop box. Jerry was holding that box and holding up one of the chicken bones exclaiming to everybody that listened to him down on the street that the fried chicken was what he had been eating. About that time there was a commotion around one of the squad cars, and we could hear a radio saying that an officer had been shot in Oak Cliff.

Looking back on it, and this is more amazing to me right now, all this time I had never made contact with my city desk. I did not have a walkie-talkie like they do today. They didn't know where in the hell I was! They probably didn't know where the hell a lot of the *Dallas News* reporters were because events were moving so quickly that you had to stay up with it, and you had no time to stop and let them know what you were doing and what they could do to help you.

But, nonetheless, I left the scene of where an attack, a shooting attack, had been staged against the President of the United States to go to investigate, as a reporter, the reported shooting of a Dallas police officer. Now keep in mind, in 1963, you DID NOT shoot policemen! You DID NOT strike policemen! Only in very rare cases did you strike a police officer. Look at what's changed since then! And yet, I left the location at the School Book Depository and jumped into a car driven by Captain Westbrook with Sergeant Stringer. I rode in the back seat as we sped across into Oak Cliff by taking the Houston Street Viaduct right beside the *Dallas News*.

When we arrived in Oak Cliff, I got a chance to go into a convenience store, McCandles' Minute Market it was called in those days, just down from the Marsailles Public Library, and I did get to make a phone call to the city desk asking them to send me a photographer. They didn't know what I was doing in Oak Cliff. This particular editor was too overpowered by what was going on downtown to pay any attention to what I was trying to tell him, and I know I came out saying, "You know I've got to have a photographer out here!"

As I stepped out of this convenience store, next door to it was a two story boarding house, and there I saw Bill Alexander with an automatic pistol stalking across the balcony very carefully. Alexander always impressed me because, being an assistant district attorney, he was one of those guys from the prosecutor's office that you saw with the cops. He was a squad car prosecutor. You very seldom saw the district attorney outside of his office.

From there we proceeded to a side street down from where they said J.D. Tippit had been shot not far from East Jefferson. There was another police car there as they were examining a jacket next to the curb which had apparently been located by one of the policemen after Oswald had thrown it down as he ran toward Jefferson. I had a jacket just like it. I remember it as being a light tan windbreaker. I was with Westbrook as we all went over to examine the jacket because it was the only tangible thing we had at the moment that belonged to the killer. In fact, I held the jacket in my hands. I remember that they were talking about a water mark on it that was obviously made by a dry cleaning shop.

They were discussing it when the report came in that the person they thought might be the police officer's assailant had gone into the Texas Theater. Now we were on East Jefferson, so I'm thinking that we were about five blocks from that location. Immediately, Captain Westbrook and Sergeant Stringer ran back to their car, which was across the street, and I ran to jump in the backseat. By that time, they were already turning out and accelerating. When I got in the backseat with the door still hanging open, I came out of the car hanging onto the door. They slowed down long enough for me to get back in, as I could have been flung out across the gravel into a curb if I hadn't held on.

Anyway, when we arrived at the Texas Theater, we parked right in front and everybody jumped out and went into the lobby. There were other police cars getting there, too. I was very familiar with the Texas Theater, having lived close by back when we were a younger married couple. At that time, they had some kind of stairway up to the balcony, and I remember somebody kept shouting, "Turn on the house lights! Will somebody please turn on the house lights?"

For some reason, instead of following the police into the main part of the theater, the lower floor, I went up these stairs into the balcony. And there, there must have been about fifteen or twenty high school age boys up there watching. They'd skipped school to watch double feature war movies. One of them was "War Is Hell."

Then there was a commotion. I stepped to the railing where I could look down onto this. Just about that time the house lights came up and Nick McDonald made his move on Oswald. So I'm in a position looking down on where Oswald sat, not knowing who he was. Then I saw the fight that broke out. First, Nick was shouting, and then there was just a swarm of officers that came in. What I'm describing is what appeared to be a football play from above. John Toney remembered that some officer screamed out that they were breaking his arm. Another officer, Paul Bentley, the Chief Polygraph Examiner for the Dallas Police Department, who was well known to us all, came out of there with a broken ankle. What I saw rather astounded me. Someone was trying to hold the barrel of a shotgun, or train the barrel of a shotgun down among the heads of these officers. I thought, "What's he going to do with the shotgun?" I didn't know what was going on, but this person was holding a shotgun; I did see that. And it all happened in a matter of seconds!

When the fight broke out down there, these kids stampeded out of the balcony, then I followed them down. The next thing I recall is that I was out in the street with the car that I arrived in between me and the officers bringing Oswald out of the theater as they kind of separated the crowd and made an aisle for him to come through to get to the car. I'd say that I was about ten to twelve feet away from Oswald at the time. During this sequence of events, I was distracted by the tone of a teenage girl, and we used this in the story because at that time, for teenagers, especially teenage girls to be so profane was just very uncommon. But this girl shouted, "Kill the son of a bitch!" And the *Dallas News* let us use that. Being a strong family newspaper in 1963, we still used that because it was very pertinent to describe to the readers how supercharged the area was. This was about thirty-five minutes after the shooting of Tippit, so the word apparently had already gotten out around that part of Oak Cliff that they were looking for a cop killer. Evidently this teenage girl got swept up into it to the point that she was that emphatic about what she thought ought to be done to this person later identified as Oswald. There were some other shouts and threats made right there by the crowd which had been brought there by the arrival of all these squad cars with sirens screaming and them screeching up in front and also by the arrival of squad cars in the alley behind the Texas Theater as they came in from the back as well. It was obviously an ugly crowd, but not to the point that they were going to overpower the police officers and try to get the prisoner. Oswald then took my

place in the backseat of the same car that I arrived in. So when
they left with him, I stood there, stranded. I then hitchhiked a
ride with a man in a pickup truck.

By now my mind was just a swirl because things had been
moving so fast that I was getting scrambled. It was on the truck
radio that we heard that they had pronounced Kennedy dead. That
was the first that I realized that he had suffered fatal wounds. The
next thing I remember was that I was out in the street. I was
actually standing out in the street in front of The *Dallas News*
Building on Houston Street.

I was just barely out of the truck when I saw driving up one of
our evening editors, Louis Harris, who was just coming in for the
night edition. "Louie, take me to the police station," I said, as I
commandeered his car. Louie went into the station with me, and
we went up to the third floor. At that time, there still wasn't the
congestion that later occurred with all the media coming in. We
got into the Homicide and Robbery offices there on the third
floor, and in a back room where there was kind of a small squad
room sat Oswald.

They had just put him at a table that they used to write their
reports on. The room was no larger than eight by twelve at the
most with one or two metal tables and some chairs. The
detectives normally used it as a squad room. This would have all
been just after two o'clock as they drove him straight from the
Texas Theater, and it would have taken them no more than
fifteen minutes to get him back downtown.

But that's the first opportunity that I had to get back to the
telephone and call in to let them know what I'd been doing. It
turned out that I was probably the only reporter that I remember
who was at the Texas Theater. However, Hugh Aynesworth, who
was a member of our staff, said he arrived at the Texas Theater
also. I didn't see Hugh, but I know this; all the other press had
been concentrating on the hospital and the School Book
Depository. Now the word was out that a suspect had been
arrested, and they were coming to police headquarters.

I remained at the police building until probably 2:00 or 3:00
A.M. the next morning because our final press run was starting
around 2:00 A.M. I was able to get stories out to the office since
we had a pressroom up there on the third floor right down from

Homicide and Robbery, and all I had to do was go down to the pressroom and use the *Dallas News* telephone to call in.

By the next day, which was Saturday, it was almost impossible to make your way down that third floor hallway where all the detective's offices were located because all three major networks had set up cameras there in the intersection of the hallway. They had cables running down that hallway and out the windows to their sound trucks or their power sources out on the streets. They had cables dangling three floors down!

This naturally made it more difficult for us. We were cut off from our normal sources. Of course, we had the advantage over the out of town press because we were the local press, and we could capitalize on our close-in sources that we had developed through the years. These sources would include police officers who were around the actual events that day, although really I didn't have to ask too many questions because I saw as much as what the police had seen, as far as the arrest of Oswald in the Texas Theater. But we had a very good relationship with the police.

There was a lot of news to collect. You couldn't miss it as it was happening there, and it was all concentrated in the building where we were because Oswald was there; that meant the district attorney was there and the FBI was all around us. But we relied mainly on the police sources. They were the people in front of the investigation more so than anybody else. The FBI, Secret Service, and all those people, whatever they were doing was typically out of sight of the press. But with the Dallas Police Department, it was out front.

We kept up with the investigation as Homicide reconstructed the events that led up to Tippit's murder. But one thing that could never be answered was what caused Tippit to stop and question Oswald; we'll never know. There was nobody else around to answer the question. I remember the police officers who knew Tippit said that one of his characteristics was to never look a person in the eye. When he would talk to people, he would look downward, and this might have been the case when he was dealing with Oswald. Apparently, he pulled up, rolled down the window and told Oswald to come over to the car. Then, for some reason for which I am not aware, he elected to get out of the car. As he stepped out, Oswald stepped aside to where he could fire across the hood of the car. By that time, Tippit's dead!

Over the years, questions have been raised as to the number of police who arrived at the theater and how quickly they got there. And certainly, the arrest of Oswald was not routine. But how could you compare it with anything else that I was ever aware of? There had only been one other Dallas policeman killed in the line of duty in the previous twelve years or so, Slip Mullenax, who was a Vice Squad officer involved in plain clothes undercover work. I covered that. I went out with Captain Gannaway, who was in charge of the Special Services Bureau, which included Narcotics, Vice, and Intelligence. Mullenax was in a walk-up hotel, and the manager mistook him for a prowler or an assailant and shot him. Later he was exonerated. But in the case of Oswald, the police were tracking and caught up with the alleged killer of a buddy officer. I was at the police station till about 2:00 or 3:00 A.M. Saturday morning, and then I came back out here to DeSoto. We had just built our house here after trading a house in Oak Cliff. At that time, we had boxes stacked everywhere.

Saturday morning, I went to the *Dallas News* and back up again to the police station. By then, the police building was overloaded with the press! It looked like they were covering one of the national conventions!

That Saturday morning it was hard for Captain Will Fritz, leading the investigation, to come and go to his office. Everything was so tightly packed up there that it paralyzed police headquarters even though the detectives still had to continue their regular duties. The city just didn't stop because of this; crime just didn't stop. They still had to be involved with handling crime reports. But the fact is they were paralyzed by the log jam in that hallway on the third floor where most of the detective's offices were located on the east side of the building. On the west end of the floor were the executive offices for Chief Curry and all of his staff.

It's a funny thing that nothing really moved on the story-line until Fritz or Chief Curry appeared or Oswald came out. So there was a lot of self-interviewing among the reporters. The local reporters were amused by it. But they were trying to grab on to any little thing.

I didn't have any question about their professionalism. I recognized many of the reporters by their names and knew that they were outstanding reporters. Mainly these came from the *Los*

Angeles Times, the *New York Times, Chicago Tribune*, and the *Detroit Press*. I felt those reporters stood out above everybody because they were smooth in how they handled themselves. They were not up there slugging it out. The television guys were doing that. They were always the pushy type. Of course, there's always been that rivalry or friction between the printed reporters and the television reporters.

But I think a lot of us locally were amazed and disgusted by the reports that we saw when the out of town papers came back to Dallas, or we saw the reports on national television. There were a lot of inaccuracies that we knew were inaccuracies! But you had to remember, too, that it would be the same if I went to a strange city trying to report on a story of this magnitude, not knowing the local turf. But, by and large, even though Oswald had been identified as a Marxist sympathizer and had married a Russian Communist, there were still those that didn't want to believe that the leftists or those of the liberal side had anything to do with killing Camelot.

At the time, I didn't know anything about Oswald other than he carried other identification. It was a *Star-Telegram* reporter from Fort Worth in the building there that immediately recognized the name, and he quickly circulated that this Oswald had to be the same one who had defected to Russia a number of years before. That supercharged the whole deal! Was this a Soviet assassination? Was it their way of getting back at Kennedy for his backing down the Soviets over the missile crisis?

The FBI could have answered many of our questions, but they were strictly a "no comment" organization, and they got away with it. Hoover managed to maintain such control of the FBI that the press could not penetrate it. Trying to penetrate federal law enforcement organizations just wasn't done as might be done today. But it's not much different today than it was then as far as the feds are concerned. They are still held at arm's length.

One of the major developments by the *Dallas News* was that we obtained Oswald's diary, which came later on. But, also, sometime after the initial weekend of the assassination, I obtained the report of Lieutenant Jack Revill which stated that the FBI knew of Lee Harvey Oswald and that he was in Dallas. This came from a conversation that Revill had with Agent James Hosty, who had been assigned as Oswald's case officer.

This created a major controversy! Curry had that memorandum and announced its contents to the press. As a result, it turned the blame away from the Dallas police, who were receiving all the world wide blame for allowing this to happen. The question was: How could this guy smuggle a rifle into the School Book Depository and sit there and wait for the President? I remember Jesse Curry's reply was that there were fifty thousand windows they'd have to cover on that parade route and you couldn't guard all of those. When it was learned that the FBI knew all along that here was a defector, returning to the United States, and working in Dallas in a building on the very route of the motorcade, that so infuriated Hoover that he cut the Dallas police off from attending the National FBI Academy.

Anyway, I broke that story. After a while, I noticed that Dallas police were not getting called to go to the FBI Academy. They started picking officers from some of the smaller police departments around Dallas despite the fact that Dallas always had had a special connection with the FBI Academy. In fact, the police chief prior to Jesse Curry, Carl Hansson, had been one of their instructors at the Academy.

Aynesworth picked up on the story because he knew more about the repercussions of what it all meant. I had merely gotten hold of a memorandum that said that Agent James Hosty revealed that the FBI knew about Oswald and that he could be considered a potential risk to the President and that he was capable of doing this or something to that effect. Unfortunately, I don't believe anybody got to talk to Hosty because the FBI shipped him out of town to Kansas City. There was "no comment" from any of the other local agents either. As to Revill, I don't recall whether I talked to him about it or not. I'm not sure that Curry would allow him to expand on it as this situation was handled strictly by the chief. This was a very sensitive issue.

I was assigned on Sunday morning to cover the transfer of Oswald from the city jail to the county jail on the west end of downtown Dallas. To me, that was so routine. It was an exercise that would allow the press to get some additional footage of Oswald in custody. Of course, once he got into the county jail he would have been locked off unless his attorneys would have arranged for a news conference. But once he left police custody, that would have been the last that we'd have gotten to see him until he appeared in court.

But that Sunday morning I was fatigued, so I stayed here. I had lost all my energy. We still had to have a story for Monday morning's paper, but I knew there were other things happening around the Kennedy story that would be built into the main story for Monday morning. We had a console television over in the corner of the living room, and my year and a half old son walked by and pulled on the button to the television. Immediately the focus was on the Kennedy memorial services at one of the big cathedrals in London. I stood right here drinking a cup of coffee and watched the proceedings of that service. About that time, a voice broke in and said, "We're now taking you to the basement of the Dallas City Hall." And immediately, they cut in and I saw all the familiar people. The cameras were in position; I saw Captain Fritz, and about that time here came Leavelle with Oswald. Then, all of a sudden there's this dark form that breaks in, and then you hear, POW!! And I'm standing here, helpless!

I quickly got on the phone and dialed the city desk and talked to Robbie Miller, who was an assistant to the city editor. He thought I was up there at the police station. He said, "We'll get you some help right now!"

I told him, "Miller, I'm not there; I'm still in DeSoto!"

"Get your ass down there, now!!"

The freeway not having been completed at that time was in sections, so I remember cutting in to get on the freeway where it was open so I could make faster time. And the radio was reporting, without mentioning any names, that this person was well known to the Dallas police. I remembered there was a guy by the name of Jack McDonald, who was one of those kind of guys. They called him "Motorcycle Jack" or "Bicycle Jack" because he was always riding a motorcycle or a bicycle, and he was always looking for stolen cars to collect a fifteen dollar finder's fee. So he was always hanging around the police station. But I thought, it can't be McDonald! How in the world could he..? That tells you that I had never heard of the name Jack Ruby, and I had been around the police station the better part of eight years. I had never heard of the name Jack Ruby!

When I got downtown and got back in the basement where I parked, I was impressed that even though I was well known around that building, I still had to have a special police pass displayed so I could get into the building. Now this was all really high level, heavy duty stuff because I've got to wear one of those.

I took the elevator and went up to the fourth floor, which was one floor above where CID was, and that was the Identification Division where they had all the mug shots, fingerprint files on one end; on this end was the admission desk or the public opening to the city jail. I asked them for a mug shot of Jack Ruby, and I got one. That's the first time I realized that here was the guy that they'd arrested for killing Oswald. But get this, as I walked back to the elevator, there were two elevators, and I punched the button to go back to the third floor, to my right was a lawyer interview room or public room where they could visit prisoners and talk to them by phone looking through a window. There in that room was a lawyer I recognized talking to Jack Ruby. It was Tom Howard with the western hat on, the whole bit. He was well known to the police reporters because he had an office across the street from the police department. Looking back, since I knew Tom well, I could have walked over and said, "Tom, I'd like to talk to your client," and I think he would have put him on right then and there! But I didn't. I pushed the button, got on the elevator, and went back downstairs!

I don't know who wrote our story that day. Hugh Aynesworth and I were too busy dictating notes into the newsroom. I don't know who Hugh called in to write it, but we stayed up there until we milked everything we knew to write about it that Sunday till we just dropped. On a story of that size, one reporter can't cover everything. He gets what he can, and he runs it into a rewrite man. Somebody would take your notes and they'd say, "From Ewell, 3:10 P.M." In a story like this, you then bring in one of your heavy duty writers. Bob Baskin was our Washington Bureau chief; he was in town for the Kennedy visit. He and one of our columnists, Paul Crume, combined their writing talents for the main story-line on the Kennedy assassination. So I don't know who they called in or who they had that Sunday afternoon to construct the story out of our notes because how could you continue watching everything as it was unraveling and go back and write a story? You had to unload your notes as quickly as possible so you could stay in position. By that time, other reporters from the *Dallas News* were getting there, too.

One of the big things that I remember about that Sunday was that Jack Beers, one of our photographers, had been assigned to that deadline. Originally, it had been assigned to another of our photographers, Joe Laird. But I had arranged the night before, Saturday night, before I left, who was going to be up there on Sunday morning. So Jack Beers took the assignment.

When Beers flashed off in that famous photograph of Ruby bursting through and thrusting his pistol up, Aynesworth and I kept hearing reports from the city desk that we had one hell of a picture. We had the picture of the year! It was so good that we were going to run it on almost three-fourths of the entire front page on Monday. I believe close to the bottom. Then, later that evening, we heard the *Times Herald* had something.

When Beers flashed, Bob Jackson of the *Times Herald* flashed. It was in that split second that shows Oswald grabbing at his side that got Jackson the Pulitzer Award. A split second!

Much has been made of Jack Ruby's connections with the Dallas police. If he had that many connections, I think I would have seen him sometime in the eight years that I was around the station at that time. I think those stories are untrue. I think where they had a connection with Ruby was that the Vice Squad officers went to his nightclub, the Carousel.

There was also a Vice officer by the name of Tippitt, G.W. Tippitt. I remember that he was mainly a desk officer, but he spelled his name TIPPITT. J.D. spelled it with just one "T." That's what confused a lot of these writers. The story that was written was that J.D. Tippit was killed because he knew too much; he was one of those that consorted with Jack Ruby. That's where they got confused. It just so happened that there were two officers by the name of Tippit.

If there'd ever been any connection between Oswald, Tippit, and Jack Ruby, we would be talking about it as if it happened today. It was never established! And I think that there was an all out intensive effort on the part of the press to be the first to find those connections, and there were some very good reporters in those days looking into that. Some have accused the press of cover-up. Even though we had our own office and parking privileges at the police department, to say that by having those, they were able to control us just simply wasn't the case. If any one of us had gotten in to where we could break the "story of the century," and that was the conspiracy behind the assassination of Kennedy, no lap dog reporter would have been sitting out there waiting for the story to break. We had some of the best newspapermen in the United States in Dallas trying to find those angles. You also had the best from the television networks.

Even in the *Dallas News* several reporters stayed hooked in to what they thought might be more to the story, more than just Oswald. They were assigned specifically to that role. We had reporters like Hugh Aynesworth who was accepted by the *Dallas News* as being a reporter who was still pursuing any kind of lead that came out. Aynesworth got into the bigger scene much more than I ever did. For instance, he was in the police basement that Sunday morning just by chance. So when I called in and said that I wasn't there, I could imagine that scene breaking and no *Dallas News* reporter being down there. It turned out that Aynesworth was there. Behind Aynesworth was another reporter, Earl Golz, of the *Dallas News*.

For the longest time, Golz was allowed to pursue that for the *Dallas News*. We didn't have that many reporters who could stay hooked to the story or continue to look, say, six months later. They had to get back to other things. We didn't have the luxury of the staff sizes that they have today. If the assassination happened today, with today's same numbers and players in place, the assassination would have been covered by no less than seventy-five Dallas news reporters. They sent twenty-five to thirty to the Olympics in Los Angeles. They send that many to the national conventions. Can you imagine what they would have done with the assassination in Dallas, Texas?

But after the first six months when this story started settling back, the Warren Commission Report was out and they were concentrating on Johnson's conduct of our growing involvement in Vietnam, I was very content, as a beat reporter, to fall back into my old routine as if it never happened. So when something would come up that might lend itself to another story about the assassination, I would simply pass it to the desk.

As a newspaperman, I never felt that I wanted to be involved in a story that was centered on the assassination of a president. I think every one of us felt that we had lost part of our soul by Kennedy's death. And we couldn't figure out how Dallas was going to work its way out of this. We knew that there was a lot of anger and that Dallas was blamed for his death. How could it be? Here was a guy that probably was deranged, in my thinking, that for some reason wanted to make a break in front of the American people that he had killed the President. But then Ruby has to be the most condemned player of that whole situation because he took away from the American people their chance to learn the real reason by Oswald in a trial court where all of this would have come out. He robbed the American people of those answers which has left many still doubting that one person could have killed the President. By the 1970's I think Dallas had finally come to grips with the assassination. Looking back on it, I think that if Oswald had not been arrested and identified as quickly as he was, and if Dallas had to go through a night with the assailant still at large and not even identified, I think the city would have been caught up in some serious heavy duty stuff. I think people would have blamed those who were identified as the leaders of the conservatives. There might have been actual physical assaults on those people; maybe a Tippit like assassination of public officials in an act of revenge to get back at those for what had been done against the President. I really do! I think there'd have been bloodshed, outrage, and just fanaticism overtaking Dallas. But when they quickly identified Oswald, his connection as a defector from Fort Worth to Russia, you can see how quickly it turned. By that night, there was so much disbelief that somebody with Oswald's connections, who was married to a Russian, was now the accused assassin of the President. I'll always be grateful that he was captured before he could escape from the city. Otherwise, there is no telling what kinds of stories would have been reported by that night.

I continued on the same beat with the *Dallas News* until January 1981 after twenty-five years service. During that time, I saw the maturity of the city; it became more sophisticated. After leaving the *Dallas News*, I assumed the job of a public employee in a law enforcement organization that deals with the press on the opposite side.

Jim Ewell, scheduled for retirement in 1998, currently serves as the Public Information Director for the Dallas County Sheriff's Department. He is commonly regarded as one of the top aides under Sheriff J.C. Bowles and has been extremely helpful to researchers throughout the years. Ewell and his family still reside in the same home in DeSoto, Texas, as they did on the day of the assassination.

HUGH AYNESWORTH
News Reporter

"I don't think there's a good reporter on earth who wouldn't give their eye teeth to break anything approaching a conspiracy. If I knew there was a conspiracy, I'd be a millionaire tomorrow and would be living on the French Riviera the rest of my life..."

After attending Salem College, Hugh Aynesworth started in 1948 as a newspaperman in West Virginia and later worked in Arkansas, Kansas, and Colorado prior to joining the staff of *The Dallas Morning News* in 1960.

The day the tragedy occurred I was the science editor for the *Dallas News* and had an interview set up at SMU with a scientist whose name I have long since forgotten. But due to there being a great deal of excitement in Dallas that day, I instead decided to walk over to watch the motorcade with an assistant district attorney and another lawyer. So I was there in the center of Elm Street where the police had it blocked off observing what was to be the start of a very chaotic day.

To fully comprehend the atmosphere surrounding the Kennedy visit, it is necessary to understand the political climate in Dallas at that time, which was testy at best. There was a very small but vocal cadre of arch conservatives, and these people were helped along by the editorial policy of *The Dallas Morning News,* which was to the right of Genghis Khan. It was an amazing thing because I don't think that there were over 300 to 400 of these people, but they were very vocal and did get tremendous coverage.

Of course, what received the most coverage was when they spat upon and hit Adlai Stevenson with a sign on October 24th, I think it was, which made everybody fearful for Mr. Kennedy when he came because here you had, again, the person that they thought was an arch liberal or a semi-communist, thus we had a feeling that something embarrassing would happen.

There had already been a gag order which prohibited people from shouting obscenities and things of that sort. The police department and the city council had already made sure that that wouldn't happen.

The day before the assassination I received a call from a group of people who were going to dress up and try to embarrass Kennedy at the Trade Mart. I talked with them at length and tried to fathom how many people they might have had, which seemed to be only six or eight, though they told me that they had two or three chapters in this group. I remember talking with the city editor, Johnny King, and saying, "Johnny, maybe we ought to do something on this." And he said, "No, it'd just bring on fifty more crazies if you write it." So we didn't write anything about that.

But the mood was anticipatory, somewhat fearful, and yet once he got off the plane at Love Field, remember we didn't have DFW Airport at the time, and started down Cedar Springs it was just a festive occasion. People were running to the car and shouting that they loved him which took some of the fear away in those few minutes.

There was no particular reason why I went to Elm Street other than the crowds were larger along Main Street, two or three deep, and I wanted to get a clearer view. Locating myself in the middle of the street a little toward the curb, had I looked up to my right I could have seen Oswald up there. But, instead, I was looking at the motorcade.

The first shot I wasn't sure was a shot. I thought it might have been a backfire from one of the motorcycles since there were several in the vicinity. When you hear one, you listen more closely, and when I heard a second and then a third very clearly, there was no doubt in my mind that they were shots and that they were from a rifle. I didn't know a whole lot about guns, but I knew that it wasn't a pistol. At one time I thought that one was fired closer to another in time sequence, but I can't recall that anymore.

Immediately, people started jumping and running and some were throwing their kids down. Maybe I would have run too, but I didn't know where to run. It was a strange situation where you had about forty percent of the area open and then buildings all around the other part. Not knowing where the shots really originated, you didn't know which way to run or how to protect yourself. I remember one woman throwing up while others were screaming, shouting, and running to protect their children. It was just total chaos! I'd never seen anything like it! I was never in the service or seen a war, but it was the closest thing that I could imagine to that.

People in the doorway and even others across the street where I later learned that the eyewitness, Brennan, was started pointing, even then, to the Depository Building. As a result, everything converged there and a lot of people ran into the building. I don't know why, but I didn't. Maybe I thought, "Well, if there's a gun in there, I don't want to run into it," or maybe I just didn't think till I started interviewing. I didn't have any paper with me; I just had a bunch of envelopes in my pocket, so I started filling the back of them with notes.

Time passed quickly. Then, of course, newsmen and police converged on the place along with everybody else. I remember people saying, "There's a Secret Service man that's been shot; Lyndon Johnson's been hit. I saw him fall over," and things like that. It was just complete chaos!

During that time span, I kept thinking, "He's in that building!" I remember interviewing people that said that they saw certain things: some did, some didn't. Even then there were people making up things. Even then!

I remember interviewing a young couple where the guy was telling me that he had seen this and he had seen that, and his wife said, "You didn't see that! We were back in the parking lot when it happened!" Even then! And, of course, we've seen that in abundance since.

We know now what everyone said. A lot of them heard four shots, some eight, and, of course, many of them changed their opinions on that. People disagreed. If you had five people who witnessed an automobile accident, I guarantee you that, if deposed, those five people that day, a week later, whatever, would have seen five different colored cars, a different time of day, a different number of people in the car, and you might even find a puppy dog in one of those cars as you did with one of the Kennedy witnesses.

I've always been around a police radio because you don't miss much if you know where they're being sent. There was an open mike somewhere in that location, and at that time, the word was that since so many police had run into that building that he must have been on top of the building. That's what we thought at the time. We didn't think that it was the fifth, sixth, or seventh floor; we just thought that he was on top because that's what everybody was saying at that time.

I remember hearing on the police radio the transmission: "This is a citizen" or something to that effect. "A policeman's been shot! He's hurt pretty bad, I think!" It was obvious that it was someone who wasn't familiar with using a radio since they didn't know exactly what to say. I remember seeing the regular police reporter, Jim Ewell, come in that time frame. I was the science and aviation guy, but once in a while I'd be pressed into duty, so I knew Jim quite well from covering the police.

I don't know whether Jim was standing with me or was somewhere else, but within the next two or three minutes two people from Channel 8 television station came up to me and said, "Let's get over there!"

I said to Ewell, "Well, you've got one here! This is probably going to be a conspiracy situation!" A cop isn't shot three miles away from where the President is shot unless there's something connected.

This was long before the narcotics' problems and drug addictions of crack cocaine and all that today. It was extremely rare for a police officer to be killed in Dallas in those days, and in broad daylight, rarer still. So I said, "Ewell, why don't you stay here and get this one and I'll go in the Channel 8 cruiser?" Vic Robertson was one of the Channel 8 reporters, the other I've forgotten.

The drive over to Oak Cliff where the officer was shot was precarious because the traffic was stopped in some areas, and not in others. Vic and I were screaming "Stop! Stop!" as we went right through intersections as fast as we could.

When we arrived, we talked with one of the eyewitnesses, Helen Markham, as well as to Callaway and a guy named Guinyard. We also talked to the Davis sisters who were either half-sisters or step-sisters or something. They lived in the house right there and had seen the suspect leave the scene.

That's one of the things that you don't catch in these conspiracy books: You don't really see the overwhelming case in the killing of J.D. Tippit. You just don't see that five, I believe it was, of these people picked Oswald out of a lineup that day, and one didn't because he said that he was afraid. Maybe he was, I don't know. Mrs. Markham described the suspect fairly well. As I wrote the next day, she told me that he was maybe chunky or something to that effect. As it happened, I guess his jacket was out and he looked a little heavier as he was running. But we also had descriptions on the police radio from Brennan; so we had some idea.

I remember seeing Assistant District Attorney Bill Alexander at the scene. Bill's got a good nose, and after somebody had said, "I think he ran in there," we went into an old furniture store looking for the suspect. Furniture was stacked everywhere in this old ramshackled place. I was there with Bill and five or six officers; all had guns except me. All of a sudden someone fell through the second floor. I remember screaming as I was scared to death! But it turned out to be nothing; he probably hadn't been there at all. Some have questioned why an assistant district attorney like Bill Alexander was there. While it's true that he had no reason to be there with a gun looking for whoever had shot the President, at a time like that, things do change and people run after whoever they think did something.

At any rate, I then went back to an FBI car outside that place and heard an announcement: "Suspect has entered the Texas Theater." I'm not sure how far that was, maybe four or five blocks, something like that, so I ran to that location.

When I arrived at the Texas Theater, I ran into Jim Ewell again. We decided that he'd go upstairs into the balcony since somebody had said that he'd gone there. So Jim went up while I decided to go down and under, and maybe I could see from there what was going on in the balcony. As luck would have it, I just got in there when I saw officers coming off the stage on both sides. I don't recall the exact number, but I wrote about it all 29 years ago. They paused and talked to some other people on the way up so that he wouldn't become alarmed and try to escape. But when one of the officers, Nick McDonald, got to Oswald, Oswald hit him as he came into the row. Had it not been for the other cops coming from behind and grabbing Oswald, I think that he would have probably pulled a gun and shot and killed him.

But it was over in an instant. The thing that I remember most about that is that immediately, as soon as they got him, Oswald started screaming, "I protest this police brutality!" I've never forgotten his exact words, "I protest this police brutality!" Then they whipped him out front and put him in the car.

Jim Ewell had ridden over in that car, but he didn't get to ride back in it. The strangest thing was that one of the Homicide guys, I don't remember which one, kept putting his big Stetson in front of Oswald's face as the cameramen were shooting pictures. I don't know whether this was a normal arrest or not, but it was fast.

Out in front of the theater there must have been somewhere between 100 to 200 people, a lot of them shouting, "Get him! Kill him! He shot an officer!" Word got around quickly, though I don't think that anybody thought that he'd shot the President at that time, I really don't.

After the arrest, I talked to the concessionaire, Butch Burroughs, who had been selling popcorn. I don't recall the exact number of people who had been in the theater, but the number was in the teens. I interviewed a couple of them, but most had left in a hurry after the arrest. I didn't really follow up that aspect of the story since I had seen what had happened.

Later I got the addresses of Tippit and his partner, maybe from Ewell, I don't recall. In any case, I also learned of a couple of addresses where Oswald had lived from the police officers after they had gotten back to the police station and had gone through his wallet. So I went to visit where he had lived before.

When I arrived at Oswald's rooming house, the only thing left in his little eight by eleven room was a banana peel. I was looking for anything and everything. However, the lady there, who later died, offered me the register book signed "O.H. Lee," but I didn't take it. It would probably be worth $100,000 today!

I talked to her that afternoon, but then she later changed her story tremendously when some of the conspiracy theorists got to town and started offering money. When you pay money, you get what you pay for. You word your questions the way that you want a response, and people are smart enough to know that if they disagree with you, you may not come back and you may not pay them again. Sadly, many people have made a lot of money out of this thing, and it's contorted the whole story.

She told me that day that Oswald came running in while she was watching television and that she tried to talk to him about the President being killed. He didn't want to talk, so he went in, changed his jacket and ran out. She then saw him run off the porch to the left and that was the last time that she saw him. See, there's no mention of what she came up with later that a police car came up and honked and all that crap. As we know, there was no police car with the number that she came up with for one thing, and secondly, it was at least three months later that she concocted that story.

But this is the way with so many of these witnesses. If you got to them that day, they were stunned and told you what they really saw, although, as I've said, some of them were even making up stories then. But it wasn't all devious. Some of it is just that over the years they have seen so much conspiracy and seen so many things that, in many cases, they now believe it. In the last year or two, I've had two or three public officials who were involved in this tell me that "Maybe I might need to rethink this." It's amazing to me, but it happens. I don't know how many people were in Dealey Plaza, but if they ever had a convention, you'd have 10,000 people there!

After I came back to the office that afternoon, I started writing. We all wrote most of the stuff which was put together into one major story by Paul Crume, who was a tremendous writer. After I'd written that and a couple of side-bar stories, it was 9:00 or 9:30. Then I was told that I had to go out to the Tippit home and do a story on the Tippit family. All the cops were there, and I talked to his partner and best friend all through the years. I said, "Look, I don't want to go in and bother his wife. I just don't want to do it. Tell me what you can and I'll just get out of here." I was embarrassed about having to do that.

After that, I began to think that we needed to know how Oswald had gotten from one place to another and how it had transpired. So Larry Grove, a reporter for the *News*, and I started working on escape route stories. Five days later we did a massive story about how he had gotten out of the Book Depository, where he was, what he did, the bus, etc. We didn't get any tremendous detail, but we disclosed for the first time the bus driver, the cab driver, and all the people that he encountered along the way. That was in the paper before the Warren Commission was ever formed, and it stood up quite well.

I remember that we chased down the cab driver, Whaley, who was off duty in Denton, and we had a little trouble finding the bus driver, McWatters. It took us time because the FBI and the local police were saying to people, "Don't talk! This investigation's open. It's serious. Don't talk to anybody!" So in those first few days it was really tough!

Meanwhile at City Hall, we had a press room on the third floor right next to Homicide. I was in and out that weekend, though not a whole lot. When I was there, it was just total chaos! It was horrible! With the 200- and 300-pound television equipment and cameras, people could have gotten crushed going down that little hallway. Why they brought Oswald through that, I'll never understand! Every time they took him in and out of Homicide they went through that.

I thought it was rather dangerous because anybody could have poked Oswald in the nose, and some people were angry enough to do that. I thought the police chief, Jesse Curry, who was very weak and ineffective, should have blocked off that whole damn floor. That situation should never have happened. If they wanted to bring him out for arraignment or for a press conference, that was one thing, but to drag him through there all the time was inexcusable. People actually got hurt. I know of people that actually got hit in the stomach or in the head with equipment. It was just a melee!

I called into the office once or twice, but was pretty much on my own. You know, you don't know how to cover something like that since it only happens once in a lifetime and your gut reaction sometimes takes over. But that was the strange thing about it. I did that for several days, and then after that, could never get unassigned. From then on, forget the science.

On Sunday morning, somebody at the newspaper called and told me that there had been threats to take Oswald during the night, that everybody was up in arms and that they were going to transfer him from the city to the county jail. It was about 9:00 o'clock in the morning and I said, "My God, you mean they didn't move him in the night? That's what they should have done!"

"No, he's still there," I was told. So I turned on the television and they were waiting to move him after 10:00 o'clock. I raced to my car and drove like mad to get down there.

I said to myself, "This is ridiculous! Now with the crowd anticipation, if anything's going to happen, it might happen."

When I arrived from the Commerce Street side down by that armored car, they checked my ID twice, and they started to a third time before I was let in. I had no idea how they were going to use it because armored cars in those days had turrets on top and you couldn't back it all the way down and squeeze it into the basement. I just got there in time to see three or four newspeople, but nobody knew when he was going to be moved. Then, all of a sudden, the lights went on and there he was! I had only been in the basement four or five minutes at that time.

I don't know how many people were in there, maybe 50 to 60, but as you faced that doorway where Oswald was brought out, I was standing at 7:00 o'clock behind a couple of cars.

As he was brought out, I just heard a pop and a couple of people go "Ahhh!" What followed was almost a comedy. You know how it is in the cartoons where they get into a fight with the road-runner and a couple of others and they're all in a fall going crazy; there's a foot and there's an arm? That's the way it almost was, briefly. I saw this gun a couple of times come up with someone's hands pulling it back. It was amazing! Almost like the capture of Oswald, once again, it was over before I knew it.

I tried to interview people down there but it was tough to do. They didn't want to talk about it at the time. Cops were running in different ways; newsmen were all doing their own thing. I had watched them as they had taken Oswald out, so I tried to figure where they were taking Ruby and how to get in to that situation. I remember running outside and seeing one guy who was running out of the building and somebody, BOOM, hit him and knocked him flat! He wasn't involved in it and was just running out to call his wife to tell her what had happened.

The question that developed was: How did Ruby get into the basement? I understand fully well that people say that it was a million to one shot that he could have gotten in the way he did, and I think that's true. But had it been a conspiracy, Ruby would not have slept till after 10:00 o'clock when he got a call from Little Lynn in Fort Worth. He told her, "All right, I'll eat breakfast then go down and send you a Western Union money order," and he did. He went down, left his dog in the car in the parking lot, and sent her the money order stamped at 11:17, went out onto Main Street and saw the crowd gathered around the ramp entrance. This was when they were pushing back the crowd to allow a police car out the Main Street ramp. He saw the crowd and obviously knew what it was about.

So why did he have the gun? He always carried a gun. At that time, there was sort of an unwritten rule with the police: If you were a businessman and you carried money, you could carry a pistol. But when he saw the crowd, he walked right in and couldn't have gotten in more than two or three minutes before it happened. And I'm sure, in his testimony, one of the cops saw him, didn't know who he was, but saw this guy coming down the ramp. It's been so many years that I've forgotten his name, but he had a choice to make: He could stop the one man who's running down there, or he could let the whole crowd go and go after the one man. It was a judgment call.

The word in Dallas that morning was that Oswald was to be moved at 10:00 o'clock. That's what the police chief told all the locals and the networks and everybody else. In fact, I remember his saying, "Hey, y'all go home and get some sleep. We won't move him. I promise you that we won't move him before 10:00 o'clock." He should have moved him then and not made that promise.

I didn't like Jack Ruby at all and had known him for years. He was a whiner, a show-off, a showboat, a despicable person and not a very nice man. He was also a guy who would beat up on drunks. I once saw him beat a drunk over the head with a whiskey bottle in 1962. I was actually going to testify against him but had to be in court and the charges were dropped, and I've never seen those charges since. But all this guy tried to do was bum a quarter from Ruby, and he hit him with a whiskey bottle and cut his head open.

I was there that morning when Jack came into the *News* as he often did, about once a week to see Tony Zoppi, the entertainment editor, to try to get something about his clubs or his entertainers in the paper. About once a week you'd see him in the cafeteria about the time we all drank coffee, around 10:00 or 10:30. That morning he got some eggs and bacon and went to a table or two away from me. I've often thought that I could have changed history had I just grabbed him then.

As much as I may have disliked Ruby, if he was going to be involved, he wouldn't have slept past that time unless you believe that the police chief, the Homicide chief, and the postal inspector, Harry Holmes, who just decided to question him one more time, were involved in calling Jack Ruby with the thought: "They're setting up something. We must hold him. Jack won't be up here till 11:17. Now we've got to hold up!"

And I know that there are those who would say, "Yeah, that's what happened."

As soon as I got back to the *News*, the Jack Beers' photo had been printed. My God, everybody went crazy! "Look at that!" many were saying. "Two seconds before!" As I understand from Bob Jackson and others, when they saw this damn Beers' photo, they thought that Jackson's photo wouldn't be any good because it was taken after the fact, and they almost didn't develop it immediately. See, this was on the wire long before it was in the papers. When they saw that that afternoon they thought, "Geez!"

As a reporter, I encountered numerous rumors and allegations regarding this whole story. Again, you have to consider that people were making up stories even then. I remember another reporter from Houston called me and said, "I'm on to this story about Oswald being an FBI informant. I've been told that he was paid $200 a month. I even have his payroll number." I was busy at the time and told him that I'd have to call him back. I talked to this reporter three or four times. One day he called and I was on a deadline, was also a stringer for *Newsweek* and was doing something for a London newspaper, as well. I had all kinds of telex numbers and all sorts of projects at that time and knew this reporter to be less than believable.

He had done a lot of things that I wouldn't have and was known to take short cuts. In any case, he called and said, "I've got his payroll number, and I think he's CIA."

I said, "Yeah, I've got his CIA number, I think."

"Oh, let me have that," he said. So I gave him the S-172 number which came from a combination of a bunch of things I had to mail to various publications. After I gave him the number, he said, "By God, yes! Yeah, that's his FBI number." Then he gave me the CIA number. This was the week of the assassination because I think it was printed in the *Houston Post* within days. That's where the S-172 number originated: I made it up!

Later, Bill Alexander was asked about it and a deputy sheriff said that he'd heard it, too. When Henry Wade was questioned before the Warren Commission, he said that he had worked informants when he was with the Bureau and that they didn't always have a record, but they always had a number. A rushed trip to Washington was made after this story came out in the *Houston Post*. Texas Attorney General Waggoner Carr, Alexander, Henry Wade, and I think Bob Storey, who was an adviser from SMU, were all flown up for a hurried conference.

I think that one must realize that there's never been a homicide put to this kind of scrutiny in the history of the world. Circumstances being what they are now, it's much easier to do this. In addition, we had several things in this story that you didn't have in some others: You had a very popular president killed by a fool, a nothing, and then you had him put to death by another strange individual, who at the time, dreamed that he had Mafia ties. Those two people, Oswald and Ruby, were two that no sensible organization or person would ever ask to do anything and could imagine that they would follow through on and not tell somebody about it an hour later.

You also had the specter of Russia. When we learned that he'd been to Russia, that made everybody think: "Well, how in the world? And he has a Russian wife!" In 1963, the Russian connection was really scary.

In the immediate time period after the assassination, I don't believe that I had any contact with Oswald's wife, Marina, or his mother, Marguerite, since they were ensconced at the Inn at Six Flags in Arlington until Oswald was killed. But in the years following the assassination, I had many unpaid interviews with Marina Oswald. I don't think that's possible today. I remember talking to her during the Ruby trial, a very long interview, where she said that she didn't want him to get the death penalty.

I felt sorry for her; she was scared to death, was in a foreign country and really didn't speak the language that well. But she learned fast because she was interrogated a lot and made several appearances before the Warren Commission. She's had a rough life. One of the amazing things is that she has two girls by Oswald and has raised them in fine fashion. They're good, young, smart girls, and I can only imagine the pressures that she has had in raising them. But I've only talked to her once in the last year, and she didn't want to talk to me then. She disliked me very much at one time because I printed Oswald's Russian diary.

I've never told anyone how I obtained the diary. There's been speculation that an FBI agent gave it to me, that Bill Alexander gave it to me, and Henry Wade, as well. All of them deny it. All that I will say is that it came from someone who was just a little concerned that his Russian background might not be completely given to the American people. That's where it came from!

Marina got $20,000 for the diary. I put in an expense check to *Life* magazine and told them to pay my expenses which were slightly over $2,000 and said, "But Marina owns this; you've got to settle with her. You've got to agree before I give you the copy." So they paid her the money for something that she'd never seen.

Over the years, I also became well acquainted with Marguerite Oswald, Lee's mother. She was a very bizarre woman! She said, "Lee Harvey, my son, even after his death has done more for his country than any other living American." She had that inscribed on a plaque, as well. Fifty of them were made, and she sold them to reporters that came from all over the world who felt sorry for her. Marguerite probably made Lee what he became. When he got out of the service early because of an injury to her, he stayed with her only three or four days, then took off for New Orleans and got on a ship. He couldn't stand her!

Anyone that was around her echoed the problem. She wanted money for everything. She used to call me and say, "We could go on these town hall meetings in Los Angeles. Will you go with me?" When I would tell her, no, she would then accuse me of everything under the sun.

I remember one time I wrote a book review about Oswald based on a book by one of the early French or German writers. The author said that Oswald was a CIA agent; he was an FBI agent; he was involved in the Dallas Citizens Council and all that. I said in the review, "How's that for a guy who in his diary couldn't even spell "wrist?" He spelled it "rist."

Oh, she took great umbrage at that and called me for weeks saying, "I just think it's terrible your making fun of my son because he couldn't spell "wrist!" You know that he worked for the FBI," and on, and on, and on. One of the best studies on Mama Oswald was Jean Stafford's book *A Mother In History*.

I had dinner with Jean the night before she went over to Marguerites the first time. She was scared to death! And after she got back from visiting Oswald's grave, she was still scared and called me, saying, "I've got to get back to New York!"

I asked, "When's your flight?"

She replied, "I don't know. I'm just going to the airport. I told her I was staying at the SMU Faculty club."

I said, "But there is no SMU Faculty Club."[*]

"I know and she'll still find and get me," she said. She was really scared! She said, "I'm going to leave my tapes with Braniff. Will you pick them up and keep them for me till I get back to town?" So I sent them back to her two or three weeks later. She was that afraid of her!

The news coverage came under criticism at that time, and certainly there could have been improvements. But remember that this was the first time that this had ever happened at a time when you had cameras and press people there at the scene, and I think they did a credible job. In those days, you didn't have as many really good television reporters. Now you do. And most of the television reporters had been newspaper reporters. This was sort of the beginning of the first decade or so of television influence. Now you have people coming right out of college and starting into television as a career, and they're much better qualified, and a lot more competitive. But we still see television news as a dumping ground for every conspiracy, every allegation, every false report and everything else, and I don't know how you ever get around that. I don't think you do. We have freedom of speech and freedom of the press, and we pay mightily for them.

One of the stories which lacked credibility was the mysterious deaths of witnesses which broke in *Ramparts Magazine* and was done by Penn Jones. Poor old Penn didn't know how to investigate the death of anybody. One guy was killed in a raging head-on crash which I suppose means that they have kamikazes out there to kill people. I don't think anybody ever accused that guy of being involved in anything, but I know that some

---

[*]Actually, there is an SMU Faculty Club. However, it has no provisions for lodging.

investigators in years since have said that there was no autopsy in that case, but there was.

But even then, and I can't recall whether it was 60 or 80 deaths at that time; it's probably 200 or 300 by now, but who are they talking about when they say "close to the Kennedy assassination?" They're talking about all the police, the FBI, the CIA, the State Department, the people that worked at the Depository Building and all the people that they knew, everybody that ever worked with Oswald, the Paines and the people they knew, the people at the Texas Theater, the press, the people in New Orleans, and the list goes on and on. They're talking about thousands and thousands of people who could be said to be "close to the Kennedy assassination." So the fact that a few hundred have died does not suggest that they're all that mysterious. They're talking about reporters who don't know how to report and who don't know where to go to get this information.

Mark Lane is a good example. Mark Lane came to me first when he hit town years ago. I don't know why; I guess because he saw all the stuff I'd written in the *Dallas News* early on. He told me that he wanted to be the devil's advocate for Oswald, which I thought was fine. He was a lawyer from New York; I knew nothing more about him, so I gave him 60-70 documents. The next thing I knew he was in Copenhagen, London, and Prague opening up Who Killed Kennedy Committees waving these sheets of paper I'd given him. They were actually eyewitness affidavits which are now all in the Warren Commission volumes, but at that time nobody in Dallas had them or had used them. This was in December 1963 or January 1964. Lane said to me, "Thanks a lot. Maybe you could be my Dallas investigator." Then I remember very vividly what he said, "No one will have to know." I understand that now because nobody wants to be affiliated with such trash!

I don't think there's a good reporter on earth who wouldn't give their eye teeth to break anything approaching a conspiracy. If I knew there was a conspiracy, I'd be a millionaire tomorrow and would be living on the French Riviera the rest of my life. It would be the culmination of a rather good career that I've had. But I don't care how much you might believe it, want it, need it or anything else, at some point you have to be honest and say, "I really don't have it." This is what the conspiracy theorists won't do. As long as they can make a few bucks selling a new conspiracy, they'll be with us forever. And the sad thing about it is that people that really know, the police officers who investigated it and the newsmen of those days, if they don't agree with these new conspiracy theories, they're called CIA plants, FBI informants, or cover-up artists.

If you were on the scene and investigated the crime, or you were an FBI agent, or you were somebody involved in officialdom, nobody believes you because of where you came from. There are hundreds of conspiracy books, and there are probably a hundred different conspiracies. People are raised in this country to believe that there was a conspiracy. When I tell people that I don't see a conspiracy, they look at me like, "Well, you old relic, you fool. You must work for the FBI or somebody." That's why most don't go back and talk with the people who investigated it. The theorists would say, "Well, what did you expect him to say?" It's like David Belin, who's a top notch lawyer who makes tremendously good points, but nobody believes him. He was a Warren Commission counsel, so who believes David Belin? Sad, but true.

There's another fellow here in town, Bob Gemberling, who was a former FBI agent, who actually put all the stuff together and sent it to Washington. He was the one that coordinated it. Bob is striking out in the wilderness: "Wait, but you don't understand!" Nobody gives a damn. He's an FBI agent, what do you expect?

And I've been lumped in the same way. "Well, he was with the *Dallas News* and obviously he was in on the cover-up and has made some money out of this." I'm very aware of the criticism, but I don't pay much attention to it. I don't see a lot, but people tell me about it.

Other writers like Earl Golz have fared better with the conspiracy theorists. I had already left the Dallas newsroom when Earl was writing about the assassination. Earl has better vision than I; he sees people in trees and up behind culverts and things like that. I just have never seen as well as some others.

Now I do think that there are some whom I have encountered over the years that are truly, almost patriotic in their quest in believing that there was a conspiracy. I know three or four of them in particular who believe that they are doing the right thing, and I admire them. Then there is a cadre of others out there that are purely greedy and opportunistic who are a bunch of liars; they know it and so does everybody else, and they're all on each other because they all can't make a living out of this. So there's a great disparity there and a great argument among them. But when you tell people, as I have done over the years and shown them where they were wrong, and still twenty years later, they use that same incorrect material, then I have to think that that's being dishonest. As inundated as we've been for the past 29 years with almost nothing but conspiracy, nothing else sells. I tried to sell a book years and years ago just setting some of the story straight by showing where some of the early opportunists came from and by showing how they either falsified evidence or bought the interviews or whatever, and nobody was interested in publishing it.

While at *Newsweek* a few years later, I was assigned to cover the Garrison case in New Orleans. Garrison was one of the sickest people that I've ever known. There's no doubt in my mind that the man was insane! Despite being brilliant in many ways, he knew the arts, famous things in history, and he was learned. The man was a devious, nasty man who committed more crimes in his investigation than anybody that he ever accused.

He charged Clay Shaw with being involved with the Kennedy assassination March 1st of 1967; he was acquitted March 1st of 1969. Garrison arrested Shaw mainly because he was pressured by mostly international and some *Life* magazine people to do something. When he arrested Shaw, he had one witness, one witness: Perry Raymond Russo. Garrison had known Russo eight days at that time. Russo rode in from Baton Rouge and said that he knew David Ferry, who had just died, and that he thought he knew about some pot sessions of that sort. When Garrison sent "Moo-Moo" Sciambra, his investigator, up to Baton Rouge to interview him for several hours, he came back with this long, lengthy report. Nowhere in it did he mention Clay Shaw. That only came after he was hypnotized three times the first week that Garrison knew him. If you look at the transcript of the hypnotic sessions, you'll find that they asked, "Who is that big white-haired guy, Clay... Clay? Who is that? Could that be Clay Shaw?" That is how they got him, under hypnosis, to finally say that it was Clay Shaw that he had seen. He took sodium pentothal twice in addition to the three times that he was hypnotized. On the basis of that, Clay Shaw was arrested. That whole thing was so bizarre!

Garrison did a lot to keep Perry Russo around for a while. His office had one man charged with a crime, burglary or something of that sort, when they knew they'd never be able to prosecute, but they were trying to keep him from going into the Army because he was Perry's best buddy. Perry told me that himself, and I researched it, as well.

They also tried to get a man to plant evidence in Clay Shaw's apartment. This man, who was a cat-burglar, passed a polygraph test. They took him out of jail; the reason being that Garrison had something on the sheriff at the time, as well as the governor. Strange case, Louisiana politics. But he was a total fraud and a criminal!

He had nothing at all! There was nothing there that withstood any cross-examination. He made it up! The jury came back with an acquittal after one vote after almost a two week trial, longer than that counting the hearings. Almost all the witnesses have since agreed, "Yes, well, they did ask me to say that."

Garrison didn't have the emotional ties to the assassination that we had in Dallas. Dallas was in the throws of grief for a long, long time, and it cost the city not only financially, but in the spirit of the city for a long, long time. Nobody wanted to touch it; nobody wanted to talk about it. At the time, I was an officer in the Dallas Press Club, and we had this Gridiron Show every year where we would poke fun at politicians and newsmakers as well as the biggest things that had happened. I was head of the script committee in 1964, and we had to do one of those shows without mentioning the assassination. Think about that! It was one of the hardest things to do that I can recall. It was a real toughie because there was nothing else of any value newswise that went on at that time. Everybody acted as though it didn't happen, and those that did talk about it were castigated by others. Then there was sort of a cleansing period. After Memphis and Los Angeles, people saw that it could happen elsewhere. They didn't make the same mistakes, but it was in hindsight, and Dallas helped in that respect.

Now there is new leadership here along with a new influx of people, and it's gone almost to the opposite extreme. They laid down for Oliver Stone. I used to hear people say, "Well, my God, there's nothing to hide. He's just going to do a legitimate story on this." But when I learned that he was doing the Garrison story, I knew there was no way that anything legitimate was going to come out of it.

I think there'll probably be more films made because people see that they can make money out of it, but they'll never get the carte-blanche that Stone received. They opened everything to him by stopping traffic for days for three or four hours a day in about a fourth of the downtown area, and I think they learned their lesson on that, but too late. Martin Jurow, the famous producer of "Breakfast at Tiffany's" and several other good movies, warned them: "You should see the script before you open up your wallet, your life, and your heart to these people."

I was amazed that Oliver Stone, whom I don't care much for but thought had some sense, would choose Garrison as his vehicle in the making of his movie "JFK." I was really amazed! I've always said that Stone got two things totally right: the victim and the date. After that, it goes downhill.

What Oliver Stone and the other theorists fail to realize is that everybody makes mistakes. Several years ago I talked to Mr. Kelley, who was the head of the FBI at one time, and we discussed why the FBI, and Hosty in particular, didn't inform the Dallas police that Oswald worked along the parade route, especially since the Dallas police at the time were going as far out as 75 to 100 miles to visit known dissidents to tell them not to come here and not to cause any trouble on this trip, but Hosty just let this information sit on his lap. Kelley told me, "Well, as I recall, we didn't want him to lose his job."

I said, "Well, Mr. Kennedy lost his!"

Everybody makes mistakes: the FBI, the Dallas police, etc. There was no way that Oswald should have been pulled through that crowd; no way that he should have been moved in public. None of that should have happened. You didn't see it happen in Memphis or Los Angeles or in any of the other assassinations. But people learned from Dallas; this was the learning ground, unfortunately.

The mistakes we now make are different. However, we still allow a president to walk among people where it isn't safe, but what do you do? You can't put him in a glass cage; this is America. And I'm sure that we'll see the shooting of another famous person again because this nation is in some chaos now, both economically and philosophically. In many ways, we're at a turning point. I think the fact that every time someone shoots someone that coverage is far more than these nuts would ever get in any other way brings out a lot of crazies. They see themselves on the cover of *Time* and *Newsweek* and the subject of documentaries for years afterward. This, to a deranged person, is a real opportunity!

I didn't pursue this story and wasn't assigned. I did what typically a reporter would do: I reacted, followed it, and went after it for a few months. And all during this time, I covered every manned space flight that we had in the '60's, everyone, as well as many other things. This was not a career for me, but I was always pressed into it. I went to *Newsweek* for several years where I was a bureau chief and had to cover the Garrison case and everything else. Then I went to the *Washington Times* and had to cover it there. I'm still with the *Times* and every time something comes up about Kennedy I have to cover it. People come to me all the time. I just have to beware because it's such a charlatan's game. I haven't done it by choice. That's why I have never really written a book on the subject. I'm sick of it and would love to just say, "This is the last thing I'm ever going to do." But as long as I'm a working newsman and people are buying my expertise and I'm told to cover this, I have to do it. But I'd love to walk away from it, and I've felt that way for many years.

Hugh Aynesworth lives in Dallas and still covers national events as the Southwest Bureau Chief of the *Washington Times*. He has also co-authored five books on true crime.

JAMES W. ALTGENS
Eyewitness

"I think that the majority of these people who spend their time writing books on this particular episode of history are fiction writers. They don't know and cannot evidently stay with the facts..."

Born in 1918, James W. Altgens is a native Dallasite who earned a degree from Southern Methodist University after his discharge from the Coast Guard in 1945. For several years following the war, Altgens supplemented his income by doing television commercials and working as a model for newspaper and magazine ads. By 1963, Altgens had worked as a photographer for the Associated Press for about twenty-five years. On the afternoon of the assassination, he was standing on the south side of Elm Street near the presidential limousine.

Being in Dealey Plaza that day was an act on my own part. At that time, we had a large number of people that we could use as photographers, and we had them scattered all over the city. My duty was going to be as photo editor which meant that I would be in the office. I would have helped the other people bringing in their film, processing it, printing it, putting it on the wire, and writing the necessary caption material for it. A number of the newspapers in Texas and surrounding states who could not afford wire photos were given a mat service, and we had a deadline in which we had to do this because, otherwise, we might miss the deadline of the newspapers themselves. We had to check the post office, make sure about the pick up time and, of course, you've got engravings to be made and mats to be pulled. So, my suggestion to the bureau chief was that someone ought to be down at the Triple Underpass because we had no one there; my reasoning being to make something pictorially graphic like a scene with the city in the background and making it from atop the underpass. It didn't sell too well the first time around. But after some consideration, he said, "Well, I tell you what we can do. We can bring the night photo editor in early and that would release you around eleven o'clock to go over there and shoot whatever pictures you can and then come back and help at the office."

It was necessary for me to make news picture selections and get them off to the engraver before I could leave for my assignment at the Triple Underpass which would be somewhere between 10:30 and 11:00 A.M. The night photo editor then relieved me, as promised, at that time so that I could make my assignment.

So, my original intent was to make my picture from the triple underpass, and I would have done that. That was the first place that I went. But the police chased me off because they said that it was private property: It belonged to the railroad and unless I was a railroad employee, I would not be allowed to stay up there even though I had credentials. At that time there was no one up there other than the police: one on each side of the underpass. I tried to argue my case, but they wouldn't listen. I showed them my badge to show that I was accredited which would allow me on the parade route, but they said, "Sorry, but it's still private property, and no one's allowed up here unless you're with the railroad." So, I went on over, came through the School Book Depository parking lot area and came on through Dealey Plaza and down to the corner of Houston and Main Street because I knew that the caravan was coming down Main Street, would make a turn at Houston, and then go to Elm, and Elm under the Triple Underpass on out to the Trade Mart where he was to speak.

While I was at the corner of Main and Houston, there was a young man who suffered what appeared to be an epileptic seizure. It was a most unusual time because there was a civilian and a policeman that came to the fellow's aid as he was rolling around, and they thought he was going to roll into the lagoon. Should he have done that, he probably would have drowned. So they held him down, and somebody produced a stick or something to put in his mouth so he wouldn't bite off his tongue. The policeman* near where I was standing, who was on a three-wheel motorcycle, said, "We'd better call an ambulance!"

"Not a bad idea," I said. So, he called for the ambulance, which a short time later came up the wrong way on Elm with its sirens and lights going since I guess they knew that it would be difficult to come through all the crowd up town. As they picked him up and as the ambulance was leaving, you could then see the red lights of the President's caravan making their turn onto Main Street headed our way. So it was good timing on their part to get there and pick the guy up and take him to Parkland Hospital, as it turned out, the same hospital where Kennedy was taken.

At the time, I didn't realize there was any kind of news interest involved in the incident, and there would not have been had the President not been assassinated. Epileptic people are all around us and these things do happen, and they're not newsworthy. I don't think the seizure was contrived as some have speculated to create some type of diversion.

Later, the FBI came out here, and one of the questions I put to them was about this fellow that had the epileptic fit. And they said, "We had a hard time finding him because when they took him out to Parkland Hospital, he had recovered from his epilepsy, refused to be treated, and just got up and walked away." So, he said, "We had a pretty hard time finding him, but we finally did get in touch with him." I've heard stories about this incident, but they don't make any sense. I would say this fellow certainly had a very dynamic case of epilepsy because I know I wouldn't care to go through what he went through. I could tell that he was in severe pain. Anyway, I didn't do anything in particular as the motorcade approached. I just started getting into position. I was standing there where this policeman was also stationed, and you could hear on his radio all the things that were being said back and forth in connection with the caravan and instructions to various officers and such as that.

I had two cameras but time to use only one. They were hand cranked Nikorexes, which is a product of Nikon, and I had all my lenses: one, I think, a 50 in one pocket, a 28 in another, and then

---

* Sgt. D.V. Harkness

I had the 105 on the camera. As it turned out, I didn't have much time to do any changing of lenses. If I'd had a zoom lens, that would have been much better. But I didn't, and the 105 is what I used throughout.

The first picture I made was down Main Street. Sometimes those don't always turn out very well because of the shadows of the buildings, but I thought I captured them pretty well as they made their turn onto Houston Street even though there was a wind blowing about that time. We had had a bad day up until the President's party arrived, and the sky was clearing and, usually with this, you get strong winds to push the clouds on to a different area. So you had a pretty strong wind and, as the President's limousine came around the corner, I had what I thought was the perfect picture. Before I could snap it, Jackie Kennedy raised her hand to catch her hat because it was about to blow away. So I had everybody looking right into the camera except for her. In fact, I got a picture which shows John Kennedy actually waving into the camera. That was the last good picture that I made before the assassination.

After I had made my pictures at Main and Houston, I ran down to get ahead of the caravan again to make additional pictures. I happened to look up at the Triple Underpass, noticed that it was loaded with people, and I thought, "Well, there sure are a lot of railroad people out there on that underpass." How many were legitimate railroad people I don't know, but the police were still up there. It would be hard to say how many people were there. It was just a blob. You could grab any kind of figure and go with it because there were some people behind people, and it would be difficult to come up with a number.

But anyway, I took a diagonal run right across Dealey Plaza, as I mentioned, so I could shoot additional pictures of the caravan. I thought I could have possibly still been able to get the scenic picture I wanted but that never developed. Instead, I was able then to make the picture that turned out to be the first shot that Kennedy received. What prompted me to make that picture was that I heard a sound which sounded like fireworks. I couldn't see because it was some distance up away from me. So I thought, "Well, I'm going to make the picture; the picture then will show if it is fireworks up in that area."

I was using a 105 millimeter lens, which magnifies; it compresses the action; it brings the cars closer together, so there was more space between them than what the picture indicates. But using the 105 millimeter lens gives you that kind of distortion, and yet, it was all I had on the camera at the time. So I just put the camera up in that direction and made the picture so I would have some idea of what was taking place up there since I was downhill and couldn't see from that vantage point, as Elm Street slopes downward.

The picture showed the School Book Depository; it showed the officers on motorcycles there flanking the caravan and the lead car. Behind that is the President's limousine with the Secret Service men standing on the running boards. And as you look on back in the caravan, there's LBJ and Lady Bird and another car back behind which I think had some of the politicians in it. You can see the School Book Depository on the left hand side, and on the right hand side, the building across the street from the School Book Depository and some more people out on the fire escape wanting to get a look.

That picture created a great deal of controversy. There is a man standing on the step of the School Book Depository, and I am told that they enlarged this because they wanted to make sure that it was not Lee Harvey Oswald that was standing out there on the step. A strange thing about this: This man was wearing a sports shirt that some of the so-called experts believed was the same kind of sports shirt that Oswald was wearing. It created a rather strange situation because CBS, Walter Cronkite of CBS, came down to Dallas and did enough material to do four nights on the assassination coverage, and they had me down at the television station for over four hours that evening.

They were really nice to me at CBS. They sent me some things to thank me for spending my time down there; I think a bowl and some things from Neiman Marcus and so on. I didn't ask for it, but I was glad to get it. And yet, when this thing appeared on CBS, I don't suppose I was on there for more than five minutes. And I thought this was rather strange because they had four hours of information on me somewhere in their files. But I didn't question it; I sort of let things go. And then one day I got a phone call, it was on a Sunday, and this man identified himself as Lovelady, the very guy that's pictured in that particular picture.

I had made every effort to get in touch with him after this matter surfaced about him looking so much like Oswald, and he wouldn't even return phone calls. But the office said if I was ever able to set it up, do it. But I was never able to do so. Anyway, Lovelady called me, and he was telling me that he would like to have a print of the picture that showed him on the step of the School Book Depository. He said, "I've written to the Associated Press to get a copy, and they will sell it to me for $100, an 8x10 print." And he said, "I can't afford that much." I told him, "Well, Mr. Lovelady, I cannot get you a print off of the original, but we have what we call a monitor negative from the wire photo. If you will tell me how many prints you would like to have, I will give you those prints in exchange for an interview and a picture session with you."

"No way! No way!" But, he asked, "What would it cost me to get one of those prints?" I said, "It would probably cost you about five dollars plus sales tax." "I would like to have it. Deliver it to the Houghton-Mifflin Publishing Company," which was located here in town. He said, "My wife works for them and just go in and tell them that you've got a package for me. The money will be there, and they'll take the package from you." And I told him, "Well, I hate to lose touch with you here because you're a very significant part of this story. You had a lot of people asking whether that was Oswald on the steps of the Depository." I remembered that the *Oakland Tribune* was one of the very first newspapers to notice the similarity between he and Oswald. He absolutely refused!

When I went to deliver the print where Lovelady said his wife worked, I approached a woman who appeared to be a receptionist. "I have this package for Mr. Lovelady," I said. "I've been expecting it," she smiled. "But," I inquired, "I have a little request of Mr. Lovelady. My nephew collects autographs, and he has given me a postpaid envelope for his autograph."

"He won't do it, Mr. Altgens," she said firmly. "Well, it won't hurt to try," I pleaded. "He won't do it, Mr. Altgens. I'm Mrs. Lovelady, and I know he won't do it!" "Now, Mrs. Lovelady, I'd like to have some more information about you folks," I responded. "The very short information I got on the telephone with Billy Lovelady didn't tell me too much about him. What is the hang up here? Why are you being so secretive?" She said, "Well, I'll tell you, we've been run out of so many places where we have lived, and it's all because of that shirt he was wearing. At this time, I've got it locked up here in the safe at Houghton Mifflin Publishing Company. People break into our home looking for that shirt. We have moved to about five different places, and they find us every time. Another thing about our privacy," she said, "I'm divorced from a big old Swede up in Montana, and he didn't like the idea that I got a divorce and married Billy Lovelady. And he has threatened that if he ever catches up with us, he's going to kill all of us. That's another reason why I would like to be very quiet about where we are and what's going on."

So the Loveladys wanted to keep a low profile since she felt the threat was real and was certainly not interested in putting themselves to the test once he learned where they were living. Lovelady had told me when we were talking on the phone about the CBS thing. He said, "I had to get a judgment against them. They had promised me when they came here that they would pay me for the two days I took off work; they promised me they would give me a copy of every movie or video tape that was made. They didn't do any of that! And they never paid me for those two days when I took them around and answered their questions." And so, he said, "I had to get a judgment that would restrict them from using anything that would relate to me in the production."

So that explained why, after all the four hours that I spent down there at that television station, that only five minutes of that appeared on the program because Billy Lovelady had this judgment against CBS. So, CBS still has an awful lot of material in their files up there and are unable to use it because of this judgment. Bob Jackson, whom I knew quite well, was given permission to photograph Lovelady. Jackson was the Pulitzer Prize winner who made the picture of Oswald being shot. I think the *Times Herald* put a strong bit of pressure on Lovelady by offering him money if they would permit Jackson and a reporter just to have a few minutes with him. And that, to my knowledge, was all that ever made print.

Whatever the *Times Herald* paid for that bit of information and the picture, I don't have the foggiest idea. I only saw one picture, a mug shot, with a very brief story, but I'm sure that they made more than one. As to that picture, I couldn't see that it showed too much of anything. The shirt itself was sort of like a black and white pattern, and if you're using a flash or making the shot at a distance, it doesn't show up very much for what it really was. Mrs. Lovelady told me, "I hated that shirt with a passion. I told him if he don't throw that shirt away, I'm going to burn it." But she said he still would wear it. She said the shirt wasn't worth two cents, but it was his favorite shirt. That's why he wouldn't throw it away. Later he may have realized there was some kind of value to the shirt. He also may have been trying to make money judging from the statement he gave CBS.

When the Loveladys, including the two daughters by the previous marriage to the Swede, moved from Dallas to Colorado, the often sought shirt that he was wearing on November 22nd, 1963 went with them. Within a year Billy Lovelady died from a heart attack. I suppose his widow still has custody of the shirt that she never liked, especially now that it has some historical significance.

In any case, when I saw that there was nothing else that I could photograph, I ran back to the AP office. As I went in, they said, "Let us have your film." And I said, "Here's the camera." I called the bureau chief and told him what had happened.

He replied, "How do you know the President was shot?"

And I told him that I was there and had been taking pictures. He said, "What else did you observe?" I replied, "Well, I was waiting for Jackie Kennedy to turn my way so I could get a picture of them together when the President was hit with the bullet, but I never took that picture. I was all prepared to take it, prefocused and everything, but I was so shocked at what took place that I never took it. When Kennedy was shot, and as some of the flesh parts came over in my area, Jackie Kennedy, then seeing what had happened, said, 'Oh, no!' and she jumped up and started going around in circles on the deck lid of the limousine."

So the bureau chief said, "That's all I need," and he put a flash out on the Kennedy shooting with the fact that Jackie Kennedy had said, "Oh, no!" That lead on the story held, I guess, until the Oswald shooting. So, I was the first to report the story, and an eyewitness at that, and also the first with the pictures. Our pictures were on the wire within fifteen minutes after I got back to the office. The reason they moved so rapidly around the world was because, once it was known that there had been an attempt on Kennedy's life, they tied all the world's networks together. When you moved the one picture, it not only went to the USA, but it went all around the world simultaneously. Later that evening we were getting pictures back from Africa and London showing headlines of the newspapers and using the pictures that I had made of the assassination: very rapid transmission of pictures and story.

But the events were happening so rapidly. The key pictures that I recall making included the turn at Main and Houston, and then the picture where the Secret Service man is going over the back of the Presidential limousine to help Jackie Kennedy back into the limousine. It was a rather startling thing to see happen. It is my recollection that it was that same agent (Hill) who reached down into the floor of the car and came up with a machine gun, and I thought, "My God, don't start spraying all of us around here!"

At that point, from the car radio came the report: "We've been hit! Get us to the nearest hospital!" And they took off like a bullet, cleared that Triple Underpass and headed on to Parkland.

I only recall seeing the President hit once that I can vouch for because that first camera shot, due to the distance, and since I was taking that picture just to verify what was going on when I heard what I thought was a firecracker, made any definitive conclusion uncertain. But this particular one where he was hit, the head shot, was obvious to everyone that it was a shooting, not fireworks.

I don't know how many shots there were. If I were guessing, I would figure that was probably the third shot. In other words, he was hit when I was taking the picture, and the fatal shot should have been somewhere around the third shot, and that should have been the last. But the head shot is the one that I recall because it was very graphic.

The tissue, perhaps bone, a lot of fragments, all came my way. It came in my direction because I was standing right by the curb area on the south side of Elm Street which means that it came right across Jackie Kennedy, perhaps fifteen feet from the limousine, some of this, of course, falling in the car, some out of the car. But the majority of the mass that was coming from his head came directly like a straight shot out my way on to the left in a straight line. When he fell over into her lap, the blood was on the left side of his face. There was no blood on the right hand side which suggested to me that the wound was more to the left than it was to the right.

I've had any number of people ask me if the President was dead at the time? Well, you'd never know because this is a technicality. Brain dead is one thing that they seem to use as a means of determining whether or not a person expires. No one would know that unless you're a doctor. I would say, from the damage that was done, he would have to be dead or in the process of dying because that was a very severe injury, especially with the loss of all the cranium and blood. What happened at that particular moment was utter confusion within the car. I didn't know that Connally had also already been hit by that time.

There was no other reaction inside the automobile that was visible except for Jackie Kennedy. And since Jack Kennedy had a back brace on, it made good sense to me, as I learned later, that he didn't fall over when he was shot the first time because the brace would have held him in place in that seat. So the brace really did him a disservice; it held him up as a target so he could be shot again and again. That impact to his head was quite powerful. It was like on contact it exploded and drove him forward and released him from the cushion as he fell toward his wife.

I'm sure that Jackie Kennedy went right out of her mind at that particular time because of seeing John Kennedy with blood on his face falling down into her lap. There was an awful lot of blood coming out, and she must have felt that she was in the middle of a disaster, and on impulse from fear, attempting to save her own life, she went crawling out on the car's rear deck in the hope of escaping danger. Obviously, she was scared out of her wits. It's peculiar what runs in your mind at times like that. That's got to be a terrible time. I would think, if you're normal, that's something that you would always have to live with.

At the time the President's limousine took off, there was confusion. I saw some officers in uniform, some in civilian clothes, some with drawn pistols, some with rifles come running toward what they call the knoll which is close to the railroad track. I was across the street from this activity and thought, "Well, I'm here for the purpose of making pictures. If they've got some suspect cornered, I want to get his picture." So I ran across the street and started up after them and met the whole gang of them coming back down. Somebody had evidently said, "There goes a suspect!" or something, and these guys took off running. They never had a suspect, but they didn't realize they had no suspect till they got up there and there was no one around. So there was quite a bit of confusion immediately following the shooting because everybody was looking for the assassin.

Immediately across from where I was standing there was a man and wife with their two children.* When Kennedy was hit with a bullet, he just turned around and swept the whole family down on the ground, and he went down with them. I imagine this was good thinking. If there are any bullets whizzing around, you don't want to be a standing target. I think most of the other people were just stunned. They stood around; they didn't move. It was just unbelievable what had taken place. Not that many went up the knoll. I think at that point in time people were scared. They didn't know where the gunman was; they didn't know if there were going to be additional firings, and soon they just began to drift away. The only ones that were left around there were the newspeople.

I didn't remain in Dealey Plaza any longer than I had to since I realized I was sitting on some pretty hot stuff and, after running after those policemen up to the knoll and back again, and seeing nothing of importance that I needed to, I grabbed my gadget bag and headed back to the office because I knew if the pictures I had were of any value, we needed to get them on the wire just as quickly as possible. As it happened, I made it back to the office in ten minutes or less, running all the way. I had a green light at every intersection, and the elevator was waiting for me at the first floor as I got into the building. So everything worked out really well. In addition, I later received a $500 bonus not only for just the pictures, but it was also for being first to report the story because it gave us a very good edge. I'm sure they made that back in the first one or two pictures that they sold.

I was sent back over to Dealey Plaza later that evening to make pictures of the School Book Depository so our New York office could diagram the movement of the vehicle, where the assassin's nest was located, and all of that information was fixed by the art department. In that way you could take a look at this, and you could see exactly what had happened. I even had to

---

* Bill and Gayle Newman with their two sons.

correct them on that because they had the Presidential limousine traveling in the right hand lane when, in fact, it was traveling in the middle lane. So they had to redo their art work on that. But it made a very good graphic display for the benefit of those who were not familiar with the area.

As many know, Abraham Zapruder made a movie of the assassination. Eastman-Kodak, at the urging of the Secret Service, offered to screen the movie for the news media. New York AP had the local photo editor and another photo editor brought in from Los Angeles to see the film and bid on still rights of the film. AP was out-bid, but an AP member, *Life* Magazine, was successful, and they, in time, allowed AP a one-time use of the pictures.

On that same night of the screening, I returned from City Hall with film made by our Austin photographer of Oswald being interrogated and was greeted by the Los Angeles editor. "We are lucky to have you on the payroll," he said. I asked what he meant, and he said that in looking at Zapruder's film, "The trajectory of that bullet: had it gone just a bit to the left of Kennedy's head, you would have been the victim." I replied, "How about that; an unknown newsperson dead instead of the President!" So, you get to thinking about things like that. It's just one of those narrow escapes.

When the Warren Commission convened, I thought it was rather strange that they waited so long to interview me. Matter of fact, I had touched base with my bureau chief two or three times asking him if perhaps I ought to call the FBI or the local police or someone. He said, "No, your pictures, all of them bear credit. We have put out a story on you and where you were and what you did. It's no secret, and if the FBI, Secret Service, or any of them want to get in touch with you they know where to do it because you work with us. We don't volunteer information. If they want information, we're available, but we don't go volunteering."

In May 1964, while the Warren Report was still being assembled, Don Bonafede, a reporter for the now defunct *New York Herald Tribune*, called me from here in town and said that he was in Dallas to do a story on a very controversial photograph I had made at the time the President was assassinated. All he wanted to know, he said, was the information I had already given the authorities, and he would be satisfied with that information. I told him that no authorities had questioned me, including the Warren Commission people. "That's my story!" he shouted. Of course, he was referring to the picture showing the questionable person, thought to be Oswald, standing on the steps of the School Book Depository. As a result, after two long phone sessions, he produced a pretty good account that appeared in the *Sunday Herald Tribune Magazine* on May 24, 1964. This story set the authorities to work, and eventually even the FBI sent two men to visit and interview me. What had happened was that Bonafede's story was picked up by columnists all across the country who then began asking if other witnesses had been overlooked like the photographer who was only fifteen feet from the limousine when Kennedy was killed.

While the FBI agents were here, they asked me for certain bits and pieces of things that I happened to have. Most of the valuable information was in the custody of the Associated Press. But I had a report on my activities on that day that was sent out by the New York office and some other stories, and I had copies of some of those things which I showed them. They said, "It indicates to us you were all over the place."

And I said, "That was my primary reason for being there: trying to find the suitable place. If they had left me alone and left me up on the underpass like I originally wanted to be, then it would have been far better for law enforcement people because I would have had better pictures for you." When you're in an elevated position, you cover a larger area, and this would have been ideal. By being up there, I would have been able to show the sniper; it would have appeared in the pictures I would have been taking. But denied that, and having to work on ground level as I did, and all of the natural interferences that I encountered, it didn't come off as well as it would have had I been up on the underpass.

Following the FBI visit, I soon heard from the Warren Commission requesting me to appear at the Federal Building in Dallas to give my deposition, which was included in the official report. This was done with Arlen Specter, later the senator from Pennsylvania. I didn't feel that I was being intimidated. Looking at this from a legal standpoint, he was trying to get the facts, and he was trying to get them in some kind of order. I've had some people tell me, "I have read your deposition, and it sounded like

Arlen Specter was really hounding you, harassing you." At that time, I didn't feel that it was coming out that way. I knew that he was reaching for certain bits of information, and I was trying to provide the answers for the questions he had. The delay in my testifying may have been on purpose to make sure they didn't miss anything. You see, they had so many people on this very large board, the Warren Commission. They had an awful lot of people there that had to study all of this information to come up with a single answer. Some of the skeptics figure it was too large; you had too many people, and you could not come up with a reasonable one answer among all of those members. But it did happen, and it does appear in the Warren Report. I've heard so many of these so-called experts, I call them experts, they're authors, who try to investigate and come up with what their own Warren Report has developed. They will tell you that there were some chips of concrete off of a curb; there was a chip in the windshield of the car and various other things which don't really prove out. They do exist, but they cannot be proven as part of this particular problem. No one can say for sure that the crack in the windshield did not exist before the caravan ever started. No one can prove that the chip off the concrete wasn't there all the time, and somebody just wanted to say, "Well, this is where another shot was fired, and it ricocheted off this area." And there's also been the speculation that somebody hid down in one of those manhole cover locations and came up firing. None of this actually took place. So I think that the majority of these people who spend their time writing books on this particular episode of history are fiction writers. They don't know, and cannot evidently stay with the facts. They've got to do it as television does sometimes: They take a book of facts, and in order to dramatize it, in order to get your attention, they have to write in all of these good fictional things in order to make it sell. I think that a lot of the people that are engaged in doing this sort of thing right now are just plain fiction writers, but they refuse to accept that fact.

Many of these skeptics have said that he was shot from the front. There is no evidence that he did receive any frontal damage; it was all from the rear. Years later, Doctor G. Forrest Chapman of Belleville, Michigan, a pathologist in forensic studies, who had been called to Washington to study the X-rays of

President Kennedy and come up with the final rendition of what these X-rays showed, wrote me for my personal observations of the assassination. He had been requested by the House Select Committee on Assassinations to lend his expertise in the study of autopsy photographs and X-rays of President Kennedy. His findings, according to letters and copies he has sent me, has now been made part of the permanent Congressional Record. One thing he made clear to me was that there was no frontal impact to Kennedy's head, which certainly supports what I have always said that all the shots came from behind the limousine.

The explanation given which looks like a forward impact I think is really unexplainable. I don't know whether it's a body reaction or what it was because, from my vantage point, it was very clear he moved forward and didn't move backward. It's difficult, I know, under the circumstances, to be explicit with your details, but my argument has always been that I knew that the shots came from behind, and my problem was I couldn't find from where they came from behind. I was uncertain as to the number of shots and the spacing of the shots. It was difficult, also, to determine where the shots were coming from because of the echo off the buildings and the reverberations off of the underpass. But I looked back over in the area where the county jail is located and the building across the street from the School Book Depository and everything I could check about the School Book Depository. All I saw were some black people hanging out of windows, but I could not see where the sniper's nest was supposedly located because of that big, giant live oak tree that was between me and that location. That served as a pretty good blind for Oswald, or whoever it was that did the shooting, because it's difficult to see up that way unless you're looking at it from a different location.

I've looked out that window, and you can oversee that tree, and you can see very clearly into that area where he did his shooting. It's just that my position being where it was, downhill and looking uphill, just did not afford me that kind of advantage going back the other way. But he was in an ideal location to do what he did.

In 1965 I was invited by the University of Victoria in Canada to come and speak on the assassination. The AP authorized me to go on my vacation time, and they would pay for the air fare round trip. This university had a multi-million dollar endowment, and they were in the process of building a lot of new buildings, and one of these was this auditorium: absolutely beautiful, with the very latest in photographic materials.

We had a packed house with every seat and every aisle full. Even in the projection room the guy couldn't hardly work his equipment because of people being in there. As it turned out, that was an area where they loved John Kennedy. I spoke for an hour and received a standing ovation. They then took me out the side door where there were two television stations and three radio stations waiting. They asked me, "How in the world did you ever get the people off of the back of Texas because, as they thought, 'everybody in Texas was guilty?' "

I told them, as I have told many people since, that if it had not been for the Warren Report showing that Oswald was not a Texas native that we would probably have to live with this condition. But the fact that it was proven that Oswald was not from this area, and he was the assassin, then that took the heat off Texas.

I don't suppose anyone felt worse than the people of Dallas when this took place because every effort was made to put forth a real good effort and show the respect that they wanted for Kennedy. Whenever the word went out that the President had been shot, no one could believe it, absolutely no one, particularly the people of Dallas because they didn't realize that element was here. There had been a lot of talk, of course, but nothing of that nature.

Later, I was sent down to Houston because LBJ was there and also to take a picture of George Bush and his wife voting during his senate race. I got up early the next morning, as I wasn't that familiar with Houston, and went down to the coffee shop. A woman sat down beside me, and after I'd said good morning to her, she said, "Well, today's the big day. Who are you going to vote for?" After I told her that I'd already voted absentee, she asked, "Where are you from?" When I told her Dallas, Texas, she said, "The murder capital of the world! I've got a sister that lives in Dallas, and I will not come and visit her again! What's wrong with you people up there anyway?" Talking loud and ugly, she just berated me!

Finally I shoved my breakfast aside and said, "Ma'am, I'm sorry I said good morning to you! You've ruined my day," and got up, went over and paid my tab and left. So, you see, even within our own state we had all kinds of problems like this: everybody blaming the other party.

A few years after the assassination, my name surfaced during Garrison's Clay Shaw trial. Jim Garrison was the district attorney of New Orleans who was trying to nail Clay Shaw as a participant in a conspiracy for the assassination of Kennedy, which put him in league with Oswald and some other people. Yet, all of the information that had been made available to the media indicated he was going nowhere because, while he was making certain accusations, he couldn't prove them. So, he started fishing around and going to some other people to use as witnesses. In my case, a subpoena was issued to come to New Orleans to testify in the Clay Shaw trial.

I had heard enough about Jim Garrison at that time to realize that it would do me no good to get involved in something he was doing. Garrison's reputation had already been established, and I knew that he would use any devise at his command to find perjury charges against witnesses. I did not wish to go. After all, what else was there to my deposition but the pictures, and that was it.

So, I had to appear before a judge because you cannot be approved to go and honor one of these subpoenas from one state to another without the judge giving permission for that to happen. When I was summoned to the state court of Judge Holland to show cause as to why I should not be required to go to New Orleans, I told the judge that the Warren Report contained my eyewitness account and that I stood fast on that testimony; therefore, there would be no need for me to go to the Shaw trial. The honorable judge disagreed. After looking at my pictures, the judge was so interested in what he saw that he got down off the bench and said, "I want you to go to New Orleans and have a good time." I told him that their stated conditions of meeting me at the plane, keeping me in seclusion until my turn to testify, then returning me to the airport did not sound like a "fun time" to me. He replied, "Well, I think you ought to go. You've got a good set of pictures which proves everything you did, and I'm going to approve it." I noticed that two of Garrison's assistants seemed pleased with the decision.

Under those conditions, with his approval, they gave me a check for first class, round trip air fare to New Orleans. A deputy and two assistant district attorneys from New Orleans told me, "We will meet you at the airport and will put you up in a private location. Nobody will have access to you but the court. And then, once your testimony is over, we'll put you on the plane, and you'll come right back to Dallas."

I knew I was in for a rough time of it. Frankly, I was uneasy and made a fast trip to our AP office, copied my testimony from the Warren Report, and committed it to memory. I wanted to be sure that "Sly" Garrison would not nail me for perjury.

While still waiting to be called for the trial, I was on a brief visit in Houston and ran into Governor Connally at the Fat Stock Show, where he was exhibiting and selling some of his cattle. I had met Connally at his ranch one time when LBJ had brought some mats down and had talked with he and his wife Nellie. I asked about his arm, and he said it was good some days and bad on others; the pain would come and go.

"Have you been subpoenaed for the Clay Shaw trial?" I asked. "Hell, yes, he replied, "and I'm not going. That damn Garrison is a shyster. That was a phony thing all the way through! He doesn't have a case and is doing this just for political gain. I wasn't going over there to testify under any condition because that was a set up job."

I asked if he had received any travel money for the trip to New Orleans. "Oh, yes," he said, acting unconcerned, "but it was only for fifty bucks since my trip is short, round trip from Houston." I told him that I had been given a check for over $300 but hadn't cashed it. He said, "Cash the damn thing! I cashed mine."

About a week or two later, there was a short article on one of the back pages of the *Dallas News*, bearing a New Orleans dateline, that read: "James Altgens and Governor Connally will not be called for the Clay Shaw trial because they have become hostile witnesses. What a relief! I was never called, and they never asked for their money back, so they never got it. That's how that episode came about, and of course, Clay Shaw was found not guilty.

Since those days, I took early retirement from the AP the latter part of 1979, and I've been working for Ford Motor Company in their Display and Exhibits Department out of Detroit. I accepted their work with the condition that they just use me six months out of the year, but it doesn't always work out that way since they have people sick or something of that nature. We do auto shows, state fairs, sports vacation shows, anywhere that Ford exhibits their products. About the only holiday I get at home is Christmas. But I like the work because I have a background in radio and television, and that's how they got me. I've been working with them since that time in various places all around the country.

Whenever I'm home, I still receive calls from all over the world about the assassination. Many of these are from youngsters, some born after the assassination, who are doing this as a term paper or a thesis or something. I have felt that if my contribution of being a witness at this particular incident of history is of any value to these people, then I want to help them. I've turned no one away.

I had this one kid who came here with his mother from Beverly Hills, California. He was the head of a debate team, and they were debating the Kennedy assassination. After I helped him, he gave me credit in a letter: "Without that information, we never would have made it."

So, these are the things that are the payoffs, and it doesn't mean any financial reward or anything like that. But there is a personal thing that I like about it. If I make a contribution and it helps somebody else, then that's great since it would be interesting to talk to someone who might have been around at Lincoln's assassination because what they would have to say would be good for the history books.

James Altgens eventually retired but continued to work on occasion on exhibits for Ford Motor Company. In later years, Altgens, who never sought publicity, became more reluctant to cooperate with the numerous interview requests due primarily to having his words distorted by various writers and news media and also because of certain eyewitnesses who had changed their testimony in recent years, either for publicity or monetary gain. He wanted no part in being associated with such people. Altgens and his wife Clara were both found dead in their home in Dallas on December 12, 1995, apparent victims of carbon monoxide poisoning.

CHARLES BREHM
Eyewitness

"If the assassination had to happen, I'm glad that I was here to see it. This way I don't have to depend on other people, like the rest of the world does, as to what happened in those six or eight seconds..."

A veteran of the Second World War in the Ranger battalions, Brehm is one of the very few to have witnessed two of the epic events of the twentieth century: the D-Day invasion and the John F. Kennedy assassination. At the time of the assassination, Brehm was a carpet salesman for Montgomery Ward at the Wynnewood Shopping Center in the Oak Cliff section of Dallas.

The closest place that I could see the President was here in Dealey Plaza. Also, I was off work that Friday. I was out at the Knights of Columbus preparing a buffet for the following night where I was cooking beef which we would later cool and slice. From my house at that time, it took no more than five minutes to get here.

I parked up on the I-35 freeway, which was not completely developed at that time, and walked down with my five year old boy to the northwest corner of Main and Houston Streets. Main is a two way street as it was then. As the parade approached on Main about two blocks away, the police stopped all traffic, and we were able to move right out in the middle of the street. I had a wonderful view; the first time I had ever seen the President of the United States.

As he turned the corner at Main onto Houston, I looked over toward the Texas School Book Depository and realized that the turn onto Elm would be a difficult one as it was more than ninety degrees, and each and every car would have to make the same turn. I realized, with the slow turn, that I would have time to move down across the grassy median and get another look across from what is now known as the grassy knoll. So, with my five year old boy, and twenty-five years younger and that many pounds lighter, I was able to grab him and run across the plaza to the south side of Elm Street across from the steps on the grassy knoll and probably still see the Presidential parade turn the corner up by the School Book Depository. I ran as fast as I could and, in fact, did beat the motorcade and was down on the curb before he made the turn onto Elm.

As I was standing there, then the parade came around that corner with a wide curve toward the School Book Depository. After the car passed the building coming toward us, I heard a noise, and I say noise. If I wanted to recreate what happened, there was no shot that I could say, "God, there was a shot!" or something like that. There was a surprising noise, and he reached with both hands up to the side of his throat and kind of stiffened out, and you could see as he approached us that he had been hit. Of course, it became obvious immediately after the surprise noise that it was a shot and that he was hurt. And when he got down in the area just past me, the second shot hit which damaged, considerably damaged, the top of his head. Realizing that he was hit in the head, and from what I could see of the damage, it just didn't seem like there was any chance in the world that he could have lived through it. That car took off in an evasive motion, back and forth, and was just beyond me when a third shot went off. The third shot really frightened me! It had a completely different sound to it because it had really passed me as anybody knows who has been down under targets in the Army or been shot at like I had been many times. You know when a bullet passes over you, the cracking sound it makes, and that bullet had an absolute crack to it. I do believe that that shot was wild. It didn't hit anybody. I don't think it could have hit anybody. But it was a frightening thing to me because here was one shot that hit him, obviously; here was another that destroyed his head, and what was the reason for that third shot? That third shot frightened me more than the other two, and I grabbed the boy and threw him on the ground because I didn't know if we were going to have a "shoot'em-up" in this area.

After I hit the ground and smothered the boy, it was all over. The people were running helter-skelter here and there. They were running up to the top of that hill it seemed to me in almost sheep-like fashion following somebody running up those steps. There was a policeman who ran up those steps also. Apparently people thought that he was chasing something, which he certainly wasn't. There were no shots from that area, but some of the people followed him anyway.

In the meantime, I became surrounded with newspeople from the two buses. They selected me to talk. In that group, I was telling them that there were rifle shots and that they came from up in the corner of the School Book Depository or up in the corner of the building across from it. One of them asked how I knew they were rifle shots; was I ever in the Army? And I slid the jacket up and showed them my damaged arm here from bullet wounds and told them that I had been in the Ranger battalions. I had been in Europe from early morning on D-Day till September 16th when I was wounded, had seen considerable combat, that there had been a lot of rifle firing around me and that it wasn't a matter of figuring it out; it was a matter of second nature that the rifle shots came from that area up there.

Then I was taken to and put in a police car up to the front door of the School Book Depository. Being put in that police car was the most hazardous thing that happened to me all day long because the police took me because of my knowledge of what went on and wanted to put me in there so I wouldn't get away. This was misinterpreted by many people on the scene as they had caught the culprit. So, with myself and my five year old boy in the police car right in front of the School Book Depository, people started beating on the car and called me everything but a nice guy.

With the traffic in and out of the Book Depository, I can understand easily, without even being critical of anybody, how Oswald could have walked out of there. I was up there in a matter of minutes after the assassination and people were moving in and out of there. You didn't know the cops from the robbers: people with all types of arms from shotguns to pistols in their hands. It was like a gun show with people moving in and out of the place. From there I was taken over to the jail and kept for a couple of hours so I could answer their questions.

At this time, I might say that I did not stand there, basically, and count shots. There were events that were accompanied by shots, and the events are lodged in my mind more so than the shots because of the President's motion when he was hit, with the shot in the head and the wild shot that was going away from the place; everything that stands out in my mind was a consequence of the shots. I never thought of them as, "There was a shot! What did it do?" It was always, "What happened?" and it was because of the shot fired from up there.

Because the car was a short distance beyond me when it happened and it was moving away, I heard nothing from inside the car. I have to say this: I had tunnel vision at that time. I had never seen a President of the United States. I would not make a very good witness as to what Mrs. Kennedy was wearing or how and when Governor Connally was hit because I was concentrating on the President. He was the center of my attention. That night, when I finally got to the club I was going to, people asked me how in the world Connally could have gotten hurt. Within hours after the knowledge was given to me that Connally was also wounded, I said the only thing that I could think of was that a bullet that went through the President had also obviously hit Connally because there were only three shots fired: one went wild and two hit the President. The question then was how could it have happened? At that time, it was very easy for me to open up my shirt and show the bullet wound in what was the solar plexus, to come over here and show the exit wound where it passed through my body and came out between my ribs; then the second part of the bullet, the damage, because the bullet was softened and out of shape, tore my arm apart.

One bullet did that to me! Any questions that night about what a single bullet can do, my God, I was living proof of it that day!

I didn't see anything isolated when the President was hit. There was just an explosion. It was almost like a pond hit with water and water flew up. Something happened and something flew up, but identification or fragments, I couldn't be certain. I thought at one time that something hit the ground over nearby, but it was proved to be wrong, at least as far as I was concerned. It was proved to be wrong because I never saw anything.

Mrs. Kennedy, the poor woman, and God bless her, she was trying to get out of that car because she was scared to death. She wasn't trying to pull anybody in. She was trying to get out of it, which is to say nothing bad about her because, my God, there's her husband mortally wounded, with fragments of his body all over her, and if she wasn't frightened to death, I can't see how she could have been otherwise.

There is something else I want to mention. Since I have a history of using firearms, people have asked me what my opinion was regarding the ability to fire those shots. I have no doubt in my mind that almost anybody who had basic training like I had in the Ranger battalions would have no difficulty at all. And especially the fellow was in the Marines, who are ordinarily cracker jack people with firearms, would have no problem at all. And I understand that he had a full sling which actually melds the rifle to your body. You become one so that your re-aiming is not necessary. You have the rifle in your arms in the same position. So there's no doubt in my mind that he could have gotten off those shots.

And then you take the matter of the first shot. What happened after the first shot? After raising seven kids, I know that when one of them would act up in the backseat of the car, you turn and your foot automatically comes off the gas pedal; and the fact that when that shot went off, the chauffeur turned and his foot absolutely must have come off of the accelerator, which is further proved by the fact that a Secret Service man ran from the car behind and caught up to it. So, the car absolutely must have had a momentary lull while he looked back. But he did not come to a complete stop. No, not at all! I don't even begin to think that. I think that there was just a moment where he might have taken his foot off the gas which was probably the reason why Clint Hill, I think his name was, was able to catch up with the car in front of him. Other than that, those cars move at a fairly steady pace in a parade. You're not going to run and catch up with a car very easily. So, I feel that that had a marked difference in his ability to shoot a second time without that car speeding up or getting that much of an acceleration. It was only with the third shot that he really had to prove his metal, and he could not do it. The third shot missed because of the evasive action of the car and the speed that it had gathered.

I don't think there was any echo pattern down there where I was standing. I think if the shots would have been fired from an adjacent building up on Houston where you had an echo factor, back and forth, you might. From that spot, it's one dimensional to that window. From where I was, there was none that I could recognize. If somebody went up there now and fired a shot, maybe there would be an echo factor but it was not apparent to me at that time.

People have mentioned seeing puffs of smoke at the time of the assassination. I saw none whatsoever. The smoke that I created through years of cigar smoking would probably account for a puff of smoke here and a puff of smoke there as I went through life. But I sure didn't see any puffs of smoke anywhere; nothing other than the three shots from the same area, and that has been identified to me as that particular window as to where they came from. I would agree with it because of the sound factor. But if they told me today that I was all wrong, that they came from the fourth floor, or the seventh floor, I'd have to believe them. But there's no question in my mind that there were three shots from one source, the Texas School Book Depository, and nothing else from any of the other buildings.

There were no shots from sewers, no shots from the grassy knoll. There were no people hiding around with silencers, which in itself is laughable, because why should this person have a silencer and that person not have a silencer? And if there were nine people, as somebody advocates, why eight people with silencers shooting and only one without one. No, I feel comfortable with myself. I was very uncomfortable until the Warren Report came out because I stood by myself on November 22nd, that night. I came up with the original thought of the single bullet. I said at that time that there were three bullets, and they all came from the same place.

Then all the controversy starts. You don't know what you're letting yourself in for in a deal like this. The controversy starts about this or that extra gunman coming from here, coming from there. All of these things go on and you start to doubt yourself. You say, "Hey, am I right on this thing or what?" People are going to show me movies and tapes and things like that of what I said and they're going to cast doubts. But everything I said was what the Warren Commission said, so I felt that I was clean on it. I felt that they printed the truth of what happened. Conspiracy, before or after, I have no idea. All I know is about those few seconds where I was standing, and that I'm sure of.

I've had one experience with Mark Lane where he did the interview by asking the questions off camera. I saw his movie, "Rush To Judgment," once, and this was less than a year ago. It seems to me that he might have taken poetic justice with some of the questions that he asked or fit my answers to his questions rather than the opposite way of me answering the questions. But that was an unpleasantness because he was the type of person who made you believe that you were helping him when all he was looking for was one piece of junk in that whole new car showroom so he could say, "Ha! Ha! Here's what! The whole thing is wrong because of this!" And that's what he was! He was looking for that junk in some shining place so that he could destroy everything that was worthwhile.

I've had people, because they were from my home state, Pennsylvania, ask to please do it for me, and I came down, met a guy here, and this was just two years after it happened; he showed me a mark over there in the concrete where the third bullet hit and told me how wrong I was... some nineteen year old kid. I had a lot of fun with him because I had taken a job which gave me a new Lincoln Continental every year selling furniture, which is what I was doing all the time, traveling, etc. And I had moved to a different home, which was nice, and I was able to afford. So I told him, "Oh, you have got me! You have got me real good! Now, come on and I'll show you what kind of car I used to drive, and I'll show you where I live." My God, that guy ran back up to one of those tabloids up there in the East and that became the story. He believed it! Unfortunately, a lot of other people did, too.

I've had kids that have said, "Dad, I'm sorry you ever got into this" because somebody would get on the phone and ask if I was around and they'd say, no.

They'd say, "Well, who is this?"

"Well, this is his daughter."

"Well, your dad is a goddamn liar!" And this has gone on time and again. People call up and tell you how nuts you are, that this never happened or that never happened. I had nightmares after the things of the war but nothing related to this. I had some psychiatric care, but I think that's because I'm a little flakey to begin with and not because of anything that happened here. I got discharged from that hospital and got a piece of paper that says I'm sane. I'm one of the few people that's got one that says they're sane.

If the assassination had to happen, I'm glad that I was here to see it. This way I don't have to depend on other people, like the rest of the world does, as to what happened in those six or eight seconds. It's a very unpleasant thing to think of but, like anything else, it diminishes in how terrible it was over a period of time. I've seen people shot in the head beside me who died in a war that we thought was worthwhile. It's always hard to see those just shot, their bodies and personalities destroyed, the pleasure that they could have brought somebody is gone and the unhappiness it causes. But these are just fleeting thoughts that I get when I'm reminded like at this time. Other than that, I drive by the spot many times; I have to. For years, I passed this area twice a day on the way to work and almost got to the point where we forgot where we were passing until you see, almost any hour of the day or night, year in and year out, somebody here. The interest is still here for the tourists.

Our company has been acquired twice, not commercial-wise, but by Ragoo Foods Spaghetti Company which is a part of Cheeseborough Hahns, Inc. After the first acquisition, those people were all interested in coming down here after they looked at our plant and had their meetings. This is what they wanted to see. The same happened with the second acquisition. They wanted to see this. We were later acquired by Unilever which is out of Holland, and they, too, wanted to see this place. So I would think that, forever, this site, the same thing will be going on; people will be talking. When all of us old goats are dead and gone, there will be somebody here with some theory about the shot from up there, or the shot from up there, or over in the sewer. They'll still come up with those things, but there won't be anybody around who was here to say, "No, you're wrong on that."

At the time of the assassination, I was working at Montgomery Ward in the Wynnewood Shopping Center over in the Oak Cliff section. By golly, there was no rest! I had to have some rest because, when it came out that I was an eyewitness, people weren't looking to buy carpet, which I was selling; they were looking to talk with me. It was really bad over there for awhile.

I hate to say this, but I made money out of this thing a few years ago when they were making a film over in London. They took my wife and myself and flew us over there in style, put us up in a nice hotel and gave us $75 a day for meals with a nice cash stipend. It only took me about three hours from makeup until the time I left the studio, which was on the day of the Prince and Fergie's wedding. I didn't get to see it, but my wife did. But it was a very, very nice first class trip. They didn't attempt to coach me for that movie.* All they asked was to tell what I saw and how it was. And in this particular case, they had an adversary there who was going to try to prove me wrong. This was the first time anybody had directly confronted me, and really it frightened me because he wasn't about to take what I said. It wasn't that he had anything that he could disprove what I said, but it was to try to knock down my credibility.

Officially, I was never interviewed by the Warren Commission. I was surprised, especially after I saw all the people that were. I gave only a deposition. Two FBI people came out to my house on the Sunday after the assassination. One of them I happened to know, Joe Hanley. His son and my daughter were keeping company at the time. The Hanley interview was a friendly situation. It wasn't that he was going to try to brow beat me or that I was going to try to fool him. We sat down as people who knew one another and went to the same church, so it was done thoroughly and in good hands. I don't know how I could have covered any more. I was satisfied that I didn't have to go before the Warren Commission. I think possibly some people have been critical of them because I didn't, but I really don't think it was necessary. I don't know how I could have helped them further in any way. Despite all those who have criticized the Warren Commission, I do know this: I was here, and it happened the way I've said, and you can take that to the bank!

---

* Brehm is referring to the docudrama, "On Trial: Lee Harvey Oswald," produced in London in 1986 by LWT International.

Soon after the interview was conducted in Dealey Plaza in the summer of 1988, Brehm retired and remained active in veterans activities for many years. In 1984, he was among the honored Ranger battalion members who met with President Reagan at the 40th anniversary of the D-Day landings at Pont-Du-Hoc in Normandy, France and again in 1994 with President Clinton at the 50th anniversary. He and his wife Evelyn continued to live in Carrollton, Texas until his death in 1996.

RUTH DEAN
Eyewitness

"I was standing there with Madie Reese and Billy Lovelady and several other employees. I remember Billy being there because we were joking before the motorcade arrived. Lee Harvey Oswald was not on the steps as some people have claimed..."

Born and raised in Little Rock, Arkansas, Ruth Dean attended classes and met her future husband at West College in Mississippi. After moving to Texas, she was employed by the MacMillan Publishing Company, the only job she ever held.

I was the bookkeeper and cashier for the MacMillan Publishing Company in 1963 here in Dallas. Our offices were located on the third floor at the Texas School Book Depository. I think there were about seven or eight publishers that were in the building then, but there were other publishers who had their books there but did not have offices in the building. If you wanted the Texas School Book Depository to handle all your shipping for you, you deposited your books with them, when we had sales, and they did the shipping for you.

I had advanced knowledge of the President's visit, but I had not planned to watch the parade. I had seen President Roosevelt probably in 1936 or '37; seeing President Kennedy just didn't mean anything in particular to me.

At lunch-time, one of the ladies in the office and I were going to lunch and were going to stop by the bank and make the deposits for the day. We just happened to be standing on the steps of the Texas School Book Depository when the parade came by. I was standing there with Madie Reese and Billy Lovelady and several other employees. I remember Billy being there because we were joking before the motorcade arrived. Lee Harvey Oswald was not there on the steps, as some people have claimed.

The motorcade, of course, came down Houston Street and then made a left turn onto Elm. The view where we were was very good. But the motorcade went a little bit beyond us before the shooting started. I heard three shots with two being close together and one a little further apart. They weren't evenly spaced.

I remember seeing Jacqueline Kennedy climb over the back seat and on to the turtleback of the car, and the Secret Service man jumped up and made her get back into the car. That's about the most vivid recollection I have of it. I was able to see that reasonably clearly from where I was standing, although when the President was hit, apparently I wasn't able to see that because some of the tree trunks were at that point.

I wasn't able to tell where the shots were coming from. The sounds seemed to reverberate from the buildings around that particular location. I remember saying at the time, "Oh, somebody's going to get into trouble."

It sounded like firecrackers, and Mrs. Reese, who was standing next to me said, "No, that was a gunshot!"

We continued to stand there because it was so quick when all three had been fired, and then we decided we needed to hurry on because the bank was going to be closing. So, we went on to the bank, made the deposit, had our lunch, and came back. But we did talk about it.

As far as the employees of that building, very few of them really knew Lee Harvey Oswald. He stayed to himself. He did not carry on conversation with the people. The only time I ever saw him was when we went from the third floor to the fourth floor in the freight elevator which he was operating for us to pick up some of our books to be shipped from our office. He didn't operate the elevator on a regular basis. We usually just called down to the Depository and said we needed an elevator.

Since it was just a short period of time that he had been there, we felt sure that it had all been prearranged. After that Sunday morning when he was shot, we just felt like we probably would never know exactly what took place or who really was behind all of it. I don't know all of the theories, but I think that it all originated from the Depository.

After all this happened, the Texas School Book Depository continued to operate. In 1971 the Depository bought property off of Ambassador Row and built a building and a warehouse, office space, and all of those who wanted to move to that location went to the new Depository. My particular company decided it wanted to become a regional office, so we built an office building, warehouse, in Carrollton, and we moved out around 1981. The Depository was still operating when we moved.

For a long time after this happened, we would go out to lunch or for any other reason, and there would be tourists out there, and I have heard anything from "They ought to tear the building down and sell the bricks and build a memorial to Kennedy" to "It's terrible that Dallas is such a horrible place that they would have something like that happen in their city," as if it were the fault of the city. This irritated me greatly. I think it was grossly unfair because I know that the majority of people in the city of Dallas loved Kennedy. I think a lot of it is still there because on trips, when they would find out we were from Dallas, that would be one of the first things they would want to know: "Did we see Kennedy assassinated? Tell us something about it."

But I don't know that it has affected me in any way. I was terribly sorry to see something like that happen, and it could have been anybody. Whether it would have been the mayor of Dallas or anyone else, I would still have felt terrible about it. But it was something that I could not prevent, and it really hasn't affected me in any way that I am aware.

Mrs. Dean retired from the MacMillan Publishing Company in the early 1980's. Now widowed, she remained in Dallas enjoying her two main hobbies, dancing and gardening, until her move to Katy, Texas, in the early 1990's.

RUTH HENDRIX
Eyewitness

"It was a terrible thing! I knew he'd been shot, but I didn't want to believe that Mr. Kennedy had been killed. But in my heart, I knew he had..."

Ruth Hendrix began working for Allyn and Bacon Publishers at the age of 18 in 1930. She witnessed the assassination standing on the north side of Elm Street west of the School Book Depository.

Our offices were on the third floor of the Texas School Book Depository at 411 Elm Street as were those of MacMillan and many other companies. For many years prior to the assassination, I was the head bookkeeper and eventually was the office manager.

Texas and California were states that furnished free textbooks which were selected by committees and adopted by the states. The Texas School Book Depository handled our accounts both for the state adopted books and for books that were not state adopted. The non-state adopted books were kept in the building at 411 Elm while the state adopted books were kept at a large building about two or three blocks beyond the railroad tracks at the end of McKinney Avenue. The Depository did our shipping and accounts, receivable billing, and collections.

The Depository had books on the first, fourth, fifth, and sixth floors with its offices being on the second. Our offices and many others were on the third. Ours' were really just promotional offices for their companies. We handled correspondence with the customers and had one of the few offices which did its own bookkeeping. My boss, Steven F. Wilson, called Dutch, had the corner office with windows facing on Houston and Elm, and my office was in back of that. It was an inside private office.

We had all known for days that the President was coming and that he would be out at Love Field. Some of the people in the building had left their jobs and had gone out to see him there when he came in. The other girls who were working out in the front office wanted to go downstairs to see the parade. I hadn't planned to see it as I was busy. It was mid-year which was the time when we determined our profits for the year because the fall was when we did most of our business, and the end of November would tell us about what we had done. I was working hard to get my reports out, and I really didn't have time to go downstairs and watch the parade. I thought I would just look out the window, and then, suddenly, I thought I'd like to see what Mrs. Kennedy was wearing. I didn't think that I would have an opportunity to see it later. So I decided to go downstairs while my boss stayed up in a window and watched it from there.

The other girls had already gone down, so I went down an elevator and out on the street. We knew that the parade would come down Main Street and that it would turn onto Houston, then it would have to turn again onto Elm to go down under the Triple Underpass. The girls were up on the embankment west of the Depository looking down. I stood near a lamp post on the sidewalk near the street about even with the west end of the Depository. I just went down there and was standing on the street like hundreds of other people.

There were people over in the Terminal Annex watching, and there were others in the Criminal Courts Building, the Old Red Court House, as well as the building at 501 Elm. They were all around besides the people on the street. The police had blocked traffic at Elm Street and Houston there beside the Book Depository.

At the time, there was just a lot of pleasantness. We were all happy to see the President, his wife, and Mr. and Mrs. Connally. I don't remember seeing Mr. and Mrs. Johnson. I had seen all of them before and wasn't particularly interested in any of them other than seeing what Mrs. Kennedy wore. I had walked for blocks beside a parade Mr. Kennedy was in years before, and I had seen him for blocks and blocks, so I wasn't trying to see him, but I was trying to see his wife.

But anyway, when they turned onto Houston and then Elm, people were just really happy. The parade itself was going rather slow, maybe seven or eight M.P.H., certainly not as much as fifteen. But it was going fairly slow. When that first shot rang out, I thought it was a firecracker; I really did! I didn't expect anything else. But I knew there had been talk about some tension, and I thought he had gotten through without any problems.

When I heard the shot ring out, I thanked God that he had gotten through without getting hurt. But as I looked, he fell over, and about that time, Mrs. Kennedy raised up and pulled the man up over the back of the car. I saw all of that very clearly, and I saw Mr. Connally when he fell over. With that, they were out of my view and in an instant they were gone! It was just like a streak of lightening! In the meantime, there had been two other shots and everyone knew that somebody meant business. But we didn't know at first that they were targeting him anymore than they were just shooting at random. In all, I heard three shots, and it seemed to me that there was more time between the first and second and less between the second and third shots. I wasn't sure where they were coming from, but I knew they were coming over my head from a high location. You don't have time to analyze a whole lot of things when shots are firing!

It was horrible! People across the street on that triangular parkway just fell to the ground to get out of the line of fire. It was a terrible thing! I knew he'd been shot, but I didn't want to believe that Mr. Kennedy had been killed. But in my heart, I knew he had.

After the shooting, I ran back to the building. I wanted to get to the telephone and call home. As I rushed back to the building, Mr. Campbell, one of those who ran the Depository, was standing outside, and he asked, "Miss Hendrix, what happened? What happened?"

I replied, "I'm not sure, Mr. Campbell, but it's awful!" With that, I got into the building, got on the elevator and went back to the office. That's when I called my mother.

When I called, I asked her if she had been listening to the radio. She replied that she hadn't. I said, "Well, turn it on.

Something very, very exciting has happened. You'll hear about it, but I won't tell you." It hadn't even come out on the radio when I called her because in a short time they had blocked the telephone lines.

A while later we were called in, three of four at a time, and our names and addresses were taken. I don't recall an actual lineup. I guess they did for the Depository people, but I worked for one of the publishers. There was a lot of difference between working for the Depository and the publishers. The Depository didn't have any authority over any of us.

I guess it was the Monday after that that Herb Junker, who worked for one of the publishers at that time and was a good friend to all of us, asked us, "Wouldn't you like to go up on the sixth floor and see where Oswald shot?" Of course, we didn't always say "alleged" because we were so sure that it was Oswald. We went up there and the gun was in place there. He said that Oswald had used an Italian gun. And there was a gun there.* He said, "Look through here." I had never handled a gun, but at that time, you could look from that sixth floor over those trees just like they were shrubs. You had a clear view of the street. Honestly, I believe, with the car going as slowly as it was, that I could have targeted a person and fired a shot, and I'm not a sharpshooter.

They kept a guard at the door of the Book Depository for about two months after this happened. Of course, the guard got to know those of us who worked there in the building. I assume this was just a private security guard who was hired by Mr. Cason. They had a lot of school books on the first floor, and if you didn't have a guard there, with all the curiosity that people have, people would have just been streaming in there. We couldn't have carried on business, and they could have carried out books. They could have been all over the place and no telling what else might have happened. There was even a guard at the elevator for a while and another on the third floor where our offices were.

Roy Truly was one of those who was especially affected by all of this. He was the shipping clerk for the Book Depository for years and years, even back when they were in the Santa Fe

---

* The origins of this gun are a mystery. Apparently, the "gun" referred to by Miss Hendrix was a rifle with a scope.

Building. That was a long time ago. I talked to Mr. Truly several times about this. He told me that he had just said to himself a few days before this happened that, "Oswald is such a good worker. I just wish I had a dozen like him."

They had a lot of young men that they hired for part-time work in the fall when they were real busy, and he was one of them. He'd only been there for a couple of months or something like that. Apparently, Oswald kept to himself and he kept busy. He didn't idle around and he wasn't always playing off on the job. He was busy. Of course, Mr. Truly didn't know about all that he was doing. Part of the time he was setting up that little place for himself up on the sixth floor. There were some Scott-Foresman books there that said "Think and Do." But he had those books set up. He was right in the corner with the window looking across Houston Street, and the people could have seen him from windows in the other buildings. So he had this stack of cartons of books there and then he had a few at the front.

Over the years, many people went up to the sixth floor and then, finally, they just blocked it off and wouldn't let anyone go. They had to; they had to. So many people questioned Mr. Truly about it, and he was so nice and cooperative with them. They ran him up and down those back stairs I don't know how many times to see how long it would take if Oswald ran down the steps. Poor Mr. Truly wasn't as young as Mr. Oswald, and it was hard on him. Mr. Truly really bore the brunt of it and it wasn't fair!

There's been so many people that have come there visiting that you just wonder why they come. Why do they come? Why do they come? They'd stop me when I'd be coming out of the building, and I nearly always had to work late. I just couldn't get through. I had just been delayed and disturbed enough to make it hard. I'd have to get down on my hands and knees to lock the door down at the floor and people would come up and ask, "Did you see the assassination? Oh, where was it?" Sometimes I would tell them and sometimes I was just simply too tired to tell them anything. It worked a real hardship on a lot of us.

Geraldine Reid worked for the School Book Depository. She was a lovely little woman who had a tremendous amount of responsibility. She needed a private office but didn't have one. As I recall, she told me that that day, after this happened, Oswald came out of the lunchroom with a coke in his hand. As he came

by her, she said, "I hear the President's been shot!,," and he
mumbled something and went on out. Geraldine Reid bore a great
brunt of this assassination problem, too. She died a few years ago,
and I think this helped contribute to her death.

Obviously, all of this was very disturbing, especially to the
city of Dallas. But it happened, and you just have to bear it and do
the best you can. I think many of these stories that have been
written about the assassination are morbid. I never did believe
there was anything to them. I think Lee Harvey Oswald acted
strictly on his own. Now, where Ruby figures into this, I don't
know, and I don't know that it matters. It's all over!

At the time of the assassination, the School Book
Depository's lease was about to run out. I think that's why they
built a new building out on Ambassador Row and moved out there.
That way they had room for their state books and for the
miscellaneous stock in the same building. It seems to me that we
moved out there about 1970 or 1971. But I worked out there for
several years until 1977 when I turned sixty-five and retired.

Never married, Ruth Hendrix did volunteer work for the Lakewood
Republican Women's Club and for her church, the Lakewood Assembly of
God. She still resides in Dallas, Texas.

CLEMON EARL JOHNSON
Eyewitness

"You could tell that the whole top of his head was probably missing, and you could see blood and maybe brains and bone. It happened so quickly that you couldn't tell exactly..."

Born in Hopkins County, Texas, one hundred miles east of Dallas, Clemon Earl Johnson moved to Dallas in 1922. After working at various jobs, including the Dallas Gas Company, Sears-Roebuck, a furniture company, Greyhound Bus Company, and as an undertaker, Johnson was hired on April 16, 1946, by the Union Terminal Railroad. After working on steam engines for many years, he was the first man to work on diesel engines for the Union Terminal Railroad in Dallas. It was while working for the railroad that he observed the assassination from the Triple Underpass overlooking Elm Street and Dealey Plaza.

There were between four and six of us that would eat lunch at a place on Jackson Street, and we hurried back up over the underpass where we could see the President come by since we knew the route he'd take, and that he'd come under the underpass. That was maybe ten minutes before he arrived.

At that time, there were only two or three others there but not enough to notice. It was pretty hard for people to get up on that railroad because the police would run them off. But since we worked there, they let us up with no questions asked. By the time the President arrived, I can recall eleven that I worked with that were up there along with two that were supposed to have worked over in the post office that were there with us. I was standing with a man named Simmons, who was a car man. A policeman was also there.

Even though no one was allowed in that area at that particular time, I don't think the police would have run anyone off. They didn't crowd up there. If there'd have been a big crowd up there, he'd have probably made some of them get off. All of us up on the railroad had a perfect view because we were right there at the time this happened.

Just off of the railroad on the side street that comes down in front of the Book Depository, there was a bunch of people. There were quite a few trees, bushes, and hedge, and that's where everybody for a long time thought the shots came from as they saw smoke coming from there.

The President was headed toward the underpass at the time the shots went off. First, you think of firecrackers going off, then, when you see all the motorcycles buzzing around, falling down, turning around, and running into one another, then you could see plainly that the President's head was shot off. Being that I had been in the undertaking business, I could realize just what happened because I had done a lot of post mortems with the head lifted off and the stomach opened up and all that. You could tell that the whole top of his head was probably missing, and you could see blood and maybe brains and bone. It happened so quickly that you couldn't tell exactly. It was just a few seconds and they were gone, but he was right close, and you could see plainly what happened.

I heard maybe three shots; I know two plainly. After the second shot went off, you could tell distinctly that it wasn't a "Baby John" firecracker. You could tell it was a rifle. They seemed like they were spaced almost like you'd expect two shots from a rifle with a bolt action.

The whole affair seemed like it was drawn out, but it wasn't. It all happened so quickly. The car they were in, of course, didn't have a top on it, and you could see four or six people in it. You could see it speed up and then stop, then speed up, and you could see it stop while they threw Mrs. Kennedy back up in the car. Then they just left out of there like a bat of the eye and were just gone.

After it happened, I said, "Well, it's all over now! Let's get back to the engines, because if we don't, they'll all have us in jail right quick!"

They were gathering everybody up, and a fellow by the name of Dodd, and at that time our boss, Holland, went running around to some bushes. They kept saying, "The shots came out of those bushes! The shots came out of those bushes!"

They had turned to their left around into the street that came up beside the Book Depository Building which was put there for the benefit of the railroad. It was there because that's where two of their towers that throw the switches for the trains were located, and that street always had to be there to give an opening in and out to the railroad as they owned that property all around there.

Anyway, Holland was our foreman out on the railroad. He and Dodd went around to those bushes and were taken into custody. And for that, I understand they kept them in jail until around midnight or after before they let them go. But Holland and Dodd, if both were living today, they'd almost fight you that they saw smoke coming from out of those bushes. They swore that they were looking right at the bushes at the time. You couldn't talk to them. Those guy's head's were set.

I didn't have any idea where the shots came from, not even a guess. I was looking down at the President as they came through, and I didn't hardly look up till he was gone. I wasn't looking up at those bushes. I did see smoke, lots of puffs of smoke, but I was of the opinion that the smoke was coming out of those motorcycles. The smoke was coming up off the ground out where the motorcycles were, not on the grassy knoll. A lot of them said they saw smoke come out of the grassy knoll, but I didn't. Maybe it's because they were looking that way, and I was looking down on the car. But the smoke cleared up pretty quick after all the cars and motorcycles left. I've always thought the smoke came from those motorcycles.

After the shooting, we stayed maybe just a minute. We then ran back towards where the engines were as they were leaving at one o'clock. I was supposed to always be there when the engines left to be sure they functioned right, and I had to ride them out. I guess the others were of the same opinion I was: They figured they might carry them in because the police came running up on the railroad and just picked up everybody they could.

Later, they were digging around down there where a woman and a little child were sitting. I think the woman said, "It's a wonder we didn't get shot because the bullet went in right there." They kept digging, and they finally found the bullet. I never saw the bullet dug out of the ground, but I heard a lot of people talking about it.

Day and night for almost a month there were FBI men all over the Union Terminal railroad yards. They stopped every train coming and going for a couple of days. They would shake them down and make the hobos get off. Dallas was full of hobos because they made them all get off in Dallas.

About a week or two later they had all of us that were on the underpass come upstairs in the Union Terminal Building for an interview. That would include two boys named Potter, Dodd, Holland, Simmons, Cox, Doc Halbert, myself and several others. We went up maybe as many as six times to testify. The FBI conducted the investigation upstairs, as I remember. When we went up there, there were three or four or five men. All of them would ask us questions, but not one in particular. They were double-checking our stories.

Sam Cox was a coach cleaner foreman. My chief clerk, Dudley Neath, said that Cox was, at the time of the assassination, down there at the roundhouse in our office way down at the south crossing, which was a long way from there. But by the time everybody told their stories, he knew more about what had happened than everybody else. I think they had him up there two or three times and finally found out that he wasn't even out there at the time this happened.

Sam was a guy that nobody understood. Even Sam didn't understand Sam Cox himself. Later, Sam and his wife were mysteriously killed by gas in their house. But he apparently got his information by talking to everybody about what had happened.

We didn't think much about what the outcome would be. We talked among ourselves about it, then all of a sudden we were warned by somebody to dummy up, that everybody was knowing too much. So we just decided to quit talking about it because we were liable to say the wrong thing. In those interviews, we had to stick to our stories. They figured we were withholding evidence if we didn't tell the same story every time we went up there.

After this happened, I would get an awful lot of telephone calls, and they'd want to come out and talk to me. But I never let anybody come out and talk. I didn't know whether I was talking to the right person or not because of about nine people mysteriously coming up dead over a period of two or three years after that. Maybe that would have happened anyway. But one or two hit highway bridges and were killed; one or two died in their homes like Sam Cox. Nobody knows who came in and turned the gas on. Surely they didn't turn it on and then go to bed with it on. I always wondered if the Mafia was behind that or if there was still somebody else in with Oswald behind that and didn't want any evidence left. I just never could figure it out or why Ruby was in on it. It looks like there had to be somebody in on it besides just those two.

Anyway, I just figured that it would be better not to take any unnecessary chances. But I'm 81 years old, and the Lord has let me live my life span. I have nothing to worry about now. If somebody were to come here and knock on the door and say, "I'm Oswald's friend; I'm going to kill you," I'd say, "Well, you came at a good time. I'm ready."

After retiring from the railroad in 1966, Clemon Johnson later worked as a maintenance man at an apartment complex. Johnson died in November 1996 at the age of 90 after living the last six years of his life with one of his daughters, Inez Roe, in Nashua, New Hampshire.

ROY E. LEWIS
Eyewitness

"Unlike some witnesses, I didn't see any smoke or smell any gun powder, nor could I tell the direction of the shots because it was like an echo there. But no way did I suspect anything coming from the Texas School Book Depository..."

Originally from Carthage, Texas, Roy E. Lewis was married in 1962 and went to work part-time that same year at the Texas School Book Depository. His work eventually evolved into a full-time job. Lewis was an eyewitness to the assassination while standing on the front steps of the School Book Depository.

I was sixteen when I started working there in August or September of 1962 but had told the man, Roy Truly, that I was eighteen so that I could get the job. The peak working period there was mainly in the summer when school ended or right before it started back. But even after that we didn't have any layoffs.

At the Book Depository, we had order pickers and packers. Order pickers would get their assignment orders, take a clipboard, go up on the floors to pick their orders then bring them back down on a cart to put in the packing tape. The packers would then pack them, wrap them, and ship them out.

As I recall, Junior Jarman was the shipping and receiving guy which meant that he would check things out then pack them. Sometimes he would need to fill orders, so we'd all go up on the different floors and bring them back to the first floor. We had access to the fourth, fifth, and sixth floors where all the stock was

located. Our offices were located on the second and third floors
but we never went into the office unless they asked one of us to
come up for something. Besides, the book publishers' offices were
located on the second and third floors, and we didn't have any
dealings with them since they were a totally separate operation.

The main lunchroom was on the first floor, which was also
referred to as the domino room. There was also a breakroom on
the second floor where they had a vending machine and a pop
machine. However, we hardly ever went to that floor, though,
since that floor was considered for the publishers' office people.

Altogether I'd say there were twelve to fifteen who worked in
the warehouse. Mostly the packers stayed on the first floor while
the order pickers were the ones that had access to the upper
floors. Occasionally the packers would go to the upper floors if
they had a mistake or if they couldn't find us, in which case they
would go up and straighten it out themselves. But mostly the order
pickers would go up and fill the orders.

The upper floors were filled with stacks and stacks of books
from various publishers: Southwestern, MacMillan, and Scott-
Foresman. They were mostly all school books.

As I recall, Eddie Piper was the oldest worker there. He was
black as were Troy West, Hank Norman, Junior Jarman, Charles
Givens, Bonnie Ray Williams, and myself. The white workers
included: Jack Dougherty, Billy Lovelady, two brothers named
Frank and Fred, Wesley Frazier, and Lee Harvey Oswald.

Bonnie Ray was a really nice guy who was very quiet. He was
an order picker like me, but he always had the ambition some day
to leave and get another job. He was an ambitious guy and I liked
that about him. Next to me, he was the youngest black worker
there. Wesley Frazier was the youngest white. Junior Jarman was a
little older, probably in his '30's while Hank Norman was a little
younger. Charles Givens, we called "Slim." I imagine that he was
in his late '40's or early '50's when I first met him.

Oswald was quiet, hardly ever talked to anybody, and kept his
head in a newspaper all the time. Even when we were in the
lunchroom together he'd hardly ever talk to anyone. If you'd ask
him to pass you something, he would, and if you spoke to him, he
would speak to you, but that's as far as it went. Nobody made fun
of him; they just joked with him a little. Givens used to tease him,
but he didn't seem to care. He just gave a little smirky smile and

went on about his business reading the paper or something else. Usually he brought his own lunch, hardly ever went out, and he almost never played dominos or talked with the rest of us. We all thought that he was very odd.

He never wanted to get a haircut. We would tease him about it because hair would be growing down his neck. We told him a week or two before the assassination that we were going to throw him down and cut it ourselves, but he just smiled. But he was a good worker, and I don't remember his getting into arguments with anybody.

I've been told that some people confused Billy Lovelady with Oswald, but Lovelady was much heavier, and even though Oswald's hair was thinning, Billy's was about all gone up there.

It was just like a family there. We were all good friends on the job, but after work we hardly associated. But we did have quite a bit of fun on the job racing up and down the elevators to the floors filling orders. Sometimes if you were on one of the floors by yourself somebody would sneak up and you'd never know they were there. They might go up on the floor above you where you'd hear the elevator stop, and you'd assume that they were there. But they could walk down the stairway, and a lot of times they'd be on you before you'd know it. But we did have a fun filling those orders because there was nobody to bother us. Roy Truly would give us something to do and he'd never check on us.

I learned about the President's visit to Dallas on the news and in the newspapers and had planned to see him even though I wasn't that excited about it. To me, it wasn't that big of a deal. I guess that I was kind of different since I wasn't as excited as some of the others.

Due to my lack of excitement, I was one of the last ones out of the building before the motorcade arrived. That's why I wasn't outside near the street like most everybody else. Instead, when I came out, I was standing with some ladies from up in the offices right in the middle of the steps in front of the building that led to the sidewalk beyond the glass door.

As the motorcade came by, I remember seeing Kennedy brushing back his hair. That's when all hell broke loose! I heard BOOM!... BOOM!... BOOM! with the second and third shots being closer together. The people down in front of me hit the ground then everybody started running toward the grassy knoll.

Apparently the people assumed that whoever was doing the shooting might have been over there so I followed them. But before we could get far, a policeman stopped us and told us to go back into the building and wait. They then came in and interviewed everybody and told us not to go back out anymore after that. I don't know if he did it on his own or for the police, but I do remember Truly calling off the names of everybody from a list that worked there. That was on the first floor where a few of us were gathered. But since we could come and go at lunch, you could do whatever you wanted as long as you were back in time. So not everyone was there.

The day of the assassination I don't recall seeing Oswald. If I did, it would have been early that morning; afterwards, I didn't see him at all. How Oswald got out of the building, I don't know. In fact, I don't know how he got from the sixth floor to the second. As I understand, though, he was seen in the second floor breakroom when Truly and the policeman encountered him something like a minute and a half after the shooting. I guess that's possible, but he would have had to have been boogeying. But Oswald was thin so it would have been easier for him because he could skip two or three steps on the way down. Coming from the sixth floor down to the second, four flights of stairs, would have still been tough, though. I never tried it, but I imagine if you were in good shape you could do it. After that, I don't know how he got from the second floor out of the building without anybody seeing him, but it probably would have been easy since there was so much commotion.

Truly never talked to us about it and there was very little talk among the workers after it happened. We were so stunned and hurt, and I guess everybody felt so badly about it. We just couldn't believe that this had happened, and it was especially hard to believe that you worked with someone that they said had done it.

The only one of us that I assume Oswald was friendly with was Wesley Frazier, and that's because he rode to work with him. Wesley didn't talk about him much, but he did say that he asked him what he had in that package that morning, and he said, if I remember him correctly, that it was curtain rods for his wife. He told me that long after this was over.

Eventually I think it was the Secret Service that came out to work and took a statement from me. After that initial statement, none of the law enforcement agencies or the Warren Commission ever contacted me, and I made no attempt to come forward. I figured that they had all the information they needed, and if they needed me they could find me. I guess they figured that I was a small cookie and didn't need me since they already had the most important interviews that were necessary, although I don't think they really put up a good effort to find me. They probably knew that I was on the steps and couldn't give them as much information as the guys who were on the upper floors that heard the bangs.

I'm not sorry about not getting involved. If they had contacted me, there probably wouldn't have been much that I could have told them more than I'm saying now, so my life never changed much as a result of the assassination. Now if I'd have been interviewed by the FBI or Secret Service at my home, I'd have been in the limelight and received a lot of publicity. But the assassination hasn't affected my life because I didn't go through all that like the other guys did. In fact, a lot of people don't even know that I worked there.

Unlike some witnesses, I didn't see any smoke or smell any gunpowder, nor could I tell the direction of the shots because it was like an echo there. But no way did I suspect anything coming from the Texas School Book Depository. To me, a shot coming from behind wouldn't knock your head back like that from the films I've seen. Having seen what happened at the time, too, that's what made me think about the grassy knoll when we ran toward that direction. I thought that maybe there was something or someone there. But to me, that would have been an awfully difficult shot to make the head snap back. You would think that a shot from behind would make your head snap forward. That's what I remember most!

Over the years I've really tried to block that out because it was such a terrible, terrible thing. But every now and then you think about it and it crosses your mind. He was such a good president that you hate for something like that to happen.

Two days after the assassination when Oswald was shot, though I know they didn't let it happen intentionally, I still wondered how that could happen in the police department. I was mad at Oswald at the time, but I'm a sympathetic person, and I hate to see anything bad happen to anybody. But I'm still not convinced that he did it, and because of his murder, it's for certain we're never going to get to the bottom of it. I'll never be convinced that Oswald did it or that he acted alone.

Roy Lewis continued to work at the Texas School Book Depository for three more years. From 1966 to 1970 he worked for Sears, for a trucking firm, Texas-Oklahoma Express from 1971 to 1985, then for Emory Air Freight from 1985 to 1991. After a stint at selling insurance, Lewis has returned to truck driving and still lives in the Dallas.

T.E. MOORE
Eyewitness

"The city of Dallas didn't kill President Kennedy; Lee Harvey Oswald killed President Kennedy....Dallas should not be blamed just because it happened here..."

Born on November 8, 1920, in Campbell, Texas, T.E. Moore moved to Dallas in 1922. After attending Bowie Elementary and Oak Cliff High School, he worked for Henderson Wholesale, a tobacco jobber, from 1938 to 1942 and from 1946 to 1959, interrupted by service in the Army during World War II in the South Pacific. In 1960, Moore went to work as a clerk for Bill Shaw, the District Clerk for Dallas County, at the Dallas County Records Building Annex.

Most everybody downtown planned to view the motorcade as it was advertised some on radio and television. As a result, I knew where the route was downtown. That was really all I cared about. There was a banquet being held in one of the Market Hall buildings, so most of the Dallas County officials and I don't know who else had gone to the luncheon banquet in which I believe the President was supposed to be the speaker. So most of the county officials were gone at the time, leaving just the peons, the employees.

There wasn't anything special going on that morning. Some of the clerks in the upper part of the building that could see the upper end of Main Street were watching out. When the motorcade came into view, they called downstairs so that the offices could be locked and everybody could go outside and view the motorcade.

That's when we went out on Elm Street and down about seventy-five feet to Elm and Houston. We stayed on the sidewalk till the motorcade came around the corner at which time we stepped out into the street cater-corner from the Book Depository six or eight steps so we could get a better view of the motorcade.

The motorcade came down Houston, made the turn as it ordinarily would, came down a block and then made a left hand turn to go down toward the Triple Underpass. There was a highway marker sign right in front of the Book Depository, and as the President got around to that, the first shot was fired. That's when the excitement really began! As he got down a little further, the second shot was fired, and then I believe as it got further down, a third shot was fired. I still believe there were three shots fired.

There's an echo down in that part of Industrial Boulevard. It's rather low down there, and it would cause an echo. I think that's what a lot of people heard was the echo of the shots, at least with the last one. Some people even thought shots were being fired from a manhole, but I never felt that way. Nor did I smell gunpowder or see any smoke. It was too far to smell any gunpowder, and you couldn't see the muzzle of the rifle because he was standing far enough back that it wouldn't have shown.

You couldn't tell exactly where the shots were coming from, though. If I had known, I could have looked up to the corner of the fifth floor of that building and seen him, or maybe seen him. But then, as the motorcade got further down, the echo would be a little different. A lot of people who ran up on the hilly section there thought it came from there, then the motorcade went on further out and it just echoed, I think. I feel sure that there were three shots and they spaced at regular intervals.

Not everybody ran toward the hilly section. The people that were standing along Elm Street going down toward the Triple Underpass probably ran toward the grassy knoll. But a bailiff who worked with me ran into the Book Depository at that time along with some others. I think they might have thought the shots came from there.

When the President went in front of us, you could see him as he was waving. You could also see Governor Connally, but as they got further around the turn toward the Triple Underpass, you could see less and less.

I could see the car when the first shot was fired, which was on this side of that highway marker, a small number sign, and you could still see it a little bit further when the Secret Service man jumped on the back of the President's car. We could see all the way down there.

When the shots were fired, you hoped they were firecrackers, but you couldn't tell exactly what it was. I had been around firearms in the Army for three years, so I was afraid it was gunshots by the way they echoed. I don't think firecrackers would have echoed, not that much.

After the shots, most everybody stood around a few minutes, probably fifteen minutes, and then it was about time to go back to work, which was one o'clock. People then began thinning out and police started arriving. I recall one motorcycle coming up from the triple underpass on the wrong side of the street, and then it wasn't but just a short time till police cars started arriving pretty quickly in large numbers. There was a number of black teenagers saying, "Our President has been killed!" By that time, they had traffic stopped and people kind of congregated, and then a bit later the police started cordoning that area off down there getting people out. I then went back upstairs at one o'clock.

I was working in the 68th District Court on a case we had set for trial that day involving a barber using dirty towels. As the lawyers got back to the courthouse and discussed it, everybody was in accord that they didn't want to try that case that day. So I reset the case and they left. A few minutes later, the judge came back and said, "We won't try anything today. Reset it." I told him that the case had already been reset and the lawyers were gone. About two o'clock all the employees in the courthouse were dismissed. Then, on radio and television, it was learned that the Court House would be closed on Monday.

On Tuesday, when the Court House reopened, large numbers of FBI men started coming around, and they would go to anybody that had seen the assassination, or said they had, and discuss it with them. I don't know of anybody that was pressured into saying anything. They just stood there and took a few notes, then they went to somebody else to talk to them. Of course, a large number of people in the Court House had seen it, one way or another, from the windows or from the street. I think the FBI man I talked to came from Missouri, but they came from all over the United States.

Since this happened, everybody is looking for attention. If they're writing a book or a magazine article, they're looking for something to sell that book or that magazine article. I think that's what happens when they come up with a new theory. They're looking for something. I don't believe them. I believe it was done by one man. I don't know how he got the rifle into the building without having created some suspicion, but I'm of the opinion that one man did it, and I don't think it was caused by any Russians or Cubans. I think there was just one man.

When Oswald was killed, that took care of everything. I was at church on the Sunday that Oswald was killed when they were going to transport him to the county jail. It was just hard to believe. And, of course, it was all over radio and television. It did leave you with a strange feeling.

Anytime anything happens, people, and especially the press, are looking for someone to blame it on. The city of Dallas didn't kill President Kennedy; Lee Harvey Oswald killed President Kennedy. I think most of the people of Dallas would be just as sorry that it happened as anywhere else. Dallas should not be blamed just because it happened here.

T.E. Moore later served as district clerk for two years and later worked at a jewelry store. Retiring in the early 1980's, Moore passed away in January 1994 in Dallas.

BILL NEWMAN
Eyewitness

"It appeared to me that it hit him on the side of the head, as the side of his head came off. I can remember seeing a white mass and then just a mass of red..."

Standing near the curb on the north side of Elm Street, Bill Newman, along with his wife Gayle and two sons, was one of the closest eyewitnesses at the moment President Kennedy received the fatal head wound. The term the "grassy knoll" was coined during his interview on WFAA-TV shortly after the assassination.

I was an electrician and was married with two small children. I was off work that day as I had taken an electrical exam and was waiting for the results of the exam. I can't recall the exact day that I heard of the President's trip, but it was on the news, and the President had been in Fort Worth the day before and that morning at the breakfast. The route of the parade was published in the paper the day before, so we were quite aware of the route of the parade. That morning we all went out to Love Field to see the President and Mrs. Kennedy come in.

There was a large crowd. I remember when they landed, came off the plane and got in the car. I was able to get a real good view of President Kennedy and Mrs. Kennedy. Gayle and Billy were not able to get the view that Clay and myself had.

Since we knew the parade route, we jumped in our car and tried to get ahead of the motorcade, which we did. We parked behind the building adjacent to the School Book Depository and walked down behind the crowd on Elm Street in the direction of the Triple Underpass and simply stopped where the crowd played out. We were familiar with the area and knew that would probably be the last spot where we could see them before the motorcade picked up to get on the Stemmons Freeway to head toward the Trade Mart where the people were expecting the President.

There were a lot of people, the majority being at the corner of Houston Street and Elm. They were five or six deep from the curb, and we just went down through the crowd and walked toward the triple underpass to a spot maybe halfway between Houston Street and the Triple Underpass. We were standing there for probably five minutes or less when the motorcade appeared turning right onto Houston Street from Main.

Of course, the excitement was building because we were going to see the President. I can remember the car turning from Main to Houston Street, making a right hand turn, and then traveling that short block and making a left onto Elm Street. As the President's car started down Elm, the first two shots were fired. It was BOOM!... BOOM! like that.! The first two were much closer together in my opinion. It's hard for me to tell the time frame because my concentration was on the President's car. I'm sure the Zapruder film can tell exactly the time frame. But the first two shots were much closer than the third shot. At that time, I thought someone had thrown a couple of firecrackers or something beside the President's car. I didn't even realize at that time it was gunfire. The President's car was probably 150 feet or so from us at that time. As the car came closer to us, it was obvious something was wrong. I could see Governor Connally; I could see his protruding eyes, and I could see him more or less frozen in the seat holding himself. You could see the blood on Governor Connally and President Kennedy. When the first two shots were fired, he threw his arms up. I believe I said at the time that he raised up in his seat, which I think, in reality, all he did was throw his arms up.

I can remember him turning, looking into the crowd, and just as the car passed in front of us at a distance of ten to fifteen feet, the third shot rang out, and it hit the President. It appeared to me that it hit him on the side of the head, as the side of his head came off. I can remember seeing a white mass, and then just a mass of red. The President fell across the car away from me over into Mrs. Kennedy's lap. It was as if someone had given him a hard shove. It wasn't like slow motion. He went across the seat pretty quick. Mrs. Kennedy jumped up and said, "Oh, my God, no, they've shot Jack!" Then I recall her on the back of the car when the Secret Service agent ran toward the car and pushed her back in.

When the third shot rang out, I turned to Gayle and said, "That's it! Hit the ground!" because at that time I thought the shot came from directly behind us in the grassy knoll area. The only basis I had for that was what I visually saw: the President going across the car and seeing the side of his head come off. The sound played little factor. I believe it was a visual thing at that time. We turned and hit the ground and threw our children down and covered them. We were not on the ground more than a minute or two at the most.

One of the two men in the front seat of the car had a telephone in his hand, and as I was looking back at the car covering my son, I can remember seeing the tail lights of the car, and just for a moment they hesitated and stopped, and then they floorboarded the car and shot off.

It was a little embarrassing being the only two people down there on the ground, although there were others that hit the ground momentarily. I can remember people running past us up over the grassy knoll and back behind the School Book Depository. I remember the men coming off of the car behind the President's car, and I thought they had submachine guns or some type of weapons. Some of them went up on the grassy knoll immediately after the third shot was fired and went back in that direction.

It was very obvious that the President had been shot, and to me, it was obviously a fatal shot. Just a few minutes after the assassination two men came up to us and asked us what we saw. One of them was Jerry Haynes, a local radio and television personality, who was known as Mr. Peppermint. We said that we had seen that President Kennedy had been shot. He asked us if we would go to WFAA, and we left with him at the time. He stopped a car in the street and asked the man, "Would you take these people to WFAA? They just saw President Kennedy being shot!" So we were in Dealey Plaza just a very short time after the assassination. In fact, I would say that we were there less than five minutes.

We didn't run up towards the grassy knoll like the rest of the people. We had started walking up there when they stopped us. A lot of people did run up the grassy knoll in that area afterwards, but we were not as anxious as most of the crowd to try to find someone. I don't know why they were running up that way. Maybe the Secret Service men or whoever initiated it, but I just think it was more or less a crowd reaction. I doubt if the people saw or heard anything up there.

My attention was on the President's car. Actually the action was going on behind us somewhere, so I didn't see any smoke or anybody sticking their head up out of a sewer as some have said. Many people ask me when I say I thought the shots came from behind if I thought they came from behind to my right or to my left, which one direction would put it in the direction of the School Book Depository and the other would put it in the direction of the fence area. I've always just stated that I thought the shots came from behind, and really that holds true with the third shot. It was a visual thing. My opinion is based on seeing the impact of the bullet and its results and also the movement of President Kennedy going across the seat. The main thing for people to remember about us is that our focus was on the car. We saw what happened to the President, but we really didn't see what happened around us. The fact is we were just there.

As to the sound, I couldn't answer as to whether they all sounded the same. I considered the first two shots to have been firecrackers. If I hadn't seen the visual results of the third shot, I might have considered that a firecracker. I wish I could, but I can't really answer if the third shot sounded different. But I want to believe that that third shot came from behind me, and coming from behind me would not necessarily be in the direction of the School Book Depository. There is certainly a reasonable doubt. But I'm also influenced by what I've read over the last twenty-five plus years, so I'd rather not try to lead people in one direction or the other because I think being a witness to the assassination and what I saw, it was more of a visual thing.

Anyway, we were taken to the television station and put on the air. There weren't a lot of people there, nor was there a big crowd reaction, but the people were really moving around.

Everybody was excited and not quite themselves. We were all concerned and excited at the time. If I'm not mistaken, the Julie Benell Show was on. It was probably a typical studio scene or what you would expect a studio to be. Jay Watson, the man who was doing the interviewing, was quite nervous and was smoking one cigarette after another. He seemed to be more nervous than anyone else in the studio.

I still remember the reports coming in that the President had been shot through the back or through the neck and that he was at Parkland Hospital, indicating that he was still alive. When I heard that, that was something entirely different than what I had witnessed. But I found out later that the first shot did in fact go through the President's back. His arms coming up was probably a muscle reaction reflex to that first shot. But I can remember to this day that I was a little confused from what I had seen and what I heard at that moment. In fact the station had to wait for clearance to release our interview. I assume this came from some government agency in Washington, D.C., but there was a time lag before they put it on the national news. Of course, later the report did come in that the President was dead.

After that, we were interviewed on the radio by a big, tall fellow who later played Lurch on "The Addams Family," Ted Cassidy. He seemed like he was seven feet tall. An officer was waiting for us when this was over and carried us to Sheriff Bill Decker's office where Gayle and I then gave an affidavit.

The whole time our two boys, aged two and four, were with us. Of course, they wanted to go to the bathroom several times and Gayle carried them. Each time she had to have a guard with her to go to and from the bathroom.

I believe there were sixteen of us that gave affidavits. We were detained, as I understand, for the purpose of comparing these sixteen affidavits to see if there were any discrepancies or if they had additional questions to ask us. We were there for several hours.

At the sheriff's office, an officer took the deposition; it was just one on one. It seemed like I was in some type of cubicle or small area off to one side. It was not a situation where a lot of people were standing around, though. But the entire group of us was held in the sheriff's office. I remember one gentleman that had walked out of the building next door; he was a businessman trying to catch a plane, and he'd gone inside to see if he could find a pay phone to call and let someone know that he was going to miss his plane as he was going to be delayed in getting back to whatever his destination was. Apparently the crowd thought that he was the one who had shot the President. The way the story went was that they turned on him, and he had to have the protection of the police officers to get away from the crowd.

I won't say that I was in a state of shock, but I was very uneasy at the time. And I was uneasy for several days afterwards because my concern was that someone may have thought we saw something we shouldn't have seen. You know, we could sit on a witness stand and pick someone out or testify against someone, so I had a concern. That we might be in danger was one of the first thoughts that went through my mind. Of course, we have never encountered anything that I'm aware of that would make me uneasy.

On Sunday, the day that Oswald was shot, we were interviewed twice by the FBI in our home. They were very straight forward and very courteous people. They were just seeking information, and there was no rudeness or intimidation at all.

It surprised me that we weren't called to testify by the Warren Commission. Vincent Bugliosi told me in a phone conversation that there were actually witnesses that said the same thing that I said that did go before the Warren Commission and testify. That made me feel a little better because I'd had individuals tell me the reason I did not go before the Warren Commission is because they wanted everything to focus on the School Book Depository, and I would have taken away from that direction.

I wouldn't go so far as to say that there was a cover-up, but you wonder sometimes what the purpose of the Warren Commission really was. I'm so close to the Kennedy assassination, and I've talked to so many people over the years that you just tend to believe that it had to be the act of more than just one individual. I was surprised to find out that all the shots came from the Book Depository. I don't mean to say that when I heard the shots that I thought something was wrong. But never once did I think that the shots had come from the direction of the School Book Depository. I never looked in that direction, and we were standing in the place where it would have been very easy for us to look up towards the sixth floor window. So it raises a reasonable doubt in my mind as to what the sole purpose of the Warren Commission was.

Later Gayle and I were involved in the Clay Shaw trial in New Orleans. I had a very good experience with Jim Garrison. He interviewed me before he put me on the stand. In fact, I was the first witness that Jim Garrison himself examined on the stand. What caught me by surprise was the number of people in the courtroom. I remember telling myself, "Now, you're not going to get excited, and you're going to stay cool, calm, and collected." But when I walked in that courtroom, there were so many reporters and so many people in there I don't believe that I stayed cool, calm, and collected, even to the extent that I don't recall even seeing Clay Shaw in the courtroom. That's something that I look back on and wish that I would have gotten a good look at the man because I was in the same room with him and so close.

As far as the theories are concerned, I'd rather not contribute or speculate. I'm sure that my thinking has been swayed over the years by hearing different versions. The one thing I do want to believe is that it was not the act of a lone assassin, so I tend to believe it was a conspiracy. Whether it was the act of two individuals or how many, I don't know. It's very possible that there was just one lone assassin at the site. I can't tell you how many assassins were at the site; I can't say that someone was behind the fence, and I'm not trying to discourage that theory, that's very possible. But even though there might have been just one person at the site, it does not mean there were not other people behind the scenes.

Overall, I'd say this event has had a positive effect on my life. It's made me realize how vulnerable we all are, even the President of the United States. It's also made me realize that the country can carry on. I remember the first few days how down the country was and really how down Dallas and Texas were. It was a great shock and a great embarrassment for Dallas and for the state of Texas, but we lived through it and the country, I wouldn't want to say is better for it, but I don't think we're any worse for it. It's just part of life. I've met a lot of nice people over the years. I hope that it's had an effect that's broadened my thinking. I try to keep my mind open when talking about the Kennedy assassination, and I'm proud that there are people who are willing to give of their time and their talents to research the assassination.

In the early days, we didn't know what to expect from people. Some of the people we had interviews with were very nice, some of them were a little "kookie." But over the years, the interviewers, I think, have become a different class of people: they're serious research people. It's my understanding that there's still people researching the Lincoln assassination, so the Kennedy assassination is going to be an ongoing research project probably for many, many years. And it was hard for me to understand why, so many years after this assassination, that people just kept trying to dig it up, dig it up. But now I've come to understand that the Kennedy assassination research will be an ongoing project, and no one knows when it will end.

It's easy for we Americans to be cynical about something like this and to get down on ourselves and on the country. But I think it's important for our young people to know that this is a great country and that our system is a great system. It's got its weaknesses and faults, but it's important for them to realize that they live in a great land and for them to strive to be the best that they can be and not to become cynical because this is a great country and a country with many, many opportunities.

In the intervening years, we've raised two sons who are college graduates and we're very proud of them. We've been in the electrical contracting business since 1964. Gayle really runs Newman Electric; she's the backbone of the company, as I'm on the city council here in Mesquite. We're older and I hope wiser than we were then; we've prospered and really had many good things happen to us in our lives.

Bill Newman, now retired from the city council in Mesquite, Texas, still runs Newman Electric in Mesquite, along with his wife, Gayle. Two of the most visible of the eyewitnesses, the Newmans have always made themselves available to researchers and others who are interested in the Kennedy assassination.

MALCOLM SUMMERS
Eyewitness

"I thought it would have been hard for one man doing it all. You hear that many shots that close together, you just don't think about them coming out of one gun..."

Born and raised in Dallas, Summers graduated from Crozier Tech High School, joined the Aviation Cadets in 1944, and after the Second World War, was placed in the Reserves. Called to active duty during the Korean Conflict, Summers served eighteen months in the Air Force. At the time of the assassination, he worked at his own mailing business which he established in 1960.

Prior to the President arriving, I was at the Terminal Annex Building depositing mail. I'm in the mailing business, so I happened to be carrying a load of mail that day. Because of all the people lined up to see Kennedy, I ran over to watch him come by also. I left my vehicle there at the Terminal Annex and then just ran across the knolls and stood on the island right beside the street on the south side of Elm out in the clear and open area till he came by.

I went over just to see the President and to wave to him. It was so close to the time I got there and the time he would be turning the corner up at Elm Street toward my direction that I was hardly there any length of time before they were ready to come down with the advance vehicles in front. In fact, I would have been standing there not more than two or three minutes at the most. I was just barely on time to see it get ready to come around there. I was pretty much alone in that area except maybe two or three feet over was a couple and some people holding their kids. Then up toward the corner, at the intersection itself, there were quite a few people all around. It seemed like a lot of people were getting ready to cheer, but I don't remember anything or anybody in particular. There was a lot of noise with the motorcycle sirens and all that.

The first shot I heard was just after they had immediately turned the corner headed west on Elm Street. The first reaction that I saw when that first shot was fired was the Secret Service men kind of looking around and down at the people. I was of the impression that someone had thrown a firecracker down on the ground and thought maybe it was a prank of some sort. As a result, my attention was diverted away from looking at Kennedy, and I didn't see him reach for his throat. But then it was such a short time that the other shot was fired, then you knew that it wasn't anything like that. Then the third shot came right after that also. I heard three shots altogether and was standing practically right beside the car after he had already been hit just a few feet up above me there. Then, when Jackie reached over and grabbed John, she was saying, "Oh, no! Oh, God no!" or something to that effect. I heard her say it just as plain as anything. I was that close! Then I knew immediately that he had been hit. I wasn't sure particularly at that time because I thought he might have been ducking. When I heard her say that was after the second one had already hit. Apparently, that was the head wound. I'm not sure about which one hit him where.

As to the spacing of the shots, there was much more time between the first one and the second two, the second and the third. They were real close.

When we heard the shots, I saw some people up above me begin to fall down and scream and holler. There was more noise at that time. Then my reaction was to fall down on the ground because I didn't know which direction the shots were coming from. One other thing that caused me to hit the ground was that there was a motorcycle officer who had stopped his motorcycle just a little bit past me and was looking. Matter of fact, he laid his motorcycle down or fell down on it. Probably he stopped and kind of laid it down and looked in my direction. That made me think that there was somebody behind me, and I stayed on the ground. Then there was some hesitation in the caravan itself, a momentary halt, to give the Secret Service man a chance to catch up with the car and jump on. It seems to me that it started back up by the time he got to the car, which made me think he slipped instead of diving. I later saw a picture of where one of them was diving on that car trying to jump on that bumper. He probably meant to dive over and then Jackie was reaching for his hand, the way I saw it.

I ran across Elm Street after all the traffic had passed in front of me. There were a lot of people running toward the railroad tracks which made me believe that they had seen someone going down that way or that they were chasing somebody in that direction. I ran over there also to see them catch that person or see what I thought they were doing. I was just following the crowd at that time.

I had no idea where the shots came from. It all happened so fast! I don't believe I even gave a thought to that. The crowd running in the other direction down toward the railroad tracks made me think that the shots must have come from over there because everybody was running that way. I assumed someone had seen somebody or the officer had.

I was attempting to go down to the railroad yards on that side street when I was stopped by what I thought was a detective or an FBI person dressed in a business suit. This happened right at the east end of the pergola or whatever you want to call it nearer the School Book Depository. I remember that because that was the way I was planning on circling to go down to the railroad tracks. A lot of other people were stopped, too. He stopped us and told us we could get shot up there and to go back. This guy had an overcoat or a trenchcoat over his arm which was unusual, but I also noticed a gun under that person's arm. It wasn't a shoulder holster. It just seemed to me like it would have been in a pocket or concealed under the coat itself. He didn't show any identification. It was only his dress that made me certainly think he was a detective or FBI, one of the two. His was not a suggestion; it was an order that, "Y'all better not come up here. You better stay back because you could get shot up here." Because of that statement, I didn't. I didn't go any further toward that direction, but I stayed maybe another minute or two and saw that there wasn't anything happening. I'd say it was no more than five minutes total time that it took me to run over there, and I probably did a little looking around or something before I was abruptly turned back. Maybe I was trying to look down in that direction to see if there was anybody I could see that they had. But I didn't see anything, so that's when I decided that I'd probably go back. Besides, I wanted to run back to the Terminal Annex and tell the people over there what had happened.

So I went back to the Terminal Annex and told the employees at the post office what had happened, and they were more or less kind of laughing at me. They said I was so white and so scared and were kind of teasing me about it. They thought it was funny because I was so excited and pale. I called my wife on the telephone as they were laughing in the background. My wife thought it was some kind of joke because of the noise going on. I told her, "No, it's true. You need to turn on the radio or TV. There's bound to be something come on in a few minutes." So, upon leaving there after that phone call and a couple more minutes of talking with them, I went and got in my vehicle. It was on the street there that lends itself where you got back out onto Houston Street. I had to turn south onto Houston to head toward my house. I, at that point, decided I'd go home also and see what the late news would say on it. When I got there at the corner and I'd pulled around to my right, which would have been headed sort of southwest, there was a vehicle that pulled out real fast in front of me. It was at the curb at that time. They were right beside me. As a matter of fact, I thought it was a little bit dangerous the way they pulled out when I was right beside them. Then they headed across the viaduct, also southwest. There were three people in the car. At the time, I thought they were Mexicans. I thought it was unusual that they pulled out and sped away as fast as they did.

There was another event connected with my getting home. I happened to live in the 400 block of East Twelfth Street. By the time I arrived home and pulled in my driveway, there were just dozens of squad cars in that area. Then I didn't know what the reason for all that was. Later they said something about this policeman being shot over on the 400 block of East Tenth. So that accounted for why all the squad cars had already arrived in that area. That was just two blocks away. So there really was a lot happening on that particular day, but then, of course, I didn't know about this Oswald in that vicinity or that he was supposed to have shot the officer. I didn't go over to the scene. I didn't even know at that time why they were there. That came on the news later. I had no idea that anybody was shot over there.

About a day or two later I went down voluntarily to the sheriff's office and told them about this event happening. My first reaction was not to. I wasn't involved or anything. But then the three people leaving the post office as fast as they did, I thought perhaps that could figure in some way. As I mentioned, the car was parked in front of the post office. It was a Chevrolet, about a '61 or '62, something like that. At the time, it looked maroon. I don't know what ever became of it.

I'm sure that most people are aware of all the conspiracy stories about the assassination. I don't really have any reason to question it at all. I don't profess to know whether any of the shots came from any other direction. It made me so sick thinking about it and knowing that it happened in Dallas. It didn't concern me that there was any question from where they came. I didn't have any opinion that they would have come from anywhere other than what the facts stated. I just do not want to say that the government investigation was wrong or not. I just don't want to question it.

I don't have any reason to believe that shots came from the grassy knoll. There was nothing that told me that other than those people running in that direction. I presume it was someone who saw somebody and that's the reason they did what they did at the time the motorcycle cop came off that motorcycle. I presumed he was looking at someone behind me. I feel like they were trained to know those type of things. But that's the thing you'd think about in something like that, or maybe he didn't think anything. Maybe he was looking to see if someone was shooting over there. I have no idea about that.

When the President got the head wound, he still hadn't come up to me yet. I was still looking directly at him. Then the third one, he was right beside me or something to that effect. I'd say when he got the head wound, I'm guessing that he would have been ten to twelve feet away. And then the other one came which led me to believe it was several people shooting rather than just one. I thought it would have been hard for one man doing it all. You hear that many shots that close together, you just don't think about them coming out of one gun. That's the only time that I thought perhaps there could have been someone else.

A lot of people question that they could do it that quickly, especially those last two shots. Certainly I had some doubt at that time that they were from the same gun because they were real close. And that's the only time I had any doubts. But it seemed to me like it was unreasonable that the guy would shoot that fast.

It surprised me when I wasn't called to testify before the Warren Commission because I thought they were interviewing all eyewitnesses there. I did have some FBI men come out to my place of business several months later and talked with me about it. I think the first day when they were asking people to come down to the sheriff's office if they had seen something that happened, I was concerned that I would be tied up with questions for so long that I didn't want to. I didn't want to lose that much time away from my business. So I think that was my concern until I got to feeling remorseful about the fact that possibly the information about the three guys would be some help to them.

I worked for a newspaper for twelve and a half years prior to starting my own direct mail business, and I grew slowly. Since that event, it hasn't figured in any of my business relationships with anybody, although it's certainly been a conversation piece over the years about my happening to have been there. I've got a couple of *Life* magazines where my picture appeared. I kept them because I felt that sometime my grandkids would enjoy seeing them and knowing that I was there when it happened.

I've never thought whether I wish that I hadn't been there. I certainly wish that it hadn't happened. I wouldn't want to make a statement that if it was going to happen, I'm glad that I was there because that's not my point at all.

Certainly this event was one of the most memorable events that I have seen. I was disgusted that it could happen in Dallas. It just seemed to me that it shouldn't have happened in Dallas. It could happen anywhere, but we were not happy about it occurring here. I've never had any trouble with sleeping other than the remorse that someone here would do something like that or that it would happen in Dallas. I'm very fond of Dallas because this is my home.

Malcolm Summers still lives in Dallas and has owned his own mailing business for years. He is the brother-in-law of former deputy sheriff Al Maddox.

JAMES TAGUE
Eyewitness

"I called my father and told him that Kennedy had been killed. He said, `Jim, I'm watching the TV and they said he's still alive.' I told him, `Dad, believe me, he's dead because I was there.'..."

Originally from Indiana, James Tague moved to the Dallas area in 1956 while in the Air Force, married a Texas girl, and later fathered five children. By 1960 he was employed in the automobile business. He is sometimes referred to by some assassination researchers as "the other victim."

I was working for Chuck Hinton Dodge on Lemmon Avenue in Dallas and was running late taking a friend to lunch around noon. At that point, I drove down Stemmons, turned to go east on Commerce and was stopped at the Triple Underpass. I realized that the Kennedy motorcade was coming through that area and, due to the fact that traffic came to a momentary stop in the left lane where I was, I stepped out of my car with the nose of the car sticking out of the east side of the underpass just seconds before the motorcade turned the corner in front of the School Book Depository. So I was standing to the front of the car on the cement where it narrows to go under the Triple Underpass between Main and Commerce Streets.

I could see the car turn left onto Elm Street then I heard three shots. When I heard the first shot, I thought somebody had thrown a firecracker and was standing there wondering what had happened. Then I heard another sound which was a little different. The third shot sounded the same as the second. At that point, I realized that they were possibly gunshots, so I ducked behind the concrete support and peeked out just as the Presidential limousine was passing into the Triple Underpass. In hindsight it was already over at that time.

I could not honestly tell from where the shots had originated, but the first shot I found the most interesting. A number of people described that shot as a firecracker, and it was different from the next two.

After the limousine had passed, one policeman stopped his motorcycle, drew his gun and ran up the grassy knoll while another came running. Other than a few people running for whatever reason, either toward the grassy knoll or in other directions, many people were just standing there, stunned. Veteran policemen were not reacting.

While I was standing there watching this, a man in a suit, who later identified himself as Deputy Sheriff Buddy Walthers, ran up and said, "What happened?" I told him that I didn't know, so we then walked over to the curb next to the grassy knoll on the north side of Elm where a motorcycle policeman had stopped and where three to five people were standing around. One of the men was very anguished and said his head had exploded.

When the policeman asked him who, he said, "The President's!" That was the first that Mr. Walthers and I even knew that somebody had shot at the President.

At that point, Mr. Walthers looked at me and said, "You've got blood on your cheek!" So I reached up and felt a couple of drops of blood. That was the first time that I recalled that there'd been something that had stung me, much like a sweat bee sting. So he said, "Let's go back over to where you were standing." Before we could cross Main Street we saw the mark on the curb from across the street. It appeared that a shot had hit the curb right at my feet. I don't know the exact measurements but it was on the rounded edge of the curb on the south edge of Main Street about ten to twelve feet out from the Triple Underpass.

According to the photographs and police tapes I probably stayed in the area a little over seven minutes. In fact the motorcycle policeman called in: "I have one more possibly with minor injuries." I was then told to go down to Homicide and give them a statement, which I did.

I think I got to police headquarters about 1:15 because I stopped and called the person I was to have had the luncheon engagement with and also called my father and told him that Kennedy had been killed. He said, "Jim, I'm watching the TV and they said he's still alive."

I told him, "Dad, believe me, he's dead because I was there!"

I found out years later by accident that the detective that I gave the statement to in Homicide at police headquarters was Gus Rose. I was listening to the radio one day and they were interviewing him on his retirement from the Dallas Police Department. He was asked if he remembered interviewing Oswald and he said, "Yeah, I remember very distinctly. I was sitting in my office taking a statement from a man that had a minor injury at the time of the assassination." At that time I hadn't known his name. In fact I often wondered whatever happened to that statement because it never showed up anywhere later.

In any case, while I was in Gus Rose's office giving him a statement, there was a commotion to our right as Oswald was brought in. Matter of fact, they put him in the office next to the one we were in. Mr. Rose told me, "That's the guy that shot the policeman over in Oak Cliff."

I said, "I didn't know there'd been a policeman shot."

He responded, "Yeah, killed him!" That was the extent of the conversation. There was no connection to the President.

I don't recall how long I was at police headquarters, but I left three or four minutes after they brought Oswald in. From there I went back to work. Most businesses in Dallas had ground to a halt by that time. Further into the afternoon it just stopped. I don't remember exactly but I think our business, which was normally open till 9:00 P.M., closed at 5:00. At that point I went home, took out a spiral notebook and started writing down a lot of feelings I had and what I recalled happening. The only thing on TV, of course, was the assassination.

Immediately after the assassination there was talk about three shots which was the same number I heard and that all three had hit Kennedy and Connally. All three shots were accounted for. Well, I knew that our great government, the FBI, the Secret Service, they're smart and they were going to find out the truth about what really happened. They'd dig in and be coming around to me to find out about this one shot which had missed and hit the curb near me. Later I told friends, "Hey, I was there and that one shot missed."

These people replied, "No, no, you're wrong, Jim."

After a couple of weeks with this persisting in the papers, I picked up the phone, called the FBI and said, "Hey, there was one shot that missed!"

Of course they came out and interviewed me and started asking questions. One of them asked right off, "Do you know Jack Ruby?"

I said, "Well, I've met him." So he started digging in on that then learned that my roommate, who was a guitar player, was dating a dancer who worked for Jack Ruby. He really got heavy into that.

Into the spring of the next year, the papers were saying that the Warren Commission was wrapping up its findings about three shots: two that hit Kennedy, and one that hit Connally. I was distressed and concerned about my credibility. Whenever I mentioned this thing, I was told, "You're crazy!"

One day I was talking to a man I knew in the service department at my place of business and mentioned, "You know, the photographer of *The Dallas Morning News* took the picture; there was a deputy sheriff who was there also and he brought some other police officers; I gave a statement to the Dallas Police Department and another to the FBI and this is wrong!" So he went to a news reporter who worked for the *Dallas Times Herald*, and since the *Times Herald* was only five to ten minutes away, it wasn't an hour till a young reporter named Jim Lehrer of the later MacNeil-Lehrer Report called and said he'd like to talk to me. I told him, "Hey, I'm not seeking publicity. Don't use my name, but I think this is what happened. I know I'm not crazy!" That was maybe 10:30 or 11:00 in the morning.

About noon he called back and said, "Jim, I put this on the wire service and they're calling me from all over the country. Matter of fact I've had to give them your name."

I replied, "That's fine. Of course it's not in the local paper."

So it wasn't long after that that all of a sudden it was learned that the Warren Commission was going to be reconvened. At that time, I was called for the first time to give my testimony to

Wesley Liebler of the Warren Commission. Of course I got the testimony of the photographer, Buddy Walthers, and other people who corroborated that there had been a shot which had missed. Lo and behold, all of a sudden the newspapers came out with a new theory that two shots hit in the car and one of the bullets went completely through Kennedy, the one that also did all the damage to Connally. Since all of this had become a personal thing to me, I felt vindicated.

I became very interested in this for years. At the time the Warren Commission amassed its findings, I had to accept what they concluded since I didn't know. But as I got deeper into it, by filing under the Freedom of Information Act to get information from the FBI, Secret Service, and CIA, I did not accept its findings.

If we go back into history, recall that we almost had a Warren Commission Report which would have said that all three bullets hit Kennedy and Connally. Of the many mistakes, at least that mistake was corrected. But many others were never corrected.

I had the good fortune of riding to the airport with one of the Warren Commission lawyers and asked him, "How did you happen to get selected?" This was a brilliant man and a tremendously brilliant lawyer.

He said, "Well, the government sent out letters to the top law schools in the country asking if they'd recommend the previous year's top graduates. Due to the fact that I had graduated at the top of my class and within six months of graduating was already a partner in a law firm, my professor nominated me, and I was one of seven chosen."

I asked him, "Is that how all the investigators were picked?" When he responded, yes, I further asked, "You had no investigative experience before?"

"Well, we were at the top of our class," he said. Now I'm not discrediting those lawyers at the top of their classes, but these were not seasoned trial lawyers or investigators. You can be good, but if you don't have the experience it can cause a problem.

In 1963 J. Edgar Hoover ran the FBI. Some honest retired FBI agents will tell you that fifty percent or more of their time was spent making things happen the way J. Edgar Hoover wanted them to happen. An agent would go out in the field and investigate something but would not write up his report. Instead, he turned it over to another who was a professional in writing up flowery reports that he knew would sound and read like J. Edgar Hoover wanted. Within three days of the assassination, Hoover wrote out a memorandum to President Johnson about what had happened. That was the direction the Warren Commission received. In a secret meeting in January 1964, one of the Warren Commission members said, "They don't need us. We're going to have to find it this way. The FBI will not give us any help, so we might as well fold up and go home." That was the atmosphere.

God, we all loved J. Edgar, but he had gotten too old for the job and too set in his ways. Everybody feared him. I've got a copy of a report that after this newspaper article appeared, the FBI interviewed the writer, Jim Lehrer. The report was most negative. It took what I had to say and turned it around with a different meaning which was very negative.

In my research, I have become convinced that Lee Harvey Oswald was involved but that he had some people helping him. The problem was in New Orleans. Probably the CIA had hired Oswald as an agent or an operative to do a certain job for them: namely, go burglarize an armory with some other people. He might have been told, "You do this, Lee. You'll have all the people you'll need and all the doors will open. We're going to give the guns and ammunition to the anti-Castro people. We can't just directly give them to them because it would appear too obvious, but we can say that they were stolen and your job is to pretend that you are stealing them." So this little group worked for the CIA as operatives. When the Bay of Pigs disaster happened, I think conversation in the group changed from Castro being the bad guy to Kennedy had let them down. Thus the plot to kill Kennedy was hatched in New Orleans which was described in Harold Weisberg's book, *Oswald in New Orleans*.

I think there is good evidence to indicate that the original plot was to have Kennedy assassinated in Atlanta, but the FBI became aware that a weapon was supposed to have been taken up to an office building and they changed plans. Kennedy never went to Atlanta, but lo and behold, Oswald was on the parade route here in Dallas.

If you go back to Dealey Plaza at 12:30 and get the photographs and police tapes, there was really no action taken on the School Book Depository for seven minutes. True, there were a couple of policemen who said they rushed in, which looks good on a sergeant's report, but it didn't happen that way. In those seven minutes, I think Oswald may have assisted in letting people into the building by saying they worked there or whatever. During that time, they could have moved an army in and out of the Texas School Book Depository.

In viewing the Zapruder film, there's overwhelming evidence that there was a frontal shot. They keep saying that there was possibly a neurological reaction, but if you view the film in slow motion, the Groden enhancement, the power of that shot even throws the body backward. The car was barely moving, so it wasn't from the acceleration, and I've never found anybody yet that has seen a kill of an animal where they fall toward the shot. As a result, there very definitely had to have been a shot from the grassy knoll.

After over thirty years, James Tague is still employed in the automobile business and maintains an interest in the research on the Kennedy assassination.

OTIS WILLIAMS
Eyewitness

"I remember the day he came in because I was talking with Roy Truly. Truly said, `I believe I've got an extra good help. I've got a good one, I think.' That's the first thing he said. He seemed to know more than the ordinary person they sent up to him. That was the first thing I ever heard of Oswald..."

Born in Cooke County, Texas, northeast of Dallas in 1899, Otis Williams graduated from Valley View High School in 1916, attended Metropolitan Business College and then went to work for the Southern Publishing Company, a school book publisher, where he served in numerous positions for over thirty years, eventually becoming the secretary-treasurer of the company. After the company was sold, Williams worked for Olmstead-Kirk Paper Company for four years prior to his employment with the Texas School Book Depository in 1953.

I had various jobs with the Texas School Book Depository, but my official title was credit manager. Most of our business was with the Texas Department of Education with the free textbooks, and I kept track of all the orders and everything that came in and saw that they went out on time. The department specified when we had to ship them. We also had to make sure the bills were paid; we did some outside miscellaneous business, and I'd have to pass on the credit of those customers.

The Texas School Book Depository secured contracts with the different publishers to distribute the books. A publisher, unless he had an awful lot of books, couldn't maintain a shipping department. So a group of publishers would go into the Depository, and the Depository would combine all their books to get the shipments out. We worked on a commission, and they'd pay them off at a certain designated period, usually after the state had paid us.

I just worked the general work that morning coming up to time to go, so I worked them up until ten or fifteen minutes before the parade came by. We worked on the second floor, and a few minutes later went downstairs down into the doorway entrance and waited until the President came by. Actually, they all did anyway without me saying anything. Everyone in the Depository went down to see it or looked from the windows. We had offices facing the street, and some of the workers stayed up in the offices and looked down.

We were just waiting at the entrance to the building above the steps when the motorcade came around the corner and then made that bend to get to the underpass. I had a clear view as it passed by of the President and all in the car, and then it went behind a little wall going toward the underpass. Probably five or ten seconds later is when I first thought I heard the shots.

The first one I assumed someone threw a firecracker. But soon evidently it showed that people were coming and swaying so that you knew they were shot. I didn't actually see the President hit as he was behind that little wall. It was about five or ten seconds before he was hit when he went out of my sight. I definitely heard three shots. I didn't hear any other shots or any other thing. Some say a motorcycle made a backfire, but I didn't hear that. I couldn't tell the direction of the shots. Actually, I probably heard echoes more than the actual shots because I was right under the shots, and the building covers over where we were. He was directly above us on the sixth floor.

I didn't see smoke or smell gunpowder. Fact is, as soon as the third shot happened, and everybody commenced milling around, I thought it came from the underpass. I entered the building immediately, climbed up the stairs back where the warehouse elevator was which led to the sixth floor and went up to the fourth floor, which was the first one I could see from to see the underpass. After I got up there and saw that nothing was going on on the underpass, I turned around and came back down to the office and called my wife. Soon, while we were talking, people came in, officers rushed in, and I had to get off the phone. I could have gone down the steps while Oswald came down, but he came down on the elevator. Anyway, I walked down the steps and didn't see him or anything. The first impression I had that it came from our building was that the policemen and reporters commenced rushing into our office and were getting the telephone and things like that.

Oswald worked for us only about thirty days. He worked in the stock room. Sometimes I'd have to know how many books we had or something like that, and I'd go back to the foreman. He'd call Oswald or somebody else to count them and come back and tell me. That's the only connection I know of him. I never did talk with him at all.

In fact, I didn't know anything at all about him as we didn't have a personnel file on him. Those type employees in the stock room from the Texas Employment we just called and told them to send us help. We didn't even investigate them. Most of them were temporary because they'd leave pretty quick. Their job was to stack books or to fill orders and things like that. I remember the day he came in because I was talking with Roy Truly. Truly said, "I believe I've got an extra good help. I've got a good one, I think." That's the first thing he said. He seemed to know more than the ordinary person they sent up to him. That was the first thing I ever heard about Oswald.

Truly said that he was doing well, and we assumed that he was. As far as I know, he could have stayed as long as he wanted. They kept most of the stock room workers all year round if they decided to stay. They might get extra help sometimes for certain periods, but usually they would just come and go.

I didn't see Oswald on the day of the assassination. He apparently walked back through the office, but I didn't see him. Mrs. Reid said she spoke to him and told him that the President had been shot, and he didn't respond. He just kept walking out.

I'm told that Oswald was seen after Truly and the officer came in the lunchroom. He and the officer thought the shots had come from the roof, and as they were going up steps, the officer saw Oswald with a Coke and said, "Who's that?"

Truly responded, "Oh, he works here," and they went on.

I was there when Roy Truly actually called roll and found that he was missing. He said, "Oh, it can't be one of our employees!" He had no idea that anything like that would happen.

After this happened, one of our employees, Joe Molina, ran into a problem. Joe and I worked desk by desk. He was the credit manager at that time, and I worked more with the state department getting out orders and watching them go through. We received the orders from the state department, and we'd have to run duplicates of them to give to all the publishers for their records. The records would show the date we had to ship the books, and we'd extend them and that was part of my job. I had people helping me do that, and we'd see to all of them, and if there were back orders, we'd have to do special things for those. Joe would OK all the orders when they came in and keep records of that.

That night, officers went out to his house and wanted to search it. He agreed and had them come in and search. I guess it was from the history of this club that he belonged to which they thought favored communism or whatever, but they suspected that kind of a deal. They went out and searched his house and found nothing wrong.

Soon after, Joe was let go by the Texas School Book Depository because they said they were going to put in new equipment which would cut out a lot of the work. They talked to me previously about how long I was going to work because they knew I was getting near retirement age. So they turned everything over to me and let him go.*

Actually, the reason they let him go was not particularly that they didn't need him; it was because the publishers that we did business with thought it would have some effect on their sales because people would connect them with being associated with that leaning. As a result, they put enough pressure on them to make the change just to keep out that kind of effect.

People have asked me about my opinions on the assassination for years. As far as I'm concerned, there was only one gunman. I didn't hear any extra shots that came from the terrace. I'm convinced Oswald did the shooting because the boys on the floor

---

* The controversy regarding Joe Molina occurred when his name was linked with an alleged subversive organization, the American GI Forum, by Dallas Police Chief Jesse Curry on television and in the newspapers on Saturday, November 23rd. For additional details see Hearings Before the President's Commission on the Assassination of President Kennedy, CE 1970 and CE 2036.

below him, watching from that floor, heard the shells hitting on the floor, and the shells, three shells, were still there.

Personally, I think that he and Ruby were connected. He left our Depository and went to his boarding house in Oak Cliff and got his pistol and then walked out. He was going directly in the direction of Ruby's apartment. I think he was going to Ruby's apartment to stay there for an indefinite time until all the pressure was off where he could leave. When the policeman stopped him, that killed everything. I think Oswald and Ruby were connected in some way with Cuba through Mexico and that he intended to go to one of those two places.

Upon his retirement in 1970, Otis Williams and his wife began a series of travels throughout the world until her death in 1985. After living a number of years in a retirement home in Dallas, Williams is now deceased.

THE POLICE: INITIAL REACTIONS

Marrion L. Baker

James W. Courson

Bobby Joe Dale

Stavis Ellis

W.G. Lumpkin

H.B. McLain

James C. Bowles

Joe Murphy

Edgar L. Smith

David V. Harkness

J.W. Foster

Jack Faulkner

Luke Mooney

MARRION L. BAKER
Solo Motorcycle Officer
Dallas Police Department

"What attracted my attention was this huge bunch of pigeons that flew off; fifty to a hundred of them were flying off the top of this building. I just knew that it had to be close to them or they wouldn't be disturbed like that..."

Patrolman Baker was born in the small town of Blum located in Hill County, Texas. After moving to Dallas in 1940, Baker later graduated from W.H. Adamson High School, located in Oak Cliff only a few blocks from where Officer J.D. Tippit allegedly was slain by Oswald. Baker worked at a variety of jobs after high school, then joined the Dallas Police Department in 1954. After nearly two years in Radio Patrol, he joined the Solo Motorcycle Division and had ridden motorcycles for seven years prior to the Kennedy motorcade.

———————————

I think that morning we were already assigned locations when we arrived at headquarters. They didn't want anyone around the Presidential car, so they told us to follow in behind the news media. We didn't know whose instructions those were; it might have been from the Secret Service. I know Johnson didn't want anyone around him, especially a motorcycle officer. He never liked that motorcycle noise beside his car. In fact, he didn't like police anyway.

As we made it all the way from Love Field to downtown, it was a pretty routine motorcade till we got to Main and Houston, then we cut over north on Houston. Most of the front of the motorcade had already turned west on Elm Street down toward the triple underpass. At the time, I was approximately 150 feet south of Elm Street traveling north on Houston on the right hand side of the street. Suddenly, I heard these three shots. It was my impression that they came directly in front of me and high. I just assumed that they came from the top of the Texas School Book Depository Building. The shots were very distinct. The first two were pretty evenly spaced, and the last was a little bit closer. It was kind of BOOM! . . . BOOM! . . . BOOM! I wasn't sure what kind of gun it was. I just heard three distinct shots.

What attracted my attention was this huge bunch of pigeons that flew off, fifty to a hundred of them were flying off the top of this building. I just knew that it had to be close to them or they wouldn't be disturbed like that.

I immediately rode to the corner of Houston and Elm and parked my motorcycle. At that time, there was just mass confusion down there. I remember one woman standing on the corner screaming, "Oh, they shot that man! Oh, they shot that man!" I didn't know what man they had shot. I was assuming. So I ran into the building, and at that time, it seemed like everybody else was, too.

Most of them that were standing in front of it were going into the Texas School Book Depository Building. When I got there, I asked which way were the stairs or the elevator, and this man stepped up and said, "Officer, come on! I'm the building supervisor." So he led us into the back, and we tried to get the elevators, the freight elevators. For some reason he couldn't get them down so he said, "Come on, we'll take the stairway!" So we started up the stairwell at the back. I later learned that this was Mr. [Roy] Truly.

Mr. Truly was ahead of me. As he had turned the corner and started on around toward the third floor stairwell, I happened to look over in front of me, and about twenty feet away there was a doorway with a small glass. I caught a movement behind the glass, so I went over, opened up the door, and saw this man standing approximately twenty feet in this next room. At that time, I didn't know if it was a coffee room or what. By this time, I had drawn my pistol on the first flight of stairs. I called to him, "Hey, you!," and he started turning around toward me. He didn't have time to respond; it was momentary. He didn't have time to say anything, and I didn't have time to observe him.

About that time, Mr. Truly was beside me. I asked him if this man worked for him or if he knew him, and he said, "Yes, he works for me!" So we continued on up the stairwell to the sixth floor and to the top. Later it was learned that the man I had encountered was Lee Harvey Oswald. But at that time, the name Oswald would have meant nothing to me, especially after being told that he worked there.

When we went out on the roof, I saw immediately there was no way anyone could shoot from the rooftop because the ledge around it was too high. You'd have to stand up on top of the edge to be seen. There was also an old neon sign up there, so we climbed up on that sign, but there was no way that you could shoot straight. We also checked an old motor house that covered a motor or something, but it wasn't very big and there was nothing in it. You could see that no shots could have come from up there just as soon as you got up there and looked around. I then went to the edge and kind of raised myself up to get up high enough to look over. Most of the people had gone by that time and very few were moving around. Really, I didn't pay any attention to those people down there. There were very few, and it looked to me like I saw some police officers going somewhere around those tracks. So, after several minutes on the roof, we turned around and came back down.

After I came back downstairs, I went outside. My motorcycle was the only one sitting out there. So I continued on out to Parkland. When I arrived at Parkland, it was all sealed off. The police had the hospital cut off at the entrance: no one came or went unless it was an emergency. So I checked in out there and was told to work crowd control.

In regard to all this, I don't consider myself an important person, especially when you're doing your job! I don't understand people's reasoning on that. We do it because we're a paid officer and it was involved in our work. Nor was I badgered by the Warren Commission. They asked me the questions and I answered them, and if they didn't understand, they'd ask again. And we went through it until we cleared up whatever was misunderstood.

One of the questions was whether Oswald could have made it from the sixth floor to the break room before I saw him. One day we ran some tests close to what I did, a reenactment of it. They determined that it was possible that Oswald could have gotten from the sixth floor to the second floor in the time that I started from where I was and got to the second floor. There was somewhere around five to ten seconds difference in each time we did it. We did what we assumed he did, and it was five to ten seconds off.

Since the assassination, basically, I've tried to forget this incident. I resent anyone saying it was Dallas that was at fault or anything like that. We did what we had to do under the circumstances, and I feel like we did a good job.

Officer Baker retired from the Dallas Police Department in 1977 and now lives on a farm outside Lancaster, Texas.

JAMES W. COURSON
Solo Motorcycle Officer
Dallas Police Department

"We were taught in the Marine Corps on the rifle range to count your shots, then on the police department the same thing on the pistol range: count your shots! That's one reason that I know there were three shots, and they probably came from the same gun..."

Jim Courson served in the Marine Corps during the Korean War and joined the Dallas Police Department after his discharge in 1954. Two years later, in 1956, he became a solo motorcycle officer and was assigned to escort the Kennedy motorcade on November 22, 1963.

The Kennedy motorcade was much the same as many others which I had escorted. We went to work fairly early that morning and spent a lot of time getting our equipment shined and polished since we always wanted to look sharp on those escorts. At that time, we were riding Harley-Davidsons, which was a tradition with the police department. We were given our assignments that morning through our sergeant which had been coordinated between the Secret Service and the police department.

It had been raining that morning, so we had to wear our yellow slicker rain gear out to the airport. Just as we pulled in to Love Field and just as the plane arrived, the sun came through making for a beautiful day. We then stripped off the rain gear and put them in our saddle bags.

After the President had met with many in the large crowd, we all left the airport, made a left turn on Mockingbird Lane, then a right on Lemmon Avenue. There were people scattered all along the route. In the early stages of the escort, they were not big crowds, but as the sirens were heard, businesses let their employees out and it appeared to be a good turn out. It was all fairly routine for us.

The motorcycle officers were concerned with the traffic, with side streets and driveways, and making sure that no one ran out into the motorcade. Tactical officers and patrol officers were stationed at all the intersections including all railroad trestles and overpasses throughout the entire route. There was a lot of security out that day. No traffic was moving except for the motorcade.

The motor jockeys in the escort were all experienced and were graduates of the Motorcycle Training School. When they got through with you, you were ready for just about anything. The newer, less experienced men were stationed further back in the escort. The ones in the front and around the President's car were the more experienced.

The route itself was fairly straight, with the exception of a few turns, and was designed for convenience and quickness. It would have been shorter and safer to have gone a more direct route between Love Field and the Trade Mart, but Kennedy wanted to be exposed to as many people as possible, so the route included the downtown area which was out of the way.

By the time we arrived in the downtown area at Harwood and Main, many of the City Hall employees and policemen came out to watch. On Main Street, the crowds were very heavy, three or four deep.

All was going well until we had just made a right turn from Main onto Houston Street due to the limousine having to make the sharp left turn up ahead on Elm which slowed the motorcade. We had to stop, thus I was sitting on my motorcycle in the left lane on Houston looking more or less at the Book Depository. That's when I heard the shots!

I couldn't tell exactly from where the shots came because of the echo pattern, but there were three very distinct shots. The first two were fairly close together then there was more space between the second and third. I could tell that they came from one location, but really I was concentrating more on the President and seeing if they needed help up ahead. People near me were just astonished: there were surprised, shocked looks. They didn't know what had happened.

I looked to my left and tried to see down across Dealey Plaza what was going on then sped to catch up with the President's car. At that point, we forgot about the rest of the escort; we were just concerned about the President. We had orders if harm came to him to get him out of the area and to the nearest hospital, in this case Parkland.

The limousine came to a stop and Mrs. Kennedy was on the back. I noticed that as I came around the corner at Elm. Then the Secret Service agent helped push her back into the car, and the motorcade took off at a high rate of speed.

I caught up with them as they entered the Stemmons Freeway ramp but had to back off some to make the turn because the limousine was taking up much of the lane of traffic. The driver immediately got out into the center lane with me on his left rear and another officer on the right. Mrs. Kennedy had, by that time, gotten back down in the seat and was holding the President's head in her lap. I was able to see that his head was horribly mangled. Skull, brain, and blood material was all along the seat. She looked up at me a couple of times with a blank expression as if she were in shock, which I imagine she was, then she'd look back down at him. Flowers were scattered all around the car.

At that point, on Stemmons, we were riding wide open, probably 85-90 miles per hour. It was dangerous for everybody concerned. We knew that the limousine driver was experienced; otherwise, he wouldn't be driving, but we couldn't anticipate his reactions. As we exited from Stemmons onto Industrial, you could hear the tires squealing on the limousine as it turned the corner faster than it should have.

There were officers everywhere at that location since that was our original destination: the Trade Mart. They were staring, not knowing what had happened. Sergeant Striegel was trying to motion us in as we sped by and must have thought that we had missed the turn.

Just before we reached Harry Hines Boulevard there was a railroad track on a small incline. All the motorcycles left the ground at the same time, and it appeared that the wheels of the limousine came off the ground as well. Of course, the driver was doing all he could to handle the car after jumping the track and then preparing to make the sharp left turn onto Harry Hines. He wasn't paying any attention to me to the left rear, and as he made the turn, I heard a scraping noise on my crash guard and realized that he had shoved me over into the curb. Fortunately I managed to maintain control and followed him to the hospital.

There must have been eight or nine motor jockeys who made that ride to Parkland. Two other officers and I helped take the President out of the car and put him onto the stretcher. From what I was able to see of the wound, the damage seemed to be in the right rear of his head, but it was hard to tell because there was so much blood. The back part of the skull seemed to be laying over the forehead. I didn't actually see an exit wound since I saw only the back part of his head.

While I was on duty there, there was a man in the hallway near the emergency room who was evidently causing some concern with the Secret Service. I was told by the Secret Service to get him out, which I did. As I caught hold of him, he told me that he was FBI. I said, "I don't know who you are; I don't care who you are! The Secret Service is in charge here, and they say to get you out, and you're going out!" As I edged him back, under his coat I felt what I thought was a gun on his right hip.

"Don't disarm me!," he said. I just kept hold of the gun with one hand and marched him to the door. Chief Curry himself was at the door of the emergency room and wondered what was going on as he opened the door for me.

I told him, "The Secret Service said get this man out of here."

Curry responded, "Get him out!" Later I heard that he was an FBI photographer.

One of the images that has stuck in my mind over the years was that of a young boy about nine or ten years old with a box camera there at the hospital. Right after the President was taken out of the car this boy walked up and took a picture of the inside of the car. Some man, whom I later learned was a Secret Service agent, took the camera, opened it up, and shelled the film out and handed the camera back to the boy. Tears rolled up in his eyes as if he'd been slapped away from the table.

Later I went to Love Field and was there when Judge Sarah Hughes swore in Johnson. Eventually, after I returned to the hospital, the motor jockeys were told to report to City Hall where Oswald was being questioned. While on duty in the hallway, I saw him a couple of times as he was being escorted to the restroom or to lineups downstairs. Part of our job was to clear a path amidst the press and people from all over the world. The hallway and the room where he was being questioned were completely crowded.

Late that night Chief Curry came to the motorcycle officers and told us that we had done our job well: that we had done what we had been instructed to do which was to escort the President from Love Field to the Trade Mart. Our primary function was not to protect the President but to escort him from one point to another. At that time, all the men were thinking we had let the country down; we had let the city down; we had let the chief down. So what he said meant a great deal to us.

J.W. Courson retired from the Dallas Police Department in 1979 after 25 years service. Though no longer riding motorcycles, he now spends much of his time fishing and traveling. He and his wife Sue now live in Rockwall County, east of Dallas.

BOBBY JOE DALE
Solo Motorcycle Officer

"I caught up to the limousine on Stemmons somewhere around Continental.... Your mind runs wild at a time like that. Maybe he's hit; if he is, maybe it's an impersonator. Maybe it's not really happening....Your mind just runs loose..!"

Born and raised in Dallas, Bobby Joe Dale served in the Navy as a boilerman during the Korean Conflict. Following his discharge in 1953, Dale considered working in boilershops, but remembering the heat involved with the job, he instead joined the Dallas Police Department in 1954 as a patrolman. By 1960 he transferred to solo motorcycles and was part of the motorcycle escort for President Kennedy on November 22, 1963.

Two or three days prior to the President's visit we'd ridden with the Secret Service checking to see where the turns and problem areas might be. We had three possible routes, but we didn't know which one we were going to take, and we were not briefed on it. But by riding during the week, I kept hearing the phrase "escape routes," which dawned on me later that should something happen to any part of the motorcade we had an escape route to either Baylor or Parkland Hospitals. I was impressed with the details in covering all emergencies should they arise.

I assume the assignments were drawn up in a joint meeting of the sergeants, lieutenants, and captains. We had our assignments prior to the 22nd. It was to be a routine escort with experienced riders. At the time, I didn't consider it an honor to be included since I had been on VIP escorts several times in the past. To me it was just another assignment.

That particular morning it was raining and everybody had on their rain gear, so it really didn't matter whether your boots were polished or shined. Everybody was either assigned to the escort or at Market Center whether you were working late nights, evenings, or whatever. We all assembled at the motorcycle shed at the police department downtown; those of us who were in the escort were to meet at Love Field at a particular time.

We rode casually out to Love Field in groups of four or five together riding slowly since it was raining and we were being careful. While we were waiting in the restricted area at Love Field for the plane to arrive, it cleared off, the streets dried, and everybody came out of their rain gear.

Once we were assembled and the President was ready to go, we started the motorcade by going out a gate at the far end. At that time, we didn't know which route we were taking; we had three: right, straight, or left. As we were leaving, the word came over the radio that we would use the particular route that went left. As soon as we heard that, we knew where we were going. That meant that we would hit Mockingbird at the entrance to Love Field, make a left and go up to Lemmon Avenue, then turn right to Cedar Springs, which then changes names to Turtle Creek, then Harwood to Main.

They seemed to be concerned with the timing element in this motorcade more so than in others I had been in. Time was given continually over the radio to check the progress of the motorcade. We'd give a certain check point and time was given. We were held up a little as we got to Lemmon and Loma Alto, and after this was cleared, we were told that we were running forty-five seconds to a minute behind, so we picked it up a little to be on schedule. There was no reason given for the concern about time but, in retrospect, probably what they were doing was trying to shuffle those with multiple assignments so they could cover those assignments.

Nothing was noteworthy about the motorcade; it was jovial and everybody seemed happy till we got to Lemmon and Loma Alto. There the crowd was lining the sidewalks and seemed to move in, narrowing the street, creating congestion. People ran to the car to greet the President once it slowed down which created a nuisance for us because we had a schedule to keep. It was about that time it dawned on me just how important he was.

My particular assignment was behind the President's car where the motorcade had the VIP's and press buses. I was at the end of the car just in front of the press buses.

Our job specifically was to keep intervals, to keep the motorcade altogether including the press buses and cars behind: no lagging, no gaps, certain distances between each vehicle. If they began to lag, we were to speed them up. This could be done usually by looking at the driver and telling him or giving him some indication. Normally the indication would be through hand signals since the Harleys we were riding made quite a bit of noise. When crowds moved in, you could usually engage the clutch so it would slip, race the engine and create more noise. We'd use that as a psychological method to move the crowds back. You could even cause them to backfire if you retarded the spark. Mine was a '62 model which was relatively new since the average lifespan on the police department of the Harleys was between thirty and forty thousand miles, or three years.

I noticed as we started on Harwood that the crowds became heavier and, by the time we got to town, the streets were full, much like a parade, with everybody upbeat, hollering, and a great deal of enthusiasm.

I had just made a right turn off of Main and was probably about forty feet onto Houston in the right hand lane as the President's car turned left onto Elm when a round went off, but it didn't dawn on me that it was a shot. I noticed the crowd looking and moving and becoming congested. At first I thought it was a backfire, but then I heard rapid succession. I didn't pay much attention to counting them because you couldn't tell where they were coming from in that low area, bouncing off all the walls and buildings. It just wasn't possible to tell where they were coming from!

After the shots were fired, the whole motorcade came to a stop. I stood and looked through the plaza, noticed there was commotion, and saw people running around his car. It started to move, then it slowed again; that's when I saw Mrs. Kennedy coming back on the trunk and another guy pushing her back into the car. I didn't know what she was doing. At that time, I figured that she was fleeing rather than helping. It looked like a camera out of focus or the film jumping its track. I had no idea what had happened.

About that time it was on the radio that he'd been hit. If I'd speeded up, the press buses and everything else would have gone with me, so I got the driver's attention of the bus behind me and told him to stop, then I accelerated to catch up to the limousine. As I turned onto Elm, a motorcycle which had fallen over caught my attention, and Hargis was going up the grass. Other than the general commotion, that was all that I noticed since my attention was focused on catching up to the motorcade. I caught up to the limousine on Stemmons somewhere around Continental. From there it was north on Stemmons to the Industrial exit running fast. I wasn't paying any attention to speed, but by the way the motor was acting, I'd say it was doing 70.

Your mind runs wild at a time like that. Maybe he's hit; if he is, maybe it's an impersonator. Maybe it's not really happening. Even when we got to Parkland, while he's being taken out of the vehicle, you're thinking maybe it really wasn't him; it was an impersonator riding in the parade. Your mind just runs loose!

As we passed Market Center, one of the officers, Sergeant Striegel, thinking the motorcade had arrived, came out to direct us in, but we sped on by at a high rate of speed. It was hectic! Looking back, it didn't seem like it took that long. After passing Market Center, I knew there was a railroad up ahead and was hoping a train wouldn't be coming by. I had no sense of the speed we were making until I hit the incline at the railroad. At that point, the motor left the ground and I said to myself, "Hey, don't lose it." Of course, if I'd lost it, then probably I would have been run over by somebody behind me; that occupies your mind! I'd been airborne before on a motorcycle, but it was intentional; this was unintentional. There's a big difference!

Apparently we'd beaten the news there when we arrived at Parkland. Just as I pulled up and parked my motor the President was on the gurney beside the car, and they were wheeling him in. At that time, it was obvious that nobody could have survived a wound like that. As I recall, Mrs. Kennedy had already gone into the entrance of the emergency room prior to them bringing him in. There were quite a few people that went in ahead of him either clearing the way or getting him ready.

It was a fairly routine operation for us. We knew to keep the crowd away, that the sooner we could block off the entrance to Parkland up to Harry Hines about half a block away the better off we'd be. The problem was clearing the emergency entrance. Everybody began showing up as the news got out while we were trying to gain control of the scene. It was hectic there for two or three minutes! At that time, some three-wheelers arrived and helped clear it all the way to the street. Meanwhile it was hard to tell somebody that needed to go into the emergency room that was sick or injured that the hospital was closed.

It was so hectic I can't remember everything in sequence. I went over to the limousine and saw a Secret Service man starting to put the top up. "Help me secure this," he said, since it was heavy and in sections. Blood and matter was everywhere inside the car including a bone fragment which was oblong shaped, probably an inch to an inch and a half long by three-quarters of an inch wide. As I turned it over and looked at it, I determined that it came from some part of the forehead because there was hair on it which appeared to be near the hairline. There were other fragments around, but that was the largest piece that grabbed my attention. What stood out in my mind was that there was makeup up to the hairline. Apparently he had used makeup for the cameras to knock down the glare. It was fairly distinct where it stopped and the wrap of skin took up. Other than that, nobody messed with anything inside the car in any manner, shape, or form. Nobody said, "Clean this up!" We then put the top up and secured it.

After that Chief Curry came back out and said that he wanted me to monitor the radio from my motor sitting right outside the emergency entrance. My job then was to relay information to him and then from him back to the dispatcher's office. Later he told me to advise the people at Market Hall that he would not be there. When they inquired why, I just repeated what he told me. I wouldn't tell them that the President had been hit.

Later on Curry told me that he was going to back his car up and move LBJ back to Love Field and for me to get somebody else to help escort him but not to use sirens. We were to pull the escort at a steady speed, use red lights and whistles and not to attract any more attention than was necessary. He said, "When you see us load, I'll give you a signal and we'll leave. Go through the crowd!" He didn't want to have to stop. So I got Brewer and told him that we were fixing to take some people back to Air Force One and that it was to be a guide escort only, braking at intersections with whistles and no sirens.

We started up, took the entrance to Mockingbird and about that time Striegel showed up. He saw what we were doing and ran off ahead using his siren. When Curry heard that, he said, "Motorcycle officer using his siren. Tell him to discontinue!" It took about a three-block chase trying to get him to shut his siren off. I guess he was embarrassed because he made a right turn, and that's the last I saw of him.

As I recall, there were two vehicles that went back to Love Field: Curry's and another. Somewhere in the time between Parkland and Love Field the U.S. borders had been closed, and then it dawned on me: Why have they not said the President was dead? It was obvious; we knew what had happened. But then it all came to me as to why things are done that way. If there had been a conspiracy, the United States was vulnerable to attack and there would be nobody to order retaliation. I guess I didn't realize the magnitude of all this until that time.

We went back into the same entrance we'd exited earlier and pulled onto the tarmac. Air Force One had pulled right up to the ramp. Brewer and I stayed there at the bottom of the ramp as an ambulance pulled up and unloaded while they went up. Then the driver got back into the ambulance and backed it over next to the fence and just left it. I realized then that the owner of the vehicle was not driving; it was the Secret Service. About that time there was a DPS trooper taking pictures, and the Secret Service hollered at him to get his camera out of there.

We didn't know what we were waiting for, and about that time another car drove up carrying Judge [Sarah T.] Hughes. They had found her and escorted her up into the plane for the swearing in. All the while I kept wondering who was going to come and get the ambulance. After the plane took off, we were then sent downtown to City Hall.

During the time I was monitoring the chief's radio at Parkland, it had come in that an officer had been shot in Oak Cliff. The chief was saddened and wanted to know who it was. I ascertained that it was Tippit, but at that time we didn't make a connection between the shooting and that of the President.

When I arrived at City Hall, Oswald had already been arrested and brought in. I was told that they needed help up in the homicide office on the third floor, so I went upstairs to help clear the halls.

You plan for the motorcade and everybody's on assignments; you plan the visit and covering the hospital; everything's covered with the exception that you don't anticipate an arrest being made or the third floor being a problem. Everybody else is on assignment; the only thing that's left free is the motorcycle officers. They're no longer on assignment, so that's the reason we ended up up there. It was strictly that there was no other manpower allocated or preplanned to be up there.

At that time, Oswald was a suspect in the killing of the police officer. They hadn't made the connection with the President at that time. When that connection was made shortly thereafter, it became rather hectic. Generally it was fairly orderly with the exception of the reporters, and we didn't have the right to keep them out. We tried to stop them, but the press was pretty innovative. Being frank, they made an ass out of themselves! We had more problems with the press and the reporters than we did bystanders or civilians.

When Oswald would come out of the office and down the hall, what I observed was that he seemed to be toying with everybody. He was way ahead of everybody else. He knew what he was doing and seemed very confident. He acted like he was in charge and, as it turned out, he probably was.

I was off the following day, as I had already made arrangements to attend the wedding of a friend of mine in Oklahoma. In fact many of the motorcycle officers were off duty.

About the only time this subject came up with the motorcycle officers after this was over was when an officer was asked to come to the Warren Commission or be questioned elsewhere. It wasn't something that we sat around and talked about. I guess we thought about it, but we didn't talk about it unless somebody like Baker was called to Washington. Coincidentally, on one of those flights, my wife, who was a stewardess for American, ran into P.T. Dean, who also was going to Washington to testify. Since American had a policy about stewardesses not being married, she passed him a note saying, "I'm Shirley Weir, but I'm not supposed to be married." She figured that he would say something since we all knew each other. Before we were married, she also lived in an apartment at Thornton and Ewing above Jack Ruby, though she didn't really know him.

Regarding the assassination, I didn't think the police department was treated fairly by the press or the writers for at least a year after it happened simply because there was too much "Monday morning quarterbacking." Certainly you could find a lot of things that should have been done differently, but that was after the fact; you can cut it all kinds of ways. In living an incident, you don't think about all these things. Policemen very seldom act; they always react. That's their training. You play the hand you're dealt. That's what the Dallas Police Department did, and they reacted in a normal manner.

We also don't put much stock in speculation or theory. In the late '70's, there was speculation that a stuck microphone on one of the motorcycle radios in Dealey Plaza picked up the sounds of the shots. At that time, we had two channels on the radio: one channel was for Oak Cliff and the other for the rest of Dallas. But that day, they cleared one channel for those events pertaining to the motorcade. We were on that channel, but you could flip the switch and go to the other channel.

At the time, what I was thinking was that there was a mike stuck on that particular channel which garbled other transmissions from other vehicles, but the dispatcher could override it. In fact, I think he said two or three times that there was a mike stuck open and to check it. You could pretty well identify what the sound was on the radio. It seemed at the time, and it's still in my mind, that it was a three-wheeler. They had a flat-head engine with a distinctive noise, so you could tell them from a solo motorcycle. Stuck mikes were a fairly common occurrence, especially among three-wheelers. With the solo, you didn't turn on your transmitter until you got ready to talk; three-wheelers left their's on all the time due to the fact that they had bigger batteries.

Under ordinary circumstances if your mike became stuck, you had officers close to each other all the time and it could be cleared up quicker by somebody saying, "If your mike's stuck, you can't hear anything. Check your mike! Check your mike!" Usually the problem would be located and quickly corrected if it were a solo motorcycle. However, had a three-wheeler been on assignment in a parking area with his mike stuck, he might go an hour with it stuck. Of course, he'd have no knowledge of this unless somebody told him to check his mike. Again, if your mike's stuck, you don't hear it.

In 1975 I became an instructor at the Police Academy at the pistol range. By coincidence, that's when the acoustical test was being run to check for shot noises on the tapes. The pistol range personnel reenacted it with one of the instructors using the same type weapon firing the same distance into sandbags. It was sort of interesting just sitting there watching the technicians and so-called brains attempting this reenactment. It was half funny and half absurd to come by fifteen years later firing a gun with the same sounds without taking into consideration that all the trees in the area had grown during those fifteen years and would absorb more sound, thus the sound's going to be different. It was absurd because, in my mind, the stuck mike was never anywhere in the area of the assassination, so they were basing all these tests on a false assumption.

I've heard the tapes of the radio traffic and could even hear a train which was in the vicinity of Market Center. You can hear the motorcade with the sirens going by the stuck mike which indicates that the mike was on a stationary vehicle, most likely a three-wheeler at Market Center. If you listen past where the "experts" checked the tapes, you can hear the motorcade with sirens in the background, and you can hear them pass the mike. The time element was two or three minutes after we would have left Dealey Plaza.

Several of the TV people came by at the time of the acoustics' tests and even said that they had heard that the stuck mike was mine. I knew that wasn't true! I could hear the mike stuck. I could hear all these sounds coming over the mike and therefore concluded at that time that it was a three-wheeler at Market Center. Had my mike been stuck, I wouldn't have heard anything. If your mike's stuck, your radio's dead. There's no doubt in my mind that mine wasn't stuck!

You tell them it wasn't, then they continue talking like it was. To me, once you say it wasn't my mike, that it wasn't stuck because I could hear the mike stuck and could hear all the background noises over my radio, then it wasn't stuck! At that time, whoever it was that I was talking to, the conversation should have been over, but they persisted! I resented that! They should have concluded that it wasn't mine and gone about their business to find out whose it was. But it was typical.

People who have written about the assassination voice their opinion, and they'll include just enough truth to give it credibility. A lot of these people who are gifted with words have made quite a bit of money on their ideas and theories, not the facts of the case. I don't think there's a whole lot of truth in their books. They seem to interview only those that will give credibility to their theories. It bothers me that some of these people are so far out in left field. It's a little upsetting when you look at what kind of following they have for their theories. You just want to grab and shake them and say, "Hey, don't you know better than that?"

Bobby Joe Dale retired from the Dallas Police Department in January 1981. With the election of Don Byrd as sheriff of Dallas County, Dale became one of his assistant chiefs. He remained in that role until 1985 after Byrd lost his bid for reelection. Dale is now retired, living in Cedar Hill, Texas.

STAVIS "STEVE" ELLIS
Solo Motorcycle Officer
Dallas Police Department

"Sarge, the President's hit!... Hell, he's dead! Man, his head's blown off...!"

Born in 1918 in Laredo, Texas, and raised in San Antonio, "Steve" Ellis* graduated from Brackinridge High School and later attended college in the military. During the Second World War, he joined the National Guard and served as an MP. Ellis began his career with the Dallas Police Department in 1946 as a patrolman and became a solo motorcycle officer fifteen months later with promotion to sergeant in 1952. Sergeant Ellis was the officer in charge of the motorcycle escort for the motorcade through Dallas.

I always liked riding motorcycles and had ridden them half way around the world in the Army. I guess I liked that kind of work. You work on your own; you're out there by yourself; you

----

* The name Stavis has been a curiosity to a number of researchers, including the author. Sergeant Ellis's father was a Greek immigrant who entered Ellis Island at the age of thirteen. His surname, Heliopoulis, was eventually changed to Ellis either as a shortened version of Heliopoulis or for Ellis Island itself. Stavis is the Anglicized derivation of the Greek "Stavros," while "Steve," as Ellis is known to his friends, is the Americanized version of Stavis.

don't have a partner that will do the driving for you. When I was a kid, my father owned a restaurant in San Antonio just a block or so from the Municipal Auditorium. Whenever the San Antonio police officers came to work traffic in and around the auditorium, they'd stop by the restaurant and drink coffee with my dad. Since I was there quite often, they became my idols. That's why I had it in my mind to become a motorcycle officer, and it's what I did for almost thirty-one years.

The motorcade assignments were, I believe, made up by Captain Lawrence and Chief Lunday. I'm just guessing at that because Lawrence had been making up all the assignments, and they'd ask me a question or two about who should be put here or there in the motorcade. I recommended the four guys that I had to ride immediately to the rear of the President's car: Chaney, Hargis, Martin, and Jackson because they made a neat appearance, and I knew that I could count on them and the job would be done properly.

That morning was rainy. It wasn't raining hard, but hard enough in riding your motorcycle that you needed a rain suit. So, as we left the garage on our Harleys, we put our rain suits on and headed out to Love Field where we racked our motorcycles and waited for the motorcade to begin. A few minutes after we arrived, the rain quit, the sun came out, and we pulled our rains suits off and put them in the saddle bags.

Kennedy had arrived but there was a bit of a holdup. There was a huge crowd and he wasn't ready to go right away as he had walked over to a little fence and was talking to everybody and shaking hands. Some of the Secret Service boys seemed worried about this while other agents were taking the bullet proof top off the car. When that had been rolled up, he got in, and we took off on the escort.

We didn't have any idea that anything was going to happen. Our job was to look for any kind of interruption en route: maybe some radical might run out and holler or otherwise try to stop the motorcade. We were always on the alert for that and were prepared to take quick action to get them out of the way.

I was in charge of the actual escort of the President's car. All the other officers had their assignments, but some were just assigned to us as surplus. At the airport, Chief Curry told me, "Look, you see that double-deck bus up there? That's full of news media. Now they've got to get to the Mart out there where the President is going to talk, but we don't want them messing up this motorcade. Just give them one of your men back there and tell him to escort them there on time but to keep them out of the motorcade and not to mess with us." So I got M.L. Baker and told him exactly what the chief had told me. That put him behind us quite a bit.

This motorcade was no different than many others that I had helped escort. I was riding between Curry's lead car and the President's. There wasn't anybody close to me. I'd slow down and let them catch up then check to see if the interval was right in town and so forth. You want to increase the interval between the cars on the freeways and keep it tight in town; that's your usual operating procedure. When we came through the traffic along Lemmon Avenue from Love Field, I gave them a sign to close it up tight.

Everything went smoothly except for one time on Lemmon Avenue when a group of little girls from a Catholic school, dressed in those little uniforms, standing out there with the sisters, got too far out in the street. When Kennedy approached, they naturally ran out into the street, the car stopped, and Kennedy was shaking hands and touching them. While this happened, the rest of the crowd moved out in the street against the car so that it couldn't move anymore. I made a U-turn and came back down the left side of the car to clear everybody back to the side so we could move on. Some grown people got back when they saw the motorcycle coming. Meanwhile, Curry, in the car in front of the President's, was waiting for me to get it clear. As I approached the disruption, I looked up and saw Secret Service agents grabbing those little girls and slinging them out of the street like they were sacks of potatoes. By the time I got there, they had the street cleared and said, "OK, let's go!"

As we turned off Harwood onto Main, the crowds were bigger. Many times when I've escorted other presidents, there wasn't but a handful of people on the streets and we were able to move quickly. But Kennedy wanted people to see him and he wanted to see everybody, so we traveled slowly.

We came west on Main Street to Houston Street and took a right, facing right into that building. The building with the window was looking right at us as we came up to Elm Street and made a left, heading back toward the Triple Underpass. Midway down Elm I remember waving at my wife's niece and nephew, Bill and Gayle Newman, who had apparently come out to see the President. About the time I started on a curve on Elm, I had turned to my right to give signals to open up the intervals since we were fixing to get on the freeway a short distance away. That's all I had on my mind. Just as I turned around, then the first shot went off. It hit back there. I hadn't been able to see back where Chaney was because Curry was there, but I could see where the shot came down into the south side of the curb. It looked like it hit the concrete or grass there in just a flash, and a bunch of junk flew up like a white or gray color dust or smoke coming out of the concrete. Just seeing it in a split second like that I thought, "Oh, my God!" I thought there had been some people hit back there as people started falling. I thought either some crank had thrown a big "Baby John" firecracker and scared them causing them to jump down or else a fragmentation grenade had hit all those people. In any case, they went down! Actually I think they threw themselves down in anticipation of another shot.

As soon as I saw that, I turned around and rode up beside the chief's car and BANG!..BANG!, two more shots went off: three shots in all! The sounds were all clear and loud and sounded about the same. From where I was, they sounded like they were coming from around where the tall tree was in front of that building. Of course, I'm forming an opinion based on where I saw that stuff hit the street, so I knew that it had to come from up that way, and I assumed that the others came from the same place.

But all the time I was moving up, I still didn't know it was shots until Chaney rode up beside me and said, "Sarge, the President's hit!" I asked him how bad, and he replied, "Hell, he's dead! Man, his head's blown off!"

"All right, we're going to Parkland," I said. This had been the prearranged plan in the event that someone was shot or injured; it was normal procedure. Chaney and I then rode on up to Curry's car. Curry was driving with the Chief of the Secret Service, Forrest Sorells, in the front seat with him. "Chief," I said, "That was a shot! The President was hit and he's in bad, bad shape! We're going to Parkland!"

He said, "All right, let's go!"

Chaney and I then got in front of Curry's car and I told him, "All right, we're going to Parkland, I'm going Code 3, everything we've got!"

"All right, hit 'em," Chaney said. So we took off and headed toward Parkland with the President.

Of course there was a lot of transmissions on the radio. Chief Batchelor was asking one of us if he was dead. Well, we couldn't tell him that for security reasons. We knew that this was far-fetched, but it could have been a Russian bombing raid in flight and we couldn't retaliate if they knew our president was dead. They could make their drop in safety because we couldn't retaliate with atomic weapons without a president. These things were going through our minds at that time. Curry, more or less, told Batchelor to shut up.

But really, in a situation like that, you don't really have time to think. All you're trying to do is not do something wrong to fall or hurt yourself on that motorcycle. You know that you've got a mission to accomplish and you know that if you fall, you're not going to do them any good because they're not going to make it either. So you're just sitting there tight trying and hoping that everything goes right.

But it was tense, real tense. We were under terrific pressure. We knew Governor Connally had been wounded; we knew that Kennedy was dead, but we also knew that we had to get there as quickly as possible, so we gave it all she'd take. I don't remember looking at the speedometer, but we were going way too fast!

Chaney and I took the Stemmons Freeway and exited onto the service road to Industrial. The service roads hits Industrial right under Stemmons, and we took a right heading toward Harry Hines where the hospital was located. As we sped by where he was to give his speech at the Trade Mart on Industrial, Sergeant Striegel was out there trying to flag us down and Batchelor was there telling him, "Stop 'em! Stop 'em!" Of course, we were going Code 3 and they didn't know that we were headed to the hospital.

As we approached Harry Hines, it was almost a square turn; there was a high bank over on the side. All I could see was that big, tall, green bank and hoping that I'd stay on the ground going around that. Chaney and I were side by side with Martin somewhere behind us and the President's car right on my tail. I was kind of teed off at that agent for staying so close. Chaney would look back, and I'd look back; we'd speed up and look back and there he was on our back bumper. I don't care how fast we went the bumper of the President's car looked like it was right behind us. He was directly behind us all the way to Parkland! They shouldn't ride that close on an escort because if we had to take some evasive action or brake, they'd run over us. We didn't like that too much but it couldn't be helped under the circumstances.

Fortunately everything fell into place just beautifully! Nothing got in our way. After we turned onto Harry Hines, the first signal light we caught was Amelia which led to the emergency entrance. We went right through without having to shut down our engines. We just went right on in.

As we entered the emergency entrance, we pulled to the left to let the car go on in where they unloaded. Curry hollered to me when he went by, "Cut 'em off right there! Don't let anybody else in that's not in that motorcade!"

So when Martin rode up, I told him, "Bubba, when that car gets in, cut it off! Don't let anybody in!"

Man, in just a matter of minutes that place was just swarming with people around in back of the hospital. It seemed like everybody was trying to get in closer to the emergency area where they could see. There were just oodles of people climbing over high places like a bunch of ants toward the back of that hospital. That's when the perimeter was set up.

When the President's car was unloaded, I was maybe fifty feet away. I wasn't able to see much because there was a lot of people from the hospital around him. I don't remember seeing Connally at all. But when the car pulled up, the hospital people were coming out the door like a bunch of ants. They were right on him.

I walked by the limousine after they were taken in. The thing that impressed me was in the seat and on the floorboard there were puddles of blood. Right in the middle one of those puddles lay a beautiful red rose. I never forgot that! I can still see it, that red rose in that blood!

Some of the jockeys around the car were saying, "Looky here!" What they were looking at was the windshield. To the right of where the driver was, just above the metal near the bottom of the glass there appeared to be a bullet hole.

I talked to a Secret Service man about it, and he said, "Aw, that's just a fragment!" It looked like a clean hole in the windshield to me. In fact, one of the motor jockeys, Harry Freeman, put a pencil through it, or said he could.

I remember a little kid I had first seen out at Love Field who had a little home camera with the old reel type of film, and he had taken some pictures there. I saw him again on Lemmon Avenue where he had taken more pictures, and again in town. Well, he also showed up at Parkland and was taking some pictures of the hearse that they had brought in. He was one of a bunch of people in the back of the hospital taking pictures. A Secret Service man ran up, grabbed that camera out of his hand, opened it up, shook the film down and gave it a kick. You know how those reels of film unroll? I'm sure it exposed everything he had. I felt sorry for him. I got into a little hassle over it and told the Secret Service man, "I don't think that's right the way you did that. That poor kid's been taking pictures ever since we left Love Field and now you've exposed every one of them!" He made some smart comment to the effect that he didn't think it was right for me to say anything to him about it. But I didn't appreciate it a bit! I understand that they were under pressure, but they were awfully uncouth, all of them!

After staying at the hospital for a short while, we were told that we had to take LBJ to Love Field immediately. Chaney and I took him, and maybe Martin, Code 3. As I recall, two or three others escorted the hearse. Shortly after we got to Love Field a squad car brought Judge Sarah T. Hughes for the swearing in of Johnson. We were standing there by our motors when the swearing in took place. I'm not sure of this, but I was told that it was only thirty-eight minutes from the time the President was killed till we had Johnson out there and sworn in.

Upon completion of our assignment, we then went back into service. That evening, after Oswald had been arrested, and all the news media was trying to talk with him, most of us motor jockeys were assigned to the third floor of City Hall for security where we remained until our shift was over. Since I had enough seniority, I was off the rest of that weekend. That's when I saw the shooting of Oswald on TV, and that's when we got a lot of unjust criticism from the news media.

One of those high powered news reporters made me mad several times by putting it on us that we were a bunch of dummies because Oswald was killed. But, before that, the President was killed in our presence, and in just a few minutes, an officer sacrificed his life trying to arrest the guy that killed the President. The Dallas Police Department was back on top of the world for being a good, efficient outfit. Then, when Oswald was shot, our stock dropped right to the bottom again, as if it were our fault. But it wasn't our fault; we had orders to move him like that!

Chief Curry told me late that evening, "I want you and one jockey to come down here, and we're going to move Oswald to the county jail at two o'clock and nobody will know about it." Then what happened?

Elgin Crull, the city manager, and Earle Cabell, the mayor, eventually gave Chief Curry direct orders, "No, you will not do that! You will notify the news media and the press so that they can be in the basement with their lights and cameras set up before you move him." That's what got him killed! But we took the blame for it, and all of us were called a bunch of dummies. It eventually cost Curry his job because somebody else laid it on him and it wasn't him at all. But he wouldn't speak up!

Curry was a very close friend of mine. After he lost his job as chief, I ran into him later at Fair Park when I was getting my radio fixed. Curry was driving a van picking up parts and other stuff for a former policeman named K.K. Stanfield, who was in the building business. That day he was wearing old clothes driving that van. I made a U-turn when he flagged me down. As we talked, I told him, "I'm not going to be one to say I told you so, but I warned you ahead of time about what was about to happen, and you said you weren't worried about your assistant chief. All right, why don't you do this for us? Get on national television and make a statement or be interviewed where all the people in the United States can see it and tell them that you were ordered by Mr. Elgin Crull and Mr. Earle Cabell to do what you did and get the pressure off of you and all of us?"

"Oh, I can't do that!" What had happened was that they had already offered him a job to keep his mouth shut because it wasn't long after that they put him in charge of security for One Main Place, which was owned by all the big wheels in Dallas when it opened.

In 1961 I had been recalled to the military and was in charge of counterintelligence work stationed in Columbia, South Carolina. One of the agents who worked for me in my field office was Curry's son. Batchelor, his assistant chief, and several other chiefs at that time were trying to undercut Curry, and I told his son about it. In a couple of weeks, he came back and said, "I got a letter from dad. He said to tell you thanks, but he thought he could trust his assistant chief." Curry, who had a drinking problem, was asked to resign after the assassination. But we wanted him to at least tell the world what really happened and why we moved Oswald in front of all the lights and cameras and to tell how Ruby got in. But he wanted to keep the pressure off the people who were going to hire him for security at One Main Place.

I know how Ruby got in according to what our reports showed. The orders were the same on Sunday morning as they were on Friday night when I was up there on the third floor. If a cameraman came up and said, "This is one of my crew," I let them in as long as he identified himself as a cameraman. Ruby knew all those guys just like he knew some policemen from the Silver Spur. Wes Wise, a reporter who later became mayor, went up there. They all knew him.

I'm sure that he probably talked to some of those cameramen and said, "I sure would like to see what a guy that would do something like that would look like."

And one of the cameramen probably told him, "Here, carry this can of film in," and that's how he got in.

The news media turned it around by saying, "Well, a lot of policemen drank downtown with him and, on account of that, they knew him and let him in." That's not true! The officer that was there, Roy Vaughn, was one of the strictest and most efficient officers that we had. I'm convinced that he came in just like I said: carrying a can of film. What they should have done was to have had each one of the news media identify every one of their people with a badge or a button.

What brought about this lenient attitude toward the news media was that shortly before I had escorted Adlai Stevenson into town on the day shift. My men and I had him all day and nobody messed with him. We guarded him closely because we had heard that people were going to try to stop him. We got off at three o'clock and left him at the auditorium when Sergeant Bellah relieved me. That evening a woman spit in his face, and the news media told everyone what a bad bunch of people Dallas had. So we felt that the city fathers were trying to bend over backwards to be nice to the press to try to get a decent write up from the President's visit to Dallas. As it turned out, the President was killed, then we really bent over backwards to be good to them, especially on the third floor of City Hall. In the dispatcher's office, some news media guy came in, used the phone, climbed up on the table and began taking pictures. That shouldn't have been possible!

There's a guy I know out here in Oak Cliff who believes that all this was a conspiracy: Oswald didn't do all this; we did Oswald in; the Secret Service and the FBI put it on him because they couldn't get anybody else. You hear people talk on the street that wonder if Oswald killed him or not. These are people who are supposed to have good common sense! Then you have those that saw it happen like those motor jockeys. They know where the shots came from. They know that they didn't come from the top of a building or the grassy knoll. If there had been any shots fired from the grassy knoll, I couldn't have missed it since I was right even with that area when the shots were fired.

Baker said that he saw something that would indicate that somebody was shooting out of that window. When he got off his motor near the front of that building, he told the man in charge of that operation and they went inside. They couldn't get the freight elevator down, so Baker and the man went up the stairs. That's when they encountered Oswald drinking a coke on the second floor. Baker was told that he was all right, that he worked there. That's where Baker messed up! He should have sealed off the building and not let anybody out till it was ascertained that nobody there had anything to do with it. He could have saved an officer's life had he arrested him there, had he done what he was supposed to have done. We don't say anything to him about it; officers make mistakes just like everybody else.

On the other hand, Baker wasn't real bright either. Before he went to Washington to testify to the Warren Commission, he went into Captain Lawrence's office and said, "Captain, I've got to go to Washington. Don't you think the city ought to buy me a suit?" Ain't that some bull crap? I don't know why, but the boys called him "Momma Son." But he was always slow. That's the reason I didn't have him in a responsible position on that escort. When I got the assignment from the chief to put somebody on that press bus, I put him there to just trail along.

We had similar case with another officer named McLain. We had a guy come to Dallas several years ago with a sound device listening to some noise on one of the police radios. He said that he counted seven shots. McLain told them it was his radio making the noise, so he was taken to Washington and questioned. Mac didn't know what in the hell he was talking about. He was kind of a nit wit, and when he went up there, he made an ass out of our whole department. It was disgraceful! I think he just wanted a trip to Washington.

In a way, the Tippit shooting was closer to us than that of Kennedy. It was like family to us. If you heard about a guy being killed, that would be real bad, but if somebody from your family was killed, that would be even worse. That's the way it was.

I knew Tippit, though not very well. He wasn't known much outside his patrol unit because he was so quiet. Right after he was killed, his captain, Captain Solomon, told me that the reason he was killed was that when he talked to somebody he wouldn't keep his eyes on him; he might look off and question them. He said that many times when Tippit worked for him he had to correct him about that. It may have been the reason that Oswald was able to kill him.

Some have suggested that it was unusual that Tippit was never promoted. It wasn't. A lot of guys didn't get promotions for more than ten years. Jim Chaney was about as efficient an officer as you'd ever find in all aspects of police work. He was good; he was great; and he didn't make it. He made the sergeant's list once after taking the promotion exam. I'm not sure how they do it now, but in those days they'd pick those who scored the highest on the promotion exam for promotion. Chaney worked himself up to number one on the list and was waiting for one of the other officers to retire. Unfortunately, the officer didn't choose to retire and since an opening didn't come up on the list, it was canceled and a new exam had to be given. It disgusted Chaney to the point that I don't think he ever took another one. So there was nothing unusual about Tippit not being promoted.

After the assassination, the FBI did their investigative work on the curb where I had seen the shot hit and cut off the section to analyze. However, they cut off the wrong section. We later found the place where it hit. Sergeant Harkness knows. He was a three-wheel sergeant who worked traffic downtown.

He first became involved in all this several months earlier when one of his three-wheelers apparently saw Oswald passing out pamphlets about Cuba, which was illegal in the city of Dallas without a permit. Harkness was called in to investigate and, of course, Harkness was also in the downtown area when all this happened with the President.

Most of the officers I knew spoke in favor of Kennedy, though a few didn't. I had a great deal of respect for him because I thought he had a lot of guts, especially in regard to the missile crisis. What teed me off was that somebody like Oswald, who was so sorry that he wasn't worth the powder it takes to blow him to hell, kills a president, a young president, who was doing a good job for us.

Oswald went to Russia, stayed over two years, denounced our type of government, married a girl from over there whose uncle was in Russian intelligence, then comes over here and kills the President. The people of the United States made a big deal out of her and made her a millionaire. I was really teed off about that! And still there are these people in the United States who believe that Oswald was all right. It's ridiculous!

Ellis continued to ride motorcycles until his retirement from the Dallas Police Department in 1976. After twenty years of service, he also retired as an Army major and still lives in Dallas.

W.G. "BILL" LUMPKIN
Solo Motorcycle Officer
Dallas Police Department

"We were going fast, very fast! I'm going to say we might have hit speeds up to 80-85 M.P.H. on Stemmons... I saw the limousine behind us, and I noticed this Secret Service man hanging on the back of it with his coat hanging, and I was amazed that he could hang on.... When we got to Hines, there was a railroad track, and I know that I got airborne....I knew that if I went down I'd probably get run over..."

Born and raised in Avery, Texas, Bill Lumpkin worked at General Dynamics as an aircraft electrician after serving a hitch in the military. He joined the Dallas Police Department in 1953 and was assigned as one of the lead motorcycle officers in the Kennedy motorcade.

I don't know what time we went to work that day. I remember having a detail with all the squads of the motor jockeys together, and we were all given our assignments. We knew the route and where we were going and approximately how long we were going to be. We were told what to do in case things happened, what hospital to go to if an emergency came up. That would be the only time we would use the siren.

I was one of the people that led the parade along with Leon Gray, Ellis, and McBride. There were quite a few of us in the parade, but some of the motor jockeys weren't assigned to the parade. Some of them were sent to stand-by stations. It wasn't considered necessarily an honor; you just did what they told you. I escorted a lot of parades, so it was just an assignment. Probably if I hadn't been in the parade, my feelings would have been hurt. But we used to have a lot of parades in town and there had been times when the other jockeys had gone out of town on assignments, and I'd stayed in to lead a parade because I had done it so many times. I was used to doing it.

There was nothing special about that particular morning. We spit and polished our equipment and our uniforms and were told to assemble at Love Field. There were a lot of folks there, a lot of folks!

We had no problems with the parade except one time, I believe, the President got out of the car on Lemmon. The Secret Service got on the back end and proceeded again. When you lead a parade, you limit your speed to whatever speed they want to go. And so we really had to keep our eye on his vehicle by turning around and looking because he was slowing down.

My job in leading the parade was to make sure the crowd was back out of the street in front, and then, of course, you alert the officers up on the parade route that the parade is behind you. But the main thing is, when you're four abreast like that, you keep the street clear for the parade. You look back and try to be sure that the parade is in a group, that it hadn't straggled out. And you can slow them down for that. But nothing stands out. It was just a presidential motorcade.

We were in front of the President's car when the shooting took place. We were stopped on Elm Street between Houston Street and the Triple Underpass. There were only three of us at the time. McBride had already gone over to Stemmons to notify them that we were getting ready to come through since they were going to close Stemmons northbound. Sergeant Ellis had asked him to go on up and notify them that we were en route. But we had turned off of Main Street onto Houston for one block, then over to Elm Street, then turned back left, and we were stopped at the time before we heard the shots.

When the shots occurred, I thought it was a motorcycle backfiring. The motors were running really hot because we had been going slowly for so long. They would have a tendency to backfire when they were running hot, and running slow for a long period would cause them to run hot.

I heard three distinct bangs with none of them being together or anything like that. There's been conflicting reports where all the noise came from. From where I was it was behind me. I've heard people say a lot of different things over the years, but when you have buildings and other obstructions, you're going to have an echo factor and different opinions.

The shots came from behind where I was and, as I mentioned, I thought it was a motorcycle backfiring at first, till I turned back and saw the commotion in the President's convertible. I wasn't sure at the time what it was, but it later turned out that it was his wife on the back. There was no problem seeing the car, but at the time, I just saw a figure. Then Chaney rode up to Curry and probably told him that the President had been shot.

We were still stopped at that time, and then Chief Curry comes on and says, "Let's go boys!" I'm not sure that there was anything said other than that and, of course, we headed for Parkland because we knew in case something happened, that was where we were supposed to go.

We went under the Triple Underpass and took the entrance ramp to Stemmons Freeway. At that time, Sergeant Ellis stopped there at Stemmons. Leon Gray, Chaney, and myself escorted the parade on to Parkland Hospital by way of Stemmons, to Industrial, Industrial to Hines, Hines to the entrance into the back of Parkland.

We were going fast, very fast! I'm going to say we might have hit speeds up to 80-85 M.P.H. on Stemmons. We were going just as fast as we could get the car to go. I saw the limousine behind us, and I noticed this Secret Service man hanging on the back of it with his coat hanging, and I was amazed that he could hang on. When we got to Hines, there was a railroad track, and I know that I got airborne. I'm sure that I was out front and Gray and Chaney were behind me. More than likely they got airborne, too. You didn't have a lot of space over on the other end, and when you land to turn, I knew that if I went down I'd probably get run over. But you train and you know that you can drag your footstand without going over as long as you don't go over too far. Oh, you're going to get some sparks and some noise when you go over that far, but unless you get on some oil or sand or something like that, you can stay up. But it was a fast ride!

Nothing much goes through your mind at a time like that. You know that you've got a job to do, and you want to do your job well. When we came off of Stemmons, we were supposed to turn into Market Hall. Sergeant Striegel and some other officers were there, including some other jockeys, and he came out into the street waving because we were going too fast and that we were supposed to pull in there. I guess he hadn't heard that the President had been shot, and you have to worry about him not getting too far out into the street. But you're concerned with just doing your job when something like this happens. After it's over, then you have time to think about it.

When we turned in to the hospital, there was only a certain amount of parking space back there. Since I was in the lead, I stopped to get off my motor to make sure that cars that didn't belong there didn't come in because I was in a better position to react. So I stopped probably a couple hundred feet from the emergency entrance. When the last cars that I knew and the last jockeys came in, I stopped traffic. We had to get all that secured. I was the only one right then. Later some people came up to help me, but it wasn't any big problem then. You just stepped out and stopped them. That was the main thing you wanted to do was to just get more cars in there so you could maneuver the other vehicles.

I was probably still in the process of just getting off my motor when the limousine came by. I saw the President slumped down, and I saw Lyndon Johnson. Johnson was like a ghost; I thought he was shot. He came by after the President riding in a different vehicle, if I remember right. His face was familiar to me because I had had some problems with him in the past back when he was running the year Kennedy got the nomination.

Leon Gray, at that time, was my partner. Our assignment was that we were to ride on each side of his vehicle for his protection to keep people from rushing it. On this occasion, it was already past our time to get off, but we had to go ahead and finish the escort. Johnson didn't have any good things to say about motor jockeys, and he told his driver to force Gray back to the side of his car, which he did. He forced Gray into the curb on a bridge on Zang and nearly caused him to wreck. I had some words with his driver, so I guess that's why I knew Johnson pretty well.

Anyway, I didn't see much of the President other than he was just slumped down and that he had been shot, and that his brains had been blown out. I must have seen that somewhere along the way. I know they kept wanting to know whether Kennedy was going to make his speech at the Market Hall, and finally this three-wheel officer came on and told them that his brains were blown out, and he wasn't going to be there. But nobody would make a decision to tell them that he wouldn't be there, and this kept coming over the radio: "Well, is he going to be able to make the speech?" We knew that he was dead.

We stayed out at Parkland for a long time, and then they sent us downtown to guard Oswald. We were on the third floor where they had him. There were quite a few of us up there and, of course, there were newspaper reporters and cameramen from all over.

The scene up there was wild! Absolutely wild! Forcefully, you had keep them back. It was hysteria! Just asking them to stay back wouldn't do. They weren't responding! I can remember the cameras back then had big battery packs that looked like they weighed eighty or ninety pounds. I imagine they probably weighed a lot less than that, but they were big things, and their TV cameras were monstrous. Anyway, I can remember this guy that must have weighed over four hundred pounds who wouldn't stay back, and finally, I just had to put my fist into his stomach because I weighed only about 160. Manners were a thing of the past, or courtesy. You could ask our own people to do something and they would try to cooperate with you. In fact, we knew quite a few of them personally. But the national people, a lot of them just didn't want to do what you asked them to do. They decided that they knew how close they could get a lot better than you did. But there was such a rush and, I guess, everybody wanted a story. I've been involved in escorts for Elvis Presley and the Beatles, and those were wild. But the crowds were young. These were adult people that you expect more out of.

I saw Oswald a few times. He was screaming and hollering and all this. He was like a wild man claiming his innocence. I don't remember what all he was saying, but I think he was talking about conspiracy. They didn't move him any more than they had to, I'm sure, but they brought him out of Captain Fritz's office,

Homicide Division, and down a private elevator where I think they took him down to the lineups or details.

I think I got home around midnight that night as we stayed fairly late till they got some of the photographers out. I was off duty the next day because I had Saturdays and Sundays off then. Fortunately I wasn't there when Oswald was killed.

That was an hellacious mistake! It should never have happened even though I can see how it did happen. To me, that was a lot worse to Dallas than the President being killed.

I knew Jack Ruby, and I know that a lot of officers knew him. He owned nightclubs, and if you went in his place you didn't have to worry about the establishment. If you wanted to arrest somebody, you did not fight the establishment; you only had to worry about the person you were arresting. I had made some arrests up in his places and knew that you didn't have to worry about him if you were given a hard time by his enticing the crowd of people in his club not to let them arrest this person; in other words, trying to turn the crowd against you. He liked officers. I think he appreciated the job that they did, so I can see how he could have gotten down there and shot Oswald.

But I didn't know him that well and didn't know that much about him. I'd been in the Vegas Club out on Oak Lawn and the Carousel downtown, but I didn't drink, so I didn't go into those type places other than to make arrests or on some police matter.

Like I've said, City Hall was a mess that weekend which definitely contributed to what happened to Oswald. Jesse Curry probably was responsible for that, but he had bosses, too, and any chief has a certain amount of politics to play. I'm just speculating, though, because I was just a patrolman. They gave me a job to do and I did it. But City Hall belonged to the public, and I guess they were trying to let the public have as much freedom as they could.

Personally, I'd like to have seen the press cleared out, but I do know that you have to let the press know. It would have been a whole lot easier if we could have just stood at the door and not let anybody in and had all the fighting there instead of having this whole hallway full of people pushing and shoving and trying to get room for more.

I think the Dallas Police Department handled it about as well as any department would have. Regardless of where it happened, you're going to have to let the press have access, and then you have to let more in than you really like. But I think Dallas did as well as anybody would have and maybe better than a lot.

Looking back, the motorcycle patrolmen were an independent bunch back then. When I went into the Motorcycle Division, you were voted on before you got in. If the other jockeys thought you had an attitude that they thought was going to create problems, you wouldn't get on motors. That way the people knew you. You had to have a vote of confidence for you to get on. And you had good and bad motor jockeys just like you have in anything else. But it was like a club, and we were real close. I don't think that closeness prevailed in Radio Patrol. I know we had some jockeys that would kind of brag to the Radio Patrol about how great it was, and I chewed a lot of them out for that because, if you've got something good going, if you're going pretty smooth, don't rock the boat and brag to somebody else that you've got it made a whole lot better than them. But we're like kinfolks. Some of the new motor jockeys I don't know, but I still have coffee with some of the older ones today.

A couple of asides... Officer J.D. Tippit and I were from the same Red River County up in Northwest Texas. I knew him, but I never worked with him. Tippit was in Radio Patrol, and since I stayed on Radio Patrol only about nine months and then went to Traffic Division, I never worked with him. I went on a three-wheeler then, from there to solo, and I knew a lot of these people because we didn't have substations back then when I went to work, so we all met at the same place. But you'd just speak to them and that was it. Some of them you knew better than others. Some of us were loudmouths, and some were pretty quiet. Tippit was fairly quiet. When I heard that Tippit had been shot, we had a traffic hit and run investigator named Tippitt, and I thought that's who it was that got shot. But you just wonder how he got shot because he was a pretty strong guy.

I also knew Mary Moorman. She and McBride went to school together, I believe it was. That's how I met her, and she was down there with another lady named Jean Hill, so I knew them both. Mary took a picture of me sitting on my motorcycle there in front of the Triple Underpass just before Kennedy arrived. Then she took a picture of Kennedy and received a cash settlement for quite a bit of money. I've seen her a number of times since then.

She gave me the Polaroid picture of me straddling this motorcycle, but I don't know where it is now. I knew where it was for a long time, and some years ago, somebody wanted to look at it, and now it's misplaced. I've been asked about that picture a number of times, but I just remember it had me being on a motorcycle. It didn't show anything suspicious that I recall. I didn't pay that much attention to it since I don't care much about getting my picture taken.

I retired in 1981 after twenty-seven and a half years on the department. When I retired, another man and I had a business selling and repairing lawn mowers, chain saws, garden tractors, and tillers. We sold that business, and now I'm helping raise grandchildren.

———————————

Bill Lumpkin now works on a part-time basis as a bailiff for the Dallas County Sheriff's Department and lives with his wife in Mesquite, Texas.

H.B. McLAIN
Solo Motorcycle Officer
Dallas Police Department

"Unfortunately all their accusations that it was my microphone that was stuck open and the shots were heard on it were printed in the newspapers, and it'll be that way from now on. They'll never be convinced otherwise, regardless of what I say..."

Born in the piney woods of East Texas in Nacogdoches County, H.B. McLain moved to Dallas in 1942, attended high school for six weeks, then joined the Merchant Marines during the Second World War. After joining the Dallas Police Department in 1953, he worked in the Patrol and Burglary and Theft Divisions until he became a solo motorcycle officer in November 1955. McLain was one of the escort officers in the motorcade on November 22, 1963.

––––––––––––

It was a hazy morning as we went out to Love Field to wait for the President to come in. When we arrived, we parked our motorcycles on the outside of the fenced area until he arrived. Then, as the motorcade began, we met it at the gate and came on out.

The escort route had been picked out for him by the Tactical Group. Normally we had done our own scheduling, but they took it upon themselves this time. It was rather unusual because they had people working in positions they didn't normally work. We usually rode side by side with the senior man riding on the left and the junior man on the right. In this case, they had it reversed.

My assignment was to ride alongside the procession mostly between the President's car and the press buses five or six cars behind the President on the left side. There was nothing extra special about the escort as we had done many of them. It was routine.

Our job was to keep the pedestrians back out of the way so they didn't get run over. We'd just ride alongside, and if anybody was too close, we'd tell them to move back. If that didn't work, we might bump them.

There were a lot of people along the motorcade route, especially in the downtown area from Akard to Houston Streets. When I made the turn onto Houston on the left side, we had caught up with the cars in front of us, and I had stopped right by the side of the entrance to the old jail, which is about midway between Main and Elm Streets on Houston. I heard one very clear shot. Evidently I must have felt like it was coming from straight ahead because at that instant I was looking down, and when I heard the shot, threw my head up and it appeared that about 5,000 pigeons flew out from behind that building (the Texas School Book Depository) straight ahead. In fact, I thought to myself, "Somebody's shooting at the pigeons!" But I could see the limousine off to my left on Elm and saw Mrs. Kennedy crawling on the back of the car. I had a good idea that somebody had been shot at but didn't know which one.

About that time the chief came on the radio and said, "Get to Parkland Hospital!" and the race was on.

As I sped through Dealey Plaza, the only thing I noticed was Hargis with his motorcycle laid down crawling on his hands and knees across the grassy knoll. I didn't have any idea what he was doing. You think maybe he might have fallen or that he lost his footing when he stepped off and slipped on the grass.

In any case, I caught up with and got in front of the limousine on Stemmons somewhere around Continental. The ride was wild! You know in your mind that you're going way too fast, but if you slow down or fall, the cars behind are going to run over you. But you don't think about those things, though, at the time; it's all instinct.

We had to slow down when we got off Stemmons at Industrial. Along Industrial there was a railroad track which was located on a small incline some twenty to thirty feet before we were to hit

Harry Hines Boulevard. Chaney, myself and another officer went airborne up the incline, hit the ground, and made the sharp left onto Hines.

When we arrived at the hospital, I parked my motorcycle and came back to the limousine about fifteen feet away. As the hospital orderlies approached to take him out of the car, Mrs. Kennedy was still laying over him, covering his head, and wouldn't get up. So I took it upon myself, reached over and caught her by the shoulder, pulled her and said, "Come on, let them take him out." Somebody threw a coat over him just as she raised up, and they took him out on the right side of the car. She then stepped out on the left, stunned, and walked with me in a daze into the emergency room.

I figured at the time that the wound was fatal. Part of the skull was laying on the floorboard. Blood and brain material was splattered all over as if a ripe watermelon had been dropped. It was a pretty gory scene.

As I left the emergency room and was walking down the hall, one of the Secret Service agents told an FBI agent to get out of the building. "I'm with the FBI," and he started to ask him something. "I want you to get out of here!"

"But I'm with the FBI," he said.

"I don't give a goddamn who you're with! Get out of here!" The Secret Service agent then grabbed him by the nape of the neck, carried him to the door, and told the officer on the door, "Don't let this man back in here!" As a result, the FBI agent became belligerent. He seemed to think that because he was with the FBI that he could butt in and do whatever he wanted. Other than that and with everybody moaning and crying, the general scene at the hospital was under control. Later the motorcycle officers were then assigned to City Hall to control the turmoil there while Oswald was in custody. All I did was to stand in front of Homicide's door and keep people out. The following days, Saturday and Sunday, all of the solo motorcycle officers were off duty.

We tried to put most of this behind us as much as possible until it all came up again in 1977 when the House Select Committee on Assassinations began re-investigating all of this. The best I can figure is that the people doing it didn't know what the hell they were doing. They were jumping to conclusions. They sent one investigator down here to talk with us, and he began telling us what had happened and how it happened. We said, "To hell with you; we ain't telling you anything!" So he left and the next thing we knew the acoustics stuff was coming out.

The police department recorded on tape all radio transmissions on the two channels operating that day. We used Channel 2 for special assignments such as the motorcade and Channel 1 for regular assignments. We were all tuned in to Channel 2. At the time of the assassination, a mike on one of the motorcycles was stuck in the on position on Channel 1. Somehow the investigators concluded that one of our mikes was stuck, even though we weren't on that channel, and therefore the sound and number of shots would be recorded on the tape.

I talked to them several times to pinpoint where I was sitting, where the mike was on my motorcycle, and which way I was headed. I was surprised that I was being accused of being the one with the stuck mike because if mine was stuck, I couldn't have heard any of the other stuff that was going on.

To operate the radio, you had to press the button to talk on it. As a result, you couldn't hear anything and most of the others couldn't hear anything either other than what you were saying. Once you let off the button the channel was open again. But you wouldn't necessarily know if your mike was stuck open until you began to notice that you were hearing nothing on the radio. You could still transmit but you couldn't hear anything.

Eventually I was called to Washington. When I got up there in the late afternoon, they whisked me over to the hotel and asked me a bunch of questions. They told me what they were going to do, what they were going to ask, and what they were trying to prove. Something was said about the tapes and they said, "No, you don't need to hear the tapes."

The questions they asked couldn't be answered with a yes or no answer. They worded the questions so that the answers I gave fit their way of thinking because they were trying to reopen the investigation. The questions were hypothetical like: "Could this have happened?" or "Is it possible?" The only way I could answer was, "It's possible. Anything's possible." But I don't think I answered them with a yes or no. In fact, I really didn't know at the time what they were getting at.

When I got back from Washington, J.C. Bowles, who was the chief dispatcher and who had studied the tapes, called me and asked if I'd heard the tapes. When I told him, no, he said, "Can you come by my office when you get off work?" So I went by there and was told to take two tapes into the other room. He set up a cassette recorder and told me, "Play this one; listen to it; then play this other one and listen to it." When I came out, he asked, "Is that your mike that's stuck?" and I replied that it wasn't. "Why?"

I told him, "It's a three-wheeler that's stuck."

You can tell very clearly the difference between the sound of a solo motorcycle that we rode and a three-wheel motorcycle; it's like daylight and dark. The solo engine has kind of a thump to it: CHUKE.. CHUKE.. CHUKE.., while the three-wheeler has more of a thrashing sound.. AAANG.. AAANG.. AAANG! You could hear this all on the tapes, but the people in Washington didn't listen. They were trying to tell us what it was.

While in Washington, they commenced to ask all kinds of questions: "Well, did you hear Curry say this, or did you hear that?"

"Yeah, I heard it!" I said.

"Well, how can you hear it if your mike's stuck?"

My mike ain't stuck," I responded. If they'd have let me listen to the tapes before I went up there, I could have told them right quick that it wasn't my motorcycle but that it was a three-wheeler. In fact, that three-wheeler was three miles away at the Trade Mart, thus they didn't hear any shots on the tapes and their theory was not valid.

The noise they heard was the radio popping. Those old radios popped all the time. Sometimes it sounded like a gun going off. But their investigator didn't listen to any of that; he didn't listen to the motors running.

Basically I didn't think they were honest with the whole situation. They sent some guy down here to investigate something, and he didn't know what the hell he was doing. You don't start investigating by telling people how it happened; you ask them how it happened. We tried to tell him but he said, "No, it happened this way!"

So we told him, "To hell with you! We ain't telling you anything!"

Dallas Police Chief Jesse Curry

Dallas Police Officer J.D. Tippit

Lee Harvey Oswald is surrounded by Dallas police officers as he faces the press on Friday night.

Jim Ewell, reporter, then and now (pages 3-20).

Hugh Aynesworth, reporter (21-40)

James Altgens, photographer (41-59)

Charles Brehm, Dealey Plaza eyewitness (60-69)

Ruth Dean, left, and Ruth Hendrix, right, Dealey Plaza eyewitnesses (70-72 and 73-79)

Clemon Johnson (79-83)   Roy E. Lewis (84-89)

Malcolm Summers, eyewitness, then and now (102-108)

Otis Williams, eyewitness,
then and now (116-120)

T.E. Moore, Dealey Plaza eyewitness, then and later (90-93)

Bill Newman (94-101)

James Tague (109-115)

James W. Courson (127-131)   Marrion L. Baker (123-126)   W.G. Lumpkin (154-161)

Courson, Baker and Lumpkin were motorcycle officers escorting the president.

Bobby Joe Dale, motorcycle patrolman, then and now (132-141)

Stavis Ellis, motorcycle patrolman, being greeted by the President, and now (142-153)

H.B. McClain, then and now (162-68)   James C. Bowles, then and now (169-94)

Joe Murphy, police officer at
Dealey Plaza (194-96)

Edgar L. Smith, police officer at Dealey
Plaza, then and now (197-203)

David V. Harkness, police officer
at Dealey Plaza (204-210)

J.W. Foster, police officer
at Triple Underpass (211-214)

Dallas County deputy sheriffs Lummie Lewis and Jack Faulkner

Jack Faulkner, deputy sheriff (215-223)

Carl Day, lieutenant, Dallas Police Crime Lab (231-244)

Luke Mooney, deputy sheriff (224-28)

Vincent Drain, FBI agent (245-262)

Elmo Cunningham, Dallas Police
lieutenant (263-284)

Paul Bentley, Dallas Police polygraph examiner, then and now (285-291)

Gerald L. Hill (292-305)

John Toney (306-312)

W.R. Westbrook (313-325)

Roy Westphal (326-335)

Gus Rose, homicide detective, then and now (336-350)

Harry D. Holmes,
U.S. postal
inspector (351-371)

Jim Leavelle and L.C. Graves, Dallas Police homicide detectives (375-385 and 386-409)

Jim Leavelle, left, playing himself, an actor portraying Oswald and an actor portraying L.C. Graves in the film, "Ruby and Oswald."

L.D. Montgomery, Dallas Police homicide detective,
then and now (410-418)

Orville Jones, Dallas Police captain
(423-435)

Rio S. Pierce, Dallas Police lieutenant,
then and now (436-442)

Charles O. Arnett, Dallas
Police Reserves
captain (419-422)

Roy Vaughn, Dallas patrol officer (443-455)

Don Flusche, Dallas patrol
officer (456-466)

Bill Courson, deputy sheriff, then
and now (481-506)

Joe Cody, Dallas
Police
detective (467-480)

Al Maddox, deputy sheriff (507-517)

W.W. "Bo" Mabra, deputy
sheriff (518-529)

William F. (Bill) Alexander, assistant district attorney (530-555)

Unfortunately all their accusations that it was my microphone that was stuck open and the shots were heard on it were printed in the newspapers, and it'll be that way from now on. They'll never be convinced otherwise, regardless of what I say. "Well, sure that's the first thing he's going to say; he's going to deny it." To hell with them!

Bowles, who is now the sheriff of Dallas County, and I have met several times and talked about it. On the tapes, some investigators have made a big deal out of a sound that they claim is a church bell. It wasn't anything but a loose manhole cover in the street. One day when I'd left his office and was walking across the street, just as I stepped up on the curb on the other side of the street, I heard a BONG... BONG sound. I turned around and noticed a pickup truck making a left turn onto Jackson Street. The front wheel ran over the manhole cover, then the back wheel. It was loose: BONG... BONG! So I went back to Bowles and told him what I'd heard, and he said, "That sounds logical." After a period of time, we figured out where the motorcycle with the stuck mike was and who was on it because the tapes indicate the rider whistled. We only knew one officer who whistled all the time that rode motorcycles. After doing some checking, we found that he was assigned to the Trade Mart at that time three miles from Dealey Plaza. Also you could hear the sheriff's car radio on the tapes. There was only one sheriff's car radio, and it was also assigned to the Trade Mart, so the stuck mike couldn't have been anywhere else. So, if the investigator from Washington would have listened to us, the whole matter would have been cleared up without all the controversy.

As a result of adverse experiences like that, most of the motorcycle officers don't want to get involved any further in the subject. I don't dwell on it; I just let it go and keep going. It's similar to someone in your family dying: you grieve for a while, then eventually you get to where it gets a little further back in time. It's always still there, but you don't think about it near as much as you do the first two or three years.

Officer McLain, after 27 years, retired from the police department in 1980. The following year, after J.C. Bowles was elected sheriff, McLain then joined the sheriff's department and eventually was promoted to sergeant in the Warrant's Division. H.B. McLain retired from the sheriff's department in 1996.

JAMES C. BOWLES
Communications Supervisor
Dallas Police Department

"McLain assumed, since they were government lawyers working for the flag, motherhood, and Chevrolet coupes, that they wouldn't lie to you. McLain had no idea, in his naive innocence, that they were trying to concoct a tale and that he was a vital validator to their chain..."

After serving a stint in the Navy and later operating a small business, James Bowles joined the Dallas Police Department in 1951. In 1963, Bowles was the communications supervisor of the dispatch office. In the years following the assassination, Bowles transcribed the so-called Dallas Police Tapes and later wrote a manuscript titled "The Kennedy Assassination Tapes: A Rebuttal to the Acoustics Evidence." Based on his background with the police department, he is recognized as the authority on the inner workings of the radio communications of the Dallas Police Department and corresponding events at the time of the assassination.

I was at Love Field as part of the reception for the President while my dad, Major, was at Baylor Hospital after suffering a stroke. Before the President arrived, Chief Fisher* came over to me and said that Major had taken a turn for the worse and that I'd better take his car over to the hospital before it was too late. So I

---

* The title "chief" is an umbrella term used by Dallas policemen for
assistant chiefs and deputy chiefs as well as the chief of police.

took his car, rushed to the hospital, and returned as soon as I could. By then the reception at the airport was over. My dad passed away about the same time as Kennedy, so I had to divide my attention between family and department matters for the next couple of days.

Since I was the communications supervisor in charge of the dispatch office, I became involved with the tapes of all radio communications of the Dallas Police Department that day, the same tapes which were analyzed by the Warren Commission and later the House Select Committee on Assassinations. There should be no controversy about the tapes. The tapes are very simple and self explanatory if you accept them for what they're worth. Now, if you have a bit of imagination, you can use all kinds of dreams and concoctions to try to fabricate anything you want with them. Very simply, the tapes are recordings of the two radio channels operating at that time.

Regular police operations were maintained on Channel 1. All personnel assigned to the Presidential motorcade, which ultimately became involved in the assassination scenario, were on Channel 2.

It's hard to say whether they operated continuously or not. What we had in there was a sound activated recorder with a delay so it would pick it up and hold in the record mode for four seconds after the sound or noise level dropped, and there were two recording systems, one each on the two channel operations. On Channel 1 we used a two phase dictaphone voice recording. I stress voice recording because it was not a precision quality; it was a stenographic type recording. You had a comparatively dull stylus making a simple impression on a thin celluloid belt.

The Channel 2 activity was a little better in its potential but not as good in reality because of its age. We had an old Gray recorder; I think they called them Gray audiographs. Anyway, it was a thin flat disk with the stylus cutting a groove in the disk much like in the typical phonographic recording. But the machine was old and worn. It was prone quite frequently to repeating itself, picking up transmissions and not letting them go. There were times when it was repeating itself that it didn't pick up what someone was saying. Then there were times that it didn't pick up anything. In other words, it just didn't work. So we have no way of knowing what traffic would have been on Channel 2 had we had a more sophisticated, state of the art, by today's standards, recording capability.

One point that needs to be clarified which some folks, qualified and unqualified, who have tried to pick up and run with the assassination investigations, don't seem to understand. They use the words "voice activated" very generally and inaccurately. More correctly it's not voice, it's sound activated. Sound would turn it on if the decibel level was sufficient. They were sound activated, not just voice activated.

At the time of the initial investigation following the assassination, we impounded the tapes and held all records for just that purpose, the ensuing investigation. When the FBI took the tapes and tried to make audible sense out of them, they found that they couldn't comprehend the tape traffic because they couldn't understand the speech style used on the radio. The things that were said by the officers on the radio made complete sense to the officers, but they didn't make a bit of sense to the transcribers. So an FBI agent brought the tapes back to the department, and the chief gave them back to me and asked me to transcribe them for him; of course, understanding that we didn't have a lot of conspiracy theorists in our midst at that time. It was fairly obvious that Oswald had killed the President; Oswald then killed Tippit; we captured Oswald, and then Ruby killed Oswald. By the time we got a chance to run the tapes, it was just a matter of organizing the information to support the empirical things that we had before us. So I didn't go into any effort; in fact, I couldn't. We didn't have the scientific measuring devices then to put the tapes on the digital analysis machine, nor did we have good recorders then. Today the voice can be analyzed by voice measurements.

This is no reflection on the dictaphone people. In fact, they laughed when I told them what the Assassination Subcommittee was trying to do with the dictaphone belts. The head of the company and their chief engineer said, "I wish we could take credit for being that good. We'd love to run an advertisement, but I don't think it would be supportable."

The general capability, for example, for both those recording systems is what is generally referred to as being voice quality, which is also generally applied to telephone level voice quality: somewhere between 200-250 decibels on the low side to maybe

172 NO MORE SILENCE

2400-2500 on the high side. This doesn't mean that anything less than that or greater than that was automatically, at that point, eliminated and cancelled. The machine tried to hear anything that presented itself to it via sound waves, but it was most specifically designed to hear and translate those that came within the frequency range it was designed to handle. It would try to respond to the other sound sources, but it didn't do so quite faithfully. The reason I draw that point is that when you start making precise scientific measures of a machine that can't pick up more than about 2500 cycles recording supersonic frequency indications on the belt itself, they had to be induced from outside; they couldn't have been produced by the system itself. This was especially true when you consider that we used regular telephone company land lines to transmit radio traffic between field units and radio transmitter tower, receiving tower, and the radio transmitting office from downtown.

What we had was any sound coming from the field came to the radio transmitter tower, then through telephone lines to the dispatcher's office to be received and to be transmitted, or monitored and recorded by the dispatcher's office. And all radio traffic from the dispatcher went through the microphone over telephone lines to the tower and then by radio out to the field units. So radio traffic was filtered several times in the process. Both signals originating in and being dispatched to the dispatcher's office went through telephone company equipment, which again, it was incapable of handling and was designed to filter out any conflicting frequencies below and above the normal voice range. This was what the equipment was designed to handle, and this is what the equipment did handle.

Not having any indication that we should be looking for some mysterious, covert conspiracy indications and not having the equipment to look for it if we did have suspicions, I just made a recording of it with a nice reel to reel tape recorder which the FBI furnished to me and then set about from the original tapes and the original Gray audiograph disks to transcribe the tapes using the originals because, according to the law, that's the best evidence. The tapes were in as good a condition as you would expect considering the fact that the FBI had tried to transcribe them using a single stylus.

When playing back the original disk, which had a dual control head on it which you just flipped to one side and it recorded, and the other side was playback, if you put it on record, it recorded. When you flipped it to playback, you set it back over and it would play back what you'd recorded. The belt was different; you put the belt on a machine and it used the same stylus. You had a little up, down and neutral position on it; put it one way and you played back, the other way it recorded.I also made backup tapes since it was obvious that there would be damage to the original tapes during the process. They couldn't take that kind of wear, after wear, after wear and still be considered unaltered. Every use of them has the potential, the probability, the inevitibility of alteration.

The tapes themselves were in our custody until we turned them over to the FBI, which would have been in late November or early December, right after the assassination. I believe it was around March of the next year that they returned them to us where they were placed in a safe, probably in Chief George Lumpkin's office. Eventually they came under the custody of Paul McCaghren within the police department. I have no reason to suspect that the FBI did anything with them because the conversation on the tape is wholly consistent with what people who were actively present remembered from that day. No one determined anything. But here you would have to impeach the integrity of the FBI and their laboratory if you want to question whether or not there was an alteration of the tapes. Remember, even the House Select Committee and the National Academy of Sciences put in computer monitors on the belts and on the tapes so that the consistency of the tapes used indicated no interruption, alteration or changes. Both agreed as well as could be that the tapes at the last instance are the same as the original tapes in the first instance. No hanky panky!

Engineers say that anytime you induce some change there's liable to be some evidence of difference. There'll be a frequency change enough that even using similar equipment that there would be an induction of however many cycles it runs on, that you'll hear a certain amount of interference, a certain noise on the line, and that that noise wasn't present. The noise that was present was there all throughout. The tape showed no interruptions which would indicate no alteration.

This is what I believe happened to the tapes whenever the House Select Committee felt it convenient to find these supersonic impressions: sound impressions, which were sounds without making sounds. They acknowledged that they found similar impressions throughout the entire belt. Suddenly, when you got within that small parameter, which would be the approximate place to try to look for something that would tend to support shots being fired, they found no such. But they found a convenient array where the approximate separation in time would be the equivalent to the order of the three shots fired, and then they found some others and identified one of those as the fourth shot. All other sound impressions that they found were discounted as having any relevance. This is called selective evidence.

These impression points were all through the tape. What I believe the House Select Committee was doing was trying to look at them as line or transmission originated, which they were not; they were systems originated. You raised and lowered the stylus to listen to it. You had your earphones on, and you had to listen through a transmission with the stylus set in playback, and you'd throw it to neutral, tap it back, put it back down and listen, throw it back to neutral, tap it back. It might be necessary to try ten or twelve times through one small segment to try to differentiate, say, two different people who spoke approximately at the same time, or someone might have said something over someone and you'd try to separate the two. You might go back and forth any number of times, raising and lowering the stylus, and each time you raise and lower it, you'd put a little peck mark on the disk. I don't know how those read on a computer and the House Select Committee wouldn't tell me. It might be that they would have no effect. But for some reason, they didn't want to explain to anyone's satisfaction, scientific or layman, how you can look on 100 percent of the belt and find similar injections of a sound source, as they called it, and say that these four, because we need them to be exactly there at that time and in exact order, are shots and all the rest are nothing? Now, that's fantastic! I had my findings ready for them but they declined. They rebutted what they must. But you have to understand what they wanted: a conspiracy. They wanted someone else to be shooting at the President. It was important to them to have someone besides Oswald as the assassin. So they had the difficult situation of absolutely removing Oswald from a solo shooting situation and inserting someone else and being able to prove it or at least open the elastic consideration: someone else must have been shooting, too. To prove this, they needed some kind of scientific corroboration that a second person at least fired at the President. Thus, you can suggest a conspiracy.

In the end, when the House Select Committee made its famous announcement on the afternoon of New Year's Eve, "Our clock has run out. Our committee is adjourned right on time," they didn't determine anything: they concluded. Determination implies a bit stronger qualification of evidence. I don't use words casually if I can avoid it. They didn't determine anything other than what they decided to determine. They concluded from the processes they chose to use certain conclusions which were wholly inaccurate and unsupportable. As a dedicated career police officer, the thing I am most concerned with is to always be honest and keep things clean. I don't know whether there was a conspiracy, but as a peace officer I would be a corrupt officer to try to let my personal beliefs inject something as supposed evidence for or against conspiracy because it would compromise any later development. Take for example this mockery of evidence that says a fourth shot was fired from behind the fence on the grassy knoll. The House Select Committee was a very expensive federally funded investigation. If some evidence subsequently turned up that a person was identified as an assassin, and that person did, in fact, fire at President Kennedy but not from the grassy knoll; they instead fired from some other location significantly apart, then they have a multi-million dollar defense built in because the government, through this federally funded investigation, has stated that the only other shot came from the grassy knoll. There was no other shot fired from here, or there, or somewhere else. Absolutely not! So what they've done is to let conjured evidence adulterate the purity of an ongoing investigation. It's a murder and will never be closed statutorily. It's open forever!

I don't know why some people have claimed that the tapes have been altered or how these stories have appeared. Why does anybody ever tell a story different from the truth? Is it a mistake? Is it a belief they have and just don't know? Is it ignorance on their part of reality, or are they just liars?

I haven't had the tapes back since 1964, but I've seen the tapes since then because the subsequent investigation questioned whether the tapes were in the right continuity or whether somebody might have made substitute tapes and stuck them in. A visual survey of the tapes indicated that they were wholly consistent with what should be there. I even took them to the retired telephone clerk who had signed on the belt, and she confirmed that that was, in fact, her signature and that the belts appeared to be the legitimate originals. That's the only time I've seen the belts since then.

I've got a first generation reel to reel of the original tapes after the FBI tapes were made. They are only as clean as they could be after they were recorded and handled by the FBI and then handled for two recordings by myself. Now, from those reel to reel tapes, I have made cassette tapes with a filter and without a filter, and if evidence exists on any true recording, it would be on those tapes. If somebody has a tape that has something that's not on those tapes, they're going to have to explain why it's there. I can't.

Because of my familiarization with the transcripts of the tapes and because the House Select Committee was leaning so hard on the radio tapes to try to make their case, and since I knew that the tapes could not make their case; in fact, truth was to the contrary, I was assigned to work with them. But instead of working with them, they opted to take Officer McLain to Washington and gave him only minimal information and asked him very carefully couched questions—"Is it possible? Could it be? Is there a chance that?"—and never gave him anything to the alternative.

McLain assumed, since they were government lawyers working for the flag, motherhood, and Chevrolet coupes that they wouldn't lie to you. McLain had no idea, in his naive innocence, that they were trying to concoct a tale and that he was a vital validator to their chain. He was their missing link.

The day McLain returned I called Chief Warren and told him that I needed McLain and any person McLain felt comfortable with, and to send them to me. So Chief Warren got in touch with McLain, and he brought Lieutenant Sword over with him. He had no idea what it was about. By this time, Jerry Cohen, of the *Los Angeles Times*, coincidentally came in to my office, joining several other newspeople who were there. I said, "No, you can't talk to him yet. Mac, I want you and Lieutenant Sword to go into that office. Here's a recorder and here are some tapes. Don't phone anybody; don't take any phone calls; don't talk to anybody, and don't let anybody talk to you. Sit down in there and listen to these tapes all the way through. Don't say anything till you're completely through."

They were in my office for about four hours listening to the tapes. When they were finished and opened the door and came out, McLain looked at me and said, "J.C., ain't no way in the world that was my radio stuck open!"

I said, "How do you figure that, Mac?" He replied, "Well, after listening to all this traffic on Channel 2 tapes, it just comes back like it was yesterday. I remember all that conversation."

I asked, "Well, is there any reason why you didn't relate to that as fact in Washington?"

"They didn't let me hear those tapes! They just gave me what they wanted me to hear. They let me listen to a little of this and a little of that, and they would ask me if this was possible. I didn't know whether it was or it wasn't! I'd have to admit the truth is, it might be; I don't remember. So that's what they told me to answer."

As a result of that type of an absolute 180 degree back away, Jerry said, "I think what you need to do is take the information you have and write it down. We're this many years down the pike and twenty or twenty-five years from now there's still going to be inquiries about this, but your memory and everybody's recollections are going to be slim as the years go by, and frankly, when you people die off there'll be no track record if you don't create one." So he said, "I really urge you to take what information you gather, organize it into a manuscript format, and then we'll have one." So I did and entitled it *The Kennedy Assassination Tapes: A Rebuttal to the Acoustical Evidence*. And I'm glad I did because we subsequently passed it on to the National Academy of Sciences through the FBI, and they were able to reach the only conclusion that should have been there in the beginning.

Something a lot of people really got their lather up about was whether something was or wasn't at a certain time. Some people tried to use stop watches to time that belt to say something happened after a certain minute, second, or fraction of a second. That is nonsense, utter nonsense!

My office in communications was off to the side and then there was a larger office which was the telephone room. The conveyor belt went through behind two rows of desks. Behind a glassed partition there were two dispatchers, Channel 1 and Channel 2, and then behind them was the radio equipment.

The dispatcher had two types of clocks: He had a time stamp clock that didn't show seconds, just minutes, and he had a digital clock in front of him which had the numerical hour and minutes. That was the usual clock for general sight and time statements. At the same time, the same dispatcher might use the digital clock. There was no way in the world that some six clocks in the telephone room and the two clocks in the dispatching room were synchronized. They could be as much as a minute or two apart. Usually we didn't change them until they became at least two minutes or more out of synchronization of each other. There was one clock in the office that had a generally reliable time. It was on the back wall of the telephone room. The only trouble was that it was way back in the corner which you could hardly see, and nobody ever looked at it. It was just there. They'd use it only when they wanted to check its time versus the other time.

An officer, depending on the individual circumstance at an individual time, might use either the digital clock in front of him, or he might use the time stamp on the other clock. Using a headset, let's say the dispatcher turns away to do something and in the process sees the digital clock and says, "224, a disturbance at such and such location—2:13." He used the digital 2:13. By now the time stamp clock might be reading 2:15.

He puts it in the slot, turns around, and now 125 says, "I'm clear."

The dispatcher says, "125 clear," and he looks at the time stamp - 2:15, "2:15 KKB364." Now it would look like to all the righteous world that 125 cleared two minutes after the radio operator dispatched the call at 2:13, but he didn't. It was almost in one breath. So, under no circumstance could you put any stock in the real world time or any continuity on time references by the belt because there were no time references on the belt; they were only spoken times, and those spoken times had no faithful validity.

More specifically, at the time of the assassination, when Gerald Henslee, who was operating Channel 2, said, "12:30 KKB364 Police Department, Dallas," it really wasn't 12:30 by all that I can reconstruct by all other parallels. I used several indices to try to correlate that. There were certain places you could tend to lock Channel 1 and Channel 2 together such as things that transpired where there's cross talk between the channels or where they used a simultaneous broadcast and went on both channels. I made a big, long sheet of paper where Channel 1 was on one side and Channel 2 on the other and slid these papers back and forth to try to line up conversation in a reasonably faithful lineup. A good close proximity is the best I could do—no one can do better.

One of the things in the rebuttal I wrote was to construct the validity: a conclusion that would self sustain rather than reach a conclusion, and then trying to construct myself into that as my way of proof. And a lot of this happened to fall into place only after all the people who were participants provided information, and then to lay those over and see how well they fitted. So, for a period of three or four months after that, I located a lot of these officers, some after they had retired, to interview them. I included in the manuscript the report of one officer who had gone home that day and wrote down what had happened while the events were still fresh in his mind.

Jim Chaney was the officer who was immediately next to the President, but for some reason didn't get interviewed by many people. Chaney was a good friend of mine. I helped his sister through physics in high school and, periodically, when Jim was assigned motorcycle duty out in the northeast corner of town, when he had finished what he was doing, he'd stop by my house and sit there in the kitchen at the breakfast table, drink some coffee and talk. Jim wasn't given to a lot of talk. But by sitting down friendly and quietly, he had some things he wanted to talk about, and I provided him a good listening ear and learned as much about the immediate assassination of President Kennedy from Jim as I did from anybody. This was long before anybody started to talk about a fourth shot or whether or not the head shot was a front or rear shot.

There's so much proof that there was a rear shot that I really find it hard to even listen with any degree of good manners to people who talk to the contrary. It's such an absurdity! If the shot, for example, came down from the grassy knoll into the President's limousine and hit him in the head from the front, how did it get turned around so that it went up in the air because it sure as heck didn't hit the back of the car anywhere? And if the car is going forward, and the bullet hits traveling to toward the rear, why didn't the brain matter fly to the rear of the President instead of forward? The brain matter was hit by the fatal shot which hit in the back of the head and came out the front as evidenced by the spray forward in the Zapruder film.

Also, the limousine was not driven at a constant speed. This is another one of the things that was an inherent error in the House Select Committee's scientific analysis. They calculated that the motorcade ran at an average speed of about 11 M.P.H. I can show places in the Zapruder film where it went faster or slower. It did not travel at 11 M.P.H. at a constant rate. You can't make averages serve you like a master. It's a point of reference. In this type of situation, you had to deal with each occurrence as a matter of fact at the time it occurred. There were times the limousine almost stopped. When Mrs. Kennedy started out the back and the agent jumped on the back to put her back in and covered them up, it almost stopped.

From what I gather, part of the motorcade stopped briefly before it entered the Stemmons Freeway, although the limousine itself did not. Apparently the lead car driven by Chief Curry and two motorcycle riders, Ellis and Chaney, for a very brief period had a meeting of the minds ahead of the limousine after the shots. This was where Chaney told Curry and Ellis that the President had been hit just prior to their entering the Stemmons Freeway ramp where Sergeant Bellah was waiting for the signal to stop the north bound Stemmons traffic.

Another direct rebuttal to the House Select Committee's observations, not their findings, concerned the microphone which was stuck in the open position on Channel 1 at approximately 12:28. They wanted to have, running at 11 M.P.H., McLain coming down Houston Street, make a left turn and reverse back, and be so many feet down Elm Street. They took great pride in their revelation until they realized that one of the errors they had was the fact that the motorcycle had a windscreen that filtered the noise from the microphone, and it didn't square with where he had to be when he turned the corner until suddenly they remembered, "Well, the motorcycle turned this way, the screen is here. His mike didn't go through the screen." So beautifully scientific and so utterly absurd! It just didn't happen that way!

What had happened was that the crowd encroached on the President at the corner of Houston and Elm. This was the last place where there was a large crowd, and it's also a sharp reverse left turn onto Elm. Making the turn at Elm, the motorcade almost halted, to the point that the next car behind where McLain and Baker were, had to stop for a second. By the time the President got around the corner and the motorcade started to move again, McLain heard what was presumably the first shot because he noticed pigeons jump up from the Texas School Book Depository. Then, in looking around, he was not consciously aware of hearing, in his recollection, any other shots. But he was attracted to his left where there's an opening in the backdrop to the little pond there in Dealey Plaza. Through the opening in the wall behind the pond, he saw the agent running up behind the limousine. As the limousine almost stopped, the agent jumped on, and he saw Mrs. Kennedy trying to get out and being pushed back in, then the limousine took off. Moments thereafter, almost simultaneously, he heard Chief Curry say, "Go to the hospital! Go to the hospital! Code 3!" At which time, McLain accelerated, turned on his red lights, turned the corner, and started trying to catch up to the motorcade. When he pulled around the corner, he saw Hargis's motorcycle down and thought something had happened to him. But he noticed at the same time that Hargis was getting to his feet and was trying to run up the hill. Meanwhile, Hargis had heard the chief say, "Get somebody up on the hill!" He didn't know what it was, but he tried. Curry later said, "No, I didn't see anything up there. I just didn't know. It was just a spontaneous reaction."

At a certain point on the tapes, just after the shots were fired, the President's hit, and the motorcade's on the way to Parkland, the open microphone picks up three distinct and one straggler sound of sirens passing the open microphone. The reason I say sirens passing the open microphone is because, in acoustics, there is the Law of the Doppler Effect. Simply stated, this is when a recording source and a sound source pass a certain point the sound blanks itself out and cancels and then picks up again. It's not a continuum. There is a stop. The microphones had the ability, generally, to pick up sound at a distance of about 300 feet maximum. That didn't mean that anything 301 feet away could not be picked up and anything 299 feet away would be recorded, but it was just the outer range limits. With that, there must be considered the loudness, the quality of the sound, the atmospheric conditions, and the condition of the microphone itself. But we're talking about an optimum thing. A siren is a high pitch, high frequency sound certainly in excess of the normal 2,400 peak range of the voice grade recording.

Projecting by speed, the ability of the motorcade to travel certain segments because of the physical layout, the turns, the ability to get on and off the freeway; and depending on the recollections of the motorcycle operators themselves as to how fast they were riding at given points, indicates a continuum projected long away. It would take them from where they started to where they were at a certain point after the shooting. At the same time these officers would be making the turn off of the service road at Stemmons onto Industrial Boulevard, it's exactly the same time that the sound on the tapes record the sirens.

There is a distinct recollection by the motorcycle officers that the motorcade came by in three separate groups. There was a front group, middle group, and a tail group. In addition, one special agent who got off to a late start had an old siren on his car and came through after all the rest as a straggler. At the same time, when you position where the open microphone was by previously determined acoustical information, this is where the guy who had the open microphone parked his motorcycle. To check this out, if you place two points on a map representing Industrial Boulevard in front of the Trade Mart and figure the distance between the two at being a couple hundred feet around the corner, this is where they would have picked up their speed after they'd made their slow down off the service road from Stemmons and turn onto Industrial. There was a crowd there at the Trade Mart, and this crowd was curious because they thought the President was coming to speak. They didn't know that he was going to Parkland.

Most of the motorcycles didn't have electric sirens; they had foot operated sirens, and you had to have a certain amount of speed before they would operate. Navigating the turn onto Industrial would not allow the sirens to work because of the deceleration, but once on Industrial, the 200 feet gave them the opportunity to speed up again and operate the sirens which were picked up at the point of the earliest capability of the open radio microphone from a distance of 282 1/2 feet. Once the 282 1/2 feet had been traversed to a point at a 90 degree angle with the open microphone, that's where the Doppler Effect occurred. The siren's blank! When the tape is run to the point where another 282 1/2 feet elapse, then the first range of sirens quit because they are out of range of the open microphone. The second group of motorcycles, the same thing: The sound was picked up and lost where it should have been. It Dopplered where it should and dropped off where it should. The same with the third group.

I didn't write the law on the Doppler Effect; I didn't park the motorcycle there; I didn't sound the siren. I'm only reporting on what happened. The motorcade turned onto Industrial, and in 200 feet, accelerated to 50-55 M.P.H. Fifty-five M.P.H. travels 80.66 feet per second. The siren sounds passed in seven second intervals. The source travelling at 80.66 feet per second for seven seconds will travel 565 feet. That's 282 1/2 feet in an approach segment and 282 1/2 in a departure segment. The middle of that mark is exactly parallel to the motorcycle with the open microphone, exactly where the Doppler would occur.

This particular motorcycle had a defective transmitter which had stuck open intermittently several times during that morning on Channel 1. At the particular time of relevance, though, at 12:28, approximately three minutes prior to the assassination, there was another block of transmission.

During that period beginning at 12:28, we have the dispatcher talk to 83, check him out; 56 asked for traffic checkout on a '56 Chevrolet, didn't see the license; 75 said he was in service, and the dispatcher acknowledged that. Then, in the microphone at the same time, he said, "75 clear, 12:28," then the microphone stuck open for 17 1/2 seconds. At that time, it was transmitting the sounds of a running motorcycle, not sitting still and idling.

Then the dispatcher answered 38 when he came on the air, "Might tell some of those people out here at Market Hall that there's people walking across southbound Stemmons here in front of the Marriott Hotel and all the way down south." As soon as he finished that, the microphone stuck open and continued open again.

During the conversation, the dispatcher said, "10-4, 38. Are you still en route to court?"

And 38 acknowledged "10-4" into the microphone. They're able to talk over the microphone stuck open because the signal was strong enough and clear enough to come in. So, sometimes you could hear transmissions and sometimes you couldn't. In this case, 38 overloaded the open transmitter. When he says "10-4," the microphone continued to stay on for five minutes and the motorcycle's engine is running.

Then someone came on and said, "Market office."

And somebody else said, "All right." Just after that, at about 12:30:55 is when the first shot was fired. The motorcycle engine at about 12:31 then slowed down its idling noise. Apparently he had gotten to where he was going and was running much slower. Then, at 12:31:03, just about three seconds after slowing down, the third shot was fired.

Someone else came on the air about 12:31:02 on Channel 2 and said, "I'll check it." That was a bleed over from Channel 2.

The same thing had happened at 12:28 when on Channel 2, 125 said, "I'm at the Trade Mart now. I'll head back out that way." And 4 responded, "Naw, that's all right. I'll check it." At that instant is when we have the same "I'll check it" being said on Channel 1. The reason this happened, very likely, was this motorcycle slowed down and pulled up close to where a P.A. speaker was tuned in to Channel 2, and the operator had flipped on the outside speakers so the officers could stand by the motorcycle and hear it. This occurred just as the "I'll check it" comment was made. This bleed over is what is called crosstalk which put Channel 1 and Channel 2 within a second of each other. Anytime you can bring them within fifteen to thirty seconds, that's pretty darn good. In this case, it is within one second.

At 12:31:12, 91 said, "Check wanted on P-Pecos." Following that was the single tone of a bell. This has caused a great deal of confusion for which I have a simple explanation which I can't prove. A group known as the Young Democrats or the Sons of Liberty, or something like that, was out at the Trade Mart, and they had a replica of the Liberty Bell on a trailer. My best guess is that since it was in close proximity to where the microphone was stuck open on the parked motorcycle, maybe somebody just walked by and went "Bong!" There is no other explanation that I know of to explain a bell. However, it could be an electrical sound caused within the electronics of the system.

The most telling rebuttal to the House Select Committee's conclusions that McLain's microphone picked up the shots in Dealey Plaza is that the stuck open microphone was on a three-wheel motorcycle, not the two-wheel solo motorcycle which McLain was riding. It's easy to tell from the tapes because of the difference in the engine sounds.

On a three-wheeler, the radio is beside the back part of the operator's right knee near the engine. Any change in engine speed can be heard. Besides that, you can put a strobe cycle on that and measure the throbbing beat. The small flat-head, three-wheel motorcycle engine doesn't run the same way; they are not nearly as sophisticated, nor do they have the muffler capability that the over-head 74's had on the Harley two-wheel motorcycle. In addition, on a two-wheeler, the motorcycle radio sits up higher with a crossbar and gas tank arrangement, and the engine is down lower between the officer's legs. You could sit there with this motorcycle mike open and it would not pick up near the same engine definition. Besides that, when it runs, you would hear a different sound between the two. The engines sounded nothing alike. Thus, it was obvious that the so-called shots in Dealey Plaza were actually recorded at the Trade Mart on the three-wheeler, which meant, absolutely, there were no shots picked up by McLain's motorcycle radio. In fact, we even know whose motorcycle it was! The House Select Committee was aware of this, but that information didn't fit their scenario of a conspiracy, which was what they were trying to prove. Remember, if it doesn't fit to your satisfaction, discount it, explain it away, and maybe nobody will be smart enough to catch it.

Another thing the House Select Committee didn't want to explain was whether the existing communications' network that we had back then would record such an audible sound as a shot. Over the years I have heard several shots broadcast over the police radio during the course of our business. These were easily identified as shots. When the House Select Committee came back down here in August of whatever year it was, they blocked off the street one weekend and ran those trials, including shooting a gun from behind the stockade fence. Guess what the recording sounded like? BANG!... BANG!... BANG! You heard gunshots! Now, we heard gunshots in years before the assassination, and we heard gunshots in years after the assassination, but for some strange quirk of fate, the shots fired during the assassination were inaudible sound impressions. The quality of the sounds of the microphone would not change whether it was stuck open or if it were turned on deliberately.

If you were talking to someone on the phone and someone fired a shot on the other end of the line, would you hear a shot? Of course, though, you might not recognize it as a shot because there is an adulteration of the sound. Unless you were expecting the shot, you might not perceive it to be a shot, but there would be the distinct BANG. But again, the House Select Committee found only sound impressions.

Other allowances were not made by the House Select Committee which further made the tests invalid. The firing tests were made in August on a clear, dry, hot day. In November it was a cool, moist, windy day. It'd been raining and the air was fairly heavy, and it was fairly cool. That makes a difference. There was an additional fifteen years of foliage on the trees; there were modifications to the buildings; signs and posts had been moved or removed. For example, the Stemmons sign that the President passed near the grassy knoll is gone. According to their logic, if there were ten objects sticking up from the ground and they found an echo that didn't connect with anything, "Well, maybe someone was standing there at the time." Maybe, maybe, maybe! Again, if it doesn't fit, ignore it!

Let me put it this way: They tried to construct the validity by saying that they ran those tests that August and proved a perfect match on their scenario from a gunshot at the President from the grassy knoll behind the stockade fence; that it was, in fact, the third shot, and from the School Book Depository were shots one, two, and four. No one, again, ever mentioned where the bullet went if you fired down into the car from the front, but they made a sport as to how the so-called "magic bullet" changed directions when it hit the President as it went through his neck. How did it change directions and then change directions again to hit Connally? Equally fantastic would be this bullet which flew down and hit the President, then maybe had wings and ZOOM! They also didn't explain why, when the President was hit, the residue matter went forward, the same way the bullet would carry it. It reminds me of those Dick Tracy cartoons when I was a kid where they'd show the impact and they'd show these little marks away from it. Maybe the House Select Committee thought that Dick Tracy was an authority on ballistics: that if a bullet hits you the residue bounces back at you. It doesn't! It goes the way the impact carries it. There was also a jerk in the President after he was hit. If you talk to true ballistics' experts, not mystery buffs, the jerk is not inconsistent with ballistics.

They also wondered why the hole through the President's coat was lower on his coat. It's hard to keep your shirt tail in, and it's hard to keep your coat down when you sit for a period of time. They tend to creep and crawl. If you're waving, and waving, and waving as was the President, that hard back brace that he was wearing also tends to encourage the coat to creep up. I know from personal experience that ever so often in a parade you have to pull your coat back down. I don't know if, or when, he pulled his coat down, but suppose that his coat had hiked up about four inches in this last bit of maneuvering before the shots, and it happened at a time when he had not pulled down his coat; then his coat would be bunched up to about his shoulders. If his coat was hiked up about four inches, and the bullet goes through, when you lay the coat out over the body, the holes don't align properly. The hole in the body is in one place and the hole in the coat in another. Does that mean that someone has messed with it? No! The law of physics messed with it. The man was waving and his coat hiked up in the rear. Why try to find spooks and mystery when simple reality can occur?

But naturally, you have these mystics who say that obviously he had been shot at a lower spot, and obviously, since the hole was supposed to have been somewhere else, someone must have doctored the evidence. Some people even feel that the President's body was detoured on the way to Washington and somewhere, someone made changes in the wounds. With what Jackie Kennedy had been through, is one expected to believe that she would sit still for that? I hardly think so! She just didn't show that kind of a lack of mocksey. I think she would have gone absolutely bananas and had a fire fight if somebody had tried to mess with her or the late president.

In addition, there were twenty people who were present, and there were obvious suspicions and emotions present. Remember, the relationship between the Vice-President and the President was somewhat strained. I don't think that was a secret. I won't attribute hostility at a measured level because that's not my business. But we do know that there was not the greatest accord between the two. There was the emotional connection as to when Kennedy ceased being the President and when Johnson suddenly become the President. Obviously it was technically when the President was pronounced dead at Parkland; ceremonially it was when Judge Hughes swore him in. But in the emotional mind, President Jack Kennedy left Washington, and until they could get out of this mess and back to Washington, till they could ceremonially, appropriately, and with dignity dispose of that which was Jack Kennedy, he was still, by honor, the President. And Johnson, well, who knows? So there was this turmoil. With that scenario in the plane, does it seem logical that the plane was detoured somewhere? Check the flight log. Does it seem logical that something like that could have happened and everybody involved could have kept quiet for all these years? No chance!

Let's look at the assassination from this perspective, and it's a very simple thing. Here's this poor bedeviled individual, Lee Oswald, who gets up in the morning without wakening his wife and leaves almost all his money in a dish along with his wedding band. He then gets his curtain rods, somebody else must have gotten his gun, and takes this package to work. The paper's found where he took it, or where somebody took it; the grease on the gun and on the paper were the same. No one knew where the curtain rods went; they never turned up, but the gun did: the same gun that Oswald had purchased. But this poor bedeviled little individual, after having probably carried the rifle in this paper up to the sixth floor, didn't shoot the President. Instead, he goes downstairs just after the shooting, drinks a Coca-Cola in front of his boss and Officer Baker. Poor as a church mouse, he saunters out the front door, goes down the street, gets on a bus, then realizes that it's not going anywhere. Poor as a church mouse is he jumps out of the bus, runs over to the Greyhound Bus Station, gets in a taxi cab, then tells the driver to take him to a corner address near his house. He goes by his house for some reason. Maybe he just loves mysterious behavior. He then pays the cab driver, walks back to his house, runs in, changes his jacket and shirt, picks up his pistol, sticks it in his belt and runs down the street to the Texas Theater to watch a double-feature movie that he can't afford to go to because he sneaked in. Now, is that congruent behavior? That's consistent with what? Doesn't everybody do that all the time? When in his past had Oswald been a movie fan? He hadn't. But now, with the crime of the century happening in his presence, the most natural thing to do is go to a movie!

It was a diversion. The man went home not knowing what to expect. He bypassed his house, knowing that he got away from Baker but not knowing how long he could continue to get away. Rather than be caught by the police and held, then be identified and paraffin tested and made with his gun, he did what any person would have done given the chance: he ducked out. Getting on the bus was his natural behavior because that's how he had normally traveled. Realizing the bus wasn't going anywhere, he had to take the expense of the cab. He then bypassed his house to be sure that he hadn't been rapped. Seeing that he wasn't, he ran back to the house, got his pistol, changed his top clothing and started out. In all likelihood, Officer Tippit saw his furtive movements, and being a good officer, was attracted. When he saw Tippit, and Tippit saw him, that electric moment happened, that "click." You can't put it in a bottle and sell it, but if you're a real police officer, or if you're a real suspect, you'll know it and you'll feel it. You'll feel the officer's eyes riveted on you; you'll feel the suspect's eyes riveted on you. So he turns around and plays a little cat and mouse.

Anyway, Oswald had been walking along at a fast pace. Others tried to measure the distance and said that you just couldn't walk it that fast. You can when you're in a hurry! When the Devil's behind you, it's not that hard to do. He's on his way, remember, to the picture show. He gets as far as Tenth and Patton. Before then, Tippit came on the radio with a very unobtrusive, "78." The dispatcher was too busy to answer the low profile interrogatory. If he had said, "78!!!," the dispatcher would have probably answered and Tippit would have asked, "Do you have a description on that suspect at the School Book Depository?" Wouldn't it have been wonderful? But Tippit, being kind of a low profile, easy-going, hard to stir up sort of guy just said, "78." He probably figured the dispatcher was too busy for him. So he pulled up and said, "Fella;" Oswald walked over to the door and looked in. Tippit might have said, "Like to talk to you for a minute." Some words were exchanged which was corroborated by a cab driver nearby. Tippit opened the door and started out around to the front of the car. Oswald, in response, walked around toward the front and BAM! BAM! BAM! BAM! He walked off saying, "That damn cop" or "That dumb cop" according to the cab driver.

Oswald then stopped in the yard, spitting distance from the cabbie, dumped his dead brass, reloaded his gun, put it back in his belt, and started walking south on Patton Street. Eyewitness Callaway said, "Hey, what's going on down there?" Suddenly Oswald made a turn. Then, realizing that he'd probably been made with that khaki jacket on, he peeled it off behind a business while going west on Jefferson. Then he was eyeballed slipping into the Texas Theater. Others say that Oswald was in the Texas Theater when Tippit was shot. Too many eyewitnesses put him slipping in. The cashier knows she didn't sell him a ticket. The shoe salesman saw him slipping in, found him in the theater, and watched him till the police got there. There are too many physical facts that square. Why in the name of all that is holy would Oswald have suddenly decided to do those funny things like run home and get a pistol, change clothes, and go to a movie? The man's too poor to ride in a cab unless he's trying to get away from the Devil. The man's too poor to jump up off his job, run home, pick up a pistol and go to the picture show. What kind of a psycho would do that sort of thing? My little grandson might want to take his cap pistol with him if he was going to see a cowboy movie, but reasonable people don't take real pistols to movies.

Some have said that it couldn't have been Oswald who shot Tippit because there was a slight discrepancy in the physical description. Anytime you take five, ten, or twenty people and let them see somebody then ask them to describe what they saw, there will be notable discrepancies.

The Rand Corporation recently conducted a survey which stated that there is about an 89 percent error margin on eyewitnesses. Now, this does not mean all of a sudden that as a potential juror you should discount anything and everything to the 89 percent factor that a witness testifies to, but it does reveal that obviously there is a reasonable potential for error in what an eyewitness might say. You've got to consider the accuracy of observation. For example, weight is hard to understand. You don't say, "How much did he weigh?

The reply, "He must have weighed 200 pounds."

"How much do you think I weigh?"

"You weigh about 180."

"Well, I weigh 220, so apparently this person weighs closer to 240" because you have a skew. Or you could ask, "How tall was this person?"

"He was well over six feet tall."

"How tall are you?"

"About 5'8."

"Well, then, this guy must have been 6'6" because I'm six feet."

You don't generally do this.   But the other part of this was that Oswald couldn't have done it because Oswald wasn't there; he was at the theater. Malarkey! Oswald was there. But, they might say, this waitress, Helen Markham, said exactly this. The waitress obviously lied. But did she lie deceitfully, or did she inadvertently? The funny thing is she was standing there, after holding a man in her lap, trying to understand what he had been saying, after he had taken four shots, and she hasn't got a drop of blood in her lap. Now, something has missed the target. In her mind, even today, she might think that she talked to the man, but all the pathologists will tell you that Tippit was dead before he hit the ground, which is why there was so little blood. The blood seepage that was there was gravitational flow before coagulation. His vital functions had ceased. Gravity bleeding was all that was left. Those are physical facts, and when you take the facts and take the conversation; where the conversation is inconsistent with the facts, you've got to go with the facts.

Take, for example, the ballistics. The Smith and Wesson pistol that Oswald used was not a standard generic American made Smith and Wesson .38 caliber pistol, so there was no pure ballistics capability because of that unique feature. It was specially made for the British with a resleeved barrel to handle British ammunition, and there weren't too many made. It isn't impossible, but what is the likelihood of a person of an approximately similar description within such a close distance and exact time frame having not only the same type Smith and

Wesson pistol, but also the same mismatched mess of ammunition both in the pistol and in their pockets? There were two different kinds of cartridges in Oswald's pocket and in the gun. Ballistics of the hammer fall was approximately identical on both, but because of the looseness of the cartridge in the case, the tests were not the best. They were certain beyond a reasonable doubt that it was the same. Also the ballistics of the bullets fired through the death gun and the bullets fired in tests from the gun taken off Oswald had the same exact similarities, but you couldn't put them on a perfect match because the bullets didn't fit the land and grooves.

People stop by the office or call quite frequently to discuss these issues. We've had some funny ones, too. One morning my phone rang at home somewhere between 1:00 and 4:00 A.M., and I answered rather sleepily. It was a talk show from Australia, live! I asked, "Do you realize what time it is?"

He responded, "Well, it's 11:00 A.M. 'fore noon in Brisbane!"

I said, "Well, it's sure isn't 11:00 A.M. in Dallas!" But he was a congenial fellow, and we went ahead and talked about it.

On another occasion a lady from the New York Democrat Women's Club called several months after the assassination and asked, "Could I speak with someone who could discuss the assassination with me?"

So I said, "Well, depending on what you'd like to know, I'd be glad to try to answer your questions."

"Are you permitted to speak about it?"

I said, "Certainly. We don't have censorship." So she started asking about a lot of questions, much of which came from the Eastern press coverage which was rather tainted, slanted, heated, and emotional. I'm not faulting them because they had their jobs to do. They had a constituency to serve, editors to please, and reputations to live up to, though I think they, at times, were carried away with events. She asked some rather pointed questions without any effort to interfere with the answers.

Eventually she said, "This isn't consistent with what we've been told. Why haven't you people told us this?"

I asked her, "Why hasn't someone asked? We don't own a newspaper up in New York. Anyone who cares to know our side of it, we're glad to discuss it with them."

Certainly I'm concerned about how we are perceived; as to how we performed our jobs on the weekend of the assassination, and I think, in general, those people of significance and relevance have treated the Dallas Police Department fairly. As for those weirdos who don't know from which side of the pot to pour the coffee, I don't concern myself with their evaluations.

James Bowles retired from the Dallas Police Department in 1981 and assumed the role of administrative chief deputy for the sheriff's department. He has been the sheriff of Dallas County since 1984.

JOE MURPHY
Traffic Division
Dallas Police Department

"I could see that something was wrong in the car as it got nearer to my position because the President's wife was leaning over toward President Kennedy, and as I was standing right above them, I heard someone say, "Get us to the nearest hospital!"

Born and raised in Dallas, Joe Murphy was offered a contract to play baseball in the Chicago White Sox organization. After playing a year at Midland in the West Texas-Mexican League and later for a semi-pro team in Baytown, Texas, he returned to Dallas and upon the advise of an uncle, joined the Dallas Police Department in 1942. Interrupted by service in the Army during World War II, Murphy returned to the police department in 1946 where he served most of his career in the Traffic Division. He is reputed to have given the most traffic tickets in the history of the Dallas Police Department.

I was assigned on the Stemmons Freeway over Elm Street about 150 yards from the School Book Depository. My job was to keep traffic moving and not to allow anybody to stop on the bridge or park their car anywhere on the shoulders so that they could watch the motorcade from the bridge. I was facing west by the way the motorcade was traveling, and it was to go up the service road to my right and onto the freeway. Several motor jockeys and other officers were there to stop traffic completely when the motorcade was to pass. That was the only time that traffic was allowed to stop on the freeway. Many of the officers were north of the overpass as much as a quarter of a mile from the overpass where the Elm Street entrance entered the freeway. Others were just riding the area stopping with messages they had for me. We were all channeled to listen for any information from the office or from the dispatcher.

Prior to the arrival of the motorcade I saw some men walking up on the Triple Underpass. Based on how they were dressed, I assumed they were railroad people. There was also at least one officer there as well.

I could see the motorcade when it came down Main and turned right onto Houston and over to Elm. But there were some trees that obscured my view at Elm and Houston, so I lost sight of it for a moment or two. As it approached my position, I heard the shots and a flock of pigeons took off flying in circles. I couldn't tell where the noise was coming from due to the reverberations. In fact, I didn't realize they were shots at first. But I did hear three, what were later defined as shots, and they were about evenly spaced. I could see that something was wrong in the car as it got nearer to my position because the President's wife was leaning over toward President Kennedy, and as I was standing right above them, I heard someone say, "Get us to the nearest hospital!"

I waited to hear something on the radio and had difficulty hearing due to all the noise. By that time, traffic had been reopened north on Stemmons so the noise factor had increased.

I wasn't able to tell much about what was going on in Dealey Plaza. I saw a number of people on the ground, then some began to move back up toward the hill. Most were headed toward the intersection at Elm and Houston. I didn't see anybody below me or in that grassy area. I've heard so many tales about that grassy area, but I don't recall seeing anybody over there either running or walking.

After the shooting, the order was given for all us three-wheelers to come to the School Book Depository. We were told that some people were supposed to have been running behind the building. So we circled the area looking for anything and yet nothing in particular.

I remember talking with several people just to see if they had seen anything, but there was nothing of any value that I recall that concerned the shooting.

I wasn't involved in anything further in the investigation. My usual hours were 6:00 A.M. to 2:00 P.M., but they held us over late that afternoon. I had to referee a football game in Burkburnett about a hundred miles away that evening and was barely able to make it. Monday morning I was back on my three-wheeler patrolling the downtown area as usual.

Murphy continued his second job routine of refereeing football and basketball games as well as umpiring baseball games. Upon retirement from the Dallas Police Department in 1986, he kept busy painting houses and doing general repair work. Murphy is now deceased.

EDGAR L. SMITH
Accident Investigator
Dallas Police Department

"As the motorcade passed right by me and made its left turn onto Elm Street going toward the Triple Underpass, my eyes were primarily on the motorcade. I was fascinated with John Kennedy and Jackie and felt that they were just larger than life. Seeing them really made an impression on me..."

Born in Myrtle Springs, about fifty miles east of Dallas, Ed Smith moved to Dallas at the age of ten, graduated from Crozier Tech High School in Dallas in 1950 and joined the Dallas Police Department in 1956. Beginning in Radio Patrol, Smith went into the Traffic Division in 1960, and at the time of the assassination was an accident investigator.

I worked the evening shift as an accident investigator and was working overtime stationed at Houston and Elm Streets when the Presidential motorcade came through town. In fact, I was situated on the southeast corner of Houston and Elm in front of the Criminal Records Building.

Prior to the motorcade's arrival, I had approximately an hour and a half to stand on the corner and, at that time, I believe that I might have looked up at the School Book Depository and all those windows and sort of fantasized about how easy it would be for someone to shoot out of one of those windows. I had a completely unobstructed view; unfortunately, I didn't look up there during the event itself. But there were a lot of people and they were in a great mood. Everybody seemed really happy and looking forward to seeing the President.

I was like many of the people that were lining the streets; I was there more as an observer than as a police officer, despite the fact that, by nature, I'm not a very observant person. My job was to keep the pedestrians back and to look for any kind of suspicious events that might take place. As the motorcade passed right by me and made its left turn onto Elm Street going toward the Triple Underpass, my eyes were primarily on the motorcade. I was fascinated with John Kennedy and Jackie and felt like they were just larger than life. Seeing them really made an impression on me.

It seemed like a short time, maybe ten or fifteen seconds after they had made the turn, that the first shot rang out. At the time, I didn't think much of it; in fact, I thought it was probably just firecrackers. The thought ran through my mind that this was really a dirty trick to be playing on the President. Then the next two occurred. It seemed like a lot of time elapsed between the three shots. I couldn't really tell where the shots came from, but they sounded like they all came from the same location. Certainly it didn't seem to me that they came from the sixth floor, but things seemed to just echo around there.

At the time of the shooting, I was looking more toward the grassy knoll; however, it was sort of obstructed because there were other cars passing by. I looked down there and was able to see the Presidential car lurch off. That was the first time that I realized that something really had taken place; I didn't know what, but I knew that something was wrong. Meanwhile the crowd got quiet and then it became loud.

I reacted by running across the street from the south side of Elm toward the underpass, then cut across the street and saw that something had happened as the crowd started moving toward that location. I ran in that direction because of the crowd reaction and from what I overheard since I had no idea where the shots originated. I followed the crowd with my pistol drawn but holstered it before I crossed Elm headed toward the grassy knoll. I don't recall the amount of time that elapsed, but we did check out the area behind the grassy knoll. There was a tremendous amount of confusion! We had no earthly idea what was going on, and we had very little leadership out there. It was chaos; at least it was for me. It didn't seem as though anyone was in charge as we had police officers from different divisions there. There were also, what I assumed, Secret Service and FBI agents there simply because they had loaded carbines and were in civilian clothes. They ran with me over toward the grassy knoll, so I'm assuming that some of them came off of the cars that followed the Presidential limousine.

When I got into the parking lot, there were a number of other officers there also. I didn't spend a lot of time back there, but there was a search, which was very unorganized, that took place. I recall looking in some of the cars, but I don't recall going into the cars or looking in the trunks. From there, I was in the railroad yards for just a short time, then I reported back to the front of the School Book Depository. That's where I spent most of the afternoon. I was there when we heard that Kennedy had been hit, which was not until twenty-five to thirty minutes after the shooting. I was also there when the rifle was brought out and when we heard that Officer Tippit had also been shot in Oak Cliff. Some of the information came from the police radios and other transistors that were there.

I didn't know Tippit very well, but he impressed me as what we called a "country boy." He was not from the Dallas area and seemed to be an efficient officer, but not well educated. Many officers had gotten on the department with a GED.

When I joined the Dallas Police Department, it was really hard to get on. You really had to have a clean record, as did your family, and you had to be God fearing. I'm sure that an atheist could not have joined the Dallas Police Department. In addition, you had to be a certain height and a weight commensurate with that height. It was still the big guy, the Irish police officer image, that they were still trying to fill in Dallas. The police department recruited from the small towns because most of those people had never come in contact with police, so they hired a lot of those guys. Fact is, by far, there were probably more people from outside of Dallas than within on the Dallas Police Department at that time.

I felt that the people who went through the Dallas School System were a little smoother than the farm boys, as we called them. They were nice people; they were wonderful people, but they really didn't fit into the city life. With so many of them, when they came to town, it was the first time they had been noticed by anyone other than their high school sweethearts, and it resulted in tremendous divorce rates. There was a lot of promiscuity, which was sort of a fact of life. You put that blue suit on people and, just automatically, there's a certain group of females out there that just follow the police officer.

One of the real lady's men on the department was P.T. Dean, Patrick Trevore Dean. The women just went for P.T. He was a nice looking guy, but he looked better in his uniform than he did in his regular clothes. He had a really high opinion of himself as a lady's man, and he really was.

Pat was a good friend of mine, but he was also my trainer when we were working in Oak Cliff. He was a special guy, sort of wild, and quite a drinker. We got into all kinds of escapades. I remember that we'd drive down the street and he would sing Elvis Presley songs, and he'd sound just like him. We did very little police work, but we did a hell of a lot of running around and having a good time. It was one big party working with him.

I have learned that some have accused him of being involved with organized crime elements in Dallas and that he was a friend of Jack Ruby. I would doubt very seriously if P.T. had any contacts with organized crime, and he probably knew Jack Ruby like a lot of us did and that was to go to his nightclub and see some of the strippers. He liked to have a good time, but certainly I never knew him to do anything dishonest or dishonorable. I knew him really well, and I would not think that of him at all. Later he became a supervisor, and he really took his supervisory job seriously. I saw a big change in him. He wasn't near the hell-raiser that he was back when he was a patrolman after he became a sergeant. In fact, I considered him a very good supervisor.

I had spent some time at City Hall that weekend when Oswald was in custody but was off that Sunday morning when he was killed. I saw it shortly after it happened on television after my wife woke me up and told me about it. Of course, I wish it hadn't happened down there, but I'll be totally frank; it's amazing that more things like that don't happen. It seemed like everybody in the world was in there, despite how much it was really stressed on them not to let anyone in. It looked like most anyone could come and go if they wanted. I really didn't see anyone holding anybody back nor did we have much security when I was at City Hall earlier in the weekend during the questioning of Oswald. It just seemed like we had allowed the press to come in and take over. The whole department was never all that tremendously organized, but I don't think police work anywhere in Texas was at that time, either.

Despite that, I think we were probably as effective as any police organization in the country. I had taken trips and was always appalled at some of the Eastern cities and their police departments because, even though they may have been effective, they certainly didn't look as sharp as our guys, especially in regard to physical appearance. Even though we were not that great on security, I really feel that we knew what we could do. We had a tremendous academy which, at that time, did not stress sociology and psychology as much as they did later. But I think we were a very good police department. Later, after the assassination, not because of it, we probably became one of the finest police departments in the country. Certainly the procedures and electronics we used were second to none. A number of years later, after I was a lieutenant, people from all over the world came to see our robbery and reporting systems.

But that weekend was terribly exciting and we were in the headlines. Even though they were negative ones, I didn't realize that at the time. Then, after Oswald was killed, it finally dawned on us that people were scrutinizing us from all over the world. But I don't think that it's been necessarily a negative thing to Dallas. I don't think it's a stigma. There was a period that in the pulpits of the city they preached that, that we caused it in some way, but I never did buy that and still don't. It was a quirk of fate; it could have happened in any other city of the United States. Probably the police department and the Secret Service were as effective here as they would have been anywhere else. It just so happened that Oswald lived here and it happened here.

I don't talk about the assassination much. In fact, the people in my office were surprised to find out that I had testified to the Warren Commission. But I've often thought that I might have gotten myself killed because if I'd seen him in that window of the School Book Depository and tried to fire at him with a pistol, there's no way that I would have hit him because I was a lousy shot, and he probably would have shot me. In fact, I think that ran through my mind when I was running down the street with my pistol drawn, that "You're a damn fool. What are you doing out?

You'd better find a place to hide!" In addition, had I pulled my pistol out and fired a couple of shots up there, the Secret Service would have probably shot me. Those people were about half crazy anyhow.

As far as the assassination goes, I do feel that Oswald fired the rifle from the sixth floor, that he fired three times, and he is also the one who killed J.D. Tippit. I do accept all that as reality, but I do believe that there could have been other outside parties that induced him to do it. The conspiracy books sound very authentic as though they contain a great deal of research, but much of it is speculation. I would certainly hope that I would find out in my lifetime and not have to wait until 2039 when the records are opened if, in fact, there's anything in there worth waiting for.

During my career, I worked in nearly all the sections of the Dallas Police Department. Usually it was by my design, as I would become bored with the job I had, so I'd ask for another one. From 1963 until 1983, I served as an accident investigator, school safety officer; I made sergeant with the Patrol Division and then became a departmental safety officer. I thought I had found my niche there when I was promoted to lieutenant and became a member of the Executive Committee of the National Safety Council and was going to become a certified safety expert. However, I was transferred to Planning and Research, then as a watch commander at the Southeast Division. From there I went to the Report Division and ended my career in the Property Division.

After I retired in 1983, I eventually became the Director for Facilities for the Dallas Historical Society in Fair Park. I was in charge of making sure that the building was operated properly which included maintenance. In fact, I was the liaison between the Historical Society and the City of Dallas.

It was during this time, when I had a part-time real estate job, that I first met Marina Oswald Porter. My wife, Sue, and I were checking out some property east of Dallas in Rockwall County and our vehicle became stuck. We knew where she lived, and we passed a couple of houses that were dark along the way until we saw her lights on. This was approximately two miles from where we were stuck. She invited us in, and I noticed through the door a man who ran through there wearing a robe and carrying a shotgun. As it turned out, everything was all right, but I thought, "My God, what have we got ourselves into?" It had been Kenneth Porter, her husband, who had been shooting rabid skunks, or at least what he thought were rabid skunks. They were very cordial as she put on a pot of coffee, had a nice chat, and I mentioned that I had been there when the President was assassinated. She's a small, thin, chain smoking lady who looked rather hard. She's certainly not the beauty she was in some of her earlier pictures, but not really a bad looking person either, just hard.

That night, I made the mistake of calling her Marina Oswald and did so again the other time Sue and I met her at an estate sale. On both occasions she corrected me very abruptly. Ironically, she now lives just down the road from us but we seldom see her. It's a small world, isn't it?

Ed Smith and his wife still live down the road from Marina Porter in rural Rockwall County, Texas. Smith now serves as a probation officer in Rockwall County.

DAVID V. HARKNESS
Sergeant, Traffic Division
Dallas Police Department

"Even some of the people, immediately after the assassination, were angry at the police. They assumed we'd let the President get shot. Some of them were real abusive."

After having served four years in the U.S. Coast Guard during the Second World War, Harkness joined the Dallas Police Department July 8th, 1946. Prior to 1963, Harkness had worked in the Patrol Division, as an accident investigator in the Traffic Division, in school safety, and then as a downtown traffic sergeant.

I was assigned to the parade route as a three-wheel officer supervising point control and three-wheel officers. My assignment was to keep the parade route open from Main and Field to Elm and Houston. At the time of the arrival of the President, I was at the intersection of Main and Houston because I could see all of my area. If there were any problems, like congestion or anything, I could get to it quickly. So I had a good view all the way up Main Street and over to the Book Depository.

Just about the time the parade was at Elm and Harwood, getting ready to turn west on Main, we had a person who had an epileptic seizure over on Houston Street across from the county jail in Dealey Plaza. So I asked for an ambulance to get him to

Parkland and get him out of the area. It just seemed to be a person normally having an epileptic seizure. He did strike his head on the concrete retaining wall right there near the curb, and he was taken to Parkland. We got an ambulance and got him out of there, so it didn't interfere with the parade. I radioed to the officer assigned to Parkland to get the information because we didn't obtain any information at the scene. We were interested in getting him loaded and getting him out of the way. All this happened just four to five minutes before the parade arrived.

I was on the northwest corner of the intersection when I saw the parade coming west on Main and making the turn onto Houston. I was looking at the President, made eye contact with him, and he waved at me.

As soon as the motorcade passed, the people that were standing near the intersection where I was kind of walked back. So, when the motorcade made the turn to go down Elm Street, they went back to the grassy area there in the median between Main and Elm to get a better view of him. So I kind of followed the crowd. As the first shot rang out, then the second, I saw the President's head jerk. Then, as the third shot was fired, Mrs. Kennedy came out of the car and was on all fours on the trunk lid of the car.

At the time, I was probably 150-200 feet from the car at the edge of the grassy median between Main and Elm, not far from where my motor was parked at the intersection. The sounds were loud reports. It seemed like there was more time between the first and the second shots than between the second and the third. The second and the third were pretty close together. Due to the echo pattern in Dealey Plaza, though, I was unable to tell the direction of the shots.

After they heard the shots, some people fell down. My first observation on this, if I would have been suspecting where the shots came from, I would have picked the building across from the School Book Depository because I looked up and there was a huge flock of pigeons that flew up from that building. You know how pigeons congregate on top of these buildings; well, they flew up from over there, so I focused my attention to that building. I couldn't see the sixth floor window of the School Book Depository because the colonnade structure in Dealey Plaza was between me and the sixth floor at the level where I was. I was right behind that structure. What I could see was the outline of the President's head, and I could see it jerk.

I tried to find someone. . . an escape route. I knew we had people stationed all around the place, so I got on my motor and went down to Industrial because there was an open area back behind the railroad to see if I could see anything or anybody trying to escape. After I made a quick turn down there and could see nothing, I came back to the area and started searching behind the railroad yards, not because I thought shots had come from there, but because we were looking for an unknown, somebody running, trying to get away.

I didn't smell any gunpowder. I think there was a car that started up over there that smoked a lot, and a lot of people seemed to think that was a distraction. But I believe it was just an old car that started that was burning a lot of oil. After the shooting, a number of people fanned out into the area behind the School Book Depository, and I assumed some of them to be Secret Service. But I understand later they weren't. I didn't see anybody's identification, but I could tell they were law enforcement officers dressed in business suits.

When I came to the front of the building, after leaving the railroad yards, immediately after that, I found a witness, a Negro boy named Amos Euins. He was a high school student out here at, I believe it was, Roosevelt High School. He told me that he definitely saw the shots come from the sixth floor window up there and that he saw a gun barrel out of the window. I went to the front of the building and told Inspector Sawyer that the shots definitely came from the building, and I asked for a couple of squads to seal off the building. So it was probably within five minutes that the building was sealed. Elm Street itself was not sealed off. I think if we'd have sealed it off, it would have caused more problems than if we would have left it open because there was no reason to seal it off. The President went to Parkland Hospital, and the building was our main crime scene, so we sealed the building off. I felt that was sufficient.

I was then assigned to go down to the railroad yards and check the boxcars. So we went down and pulled several people off and sent them to the sheriff's office to check them out. In this particular case, there was a freight train which had a lot of boxcars on it. Everybody that we found back there behind the Union

Station and around the overpass we took with us that was unaccounted for. We found a train which was probably two or three hundred yards to the south of the Triple Underpass; everything was stopped when the parade was going by there. These so-called tramps were in a boxcar. Anyone that was loitering around near this train was picked up. We just started with the engineer and went all the way to the back of this train. It was the only one that was in the yard.

There were several officers out there. Every time we'd get one, we'd send a couple to take them over to the sheriff's office. I think Officers Wise and Bass took the ones over that were in the pictures in a magazine. There were several taken off and sent to the sheriff's office, but I don't remember how many. I don't recall all the officers that were there, but I took six or eight down there myself. There's been a lot of talk about these so-called tramps, but these were just ordinary people, transients, most of them. We had those type of people come through the area all the time. Usually, when we took them in, because of the overpass and the construction of Dealey Plaza, we'd come over close to the School Book Depository since the sheriff's office was kind of diagonal across the street from there. The sheriff's office at that time was on the first floor of the Criminal Courts Building.

Later, I reported what could have been a bullet scar on a curb. I reported it because I noticed it was in line with where the Presidential car was from the window up there and was in direct line with where the President was hit. One of the bullets, I understand, had gone wide, and I thought maybe it could have possibly nicked the concrete there. But it could have been where an edger had clipped the curb since they had manicured that area pretty well for the parade. In any case, I called it to the attention of the investigators. The scar was located near a manhole cover on the south side of Elm Street, near the curb. There's a manhole cover and then there's about two feet of concrete surrounding the cover. As best I remember, it's about two feet by two feet, and the scar was on the edge of the concrete. I didn't know whether it had anything to do with the assassination or not, but I think they investigated it pretty thoroughly.

While all this was happening, I didn't know what was going on up on the sixth floor of the School Book Depository. I never went up there. Whenever I went to the entrance of the building, they would give me another assignment such as shaking down the boxcars. However, I do remember that there were some leaflets passed out earlier that morning: "Wanted For Treason." I found a stack of them over on Pacific when I was on my traffic run, and I turned those over to Officer Hart in the Intelligence Division.

The rest of the day I wasn't assigned to any of that down there. I just worked routine traffic problems downtown. Of course, everybody was feeling pretty low. I mean everyone felt terrible about having the President of the United States killed in our city.

Saturday, I was traffic sergeant. At that time, we had Oswald in the city jail at City Hall down on Harwood and Main. They were anticipating moving him to the county, and there was a large crowd that had congregated down at Elm and Houston that morning which was close to where the sheriff's office was. We wanted to keep all the pedestrians off of the east side of Houston Street which would be next to the jail. That's where they brought the prisoners in. We didn't know when Oswald was going to be moved, so I had a no parking area across the street, put up some barricades, and assigned some officers there to keep everybody back. Some newsmen were there including Wes Wise, who later became mayor, but we wouldn't let anyone next to the area where they would back him in to the jail. I also noticed that Jack Ruby was down there at Elm and Houston, and I wouldn't let him in the area either. But I did see him there that morning. I didn't know him very well, but he had a nightclub downtown, and when I was working downtown I'd see him there at night. He had a couple of little dogs that he'd walk in the area around the hotels. But when I saw him in this restricted area, I just told him that we wouldn't allow any pedestrians on this side of the sidewalk. I don't recall whether he said anything, but he left.

There was also another incident that happened sometime before the assassination; I don't recall exactly when. But we had a person that was passing out pro-Castro literature downtown at Elm and Ervay, and a lot of citizens were getting pretty disturbed about it. So they asked the traffic officer who worked for me, Walter Finigan, who was the officer there, and he called me and said, "There's a fellow down here putting out pro-Castro literature, and they're getting into some pretty heated discussions." And so he asked me to come down. So, I got on my motor and went down, and as I parked across the street, the fellow broke and ran. I didn't get a good look at him and didn't know who he was.

So I told the officer, "Let him go. He hadn't done anything, so just let him go." It wasn't a violation that I was aware of. If a person wanted to disagree with someone, we certainly weren't going to deprive him of that right. As I understand, there was a witness to this who is now a magistrate here, Madden Hill. He got into a heated argument with the man from what I've heard. All I could see was the back of his head.

Over the years I've been interviewed many times about what happened with the assassination. There was an investigative committee that came down here on that, and then I've had several investigators from Washington come and talk to me. But I feel like the Warren Commission was thorough. Now, as far as the motives for the assassination, I don't know anything about that. But I feel that everything was pretty thoroughly investigated.

One thing that I'm always asked about are the men who supposedly showed me Secret Service credentials by the School Book Depository after the shooting. I'd like to clarify that. I saw no identification. I could have been mistaken on their identities because anything like that that happens you've got to stay with the facts, and I probably had an assumption that everybody that was with the parade was Secret Service. For instance, I think they had a member of the Texas Department of Public Safety driving one of the cars. So, everybody in the parade wasn't with the Secret Service.

But things like that get into the conspiracy theories. I have received a lot of inquiries, and I don't answer them because a lot of these people are trying to write a book, to exploit, and to do it for profit. I'm not interested in that. Probably some of the people have had good intentions, but I believe in letting the investigating authorities handle it because everybody that gives their version of it will be different. One of the problems is that many have had their words turned around or taken out of context. I thought the police department should have had one spokesman that would get all the information and then release it altogether, so that way we wouldn't have so many conflicts because everybody expresses themselves differently. Glen King acted as public information director, and he let everybody tell their own story. I told all my men to give all their information to him. But he said, "No, let everybody talk if they wanted to." And that's why you have so many different versions. I think if you have one spokesman it's better.

Locally, we had good press relations. However, on the national level, people like Eric Sevareid and Harry Reasoner made some rather cutting remarks. They put out a lot of information before they had the facts. They and some of the other newscasters were pretty harsh on Dallas and the police, and we felt terrible about that. Even some of the people, immediately after the assassination, were angry at the police. They assumed that we'd let the President get shot. Some of them were real abusive. Actually, Chief Curry gave the FBI and the Secret Service everything they asked for, and then he called in fifty more men and had them at designated locations in the event they were needed. He did everything they asked him to do.

I really didn't have a very active part in the assassination. I just had a small part and that's about all. Now, I did testify in the Ruby trial about him being down there in that area, and that's all I knew about it. I played a very small part in this assassination. I was just a small cog in a big wheel.

I retired from the police department and then joined the probation department in 1973. I've now completed forty-four years with the criminal justice system: seventeen with the probation department and twenty-seven with the police department. I'm now on my forty-fifth year, but I'll probably retire from here before next year.

Harkness was well known within the police department to stand up for his men, and in the opinion of many fellow officers, his outspokenness resulted in his lack of promotion above the level of sergeant. D.V. Harkness retired from the probation department in 1991 and now lives with his wife, Ellie, in Dallas.

J.W. FOSTER
Accident Investigator
Dallas Police Department

"You could see about where the bullet had come from by checking the angle where it scraped across the concrete and the column where it struck the pedestrian. It appeared to have come from the north-east, approximately from the book store area, but we were never able to find the slug..."

J. W. Foster was born in Italy, Texas, and was raised in nearby Hillsboro. After serving in the military, he worked at construction jobs for ten years prior to joining the Dallas Police Department in 1955. For the next seven years he worked in Radio Patrol, and at the time of the assassination was an accident investigator.

I was assigned to patrol the triple overpass over Elm Street and arrived down there about 9:30. Our orders were to keep all personnel off the railroad overpass. During the morning, there were several people who came up, and I told them they had to leave. I checked the ID's of the railroad people and tried to get them to leave, but they had the idea that I couldn't do that. If I'd have gotten them off, they would have probably pulled the engine up right behind me, which would have created a noise problem. So there wasn't much I could do about that.

At the time the motorcade came through, there were about seven or eight people up there. As you looked down, I was standing over the third lane from the north curb of Elm Street. Four or five were standing right in front of me, and there were several on down the trestle away from me. Just prior to the shots, a three engine locomotive went by, so there wasn't a lot that you could see or hear from up there even though the locomotive had already passed and just the boxcars were going by at the time the motorcade passed through.

At about 12:30, I saw the motorcade as they came around the corner off of Houston onto Elm proceeding west. When they got about halfway between Houston and the Triple Underpass, I heard three distinct, evenly spaced shots. I could see into the car but couldn't really determine anything, but I did see Mrs. Kennedy crawl up on the back of the car and the driver of the vehicle swerve to his right and a Secret Service agent push her back into the car. From that point, they proceeded west on Elm Street to the Stemmons Freeway. At the time, all I could tell about the shots was that they all sounded about the same, and they came from back toward Elm and Houston Streets. None of them came from the grassy knoll.

After the shooting, one officer ran up and said the shots came from the overpass, and I told him they didn't. Then I moved around to the end of the viaduct where somebody said some man had run up the railroad track from that location. So I proceeded up to the yards to check the empty boxcars to see if anybody had run up that way.

I was in the yards maybe ten to fifteen minutes looking in the cars, but I didn't find anything. Nor did I see anything suspicious behind the picket fence or see anyone with Secret Service or FBI identification, as some have stated. From there I moved on down to the book store and walked on down to the south side of Elm. The plaza had been freshly mowed the day before, thus I noticed this clump of sod that was laying there and was trying to find out what caused that clump of grass to be there. That's when I found where the bullet had struck the concrete skirt by the manhole cover and knocked that clump of grass up.

Buddy Walthers, one of the sheriff's deputies, came up and talked to me about it, and we discussed the direction from which the bullet had come. It struck the skirt near the manhole cover and then hit this person who had stood by the column over on Commerce Street. He came by and had a cut on his face where the bullet had struck the column. You could see about where the bullet had come from by checking the angle where it scraped across the concrete and the column where it struck the pedestrian. It appeared to have come from the northeast, approximately from the book store area, but we were never able to find the slug.

When I first found the scraped concrete and torn up sod, I contacted my sergeant, C.F. Williams. He told me to remain there until they got down there and had some pictures taken, which they did. I don't know what went on from there in regard to that other than the FBI was supposed to have gone down there and taken out a section of the curbing. I probably got away from there about four o'clock.*

While I was guarding the manhole location, I wondered why all the squad cars and most of the supervisors had left the area. Then somebody told me that Tippit had been killed.

I knew J.D. about as well as anybody in the department since I rode with him for some time when we were working squad years earlier out in West Dallas. I found him to be pleasant to work with, very quiet, and went about his duties. Knowing Tippit, I wondered how it could have happened and why he got out cold-turkey without some protection, especially since he was not one to take unnecessary chances. I went to his funeral, as did many other officers. Tippit was only the third officer killed since I had joined the department. Prior to that Johnny Sides in 1951 had been the last before I joined the force. So the killing of a police officer was a serious thing. It wasn't like it is today where policemen's lives seem to be a dime a dozen.

After I left Dealey Plaza, I went on to City Hall up on the third floor and worked crowd control there for a while. The hallway was full of newsmen and officers. The newsmen generally weren't giving us too much trouble. You could ask them to do something and they would disperse a little. From there, I went

---

* This episode has created controversy among researchers. A man dressed in a business suit is seen in photographs near Foster and Deputy Sheriff "Buddy" Walthers allegedly picking up something in the grass near the manhole cover. Did he discover a slug? Who was he? The answer to both questions has never been conclusively resolved.

back in my squad car to my regular job as an accident investigator. As I recall, I got off work at about 2:30 the next morning and had nothing further to do with the events the rest of the weekend.

Overall, the assassination and the shooting of Oswald had a severe effect on the police department. We got some pretty nasty phone calls and, of course, all the officers hated it because of the strain it put on the city. But it's something you have to get away from as soon as possible and get on with everything at hand. But I think much of the criticism was unjust, especially because the FBI knew that Oswald worked in that building and we didn't know anything about it.

I finished my career with the police department in 1976 and went to work as a production supervisor for a plastic's company and worked there for about ten years building tanning beds. Currently, I'm working part-time in floor sales for a lumber company which keeps me away from the house.

J.W. Foster still is active with the lumber company and resides in Cedar Hill, Texas.

JACK FAULKNER

Deputy Sheriff
Criminal Investigation Division
Dallas County Sheriff's Department

"We had many people inside the Texas School Book Depository tell us that those shots didn't come from that building. That was understandable since I have seen deer shot at and, not knowing which way the bullet came from, they would look all around not knowing which way to run. It's hard to determine where a shot comes from a rifle..."

Born and raised in Dallas, Jack Faulkner lived next door to Bill Decker, who was elected sheriff of Dallas County in 1948. Faulkner then joined the sheriff's department on January 1, 1949.

I was a criminal investigator working out of the sheriff's office downtown and was standing outside the office waiting to see the President, as were many of the other deputies, since the sheriff's department had no role in the security for the parade. This was not unusual since the Dallas police were responsible for events inside the city, while the sheriff's department dealt with matters outside the city, but still inside Dallas County.

Much has been written about how unpopular John Kennedy was in Dallas, but as the Presidential parade came down Main Street right in front of the office where the deputies were standing, that obviously wasn't true because I saw the crowds cheering him as he drove by. I certainly didn't see anybody that hated him. The sheriff was in the parade along with Chief Curry, who was driving and leading the parade. But, of course, everybody wanted to see the President of the United States. I recall very well Jackie wearing the pink outfit and the smiles that John Kennedy had when they turned the corner off Main onto Houston. It was all very inspiring!

When they turned back onto Elm Street and headed toward the Triple Underpass, then I heard three very distinct shots. I'll never forget the sequence: there was a pause between number one and number two, then number two and three were rapid. At that time, I actually thought that someone had attempted to shoot the President and possibly the Secret Service had shot back. It was that fast!

A.D. McCurley and myself moved down the knoll that's just west of Houston Street between Main and Elm Streets. People were pointing back toward the railroad yards, so we headed in that direction. As we were crossing Elm Street, McCurley picked up a white piece of bone near the north curb. He asked me, "Do you suppose that could be part of his skull?"

I said, "There's no blood on it," and he put it down. Later, we got to thinking, and somebody said your skull doesn't necessarily have to be touching something that's bloody. We went back and looked for it later but never found it. To this day, I believe it was a piece of John Kennedy's skull. In any case, when we reached the grassy knoll, people were lying down trying to dodge the bullets.

There were quite a few people and officers searching the parking lot and going through railroad cars in the railroad yards, but of course, there was nothing. I really didn't do that myself. There was probably as much mass confusion as you can imagine because no one was in charge, but everyone was doing what they were trained to do. I know my partner, who was on the other side of the street, started gathering people to take statements.

We then went up in front of the Texas School Book Depository Building where a little black boy was telling a police sergeant that he had seen a man shoot out of that building. The sergeant then related that information to us. So Bill Wiseman, A.D. McCurley, Joe Lorraine, who had been a former deputy who worked for the State Labor Board, and I took it from there and went in the front door of the building. This was about ten minutes after the shooting. At that time, the building had not yet been sealed by the police. We contacted the manager who said, "Well, everybody is still here that was here when the parade went through when the shooting occurred except Lee Oswald."

We then went up the freight elevator and began searching. I was expecting to see someone with a gun, so I had my gun out as I felt that they would not hesitate to shoot me, especially since they had already shot the President. After a while, it seemed as though the building was full of officers, so we more or less concentrated the search on the sixth floor. They were even looking up in the ceiling trying to find the gun.

When we arrived on the sixth floor, there were skill saws and plywood lying around, so it was apparent that they had been working on that floor. I observed the location from where the shots were fired. Boxes were arranged like a bird's nest around that window on the corner of the sixth floor. If anyone had come up from behind, they couldn't have seen what was going on. In that area, I saw three hulls which were very close together, probably in an area ten inches in diameter. Now that's my recollection from years later. It's possible that they may have been moved by the time I saw them.

There were also some chicken bones. Evidently he had chicken for his lunch. There were people that worked with him that had left maybe at noon. I don't know where they went because I didn't investigate that part of it. I've also heard of a bag which carried the rifle, but I never saw that. It could have been there, but I didn't notice it.

I was very close to Officer Boone when he spread some books aside, which were packed in large boxes, and found the rifle. I was about six feet from the rifle when I first saw it. I wasn't able to identify it, but I could tell that it was a military rifle.

Boone never touched it, and we left it in place until a Crime Scene Search officer, Lieutenant Day, came and picked it up by the strap. It wasn't long before the rifle was being referred to as a Mauser. The '03 Springfield is a Mauser type rifle which was our standard military rifle for years. The Mauser was copied and possibly somebody saw it and said it looked like a Mauser, which it does. There is no doubt in my mind, since I later examined Mannlicher-Carcanos, that that was what was found at the scene.

When the shells and the rifle were located, by that time more and more officers had arrived to the point where there must have been 75 to 100 officers on that floor; I didn't feel that there was anything else to find.

Everybody leaving the building had to sign out, so at about 1:30 I left and walked over to the sally-port of the old jail at the sheriff's office and ran into Charlie Brown, who was an FBI agent. He was listening to the radios and said, "Jack, I think they've got him! They arrested a man in the Texas Theater that killed a Dallas police officer, and he worked at the Texas School Book Depository."

I said, "Well, it looks like that closes the case," and I still think it did.

In the meantime, while Oswald was in custody at the city hall, I remember talking to Mr. Decker about how we should transfer Oswald. It was our normal procedure that we transferred everyone after they were filed on from the city jail. We could have brought him in through Record Street, which was open then, and where the plaza is now and then bring him up to the second floor, or we could have brought him in where the crowd would have all been on Houston Street. But Mr. Decker told me, "No, this is the city's baby right now. We'll wait till they can milk it for everything they can, then we'll handle it." I understand that the Warren Commission asked Jess Curry if it was the usual procedure for them to transfer prisoners to the county and he told them, yes, which was a lie! It was not their usual procedure, though they had done it. I remember that they filed on a city police officer for burglary at one time and they brought him down. But that's the only other time that I ever remember that happening. I think the reason the city handled the transfer was because Elgin Crull, the city manager, who was an ex-newspaperman with *The Dallas Morning News*, had promised all these newsmen their pictures, and they gave him the best news pictures that's ever been shot. I recall the next day in *The Dallas Morning News* that there was a full page picture of Ruby with his pistol almost in Oswald's stomach, firing, and you could see the anguish on Oswald's face.

I worked through Saturday but was off that Sunday when Oswald was shot. Naturally I was surprised! Evidently no one who worked up there that knew Ruby expected it. They let him come down that ramp. But Dallas was a smaller town then; it was not the metropolitan center that it is today. Everybody that was in public life knew each other then, and everybody knew Jack Ruby.

He was a character, very volatile, they tell me, around his clubs. He had the Vegas Club out on Oak Lawn and the Carousel downtown. I never ran into Jack Ruby anywhere that he didn't say, "Come on out; have a good time; won't cost you a cent!" But the only time I was ever around his clubs was on business. I wasn't about to go to any of those darn clubs because it wasn't my cup of tea. But he was always very friendly to the officers.

After he was transferred to the county jail, he wasn't ignored as some have claimed. We kept a man with him twenty-four hours a day because Sheriff Decker said he wasn't going to be embarrassed by his being killed. When he went to court, he had at least six people shielding him from the elevator to the courtroom. Of those who guarded him in the jail, most of them didn't like him. They were with him for eight hour shifts and said that his personal habits were very filthy.

Ruby more or less indicated to me that he was a homosexual, and I think he was. He was talking to me one day and said that one of his strippers was telling him that she was pregnant. He apparently told her, "You can't blame it on me! I don't think you can get that way from spit," or something to that effect. At that time, Ruby was living with another fellow named George Senator who, through my observation, also appeared to be queer.

I think something just snapped in Ruby when he shot Oswald. But who's to say? You'd have to know him. He claimed that he loved the President so much, but he was at *The Dallas Morning News* at the time of the parade taking out an ad for his club. He also said that he thought about Jackie and the kids, and maybe he did. But I don't think that either he or Oswald were involved in any type of conspiracy.

One of our own deputies, Roger Craig, got wrapped up in all this conspiracy business. In fact, he went off the deep end on this thing. Roger was running the radio room when this happened working as dispatcher, if I'm not mistaken. Personally I don't remember seeing him up on the sixth floor, as he claims. He wrote a manuscript making wild claims about what he alleged to have seen and heard. Roger went down to New Orleans a few years later and got involved with Jim Garrison and then later with Penn Jones, who helped him become Justice of the Peace in Midlothian.

Then Roger committed suicide. Unfortunately, he went nuts over this. He was, what I call, just squirrelly.

Penn Jones is one of those who has made a lifelong ambition of trying to prove a conspiracy. For years he sold a paper with an update on all this. But most of the critics were in New York when it happened. They've come up with all these theories: it's not Oswald that's buried in Fort Worth, and they dig him up and it is; there were four shots; and Penn Jones says a man raised up out of a manhole and fired. They're all just theories! A lot of them have tried to write things for profit that would be spectacular, and they have probably confused 25 to 50 percent of the people in this country into believing that there is more to the assassination than there really was, [asserting] anything that was contrary to what the Warren Commission said or anything to keep things stirred up, and for that reason, I imagine a hundred years from now there will still be people saying that that isn't the way it happened.

Lyndon Johnson appointed both Democrats and Republicans to the Warren Commission, and I was satisfied that they made an excellent investigation and came to the right determination. Unfortunately, anytime the police are involved in anything there's probably 25 percent of the people who are willing to believe that they're not telling the truth. They'll tell you that they got a ticket for speeding when they claim they weren't. It's just a hate of law enforcement. Who has benefited by what the Warren Commission said except some of these writers out of New York? They can profit because they can sell books. But where does the Warren Commission profit?

I think that I have as good a picture of the assassination as anybody, especially since I was involved in the investigation. Personally, I think the whole thing was quite simple. I think that Lee Harvey Oswald was a misfit, and his thinking was probably that if he could kill the President of the United States he would become famous. Of course, he did, but he died in the process. He had shot at General Walker prior to this, and then he told his wife about it. What was his reason for this? What threat was General Walker to him? He was just a very small person who wanted notoriety.

We know that Lee Harvey Oswald was working on the sixth floor of the Texas School Book Depository, that he ordered that gun, and that he brought it in with him that morning telling the guy he rode with that it was curtain rods. His wife still thought it was out in the garage when the police went out to interview her that evening. But she saw that it was gone and that there was only an imprint of the rifle on the blanket. They proved beyond a doubt that he killed Tippit, and I think they even had four or five witnesses that could identify him. Why did he do this if he was innocent of killing the President? What was his reasoning? They very seldom bring that up! There was a connection with his killing Tippit and his leaving the Book Depository immediately. I can testify to that because that's what the manager told me not ten minutes after the assassination. Why'd he leave?

What was his motivation? Who knows? Prior to the assassination, he went to Mexico for some reason. I think he may have contacted some of Castro's people and they might have said, "Why don't you kill the President?" Another thing that has not come out, and I think it's the reason why some of the files would be kept in a closet for 75 years; I think the FBI was paying Oswald as an informant because they will do that to anybody that they think will help them. I think he was getting a little money from them. I know all kinds of people who did nothing but hang around bars that were on the FBI's payroll. Agent Hosty made the statement to the effect, "I knew he was a Communist, but I didn't think he'd kill the President." So I think they felt if the information ever came out that they had given him money that it would look like they paid him to kill the President, which wasn't their intention at all. As a result, Hoover had Hosty transferred that day.

There were quite a few of the agents that came down to the sheriff's office every day, and we always worked well together. I was captain of CID for seven years after Mr. Decker died, and we worked on several kidnappings in Dallas with them. I had lots of friends among the agents, but it always seemed that they wanted to know what you knew, but they didn't want to tell you anything. I think that's the major complaint that local officers have about the FBI. They just don't trust everybody, which is good business, really!

I worked for Sheriff Decker for twenty-one years until his death from emphysema in 1969. He was to have resigned on August 31st, but died on August 29th. Decker was a fine man who had as much respect among the convicts down at Huntsville that he had had sent there as he did among the people of Dallas because he didn't lie to them. He always treated every man with respect. Bill Decker was a very dedicated person to that job and anybody, even if they were the poorest, raggediest person in Dallas County, could go down there and ask to see Mr. Decker, and they would get in to see him about whatever their problem was. There were a lot of people who felt that Bill Decker was the only friend they had in the world. On the other hand, he could be as tough, as bad, and as mean as anybody that you ever saw if you wanted to argue with him or give him some reason. But he was also one of the most charming people I've ever seen.

The whole time he was sheriff from 1949 until his death, he never had an opponent. He had been chief deputy for fourteen years, and when he was elected, no one ever ran against him.

He seldom took a vacation. If he did, he'd call the office five times a day to find out what was going on and give advice on how to run things. He practically lived at the sheriff's department. He'd come in the morning and go home for dinner, then he'd come back around 9:00 o'clock and stay until 2:00 or 3:00 o'clock in the morning.

He was also progressive about anything that would help law enforcement. We had polygraphs, computers, and the first color photo lab in the country. If it was beneficial to law enforcement, he was for it. He wasn't from the old school as far as that was concerned. But he ran that department! When I went to work there, there were only 90 people, now there's about 1,500, and you don't know anybody. It was more of a homey atmosphere back then because you knew everybody you worked with, and the people were more interested in their work and more dedicated. We used to work sixteen and eighteen hours without overtime. We certainly didn't make that much money, but to those of us who knew Bill Decker, we considered it an honor and a privilege to work for the man.

Faulkner served another nineteen years with the Dallas County Sheriff's Department following the death of Sheriff Decker and attained the rank of captain of the Criminal Intelligence Division and acting director. At the time of his retirement in 1989, he was a lieutenant serving out of the patrol headquarters near Hutchins, Texas. Faulkner continued to reside in the house that was next door to his former employer and friend, Bill Decker, until his death following a fishing trip in October 1996.

LUKE MOONEY
Deputy Sheriff
Writ and Execution Division
Dallas County Sheriff's Department

"While we were standing there, someone brought the word that the President was dead... There wasn't a sound. I then looked over between someone's feet and there lay a carton of books broken open with the lid flapped back. Inside the carton was a paperback book, and on the cover was Christ Leads the Way *with a picture of Jesus..."*

A native Texan, born in Hopkins County, eighty miles east of Dallas, and a veteran of the 764th Amphibious Tank Tractor Battalion in World War II, Luke Mooney, upon discharge in 1946 attended a business college and later worked in the automobile business. After declining a transfer to a new office in another state, Mooney, due to his background in legal matters, was asked by Sheriff Bill Decker in 1958 to join the sheriff's department in the Writ and Execution Division.

I was merely a spectator with a number of other plain clothes officers on Main Street just north of the Old Red Court House. We in the sheriff's department had nothing to do with security. That had all been arranged by the Dallas Police Department, the Secret Service, and the FBI. I hadn't been out there long when the motorcade came by with the President and his wife, Governor Connally and his wife, along with all the Secret Service agents following on the running boards of the follow up open top vehicle.

The crowd was very enthusiastic. I was close enough to have shaken hands with the President. As the motorcade passed by us, we never attempted to follow it around the corner at Houston and were still standing there when we heard a shot ring out. I knew immediately that it wasn't a backfire because, if you've ever been around weapons, you knew from the echo that it was a gun of some kind.

Several of us started moving toward Houston Street at the moment we heard the first shot. By the time we reached the street, the second shot had been fired, then there was a slight hesitation between the second and the third. We had already heard all three shots before we had reached Houston Street.

We then ran over into Dealey Plaza, crossed Elm, jumped over the wall of the embankment on what's now called the grassy knoll and headed toward the railroad yards. At that time, it seemed to have been the most logical place to begin looking unless you had actually known from where the shots originated, which I didn't.

People were scattered in every direction. By that time, the motorcade was en route to Parkland up Stemmons Freeway and thus out of sight. Other officers were everywhere already checking the parking lot behind the fence. We looked around and into some of the vehicles but didn't see anything unusual. If we had seen anything that was obvious, we would have checked it out.

I'd estimate that I was in the parking lot area less than ten minutes; whereupon, I noticed a big open wire gate near the freight area of the Book Depository. I saw a citizen there and said, "Let's close this off, lock it, and don't let anybody in or out unless they're an officer with identification." I then went into the back of the Book Depository where the freight dock was located where there was also a back entrance to a series of offices. I knew how to operate a freight elevator, so we pushed the button and went up one floor. But after one floor, the power was cut and the elevator quit operating, so we took the stairs and went toward the upper levels.

I got off on the sixth floor while some of the others went to the seventh. All you could see were books stacked about head high. At that time, I didn't search the area thoroughly, but I noticed that everything was quiet and nothing seemed disturbed, particularly over on the southwest corner where nothing was stacked. It appeared as though some carpenter work was being done.

Noticing nothing out of the ordinary, I then went on up to the seventh floor. By that time, the others had already left that floor and it was dark, so I sent out the word to get the search light from the sheriff's office. Since it was so dark and the high powered battery lights were on the way, I decided to return to the sixth floor to search it more thoroughly. I found an opening near the northeast corner and worked my way through this passageway where there was a small space between the stacks of books. It was a tight squeeze for me considering, at the time, I weighed about 185-190 pounds. As I wound my way through the stacks, I noticed at the southeast corner of the building, overlooking the corner of Elm and Houston, a small area that was big enough for a man to sit, have room, and the window was half open.

The first thing that I saw were the spent shells: that immediately captured my attention. There, apparently, was where the shots had been fired from because I had heard three distinct shots and there were three distinct spent shells laying on the floor. In addition, there were a series a book cartons stacked two or three high, one with a crease for the rifle to lay in.

As I recall, the shell casings were laying in the area of where he had rested the rifle on the carton. They were not right against the baseboard under the window sill: one was about a foot from the other and the third was further away. It appeared as though they had been ejected from the rifle and had possibly bounced off the cartons of books to the rear.

After I located the spent shells and I knew that that was the location of the assassin, I hooked my elbows over the window sill so that I wouldn't leave any fingerprints or disturb any evidence and called down to Sheriff Decker and Captain Fritz, who surprisingly happened to be down on the street, to send up the Crime Lab.

Fritz arrived a few moments later taking the same route through the stacks of boxes that I had. He was the first man to reach down and pick up one of the shell casings to see what caliber it was. I had secured the area before he had arrived, thus nothing had been disturbed until that time. After that, I don't know what happened to the casings.

I left Fritz in charge while Deputy Boone and I began looking for the weapon. We didn't know what it was at the time. Searchlights had arrived by the time we approached the northwest corner near the staircase. Boone was about six to eight feet from me when he said, "I see it!"

I stepped over and looked between the cartons and said, "Sure, that's the weapon!" Fritz and others then came over and pulled the weapon from where it was laying. At that time, there were bunches of officers on the floor; it looked like Coxey's Army. I saw the rifle close up but still didn't know what kind it was. It appeared to be a bolt-action military type much like the old carbines we had in the Army.

While we were standing there, someone brought the word that the President was dead. Even with the large number of people there, you could have heard a pin drop. There wasn't a sound. I then looked over between someone's feet and there lay a carton of books broken open with the lid flapped back. Inside the carton was a paperback book, and on the cover was *Christ Leads the Way* with a picture of Jesus.

With the weapon being found, we assumed the suspect had left the building by going down the stairwell, since that was where we found the rifle. I then left and went back to the sheriff's office. It was during this time that we heard that a police officer had been shot and killed in Oak Cliff. After that, I had little to do with the investigation.

Since the assassination, all kinds of books have been written and movies made, largely for the purpose of promoting theories and making money. I've never made one penny off of it and don't intend to. All I know is what I saw. Oswald was apprehended, and all indications are that they found prints of him up there where I found the spent shells in the area where the shots came from. I know that they had to have come from that area. If you go up there and look down, you'll see that it's a lot closer to the street than it looks from the street upward. When you're on the sixth floor, you're right on top of him. It was not that hard of a shot, especially with a telescopic sight.

————————————

In the years following the assassination, Mooney headed the Writ and Execution Division of the Dallas County Sheriff's Department which handled seized property, real estate, and executing on judgments. He also taught civil law procedure at the academy and conducted seminars in the surrounding Dallas area. Mooney retired from the sheriff's department in 1980 to join his wife in joint ownership of a cosmetics firm, Superior Products Company. Now retired, Mooney lives in Farmer's Branch, Texas.

THE INVESTI-
GATION

J. Carl Day

Vincent Drain

Elmo L. Cunningham

Paul Bentley

Gerald L. Hill

John Toney

W.R. Westbrook

Roy Westphal

Gus Rose

Harry D. Holmes

CARL DAY
Crime Scene Search Unit
Dallas Police Department

"When I came out of the Book Depository, walking with the FBI man who was taking me to the office, somebody asked me, `Is that a Mauser?' or words to that effect. I didn't answer them... I didn't know what I had other than it was a gun..."

Born and raised in Dallas, Carl Day graduated from high school in 1932. After working for a machinery company during the Depression, Day joined the Dallas Police Department in 1940. Interrupted by a three-year stint in the Navy during World War Two, he returned to his patrol assignment and was promoted to detective in the Homicide and Robbery Bureau in 1947 under Captain Fritz. The following year Day transferred to the Identification Bureau. Upon promotion to lieutenant in 1954, he joined the newly formed Crime Lab within the Identification Bureau and remained in that position upon Kennedy's arrival in Dallas.

I was in the office of the Crime Lab on the fourth floor of City Hall when the parade passed City Hall at Harwood and turned west on Main. I was busy and didn't see it. A few minutes later I received a call that the President had been shot, and I went with Detective Studebaker to the Book Depository. It took about ten minutes to get to the scene. Since there wasn't any place to park on the street, I parked on the sidewalk in front of the building where Inspector Sawyer was standing and appeared to be in charge of the scene. There was a lot of confusion; people were running everywhere.

We went on inside the building through the front door and were directed to the sixth floor where we were advised that the shooting had supposedly occurred. We took the elevator at the front, but as I recall, that elevator only went to the second floor. There we met Mr. Truly, and he directed us to the elevator at the back which took us up to the sixth floor to a window at the southeast corner of the building. There, behind some boxes of books stacked up, were three spent hulls, apparently ejected by a gun, laying around on the floor under the window being guarded by a detective. That's all I found, just three.

We put powder on them but were unable to find any legible fingerprints, which was understandable because it's hard to have prints on hulls or shells because of the skewed area there. Sometimes you can find them, most times you don't, so I wasn't surprised that we didn't find any. I turned one of the hulls over to one of Captain Fritz's detectives and kept the other two. Later I marked only the two that I kept at that time.

We hadn't been in that area taking photographs and processing the hulls more than ten minutes or so when Captain Fritz called me back to the opposite corner of the building from where the shooting occurred, diagonally across and close to the freight elevators, where they had found the rifle. It was laying flat stuck down in the crack between some boxes. It had apparently not been located prior to that. No one had picked it up, so I'm reasonably sure that I was the next person who handled it after Oswald. We made photos of that and then I picked it up.

Through just a casual examination, I didn't see any markings on it at that time. All I was trying to do was to get it up without destroying any fingerprints to see if there was a live round in it. I wasn't making a close examination on it there; there just wasn't anyplace to do it.

I had examined lots of rifles, picked them up and so forth, but I wasn't familiar with that particular gun. It appeared to be a cheap wartime gun with a telescopic sight and kind of a worn leather strap on it. There were a lot of those flooding into the country for many years after the war. You could tell by looking that there could be no fingerprints on that strap. I'd been handling those for a long time, and you could tell just by looking at it that it was too rough to get any fingerprints. So I picked it up by the strap, took fingerprint powder and tried to put it on the little knob on the bolt. It was just a small area; the chance of getting any fingerprints off of it were practically nil, but you couldn't do anything but try. I put powder on the knob and examined it with the glass, but there was nothing visible at all. So I held the rifle by the strap in such a way that Captain Fritz could open the bolt. When he opened it, a live round fell out.

Just looking at it I thought the chances were slim that we'd find any prints on the rifle itself. It had what we call a wartime finish on the barrel which would lift out of the stock. That type of surface didn't take prints well, nor did the wood stock which was too course or rough. You've got to have a smooth, fairly clean surface before the ridges will leave an impression. If it's rougher than the ridges of the finger, you're not going to find anything there.

At that time, just through casual observation, it didn't look too promising. It wasn't the place to try to do any fingerprint work since it's a rather lengthy process and we had other things to do. So I decided to carry the gun back to the office at City Hall, store it under lock and key, examine it under ideal conditions, and get to it when I could. I didn't have anything to wrap it up with at the time, so I carried it out making sure that I didn't touch anything other than the strap. Besides, you had to be careful in wrapping stuff because if there were any prints, you're liable to smear them just from the wrapping.

By that time, there were photographers and newsmen running all over the place. When I went out the door, there were a lot of cameras flashing. I told Inspector Sawyer, who was still there, that I needed a ride to City Hall. An FBI man, whose car was parked nearby, volunteered to drive me. Up until that time, I was unaware of the condition of the President, only that he had been shot. During the ride back to City Hall I asked the FBI man, "How bad is he hit?"

He replied, "The President is dead!" That was the first knowledge that I had that it was a fatal shot. Of course, I was very depressed, but it was just another shooting. We had hundreds of them which required investigation and speculation. Meanwhile, he transmitted the numbers which were found on the rifle to the FBI office and took me on to City Hall. There was hardly anybody there at the time. We drove in the basement, and I went up the jail elevator to my office.

The Identification Bureau was located at one end of the fourth floor which was not accessible to reporters or the general public. Within the Identification Bureau, we had an evidence room which had individual boxes where you could lock things up. The key to the whole room was available to all the officers in the bureau, but only Captain Doughty and myself had a key to the evidence box. It was there that I locked the rifle up and returned to the School Book Depository where we tried to continue our investigation.

Primarily, Studebaker and I were taking photos and checking for prints on the sixth floor. There were two boxes side by side aligned which would be just right for a man to sit on them and look out the window down below where the parade went. I don't know whether they were there prior to the shooting or not, but they were in a position that it was convenient to sit on while he was looking out. There were other boxes which were stacked on ends. It looked like they made kind of a shield around the window so that they blocked off the view of the window from the other part of the floor. Supposedly that's the way it was at the time of the shooting. I don't know whether anybody had moved anything or not; however, there had been a lot of prowling around up there. Of course, hindsight is always better than foresight; certainly nothing should have been moved, but it's possible that some of the stuff could have been moved while they were searching before I got there.

When I talked to the Warren Commission, they showed me a picture that had been taken by somebody, and it showed that those boxes didn't seem as though they were in the same position that I found them. That picture was taken from the outside and didn't exactly jibe with what I found on the inside. But the whole building had officers running all over trying to find where the shots came from. There were too many people running around!

One of those boxes near the window had a palm print on it. Looking out the window, it was in just the right place where you'd rest your palm if you were sitting on a box. We used a metallic powder and got a palm print which later turned out to be Oswald's.

All those boxes which had his fingerprints on them didn't mean that much to me at the time because the man worked there and handled the boxes. I didn't take all those with me. The prints that we got from the box he was sitting on meant something to me because there weren't any prints on the side of it, just on the top of the corner, indicating that he had not picked it up during the normal course of work. We just tore that off and didn't take the whole box with us.

Also found on the sixth floor, as I recall, near the shell area, was a paper bag. It should have been photographed, but for some reason, apparently wasn't. The story that I received later was that when this man came to work that morning he was carrying something wrapped in shipping or wrapping paper or brown roll paper. In the shipping room on the first floor, there were one or two rolls of that paper. We took the end pieces off those rolls for possible comparison with the bag that was found. It would have been a tedious job, but on other cases I've had occasion to match the ends of two pieces of paper. If you can find the right place, they'll match up, even if it's torn off. We had possession of that bag, but I didn't have a chance to work with it due to events that later occurred.

During the course of the investigation at the School Book Depository, an officer came in and said they'd found a skid mark close to a manhole cover on Elm Street directly in line of the shots. So I went down there maybe 150 or more feet from the window. Then there was a rumor that somebody was supposed to have heard a shell zipping by on that railroad track. In any case, one of the officers found a place by that manhole cover that looked like something might have either hit or bounced. It could have been a skid mark from a slug; it could have been some other kind of mark; it could have been a tool of some sort. Whatever it was we took a little sample of the concrete and sent it to the laboratory to see if there might have been any trace of lead from a slug. If I remember correctly, they found nothing. Several months later I think somebody went down there and cut that chunk out.

It was around 6:00 or 7:00 o'clock by the time I got back to City Hall. Captain Fritz, of course, was wanting information about the rifle. So I got it out, made photographs, and started examining it as well as I could to see if there were any fingerprints on it. It was pretty rough. I applied powder to it; there was nothing on the stock. Around the trigger guard there was a trace of a print which showed. It wasn't very legible, just traces there. While we were trying to photograph that, Chief Curry came in and wanted to know what we were doing. I explained and told him that it didn't look too promising, or words to that effect.

During the process, lo and behold, thirty minutes later somebody said that a radio report said we had found a fingerprint on it. I don't know where that came from because I hadn't found any fingerprints to tell anything about. Then, when I was adjusting the thing, down under the bottom of the barrel, right at the edge of the wood stock where the barrel projected beyond the stock, there was a trace of a print. I could see it when the light shined just right. It was an old print. The powder wasn't sticking to it, so the print apparently had been there a long time, or at least long enough for it to have dried out.

I got the barrel removed from the stock and applied powder to the bottom of the barrel. The print still had a small amount of oil on it because the powder clung to it a little. When the barrel was removed, I noticed more of that print which had been concealed by the stock. Obviously someone had had the mechanism out of the stock laying in his hand. I tried to lift it with scotch tape and it came off dimly. By then I had Oswald's palm prints, and just at a quick glance, it looked like it was his. I didn't go far enough with it to get on the witness stand and say absolutely that it was his print, but it looked like it was through the preliminary examination.

The procedure that we used to lift prints was fairly simple. The best way to check anything that is not a porous surface is with powder, which clings to the oil that might be present with the fingers. You just brush it on and it'll float all around. But it was also very messy. I'd come home after answering calls with powder all over my shirt, in my nose and ears, and everywhere else. But you'd take some black powder and brush it over the area where you hoped there was a print. You don't always leave prints. If you've got dirty hands or a dry hand, you won't leave a print. Many people don't leave prints when they touch something. When you locate the print, after the powder has been applied, you put scotch tape on it, mash it down, and the powder will cling to the tape. Then, when you pull the tape off, put it on a card with a white background, and then you've got the print where you can take the tape on the card back to the office for examination with a glass. That's the procedure I used when I lifted the print off the bottom of the barrel.

But I still wasn't satisfied with the lift because it was pretty dim. By turning the rifle and letting the light shine on it, I could still see that print on the barrel. To take the proper pictures, you have to set a time exposure on the camera and move the light which reflects around the barrel because you can't twist the barrel while you're taking pictures. I was in the process of doing that when I got word from one of my captains, which came directly from the chief's office, not to do anything else. Right in the middle of the stream I was told not to do anything else with it! So I slipped the barrel back on the stock and put it back in the lock box.

Of course, I was dealing in a vital area here, the physical evidence. It was very important to do all you could to do the work properly. Hundreds of times, in other shootings, it was just another shooting as far as the investigation was concerned. But the difference here was the national publicity and the confusion surrounding it which limited our opportunity for doing our work exactly as it should have been done.

Somewhere in the course of time, Captain Fritz came in needing information badly down on the third floor. He said that he had Marina down in his office and wanted her to look at the gun to see if she could identify it. He said, "There's a lot of people down there, and I don't want to bring her out into the crowd." Well, that meant that I had to take the gun through the crowd. I didn't want to wrap it up and really didn't realize what kind of crowd he was talking about down there. I thought there were just a few people hanging around like there usually was. So I just picked the gun up by the strap again and went on the elevator with him down to the third floor.

When we opened the door, man, there was a mob out there! I didn't know whether to run back upstairs or what! If I had realized how many people were there, I would have done something besides show that gun. It was definitely a poor way to handle evidence! But I was already into this, so he cleared the way into his office which wasn't far. She was sitting across the room while I held the rifle and was answering some questions which I couldn't hear. Then I took the gun back upstairs through the crowd. There was nothing harmed, but again, it wasn't the proper way to handle it. It was just one of those confusing things that was happening at that time.

Captain Fritz came back a little later and had run across the chief of police. He told me to go ahead and start again on what I had been doing with the gun, which I did. Before I got the picture made, another message came in: "Drop everything! Don't do anything else!" It must have been 9:00 o'clock or later. "Drop everything! Don't do anything else!" This came through my captain, Captain Doughty, but it probably came to him from Deputy Chief Lumpkin. So we didn't complete what we were trying to do. I'd have probably been working on it all night if I'd had the time.

Around 11:30 that night I received orders which merely said, "Release the rifle to the FBI." Shortly thereafter I handed it over to Vince Drain of the FBI.

I told him, "There's a trace of a print here" and showed him where it was. It was just a verbal communication to him. I didn't have time to make any written reports; I just gave it to him and he signed for it without saying anything. I don't remember whether he wrapped it up with anything or not, but he took it on to Washington that night.

It's a funny thing about that. We had a few other items around such as some of his clothes and paper off the roll at the Book Depository that we didn't do anything else with. I didn't send the card lift either. They told me not to do anything else, so I didn't even look at it again. There was some friction somewhere. I never quite understood how all that happened, but it was a confusing thing.

Later, all the stuff that was sent to Washington came back to us. The rifle came back in a wooden box but we didn't open it. We were told just to hold it, so I put it in our evidence room and locked it up. We held that stuff a few days then we got an order to release everything to the FBI: the gun, the box, everything we had. At that time, I then released the card with the lifted print. So they took it all back to Washington

Included in what was released were the two hulls I had collected at the School Book Depository. I didn't have in my possession the third hull, and there was some confusion there when I testified to the Warren Commission. That was the one which Captain Fritz retained and did not have my initials on it.

The other two I could identify, but I couldn't identify the third since my initials were not on it. There were the initials GMD there, which were those of Captain Doughty, my captain. I later learned that what had happened was that he had marked it when it was released. There was nothing out of the ordinary about it: there wasn't a substituted third hull. It was just one of those slips in the confusion.

About four or five days later, an FBI man rolled up at the house and wanted to know where I had gotten the palm print. In Washington, they didn't find any prints on the gun at all. I don't know why they didn't locate that piece of print that I thought was still there. However, if I had received it with powder all over it, I probably would have thrown up my hands because somebody else had been messing with it. I suspect that's what happened with the man in Washington. There were too many irons in the fire, too many fingers in the pie! But anyway, they didn't find any prints, or didn't find that one or were unable to do anything with what I thought was on there. It may have been that there wasn't enough there, but I thought I could still see it.

But anyway, I sent this palm print on the card to Washington. Of course, they identified it as Oswald's, but they thought that I had gotten it off the gun after it had been sent back to us, which wasn't true. So they were in kind of a stew. They thought their man in Washington had missed the print. After I explained what had happened, I guess that got him off the hook.

Prior to the assassination we had always had excellent relations with all the FBI men. Some of them I'd worked with for years. But there was friction between the police department and the FBI for a year or two after that. During the early course of the investigation, they couldn't make up their minds who was going to do what. I still got along fine because I worked with them, but with the higher-ups they seemed to have gotten crossways. Chief Curry was supposed to have been perturbed with the FBI for not letting them know that Oswald was in town. Hell, I don't see any reason for getting crossways with anybody about it, but it did happen. I never quite understood how all that happened; it was a confusing thing.

The great problem with the investigation was that there were too many people involved. The Dallas Police Department and the Texas courts had jurisdiction. Since it was not against federal law to shoot the President at that time, the FBI, the national police force, didn't really have any jurisdiction, and as a result had not been in on the original investigation. Taking it up after it had already started, it looks to me like they would have been at a handicap getting the evidence second hand. To me, it would have been much better if this investigation would have been handled in a routine manner all the way through without all the confusion. But other people such as the Secret Service were also vitally interested. We tried to cooperate with them, especially Forrest Sorrels, in every way we could. But there were too many sitting on the side just trying to get information for their future. But again, there were too many fingers in the pie. It was hard to conduct an investigation where you had such confusion.

Captain Fritz was frustrated in trying to make his investigation because he wasn't allowed to handle it the way it should have been handled. The old man was an excellent investigator, an excellent interrogator, and had been doing that work for many years. He wasn't very good with filling out reports or other paper work; he had somebody else do that for him. But I think that he would have worked things out and that we would have had a case to present in the trial. We had the facilities here to make the investigation, and if we didn't, we used the FBI laboratory or the state laboratory in Austin. It would have been a convincing case and would have gotten a conviction as far as the murder was concerned if Oswald hadn't been killed in their custody.

Another story of note was the slug recovered at General Walker's house. Several months prior to the assassination one of our men got a call at the office and went to Walker's house. Someone had fired a slug, apparently at his shadow, through the window from the grounds outside. The slug was dug out of the wall and brought back to our office as evidence. It had been in our possession from that time until the assassination. We didn't have any idea who had fired it or what gun had been used. We could do nothing else with it until something else developed. Of course, we didn't know about Oswald at that time, but it was apparently the same type ammunition as Oswald's. That was eventually turned over to the FBI, which ran the tests, and as I understand, was identified as having come from that gun, though I have never seen the written report.

Paraffin tests were also run on Oswald, which was standard procedure at that time. Theoretically, back in those days, if you fired a gun, nitrates will come out and get on your hands, especially from a revolver. With a rifle, you don't have that. As the bolt moves down in the barrel, you don't have the spraying of nitrates. But, to be on the safe side, especially since he had fired a gun at Tippit, we did make the paraffin test. One of the boys became overzealous and also made a test on the side of his face. But you wouldn't expect to find any powder there from shooting a gun. Now they've done away with those tests because they figured they weren't reliable since nitrates could come from other sources such as urine or fertilizer. We used it for many years and, to me, it's still a fairly valid test. If you take a man, for instance, who has specks of nitrates on his right hand and that's the only place, and he's supposed to have shot a revolver with that right hand, then that test means something to me. It's entirely probable that he did fire a gun. Now they have another type of test which they claim is better. In the last years I was there, we were furnished a small kit that we put something on their hands instead of paraffin.

I didn't work on Saturday, but that Sunday morning, the 24th, Mr. Truly had given me a key to the School Book Depository so that we could take measurements of the whole floor and make diagrams of everything. I had one or two detectives with me. We were the only ones in the building, so it was pretty quiet, but I noticed that somebody had been taking pictures up there sometime between Friday and that Sunday morning as there was film all over the floor. About 11:15 or a little later I saw we were going to be up there a long time, so I called my daughter and told her to tell momma to take the beans off the fire because I wasn't going to be there. She said, "Daddy, they done shot him!" I asked her what she was talking about and she replied, "Shot Oswald at the police station!"

I turned around, looked at the others and said, "Well, hell, let's quit and go home." We just threw up our hands and stopped what we were doing. I didn't take any more of the boxes in for fingerprints. The Warren Commission had all those boxes that were stacked up there. Apparently they went back later and got them and prints were developed, some of them Oswald's. But again, I don't know what they proved. He worked in the place and handled the boxes during the normal course of work.

Another problem with the investigation, especially that weekend, was that there were reporters there from everywhere, all over the world and all of them wanting a story. They were printing anything that made a story: rumors or anything else; it didn't make any difference what it was. And after it gets in print, many people accept it as fact.

A woman wrote me a letter from New York not long ago referring me to some newspaper account from the *Dallas Times Herald* which said something about a shell being found by a motorcycle officer or hitting a motorcycle, whatever it was, and she wanted to know about it. I told her that there wasn't any such thing, that it was strictly a newspaper story. But it's things like that that cause you to wonder what to believe. If you've ever been involved in anything that becomes a big story, sometimes you'll have trouble recognizing the newspaper's account from what you actually saw out there. They get all those things so fouled up!

When I came out of the Book Depository, walking with the FBI man who was taking me to the office, somebody asked me, "Is that a Mauser?" or at least words to that effect. I didn't answer them. Thirty minutes later somebody on radio or television described it as a Mauser. Where that came from, I don't know; it didn't come from me. The only place I can figure was from some overzealous reporter. I didn't know what I had other than it was a gun. I don't remember any name being on the rifle. I never learned who identified it other than possibly it was through some FBI report about Oswald's stuff that had been found and where he got it.

As far as I was concerned, there was no question in my mind that he was the man. The evidence stacked up, and I don't think that there would have been any problem at all getting him convicted in court. We had the evidence necessary. But as far as conspiracy was concerned, I didn't have much to do with that, though I don't think there were any connections between Oswald and Ruby, nor could I see any credible evidence of a conspiracy. Oswald was too unreliable to work in a conspiracy. I got the impression that he was wanting to be a hero, or trying to, if he thought he could shoot the President and get to Cuba. He'd be a hero down there because they were having trouble with Castro at that time.

Rumors were flying at that time. One had it that the rifle was deliberately placed there to implicate Oswald. I don't see how it could have been planted in the short time length there after the shooting. I do know that the gun that was delivered to the FBI and was at the Warren Commission was the same gun that I picked up on the sixth floor. It had my markings on it and was in my possession from the time I picked it up until I released it to Vince Drain. There's no question whatsoever that it's the same gun.

There was another rumor that Oswald got a job there to shoot the President. That won't hold water! They know that he was having financial problems and people out in Irving felt sorry for him and helped him get a job at the School Book Depository. That was about six weeks before the assassination. If I remember correctly, the President was not scheduled to have a parade through Dallas when he came here. He was scheduled to go from the airport directly to the Market Hall where he was to give his speech. Oswald couldn't have known that the man was going to come by the School Book Depository since it was just a few days before the arrival of the President that the plans were changed. I know that the police department was contacted and wanted to set up security for the parade route. This was just a few days before the assassination. The President was not scheduled to go by that building. So Oswald could not have known at the time he got the job that the President was ever coming by. That rumor just doesn't stand up.

Some have complained about how the police department has been treated in regard to this case, but I haven't noticed it. People in Paris and London and other places have written stories, and I can understand how they might feel about our local authorities. When Oswald was shot, it was just a series of unbelievable events. How in the world could a man just walk down into that basement and shoot the man when all the reporters were supposed to have press passes? Even now, when something happens, we wonder whether the police departments might be involved, so I can see their point.

But again, despite all the rumors and speculation which have spread, I think we had enough convincing evidence to have gotten a conviction if circumstances hadn't dictated otherwise.

Carl Day continued his work as a lieutenant in the Crime Lab until his retirement in 1977 and still lives in the Oak Cliff section of Dallas.

VINCENT DRAIN
Special Agent, FBI

"We had no indication that Oswald was dangerous...I didn't consider him a threat then, and it was my responsibility to notify the Secret Service of any potential problems. I would have gotten the information from Hosty's supervisor but didn't and, of course, that's part of history..."

Vincent Drain attended what is now the University of North Texas in Denton then took civilian pilot training for the Air Corps. After being washed out due to imperfect vision, Drain taught school and coached football prior to his joining the FBI in 1941.

The last time I had seen the President was when I sat with the Rayburn family at the funeral of Sam Rayburn in 1961. I was with the President at the church, at the cemetery, and then at the Rayburn home before he left for the West Coast.

On November 22nd, 1963, I'd gone down to get a sandwich for lunch and had returned to my office at 1114 Commerce Street after the parade passed to continue doing dictation. As was the usual manner, we monitored the police radio. From that it was flashed that the President had been shot and that they were en route to Parkland Hospital. I knew where they were taking him because I had been privileged to sit in on some meetings with the Secret Service the previous four or five days in the event that either he or the Vice-President were shot. Quickly I took my car and went to the basement and arrived there maybe ten minutes after the President had arrived. The Secret Service had sealed off the area making it somewhat difficult to get in unless you had some assistance. Knowing the personnel at Parkland, particularly the security chief and the doctors, I was fortunate to have run into the security chief and a doctor, so I was able to go directly into the trauma room without any problem.

When I arrived in the trauma room, the doctors were working with President Kennedy. They were trying to do what they could to stop the gurgling sound he was making by performing a tracheotomy on him. Despite the fact, as I later learned, that he was dead, his body reflexes were still working.

I wasn't up close to the body, but I could still see fairly well the large amount of blood from the head wound. The head was badly damaged from the lower right base across the top extending across the top of the ear. It appeared to me as though the bullet traveled upward and had taken off the right portion of his skull. It may have been the security officer or one of the other officers who gave me a portion of the skull which was about the size of a teacup, much larger than a silver dollar.* Apparently the explosion had jerked it because the hair was still on it. I carried that back to Washington later that night and turned it over to the FBI laboratory.

Apparently a problem developed at the hospital when a fellow arrived without knowing exactly where he was. He was in a restricted area and had gone through the swinging doors where he was confronted by the Secret Service. They then grabbed him and removed him from the building. I didn't know what was going on at the time because I was already in the trauma room where the President was. At the time, I was able to talk to the doctors the minute I got there. One of them told me that the President was dead and that it was just a matter of time to make the announcement. Maybe I'm assuming something here, but as I recall, a Catholic priest had been sent for, and I was under the impression, or someone told me, that he hadn't been pronounced dead because they wanted to give him the last rites before and

* This skull fragment sounds very much like the fragment discovered by motorcycle patrolman Bobby Joe Dale. See Dale narrative, page 136.

after death. At that time, I believe there were three Secret Service agents, Mrs. Kennedy, and later the priest who were in the trauma room. I left as the priest was administering the last rites.

I was then busy trying to communicate with my office which was difficult because the White House Press Corps had gotten there and was tying up the telephones. Somehow I managed to talk to my office, and they talked to the director of the FBI in Washington, who, in turn, called the attorney general at his home.

After I learned that he was dead, I proceeded to leave the area and went outside where I talked with Senator Ralph Yarborough and two friends of mine: Congressmen Jim Wright and Ray Roberts. I'd called the office for some walkie-talkies since I thought that we'd be unable to use the telephones, so as I waited, I talked with them.

It became apparent that they were getting ready to pack the President for transfer to Washington, so I began to leave because in Texas, when a person was shot like that, back then the justice of the peace had jurisdiction and normally there would be an autopsy. But in this case, the Secret Service said there wasn't going to be any autopsy. As a result, it was a Mexican standoff at the hospital. Finally the Secret Service prevailed and the body was taken to the airplane where later President Johnson was sworn in. I then followed them in my car.

Johnson hadn't been sworn in yet when I arrived at Love Field. Twenty or twenty-two seats had been taken out of Air Force One to make room for President Kennedy's body for the flight back to Washington. Many people were there, all of them trying to get the best vantage point including reporters and cameramen.

I went to the steps of the plane and no further because it was too crowded inside, and they needed all the area there as they were waiting on the federal judge to arrive to swear in Vice-President Johnson which occurred shortly thereafter. When the body arrived, they had to take the coffin with the end up, straight up, to get it into the plane, which is really a difficult thing to do. Finally, when that was accomplished and Mrs. Kennedy and the Kennedy aides had boarded joining President Johnson and his aides, they took off for Washington.

A rather unusual thing developed out there: They had trouble locating the lady who was a federal judge to get out there to swear in Johnson; secondly, they had trouble finding the Bible. It is my understanding that they ended up swearing him in with Jackie Kennedy's prayer book.

All this occurred in, I'd say, a matter of 45 minutes. I just stayed long enough to watch it taxi down the runway and take off then returned to the Dallas Police Department because one of my duties was liaison with all the local departments which included the district attorney, the chief of police, and the local head of the Secret Service.

At the police department, I was with Henry Wade, the district attorney, and the chief of police during the rest of the afternoon. There it was a three-ring circus because the White House Press Corps was there and, if you've ever dealt with them, you've really got something to deal with.

Later that evening Oswald attended a so-called press conference. The reason that he was brought to the show-up down in the basement was really more for the purpose of demonstrating to the press that the allegations that the police had beaten up Oswald were untrue. I first knew about it when the District Attorney Henry Wade and I were talking to the Chief of Police, Jesse Curry, and Curry said, "Let's go down to the show-up." So Wade, Curry, and I walked down to the basement where it was being held and stood partially in the doorway. The press was already there including Jack Ruby, who was sitting on the second row. That was on Friday night, the night of the assassination. I can't recall just what all he was saying other than his shouting some remarks and throwing his fist in the air and that sort of thing. It's hard to say what kind of opinion you'd have of a fellow that you'd just observed there, but considering the stress he must have been under, he seemed pretty cool and not overly excited. He seemed to be very sure of himself with a feeling of a sense of accomplishment.

Earlier in the evening, about 8:00 o'clock, the division chief had talked to me on the telephone and informed me that the FBI in Washington demanded that we bring to them for examination the rifle, the revolver that was used to kill Tippit, as well as the different paraphernalia such as identification cards and other small items that Oswald had on him. I discussed it with the police chief and told him that we'd keep the chain of evidence intact and that I would pick them up there myself and wait for them until they were examined in Washington then bring them back. So it was turned over to us.

By the time we got it all boxed up, it was near midnight. Meanwhile Washington was calling down about every fifteen minutes wanting to know where the material was. All of a sudden I learned that neither American nor Braniff had any flights to Washington out of Dallas after midnight. We were told that the FBI in Washington wanted the material by morning if we had to walk it up there. That's being facetious, but...

Fortunately the commanding general over at Carswell in Fort Worth happened to be a good friend of mine and was head of SAC (Strategic Air Command) at that time. So I called him and was told that the President had asked him to give us all the help that we needed. Another agent took me to Fort Worth where they had a C-135 tanker plane and crew ready.

It was a little scary on the way up because I was sitting up on the deck with the pilot, the co-pilot, and the engineer. This was an empty plane, and they were flying high and really letting her go. During the flight, they let me listen to all the short wave broadcasts about the British, French, and Canadians calling their troops and the submarines going to sea because they were afraid the Russians might attack.

When we landed at Andrews Air Force Base, an unusual thing happened. I had never been in the military service since I had joined the FBI prior to the war and had stayed continuously through then. When I had arrived at Carswell, the commanding general was at the plane with two of his aides. As I got out of the car, they all saluted, so I told myself that I'd better salute back. When I arrived at Andrews, the commanding general there also saluted. I'd gotten used to saluting by that time, so I saluted back.

The commanding general said, "Mr. Drain, we wondered if you would relinquish this airplane for us if we'd furnish you a good airplane to go back in when you're ready to go?"

Of course, I didn't know that it was my airplane to relinquish in the first place, so I said, "Sure, I'll turn it over to you now if that's what you want me to say. But I need one when I get ready to go; I mean really go!"

He said, "We'll give you a good fast airplane," which was an understatement. He gave me his card and I was taken by helicopter over to the Justice Building and landed on the White House lawn. During this time, I had an armed guard from the Air Force until I got safely into the Justice Building.

I talked to Mr. Hoover briefly and then watched them do a lot of the experiments such as firing the rifle, looking for prints, ballistics markings, hairs, fibers, blood stains and anything else that later, down the road, might be relevant to evidence which could be used in the prosecution.

By around midnight on Saturday night, they had the plane ready to go, so I called the commanding general. He sent a helicopter which then flew me to one of those fast F-104's. When we came back, we came back in a hurry! Upon arrival in Dallas, I went directly to the police department and had just turned over the evidence to the police chief on Sunday morning at the time Oswald was killed by Ruby. They then had full custody of it.

The next day I was the representative of the FBI at Tippit's funeral. I remember riding back from the cemetery in the Oak Cliff section of Dallas to the police department with a newspaperman named Jerry O'Leary of the *Washington Star*. As we were talking and listening to the radio, Waggoner Carr, who was the attorney general of Texas at the time, said that he was going to open up a hearing himself. Put it this way: There was quite a bit of competition at that time between the police department, the local district attorney's office, and the Texas attorney general. As a result, after Oswald was killed, the FBI wanted to get all of the evidence and have it brought back to Washington because I think they wanted to preserve it for posterity's sake.

At that time, the police had a homicide captain by the name of Will Fritz who didn't like to turn anything over to anyone else, particularly the FBI. So when we arrived back at the police department, I knew better than to go to the captain. I knew that he wouldn't turn the evidence over because we really didn't have much of an argument for them to turn it over other than for the National Archives since Oswald was dead and Ruby was in jail. But the city manager, Elgin Crull, who was over the police department, was a good friend of mine. I lucked into him when I went back into the police building and said, "Elgin, I just heard that Waggoner Carr is going to open up some hearings on this thing and subpoena this evidence. Why don't you turn it over to us and let us take it to Washington so that we can preserve it up there?"

He said, "I think that's an excellent idea. Let's get it out of here within the hour." So I picked up the phone, called the office, and got eight agents and headed out of there within the hour. That was, I believe, on Tuesday. Then on Wednesday I took it back to Washington with a visiting agent who had been sent in to help us out, Warren DeBrueys, the head of the New Orleans Crime Commission.

We had four or five baskets full of that stuff, every bit of paper that they had, which was located in a section of the ID Division; a fine fellow by the name of Carl Day was there. Some of it was evidentiary and some of it wasn't. But we weren't taking any chances. I went back to Washington on several occasions and went before the Warren Commission to identify this as to what it was for their benefit.

I spent a considerable amount of time in Washington following the assassination, and I talked to Mr. Hoover quite a bit. All these reports were going in and they were going over to the Warren Commission and to the attorney general about all this business about Hoover having his mind set on one assassin. I never heard this around FBI headquarters. They would brief Hoover on what was being said to the Warren Commission, but I can say that I saw it after it was at the Warren Commission, and it wasn't altered or changed at all. I went over several times as did several of our agents and testified and none of us ever got any instructions from Hoover as to what or what not to say. This is what really bothers me. I read all of this stuff that this happened and that happened, when it didn't happen at all. Why, I think they'd skin your hide if you started instructing somebody to go over and testify a certain way. We had hundreds of agents working on this thing who covered every lead in the book. I don't see how anyone can arrive at any other conclusion than what they arrived at, really!

Of course, time dims your memory a bit, but as I understand it, Oswald was sitting there looking through the scope with the target moving away at 10-12 M.P.H. It was a very easy target. He had one cartridge in the chamber ready, so he only had two more to put in to fire. The best we could tell when we reenacted it, and we went over this thing from all angles with the finest ballistics' experts in the country, the first shot went wild which was found down close to a water outlet in the curb. The second shot hit the President in the fatty part of the neck and went through completely hitting Connally in the rib cage driving the bone ahead of it, came out, and part of it hit him in the wrist. The third shot is what caught the President in the back of the head. Now that's the best that all the scientific people could come up with that happened.

I've talked to a lot of different writers both here and abroad. One of those, Jim Bishop, told me one day, "I've looked at this thing from all angles, and the one thing that I'm not going to do is commercialize on something that I know is not true. I could just start this thing and make a lot of money, but I'm not going to do it."

The whole thing boils down to this: If this had been a plain homicide, all these questions wouldn't be raised. This is not my phraseology.

I was in London visiting with the head of the special branch of Scotland Yard, whom I had known during World War Two, Elliot Jones. Elliot said, "If that had been a plain Joe Blow out there, the situation wouldn't have arisen. But it was the President of the United States and people have the idea that one man can't kill the President of the United States. Over here 75 percent of the people think it had to be a conspiracy."

Then in 1969 I was in Munich and the director of the police there called. We had met prior when he had visited the FBI school in Washington. He told me, "I believe what the Warren Commission said, but the people around here are so conspiracy minded that they think it just can't be because one man wouldn't have the power to kill the President of the United States."

It is always customary to interview all people who had tried to defect to the Soviet Union when they returned. When Oswald came back, he was bitter, very bitter, and you must remember that from the time he was a small child that he was a loner who had mental problems. But he had great ambitions to be someone that the public would take notice of.

According to his wife, Marina, he was so desperately wanting to be "notorized" that he decided to kill General Edwin Walker. When he missed him, he walked and ran all the way back home and told her about it. Then she said that when Nixon came to town prior to Kennedy's arrival to speak to the National Bottler's Association, he had entertained the idea of trying to track him down because he knew that would put him on the front page of the paper and secure him a place in history. I think that he saw the Kennedy itinerary in the newspaper, and he had an ideal location.

The Apparel Mart originally wasn't where they were going to have the speech. It was going to be at the Women's Building at Fair Park, but the Democrats began yelling that the Republicans were trying to steal the attention of the President, that the little rich people were going to get to see the President. So Connally said, "Well, we'll just have a parade and we'll bring him right downtown and take it out to the Apparel Mart." So it was changed and the newspapers had the parade route and everything.

I stayed completely away from anything dealing with Oswald's trip to Mexico City. Not that there was anything culpable, but that got into sensitive technique areas which I didn't want to get into. However, I knew James Hosty real well and was here in this office when he came, and I was here when he left. He was more or less just a victim of circumstances. Hosty was always a very determined agent and a very good agent. As they say in the Navy, "The thing happened on his watch." I don't care whether it's the FBI, the United States Navy, the United Nations, or where it is, when something like this happens, there's got to be somebody that pays a high price. Hosty just got caught in that dilemma since he was the case agent handling Oswald.

I don't want to sound trite or facetious when I say this, but this often reminds me of the quarterback who had lost the football game, and he's sitting in the barber's chair on Monday and the barber told him, "I wouldn't have thrown that last pass if I'd have been you."

And the quarterback said, "If I'd have had 48 hours to have thought it over, I wouldn't have thrown it either." That is very similar to the way it was with Hosty. Hosty was a victim of the system at that time. He was following what the system required which was kind of a profile situation.

The system at that time was that if you fell into this category you were considered suspect, and if you were in another category you were considered just another of the dozens of people who were harmless.

We had no indication that Oswald was dangerous. He wasn't considered a threat because, as a matter of fact, Sam Rayburn was the one who got him a hardship discharge out of the Marine Corps. Then, under the Kennedy administration, the State Department furnished the money, I believe, to get him back. I didn't consider him a threat then, and it was my responsibility to notify the Secret Service of any potential problems. I would have gotten the information from Hosty's supervisor but didn't and, of course, that's part of history. It was the system that broke down, not Hosty.

Just after the assassination, Hosty was alleged to have told Jack Revill of the Dallas police that he had known about Oswald and that he was capable of the assassination. The only thing I know about it was that the Dallas Police Department was getting a lot of heat on this thing. Hosty says that he didn't say it; Revill says he did, and Revill knew that Hosty handled security. Hosty may not have said it, then again he may have. I knew both men very well and liked both of them very much.

Revill was a very fine officer, but I think that naturally he would try to protect his chief. What would make me question this to a degree, and I'm not defending Hosty, is that Hosty was one of the most conscientious, dedicated individuals that I've ever seen in the FBI. He was a very dedicated Catholic and was very, very pro-Kennedy. I believe that if Hosty had thought that Oswald was capable of an assassination that everybody in the town would have known about it. But only the two of them know whether or not it's true. I wouldn't say that it is, and I wouldn't say that it isn't.

Supposedly, on Sunday, the assassination being on Friday, Hosty was called in to the SAC (Special Agent-in-Charge) Gordon Shanklin's office, and ordered to destroy a note which Oswald had left for Hosty. I was in Washington during that period and, of course, didn't know anything about it. As a matter of fact, I didn't know about it for some time.

There is controversy about that which was discussed by one of the Congressional committees. I think they finally concluded that it really didn't have any bearing, one way or the other, as I understand it. I also understand that Shanklin didn't recall any such matter. It could have happened, and he wouldn't have thought of it because there was a powerful lot of things going through his mind at that particular time. In addition, Shanklin was not the supervisor of security. As I understand, what it was supposed to have been about was that Oswald was antagonistic toward Hosty for bothering his wife. But again, I didn't know about this incident for some time.

Following the events of that weekend, I think there were fourteen or fifteen agents who were censured. In laymen's talk, you would get a letter of censure from Mr. Hoover, and it would go something like this: "I'm amazed, astonished, at a loss to understand your handling of this matter, and I will not tolerate this sort of investigative effort." They weren't that uncommon. During my career, I'd received several of them and very frankly never paid a whole lot of attention to them. I'd had several meritorious commendations and that sort of thing, so I always thought that it went with the territory. I don't think I've ever known an agent that didn't have one of those in his file. If you ever did anything, you had something in your file. In fact, I'm one of those agents that was censured in the Oswald case.

That came about as a result of the second trip to Washington. I had had about eight agents sent up to help me get all the evidence, and we took all of it, largely paper. That's when they took all that paper and compared it with other paper. A lot of this had been dusted for fingerprints by the Dallas Police Department and it was black. If you've ever been around fingerprint ink, it's powdery, nasty, and black. Anyway, these agents got it all together and wrapped it with string and were able to carry it down to the office for packing. We had just a limited amount of time to get it to the airplane and fly to Washington. There were a couple of clerks in the office that we had recruited who normally packaged this up as normal FBI book mail going out, so they were all involved in helping pack all this stuff. We took it to Washington and turned it over to the FBI there and left it.

Then, in about three or four weeks, we began receiving these letters from Washington saying, "Do some elimination fingerprints because we're finding prints on the newspaper on this wrapping paper that we can't identify." So I got all the agents together who had helped wrap it, took their prints, and sent them up. Of course, they eliminated those. Then I got elimination prints from the detectives that I knew who had examined it and we eliminated more prints.

But in the long run, about eight months later, we still had one set of prints on this paper that we couldn't identify. The Warren Commission wanted to know who those prints belonged to, if it was a third party or whoever it was. So the division chief and I were sitting here one night talking and he said, "Can you think of anybody that this might be that we might get the elimination prints?"

I told him, "Well, you know, I hadn't thought of it but those two clerks back there might have gotten their prints on that paper when they were wrapping it." So we took the elimination prints and, sure enough, one of them belonged to one of those clerks. Well, it went up to Washington and Hoover had to tell the Warren Commission that the mystery prints really belonged to one of our own clerks down here.

In a few days, I received quite a nice letter from the Director giving me a meritorious raise and telling me what a great job I had done and that sort of thing. In the same mail was a letter of censure castigating me for permitting inexperienced clerks who had no training to even touch this material, and why I hadn't seen to it that the clerks had had training, and it went on and on. This was the type censorship that came down. I paid no attention to it because it didn't affect me. The assistant directors were friends of mine back in Washington, and I knew that all of them had even gotten letters of censure. When Hoover got mad at you, he'd just write you a letter of censure. I didn't mind as long as he didn't cut me in salary.

This was the basic type of punishment, but it wasn't for Hosty. Hosty was busted and sent to Kansas City along with one or two others. But none of the Secret Service were censured.

In the early period after the assassination, you could get any rumor that you wanted: Oswald was an FBI informant; Jack Ruby was a PCI for the FBI.

I did get into the rumor about Oswald being an informant when I was asked that question when we were in Washington. I said that I didn't have the answer but that I would find out. This was no cover-up; he was never an informant.

Now, Ruby, I don't know from my own knowledge, but I wouldn't doubt that he might have been an informant because he was just crazy about being around police officers. He would give them tickets to his shows and that sort of thing.

But he was a harmless individual who, I think, just shot Oswald on the spur of the moment. I heard Ruby say, "I didn't know they'd condemn me for this. I thought that I'd be a hero and I'd be able to have a big restaurant like Jack Dempsey." You couldn't help but like Ruby if you were around him.

On the night of the assassination, when they brought Oswald out for the press conference, ironically, I saw Jack and talked to him there and really didn't think anything about it. In fact, no one really thought much about Jack. But an unusual thing developed there. We had already opened our own investigation into the assassination by Executive Order of the President. Then, the minute Oswald was shot by Ruby, we then opened a civil rights investigation against the police department for negligence and also the ability of Ruby to penetrate the security area. So, you see, we had a dual investigation going. We had one squad of agents investigating the assassination, and the second one the civil rights investigation to see if Oswald's civil rights had been violated.

You would have to understand that Ruby was in the Western Union office after 11:00 o'clock sending this telegram. Because they needed to talk to Oswald a little longer he wasn't moved till some twenty minutes later. Ruby left the Western Union office walking, saw this crowd gathered and walked right down the basement ramp. Again, if you saw Ruby around, you wouldn't think anything about it; I didn't, nor did any of the other police officers. It was just one of those ironic things that happen.

You couldn't condemn the Dallas police for what happened because they weren't prepared for this sort of thing. It was something that was suddenly thrust upon them out of the blue which no one could have foreseen, including the overwhelming presence of the White House Press Corps.

I knew Jesse Curry from the time he was a lieutenant in the police department and watched him rise through the ranks. I knew all the top level people and they were friends of mine, and the ones who are still living are still friends of mine. But they didn't have the training that they do now to handle a catastrophic situation like this. By the same token, the FBI didn't have the training at that time either.

When I came back here, arriving on January 1st, 1949, Carl Hansson was chief of police, one of the great chiefs. I worked with Hansson and helped him get nominated as fifth Vice-President of the IACP, the International Association of Chiefs of Police, so that he could rise through the ranks. I used every bit of influence I had and got the Dallas Police Department admitted into every session of the FBI National Academy to train their totally untrained police.

In 1952, they had a burglary ring inside the police department and a Lieutenant Gurley, who was in charge of the Burglary and Theft Bureau, was one of the burglars. I helped the police department eliminate that then assisted them in setting up a special squad which later became the Intelligence Squad. I also helped them set up the unit that investigates civil rights violations.

I think that all the brass would agree that we had a channel that we went through. The normal police officers weren't given the information because we went through a chain of command to protect our sources. That's the reason that the average policeman might get the idea that maybe they weren't getting it, which apparently was a common complaint. The relationship between the Dallas Police Department and the FBI was outstanding. Even though there was some outward recrimination between Hoover and the chief during that period, I was able to keep our relationship open since I was the liaison between the FBI and the Dallas Police Department, thus it was never really affected that much. Neither was it affected with the district attorney, Henry Wade, who was a former FBI agent.

The first time that I saw Marina Oswald was the night of the assassination. She was in the police department along with Mrs. Oswald and Robert, her brother-in-law, while they were interrogating her husband in another room. At that time, she appeared to be very frightened because she couldn't speak English well and hadn't been in the country long. But as time went on, and as the Warren Commission, the President's commission, started its hearings, Marina was able to speak better English because she was attempting to get a better grasp of it.

At the time that I had contact with her, she was very frail. She was more attractive in the photographs than she was in person. She was then living on Belt Line Road out in Richardson and seemed very cooperative with us.

I had previously sent in the blanket that Oswald had wrapped the rifle in in Irving among other things to the laboratory to be examined. Marina had initialed the blanket when she had previously turned it over to us, but the laboratory wanted to have her re-identify it and put her initials in bolder print. So I called her attorney, William McKenzie, and asked him for permission to interview her. He agreed and called her and told her that we'd be out at a certain time of the afternoon.

When we arrived (I took a younger agent with me as a witness) and knocked, Marina came to the door. After I identified myself, we were invited in. At the time she had two children; one of them was still in diapers. She picked the small one up that was in diapers and set her over in my lap and said, "I'll be back" and went into the kitchen.

After about five minutes, I realized that I was going to have to put the kid down on the floor because she was gone too long. Finally I told the other agent to watch the kid, that I was going back to see what had happened to Marina. Lo and behold I went to the back door and found her in the back yard being photographed by *Parade Magazine* and doing an interview there. I explained to her that I was out there on business, so we concluded our business and let her go back to her interview and photographs.

I interviewed her from time to time and found her to be friendly and outgoing, especially the more she realized that we weren't going to hurt her. I think this was a carry over from her days in Russia where there was probably a state of fear.

Later I learned from personal observation and from a friend of mine, who was an inspector with the Secret Service, that the chief, meaning Chief Earl Warren, had grown quite fond of Marina. The hearings for the Warren Commission were held in the Veterans of Foreign Wars Building in Washington, and he would accompany her to press conferences holding her by the arm and referring to her as "my child." So I knew that he liked her a lot.

Over the years allegations have been made about the way the FBI and the Dallas Police Department handled the affair. In one of the books, I was quoted in a footnote as saying that I doubted that a fingerprint had been found on the rifle as claimed by the Dallas Police Department. As I recall, I think my comment was based primarily on our experts in the Single Fingerprint Bureau. That's the real specialists in fingerprints in the FBI in Washington.

From the time they turned the rifle over to me along with other things, they were placed in a box and sealed. I then took it to the laboratory where it was taken apart and examined with different processes on every inch of that gun, assembled and disassembled. They said that they didn't find any fingerprints. Now, I wouldn't have any way of knowing from my own personal observation. My comment would have been made on what they said. As to Lieutenant Day, I've known him a long time, and I think that he's an honest individual. If he thought that there was a print there, whether there was or not, he was sincere in what he had to say. I would not want to cast any reflection on Day.

There was also a story about an alleged Minox camera. I'm well aware of what a Minox camera is because we used them. When we itemized all that material, I don't recall any Minox camera; however, the light meter would be easily mistaken for one by somebody that really didn't know and, at that point in time, I never knew the Dallas Police Department to use them. In fact, I would seriously doubt that the average officer would have known what one would have looked like. I'm not casting any reflection on them but, one must remember that, back then, those cameras were very expensive. A good one might cost between $500 and $700, something like that.

In a general sense, we tried to keep abreast of what was going on, but the General Walker case was something different; we weren't investigating him, as such. At the time that Oswald allegedly tried to kill him with the same rifle, the police investigated it, but they had no suspects. Of course, we had no reason to because he was just a plain citizen since he had resigned from the Army, though he had become somewhat radical.

My memory is vague on the specifics of the case. I believe, basically, that most of the information that he had tried to kill Walker came from Marina. You must keep in mind that Oswald didn't really have anything, as I understand, against General Walker other than this could catapult him to fame, anything that could get him in the spotlight.

Her version of it, and that's the only one that I know about, I think would have to be considered; otherwise, she wouldn't have known who Walker was. She wouldn't have known that to have shot General Walker would really put Oswald on the front page of every newspaper in the country because he was such a controversial person. So I'd have to give her story a lot of credence.

Allegations have also been made that Allen Dulles and J. Edgar Hoover withheld information from the Warren Commission, especially stories about plots to kill Castro. I wouldn't have any way of knowing that, but I knew Allen Dulles and I had spent some time with him at lunch and at various periods of recess when I was going before the Warren Commission. All of the stories about plots against Castro I'd have to take with a grain of salt because I believe these, for the most part, were hatched by some fellow that wanted to get a lot of publicity from these stories. Knowing Dulles as I knew him, I don't believe that he would have withheld anything that he thought would have been germane to the investigation. I never knew or heard anything, and I think that I am well acquainted with the material in the Warren Commission Report that would put Oswald in any position to help anybody assassinate Castro.

The FBI went into every phase available to it regarding conspiracy. It interviewed thousands of people and kept a file open for years later with any name anybody would furnish to them after they had exhausted everything they had. All of Hoover's opinions that I know of were based strictly on the investigations of what the field furnished because that was furnished directly to the Warren Commission. Now, whatever they're talking about that would have embarrassed Hoover, I'm not aware of that since I couldn't see that there's anything that would embarrass the FBI. If Oswald had lived, this thing probably wouldn't have developed like it did because I think that he would have eventually talked.

Essentially, I think the FBI did a good job in the affair. I believe that within that three days we had 90 percent of all we ever obtained down the road. It was a case of verification and confirmation about what we already had discovered, and I think they did a good job. I could look back and see some mistakes that were made, but they weren't major mistakes.

It was tough! The people were dedicated, though, and went long, long hours without any sleep. The thing about it is that FBI agents are just like school teachers, doctors, lawyers, or merchants; there's nothing superhuman or magic in the work. It's hard work and you have to face it out. You've got to have help, and you've got to have contacts. Seventy-five percent of the FBI's work is based on confidence. If you don't have the confidence of the people, you might as well take out and go home because you're not going to get anywhere.

During my period under Hoover, the FBI had the confidence of the public. Hoover had his shortcomings like anybody else, but I enjoyed my time in the FBI. I think that he built one of the greatest law enforcement agencies the world has ever known, and I, like 99 percent of the other agents, had nothing but the highest admiration for him. Hoover ran a tight ship; everybody knew the rules, and he had no hesitancy about firing you. But he wouldn't fire you unless you needed to be fired. And there was not one case of scandal in the organization in the 35 years that I was there that I know about. That's something! But as one friend of mine back in Washington who was a historian said, "Well, they're still talking about Lincoln's assassination, and a hundred years from now there'll be another hundred stories about Kennedy's assassination."

One thing that I would like to say is that Bobby Kennedy was a very close friend of mine, and he had no question with the Warren Commission. I talked to Ethel and Nick Katzenbach, and they had no qualms either. I just can't see where there's room for a whole lot of information to come from that might change the picture down the road. If it did, it would greatly surprise me.

Since his retirement from the FBI in 1977, Drain has been the executor for estates and helped run a family business in the Dallas area. His father-in-law was the founder of Ashland Oil Company.

ELMO L. CUNNINGHAM
Lieutenant, Forgery Bureau
Dallas Police Department

"I think probably the thing that registered with us most was that he was some kind of nut. He wasn't what you would normally call a normal young man trying to make a living."

Born and raised in Navarro County, Texas, Elmo Cunningham served over seven years in the Marine Corps then came to Dallas after the Second World War and joined the Dallas Police Department in June 1946. After serving three years as a patrolman and ten years as a detective, Cunningham was promoted to lieutenant, the rank he held in the Forgery Bureau in November 1963. On November 22, he was assigned security duty for the President's scheduled speech at the Trade Mart.

The President's trip to Dallas was a political object, and he wanted to be seen by as many people as possible. The turnout was tremendous! I doubt if there's ever been a president who ever came to Dallas that had a turnout such as that man had, though if you read the newspapers you'd have thought that everybody in Dallas wanted to kill him, which simply wasn't true. I suspect that if you'd have taken a poll at that time, that man was the most popular person in Dallas.

Since the President was coming to make his speech at the Trade Mart, the Secret Service had a number of people determining the final approval on the podium, the chair, and all the other places where the President was to be. They made sure that there wasn't some way that somebody had hidden a charge there or anything else that could be detrimental to his health or welfare. So there wasn't much left to chance.

We checked the building both inside and out, all the areas where he might be going near. It was a large building which included a large auditorium and a mezzanine with offices on the second level overlooking where the President was to give his speech.

We heard sirens go by and were reasonably sure that something had happened because he was late, but it was probably fifteen to twenty minutes before anybody thought to call and tell us that the President had been shot. The first word that we received was on a portable radio nearby which said that the President had been hit, then later it said that it had occurred in the vicinity of the Dallas Court House.

It was a shock, but the chief of detectives was out there with us and asked me to take some people and report to that location. He didn't know what had happened either.

While en route with Officers Toney, Buhk, and Taylor, we received word that an officer had been shot in Oak Cliff. As a result, we went straight to that scene. When we arrived in Oak Cliff, we received a report that a man had been seen running into the Oak Cliff Library about three blocks from where we were then located. When we got there, there must have been in the neighborhood of 30 to 40 armed people there, most of them being civilians, though some could have been deputies or constables in plain clothes. I thought we were going to have another Battle of the Little Big Horn right there. I don't know where they all came from!

Finally it was discovered that this kid had come across the alley and had run into the basement of the library. He had been working there that day and had gone across the street to get a sandwich. While he was in this hamburger place, he had seen the television broadcast that the President had died. So this 25-year-old ran back to tell his lady co-workers and somebody saw him.

Another thing that created a problem was that this was the start of deer season in Texas. As a result, practically every pickup truck in Dallas had a rifle in it, so we had calls from everywhere. These people would stop at service stations and they'd say, "Guy with a pickup truck just left here with a rifle sitting in there."

During that time period, we never stopped at the Tippit scene, though we drove down the street and knew where it had happened.

We were a couple of blocks from the Texas Theater when someone called in, so we arrived there within a few seconds. About the time I got to the curb across the street, a squad car drove up in front, and I asked them if they'd go around to the back and seal off the back door.

I went up to the lady cashier and said, "I had a report that some young man ran into the theater here." (I thought that she was probably the one who had called in, but she wasn't.)

"No," she said, "There's a young man upstairs in the balcony. He just went up there." So three of us went up the stairs. At the top step, we encountered a kid sitting there smoking a cigarette. I imagine we put quite a few gray hairs on his head, but he knew nothing about it and had just gone up there to smoke.

Shortly after, somebody hollered, "He's downstairs!" By the time I got there, these officers had discovered him and had him in custody. I saw Oswald as they were taking the gun away from him about 25 to 30 feet from where I was standing.

I didn't see this, but I was told that when he pulled the gun and stuck it in the officer's stomach that the officer grabbed it as Oswald pulled the trigger. As the hammer fell, it hit the primer enough to dent it. Now I didn't see the shell, but it was that close to his killing another person.

At the time I saw him, Oswald wasn't resisting much because there wasn't much that he could do. They put the handcuffs on him while I told the other officers that they should get him out of there and on the way to the jailhouse rather than let a crowd gather around.

There were about a dozen patrons in the theater which had just opened on that Friday afternoon around 1:00 o'clock. The two other officers and myself asked people what information they had which was absolutely nothing. There was nothing to cause any attention until these officers went in and turned the lights on in the theater, and he jumped up without them pointing him out or anything. When the lights were turned on and the officers started down the aisles just looking at the people, that's apparently when he reacted.

From the time that I got there until Oswald was taken out the door would have certainly been less than five minutes. We were reasonably sure that he was the one who had shot Tippit, though we knew nothing about the President. After he was taken out, I didn't take any written statements from the dozen or so people in the theater; I just talked to them and took their names down. In fact, I don't recall whether I turned the list of names in or not. In any case, there was nothing there in light of useful information.

I left after about an additional ten minutes then drove to City Hall where Oswald had been taken onto the third floor. Captain Fritz had talked to him awhile and came out into the hall and asked me if I would go with one of his officers to search his room over on North Beckley. Apparently Oswald had told him that that was where he was staying. I don't think at the time that he intended to tell Fritz where his wife was. In any case, T.L. Baker and I went over there and picked up a J.P., David Johnston, somewhere along the way, as well, in case we needed a warrant. It was unusual to have a judge with us, but it helped with the legality in this type of situation. In fact, he gave us a verbal warrant then wrote out a warrant after we got there.

The North Beckley address was located near the intersection of Zang and Beckley in the Oak Cliff section of Dallas. It was a fine home, probably 4,500 square feet with a huge living room and kind of a passageway which adjoined a dining room. This lady had several roomers. In fact, when we went in and asked her if she had a guy by the name of Lee Harvey Oswald rooming there, she told us, no. After we began describing him, she said, "Well, there's a young man and his wife who live out there," referring to a little house out behind her home. As we checked that place, she came running out and said, "They just showed that fellow's picture on television. He has this room right here. I think he goes by the name Lee."

So we went into his room, which was very small, probably not more than six feet wide and not more than eight or nine feet long which was located just off the living room and dining room area. It certainly wasn't built as a bedroom, but more likely for a hutch or something of that nature. There we found the scabbard to his gun, a city map with the parade route drawn on the map, and a little book with a hand drawing of Red Square which included a number of names and telephone numbers. This is where Agent [James] Hosty's name came in for the first time. I think probably the thing that registered with us, having already run into the fellow, was that he was some kind of nut. He wasn't what you would normally call a normal young man trying to make a living.

There was very little in the room other than several paperback books on Marxism and communism. It was very far out! The only things that we found which seemed to have any direct bearing on the assassination and the killing of the officer were the holster and the map. The rest of it was just stuff that you might find in a hundred other rooms.

The landlady was quite excited. When we asked her about it, she said this fellow had made a telephone call, and since the phone was in the living room and she was sitting there, she overheard his talking to someone in a foreign language. In fact, she had heard him talk in a foreign language on two occasions, supposedly to his wife, when he was there, but she didn't recall his ever receiving a call.

Oswald's effects were taken to police headquarters, but I don't recall our taking anything other than the map, the holster, and the notebook at that time. I don't have the slightest idea what happened to the rest of it.

I left the department about midnight that Friday night. You'd have had to have been there to believe the madhouse that we had on the third floor. You could hardly get up and down the hallway. There were newspeople from all over the world there. They had just swarmed in, and if somebody didn't stop them, they just took over. When I went to my office, these people had just absolutely taken over to the point where I almost had to threaten to put some of them in jail to get them out. They wouldn't give me my chair or my phone, so I couldn't even take phone calls. I wasn't too happy about it!

Of course, it was the police's fault that we allowed them to get in like that. But you can't be too critical of the chief of police for allowing this to happen because, after all, you had an assassination of the President of the United States, and certainly the people had a right to any reasonable information that could be gotten to them. That was the position that he took: Cooperate with them as much as you can and give them as much leeway as possible to get the story out. I believe this was Curry's doing.

Curry was a competent man, though probably not the greatest. Most of his police career had been in traffic and the uniformed area. From traffic, he moved to the academy and was in charge of it for several years. He then made assistant chief and was rather low key under Chief Hansson, who was a dictatorial type person and ran everything personally. Hansson was a good administrator, and I think probably did more for the Dallas Police Department than any other single chief that they've had since my time there. Curry was a much more easy going fellow who didn't seem to have the ambition to stay there forever. He depended more on his deputy chiefs and administrative officers to do the job. That is not to say that he didn't run the department; he did, but he did it through his lieutenants, captains, and deputy chiefs. After the assassination, he was relieved several months later, and I suspect that the assassination might have had something to do with it.

There was always a problem between Will Fritz, captain of the Homicide and Robbery Bureau, and the chief of police ever since I was in the department. Fritz would usually make the announcements to the press as to where an investigation stood and whether or not he had a suspect in custody or one in mind. This was not information that usually went to the chief. Every morning, on workdays at 9:00 o'clock, the chief would hold a staff meeting during which the chief of detectives, patrol, vice, and different commanding officers would brief the chief on what was going on. Fritz sometimes let the chief of detectives know where he stood, but not in any detail. The chief would call Fritz about a case and he'd say, "Well, we've got a suspect," or "We've got a man in custody," or "We've filed him on the case," that type of thing. But it was always brief. Most of the information they got I suspect came from the newspapers as to what Fritz was doing.

Fritz was not a great man for writing reports or letters. He didn't believe in writing, and his reports on the investigations were usually very brief. He would make up some of the case reports we filed with the district attorney which would contain a very minimum of information such as: "E.L. Cunningham can testify that he arrested the suspect and had him identified in the lineup," or something of that nature. That was about the extent of it. So all the district attorney could do was to talk to me and find out what I could testify to; it wasn't on the report.

In some cases it was rather amusing. On one occasion, he had a girl filling in as his secretary due to his regular secretary being on vacation or ill, so I asked her something about her job. She said, "Well, there's really not much to it. Lieutenant Bohart takes care of all his correspondence."

I said, "Bohart can't write!"

She replied, "Well, I haven't written a single letter for him."

I responded, "You stay here six more years and you still won't write any!" So writing was not a strong suit with him, but he could remember almost word for word conversations from ten years prior. He could also use that telephone and get information that you wouldn't believe.

As a general rule, the chiefs left Fritz alone. In fact, I suspect that he liked Curry and got along better with him than any other chief that he served under because Curry left him alone. Before Hansson was made chief, there was a lot of support to make Will Fritz chief because a lot of people liked him. He had a lot of publicity because he had cleared some difficult cases and some big cases which had gotten nationwide publicity which no one thought would be cleared. But Fritz wasn't an administrator. He was an outstanding investigator and a super interrogator, but he was not an administrator in any sense of the word. He told me that he didn't particularly want to be chief, but he said, "Now these people that's passed the word around that I turned it down are wrong. I wasn't offered the job. If I'd been offered the job, I'd have probably taken it."

To my way of thinking, Fritz was absolutely, beyond any question of doubt, the greatest interrogator I've ever heard talk to a person. He was a thorough, good investigator, and a good man. He was also a hard man and an unforgiving man. There was a saying that, once you got on his list, you stayed there. But if he liked you, there wasn't anything he wouldn't do for you. If he liked an officer that was working for him, and he thought that that officer was doing the best that he could, there was no way that he would ever fail to stand behind him. Now if he thought the officer was not doing his best, he got rid of them, and he did it himself. He wouldn't put the man down in front of or to anyone else, but he would handle it personally.

I think a lot of the techniques he used in interrogation just came naturally, and some of them he developed himself. For instance, when he was talking to a man or woman, he never let his eyes stray away from their faces. He looked them right in the eye and right in the face the whole time he talked to them so that he noticed the least little quiver of a lip and raising or lowering of the eyelid and so on.

On one occasion, he asked me if I had ever seen a sure enough amnesia victim. When I told him that I hadn't, he said, "If I ever get one in here, I want you to come in and look at him. I've only seen two in my lifetime, and in talking to these people there's something right between their eyes that looks different. I can't describe it; you'd have to see it, but it's a little bit different. If you ever see it on one, then that's the thing to look for because, if it ain't there, they don't have amnesia."

We had a case one time where a liquor store operator was hijacked by a black man. The next day this man was walking down the street and saw the black man that he thought was the hijacker. So he just threw his gun down on him and held him for the police. When they brought him down, the man said, "That's the man that did it!" The Captain sat down and talked to the suspect a bit, got up, and we went outside.

He said, "I think this is the wrong man."

I told him, "Well, that guy sure was sure about it."

So the Captain went back in and asked him, "Where were you yesterday about whenever time this came down?"

The man replied, "I was up there in a little cafe," and he told us which one.

The Captain asked, "What were you doing there?"

He said, "I was there with my girlfriend."

"Did you eat anything?"

He said, "Yeah, we ate chicken."

"How do you know about the time?"

This was back in the early days of television and every cafe had a television, so he said, "Well, I remember while we were sitting there eating," a certain program came on. So I called the station and they said that that particular program was on at that time. So the Captain had a squad go down and pick up this boy's girlfriend. Then he asked the boy about how he went about ordering the chicken and so on. He said, "Well, I just ordered one order of chicken, and I shared it with my girlfriend."

"What piece did you eat?" and the girlfriend verified each part of his story. The Captain said, "There's no way that they could have had this planned as to what pieces of chicken they ate." So we turned him loose which made the other guy so mad that he couldn't see straight. But that's the way it was: If a man wasn't guilty, we didn't keep him in jail or file a case on him. It just showed how he could just sense that a person was lying to him or not.

Now we had one case that I was aware of, a murder case, where the district attorney prosecuted a man for a murder which Fritz didn't think that he was guilty, and they convicted him. I heard him use reference to that case in talking to people. In fact, I heard one guy tell him one time, "Captain, I didn't do this, and if I didn't do it, there ain't no way they can convict me!"

The Captain responded, "Well, I used to believe that, but I knew of a case," and he cited this case. Actually the guy had pled guilty, and no doubt he thought that he had killed the man. But the pathologist said that the cut was just about twice the depth of the blade of this knife that this fellow thought that he had killed the man with, and there were several people involved in the fight. So I feel reasonably sure that the kid was convicted for something he didn't do, though he was involved in it and technically would have been guilty.

Fritz usually carried three guns: a .45 Automatic a .32 Automatic, and a .38 Smith and Wesson. Usually the .45 was fixed with a clip on the side where it would hook onto his belt. He also carried the .38 and the small gun he usually carried on various places on his body. He was also an expert shot with those guns, quite a trick shot artist, until his eyesight began to fail. He could turn the weapon upside down, use a mirror and shoot things behind him, that type of thing.

I suspect that he would have been a very difficult husband for a woman to live with because of his dedication to his work. In addition, like I say, he was an unforgiving soul. Most of the time, he lived at the White Plaza Hotel.

But I thought an awful lot of him, and he took a liking to me and let me get away with a lot of things that he probably wouldn't have from others. But all the people that worked for him had a tremendous amount of respect for him. You wouldn't find a man that ever worked for him that didn't think that he was the greatest.

I've seen people come by the office that had served ten, twelve, fifteen years in the penitentiary that wanted to say hello to him and thank him for taking care of them. Sure, he'd sent them up, but they felt like he did it fair and square, that there was no underhanded way about it with no coercion on his part. He'd just let them tell what had happened.

He approached these people more as a friend. He was not a religious man, but he was able to use religion if a person had any religious background. I have heard him say that there would be no one that he couldn't get a confession from if they had a background that was similar to his: for instance, a person that was raised on a ranch and had been around stock and horses. Will Fritz grew up on a ranch and was very fond of horses and cattle, etc.

To give another example of Fritz's ability—we had a police officer down in Tyler, Texas who had been fired, came to Dallas, robbed a man in South Dallas and killed him. He then went from here on down to Hillsboro. Apparently his conscience began to eat him up, so he went to the sheriff's office and said, "Sheriff, I want to turn myself in. I killed a man in Dallas, and that's all I'm going to tell you."

The sheriff talked to him a bit and said, "Well, what part of Dallas?"

He said, "The south part."

So the sheriff called up here, and at that time we didn't have a report of it, nor had a body been found. A while later the body turned up, so the Captain called back to the sheriff. Fortunately he still had this fellow there because he was convinced that he had killed somebody. So the Captain sent a couple of officers down there. My experience has been, as a general rule, that when you go out of town to pick up a suspect, nine times out of ten they'd tell you all about it before you got back. You would just sit there and talk to them and let them unload their conscience. But in this particular case, he told these officers when they came down there, "Now I killed a man; that's all I'm going to say. I've had seven years experience as a police officer, and I'm not going to talk myself into the electric chair. If you make a case on me, you're going to have to make it on what you've got, not on me helping you."

So they brought the guy up and put him in the jailhouse. It wasn't long before Captain Fritz came over and the officers told him, "That old boy said that he did it, but he ain't going to help you out in any way. He said that his being a policeman, he knew better than to hang himself."

The Captain said, "Bring him over here and let's try him around." So I went over and got him.

When I brought him back, the first thing this guy said was, "Captain, I don't want to be a smart aleck or anything, but I've had seven years experience as a police officer, and I have no intention of talking myself into the electric chair."

The Captain said, "Well, that's all right. I understand you worked down at Tyler, didn't you?"

"Yeah."

He said, "You know captain so and so down there?"

"Yeah, yeah, I know captain so and so."

The Captain said, "Me and that fellow cleared a good case." They just sat there and talked in a regular conversation.

After awhile, the Captain said, "Say, I know that you don't intend to tell me anything about this, and I can respect that, but, you know, that man had some papers on him which would be of great benefit to his wife. It really wouldn't hurt anything since they're not worth anything to you, so I'd like to have those papers back." Well, we had already searched the man and knew that he didn't have them with him.

"Oh, yeah," he said, "he had a billfold and some papers in there. I hid them in a cupboard."

So the Captain said, "Well, if we can get them back, I know that his folks will really appreciate it, and I appreciate your helping them out on this." He went outside and asked two guys to get this stuff, and they found it right where he said it was. When they brought this stuff in, the Captain, who was sitting across the desk from the suspect, said, "Now, you being a policeman, you know about this firearm's identification stuff, don't you? It just occurred to me that somebody could find that gun. Obviously you did something with it because you didn't have it on you when you turned yourself into the sheriff's office. You know, the wrong person could find that gun and could do something real bad with it, and it could all come back on you. So why don't you tell us where the old gun is and that way we'll eliminate that possibility?" He agreed and we found it out on Loop 12 and what is now Highway 35.

When we showed the Captain the gun, he said, "Why don't you put him back upstairs there?"

The guy then stood up, stuck out his hands and said, "Captain, I have thoroughly enjoyed talking with you. I hope that you don't feel bad about the fact that I wasn't able to tell you anything about this." Of course, in this state, I don't know how it is in others, but whenever you get the physical evidence involved in a crime, that evidence, along with the conversation, becomes admissible.

If he had just said, "Yeah, I killed a man," that wouldn't have been admissible. But when he gave him the location of the weapon and then it was found, that corroborated the verbal statements which made the whole thing admissible. So there wasn't any problem with convicting him. Now they didn't give him the death penalty, but he was sent to the penitentiary for the rest of his life. This fellow left thinking that Will Fritz was about the best thing to come down the pike. And that was the way most people that he handled felt about him.

Bill Decker, the sheriff of Dallas County, had that. In fact, Fritz and Decker were similar in many ways. They were two different types of people, but they were able to generate a lot of respect and admiration from the people they dealt with. Decker had a way of handling people and got their respect. He wasn't as good an interrogator as Fritz, but he had access to people, being in the jail down there, and I never knew of a prisoner that didn't think that Decker hung the moon. They just felt like he was a man that they could talk to, and they did talk to, and they told that man things that you wouldn't believe. If anybody in his jail knew something, Decker would find out about it.

There was never any doubt about who the sheriff was. Decker started out running the jail elevator. He was not an educated man; in fact, he came from a very poor family. But he probably knew more about human nature than 99 percent of the psychiatrists in Dallas.

Decker was more of an outgoing person than was Fritz. A man kidnapped a girl from Fort Worth and spent the night out in the little town of Irving, before Irving grew up. The next day they found blood on the step that went into the motel. A couple of days later this fellow was arrested up in Missouri. With the blood being found along with his being identified, Decker was concerned about the possibility that she might have been killed in Irving, which was in his county. So he went up to Missouri, now Decker told me this himself, and said that when he went in they had this guy sitting in the middle of the room. After he identified himself, he was told to come on in. There were about a dozen officers sitting around this room with this guy sitting on a stool with his feet being unable to touch the floor and a light with a shade pulled down like you see in these books about this type thing. As he entered, they said, "Pull up a chair, sheriff. We're just talking to this man."

He said, "No, I don't believe I need to talk to him now. Y'all go ahead. Whenever you get through, let me talk with him a few minutes, if you don't mind."

So they talked to him another fifteen or twenty minutes, and when they came out, they said, "He ain't going to tell us anything!"

Decker said, "Well, if I might have him."

Apparently this guy had dentures and they had either broken them or he had. So Decker took him across the street to a cafe and bought him a bowl of soup. After they had sat down and he had eaten about half this bowl of soup, he said, "Sheriff, there's no way I'd tell those bastards over there anything. But if there's anything I can tell you, well, I'd be happy to."

Decker said, "Well, my concern is the little girl; what's happened to her?"

He replied, "Well, I tell you, I know a lot of people think that there was some other reason for it, but this girl was my sister's only child. My sister was a prostitute and her daddy was a burglar and a pimp and so on. She started using drugs, and I could see no future for this kid there whatsoever, so I just took her. Of course, I didn't have any money, so I killed her. I intended to kill myself, but after I killed her, I lost my nerve.

So Decker said, "Well, where did you kill her?" his still thinking the body might be in Dallas County.

He said, "Oh, the body's out here outside of town where I buried her."

Decker asked, "Would you take me out there?"

He said, "Yeah, I'll take you, but I don't want any of those bastards over there to go with us."

Decker said, "Well, yes, we'll have to have at least one or two go with us out there because it's in their area." He consented and they went out and dug up the child's body and the gun. Later Decker told me, "Man, I hoofed it right back to the airport and got me a plane back to Dallas. I was through with it and didn't want no part of it." But that was the way people would talk to Decker. This guy had known of Decker, but he'd never met him or anything. But he knew by reputation that he was a good man and a good person.

I don't remember the exact date, but General Walker was working on his tax returns while living in his mother's old home out on Turtle Creek. The room opened out and there was a window that you could see into this room from the backyard. General Walker said that just as he reached across the desk for a tax form, a bullet went right behind his head. Having been a combat soldier, he knew the sound of a bullet. He told me that he then got his pistol and went outside but wasn't able to find anybody.

The bullet went through two pieces of wood on the top part of the casement window, passed through the wall, and lodged in a stack of magazines. You could look through the window to the hole in the wall. The bullet would have gone into his right ear and out his left if he hadn't reached for that tax form.

We were practically at a standstill in our investigation. I talked with Walker quite a bit and asked him if he had any gambling debts since a lot of military people did gamble. He told me that he did play a little poker but that he didn't have any types of gambling debts.

I also asked him about women and his love life. The old general was a fine looking man, straight walking military type who had quite a few admirers, but he never had any dealings with any of them that would cause irate husbands to be shooting at him. So I really wasn't sure. There seemed to be no reason for anybody to be shooting at the man. I wanted to get his reaction since I wasn't a hundred percent sure that he didn't know who had shot at him. But he showed no emotion. So after we had talked about everything, every conceivable person and reason why, I told him, "Well, I think whoever it was will probably kill you."

Oswald's name didn't come into this until his wife, Marina, told us that he was the guy who had shot at General Walker. She and Ruth Paine were brought to City Hall and placed in the Forgery Bureau right after the assassination. Marina said that he had come in that night all excited, "I just killed General Walker!"

She asked him, "How did you get away?"

He replied, "Well, all the police are looking for somebody in a car, and I just caught a bus and left."

"What did you do with the rifle?" she asked.

"I buried it in a bunch of leaves there on the ground." Apparently the next day he went back and got it.

Oswald knew of the man, though he didn't know him. But he knew where he lived and he'd read about him. But if she hadn't told us, we still wouldn't know who had shot at him because nobody would have ever thought about running the bullet to the lab to see if it had come from his rifle.

The slug that we recovered from the books or magazines was almost in perfect shape considering the fact that it had gone through those two pieces of wood and dryboard wall. It was in much better shape than either of the bullets that we got out of the President's body or car.* There was no question that it was from the same gun. In fact, the FBI lab said that there was no question that this bullet was fired by the same gun that they took from the Book Depository. It was much easier to make a match on it than it was on any of the suspect bullets in the assassination.

I don't think there was any question about Marina's story, especially since the bullet came from the same rifle. Though I never felt sorry for Oswald, I couldn't help but feel a little sorry for her. Can you imagine this young girl who comes over here, her husband kills the President of the United States, and this all hits you when you hardly know the language? It had to be a frightening experience for her.

---

* Cunningham's recollection is in contrast with the findings of the FBI Lab. According to Carol Hewett in "The Paines Know: Lurking in the Shadows of the Walker Shooting" (*Probe Magazine*, November/December 1997, page 13), "On December 2 [1963] the deformed bullet was sent to the FBI Lab which determined that the slug had the same general characteristics as the other bullets from Oswald's rifle, but was too mutilated to permit a match to the rifle itself."

Thank goodness I wasn't in the basement when Oswald was killed. I was in Gladewater, Texas visiting my wife's father and mother.

I knew Jack Ruby probably as well as any officer in Dallas. Jack came to Dallas, I guess, in 1946 and ran a little beer joint, dance hall type place on South Ervay Street which I understand was financed by his sister, Eva. I worked down there for him at least once or maybe two or three times. In those days, the city required dance halls to have a police officer, and those officers would be assigned after they had paid the city so much for the officer. Usually the guy running the joint would also give the officer a few dollars extra.

I became acquainted with Jack after working at his place those few times and then put him in jail later for pistol whipping one of his employees out in Oak Lawn. I recall putting him in jail one other time for some type of pistol offense.

But Jack was one of those people that you couldn't make angry at you. If you put him in jail, that didn't make any difference; you were still his friend. All police were his friends. Of course, the news media made a big deal out of the fact that a lot of policemen knew him. But you could take any dance hall operator in the city of Dallas, and I guarantee that there would be a lot of policemen who would know them. That was our business, and we did know him.

That Friday night, after the assassination, as the door opened when I got off the elevator on the first floor as I was leaving City Hall, there was Jack Ruby standing in front of the door with a sack full of sandwiches. I asked him, "Jack, what are you doing down here this time of night?"

He replied, "Oh, just rubber necking." Then he said, "No, I know some of those guys up there hadn't had a chance to go eat, so I just went out and got a sack of sandwiches to take over here." He then got on the elevator as I got off. The next time I saw him was on television when he shot Oswald.

Jack was a Jewish boy, born and raised in Chicago, who never had anything, but he was very ambitious. He told me on more than one occasion that he would rather run a New York nightclub such as the Copa than to be President of the United States. I don't have any doubt whatsoever that that was true. I never saw him as being a strongly idealistic person and was surprised that he showed as much emotion as he did about the President being killed since he had never mentioned the President at any time we had talked.

My thought was that when this chance came up, he took advantage of it. I think that he had in the back of his mind the intention to kill Oswald, or try to kill him, and I don't think that this was out of sympathy for the President. I think that it was a planned thing with his thought being that he would kill this man, do a maximum of two years in the penitentiary, then he would run that club in New York, which he would have if he hadn't made two mistakes: he misinterpreted the mood of the people, and he replaced the jailhouse lawyer that he had, Tom Howard, with Melvin Belli.

Certainly his name would have become a household word here, and that is all that it would have taken for him to get into the big time. He had this club out on Oak Lawn and the Carousel Club on Commerce Street, but he didn't have a great deal of money. In fact, I doubt if he could have raised $10,000 to save his name. So his thinking was probably good, and I think that this was exactly the reason that he decided to shoot Oswald if he got a chance. I think that he was completely in control of himself and his emotions.

Howard was not a brilliant lawyer by any stretch of the imagination, but he certainly could have done no worse than Belli. I think when the jury saw Belli come in to defend the man, that jury was going to convict him. Of course, he had to be convicted; there was no question about who killed the man. But generally, whenever a person was killed under those circumstances, it was very unusual for the killer to receive a very long sentence. Ten years was the maximum you could get back then for killing a person in the heat of passion and not premeditated. However, I think that he had every intention, if he got a chance, to kill him. Remember he had the gun.

There had been some threats called in that weekend that said that somebody was going to try to take Oswald and so on. So somebody came up with the thought of using an armored car. Actually they had no intention of using the armored car. Instead, it was to be used as a decoy. It was backed down from the Commerce Street side and blocked off the driveway which included the car that was supposed to lead it down. The basement was cleared of everything except a few police cars.

An officer was supposed to go down and get his car and lead the armored car. Since no left turns were permitted in the downtown area, the officer had to drive his car up the wrong way onto the Main Street ramp, turn left and then come back onto Commerce to lead the decoy van.

One officer was stationed at the top of the Main Street ramp. When this other officer comes out the wrong way going onto Main Street, the uniformed officer then stepped into the street to stop traffic so that the car could get around him to get in front of the armored vehicle. At that point, Jack Ruby, who had just sent a telegram with money to a girl, then walked down the driveway.

The telegram was dated and stamped with a time. If you go there and walk out from the counter and down the sidewalk at a normal pace and into the City Hall basement, you won't be off five seconds from the time that Ruby made it. It was just chance. There was no way that anybody knew exactly when Oswald was coming out, not even the policemen who were waiting down there.

Much criticism was focused on law enforcement agencies after the assassination regarding security surrounding the President's trip to Dallas. But the system, and this happens with all presidents, in all cities, is essentially the same. The Secret Service has the responsibility for the physical surroundings and areas where the President goes. Two or three days prior to the time that the President's coming to the city the Secret Service will send an agent-in-charge, in this case, Forrest Sorrels, to get with the chief of police to map out what they're trying to do, what route will be taken, where he will be, and the security procedures to be taken. The Secret Service is charged with the safety of the President; the FBI's job is running background checks and to have information to make sure that there's no one that's a threat to the President in the area. It's their job to know who is there and who might be a threat, and this is done in conjunction with the local police and their intelligence people. But the responsibility is definitely with the FBI. They've got the facilities for it, and all the information goes through their office.

The FBI is the one that tags people as a threat and places them under surveillance. This can happen in the following manner: The FBI might tell me, "You put so and so under surveillance and make sure that he doesn't harm the President."

As a result, I might go to so and so and say, "Let's go over here and talk a bit. They think that you might be a threat to the President, so I'm going to have to stay here with you until he leaves town."

In this particular case, FBI Agent Hosty's responsibility was to have evaluated this man and to know whether or not he was a threat to the President. I don't think that there was any way that he could have known that he was a threat because there wasn't anything to cause him to become suspicious.

Anyway, that afternoon, after Oswald was arrested, Jack Revill, the lieutenant in charge of the Intelligence Division, met Hosty in the basement of City Hall. There Hosty told him, "Jack, I knew that guy was capable of doing something like that, but I never dreamed that he would actually shoot the President." So Jack went on upstairs, and just as a matter of routine, sat down and typed the chief a little paragraph memo: "At such and such time, I met Special Agent Hosty in the basement'" and he continued the statement.

Somehow this memo, which really didn't mean a whole lot to the chief since I think he just dropped it on his desk, was picked up by some news-type person and, of course, put it on the air. This Hosty incident with Jack Revill put the FBI in a bad light which was one thing that Mr. Hoover couldn't stand. This is when he became very upset and irate over the matter and asked the chief to get rid of the officer. It's not hard to believe when I've had people in his own organization tell me that Mr. Hoover had folders on just about every congressman and senator in the United States.

You see, at the time of the President's visit we had all the right-wingers under surveillance. We knew where the John Birchers were and knew that they were not in any position or anyplace where they could fire at the President or harm him in any way. But we didn't have the so-called left covered because the FBI didn't think that they had anything to worry about from them.

On Monday, November 25th, when I came to work, Paul Wolf, an FBI agent, came by my office. After our usual conversation, I said, "Let's go get a cup of coffee." He said, "Elmo, I hate to tell you this, but you are off-limits to us."

At the time, which was a week after the President was killed, Jack Revill lived across the street from me. We usually had a small poker game every month, and it was my time to have it at my house. When Jack came in, he had two FBI agents with him, Bob Barrett and another whose name I've forgotten. I asked Mr. Barrett if they weren't taking a chance slumming with us. He said, "I don't know what you mean."

"I am referring to the memo Mr. Hoover sent your office regarding associating with Dallas police," I replied. They said they didn't know anything about it, which I knew was not true. But I did not know why they were violating the order until several months later.

At that time, Revill had an office out at Fair Park with twelve or thirteen people working for him. Of course, the intelligence chief's job was to keep the chief of police advised about any organized crime or any type of civil problems such as unrest, political problems, or anything which might reflect badly or cause problems for the police department. Jack was also the Vice-Chairman of the Law Enforcement's Intelligence Unit which is a nationwide organization of intelligence organizations, police intelligence, and sheriffs with headquarters located in Los Angeles. Captain Holt of the L.A. County Sheriff's office was the chairman and Jack was vice-chairman.

What these people tried to do was to keep a handle on the organized crime figures since they could move from New York to Chicago to Los Angeles and Dallas in a matter of hours, and they did a pretty good job of keeping up with them. For instance, if some of the major crime figures were coming to Dallas, we would usually know several hours before they got here, and we'd have somebody there to watch where they went or who they talked to. And this happened all over the country. Naturally, having a list of all these people and their connections was useful. These families actually exist; it's not all just television talk. There really is a godfather figure. We had one of those, Joe Civello, who was indicted with the Apalachin group in New York, here in Dallas, but we had very little in the way of organized crime. Anyway, these two FBI agents, the only two in the whole FBI who could talk to any Dallas policemen, were practically living with Jack.

One day these two came into Revill's office with a classified document stamped "TOP SECRET," which included a whole list of organized crime figures. They told him, "Now, Jack, we're going to bring this out here and let you look at it. It's highly classified. It's the very latest thing on organized crime in the United States. Jack thanked them and they said, "Let's go eat right now."

So Jack threw this thing over on the desk, got up, and he and these two agents went out to eat. Of course, as soon as they left, a couple of Jack's officers working there grabbed this document, took it to City Hall and Xerox copied it. Jack then sent that copy to Captain Holt in Los Angeles. Holt then took it to the most knowledgeable man about organized crime figures in the Los Angeles Intelligence Unit. As he was sitting at his desk looking through the document, he said, "What the hell is this? This marked up here "TOP SECRET," the latest thing? This guy's been dead for six months" and so on.

It just so happened that an FBI agent who was there at that moment reached over and grabbed the copy and said, "What are you doing? Where did you get that copy?"

The intelligence officer responded, "It doesn't matter where I got it, it's not worth anything anyway."

The agent said, "That's a "TOP SECRET" document, and you can tell that this copy was made in Dallas."

So they sent that copy back to Dallas to check the fingerprints all over the paper. This is when the FBI put pressure on the chief to fire Jack. I became involved in all this when the chief wouldn't fire him but did consent to a transfer. When Jack was transferred, the chief called me in and wanted me to take Jack's job, which I did. Chief Batchelor told me that Mr. Hoover, the mayor, and the city manager had all called him putting pressure on him to have Revill fired. By that time, he had around 17 years experience in the police department.

I knew, and so did most others, what was going on, that those guys were doing exactly what they were told. This was no accident. You just don't have an order from Mr. Hoover come down and two agents completely not get the word. And if one agent like Paul Wolf couldn't go across the street and drink coffee with me but two others could come out here and play poker all night, then that just didn't make sense. This thing was a setup from the word "go" because that list of names was not up to date. There was no reason for anyone to have gotten upset since it wasn't a secret document in any sense of the word. They not only knew that he would Xerox a copy, but they knew where he was going to send it. It was all a setup to get Jack Revill. Ironically, Hoover transferred the two agents that we played poker with as well, and said that it was a disciplinary move, but it really wasn't. One of them actually got a promotion.

The FBI had some good men, and I had several very close friends who worked with the FBI including the former special agent in charge here. There had been no problem whatsoever between the Dallas police and the FBI prior to the assassination. Of course, we had individuals who didn't think that the FBI gave them a square deal. For instance, if you had a bank robbery the FBI and the Dallas Police Department would be involved in the investigation because it would be both a federal and a state crime. If you went out and arrested a man, the FBI would immediately take charge if they could, and they usually managed to get control because it was considered more of a sure thing for them to make a federal case than it was for a state case. And the FBI was not noted for giving up credit for arrests and solving crimes to local police. Usually the newspapers would print all kinds of credits about the FBI, and the last sentence might read: "The FBI was aided by local police." That was commonplace. Despite that, we had a fine relationship with the FBI, even after the Revill case.

Elmo Cunningham retired from the Dallas Police Department in 1968 and now lives in Athens, Texas.

PAUL BENTLEY
Polygraph Examiner
Dallas Police Department

"As we were taking him out the front of the theater, Oswald complained that he was not resisting arrest, that the handcuffs were too tight. . . We weren't sympathetic as he was in much better shape than Tippit at that time. . ."

Paul Bentley joined the Dallas Police Department in March 1947. After successful stints with various bureaus such as the Racket's Squad, Vice, Narcotics, Burglary and Theft, and the Fugitive Squad, he was selected to attend polygraph school. From 1951 till his retirement in 1968, Bentley was the chief polygraph examiner of the Dallas Police Department.

The President had received a very warm welcome; the people were delirious. I was at City Hall at Harwood and Main and had gone back inside after the motorcade had passed when we got the information that the President had been shot some twelve to fourteen blocks away in Dealey Plaza. I don't recall whether I was in the process of administering an examination or not, but when I walked out of the office I was told by one of the clerks and was shocked by the news as were many others. I remained there and continued my work until we learned that Officer Tippit had been shot in Oak Cliff.

At around 1:30, Captain Talbert, W.E. Barnes and myself went to the scene of the Tippit shooting at Tenth and Patton to see if we could get any prints off of the patrol car. Tippit had already been taken to the hospital, and the patrol car was sitting roughly three feet from the curb with blood on the ground near the left front headlight where Tippit had fallen after being shot. When we arrived, a number of people were there who had actually seen the shooting, including several ladies that we talked with. Officer Barnes lifted prints from the passenger side of the patrol car which I understood were Oswald's palm and fingerprints.[*]

I was probably there maybe thirty minutes when Captain Talbert, the patrol captain, received a call that the suspect had been seen entering the Texas Theater several blocks away on Jefferson Avenue. As a result, Talbert asked me to go with him to the Texas Theater. As we pulled up, he let me off in front of the theater while he went to the back. When I entered the door, I was told by a man that the man we were looking for was in the balcony.

Moving quickly, I went to the mezzanine and checked both men and women's restrooms prior to getting to the balcony. In the balcony itself, there were only four or five people. A patrolman came up right after that, and I advised him to check those people and to get their names. I then immediately went to the projectionist, identified myself, and asked him to turn on the house lights. By that time, some of the officers were coming in from the stage entrance.

Retracing my steps, I came back down the same stairs and entered the theater just as you would if you were to go in and see a show. Just as I walked in, the house lights were now on, Officer McDonald and the other officers were checking people on the lower floor. McDonald walked up in the row in front of this particular suspect, who was later identified as Oswald, and, as he walked in front of him, Oswald jumped up and pulled a pistol from

---

[*] Bentley is likely in error on this point. In fact, the absence of fingerprints on the car has prompted some conspiracy theorists to state that Oswald was not at 10th and Patton streets at the time of Tippit's death. They also base their beliefs on conflicting eyewitness testimony and the alleged "identification" of hulls from an automatic pistol found in a nearby yard. (See Gerald Hill, pp. 295-96.) If Oswald's prints had been lifted from the car, it would have confirmed his presence at the scene. At least, no record of his prints on the car are known to exist.

his waist. At that instant, I dove over about three or four rows of seats and came down on the side of Oswald grabbing for the pistol. Either my finger or hand or McDonald's prevented the pistol from firing because there was a slight indention in the shell where the firing pin had come down, but it didn't explode the shell.

At the time, I had no knowledge of who he was. I didn't hear him say anything; all I saw was the action of his reaching for the pistol. I didn't see any of the officers hit him though he was resisting fairly vigorously. The whole matter was over in a couple of minutes because several officers came to our assistance and subdued the suspect. Oswald suffered a slight abrasion above his right eye on his forehead which I think came from the ring I still wear when I grabbed for him. After he was subdued, as we were taking him out the front of the theater, Oswald complained that he was not resisting, that the handcuffs were too tight and that we could loosen them. Those were the only things he said going out. We weren't sympathetic as he was in much better shape than Tippit at the time.

As I escorted him on the left and Patrolman Walker on the right, there must have been fifty or sixty people outside the theater, many of them hollering, "Kill the SOB" and things of that nature. Apparently word had gotten out that Officer Tippit had been shot. But the people weren't the only ones who were upset. When one of your fellow officers has been shot in cold blood, you are also certainly upset. Tension really builds. This, in part, explains why there must have been at least fifteen to twenty officers there at the time.

I was the first to enter the car and sat behind the driver. Oswald was placed next to me with K.K. Lyons sitting on the right side of him. Bob Carroll drove with Jerry Hill and C.T. Walker next to him in the front seat. That is the way I remember it.

We drove down Jefferson to Zang and down Zang Boulevard. During the process, we notified the dispatcher that we had the suspect in the Tippit shooting arrested and were en route to City Hall. Shortly after we left the theater I took Oswald's wallet out of his left rear pocket which contained two or three identification cards. One of the names listed was Lee Harvey Oswald; the other was Hidell. There were definitely two names, and maybe a third. When asked his real identity, his response was, "You find out the best you can!" We gave the dispatcher the names and were advised that this was a suspect in the assassination of President Kennedy and for us to bring him directly to Captain Will Fritz's office. That was the first that we knew that he was a suspect in the assassination.

Oswald kept his head bowed and did not say anything on the way back. When we were told that he was a suspect in the assassination of the President, I don't remember if I asked him or if it was Jerry Hill if he actually had shot the President, and he just shook his head "no" and didn't say anymore. Basically, I found him to be very arrogant, even up until the time that we turned him over to Captain Fritz.

When we arrived at City Hall, as we entered the police basement from the Main Street side and descended the ramp, lots of photographers and reporters were taking pictures. It was unusual to have that many there, but apparently when word spread that we were en route with the suspect they began congregating in the basement of City Hall.

We took Oswald immediately to the third floor to Captain Will Fritz, head of the Homicide and Robbery Bureau, and sat him down in the detective area outside Fritz's private office. I think it was Hill who went into Captain Fritz's office and told him that we had Oswald outside. All the while Oswald had nothing to say.

With nothing further to do with Oswald, we examined some of his belongings. In addition to the wallet with identification cards, he was wearing an identification bracelet and a Marine Corps ring. Since he had been handcuffed with his hands behind him, we didn't notice these until we got him to Captain Fritz's office. The bracelet just had "Lee" engraved on it.

Jerry Hill had possession of the gun, a .38 snub-nosed Smith and Wesson with five rounds in the cylinder and one empty chamber. One of the shells had a slight indention where the firing pin had come down but not enough to explode the shell. That was the only one that I saw. Hill had the other shells and the weapon.

Upon arriving at my office, I sat down to write the arrest sheet and a report when Inspector Chris Kockos came over and said, "What's wrong with your right ankle?" I looked down and noticed that it was swollen to the point where I couldn't hardly see my shoe. I hadn't realized that I had injured myself in any way! Immediately I was taken to Baylor Hospital to have it xrayed and placed in a cast. Apparently, I had sprained the ligaments in my ankle rather severely when I had leaped over the seats onto Oswald. I think I was in that cast for six weeks to two months though I was able to come back to work the following Monday on crutches.

That Sunday, when Oswald was to be transferred, I was surprised because I felt he would be taken out with as much security as possible. I had heard that they were going to make the transfer at two o'clock in the morning, then later I heard that some of the press had criticized us, accusing us of mistreating him. As a result, I think Chief Curry wanted the media to see that he had not been mistreated or beaten up, so the time was set for him to be taken out in sight of the media so they could get pictures of him as he was being brought out of City Hall. But I don't think this came from Curry; I think Curry was given orders by the city manager. Curry gave the orders but he was told how to do so. That was the information that we understood.

Ordinarily, Oswald would have been driven out the Commerce Street ramp, but they had backed an armored motor car down as far as it could back down. This was to be used as a decoy. Actually, Oswald was going to be transported in Captain Fritz's car. Lieutenant Rio Pierce was going to drive a patrol car which would lead the decoy armored car down to the county jail. Due to the armored car jamming the Commerce Street ramp, Pierce had to go the wrong way out the entrance ramp onto Main Street. When he pulled up to go out onto Main Street, the patrolman working that entrance, Roy Vaughn, moved out into the middle of Main Street to hold up traffic to let this patrol car make a left turn onto Main, then Pierce would make a left turn onto Harwood and another left onto Commerce to lead the decoy. Apparently, when Vaughn stepped into the street, that's when Ruby went down into the basement of City Hall.

After the shooting of Oswald, I ran a polygraph on Roy Vaughn which indicated that he was telling the truth about his actions. He did not ever see Ruby go down the ramp into the basement. When he stepped into the street, Ruby then went down the ramp. Vaughn never saw him. He was telling the truth about it based on my polygraph exam. There was no conspiracy with Ruby or any deliberate attempt to allow him into the basement. There's been a lot of criticism that the police department knew Ruby real well and that we allowed him to come in. That is not true! I'm citing this from the results of my polygraph examination.

In regard to the polygraph, in my opinion and that of many experts, a polygraph is 95 percent accurate depending on the polygraph examiner, question formulation and, of course, interpretation. It's just like an electrocardiogram. In both cases you read what the individual puts on the chart.

As I understand, Oswald refused to take a polygraph. To me, this does not indicate that a person is either guilty or innocent. Many people feel that when a person refuses a polygraph he's hiding something. I've never felt that way, and I've been in the polygraph business for many, many years. Certainly some may have something to hide, but to accuse one who refuses a polygraph is merely operating on assumption.

Despite much criticism that we received that weekend and since, I especially feel that the Dallas Police Department did an outstanding job in the arrest of Lee Harvey Oswald in such a short period of time. Naturally, it was brought on by the murder of Officer Tippit.

We will probably never know exactly what happened at Tenth and Patton in the exchange between Oswald and Tippit. Why Tippit thought he was a suspect, I don't know. He was a fine patrol officer, and a good patrol officer is a suspicious officer. If Oswald acted in any way in a suspicious manner, he would have stopped and talked to him. I assume, and that's all I can do is assume, that Tippit felt that it was important enough for him to stop and talk with him, and in doing so, to get out and apparently come around and search the man.

The question has arisen over the years as to why Tippit never got his pistol out of the holster. Back in those days, as now, the majority of officers make a lot of arrests without having to pull the pistol out of their holster. Even on traffic stops you don't pull your pistol and put it on a man because he's walking down the street, though he may be a suspicious character. Now, if you receive information over your radio with a description given and this person fits that description and he's dangerous and armed, you have a different situation. In this case, rather than Oswald beating him to the draw, I'm sure that he felt that he was going to be searched and maybe recognized at that time, thus he pulled a pistol and shot Tippit hoping maybe he could get away. Whether it would have been us or the FBI, had Tippit not been shot it probably would have taken much longer to arrest Oswald. For that reason, he did not die in vain.

Bentley retired from the Dallas Police Department in 1968 to serve as Security Director for First National Bank of Dallas. By 1979 he became Vice-President of Barker Guard Service and eventually organized a guard and investigative service for Metro Protective Services in Dallas, retiring in 1986. Bentley lives in Dallas and was the brother-in-law of retired Homicide Detective L.C. Graves.

GERALD L. HILL
Patrol Division
Dallas Police Department

"Up until Oswald was shot, we were smelling like a rose. Within a short period of time, street cops, sergeants, detectives, patrolmen, and motorcycle officers had caught the man who had killed the President of the United States, had lost an officer in the process, and had managed to do so without the FBI, Secret Service, or any of the other glory boys. Nobody could have faulted us for anything at that point..."

Graduating from W.H. Adamson High School, just a few blocks from the scene of the Tippit shooting, Jerry Hill worked at the *Dallas Times Herald*, eventually becoming the radio and television editor. Hill then covered television news for the Dallas Bureau of Channel 5 out of Fort Worth. Gradually becoming interested in the excitement of police work and the police pension plan during the course of his news work, he enrolled in the Dallas Police Academy and went into the Patrol Division upon graduation in 1955. Three years later he was promoted to sergeant.

I was on a temporary assignment, Patrol Division in the Personnel Division, which at that time, was a combination of Personnel and Internal Affairs. We were trying to hire a number of applicants, and I was doing background investigation on applicants working in the office compiling reports and getting some people ready to come in for interviews. I was working that day with Captain Westbrook.

At a little past twelve o'clock, we watched the motorcade pass by our office at City Hall at Harwood and Main. Shortly thereafter, as we were sitting around talking, one of the ladies, Bea Kinney, came out of the dispatcher's office and said that somebody had shot at the President, and she turned and walked out. Our reaction was, "Bull, this is not for real!"

A minute or two later Westbrook said, "You know, there may be something to that because she can't tell a lie and not smile, and she wasn't smiling."

So, I said, "Well, I'll go out and check."

Knowing the dispatcher's office would be bedlam if this were true, I went out to the other end of the hall to the police press room. No one was there, but they had a monitor that you could get two sides of the conversation of what squads and the dispatcher were saying. About the time I entered the room I heard Inspector Sawyer make the statement on the radio that he thought that they had located the spot that the shots had been fired from at Elm and Houston Streets and to send him some help. So I ran down to the other end of the hall, told Westbrook that it was for real and that I was leaving.

I went down to the basement and commandeered a squad car driven by an officer named Valentine. About that time I saw Jim Ewell, who was the police reporter for the *Morning News,* and yelled at him that somebody had shot or shot at the President. He quickly jumped in the squad car and went down to the Book Depository with us. On the way to the scene, the dispatcher had broadcast a description of a possible suspect: white male, 5'6" to 5'8," brown hair, 130-150 pounds. We had this information as we approached the building.

We got out as close to the Book Depository as we could considering there was a bunch of people and officers milling around. As we exited the car, I asked if the building had been sealed off and had it been searched? I was told that it had been sealed but not searched. So a plain clothes officer named Roy Westphal, a uniformed officer whose name I've forgotten, Deputy Sheriff Mooney, and another deputy sheriff and I all went toward the seventh floor as fast as we could. Unfortunately, the elevator stopped, so we went up the stairs to the seventh floor because no one had told us that the sixth floor was where the shots were fired from at the time.

After searching the seventh floor with no results, we left the uniformed officer there because one of the techniques you learn in the business is, when you search an area, leave somebody there so they can't double back on you, especially if you've got two or three stairways or an elevator that they can use. You cover your backside, so to speak, and we went on down to the sixth floor.

As we got on the sixth floor in the back of the building, Mooney went to the left, I went to the right going toward the front of the building on Elm Street. After we'd searched for a short time, Mooney hollered over that he had found some hulls. I went over to the location and noticed there were three hulls just to the right of the open window where the shots were proved to have been fired from in close proximity to the kickplate on the wall, or the baseboard as they call it in this part of the country. I don't remember whether two of them were lying right against it or if one was out away from it a bit, but there were three of them, and they were all in this immediate area.

There had also been a barricade built in sort of a semi-circle that stood up probably three and a half to four feet high so that if somebody were kneeling on the floor between that barricade and the window they would not be seen from the rest of the building. There were also two boxes of books that were in a position where a person being in a position between the barricade and the window could use it as an elbow rest while he was sighting the rifle.

I told all the other officers that were there not to touch anything and that we needed to get the Crime Lab. I went over to an open window in another part of the floor facing Elm Street and yelled down toward the street. But, at that time, fire trucks were arriving with ropes to seal off the area even more and other officers were arriving with sirens and people milling around and yelling so that I didn't know whether I'd been heard or not. So I left them on the sixth floor and went down to the street to make sure that the Crime Lab had been ordered.

I was standing beside Inspector Sawyer's car talking about getting the Crime Lab over to Inspector Sawyer with Assistant District Attorney Bill Alexander and Sergeant Bud Owens, who was the acting lieutenant in Oak Cliff who had drifted over that way, when a civilian got on the radio to tell us about an officer being shot out in Oak Cliff. I made the comment that the two shootings were awfully close together. Sawyer said, "Well, I have enough help here. You know what our suspect looks like," since I had heard that broadcast earlier. He said, "You go to Oak Cliff and assist in the investigation over there."

At that time, we did not know who the officer was that had been shot. We just knew that it was an officer that was down. Bud Owens drove since he had his own car and would have been this man's immediate supervisor. Since I was hitching rides because I didn't have a car, I rode in the front seat with Owens. Bill Alexander rode in the back.

We took a right across the Commerce Street Viaduct to Beckley, then north on Beckley. Just before we got to the intersection of Beckley and Colorado, the ambulance, which had been a lot closer to the Tippit shooting than we had, passed in front of us going to Methodist Hospital.

We proceeded to the site of the Tippit shooting and found Tippit's car with his gun on the ground on the driver's side and a pool of blood just in front of the door where the door had been opened just in front of the windshield on the left hand side. A man pointed out a spot and said, "There's some hulls over here." At that time, nobody had given us information of what type weapon had been used to shoot Tippit nor had we been informed that the suspect had stopped and reloaded. So, with four hulls on the ground, you had to assume at that point that it was an automatic that ejected the hulls after they had been fired; therefore, I went on the radio with the broadcast that the suspect was possibly armed with an automatic because we had found hulls at the scene. We later discovered that after shooting Tippit the guy had walked a few feet, stopped, and very slowly stood there and ejected his used hulls and reloaded his pistol. But at that time, we didn't know that.

If you'd have been able to look at the hulls under a microscope, you might be able to see where an ejector mark had been, but at that point you just knew it was a .38. You didn't know if it was a revolver or an automatic. Of course, it later turned out to be a revolver.

We looked at the hulls, and to make sure they didn't disappear, we marked the area on the ground where they were found. We also marked my initials inside each of the hulls, and I gave them to Officers Leonard Jez and Joe Poe because they were going to stay there and wait for the Crime Lab. Meanwhile we were going to fan out and see if we couldn't find the suspect since he had apparently left that location on foot.

Bill Alexander and I were in the process of searching for the suspect in some of the old two story houses which were being used as storage for second hand furniture stores that faced on Jefferson in the vicinity of where Tippit was shot. There were a thousand places a person could hide in them. As we were checking those, somebody came out an said that they had found a jacket in the Dudley-Hughes Funeral Home parking lot on East Jefferson in the immediate vicinity. This jacket went along with the light jacket description we had earlier on the radio, so we had to assume that this was the jacket of the suspect.

While we continued to search more buildings in that area, a call came out that someone had entered the public library on Marsalis and that that was the possible suspect. It turned out to be an employee who had seen all the excitement and was running into the library to tell them about it. All of a sudden the police came in with guns drawn and shotguns out. Some of those little old ladies spending the afternoon in the library were never the same!

After we found that that was a false alarm and that we didn't find anything in the buildings, we then began to search some of the churches in the neighborhood because Tenth Street, in the immediate vicinity of Jefferson, at that time was known to have more churches than on any other street in the United States. Being that this was a weekday, and the majority of churches were never locked in those days, that was another good place to hide.

I had just searched one of the churches and had gotten on the street when an accident investigator named Bob Apple pulled up. While we were talking, a call came out on his radio that a suspect had just entered the Texas Theater. I immediately jumped in the car with Apple and we went to the front of the theater.

Here again, as at the library, there were two officers with shotguns standing on the sidewalk in front of the theater. I said, "Okay, we've got the building covered here. Is it covered in the back?"

"Yeah," they said, "It's covered in the back also."

So, I said, "We're going to look!"

I went into the lobby and immediately went upstairs into the balcony. There was very little light in the theater; all they had on was a cleanup light and it was on. So I went over and kicked the fire doors open on the balcony to flood the place with light. We determined that there wasn't anybody that fit the description that we had up in the balcony. Basically it was kids shooting hooky from school.

As I came back down the stairs and was approaching the downstairs part of the theater, I heard Officer McDonald yell. Quickly I went in and saw McDonald scuffling with somebody who had a gun in the third row from the back of the theater. I went in to my right off of the next aisle over in the same row that McDonald and the suspect were on. Paul Bentley, K.K. Lyons, C.T. Walker, Ray Hawkins, and T.A. Hutson were all converging. Some of them were coming up from behind McDonald while others were coming across from the back. We finally managed to power the man down on the floor.

I was told later that McDonald managed to get his hand in to where the firing pin caught the fatty part of the hand between the thumb and forefinger. Several of us thought that we heard a distinct click. This could have been the trigger releasing the hammer onto McDonald's hand, or it could have been a misfire. I didn't see his hand under the hammer, but that doesn't mean it didn't happen.

Being that I was working special assignment, I had a pistol but wasn't carrying handcuffs, so I had to borrow Ray Hawkins' handcuffs. Somehow in the struggle Bob Carroll ended up with the weapon, the .38 caliber pistol.

Once we got him handcuffed, we got him on his feet and got him down to the end of the aisle he then began hollering, "Police brutality! I haven't done anything!" Here we had a suspect who was brandishing a gun with an officer killed just a few minutes earlier; our main concern was to get control of the gun and control of the prisoner. If you had to take him to the floor, and if by chance he hit his eye on the back of a seat or whatever, that was insignificant to us at that point. As far as the brutality complaint goes, I never saw anybody lay a hand on him other than to wrestle him to the floor and handcuff him. No one hit him with a shotgun, as some have charged, or with any other weapon.

In any case, we formed a wedge with one officer on the point, two immediately on each side of him, and two behind him and headed out to Lyons' and Carroll's car which was parked immediately in front of the theater.

As we came out, there must have been two hundred to two hundred and fifty people who were yelling, "Kill him! Let's get him!" These people all knew about the President and all the police activity, and being excited by all the sirens in the neighborhood, they must have assumed that it was all connected. It was crowd hysteria which was taking effect.

My first thought at that point was, "Here we have just risked our lives to try to catch him; now we're going to have to shoot somebody to keep him!" The officers out front actually had to turn and hold their shotguns on the crowd till we could get to the car.

When we got to the car, I sat in the center of the front seat, Lyons got in on the right side, Carroll drove. As Carroll got in the car, he handed me the pistol and I stuck it in my belt. In the back seat were Walker, behind the driver, Oswald in the middle, and Paul Bentley on the right.

As we pulled away from the curb, at that time I was using personnel call number 540 Car 2 and announced that we had a suspect and were en route to the station from the Texas Theater. We asked the suspect who he was but he wouldn't tell. At that point, Bentley reached into his hip pocket and came out with his billfold which had two ID's in it: Lee Harvey Oswald and the Hidell ID along with various library and other ID cards. Still he wouldn't tell us who he was. He did make the statement that he hadn't anything to be sorry for.

When we got to the station, we pulled over to the back side of the basement and formed our wedge again to go into the building. At that time we told him, "Now, we're going to hold you in such a way that you can duck your head if you want to keep from being photographed because there's going to be scads and scads of cameramen around this place." Here again he said that he didn't have anything to be sorry for. So we marched him into the station right through the same door that two days later, when he came out, he was shot. We went straight into the elevator and carried him up to the third floor to the Homicide and Robbery office and set him in the interrogation room. Walker, who was a uniformed officer, was sitting with him in the interrogation room. The door was standing open while the rest of us were talking to some of the detectives who hadn't been out there and who were asking us questions. Meanwhile I was trying to figure out who I was going to give the gun to since you had to keep a chain of evidence so you could keep track of it. Frankly, at that point, no one seemed to want it. They didn't want to have to go to court with it.

So I still had the gun and was standing there talking with Detectives Richard Stovall and Gus Rose when Captain Fritz came in. He told them that he wanted them to get a search warrant and to go out to an address in Irving, and if a fellow named Lee Oswald was out there, to bring him in. I asked the Captain why he wanted him, and he said, "Well, he was employed in the Book Depository and was there just before the shooting but had gone after the shooting and was therefore a suspect."

I told him, "Captain, you don't have to go to Irving to get him because there he sits."

At that point, I prepared to return to the personnel office because in the scuffle in the theater Oswald had received a black eye on the left side, and it was standard departmental policy at that time that if a prisoner was injured while we were effecting his arrest that you had to make a report, a "Dear Chief Report." Just as I was leaving Lieutenant Baker said he would take the weapon, thus it was marked as evidence and passed on to him so we could keep the chain of evidence going.

So I went back to personnel, sat down and started writing a report on injuring the prisoner. I had started it at that time "Injury To the Prisoner Is A Suspect In the Murder of Officer Tippit" because he was caught in the immediate proximity. While you had some thoughts that maybe he might have been the suspect in the assassination, you didn't know that, and since this was an official report, you went with what you had.

Then I started getting phone calls. Our Intelligence Division called wanting to know who our suspect was. At one time, the Intelligence Division was talking to me on one line and to DPS (Department of Public Safety) on another. When I named our suspect, they said that DPS knew him, that they were aware of him, and that he was capable of doing something like this based on their information from New Orleans and some other places.

Before I could get through with the report I was told to change the heading to "Injury To a Prisoner Who Was A Suspect

In the Assassination of the President of the United States and the Murder of Officer J.D. Tippit."

While I was waiting for that letter to be typed so I could sign it, one of my friends who was working for Channel 4, the CBS affiliate, asked me if I would make a statement about the arrest in the theater. I told him, "Yes, but it wasn't a one man show, and I wasn't going to take all the credit for it and that there were a lot of other people involved that were just as much a part of it." Just to make sure I didn't forget anybody I took a pen and wrote all their names on the palm of my hand. So I started out standing in the hall on the third floor talking to one camera, and before I got through I was live nationwide on three television networks and, I guess, every radio station in the country and maybe some overseas because, as it turned out, I was the first policeman they had interviewed about the assassination, the arrest, and who the suspect was.

I had a friend who was the night chief at the time in Milwaukee. He had been glued to the TV set but had gone to bed by that time. His wife woke him up the minute she heard about the shooting. He said that when they said that somebody was going to make a statement from the police department he said, "I figured it would be the chief or somebody. When they switched to you," he said, "Oh, poor you! They passed the buck down to you, and you didn't find anybody to pass it to so you got stuck with it!"

I had scheduled a speech at a little church on Haskell for that night at seven o'clock and, despite everything, went ahead with the speaking engagement. There wasn't more than about thirty people there that night. Instead of talking about policing police recruiting, quite naturally all the topics were about the assassination and what we did.

Saturday, there was bedlam at City Hall! Even as the TV people were relieved, the newspaper people were coming in from everywhere in the world. They had a TV cable stretched from a mobile unit outside the building up to the third floor, through the window, through the chief's office out into the third floor hall so that they could take some pictures in the third floor hallway outside Homicide and Robbery.

Chief Curry at that time saw me in the hall and told me to come into his office with him. By then he had a stack of reports

on his desk a foot to a foot and a half high. He flipped through
them and took the one that I had written the day before about
"Injury To a Prisoner While Effecting an Arrest," pulled out the
top carbon, initialed it, and gave it back to me. "Here, your kids
may want this someday," he said. I thought with all the problems
he had and the trials and tribulations the city of Dallas was going
through at the time, if he could think about my kids, he had to be
a pretty special guy.

At that time, I was the Secretary-Treasurer of the Texas
Municipal Police Association, and we were having some
membership problems in San Antonio. Since I was scheduled to be
off that Sunday, one of the other officers, who was an official in
the state organization, and myself had flown to San Antonio early
that morning. While we were on a coffee break, we heard about
Oswald being shot in the basement of City Hall. I immediately
went in and called the dispatcher's office to find out who the
suspect was or if they had caught anybody. That's when I learned
that it was Jack Ruby, who was known probably by every
policeman that had ever worked the downtown area or in Oak
Lawn because he had nightclubs in those areas. In fact, I knew
him.

At that time, the Carousel Club was on my beat when I was on
my regular patrol sector. We checked the Carousel maybe one or
two nights a week on the evening or the night shift, depending on
which we were working. Jack was kind of an egomaniac. If you saw
him on the street and commented on what a good looking shirt he
had on, he'd make a big production of taking off his coat and
hanging it on a parking meter, taking off his tie and his shirt,
giving you the shirt, tying his tie back over his tee-shirt, putting
his coat back on and would walk off down the street.

While he gave as his reason for killing Oswald that he felt
sorry for Jacqueline Kennedy and her children, I think his
calculating mind was going all the time on the assumption that
"I'll shoot Oswald. Public sentiment will get me off, and then I'll
make a million bucks because everybody'll come to see the man
that killed the man that killed the President."

His worst mistake, I think, was the lawyer he hired. Melvin
Belli was too much for the Texas courts at that time. He was too
flamboyant, too wild! He made statements which angered the jury.
They couldn't get him, so they got his client and found him

guilty. If he would have stayed with his original attorney, Tom Howard, I think probably public sentiment would have played a big factor in getting him off with a lighter sentence. Belli was only interested in writing a book and making money off the deal. Ruby eventually won a new trial, but in the meantime had developed cancer and never lived to see the new trial.

In reality, the whole incident should never have been allowed to happen. I want to defend Chief Curry because the idea of transferring Oswald the way he was was not Curry's idea. He objected to it. But in the Dallas city government, the chief of police has a boss, and that boss is the city manager; in this case it was Elgin Crull. His attitude was "because of the black eye the city of Dallas already had because of Kennedy being killed here" Crull wanted to cooperate with the press. Despite the fact that the press was crucifying us every chance they got, Crull gave the chief of police a direct order to let everybody know that he was going to move Oswald.

On Friday night, Oswald had been filed on for two cases of murder: the assassination of the President of the United States and the murder of Officer J.D. Tippit. The minute those cases were filed and accepted by the district attorney's office or a justice of the peace, then that prisoner became the property or the responsibility of the sheriff. And it was his assigned task under state law to move that prisoner. Wanting to cooperate with the press, the city manager then ordered the chief of police to do it rather than the sheriff. He ordered him to tell the press when and where. At that point, all hope was lost of being able to transfer this prisoner in a secret fashion when no one else was around; therefore, the odds increased that something might happen to the prisoner. I had been critical at times of both policemen and newspapermen because I had been on both sides and probably looked at it from a different perspective than some of the others. We didn't make the same mistake when we transferred Ruby.

In retrospect, one of the chief concerns of mine of that weekend was the shooting of Officer Tippit, especially since I knew him fairly well. Back in 1959 J.D. had worked for me in the Oak Cliff area. He was well liked by everybody that worked out there, though he was not a gung-ho type officer. He was laid back and easy going.

One of the things I've often wondered about is what Oswald said that made Tippit get out of the car because it was obvious, based on the information we had, that he pulled up beside Oswald, and Oswald leaned down and talked to him through the passenger window. Something was then said that made Tippit suspicious enough that he was going to get out of the car and walk around in front of the vehicle to confront Oswald on the street.

I think something was said that made him suspicious, or maybe he saw a bulge under his jacket, or maybe he saw a gun. Possibly Oswald had the gun in his pocket instead of in his belt. I think Tippit saw something or Oswald said something that made him suspicious enough that he wanted to check a little closer. But at that point, he didn't have enough information to pull a gun on the suspect and hold him at gunpoint until he could search him. If he had a suspect, or if he thought he had a suspect, he should have notified somebody where he was by using his radio. But he may have thought in this case that he wouldn't have time to use the radio, that it was best to get out and do what he was going to do immediately. I've always said that you shouldn't have one man squads in Texas or anywhere else because somebody will jump one man while he wouldn't think about jumping two.

Once we got Oswald into custody at City Hall, I gained the impression that he was in high cotton at that point. He was the focal point of everything that was going on. He was revelling in the glory of it. I think that he was the type that had he not been killed he would have eventually come out with all the facts just to stay in the limelight.

As we later learned, he'd been a nothing all his life and here was his moment of glory. When the spotlight would begin to fade, he would have given us another morsel to get all the interest generated again. Eventually he would have shot off his mouth and sooner or later it would have all come out.

Of course, there are many who believe that Oswald wasn't involved and was just a patsy, as he stated. Most of the people who have theories are not basing their research on fact but are merely motivated by making a buck. That was true with Mark Lane as well as Melvin Belli. It's also true with Penn Jones, who is from a little town south of here. He kept a publication going for years with one theory one week and another theory the next. He couldn't make up his mind which one of the theories he wanted to follow. Had we had a trial these conspiracy theories would have been completely eliminated. But you can't try a dead man so you've got a theory. A lot of them don't want to hear the truth.

But in all honesty, one of the things that probably contributed to the controversy for all these years was the time pressure that was put on the Warren Commission. We all made statements for the Warren Commission which were tape recorded, played back, transcribed, and given to us to be edited to make sure that names, dates, and places were correct. We worked for three or four days going over page after page of testimony, making our corrections which were to be eventually published. Unfortunately, because they were pressured by the President, they ran out of time and went with the unedited versions in many cases. Thus, names are incorrect and sequences of events are not chronologically accurate; therefore, instead of clearing up many of the problems, they added to them.

I know in my testimony there were several names which were not correct which I had deliberately corrected. This leaves doubt in the reader's mind that—Number One, it was a haphazard investigation; Number Two, that we didn't know what we were talking about; Number Three, that somebody didn't give a damn because all he wanted to do was to get the report out whether it was accurate or not.

Researchers need to accept the fact that there are errors in the text of the testimonies issued by the Warren Commission. You can't take every word as the gospel. These little mistakes, which could have been avoided were it not for the time element, have probably propagated this conspiracy mentality as well as opinions about cover-ups and the inefficiency of the police department.

Up until Oswald was shot, we were smelling like a rose. Within a short period of time, street cops, sergeants, detectives, patrolmen, and motorcycle officers had caught the man who had killed the President of the United States, had lost an officer in the process, and had managed to do it without the FBI, Secret Service, or any of the other glory boys. Nobody could have faulted us for anything at that point other than "you didn't cover that window!" You can't cover two million windows with two thousand policemen, and we didn't even have two thousand.

You could protect a man from a mob, but you cannot protect anyone from an individual who wants to do harm and doesn't mind getting caught, and that's basically what we had with this case. We had one man that was obsessed with the idea that he was going to kill the President, and you cannot police against that kind of situation.

Hill eventually was promoted to lieutenant and retired from the Dallas Police Department in 1979. In the intervening years, he has owned a bookstore, run a tax business, and beginning in 1986, worked in one of the constable's offices in Dallas County. Still active in community affairs, Hill lives in Duncanville, Texas.

JOHN TONEY
Forgery Bureau
Dallas Police Department

"It wasn't funny, but one officer was down between the seats and got under the trampling and was hollering, 'Somebody let go of my arm you SOB; you're breaking my arm!' "

Born in Mississippi and reared in Dallas, John Toney served in the Merchant Marine and later in the Army with the 1st Cavalry Division in the occupation of Japan. After his Army stint, Toney joined the Dallas Police Department, serving initially as a patrolman and then in the Motorcycle Division. Within two years he was promoted to detective, a position he held throughout the remainder of his career with the police department.

———————————

On the day of the assassination in 1963, I was in the Forgery Bureau, or General Assignments, as they sometimes called it, working under Captain Orville Jones. I was one of many plain clothes detectives assigned to be a guard at the Trade Mart working with the Secret Service while waiting for the President's arrival. The Trade Mart was a large facility which, in some cases, could pose a security problem. However, I don't remember hearing of any deep concerns over any safety factors as we had not been notified of anything of an unusual nature.

While we were awaiting the President's arrival, a broadcast was made within the hall that there had been a problem and that there would be a delay in serving the dinner. Then, through a radio that one of the people had on his belt, we were told that there had been a shooting involving the President. At that moment, we became very, very tense and, to a degree, upset. Later the broadcasting system said words to the effect that the President had been shot and, at that time, it was requested that the dinner would be canceled. Some people began to weep and all were despondent. We stayed there until they filed out to see that there was no inner disruption within the hall, then we went to our car to receive orders.

When we got to the car, the orders were for all officers to report to the Control Point, the CP, near the Book Depository. While driving to that location, I told Lieutenant Cunningham, who was with me, that it was going to be a crowded area. While en route, we heard the news on the radio that a police officer had been shot in Oak Cliff. At that point, even though we'd been asked to report to the Control Point, I stated to Cunningham that in past experiences we had never gone to a prowler call, or a call of suspicious nature, and found a person at that point; therefore, I thought we should go to Oak Cliff because, based on our experiences, I thought the two incidents were of a connecting nature. At first it was a debatable issue as to prior orders, but we just took it on our own. We couldn't get on the radio because the radio traffic was so busy, so we just diverted our pattern and went on to Oak Cliff where we found out later the officer, Tippit, had been shot.

Before we could get across the Houston Viaduct, we heard different reports of sightings of people fitting the description of the person who had shot the officer including a report on the radio that he had been seen jumping from a car, leaving the door open, and running into the basement of a library near Jefferson and Lancaster. So we immediately went to that location, jumped out of the car, joined by other officers, and surrounded the building. We were out by the door as everyone came out of the library with their hands up. However, as we learned, the suspicious person was merely an employee at the library who was off duty and had run into the library to notify his cohorts of the situation involving the President. So that was a null and void trip. As we got back into our car, we heard that someone had been seen slipping to the rear behind the screen of the Texas Theater.

Again, at the time, one thing that was going through our minds was that these two things, the shooting of the President and the officer, were of such serious nature and occurring in such a short period of time, that there was a connection between the incidents. It was not an accidental happening that both occurred so quickly together, that possibly the officer had stopped a person who was the attempted assassin. That was our thinking. That, in part, accounts for why so many officers were involved in this search, combined with the fact that anytime an officer is shot you will almost certainly have the same reaction because of the camaraderie and to aid another officer. Anyone who was anywhere in the vicinity would always respond.

It was a bright sunny day as we left the library and pulled up in front of the theater. We actually left the car in the street, not even attempting to park it, and left one man in the car to listen to the radio. Meanwhile, Cunningham and I dashed into the theater and went upstairs because we already saw officers downstairs. We didn't know if anyone was in the balcony or not which is why we went upstairs to scout it out for possible suspects and to talk to everyone to see who they were, how long they'd been there, and what they'd seen.

As I was talking to the first person for just a matter of seconds, I then heard a voice downstairs hollering, "He's down here!" Cunningham and I then ran downstairs. Someone had turned on the lights, but my eyes were still dilated from the sunlight, so I couldn't see too well. When I arrived downstairs, I ran down the aisle by the commotion where they were actually wrestling with who was later identified as Oswald, though we didn't know who it was at the time.

The first thing I saw was a pistol in someone's hand over someone's shoulder, and someone was holding the arm. They were wrestling, so I then climbed over the seats and got into the fray. It wasn't funny, but one officer was down between the seats and got under the trampling and was hollering, "Somebody let go of my arm you SOB; you're breaking my arm!" One of the other officers had another officer's arm twisting it, so it was confusing in such a small area with so many men trying to apprehend one man.

During the scuffle, I heard Oswald holler, "I want to register a complaint of police brutality!" Finally they got the gun away from him and carried him out the exit toward the front of the theater.

After the arrest, we sealed the theater to get a list of the witnesses, though there weren't many there. Someone said that they saw the image of a figure displayed behind the screen, but I don't recall many specifics. I don't know whether that's when he was supposedly entering the theater, but I recall someone mentioning something vaguely in that terminology.

At that time, we didn't know what we had. We didn't know about Oswald; he was just a person with a gun. Since these people who were in the theater had not been advised of their rights at that time, and trying to be as legal as possible, we were merely getting names for the interrogators to be used later instead of interrogating them, per se, at the scene. This information was then handed over to the Homicide Division.

Being off duty the rest of the weekend, I was driving through the countryside in East Texas on Sunday morning as I listened to this live broadcast of the release of Oswald to the county jail. Suddenly, I heard all this screaming and hollering on the radio. I thought it was a replay of us at City Hall on the day of the capture of Oswald till I heard the name Jack Ruby mentioned and that he'd shot Oswald. Then I really perked up because, being a detective, I had known Ruby during the course of my work, being in and out of his clubs on different occasions for the past several years. That was the first time I knew anything else had happened that weekend. I was quite shocked!

I found Ruby to be very congenial to officers, and to me, a very pleasant person. He had given us no problems although on one occasion I was involved in one of his arrests, a minor misdemeanor, in which he had become involved in a fight. I thought I knew him well enough, so I called and told him that I had the paperwork down at the sergeant's desk and for him to come by there at closing time before he went home and to take care of his business by paying this fine which was assigned as simple assault. So, after closing his club, he went by and paid his fine, and that was it.

I was interviewed by the FBI due to the fact that they checked Ruby's record and found out about this arrest I had on him. They were just quizzical as to why I had made a phone call to him as if implying possibly that we were more than just acquaintances. My reply to them was that any businessman in the city of Dallas at that time that committed something that amounted to around a

$15 fine, I would not have shut their business down and run all their customers off for anything that minor. I told them that I would not have done anybody that way, including Jack Ruby.

I've heard these stories about how Jack Ruby was involved with organized crime, but in my dealings with him I had no problems with his ever trying to be secretive or protective of any underworld character of any nature. He was always very cooperative as far as I was concerned, though he was not what you would call a police informant, at least not with me. In fact, I think the issue of organized crime in Dallas at that time was null and void. I never heard any of my associates speak of it.

Ruby was an impulsive individual. I'd seen him on a couple of occasions where a patron in his establishment had become unruly, and it wouldn't take him but a second to cause the patron to leave or be ejected. Just from his build and his talk I wouldn't have gone up and punched him in the nose just to have something to do. I don't think that anyone with a prudent outlook on life would have done so because he was stockily built and had apparently been a fighter in his earlier days in Chicago.

While I would occasionally stop by either the Vegas or Carousel Clubs during routine police business, I didn't partake in my off hours. I don't doubt that some officers did, though they were on thin ice. But Ruby seemed to like police officers. He might have had self-serving motivations so that the police wouldn't harass his clubs or bother his girls or dancers. But as far as being friendly to the police as a penance or for semi-bribery, I think that's incorrect. At least in my own personal observations, I never saw any such indication. He was a businessman just like other people. Nightclub owners, you take them with the rest of your duty perspectives; he was just another person.

But he never seemed to me to be the type to shoot somebody like Oswald. I've thought about his possible motives many times, as one can well imagine. The only thing I can think of is that he felt compassion for Jacqueline Kennedy. I certainly never heard him say a word about politics or anything politically at all. I can't think of any ultra highly secret motive of the Mafia, as you'll hear, or paid conspiracy. I'm a realist, and I've heard nothing that even comes close to proving such a theory. Until I do, I'm convinced that he did it just on a spur of the moment, a compassion for the wife, or a duty felt to his country or whatever.

Neither has changed my opinion that he entered the basement, as he said, down the Main Street ramp. I don't think anyone, even knowing him, would have intentionally let him in the basement. I think he got in because of the crowded, confused situation. I knew him as well as most people, and I would not have let him in even though I knew him and considered him an acquaintance. Nor would I have let anyone else in there if they weren't authorized to be there.

Chief Curry was a fine person and, in fact, too good for his own good in allowing the news media in the basement and notifying the whole world that we were going to transfer Oswald. I think that was a mistake, but that's on hindsight. Hindsight's always better than our foresight, but it happened.

One thing that is overlooked by many in all of this is that I was also assigned to investigate the attempted assassination of General Walker earlier that year. As I recall, I interviewed him three times. My first interview was after the reported shooting at him in which he told me that after the shot was fired from a darkened alley, the reason that he wasn't killed was that he dropped a pencil while filling out his income taxes and, as he bent over to get it, the bullet hit right where his head had been as he bent over to pick it up. He further stated that after the shot rang out and he knew for sure that he'd been shot at, he ran upstairs, got a pistol and ran out into the alley looking for this attempted assailant. I asked him, "Weren't you kind of leery about running into a darkened alley after someone who shot at you and not knowing where, who, or what was out there?"

And I remember his comment to me; he said, "Mr. Toney, if you had made (x-many jumps) in a parachute into combat as I have, that one shot wouldn't deter you from going out and looking for the assailant." That was his comment to me, referring to how many times he'd jumped into combat. It was nothing for him to go out looking for a man in a dark alley when it was one on one.

My impression of Walker at the time was that he seemed to like the limelight. How efficient he was in the cause which he was upholding at that time, I can't answer. He was quite well known and there were pro's and con's as to whether he was doing the right thing or not. It never crossed my mind that this might have been a setup. Due to the fact that he had had some adverse publicity about marches and his outlook on the country's perspective, a lot of people might have disagreed with him, so I never gave it a thought.

I interviewed others regarding the case but came up with nothing. I concluded that in his dealings with the immense public that he was in contact with that someone who didn't agree with his views decided they would stop him from continuing his procedures. I didn't think anything about it nationally; it was an individual thing. The first I heard of Oswald's name entering the picture was when someone interviewed Marina, and she had said that he had come home and told her that he had tried to shoot at General Walker. Prior to that I had never heard of Lee Harvey Oswald.

Over the years I have not heard one person prove one thing that we did not ascertain almost immediately after the assassination of the President. I think that everyone I've ever heard of was in it for self-fulfilling purposes with no benefit to anyone other than monetary reasons! The district attorney in New Orleans had some people indicted by just pointing fingers causing people to commit suicide and lose property and homes fighting cases, and he never proved one thing! And neither has anyone else! A man from England had inside information that the body in Oswald's grave was a Russian agent. That proved to be untrue but, of course, he probably made a million dollars in publicity off of it. We also hear that everybody involved died. I don't believe that! I think it's just a fickle of fate that it happened to them.

In my own mind, regarding this subject, I don't think the police department, by intent, had any part in any conspiracy. Those who accuse the police have no knowledge of what they're talking about. I think the Dallas Police Department did a magnificent job that weekend. They have nothing to be ashamed of!

After his retirement from the Dallas Police Department in 1977, Toney eventually joined the Dallas County Sheriff's Department and became the chief deputy to Sheriff Bowles in 1984, a position he retained until his retirement in 1997.

W.R. "PINKY" WESTBROOK
Captain, Personnel Division
Dallas Police Department

"Gerald Hill probably wouldn't know a .38 automatic shell if he saw one. Oh, he might if he could read the writing on the side, but you couldn't tell by looking at it on the ground..."

Born in 1917 in Arkansas and graduated from Benton High School, "Pinky" Westbrook came to Dallas in 1937 and joined the Dallas Police Department in 1941. On November 22, 1963, Westbrook held the rank of captain in charge of the Personnel Division.

———————————

Since I was in charge of Personnel and Internal Affairs, I had no connection whatsoever with the President's coming. We watched him come by as they turned from Harwood onto Main where my office was located. With the motorcycle escorts and people on the streets, everything was in order at that time.

Minutes later the dispatcher ran across the hall and said that the President's party had been fired upon. When we determined the location, I told the sergeant and patrolman in my office to get my car and immediately go to the scene. Then we couldn't get a straight story: The President had been shot; the President hadn't been and so on. Finally, when it was established that he had been shot, I walked to the scene, maybe a half mile away.

While I was there, my sergeant ran up and said, "They've just shot an officer in Oak Cliff!" So I went immediately to that scene. By the time we arrived, the body had been removed and quite a few people were there, including a woman I questioned who had seen Tippit killed.*

When we left to go to Oak Cliff, we got two or three rumors that whoever had done the shooting was over at the library. There were quite a few rumors at that time. I don't recall who the officers were who were with me, but as I started walking up an alley, one said, "Look, there's a jacket under the car!" If I remember right, it was an old Pontiac sitting there. So I walked over and reached under the car and picked up the jacket which eventually turned out to be Oswald's.

Then we went to the theater which I entered from the rear from the stage entrance along with Sergeant Stringer and FBI agent, Bob Barrett. At that time, it was immediately in everybody's mind that the shooting of the President and the officer were connected. Maybe it might be intuition, but when you have a president killed and a few minutes later you have an officer shot within a couple of miles, then you're going to think they're connected. A person that doesn't is an idiot! He's not normal if that's not his first thought.

Standing on the right side of the stage facing the seats, I saw this one man sitting alone, a third of the way down in the theater in about the middle seat. There wasn't anyone else around at the time. In fact, I don't think there was anyone else in the theater, and the picture was shut off. Why he hadn't gotten up and tried to get out, I don't know. He should have been aware at the time that somebody in the theater had called the police about him.

The bad thing about this situation was that I was unarmed; I had forgotten to get my pistol when I had left the office. So we started down, Sergeant Stringer on one side and me on the other. We could see a man down there even though the picture had been

---

* In his book, *Assignment Oswald*, FBI Agent James Hosty recalled that fellow agent Bob Barrett, who was with Westbrook at the Tippit scene, told him that Oswald's wallet was found beside the car. This story was not known at the time of the author's interview with Westbrook, and thus the subject was not broached. However, logically, if the Dallas police had found the wallet at the scene they would have announced it to the world at the time, and much of the speculation as to whether Oswald killed Officer Tippit could have been eliminated.

shut off. You didn't have to pick him out because there wasn't anybody else there. Now there may have been some on the left or right, but there was nobody sitting in the center section: just him. An officer by the name of McDonald came in from the other side got to him first. As I recall, Oswald said something like, "This is it!" as he came up with the pistol. McDonald then grabbed it. I think it might have been McDonald who got his finger behind the trigger when the gun was in the air. I could see the pistol and the fellow ahead of me, Bob Carroll, reach out and grab it. In fact, Carroll was really the one that got the gun out of his hand. Then I got hold of Oswald by the arm, at least I think it was Oswald, though it may have been Carroll since we were all pushing in, then he was immediately covered by everyone who was wanting to get in on it. Actually there were too many people to handle it. It seemed that everybody wanted to get in on the publicity if there was going to be any.

Since I was the ranking officer at the scene, I just backed off and said, "Take him straight to City Hall," which four or five of them did.

It was all so ridiculous, really. Everybody that could get in that car did. I guess everybody's emotions were running high, but you're supposed to be a police officer. Later, some female reporter wrote a book about one of them and gave him credit for everything, claiming that he had solved the whole case.* I just went back and got in my car, drove on back to City Hall and never had any more dealings with Oswald, nor did I ever see him again.

In the aftermath at the theater, Paul Bentley fell down and broke an ankle. McDonald at first appeared to have a small scratch on his face, but the next day he showed up and had mercurochrome all along the side of his face. It was humorous! Evidently it was to magnify the injury. Of course, I had him go to first aid as well as Bentley, too. But they really put the mercurochrome on that little scratch. I guess there's always some humor that happens regardless of how serious the situation.

When we got back to the office, the first thing I saw was Jerry Hill talking over a microphone to some reporter. He had the gun,

---

* The book was *Investigation of a Homicide* by Judy Bonner, published in 1969 by Droke Press in Anderson, S.C.

and I ordered him to take it down to Homicide, which he did as soon as he got off the microphone. Apparently he had the gun since the arrest because if he ever got his hands on it, he would never turn it loose; you can bet on it! It seemed like the biggest thing I could see around City Hall at that time was that everybody wanted publicity—at least that's the way it looked to me.

All the employees of the Book Depository were brought in and were put in the hallway. Oswald hadn't made any kind of statement when the officers came in with him. One of the girls and one of the guys who worked at the Book Depository supposedly said, "Hello, Lee. What are you doing here?" Immediately the officers concluded that he was from the School Book Depository which set off a series of conversations.

At that time, Oswald had a mark on his forehead. Some have made claims about police brutality in the arrest, and I think police brutality had a place in that particular incident. Of course, it wouldn't be in front of witnesses. There had just been a President of the United States shot down and then an officer killed in cold blood without even getting his gun out. I don't think there could be any such thing as police brutality to a mad dog like that! Maybe, but I just couldn't see it.

The way I understood it, he drove up beside Oswald, parked his car at the side of the curb, got out, and walked around the front and was killed right at the front fender with his gun still in his holster. And a person like that is going to holler police brutality!

People have questioned why so many officers converged on the scene at the Texas Theater. But when you get one of your own killed, it's just like someone killing your wife. The police department had its cliques like everybody else, and there were some that you liked better than others. There's always a lot of enmity and politics in the police department that you find anyplace else. But in this case, everybody that could get there would be there.

Tippit was a trusting good old country boy who probably should have never left the country. I'm sure that he stopped him as a suspect because they were stopping most everybody at that time. Tippit had not called into the dispatcher, but that was not unusual at that time because we didn't have near the crime then that we do now. Back in those days a lot of people hated the police, but at least they respected them. In fact, you demanded that respect.

When I gave my deposition to the lawyer from the Warren Commission here in Dallas, I just came in off the street without notes which was my usual practice when testifying. But I don't think there were any omissions. I recall that at one time he had to prompt me about the jacket. I was going to leave that out but was prompted.

People have made much about the jacket. The only thing that I remember is that it was kind of a tan, beige, or rye color, whatever you want to call it. The jacket didn't have any more to do with this case than Oswald's socks, or Oswald's shoes, or my socks, or my shoes, or my jacket.

At that time, he was supposed to be wearing a jacket and now he wasn't. I'm pretty sure it was his jacket, though it's not been absolutely proven. But again, it had absolutely nothing to do with the case anyway. These writers have jumped on every little thing they could that's not relevant. It could have belonged to the man who owned the car. It had no place in the evidence! The accusation didn't say: "Because Oswald was wearing a jacket that he killed Kennedy and then he killed Tippit, then he peeled off his jacket." This is really important evidence that they should have! I wonder if they found if he had on underwear, or if his socks were clean, or did he use foot powder?

The FBI wasted hours and hours on the jacket. Any attorney worth his salt would tell you that the jacket had absolutely nothing to do with proving or disproving the case. Why do we waste so much time on evidence that doesn't matter, including thousands and thousands of words about the jacket?

Not only that, but you don't identify anybody by the clothes they're wearing. If you're going to try to identify them in a lineup, it's much better to put them in clothes other than what they were wearing when the offense occurred. You don't identify a person by the clothes; you identify them by their face. So whether you put Oswald in a jacket is immaterial. In fact, it would probably be less sure if he was in the jacket because a witness would have a tendency to identify the jacket and overlook the face.

But no matter how much you try to explain it, you'll always have those who will question. At one time, there was a jail

318 NO MORE SILENCE

supervisor who shot himself, and I took his place for a while. During that time, which was about ten years or so before the assassination, Jack Ruby was brought in for carrying a pistol. The burden of proof rested with him, but being familiar with the pistol law that stated: "The place of business on the way home," the ruling was that he could carry it. Due to this particular ruling, I released him to appear back the next morning at 9:00 o'clock, knowing that there would be no charges filed under the circumstances. Then during the FBI or Warren Commission questioning, they paid a great deal of attention to this that happened ten years before and wanted to know why and what my purpose was in releasing Jack Ruby. I think I explained it three or four times until I finally got tired of it and said, "Well, it's on the record! Go look at it!"

I believe it was Bob Considine who connected a number of deaths with Oswald, Ruby, and the Kennedys. But one that was particularly brought out was that of a prostitute who hanged herself in our jail. He even connected that to the assassination. Much of that is mostly to make it sensational. It's the job of a reporter, I guess, to get his name on by-lines, and he does it through sensationalism. I know that a reporter has got to make a living and that we've got to have news, but there's two occupations that I rate just about the same: one of them is reporters, and the other is used car salesmen. The biggest crime, I think, of reporters is the crime of omission. They tell that part of the story which is sensational and omit the part that's not sensational, which changes the whole picture of the story about eighty percent of the time.

Let me cite an example: A man came in to the office one time and said that the police had picked up his son and rode him around in a squad car for two hours. During the conversation, I learned that his son was the same age as mine, which was sixteen. I said, "Well, that is awfully unusual that they would have done that just over a traffic violation and he still got a ticket."

"No, no, he didn't get either; he just got a warning," he said.

"Well, that's strictly unusual that this would happen."

And he said, "My son said it happened."

"Well, I have a son the same age."

He said, "Don't you believe your son?"

I responded, "Not on a stack of Bibles would I believe my son on something like this." So I told him that we would make the investigation and that I would get back with him.

As he started to leave, he turned and said, "Captain Westbrook, I feel so sorry for you because you can't trust your son."

I said, "Well, I appreciate your thoughts, but I don't."

I handled the case myself and found that his boy was with a girlfriend. I went out and talked with her and found that she had given him his walking papers because she was going to marry another boy. She was just sixteen herself. She told me, "Why, no, they we weren't even stopped by the police. We went out at Mountain Creek Lake Park, and he just wouldn't start the car again." When I contacted the boy, he confirmed the story.

See, he had gone to either the *Morning News* or the *Times Herald*, and the story had been printed in the headlines about how he had been mistreated. So I picked the boy up at school and took him home and said, "Now let's go in and talk to your daddy." We then went in, sat down, and he told his daddy just like it happened. You should have seen that old man's face!

Anyway, when I got ready to leave, I said, "Sure sorry that you trusted your boy," and went on out.

I then called the newspaper reporter who had written the story and said, "You know, you put a big lie in the paper. You didn't verify it because I just talked to the boy." I started to say, "You idiot," but I didn't. Anyway, he agreed to print a retraction, but it was printed in a small space in the back page.

Sensationalism also applies to the books on the assassination. I think the Warren Commission tried to get to the bottom of the whole thing, and I think they did. It seems like a lot of these guys that write books don't think so. They put people on a hill behind the building; they create other shots. They've even said there's no way that Oswald could have fired those shots that quickly. It's just been so sensational that everybody's trying to make a buck out of it! Now I don't blame a person for trying to make a buck, but to try to create controversy when, Lord, we already have enough; that's what I object to. Making money by creating controversy is the real purpose of the books.

As a result, the Dallas Police Department has come under close scrutiny even though most of the writers don't know much about who they were writing about. The two chiefs who were the most influential during that time period were Carl Hansson and Jesse Curry.

Hansson was completely honest and a disciplinarian. In fact, he had been a master sergeant under MacArthur in Honolulu at one time. When he came to the Dallas Police Department, he became a patrolman and worked his way up through the ranks. He didn't have many favorites and was a good solid man. Whether you were rich or influential didn't mean a damn to him. He ran a good police department. I loved him like a brother, as did the other dedicated police officers. He died an untimely death on the operating table from a gallstone operation.

Chief Curry was strictly an honest man, but it was sad that he always liked to drink. He was not a drunkard by any stretch of the imagination, but he did like to drink. It was only after the assassination that I would say that he became an alcoholic, which I think led to his retirement.

Both chiefs let Captain Fritz alone to run the Homicide and Robbery Bureau. Fritz and Hansson hated each other, and Fritz and I had the same feelings as well. I disliked him very much, and he hated me worse than that! I never really knew why, though when I was a patrolman there was a thing or two that he didn't like. The feeling of dislike was evident on several occasions down through the years. But I still have to give the devil his due; he was very competent in his job. At one time, he was probably the best interrogator in the United States. He was one of those people who, when he was convinced that a man was guilty, would say, "Well, that's it. We got him." He didn't pay too much attention to the evidence you had to have, but he did in regard to the assassination. There's no question that this case was right. He had quite a record and broke some big cases. He once shot a gun out of a man's hand who had hidden in an attic.

He was also one who overreacted on many occasions. A man who was Fritz's driver once told me that when he would knock on his door, Fritz would always come to the window first, open the curtain and look out. I guess he thought somebody was after him.

He never wrote anything about the assassination, which was strange, since he was a publicity seeker. He learned how to get his name in the papers early when he was working for a guy who was busted out of Vice Squad several years before I went to work there named John Henderson. John was a publicity seeker who knew what made a story.

After the Oswald shooting, Captain Jones, Inspector Sawyer, and I ran an investigation on the matter. We took it from what Ruby said and proved everything he said was correct. I think that people have trouble believing the incredible timing that Ruby had in getting into the basement to shoot Oswald.

One of the rumors was that two nights before when they had a show-up of Oswald, Jack Ruby was in attendance and had answered the telephone on several occasions. But the one thing, according to the police, that cinches that it was not premeditated on his part was the little ticket stub that he got in the Western Union that was stamped 11:17 while he was there: the shooting occurred four minutes later. Had it not been for that stub, the conspiracy theories would probably be a lot more prevalent.

He said that he had been at the Western Union and that he had sent a telegram, which was money, to one of his waitresses. We tried it from the time that telegram was put across the board till he walked down, pulled out the gun and shot him. He didn't have any intention of killing him until all of a sudden there was Oswald, and he had his gun, which he always carried. The timing worked out perfectly, exactly as he said. There's no way that he could have gone any other way. Someone told me that there was an old door back there that had been covered up, but I wasn't aware of it. I've been all over that basement and doubt very seriously that that door even exists.

At the top of the Main Street ramp, Roy Vaughn stepped out in the street to let a car out coming the wrong way out of the ramp. When he went back to take his guard position, Ruby walked in behind him. There's just no other way it could have happened. Polygraph tests were run on Vaughn which he passed.

Polygraphs were also run on Napoleon Daniels, who was a former policeman who had been fired for misconduct on duty. He came forth and volunteered information that Ruby stopped and talked to Vaughn and that Vaughn had let him in. Of course, he had an ax to grind and wanted to get even with somebody. Daniels, who was black, had been managing some real estate for somebody and had tried to collect rent while on duty by chasing a fellow while in full uniform. This account was supported by a fellow officer who was also black. So he was dismissed after he failed a polygraph.

Of course, when speaking of polygraph tests, many look at them as being infallible which is a bunch of bunk. They're not that valid. We had a prostitute who was thrown out of the fourth floor of the Baker Hotel. Polygraph tests were run on all the bus boys and porters. They all passed. Two or three months later on the top floor of the building just up the street from the Baker, one of the secretaries was raped on the elevator and beaten up horribly. It was assumed that it must have been somebody off the street.

Anyway, some detective got wise very quickly and checked the names against the ones at the Baker. He found the same name of one of them who had been given a polygraph. When they went looking for him, he was nowhere to be found. He made it to Terrell, where I understand that he killed a ten-year-old girl before he was finally apprehended. This was the same person who had earlier passed the polygraph at the Baker Hotel.

I knew a policeman at one time who bet that he could pass any polygraph given to him. He was a born liar! He said that he had a duck that weighed 28 pounds and a rabbit that ate a bale of alfalfa a day. He lied about everything. Polygraphs are subjective. The idea that you're going to take a polygraph can excite some people to the point that they can't even be recorded.

Jack Ruby was a typical nightclub owner who liked the women and was emotional. As I understand, he whipped two or three people at his club. He liked policemen, and a lot of policemen called him a friend. In fact, I'd say that half the police force knew him and called him a friend.

When he started mentioning names after the shooting, the name of Blackie Harrison came up. He then became very nervous, and we couldn't understand why. Harrison was given a polygraph, and it was determined that he didn't have any knowledge of his coming in. Finally, we figured out that he was one of Ruby's favorite policemen. He thought a lot of Blackie, and as Blackie grabbed Ruby just after the shot he said, "Ruby, you son of a bitch!" This was what was bothering Ruby, which showed that he was a very sensitive person.

I didn't have anything against him, but I wasn't close to him either. I'm not a nightclub person, but a lot of policemen went to his clubs. It was an open home for them. They didn't have to pay for anything because they were policemen. I never took the opportunity since I was married and just didn't go around to those places. Basically he was just a typical nice fellow who was much like myself, middle ground, except I didn't shoot a man who was handcuffed.

Ruby probably thought he would be a hero, maybe like John Wilkes Booth. As emotional as he was, I think that it was just a spur of the moment thing. I don't think that he even thought that "that son of a bitch killed my president." Generally when they bring out the temporary insanity plea, as in Ruby's case, it is nothing more than anger. Anybody is a little off when they become angry; they're not thinking straight.

You know, it's a funny thing about the way we do things at trials. The defense has three psychiatrists who say this man is crazy while the prosecution has three psychiatrists who say that he's not. So what does that say about psychiatrists? The jury doesn't understand any of them. The only thing that I sort of agree with psychiatrists is their usage of the term sociopath, or those who never develop a conscience. They don't care about anybody else. Now that doesn't mean that they will necessarily become a criminal; they might wind up being a bank president and foreclosing on old ladies, or they could become a Clyde Barrow.

Curry later wrote a book on the assassination which was more or less factual based on newspaper reports. I don't think that he felt responsible for what happened because the news media killed Oswald; there's no question about that! He'd have been moved without any problem whatsoever since they would have just put him in a car and carried him to the county jail. But no, the media caused too much trouble. They wanted the world to see him transferred, and so the world saw him dead. I don't believe you can lay his death anywhere but with the media.

The problem with the transfer was that they didn't have enough policemen really to keep the reporters out of the way. It would have taken a whole bunch of policemen. We had big names in here including the Japanese reporters. Everyone that could come in by commercial airlines came in by charter flights into Love Field. You can't imagine the cables that were running down the hallway of City Hall.

I don't know whether Curry had a sense of guilt that he just didn't disregard the city manager's orders which is what I think he should have done. I think he would have ridden the storm by doing it and moved him that night about 10:30 or 11:00 by car to the county jail. Then, the next morning, he could have apologized to the media claiming that he had misunderstood, and I think he could have gotten away with it.

Some have asked me whether Oswald could have gotten a fair trial had he lived. It's a matter of what is meant by fair. In the court system, you're going to be indicted and tried by a jury of your peers. That poses a problem. Let's say that I'm a deacon in the First Baptist Church, which I'm not, but we'll just say that, and I have jury duty. I'm sitting on the jury and there's a man whose been to the penitentiary three times and never done an honest job in his life. We're trying him for murder, but are we his peers? No. The only time he's going to get his peers is by getting people on the jury who had been to the pen three times who had also killed somebody. Then you've got a jury of his peers.

A case like this will probably never happen again. Oh, there might be another president assassinated, but the circumstances would be different. I don't think that Oswald could have gotten a fair trial in Dallas. He would have probably been transferred after all that publicity. But that publicity was all over the world.

A year or two after Oswald was killed we were in our hotel room in New Delhi one night and there was a knock on the door. There were two reporters, one with a camera, who started asking me questions about Oswald. I told them what I knew, but I never learned where they got their information, and that was in New Delhi!

But when you look back, as far as the investigation was concerned, by 6:00 o'clock that evening, Fritz made the statement that the investigation was closed. He was criticized for that. Later, investigations were conducted by the FBI, the Secret Service, the attorney general's office, and other agencies, plus the Warren Commission. After all that, there was not one relevant piece of evidence which proved Oswald guilty or not guilty that Fritz didn't have by 6:00 o'clock that evening.

So much has been written about this case that I think the whole thing has been built way out of proportion. Several years ago there were eighteen John Wilkes Booth guns which killed

Lincoln for sale at different places in the country. Probably a hundred years from now we'll have the same type thing in this case.

Captain Westbrook retired from the Dallas Police Department in 1966 and later served as a police adviser in South Vietnam. After working for Schepp's Dairy in Dallas, he then worked with District Attorney Henry Wade as a special investigator for the Dallas County Grand Jury until his retirement in 1983. Westbrook died in 1996.

ROY WESTPHAL
Criminal Intelligence Division
Dallas Police Department

"The morale on the police department also suffered because we had allowed our President to be killed. We didn't stop it; therefore, we screwed up. In addition, the Oswald shooting was a foul-up from the word go. In my opinion, we looked like a bunch of country oafs..!"

Born in Dallas in 1931 and graduated from high school in Wiley, Texas, Roy Westphal attended East Texas State University for a year and eventually joined the Dallas Police Department in December 1953. He worked in various divisions in the police department including: Patrol, Burglary and Theft, Vice, but mostly in Criminal Intelligence. Promoted to detective in 1957, Westphal continued in that role in the Criminal Intelligence Division in 1963.

I was assigned a security post, as were other plain clothes detectives, at the Trade Mart when President Kennedy was to have a big luncheon and political rally for the Democrats. Security was tight because he was the President and Vice-President Johnson was there, as well. We'd all been out there since 7:00 that morning and weren't anticipating any problems because no one was to get in without an invitation. But we had our orders: "We're not going to stand for any disruption or anything which would embarrass the President or the city."

Sometime that morning a man came up to me and wanted to know if he could wave the "Free Cuba" flag when the President came in, so I asked Captain Gannaway and Chief Stevenson if he could and was told, no. I was instructed to get the man's name and so forth, and at the end of my tour of duty that day write a report so that it could be sent through channels. So I got the man's name; he was very nice and readily agreed not to wave the flag once he was given an explanation, and that was the last that I saw of him.

Later one of our officers, Jack Brian, came by and told me that the President had been shot. I told him that I didn't think that it was very funny and didn't want to hear it because I had been on that post for several hours and was tired. He had the strangest look on his face and said, "I'm not kidding," so I knew that he was telling the truth. Shortly thereafter, Lieutenant Revill came by and got O.J. Tarver, Brian, and myself, along with Ike Lee of the FBI and all of us went in Revill's car down to the School Book Depository.

There, it was utter confusion! When we went into the building, our reasoning was to search from the top downward since we didn't know if the man might still be in the building. As we went up the elevator, I met Sergeant Flusche, and we were among other officers who got up into the attic looking for the suspect. It was filthy up there. I had on a brand new suit that day and ruined it. I was proud of that thing at the time, and it was the most expensive suit that I had, but it was never much good after that.

After finding nothing in the attic, we came down to the sixth floor. There we found rows and rows of boxes of books that were stacked as high or higher than an average man's head. Apparently Oswald had stacked cardboard boxes of school books for a gun rest. At first we thought that he had been waiting and eating because some chicken bones were discovered, but I think they found later that it was some other workman's food. Evidently Oswald had fired his shots, went down the row of books, threw the rifle over a stack of books, either went down the elevator or down the stairs, and then went out of the building.

At that time, there must have been around a dozen Dallas policemen and deputy sheriffs searching the floor. I knew a lot of them, but we didn't pass the time of day because our President had been shot. I had voted for Kennedy, though I wouldn't have the second time since I disagreed with his politics. I was sick inside because it was something that shouldn't have happened.

I was searching with the others on the sixth floor when the rifle was found. Being six or eight feet away, I was able to get a fairly good look at it. I wasn't all that familiar with military rifles, but it was a cruddy-looking rifle. I've heard that it was described as a Mauser, but I heard no one say that or that it was this or that. That was the first and only time that I saw it, though I've seen it later in pictures, and it appeared to be the same rifle. Contrary to what some have alleged, there certainly weren't two rifles found up there. All told, we were there for maybe an hour, give or take. By then Officer Tippit had been killed and Oswald had been apprehended, so Tarver, Brian, and I got into Lieutenant Revill's car, and we drove down to the basement of the city hall.

We parked and the four of us had gotten out when FBI Agent Hosty, who was either coming in or leaving, called Lieutenant Revill over accompanied by Jack Brian. Detective Tarver and I remained by the car since we weren't asked over, and we naturally didn't want to intrude. In a short while, Revill came over to us with the funniest look on his face, as if somebody had slapped him. He told us that either the FBI or the Bureau, or they, meaning the Bureau, knew about Oswald and didn't tell us. We then went up to our office on the second floor.

I marveled that the FBI didn't cover him. The people who had made the "Wanted For Treason" flyers and billboards and things like that I don't think were a great worry to us; they were covered to the best of my knowledge by maybe the Secret Service, the Bureau, or some of us.

By that time, we knew that the President was dead. Speaking for myself, I was still in a state of shock: It just didn't happen; our leader did not get killed, especially in our city.

When we arrived at our office, Lieutenant Revill, I guess, got with Captain Gannaway and informed him of the situation with Hosty in the basement. Gannaway would have then told him to write it up in what we called a "Special Report," or a "Dear Chief" letter. Apparently Curry then announced to the media what Revill had written. In the meantime, there wasn't anything else for us to do. The suspect had been apprehended, and the case was then in the hands of the Homicide and Robbery people.

We were puzzled at that time, but now it is my understanding that the Bureau, and in this case, Hosty, was trying to cultivate Oswald as an informant, mainly because he'd been to Russia, had come back, then become involved with the Fair Play for Cuba deal in New Orleans and Mexico. In my mind, it didn't happen, but it wouldn't be the first time that an informant has boomeranged on a police agency. We were angry about the Hosty incident at first, but after awhile we figured that it was just a mistake in judgment.

At that time, relations between the FBI and the Dallas Police Department were very simple: we gave, they took. It wasn't a two-way street. We fussed about how we always gave to the Bureau and didn't get anything in return, but that was an exaggeration to some extent. We did get some back, but we certainly didn't get back as much information as we gave. Of course, we didn't identify any of our informants to them. We kept that secret because we didn't want them swiping them from us because the Feds had more money than us since our budget was very, very limited, and they could pay their informants. But I didn't blame them for not revealing their sources either.

After the Hosty incident, Dallas policemen weren't permitted to attend the FBI Academy, and Mr. Hoover shut us off for information. I don't think that he was justified in doing it, but the flow of information didn't stop completely. The guys gave us what they could, and they knew that if they got caught that it was going to be their heads! But the whole affair was just a terrible mistake in judgment. They didn't know the man was capable of it. If they had, they would have absolutely covered him or put him under arrest or something. Mr. Hoover caught a lot of flak, and I was not a big fan of his, but I shudder to think what the Federal Bureau of Investigation would have been had it not been for a leader like him.

To make matters worse, I was later told that the Fort Worth police knew of Oswald and didn't tell us. Had we been informed of that, we would have had him covered like a blanket and, in my opinion, President Kennedy would not have been killed, at least not there, anyhow.

Meanwhile, after the assassination and the events following, I was numb and had forgotten to write up the report for Captain Gannaway about the man and the "Free-Cuba" flag at the Trade Mart.

After I got home, I remembered it, but with all the news about the President being on all the television stations, I was still way down. Another detective, a good friend of mine, Preston Parks, lived a few blocks from me, so I called and told him that I didn't want to go down to the office by myself to write up the report. He said, "Well, my cousin's here," whom I knew to be a nice guy.

So I said, "Well bring him along. All I'm going to do is write up the report and come on back."

So I picked them up in my car, and we went down to the office which was in a little building at Fair Park. As I was writing the report, the captain called and wanted to check the School Book Depository employee list with our files. We had handwritten, partial lists; some of them you couldn't read the names. But we did find one, a member of the American GI Forum. The captain then instructed me to bring the entire file down to his office.

When I arrived at City Hall, Preston and his cousin remained in the car as I went up to give the report to the captain. He asked, "Where's your partner?"

"He's down in the car on the street," I said.

"Get him up here!"

So I leaned out the window on the second story and hollered below, "Come on up! The captain wants to see you!" It was then that I informed Captain Gannaway of the man whose name appeared in our files.

Joe Rodriquez Molina, who worked at the School Book Depository, was the name that we had found on the list. He was a member of the American GI Forum which was an Hispanic organization. I don't think it had any Anglo members at all. We didn't keep files on the Democrats or Republicans, but we did on organizations that could cause problems. The American GI Forum was one of those that we wanted to be ready for if anything ever happened. We didn't want to get caught flat-footed, and Molina's name had been mentioned in a report that someone had submitted. That then evolved into the search warrant that Friday night.

At that time, we had no idea if there was more than one assassin or not. When we executed the search warrant on his house, Molina wasn't too happy with us being there, but he offered no resistance and we found nothing of value.

Personally, I didn't think that he was involved. I sympathized with the Free-Cubans because Castro had taken over in Cuba and had run out the good, decent people and had turned it into a Russian naval and spying base ninety miles off our shore. The few Free-Cubans that I knew in Dallas were honest, hardworking people who were not radical except that they wanted their Cuba back. I never heard any of them say anything bad about President Kennedy even though, from the reports, it sounded like we abandoned them at the Bay of Pigs.

Earlier that evening, when Detective Parks and I had gone up to the third floor where Homicide and Robbery, CID, and others were located, it was totally jammed with newsmen, still and motion cameras, and television cables running up to the chief's office. While there, I was maybe three or four feet from Oswald as they brought him down the hall to take him up to the jail elevator. But during that entire weekend, City Hall was total chaos! I'd never seen so many newspeople.

I said at the time, and I still believe, that there should have been a newsperson pool in the basement: one movie, one TV, one still camera, and one reporter. They could then share their film with other TV networks as well as their notes and still shots. Unfortunately, everybody was talking; people couldn't keep their mouths shut.

I had suggested to Lieutenant Revill that night that we seal the building and assign officers to each entrance. That way if a person came in it became a one on one deal; a uniformed officer would escort them to wherever they were going, stay with them till they left, then take them out of the building. I would have totaled the building off to the public. But they said that it was a public building and that they couldn't total it off. I said, "To hell they can't! We can do anything we have to right now!" Unfortunately, Chief Curry didn't have control over the situation. In my opinion, the fault lay with the politicians.

That Sunday morning I was in church and didn't see the transfer of Oswald. By the time I had gotten home and changed clothes, they were replaying it on TV. So I sat down by the phone and in about thirty minutes it rang, and I was called back to work where we were assigned to guard different city and civic leaders because some fools said that they were going to kill everybody.

My understanding is that they were allegedly going to take Oswald to the county jail that morning in an armored car; therefore, the exit ramp into the basement was blocked by the car. Thus everyone coming into the basement with business either in the city hall or the police building had to enter and exit off of Main Street with an officer being assigned to stop traffic to allow them to come out.

Jack Ruby is supposed to have gone to the Western Union office at the end of the block to wire money to one of his employees in Fort Worth. The officer at the top of the ramp at that particular time was letting another officer in a squad car out of the basement. As Jack walked down the street, he saw the officer stopping traffic and just went on into the basement. Now that's what I was told, that he went down the ramp. In fact, Jack may have said that himself. But he also could have come in through one of the other entrances and filtered in with the newsmen since, to my knowledge, not all the entrances were guarded.

In looking at the replays on TV, the basement was crowded with newsmen. There were enough policemen there and they had a corridor to bring Oswald out, but Jack blended in with the rest of them. L.C. Graves and J.R. Leavelle didn't see him until he fired the shot; by then it was too damn late!

As a result, we received an enormous amount of hate mail and Dallas became known as "The City of Hate." Lord, some of the mail was good! One letter that we received which I'll never forget, I don't know where it was from, began: "Greetings, Jew bastards, whore-mongers, and son of a bitches," and that was the nicest part of the whole letter!

We took these seriously, especially if they were from any local people. Then, after Oswald was shot, everybody got death threats, and Chief Curry had to move his people out of town. I spent the next two and a half months or so being part of the mayor's security, which was good duty.

The morale on the police department also suffered because we had allowed our President to be killed. We didn't stop it; therefore, we screwed up. In addition, the Oswald shooting was our foul-up from the word go. In my opinion, we looked like a bunch of "country oafs!" In fact, I've sometimes wondered why Chief Curry didn't have a heart attack and die that day. It appeared to me that he aged tremendously from the enormous amount of strain.

I knew Jack Ruby professionally and always figured that he was just a hustling nightclub owner trying to make big money, or at least as much as he could in Dallas. I'd been to his club a few times when I was in Vice. It was mostly burlesque, but there were also comics and sometimes the comics would sing and that sort of thing.

Jack seemed to like police officers, but I don't know if that was because he knew that we could close him down or what. To my knowledge, he was not a police informant. I'm told that some of the police officers received free drinks at his club, and they might have. But that didn't necessarily put them in a compromising position. A lot of restaurants would give the guys half-price meals or free meals to get them to come in. If you've got policemen coming in to your place of business, in uniform especially, then you're less likely to get hijacked. The owners figured that the cost of that meal to them was very cheap police protection. But to my knowledge, none of the police worked for him. We weren't allowed to work for any place that served alcohol. Jack could handle matters himself anyway. He was, I don't want to say, mean, but if you ran a tavern you couldn't be a Casper Milk Toast. Jack was a body-builder and very muscular.

The rumors that Jack was tied in with organized crime have been around for years. Jack was Jewish, and I'm sure that there were Jews in organized crime. But if he was, he didn't flash the big cars and the big money.

There was organized crime in Dallas at that time. They were all Italian like Joe Civello, who was at the Apalachin meeting. Joe Campisi was also suspected, but the problem was that if you had an Italian name, you were automatically associated with organized crime or the Mafia. I'm not aware that the Campisis were connected with organized crime. Carlos Marcello, who ruled New Orleans, has also been mentioned, but I wouldn't have known him if he walked up and introduced himself to me.

You see, CID was the Criminal Investigative Division which included detectives from Burglary and Theft, Auto Theft, Forgery, etc. They worked cases. But the main function of our section, the Intelligence Division, was to gather information. We made no arrests unless it was absolutely necessary. We talked to

informants, cultivated informants, found out information about
certain possible criminals, and tried to make a case on them or
supply information to other detectives that would enable them to
make a case. We liaisoned with two agents from the FBI at that
time: Bob Barrett and Ike Lee.

Our section was small, probably not more than ten or twelve
men including Lieutenant Revill. We covered all the radical
groups: right-wing and left-wing, although I was not working the
radicals at the time of the assassination. My partner, Jack Carroll,
and I were working the "subversive section," and we worked that
exclusively. I enjoyed the heck out of it. In fact, Jack was working
undercover in the American Nazi Party at the time. Most of the
other guys didn't want our job since they wanted to work on
known criminals.

We will never know for sure whether there was or was not a
conspiracy. Personally, I think that Oswald acted alone, and I
think that Ruby shot him so that he'd be a national hero, "I shot
the man who shot the President" and make a ton of money off of
it.

When the President's car came around the corner at a speed
of maybe under 10 M.P.H., Oswald had the dead wood on him and
was shooting almost straight down. He was ready with one and
popped him. I don't know which, but one shot got both the
President and the Governor, and the other I'm not sure as to
whether it went wild or what. I hunt and think that if I had the
rifle that I was familiar with that I could fire those three shots.

Some have asked how the killing of Officer Tippit could have
happened. Right after the President was killed it was total
confusion. J.D., who had to cover twice as much territory than
normal because we had so many officers on special assignment
that day, probably didn't regard Oswald as a threat. You don't
draw your pistol on someone who doesn't constitute a threat in
your mind at the time. You just don't do it; you can't do it. Also,
being that far away from the assassination site, honest people
were on the streets as well. Oswald just murdered him in cold
blood.

After the assassination, the Feds took over the investigation
and ultimately the Warren Commission was probably as thorough
as any federal investigating committee could be. We didn't
investigate any further, though I think especially those who knew

Oswald should have been investigated in depth by the Feds, not us, because we didn't have the jurisdiction to go into another city and openly investigate someone just for the heck of it.

Writers seem to emphasize the conspiracy angle, though. If I could make two or three million dollars off of a conspiracy deal, then I might be tempted to do it. Greed and publicity seem to be the motivation of many of these writers. I think that it's a hell of a way to make money by slandering your father's name, as in the Roscoe White story which was a BS deal.

Garrison, the D.A. down in New Orleans who tried Clay Shaw, I thought that was another BS deal from the start. He wasn't able to prove that the man had anything to do with it. I had no dealings with Garrison; someone else in the police department may have, but I doubt it. The general opinion in our Intelligence Division was that it was a big laugh, that he was trying to run for governor or something. Contrary to the movie *JFK*, which I have no intention of seeing, what Garrison is supposed to have said won't tell me anything because it didn't happen that way.

Following the assassination, Roy Westphal worked the radicals section of the Intelligence Division. Promoted to lieutenant in 1970, he spent his last nine years with the Dallas Police Department in uniform at the Northwest Division. After retiring from the department in 1984, he worked as a private investigator and as a part-time security guard. Roy Westphal died in March 1995.

GUS ROSE
Homicide Detective
Dallas Police Department

"I could see what I believed was the imprint of a rifle. Though it may have been partly suggestive, something was there that made me think there was a rifle there. When I picked it up, it fell limp across my arm empty. At that point, Marina let out an audible gasp. I turned and looked at her and noticed that she was wide-eyed and pale. I thought for a moment that she might be about to faint. I now believe that at that point, with the rifle not being there, the full realization had soaked in..."

Born in Arkansas, Gus Rose moved to Texas during the Second World War and graduated from Grand Prairie High School. Upon joining the Dallas Police Department in 1954, he worked in Patrol for four years, was promoted to detective, worked in Burglary and Theft for two and a half years, and was assigned to the Homicide and Robbery Bureau in 1960. Gus Rose continued in that roll at the time of the assassination.

———————————

The Homicide Division rotated every month so that half of us worked days and the other half worked evenings. As a result of that rotation, I was working the evening shift from 3:00 to 11:00 the day that the President came through. I didn't hear of any extraordinary security measures being set up thus we continued our normal rotation. The Secret Service provided security for the visit, and they'd come in and correlate the activity with the local agencies. So I assumed they had what they deemed necessary.

I was downtown at an early lunch, had left the restaurant and gone to my car when I heard on the radio that the President had been shot. So I quickly got downtown, parked my car, went to the Homicide office and reported for duty.

When I got there, there were quite a few people that had already been brought into the Homicide office from the Book Depository site. These people were witnesses, or possible witnesses, that needed to be interviewed by officers. The procedure was to interview those witnesses and then to take a written statement, thus I began to interview a man who told me that he had seen the assassination while standing at the front part of the motorcade. He said that he had heard the shot and had looked up and saw a man in the sixth floor window and felt that he could identify the guy if he saw him again. Of the last two shots that were fired, one of those struck the President in the head, and he showed me where a fragment of skull had struck him in the leg.[*]

During this interview, I had a conversation with the dispatcher who told me about Officer Tippit being murdered, and he informed me that officers had arrested the suspect and would be en route to Homicide with him. In a short while, there was a large noise at the front of the office. As I looked up, I saw officers coming in with a man handcuffed behind his back who was obviously under arrest. He was talking loudly and was sweaty looking, so I stopped what I was doing and went to see what they were doing and what they had. It was explained to me that they had the guy that had killed Tippit. Now, up to that point, I didn't have any reason to believe that there was a connection between the Tippit shooting and the murder of the President; in fact, I didn't even think about it. I just knew that he had supposedly killed Tippit.

So Officer Stovall and I took the man into the interrogation room. I asked him who he was, but he wouldn't tell me. He refused to give me a name. I then searched him and found two pieces of identification in his pocket: one had the name Alec Hidell, and the other had the name Lee Oswald. So I said, "Which one of these are you?" He gave me a real strange look and said, "Well,

---

[*] Rose probably is referring to James Tague, although the details vary from Tague's account. See Tague's narrative, pages 109-115.

you're the cop, you figure it out!" That was his term. He became pretty ugly and cussed a little in talking to me as I began to question him. He lied to me about every one of the questions. We hadn't established his identity for certain, so I then asked him where he lived; he gave me a fictitious address. When I asked him where he worked, he said, "I'm a printer. I work in a local printing company." That's the way he put it. I asked him if he had ever had any military service; he said "no." I asked him if he had any family in the area, and he again said "no." So he continually lied, though that's not necessarily a bad thing.

When you're interrogating somebody, you try to establish a rapport with them, and you set about to do that without getting into the actual case. I did ask him about his arrest and he said, "Oh, I was just sitting in the theater and officers came in and planted a gun on me and accused me of shooting somebody. I don't know nothing about that!"

So it was that type of interrogation with him. When I first saw him, he looked okay except for being sweaty and the injury over one eye. He did settle down somewhat and became less nervous in this short interrogation, though he was still combative with his answers. I found him to be arrogant and belligerent and almost in a state of confusion. He denied emphatically that he'd done anything wrong, almost overdenial. I've been involved in lots of interrogations, and it was almost overkill on his denials. His attitude was "I haven't done anything; I've been framed," which wasn't bad from the standpoint of interrogation. We might have been able to overcome that. I knew, in my mind, that he had killed Tippit, but I didn't suspect anything about the President.

Then, after a while, Captain Fritz knocked at the door and told me this; I remember it just like it was yesterday: "We just got back from the Book Depository and there's an employee that's missing. They think he's the suspect in the murder of the President. I want you to get some officers to go with you and find that missing employee."

I said, "Well, I would, Captain, but I've got the man in here that killed Tippit." He said, "Well, I'll have someone else handle that. I want somebody to go with you and y'all go find this missing employee."

"Okay, what's his name?"

He said, "His name's Lee Oswald."

At that point, I snapped real fast. "Oh, hey, I think this is him. I found some ID on him that said Lee Oswald, and I believe that'll be him." At that point he instructed me to locate any family of Oswald's that was in the area and bring them in for questioning. I didn't finish with the witness.

Immediately after that, Captain Fritz gave me an address where Oswald's wife supposedly was. That's all he gave me. So I left the witness sitting and my notes on my desk and got Officers Adamcik and Stovall to go with me to that address which was located in Irving. We also took two deputy sheriffs with us since the address was outside the city of Dallas and, as was customary with me, parked our cars a little beyond the house down the street.

As we walked toward the house, I could see that the door was open while the screen door was closed. I could also see a light flickering, apparently from a television in the room. When I approached the door, without knocking, this woman inside said, "Come on in. I've been expecting you."

I didn't identify myself, stepped inside and asked, "Why were you expecting me?"

"Oh," she said, "I could tell you were a police officer, and I knew someone would be out here to talk to us about Lee as soon as I saw where the President was shot from." Now, at that time, there was no mention made of his arrest because he had not yet been properly identified, and the name of the arrested person had not been released.

I asked, "Are you Mrs. Oswald?" "Oh, no, I'm Ruth Paine," she said. "Mrs. Oswald's here but you can't talk to her."

"Well, why not," I asked.

"Oh, she doesn't speak any English."

"Well, what does she speak?"

"Oh, she's a Russian citizen, she responded, "She speaks only Russian." I was stunned because I wasn't expecting that at all!

"Well, how do you talk to her?"

And she said, "I can interpret for you. I'm a student of the Russian language" is the way she put it.

With that, Marina came into the room, and I asked her some questions which were interpreted by Ruth Paine. Knowing that a rifle had been discovered on the sixth floor of the Book Depository right after the assassination, I asked her, "Does your husband own a rifle?" When she responded that he did, I asked,

"Can you show it to me?" She said yes and motioned for me to follow her, which I did into the kitchen part of the house.

She opened a door leading to the garage and pointed to a blanket which was rolled up and said, "That's his rifle."

I stepped out into the garage, walked over and picked it up. I could see what I believed was the imprint of a rifle. Though it may have been partly suggestive, there was something there that made me think a rifle was there. When I picked it up, it fell limp empty across my arm. At that point, Marina let out an audible gasp. I turned and looked at her and noticed that she was wide-eyed and pale. I thought for a moment that she might be about to faint. I now believe that at that point, with the rifle not being there, the full realization had soaked in.

Ruth Paine didn't say anything at that point. She was fairly cooperative until about the time we were ready to leave. In fact, she invited us to search the premises, which we did. With this invitation we didn't need a warrant to search the house. Both were visibly nervous, and I understood that, especially considering officers coming into their home.

Oswald had stored a lot of stuff out in that garage. He had a large canvas bag with numerous items in it including: pamphlets, writings, Fair Play for Cuba Committee materials, film and pictures. I also found the photograph of Oswald standing in front of a house holding a rifle and a paper in his hands. In addition to the photograph, we actually found the negatives, so this silly thing about people saying it was doctored is a bunch of nonsense. In fact, there were negatives for all the pictures that we found. What happened to the negatives, I have no idea.

We also found a Minox camera with film in it. It was a little bitty thing, and the way you rolled the film, you just pulled it apart and the film advanced. The film looked like just two little deals that just sat down in there. I didn't know much about it, but when I opened it, there was film in it. The FBI later asked me to change my report to say that it was a Minox light meter, but I never did.

It was definitely not a light meter, no question. Stovall and I initialed the evidence and dated it so that it could be used as evidence that I could identify in court as something I had recovered. Stovall, the other officers and me all saw this property, and it was a Minox camera. I don't understand why the FBI still denied this, but it was released along with all the property to the FBI after Oswald was killed.

While we were there, Michael Paine came in. I don't know that he could have seen us there since our cars weren't parked directly in front of the house. I heard the door open and close as he came in and heard him holler to Ruth Paine, "I'm here! I thought I would come out and help you. You might need some help." He didn't see us since we were in the back part of the house. Later he got quiet and didn't have much to say after that.

This was the only time that I saw Marina and the Paines. We transported them to City Hall in Dallas and never saw them again. During the trip, Ruth talked; Marina had the two children and didn't have much to say. Marina was upset with us because she wanted to change clothes, claiming that she wasn't dressed properly to go downtown. But I wouldn't allow her to change because there wasn't a female officer there to supervise her, so I made her go downtown in the clothes she was wearing. She was very upset about that.

While we were at the house in Irving, Wesley Frazier's sister, Linnie Randle, came in and talked to us. She told us, "You might want to talk to my brother. He took him to work this morning," meaning Oswald. I said okay, so when I got back to the office I turned the witnesses I had: Michael and Ruth Paine, Marina Oswald and the two children, over to Captain Fritz.

I informed Fritz about Wesley and was told, "Well, go find him and take a statement from him." So I left again to find Wesley. I learned that he was visiting his father in a local hospital, found out where, and went out and got him, then took him back to his home, and with his permission did a quick search of his room. He had a rifle which we brought in, but it wasn't the right caliber. We checked to see if it had recently been fired, which it hadn't, so it was later released.

Wesley told us that normally Oswald would sometimes ride with him on weekends to the Paine residence. Ruth had told him that she wouldn't let him stay there except occasionally to visit his wife. But most of the time she didn't want him coming out there. She had described him as a "real nut." Wesley also told me that he was a "real nut" and used those very words. He said that on Thursday, he said yesterday, of course, Oswald came up and wanted a ride out to Irving with him. Wesley asked, "Why? Usually you don't go except on weekends."

Oswald replied, "Oh, there's something out there I need to pick up."

So Wesley said, "I let him off in front of the Paine's house on Fifth Street and went on home" and told him, `I'll pick you up in the morning.' He continued, "Next morning I was getting ready to go work, and as I was starting to go out to the car I looked out the window and saw him coming up the sidewalk. He didn't wait for me to pick him up; he came there. He was carrying something large wrapped in brown wrapping paper. When I walked out, I said, 'What's you got there?' "

Oswald said, "It's curtain rods for my apartment on Beckley."

Wesley said to me, "I didn't think it was curtain rods, but I didn't want to argue with him. When we got to work, Lee got that package out, and I asked him, 'Why don't we lock that under the trunk and when we get off you can get it?' "

Oswald replied, "No, I need it here." Then he took it in with him. On the sixth floor, the rifle was later found with three empty cartridges and the brown wrapping paper.

After I took his statement, Captain Fritz told me, "Go ahead and take him home." It was late, probably around midnight, when I started to Irving with him. On the trip back, I received a call on the police radio which told me to return to the office. There Captain Fritz told me to get a polygraph examiner and polygraph Wesley to see if he was telling the truth. So I got R.D. Lewis at home and went over the statements with him after he arrived. He talked to Wesley and then polygraphed him while I watched through a one-way mirror. It wasn't an ideal situation for a polygraph, but it wasn't necessarily bad either because Wesley was a straight guy. He seemed totally straight forward and passed the polygraph with flying colors.

Most of us worked until about 3:00 or 4:00 o'clock Saturday morning. I went home about 4:00, slept only a couple of hours, then got up and ready for work. We spent the first part of the morning logging all that property that we'd brought in which we called evidence. Captain Fritz told me to get a search warrant and go back and search the house again. So I got the search warrant, went back out to Irving, searched the Paine residence, and brought in another large amount of material. One of the things I found there was a picture which showed the back of a two-story house with a '57 Chevy with the license plate having been cut out sitting in the driveway. We later identified it as General Walker's home.*

That Saturday afternoon I sat in on an interrogation session when Captain Fritz brought Oswald in for further questioning. Previously, he had told Fritz that he had never owned a gun, so I had taken the negative downstairs, had it enlarged, and brought it back to Fritz when Oswald was brought in for interrogation.#

In an interrogation session, you never just start hammering a guy with questions when he comes in; you try to settle him down with small talk. After a brief exchange, Fritz said, "Now you told me yesterday that you'd never owned a gun."

And he said, ""That's right. I never owned a gun."

Fritz said, "Okay, I want to show you this picture. How do you explain this?"

At that point, Oswald became very visibly shaken, red in the face and totally angry. "Well, that's not me," he responded, "Somebody has superimposed my face on the picture on that body!"

"Well, then it is your face?" Fritz said.

Oswald responded, "No, it's not even my face. It's just somebody that kind of looks like me." He never admitted that it was him.

He was calm until he got to that point. In fact, he was calm until you mentioned anything about the shooting of Tippit or Kennedy, then he became uncalm. He loved to talk about how great Russia was and how he loved the life there.

To me, he seemed like a real radical nut. I've talked to all kinds of people and worked hundreds of murder cases; some of them are just as rational as we are today. But he was just a radical nut. When I saw interviews with John Hinckley after he shot Reagan, it was so reminiscent of the way Oswald acted during some of his interviews. I'm convinced that they were two of a kind.

---

* This photo was reproduced in Jesse Curry's book, *The Assassination File*. However, the license tag was not cut out, indicating that the deletion occurred sometime after the photo had been in police custody.

Rose is referring to the famous "backyard photo" taken at Oswald's Oak Cliff apartment on Neely Street in March 1963.

I worked until about 2:00 Sunday morning then Fritz sent some of us home and told us to return around noon. So I went home, slept about three or four hours, got up, showered, and was having breakfast when I saw the shooting of Oswald on television. I didn't think much about it when I saw Leavelle and Graves come out with Oswald. But when I saw this figure step up and shoot him, I didn't hesitate. I immediately slipped on my coat, came to work and was instructed to obtain a search warrant to search Jack Ruby's apartment. That search revealed absolutely nothing in the way of evidence or anything that would show why he shot Oswald.

Later in the day I was present during some of the interrogations of Ruby. He seemed shocked. He couldn't seem to understand why there was such a big deal about his killing the guy that killed the President.

Ruby was homosexual and an unsavory little character. Most of the officers, contrary to much which has been written, didn't have anything to do with him. Maybe some of them went down to his club because he let them in free, but I never did, which is why I didn't know him. I knew of him because I'd heard his name mentioned, but since I didn't drink and didn't hang around those places, I didn't have good feelings for those club owners anyway.

There were some really bad things that went on at City Hall that weekend which allowed somebody like Ruby to shoot Oswald. On Friday, when I got back to City Hall with the Paines and Marina Oswald, I called Captain Fritz from the basement and told him that I had Marina Oswald downstairs. He said, "Well, I'll have some officers try to help you get them up to the third floor to our office." When the elevator door opened on the third floor, there was just a sea of people, mostly reporters, out there shoulder to shoulder. You couldn't hardly move. We were pushing and shoving to get through while they were sticking microphones in our faces hollering, "Who are you? What did you have to do with this? What's your name? Why are you here?" As we pushed and pushed, it took a long time and a lot of hassle to get through this crowd where I found two uniformed officers guarding the door to the Homicide office. I was glad to get inside out of that terrible, terrible thing. That was really a bad scene!

Looking back, the City Hall should have been secured. There should have been no one allowed on that third floor except officers on duty. Reporters should have been placed in some special area and given thirty minute updates or something, but that never occurred.

At that time, I think the chief, Jesse Curry, was way in over his head. I don't think that he had the ability that was needed to be police chief. He was probably a good officer down in the ranks, but he was way over his head in that high of an administrative position; therefore, he was attempting to do things he wasn't capable of doing. As a result, some of the lower officers probably should have secured City Hall. I'm not sure who, but it was definitely a disaster of the magnitude that would require the chief officer to be at the scene. Our previous chief, Carl Hansson, a good administrator, probably would have turned it over to those same lower officers. I think that everybody was thinking that someone else was taking care of the problem and nobody did at that particular time.

Captain Fritz, on the other hand, was ahead of his time in law enforcement. When he joined the police department, maybe forty years earlier, it wasn't common for officers to be well educated. He had a college education and was probably the most honorable person I was ever around in my life. He was a straight-laced perfect gentleman who never used improper language. Always 100 percent truthful and straight forward, he wasn't the least bit political. He was above average in intelligence and understood people really well. He seemed to be able to always know when people were not truthful with him. He had an insight into people that way.

Captain Fritz used good proper interrogation techniques which he had developed and had been so successful with. I know that it's hard to teach that since I've been teaching interrogation for 25 years. He was a good interrogator because he was able to analyze people quickly and really well. He sort of disarmed you with his manner. You try to teach that and it's difficult.

You hear criticism about how the case was handled from people that don't know anything about law enforcement or interrogation. One of the criticisms pertained to our not using a stenographer or tape recording the sessions with Oswald. Even if we had wanted to, we didn't have the equipment to do so.

First: If you have to tell him you're recording his conversation, then he's not going to confess to anything to you. Second: You don't sit down and write what he's telling you; you don't transcribe it as he talks because you still will lose him. He becomes so inhibited and careful at what he says that you don't do any good with your interrogation. Your desk should not be cluttered; it should be totally clean with no writing material being visible. Aside from that, if you were going to tape the interrogation and not tell him you were taping it, you're inhibited and careful and not as alert at how you talk to him, so you don't tape it. I've taken probably a thousand confessions and I've never taped one, never!

In addition, if the interrogations had been taped, and I'm not sure that it would have even been legal to do so, but it certainly never could have been used as evidence. He could have admitted to murdering the President and you couldn't have used it. He could have admitted it verbally to us in the room and we still couldn't have used it as evidence in court in Texas. In Texas in 1963, for a confession to be legal evidence in court, it had to be reduced in writing and signed in front of a witness. I think Oswald would have talked whenever he deemed the time was proper for him. We had an excellent circumstantial case against Oswald, but on top of that, there were witnesses who had identified his face in the window and his fingerprint on the rifle. We would have had an outstanding case on him if we'd have continued and he'd been tried. He would have been convicted without question.

Oswald, I think, was a typical political assassin who thoroughly and carefully planned to shoot the President. However, I don't think that he planned to escape, no more than Hinckley planned to escape or Lynette Fromme or Sirhan Sirhan. When he came out of that Book Depository, he seemed to be in a total state of confusion; he wasn't sure what he was going to do. He didn't get caught up there; now he was outside and he wasn't sure where he was going. He got on a bus, but it wasn't going anywhere. It sat there and didn't move. He finally got off the bus and left. You don't commit a major offense in Dallas and plan to ride away from the scene on a bus. He's in a state of confusion.

Ruby, on the other hand, acted on a spur of the moment. It wasn't unusual that he carried that gun. In fact, he'd been in jail for carrying a gun. In the back of his mind, I think he had the idea that he would be a national hero. I don't think he planned it. It was announced that Oswald would be transferred at a certain time. But at that time, Ruby was at his apartment in Oak Cliff. If he was going to kill Oswald, and planned to do it, he'd had to have been down there an hour before he was. Instead, he came down to the Western Union office, which was in the same block as City Hall, mailed a money order, and was on his way back to his car. Roy Vaughn, who was working the entry ramp off of Main Street, stepped out in the street to stop traffic so that a police car could go out the ramp as part of the transfer. Vaughn was innocent as a lamb in that whole deal. He polygraphed with the FBI twice and passed both of them. He didn't have anything to do with it. Ruby saw the ramp open, looked down and saw all those lights flashing with all those people and commotion and walked down the ramp. As Captain Fritz, Graves and Leavelle led Oswald out. Ruby then drew his pistol, walked up and shot him.

Throughout that weekend I don't believe any of us was aware of the national and international attention. I was aware of the massive job we had to do and was just intent on doing my job the best I could. We were all looking to Captain Fritz for direction. He was the boss and a good one. The Oswald shooting, I think, was a tremendous loss to him. In 1963, he was still at the top of his profession. It wasn't until around 1965 or 1966 that he began to decline. Certainly he had his detractors who were jealous or whatever. I'd beware of the guy who everybody said something good about.

He was criticized for sitting on the evidence that weekend and not sharing the information with Chief Curry and others. But in a major case, while it's still intense, it's hard to pass that along to somebody that's not involved in the case. It was probably common within the department. I'm sure that once it had begun to slow down Fritz would have briefed them. Fritz took such a direct active role in the investigation that he didn't have time to brief the chief.

During that interrogation with Oswald which I attended, there were two of us from Homicide, two FBI agents, and one or two from the Secret Service. This was very bad policy. Captain Fritz was pressured into that. An interrogator, ideally, will be alone with the subject and doesn't need another person. The subject will be freer to talk to one person, one on one, than if there's other people sitting around listening. In addition, you can't keep his attention. If I'm sitting and talking to someone, I can't hold their attention if there's people lighting a cigarette or scuffling their shoes on the floor, or coughing, or turning in their chairs. He's distracted slightly and I need his whole attention if I'm interrogating him. Captain Fritz knew that; he was a good interrogator. But he allowed himself to do that because of the press of time on that case and in the spirit of cooperation with the FBI.

Prior to the assassination, cooperation had generally been good between the FBI and the Dallas Police Department. There had always been some friction, though, in Homicide because we answered bank robberies, murder, rape, and kidnapping offenses, and Captain Fritz was very possessive of those cases. The FBI, in many cases, felt that they had equal jurisdiction. But in the President's assassination, they did not have equal jurisdiction. It was our case because it was not, at that time, a federal crime.

Captain Fritz didn't want to transfer Oswald publicly. I was present during part of the discussion when he was really adamant on not making the transfer public, but he was overruled by his boss, Jesse Curry. The majority of the time the sheriff would come and get the prisoners, but this transfer was done at the order of the chief, and it was done for show and media purposes. It should not have been. It was not unusual for us to occasionally transfer one to the county jail ourselves, especially if it were a high profile case. I'd done it before the assassination and since. But it was unusual that they would announce the time of the transfer publicly and then make a media event out of it. If Oswald had been transferred at 4:00 o'clock in the morning secretly, nothing would have happened.

Fritz was hurt over the situation badly. When Oswald was killed, we built a case against Jack Ruby and we filed for murder, but that didn't satisfy. The case hung on and everything was transferred to the FBI, thus he was cut out of the investigation at that point. Captain Fritz had a tremendous amount of pride. For example, before he was ready to fly to Washington to testify to the Warren Commission the chief ordered him to not wear his Western-style hat. He had worn that style hat throughout his whole career; it was his symbol. If you were a Homicide detective, you wore one of those white Western style hats. So he was ordered to go out and buy a snap brim hat which he had never worn in his life. He felt whipped down. His decline, I don't think, had anything to do with age; I think it was due to the tremendous,

tremendous loss and pressure over the investigation. Curry, on the other hand, had a drinking problem, and his slide downward probably had more to do with alcohol than the assassination.

Dallas itself never recovered from it, even today. There's always that lingering thing about it, and so it brought a stigma on the city, as well as the police department. Personally, I think it helped me in a way. I've used the experience in my career as an officer. From 1963 till 1981 I worked a lot of major cases, and on any one of them, there couldn't be as much pressure that offset the pressure that we'd gone through with this thing.

Unfortunately, on every murder case, especially every high profile murder case, there'll always be people that will come forward and say, "You've done it wrong," or "You've got something wrong," and they've got a better idea. It's those same people that dearly love those mysteries, especially those kind where the writer throws out all these clues so that the reader is going to believe that someone else did it. Then they'll be able to come up with some strange occurrence that proved the right one. It's too simple for those writers or film makers to believe that Oswald was a nut and a lone assassin. They like to make a mystery out of it. Some of them, I think, come up with an outlandish theory which will gain for them notoriety as well as money. Oliver Stone, with his movie *JFK* made a fortune out of it. There's only two things that I'd say were a 100 percent factual about the movie: the date of the offense and the name of the victim, and that's it.

What many don't realize is that in homicide investigations where you are relying on people to tell you things, you never know what their motives are, and thus you'll find inconsistencies. If you would take this case and lay it out like you were going to present it in court, you'd be a 100 percent happy with it. You, as a juror, would find him guilty. There'd be no reasonable doubt that he did it and did it alone. But if you're going to allow as evidence, and you're going to call it evidence, things that would never be allowed in a court of law as evidence, then you can see it anyway you want. People call it evidence when it really isn't evidence.

The police look at a combination of eyewitness testimony and physical evidence. If the eyewitness doesn't match the physical evidence, or the physical evidence doesn't match other evidence, then something's wrong. If all this ties together, you're okay. At the time of the assassination, that evening we didn't have anybody telling us that somebody else did it and probably never would have if Oswald had lived.

In the 1970's, Rose investigated the Randall Adams' Case which eventually became the subject of the PBS documentary film *The Thin Blue Line*. Gus Rose retired after 27 years with the Dallas Police Department in 1981 and became captain in charge of Criminal Investigation for the Dallas County Sheriff's Department under the then sheriff, Don Byrd. Following a four-year stint at the sheriff's department, Rose became the chief deputy constable in Garland, Texas, until his retirement in 1995.

HARRY D. HOLMES
U.S. Postal Inspector

"In the case of Oswald, I don't think that he would have ever confessed; he was that adamant. He was so direct. He'd look you right in the eye and ask you a question. He had an uncanny ability to determine or guess when I had evidence or when I was fishing... In fact, I thought in my own head that probably in Russia he had been trained to evade questions and be able to keep himself composed to guard what he wanted to keep secret..."

Born in Indian Territory in 1905, after having moved to Kansas City in 1917, Harry Holmes worked his way through his early school years in a toy factory, a bakery, and as a lamplighter. After taking an examination, he eventually became a mail handler and attended school part-time to become a CPA and later attended dental college. Following the bombing of Pearl Harbor, Holmes, who was still working with the post office, was encouraged to take the postal inspector's examination. Upon acceptance, he was stationed first in Lake Charles, Louisiana, then to Monroe, Louisiana, and eventually to Dallas in 1948. Because of his position with the post office, Holmes was responsible for much of the investigative work in tracking down the money order used to purchase the rifle which was allegedly used in the assassination. He was also a central figure in the last interrogation of Oswald shortly before he was murdered in the basement of the Dallas City Hall.

There were about five or six inspectors in town that day. My office windows in the Terminal Office Building at the corner of Main and Houston Streets faced Dealey Plaza. That morning I saw them put up barricades and saw the police getting lined up along the curbs, as well as other preparations for the motorcade. I noticed the windows across the plaza at the School Book Depository, which was maybe the length of a football field away, and remarked to one of the four secretaries, "Well, look at all those open windows. Wouldn't that be a nice place to take a crack at the President?"

When the motorcade came by, I was watching with a pair of 7x50 binoculars when all of a sudden there was a CRACK!... CRACK!...CRACK!! All of us thought that somebody was throwing firecrackers. We just never dreamed that anybody would be shooting at him.

Anyway, about the first or second crack, I wouldn't know which, there was just a cone of blood and corruption that went up right in the back of his head and neck. I thought it was red paper on a firecracker. It looked like a firecracker lit up which looks like little bits of red paper as it goes up. But in reality it was his skull and brains and everything else that went up perhaps as much as six or eight feet. Just like that! Then just a minute later another crack, and everybody fell down like they were ducking firecrackers.

If I'd looked up, I'd have been the hero of the century. But I didn't and thus didn't see Oswald in the window. I did see the First Lady as she immediately bailed out. They said she cradled him in her lap and all that; well that's a lot of hooey! She just immediately crawled over the back seat and out over the turtleback. The Secret Service agent, whom I talked to personally two or three times after that, told me that Jacqueline immediately said, "Oh, my God, they're going to kill us all!" And over the back she went!

He just grabbed her as the guys up front said, "Hang on! We're headed for the hospital!" And they took off! He just shoved her and literally threw her back into the seat as he spread-eagled on the turtleback.

As I scanned the plaza, everybody was frantic and frenzied, falling down on top of their wives and little kids to protect them. It was just as many of them have stated. I realized when they took off that he'd been shot, especially as we were listening to the same events on the radio.

I kept the binoculars around to see if anybody left the area, especially the parking area and the railroad tracks where a guy would likely try to escape. I remember also a big chain link fence in back of the School Book Depository. I also noticed a lot of people lined up on the Triple Underpass, but I never saw anybody in a hurry to get away as if they were trying to escape, and I watched the area with those high powered binoculars the whole time.

There was just a bunch of scared people there milling around and looking for debris. One of my secretaries was one of them. She was standing just 15-20 feet from where he was shot. After the cars left, then there was just a mob milling around aimlessly, not headed in any particular direction. It wasn't but two, three, or four minutes before police and detectives were running out there. In fact, the sheriff's office was right there, and at least 200 deputy sheriffs and police officers were looking out their windows.

I had an open line to Washington during that whole time. The chief inspector asked me that evening how many shots had been fired. I told him, "You know, I couldn't tell you to save my life." Upon reflection, though, I'd say it was three or four. Anything else I might say would be just from reading.

It was hard to tell because the echo would reverberate between those four buildings: the Texas School Book Depository, the courthouse, the sheriff's office, and my building. You just couldn't tell where anything was coming from. It could have even been somebody from the jail there at the sheriff's office.

Right after the assassination I called the boss in Fort Worth, who already had the chief on the phone line in Washington because everything was chaos. He told me, "Well, you're in charge of the investigation over there for whatever they need in the way of postal inspectors' help or cooperation. The entire manpower that we have over there is at your disposal and we'll send more if you need them."

All the federal agencies would band together though they didn't know what to do. Actually, for a while, they thought the shots came from my building, the Terminal Annex. So immediately we interviewed everybody on the floors on that side of the building to see what they knew or had seen because there was a possibility that it came from the post office. Of course, that was cleared up in a hurry.

I had the radio on all the time but there wasn't much that I could do. I had called Captain Fritz and told him, "If there is anything I can do, why, I'm available and I've got plenty of men available."

He said, "No, the FBI's working on it and the Secret Service has charge of it, but I'll remember, Harry." I had worked closely with Fritz; he thought that I was a good inspector, and I knew that he was a good investigator. He was one of the best that we ever had here. He was kind of an unsophisticated country-type who had different ways, but nothing got by him.

Apparently, as I later learned, after Oswald had left the Book Depository he got on a bus and the bus had gotten stalled. He then went over and caught a cab and went to his room over in Oak Cliff. Later the radio blared that a policeman had been killed off of Jefferson Avenue. A shoe salesman, who was probably the owner of the shop on Jefferson which was four or five doors down from the Texas Theater, was listening to that broadcast when he saw a man standing out in front of his door. The broadcast mentioned that the policeman had been shot by a fellow that answered the description of a missing employee at the Book Depository, and the man in front of his door looked like the same guy. The shoe salesman then stepped out of his store and watched the man as he ran up the street and ducked into the theater. He said, "I went up to the ticket window and asked the lady, `Did that fellow buy a ticket?' And he told her, "Well, he looked to me like this fellow that shot the policeman down the street."

I don't think that she even knew about that. Anyway, all of a sudden the police were all over the place. They came in the back, front, and side doors, turned the theater lights on, and there he was sitting there. As one of the policemen started going down the aisle toward him, the suspect jerked out a gun and leveled it at him. As the policeman lunged, Oswald pulled the trigger and the hammer came down on the webbing of his thumb. That's the reason the policeman wasn't killed. That was the first time I heard of Oswald.

Everybody in the post office had a little radio going, and about an hour after they had taken him into custody, one of the window clerks came up to my office on the fifth floor and said,

"Mr. Holmes, you know this Lee Harvey Oswald has a post office box right here in the Terminal Annex."

I said, "Oh, is that so?"

He said, "Yeah, we ran into him about a month or so ago." So I got the number and immediately put a postal inspector standing unobtrusively somewhere around the lobby watching that box twenty-four hours a day. They didn't leave that until Oswald was dead. That was really the first official act I took.

Nobody at that time knew what was going on. The whole country thought that this was just the thing to tee-off anarchy throughout the United States. There were all kinds of rumors. The only safeguard I could think of at the time was to put a watch on the box. If somebody came to get mail out of it, I needed to know who it was.

If somebody did open the box, he would have been apprehended, interrogated, taken to the office, identified, and his background checked and turned over to probably the Secret Service or the FBI. They would have done what they wanted with him because he would have had something to do with Oswald. But nobody ever took a piece of mail out of that box at any time until Oswald was dead, and then his wife and her attorney took charge of the mail. Actually all the mail came up to my office, and she would come in with the attorney and pick up this mail.

All kinds of crank letters came in, not necessarily addressed to her, but just to Dallas—vile letters and hate mail. I turned those pertaining to her over to her and her attorney and she signed for them. She also received packages. The Secret Service flew down a contraption nearly the size of a coffin in which they would put a package in the top drawer or something there and X-ray it or fluoroscope it. It's a lot more sophisticated now, but at that time I'd just stack the packages in that room with this contraption and they'd check them and then give them to her. All of them were just ordinary packages postmarked from the United States and they would range in size from a shoe box to smaller sizes; there weren't any big packages. A package the size of a pair of boots might be the largest we received. Each time she came in she had her attorney with her since she couldn't speak hardly any English at that time.

In fact, postal employees forwarded all the mail to my office that had anything to do with the assassination no matter how it was addressed. One particular letter was addressed to "Marguerite Oswald, Mother of Killer!" Included in the letter was a picture of Oswald on the front of *Time* magazine. It said, "Momma, why didn't you raise me like you should have? I'm in Hell forever because of you," then it got into obscenities after that.

Somebody had gotten real busy stuffing mail boxes around various parts of town prior to the assassination. Hate circulars such as "John F. Kennedy: Wanted For Treason" and "Wanted For Impeachment: Earl Warren, Chief Justice" were printed up and distributed. Those were turned in to me and lent credence to the idea of conspiracy.

Another piece of mail was sent to the employees of the Dallas, Texas Post Office. It was brought up to me and was a bunch of Bible quoting gibberish about Oswald. There were also references to Senator Goldwater. But it was all just hate mail which somehow ended up in my files. Some of the stuff wasn't addressed to anybody in particular.

Oswald had a box originally in, I think, Fort Worth, then they went to New Orleans where he opened another. When he left there, he went to the Mexican Consulate in Mexico City, but they wouldn't grant him a visa, so he ended up coming back to Dallas. During that time, the easiest way to keep up with the mail, as in Oswald's case, was to have your mail with a forwarding notice from one box to another. She had to go from Fort Worth to New Orleans to the Dallas main office, then down to the Terminal Annex. I guess there were four different post office boxes that he had.

When we opened his box at the Terminal Annex, I would take the mail to my office. It was a small box which I would say contained not more than half a dozen pieces of mail including a Russian magazine he subscribed to and some letters from Russia. But I do remember the Russian magazine which he received once a week for a while after that. Also found in his box were two softback books: *N.S. Khrushchev: To Avert A War* and *Socialism and Communism*, both being so-called review copies which were apparently circulated from Wacker Drive in Chicago.

Shortly after the assassination the FBI assigned a man to sit in my office to, I assume, second guess me. You just don't know what the FBI is up to. I never was an admirer of the FBI, not that there was any jealousy between us, but I always felt like they didn't rank. For example, in the case of a postal inspector, when I would pick up a suspect I could take him to a state or federal court, or I could turn him loose; I might even just sit on my bottom. But the FBI couldn't do anything but report it to headquarters and they would tell them what to do. Individually they didn't know themselves what they're up to; they had to ask somebody higher up. They had no independent opinion or judgment about anything. We did and would carry it to the bitter end. But in this case, I knew the guy assigned to my office, had worked with him around Dallas for a long time, and were good friends, so I didn't try to hold anything back from him.

The next morning, on Saturday, when I came in, the inspector who was on duty in the lobby watching the boxes told me, "You've got an inspector up there sitting in your office."

I said, "Well, I guess it's so and so;" I've since forgotten his name.

When I arrived in the office, he said, "Harry, if you wanted to find an original postal money order, where would you go to get it?"

I said, "Well, Washington if you knew what number it was and could identify it."

He said, "You mean it's not in Kansas City?"

"No," I replied, "it used to be. It was out on Hardesty Street in Kansas City until about two months ago. I don't know exactly why but they transferred the money order center back to Washington. Why, is there something I can help you with?"

"Well, maybe," he said. "You know, we got the owner of Klein's Sporting Goods out of bed about 2:00 or 3:00 o'clock in the morning and took him down." Somehow they had run this gun number to Italy, and this particular gun had been shipped to Klein's Sporting Goods in Chicago. He also said, "We've got another man out in California to find out where this California scope was that was on the rifle. But he says he checked his records there and they show that a money order was sent in payment, but it didn't say postal money order or bank money order; it just said a money order sent in payment. Well, he ran all that down. Meanwhile we got in touch with a bunch of agents in Kansas City who didn't know the money order wasn't still there. So, we hit a dead end."

I told him, "Well, of course, it's not there."

So he said, "Well, if it were issued, it had to have been issued if it was a postal money order here in Dallas. So I immediately put a crew to work on it.

In those days, postal money orders were issued in a book of paper money orders which, when you bought a money order, the clerk put the amount and the date, then you had a template that you put on that tore off at $10, not more than $15, or whatever. The clerk then ripped that off and handed it to the customer while the stub was retained which matched the money. All this was to be filled out in your own handwriting.

So I said, "Well, how much was it?" They didn't have a number for the money order, but they had an amount. They had me looking for a money order issued in the amount of $18.95 which we couldn't turn up. I had all the manpower and I wanted to examine all these stubs. I said, "Where did you get your information?"

"Out of a sporting goods magazine," they told me.

So I gave one of my secretaries a $10 bill and sent her next door to Union Station which had one of those rotating things they used to have in railroad stations with postcards and magazines. I told her, "You buy every sporting magazine you can find over there and bring them back." So she brought about six of them back, something like that, and I assigned each one of them to whoever was around, inspectors and secretaries, and took one myself. "Now you thumb through those," I said, "and when you come to Klein's Sporting Goods, let's see what it looks like."

It wasn't but a couple of minutes that one of the girls hollered, "Here it is!" So I looked at it and down at the bottom of the ad it said that that particular rifle was such and such amount. But if it could not be carried on a person, such as a pistol, like a shotgun or a rifle, then it was $1.25 or $1.37 extra. Shipping charges were also added, so I added those together, took that figure and called around to all the different stations and the main office where these crews were checking stubs.

It wasn't ten minutes that they hollered "Eureka!" They had the stub!

I called it in immediately to the chief on the open line to Washington and said, "I've got the money order number that Oswald used to buy this gun, and according to the records up there, they had shipped it to this box that he had rented at the main office in Dallas at that time, which he later closed and opened another at the Terminal Annex because it was closer to the School Book Depository."

So he said, "Well, we'll run that right through the correlators or whatever they do up there." In about an hour, he called back and said, "We've got it! Both the FBI and the Secret Service labs have positively identified the handwriting as being that of Oswald."

I had previously furnished headquarters, because everybody wanted them, copies of box rental applications that he had to fill out in his own handwriting. Those I had sent up on Friday night after I had gotten that information, so they had enough there on file. I figured that that was one of the very few pieces of actual evidence, not just circumstantial, that they would have been ready to go on the stand with and swear, and their testimony was just as authentic and viable as fingerprints or handwriting in federal court. Both agencies were ready to testify that that was his handwriting, that he ordered that gun in his own handwriting, and that it came to his post office box in Dallas. That's good evidence!

That Sunday morning, the 24th, I let my wife and daughter out at church about 9:00 o'clock in the morning and told my wife, "You know, I just think I'll run down and see if I can help Captain Fritz with anything or if I can be of any use to him." So I drove on down to City Hall and got off the elevator on the third floor expecting to be mobbed, but there wasn't a soul in sight; whereas, before, there had been plenty of reporters with their microphones stuck in your face. Everywhere you went they would follow and ask questions. But there wasn't a soul that Sunday morning. What had happened was that Curry, the chief of police, had promised the press that after they interviewed Oswald they were going to transfer him to the county jail, near the assassination site, which was a safer place for federal prisoners. Curry told them, "We will tell you in plenty of time so that you can photograph it and do whatever you want when we get ready to move him so that you can be a part of the move." That's the reason there was so much chaos there in that basement. They really got publicity but they brought it on themselves. They just had to be in on everything.

Anyway, when I got off that elevator and came around the corner and looked down the hallway toward Fritz's office, he was standing there motioning to me saying, "Psst! Hurry! Come here, come here!" So I hurried and he said, "You like to be in on an interview with Oswald?"

"Yeah, I sure would," I said. "There's a lot of things I'd like to ask him."

"Well, just come on in. I'm waiting here now for them to bring him down from his holdover upstairs." So we went in and sat down at this desk joining Sorrels, the local Secret Service man in charge, a Secret Service officer by the name of Kelley, who was an inspector from Washington working with Sorrels, Fritz, and me. We were the only four that took part in the interrogation. About that time Fritz said, "They're bringing Oswald down from upstairs; we're going to interrogate him for a while, then we're going to move him up to the county jail. I wanted to move him up there about 4:00 o'clock this morning when the streets would be deserted and nobody knew what was going on. But, no, the press wouldn't have it, and the chief wouldn't go along with it because the press was demanding that they be in on it and all that, see."

About that time a couple of guards came in with Oswald, who was handcuffed, and sat him down in a chair with the rest of us. I was sitting next to Fritz; Oswald was seated to the left of Fritz and directly across from me. The two guards stood beside him all the time he was there, but they never opened their mouths and didn't enter into the interrogation.

Anyway, when they first came in with Oswald, he looked around and said, "Are there any FBI men in here?"

Fritz said, "No, no FBI men."

"Well, who is that man?" as Oswald pointed to me. Fritz told him that I was a postal inspector and that I might have a question to ask in regard to post office matters. Oswald didn't have a problem with that and responded, "Okay." The FBI had interrogated his wife two or three times, and it really needled him and just set him off to the point that he had no use for the FBI. It was the FBI that wouldn't tell the Secret Service or anybody else that he should have been watched, and they really were criticized over it. But anyway, Oswald wouldn't talk until he was assured there wasn't an FBI man in the room. He just didn't want anything to do with the FBI.

This was the only time that I ever saw Oswald. To me he looked just like a normal person. You read stories about how you can look in their eyes and can see this or that, but I didn't see anything different about him. Personally, I thought that he was very intelligent. He was very positive and opinionated about what he said and never minced words. His answers were either yes or no, and he had an excellent memory. He answered all the questions put to him either truthfully or otherwise, but I knew that he was lying on certain questions because of the evidence that we had.

When he came into the room, he was just matter of fact; he just didn't know why he was there. He said, "I presume I'm here because I resisted arrest and tried to shoot a policeman there in that theater. All I know is that I was in a picture show out there on Jefferson and the police came in after me. I had my pistol on me and took it out to defend myself when it didn't fire. I wasn't successful because the hammer caught on the web of the guy's hand. If it had fired, he'd be another dead policeman. I didn't kill anybody!" He wouldn't even admit to killing Tippit, and he certainly denied any connection with the President. He didn't have any reason for it.

As the questioning gradually led up to Kennedy, he just acted like he couldn't imagine anybody thinking that he might have shot Kennedy. He never worried about going to jail or being put to death. He just denied that he ever shot the President and acted like it never entered his head that it was possible that you could charge him with shooting the President. He kept that front all the way through and never wavered from it. I asked him, "Did you have a post office box in New Orleans?"

"Yeah."

"What number?" I asked. And he just ran off the number. I'd look at my card and he'd be right. "Have one in Fort Worth?" And he knew the number. "One up here?"

"Yeah, box so and so," which is where he received his gun.

I asked, "Well, did you ever get a package in that box?"

"Well, what kind of package?" he asked.

"Did you get a rifle shipped down here from Klein's Sporting Goods in Chicago?"

"No, no, I didn't get any rifle," he responded.

"Well," I said, "one came there addressed to A.J. Hidell in this box and it was delivered."

"Well, I didn't get it."

"Did anybody else have access to that box?" I asked.

"No, except..."

I said, "Well, the box you had here you had the Fair Play for Cuba people entitled to get mail from it along with the American Civil Liberties Union."

He had already told me no, but then when he got that far down, he knew he had to hedge, so he said, "I just stuck them on. I never did get any mail from them. I tried to get involved with each of them..." That's another thing: He just did not impress anybody enough to have confidence in him to be a member of their outfit. They didn't trust him, I guess.

Finally he admitted, "Well, my wife. She didn't have a key, but occasionally I'd give her the key to check my box for me. That's before I had it moved to the Terminal Annex. She's the only one that ever got one out of there." Of course, she didn't get the rifle, he did. He admitted that nobody else could have gotten mail out of there because there was only one key issued. The same was true at the annex. There was only one key issued, and he had it in his pocket when he was arrested. So there was no evidence that he did receive that rifle. Now I don't think that he shot it before that, but he kept it wrapped in a blanket over at Ruth Paine's garage and everybody knew it. He would never admit to having owned the rifle even though I knew that he was lying, at least circumstantially. He just disabused his mind of any connection with it.

When the police went to her house looking for it, they were told, "Yeah, he had a rifle. It's out here in the garage rolled up in a blanket." At that time, you couldn't hardly talk with Marina Oswald because of her Russian language and was sort of like an Indian. She didn't express herself in her face and was rather stoic. She came into our office ten or fifteen times, but she communicated through her attorney. I didn't ask her any questions of a personal nature.

At that time, the evidence was being gathered but he didn't have to confess. They're turning them off of murderer's row because all they had was a confession. If a guy says, "I did it," that doesn't mean anything because they won't take it. But in the case of Oswald, I don't think that he would have ever confessed; he was that adamant. He was so direct. He'd look you right in the eye and ask you a question. He had an uncanny ability to determine or guess when I had evidence or when I was fishing. You would keep coming back to something such as the rifle and he'd give you the same answer. It was just like he had been trained. In fact, I kind of thought in my own head that probably in Russia he had been trained to evade questions and be able to keep himself composed to guard what he wanted to keep secret. Either that or maybe it was just his nature. He was very mannerly and only became rattled when Captain Fritz asked him about this Hidell. I was talking about the rifle coming in the name Hidell at the post office and Oswald said, "Well, I don't know anything about any of it."

"Ever use the name Hidell?" I asked.

"No," he said. In reality he had used it in New Orleans and in two or three other places, but he just plain denied it.

Captain Fritz then interjected, "Well, what about this card that was taken out of your billfold when we picked you up?" (I don't recall whether it was a Social Security card or some other kind of identification, but it looked like it was old and pocket worn, had been erased, and had the name Hidell on it or something to that effect.)

He looked at it and that's when he became testy and responded, "Now I have told you all I'm going to tell you about that card. Now just forget about it!" He would not admit that the name meant anything to him, that he had never seen it before. That was the only time that he ever got a little sassy.

None of this bothered Fritz; it was like water off a duck's back. He was too old a hand at that, so he'd just go on to something else, though he might come back to it later. There wasn't any use of his asking about it because he was just plain lying about it without any compunction and without batting an eye. But he answered all the questions put to him one way or the other while his hands were handcuffed in his lap.

During the interrogation, he was asked if he were a communist, to which he replied, "No, I'm not a communist; I'm a Marxist."

"Well," Captain Fritz said, "what's the difference?"

"If you don't know the difference," Oswald replied, "then I don't have the time to explain it to you." He tried to put you down.

That's when I asked him, "Well, Oswald, do you have a religion, a belief?"

"Yeah, I certainly do," he said.

"Well, what is it?"

He then blurted out, "Marxism. I'm a worshipper of Karl Marx. I believe everything he stands for and what he says. It's a religion." "Now," he said, "the Bible makes good reading as a novel or as literature, but as far as philosophy it's for the birds," or words to that effect. He was just that definite.

Nothing in particular was going through my mind at that time. You've got to be objective when you're interrogating someone in a situation like that so you don't form opinions. Instead, you just try to elicit opinions from him to see what he thinks about certain things, then you can think about them later and make up your own mind. Most of the time during the interrogation I was just trying to get his answers, but I don't believe that I had ever dealt with anybody like him before. He wasn't stupid, and he wasn't crazy, but he did have a twisted mind.

He made reference to his Marine Corps service only when somebody asked him about why he would want to shoot Connally, and was it because he had written him trying to get his dishonorable discharge corrected. He responded, "No, I wrote to him and he wrote me a real nice letter stating that `I'm no longer Secretary of the Navy, and I'm in no position now, but I will forward your letter on to the current Secretary of the Navy.' I had no reason to disbelieve Connally."

Oswald had a map of the city of Dallas, or at least a piece of a map, which showed a bunch of X's in ink on it. He was asked, "Well, now, what are these X's? What do they represent? Tell us about the map."

So he said, "Well, this over here is where I live on Beckley. You'll notice those X's are on bus lines between there and where my wife stayed with Mrs. Paine over in Irving, and every one of those X's are on a bus line. I had no transportation so I would check them out, ads in the paper or somebody would tell me about a possible job. Every X is where I interviewed for a job. Check them out and see if I didn't interview. In fact, here's an X on the School Book Depository and that's where I got a job." I had no reason not to believe him since he was very forthright about it and made sense.

According to Oswald the reason that he went to Ruth Paine's and stayed over on that Thursday night, which was unusual because he normally would go on Friday night, was that he learned that his wife and Mrs. Paine were having a party for the children and that it would be better if he came on Thursday night. I don't know who checked that out with Marina or Mrs. Paine or whether it was true or not, but that was his explanation as to why he went over on Thursday night rather than Friday.

Somebody in the room at that point asked him what was in the paper bag that he had the next morning when he rode to work with another employee. "Well, that was my lunch." That's what he told us! "Your lunch? Why did you carry a lunch in a big old bag like that?"

"Well," he said, "you don't always get a bag that just fits your lunch; you take what you can get." He was that quick, no mincing around, no trying to make up something.

He was then asked, "Well, where did you carry it?"

"I carried it in my lap," he said, "just like I always carry my lunch," and the driver said, `Throw it over in the back seat.' " That's what he said about it!

According to the man who drove him to work the next day he had a rather long brown paper wrapper which might have been a bag. The driver asked him, "What's that?" as Oswald threw it over the back seat.

Oswald told him, "That's some curtain rods." I've noticed in some of the literature that it was for his room, but he told Captain Fritz previously that it was curtain rods which he was bringing because he didn't need them. As they were getting out of the car, he supposedly said that the curtain rods were for a fellow at work.

There was no tape recording of the interrogation or stenographer or anyone taking notes. That was the way that Fritz operated. The interrogation itself was rather informal with Captain Fritz being in charge. He would ask Oswald various questions and pull out different things such as the map with the X's on it and the card that he had taken out of Oswald's billfold that had A.J. Hidell on it and things like that. Then he would say, "Well, Sorrels, do you have anything you want to ask him?" But Kelley and Sorrels had very little to ask; they didn't have the documentation that I had. We were free to ask or interject anything we wanted. Of course, we were all experienced interrogators, and when you went to trial in those days, especially in federal court, you had to show any notes you took to the defense. So they got to look at every note that you had against their client. But we old-time investigators would just do it by memory. I could still quote nearly every word that boy said to this day and that's been over twenty years ago. That's the way I was trained to interrogate anybody, and so was Fritz. If they're telling the truth, you'd talk to them by the hour, and if they couldn't tell it the same way twice or a third time, or a tenth time, you'd catch them because you'd know exactly what he had said the first time. You didn't need notes; you didn't need a secretary or a stenographer. Of course, you do now, but back then you really had to use your own wits to convict people.

At the time, I spent half the time in federal court, and especially through usage, I always had a good memory. You had to have to get through medical and dental school and work eight hours a day as I did. I would take post office schemes that took an ordinary person 30 to 60 days to learn; I'd learn it in five or six and make a 100 on the test which included a 1,000 or 1,200 different addresses. Much of my work dealt with memory, and memory is just training: repetition, do it and practice.

Eventually I got to where I could go into federal court maybe six months after I'd interviewed somebody without a note of any kind and quote every detail of that conversation or confession of what took place or who did what. It was just training. You practiced at it and developed a memory.

With traveling all the time and staying in motels all over the country, whenever I'd go to bed at night, before going to sleep, I'd say, "Well, let's see, I got up this morning and got out on the left side of the bed, put on my left sock first, then my right, then I went to the bathroom, came back, put on my trousers, then went back and shaved." I could tell you exactly what I ate for breakfast, what the girl looked like that waited on me. "When I got in my car, I went off to my right and the light was red and had to wait a minute." I could tell you what every light was all day long everywhere, every little detail. By keeping in practice by just reviewing what I did that day, it was just like I had written it all out, and I've done that for years.

Though I never tested him, Captain Fritz could have done the same thing. He was a Texan who was crude and had farmerish ways and mannerisms, but as far as I was concerned he was really an outstanding criminal investigator. Fritz abhorred publicity, wanted to get the job done, send the guy to the penitentiary and go on to the next one. He was the pride of the Dallas Police Department; no one need ever sell him short, no matter what the press did. I don't think this case got the best of him. He was just like me; he just got too old for the job and thought it was time to quit. As far as I know, there was no pressure on him, though there was a lot of criticism, "the stupid Dallas police," and that sort of thing. Curry, on the other hand, being chief of police, owed his job to public relations. As far as I know, that was the only cross between the two.

Bill Decker was just like Fritz. Nobody questioned anything he did, not even the criminals. When "Old Bill" picked you up, they just said, "Well, you got me, Bill." He treated them as nicely as he could, and so did I. I'd be very fatherly with them and give them advice and not gloat over the fact that they were a crook and that I was a really smart postal inspector. It just didn't work that way; Bill Decker and Will Fritz were the same way.

In any case, we talked for a couple of hours with the interrogation ending around 11:00 o'clock. In the meantime, people were pounding on the door. Captain Fritz and some of his lieutenants wanted to get him out so that the press could see him and transfer him to the county courthouse which was a federal hold-over and more secure where all the federal prisoners were transferred as quickly as possible. By that time, I assume that he had been determined to be under federal arrest.

Fritz had been adamant about transferring Oswald about 3:00 or 4:00 o'clock in the morning in the quiet streets and nobody would know anything about it. But Curry had promised the hundreds of TV people and reporters from all over the United States and foreign countries that they would be privy to the transfer. They had apparently promised, "We'll leave you alone up there if you'll let us be in on the transfer of the prisoner." That's the reason they were not up in the hall that morning.

As the morning wore on, some of those outside the office were getting impatient. They'd crack the door open and look in, but it didn't bother Fritz. "Just take your time, chief, take your time," he said. You never know whose idea something like that transfer was. Curry, being the chief of police, was quite a P.R. guy which was why he got the job. As a result, being P.R. oriented, you get involved in politics and, of course, there's a lot of really influential people wanting to be privy to the transfer such as the heads of ABC, NBC, CBS, and other powerful people.

Finally, Curry came in and talked with Fritz. However they were whispering to each other, and I could not tell what they were saying. It was during that interchange that they determined to go ahead and let him go. I didn't accompany Oswald to the basement. Instead, Sorrels and I walked out of the office to our cars, mine being on the street.

Shortly after, we learned that, ironically, Jack Ruby had a postal box in the same panel of boxes as Oswald. Immediately, I placed a watch on that box along with the box of Oswald's which was already under surveillance. In fact, another postal inspector and myself took the first watch but nobody got a piece of mail out of either box during the time they were watched. We started confiscating mail from them immediately after we were instructed but found nothing of a personal nature.

The question as to whether Oswald had ever received the rifle at his postal box was on our minds and has later become an issue. An application for a post office box in 1963 consisted of two cardboard forms that were attached and then were separated in the files. The first line on the front showed the post office, the date the box was rented, and the number of the post office box. The next line showed the name of the applicant: for example, in one of the forms I was allowed to retain, Jack Ruby. The next line was the name of the firm or corporation, to which Ruby put Earl Products. The next line referred to the kind of business, to which he put merchandising. The next line was his business address which was 223 South Ewing followed on the next line by his home address which was also 223 South Ewing. The last line at the bottom of the card contained his signature and the date of the application.

On the other side of the card was information that was kept in a different section of the post office, the delivery section. The first line showed the post office box number then it said, "Deliver mail in accordance with instructions checked below," and it had various little boxes. He checked all except special delivery mail in the box. Then, over to the right, he checked another box: "Only mail addressed to the box to be placed in it. All other mail to be delivered as addressed," in other words, to his home address. And down below it says, "Deliver special delivery mail to 223 South Ewing" and is signed below that, "Jack Ruby."

Oswald would have filled out the same type forms since they were of the same format. It would have been possible, nothing's impossible, for someone to go to their post office box, find a slip that said there was a package for them and to receive that package without having the designated person receive the package, but it wouldn't be routine. You'd have to identify yourself to the window where you would have to take the slip, but it would depend on how strict the clerk was that waited on him. Normally they would require some identification. Nine times out of ten if the clerk knows them they don't question them, but if they didn't then they would.

The slips were kind of like the ones you receive at your door if you're not at home: "We're holding a package at such and such station and we'll hold it for so many days, and then we'll return it to sender. You can call there and pick up the package." Usually the slip itself is evidence enough, but again, some clerks will require identification to determine whether you are really the person it says or not. It's really up to the individual clerk.

Actually there was no evidence that Oswald was the one that picked up the package which contained the rifle. But we did have his authenticated handwriting that he ordered the rifle from Klein's Sporting Goods in Chicago, and it did come to this post office in Dallas. Obviously, a rifle wouldn't fit in the box, so they would have to leave notice and nobody knows whether he took that notice over to the window and picked it up or whether his wife did because he admitted in the interrogation that the only person that ever got anything out of that box was possibly his wife, and he wasn't sure that she had. He just said possibly, but nobody else. So, in my mind, it's quite evident that he took the slip over and picked the rifle up at the window that was so designated for delivery of parcels.

I never interrogated his wife, but she knew all about the rifle. But, at no time, did she say anything about how he acquired the rifle or from where. She wasn't trying to hide anything. She was very open about all of her testimony and she would have said, "I know he got it because I picked it up at the post office." But she didn't say that.

Despite all that's been written, I think the Warren Commission was very factual with what they got. Being an investigator for many, many, many years, my personal opinion is that there was not any conspiracy. I say that for many reasons including the fact that he was just not high enough on the totem pole of being a spy or a double agent or anything like that. He just didn't have the knack for it, I guess, because nobody had any confidence in him. He couldn't even infiltrate himself into the American Civil Liberties Union or the Cuban outfit. They wouldn't accept him. And Russia: It didn't take them long to find out that they'd just as soon have him back in the United States because it was unusual as to how he got back and even brought his wife with him. Of course, there's no way of telling what they did with him while they had him, but most of the time he apparently was hunting a job and trying to get work over there.

And then, too, there was no skullduggery in setting him up at the School Book Depository because the people that recommended it had no interest whatsoever; they were just neighbors of Mrs. Paine that had heard about the job. In fact, I think one of them worked there. He went to work there a month before they even announced that the President was coming to Dallas. Further, the President's line of travel from Love Field to the place where he was to make his luncheon speech was in an entirely different part of the city than the School Book Depository. That was not changed to pass in front of that building until, I guess, two days before, long after he had been working there. My belief is that that's the first thought he ever had of making something out of it. I think that his mind started working and that it was a case of his finally being something, whether famous or infamous: here was his chance. And he would live on in infamy for having done this deed which was good enough for him because he had been a flop at everything else. In the meantime, there was no contact with him from anybody else, nobody. No agency or individual ever thought that anybody was trying to get in touch with him which would consummate a conspiracy.

In 1964 Harry Holmes was called to testify before the Warren Commission and presented most of the postal documents relevant to Lee

Harvey Oswald and Jack Ruby which were used by the commission in its investigation of the assassination. Holmes retired as a postal inspector on January 1, 1967. After living for several years with his daughter and family in Garland, Texas, he passed away in October 1989.

THE OSWALD TRANSFER AND AFTERMATH

L.C. Graves

James R. Leavelle

L.D. Montgomery

Charles O. Arnett

Orville A. Jones

Rio S. Pierce

Roy Vaughn

Don Flusche

Joe R. Cody

Bill Courson

Al Maddox

W.W. "Bo" Mabra

Bill Alexander

L.C. GRAVES
Homicide Detective
Dallas Police Department

"Personally, I think Oswald is exactly where he ought to be, but I resent the fact that Ruby did it under the circumstances because he definitely violated the law. Had Oswald been allowed to live, they would have made a martyr out of him, and they would have still been trying that sucker even today..."

Born in rural Camp County, in 1918, L.C. Graves left the farm at the age of seventeen to serve in a Civilian Conservation Corps camp and later joined the Army for five years during the Second World War. While in the Army, he met his future wife, Myrt, at a Cotton Bowl exhibition in Dallas. Graves joined the Dallas Police Department in 1949 and, at the time of the assassination, was a detective in the Homicide and Robbery Bureau. He is noted for being one of the two detectives who was escorting Oswald at the time that Oswald was shot by Jack Ruby.

I was working the evening shift, three to eleven, and was off that morning. My wife and I were out shopping for a piano and walked into one place and heard the news. I told her that I thought we'd better get back home because I imagined they'd be calling us right away. As soon as I hit the door, the phone was ringing and, of course, I had to go to work since all the off-duty officers were called in.

After I got to headquarters, my first duty was to take a statement from a lady named Helen Markham who was an eyeball witness to the shooting of Tippit. That took a little while because she was quite upset, rather hysterical really, but I finally got a statement from her. She was a terribly upset lady. Under the circumstances her reaction was fairly typical considering she was close by when it happened, had heard the gun and saw him fall. I had no doubt about the validity of her statement because we verified everything she said. She identified Oswald in the lineup, so that pretty well established the fact that he was the one that did it as far as we were concerned.

The lineup that Mrs. Markham observed was a typical lineup. The authorization was given by Captain Fritz, and the jail supervisor picked the lineup and brought them down. All those in the lineup were as similar as possible. The only thing different about this one was everybody that could get in got in which, in my opinion, wasn't good. But I didn't have any control over it. Other than just a lot of people being in there, though, that shouldn't have been, it was conducted in the same manner as all others.

The witness would stand or sit behind a one-way nylon screen so that they couldn't be seen by those in the lineup. As I recall, and this was the only one I attended on Friday, there was definitely shock or excitement when she saw him. She said something to the effect, "That's him! That's the one that shot Tippit!" She didn't have to be prompted; she knew him. As she identified him, Oswald remained quiet like the rest of them.

At that time, it was bedlam at headquarters! All the off-duty officers were there, and with the news media pouring in from all over the country and being allowed to have the run of the building, it was really hindering us. We just had to fight our way through it and do the best we could to keep them out and away from the essential things and continue our investigation. We didn't have time to stand still for any type of extended interviews, just yes or no and kept walking.

Saturday was pretty much routine as far as we were concerned, following our different clues. I don't recall anything specific from that day. We knew that Oswald was to be transferred the next day. We had discussed it, but we didn't plan it until the next morning.

I arrived at work early on Sunday morning. By that time, we didn't have any news media on the third floor, though there were still some cables and things around, so it was pretty quiet. We knew that Oswald was to be transferred that day but we didn't have any idea when. Around 9:30 Leavelle and I were sent upstairs and brought Oswald down to Captain Fritz's office which was rather small, probably about nine feet by twelve. I don't remember all that were in on the questioning, but Mr. Holmes of the postal service was there and probably Mr. Bookhout with the FBI and Captain Fritz. There may have been others but I don't recall offhand. We just went on out and started looking through our papers and whatever because we knew they weren't going to be in there long, and we didn't want to clutter the room anymore than necessary. Besides, you could never get a word in edgeways anyway, so we just left out. I never entered the room during the questioning. We could see in the room and when everybody got up and left, we went back in.

The plan for the transfer called for us to come out of Captain Fritz's office and come down the hall to the two sets of elevators, take the elevator to the jail office in the basement, get in the car and drive out on Commerce and straight down to the county.

Chief Curry was in the office briefly before the transfer. He had told everybody that Oswald was going to be transferred at ten and it was already eleven, so the chief was antsy. He was walking around wringing his hands. Fritz had asked him if we could give everybody the slip and just transfer him unannounced to the County, and he said, "No, we are obligated to the press. We are an hour late, so let's transfer." I don't know where he went from there, but I didn't see him anymore because he didn't follow us.

As we got ready for the transfer, Oswald decided he wanted to wear a black sweater of his, though it had a little hole in it. We weren't given any special instructions other than normal on the transfer. Leavelle happened to be standing close by, and Fritz said, "Put your cuffs on him; handcuff yourself to him." So he handcuffed his left arm to Oswald's right, and since I happened to be on Oswald's left, I just caught his left arm, hooked mine in his, and we started walking him down.

When the transfer occurred, we came out of his office, down the hallway and came to the entrance to the two sets of elevators. We came to a door on the left, opened that door, a solid door, closed it and there was the elevator, and we went down to the jail office. Oswald was very calm. We didn't ask him anything, and he didn't volunteer anything. We just told him we were transferring him to the county and that was it.

I was aware that threats had been made against Oswald. Something like that always goes around, and under the circumstances you don't pass it off lightly. You always anticipate trouble on something like that. You never, never take something like that for granted! You never, never get too lax with a situation, especially one of that magnitude. You just don't do that!

When we arrived in the basement, I expected to find other officers lined up around that wall like they told us they would be. I expected the media to be over that driveway behind the rail. There was a big camera set up there. I didn't expect them to be intermingled like they were. I wasn't apprehensive or afraid of the news media; I was just mad that they were allowed to get in there that way.

We waited for a few seconds and then somebody told us that it was all clear. I think it might have been Lieutenant Wiggins, the jail officer. But they weren't ready as far as we were concerned; the car wasn't backed in place where it should have been. I could see the rear of the car as Dhority was still trying to back it into position. People were in the way, and they were hollering at them to move over, get out of the way. One guy jumped up on the bumper trying to get a picture. Despite that, we followed Captain Fritz out with my partner, L.D. Montgomery, right behind us. About the first thing I saw after about the first three steps out was this newsman with this long microphone sticking it right over my left shoulder. That vexed me a little because he wasn't even supposed to be there. I didn't look around or say anything to him, but I knew he was there and I knew others were there. I just kept walking. When we saw that the car still wasn't in place, we continued to where it should have been, right in the middle of the opening, maybe ten to fifteen feet from the entrance to the jail office. As we made a slight turn to the right, I saw Ruby come around the officer to my left. I was already in a slight right hand turn as he came from my left with that pistol in his hand as he was making that final step just before he shot.

A second or two earlier and I could have prevented the shot, but I didn't. I caught him out of the corner of my eye as quick as I could, but he was on the downward thrust of a step coming right in front of me. When the shooting occurred, I did what I should have done; I jerked loose from Oswald and reached for the gun. Ruby was still milking on the trigger trying to pull it off, so I just reached across, took his hand, grabbed his arm, got hold of the gun with my right hand and turned my back to the crowd trying to get it out of his hand saying, "Turn it loose! Turn it loose!" and a few other choice words. Immediately, all the officers jumped on him and started pulling him away from me. I thought they were going to pull him away before I could get the gun out of his hand. Fortunately, he turned it loose just before they jerked him away from me.

If I hadn't gotten my hand over that cylinder where it wouldn't turn, in a fit of passion, he could have fired off some rounds and hit some of the officers who were all around the back. There's no question about that, plus the fact that he stated that he was going to shoot him at least three times. He made that statement to us. But it was only by the grace of God that that one shot didn't penetrate Oswald and hit another officer back there. It actually ruptured the spleen, severed an artery, and landed in the spine area.

After I got the gun, I put it in my pocket and talked with Captain Fritz as the ambulance arrived and backed up. As they brought Oswald out on the gurney and loaded him into the ambulance, I got in on the little jump seat on the right hand side, and the intern physician from Parkland hospital sat on my lap while he administered artificial respiration.

Oswald was naturally unconscious all the way to Parkland. Based on his appearance and the fact that he collapsed like he did, I thought that it was probably a fatal wound. The only noise he made was just before we got to the hospital. He stretched out and groaned and moaned, "Ohhhhh!" As far as I'm concerned, he died then.

When we arrived at Parkland, they snatched him out of the ambulance and rushed him into the operating room to start blood. Charlie Brown, who was an FBI agent, and I put on all the regalia, shoes and all that and stood by in the area just outside the door to the emergency room where no one could enter or leave and stayed there until he was officially pronounced dead. The body was then taken into custody and put in the morgue.

I was in a state of relief as much as anything when I got back to headquarters. Things were a little quieter and we started picking up some of the pieces as far as evidence was concerned, gathering more information, and running out leads that we didn't have time to run out before.

The following day, Monday, Captain Fritz, L.D. Montgomery, and myself went off, had a cup of coffee and breakfast, and decided how we would transfer Ruby. Fritz didn't tell anybody else other than to call the office and alert a few of the detectives. So we drove back into the basement, had him brought down, and drove off unannounced. Our lieutenant in our department didn't even know what we were doing; the jail didn't know what we were doing; and the county didn't know what we were doing until we got there. When we drove out of the basement, there was one lone newsman down there with a camera hanging over his shoulder just walking around looking, not even paying us any mind. He didn't know what we were doing because Ruby ran to the car, hit the back seat and lay down with his head over behind me and never raised up till we got to the county. Leavelle and I told him, "You know you don't have anything to worry about. Nobody knows you're being transferred but us, and we're not going to shoot you." He didn't say a word. Really, that's the way that we should have done the other one.

Meanwhile it had been a horrible weekend! We were all dead on our feet, tired, and about all you could hear was something about the assassination on the news and, of course, the funeral of the President, then Oswald's funeral, the transfer of Ruby and his condition. It was first one thing and then another. Certainly it was a bad situation. It was, as I told the man who took my statement for the Warren Commission several months later, "It's bad enough to get a president assassinated anywhere in the world, and it's even worse if it's in your own city."

We were taking a beating, unjustly, because had it been in New York, Chicago, or wherever, it would have been the same thing. There was no way that we could have stopped it; we just had to cope. I think we did a really fine job in apprehending Oswald as quick as we did right after it happened. He left out of the Book Depository and caught that cab to Oak Cliff. Officer Tippit recognized him from the description, stopped to talk with him and Oswald shot him. He then ran over to that theater. Some people saw him go in there, and the officer went over to arrest him in just a very short period of time. From the evidence that was secured, there was no doubt in their minds that he was the one that shot Tippit, that's for sure! Evidence otherwise pointed to him as being the one who shot the President. Now they can speculate on it till doomsday, till doomsday, and draw all kinds of conclusions, but the cold fact is that that little pip-squeak shot the President.

Basically, I think Oswald was just another radical. Knowing something about his background, all he ever thought about and all he ever studied was communism, Marxism. That's all he wanted to talk about. His own wife said that he was a wallflower. When they would go to some gathering of some kind, if he couldn't bend somebody's ear and talk about communism, then he'd get disgusted and leave. He was an eight-ball, just an outcast.

After the assassination, we drew our share of radicals and everything else. We had people drifting into the city, wide-eyed and bushy-tailed, weeks and months after the assassination wanting to tell us some wild story. You could tell first hand by looking at them that they were way out in left field, just loons, just loonies, and that's what it boils down to.

The best way to deal with those types was to find more or less what they were looking for and then console them with that thought, then they'd be happy for the moment and go on about their way. We'd listen to them when a person would come in and say, "They're after me. They're drilling holes in my brick and blowing marijuana smoke and stuff in my house."

Then we'd tell them, "Well, we've got police and helicopters out there looking, and we're going to be watching for them." That would make them happy and they would get out.

Or we might have someone come in and say, "I know that somebody's poisoning my father. He's drinking this whiskey and somebody's put some poison in it, I know they are."

So we would tell them, "You bring in a couple of samples and we'll have it analyzed." That would pacify them and they would leave happy.

I wasn't intimately associated with Jack Ruby, but I knew him because he was in the kind of business he was in, and I had to police the clubs that he ran: the Vegas and the Carousel, and earlier the little joint that he ran on South Ervay, the Silver Spur.

He was flighty and kind of an individualistic type of fellow who was a little hard to understand for most people. He had a very passionate like for police officers and the ladies, not that he forced himself upon them or even made a play for them, but he liked the ladies and respected them. He also had a high regard for the strippers. He didn't abuse them or let them be abused.

If you were a police officer, and you let him, Jack Ruby would be overly friendly with you and would give you gratuities. He'd give you things, just give them to you such as free drinks or free passes to his clubs. The proper way to handle a man like him was to be nice to him but stay an arm's length away. Don't go hanging around his joints and drink his booze or fool with his women. You just didn't if you want to stay on the up and up. You just didn't want to become vulnerable to a man like that. Just take care of business.

I think I've heard most of the stories about Ruby and how he got into the basement. He had been down to Western Union on the corner to send some money to one of his strippers that needed money, and I'm convinced that he walked right on down the street and went down the ramp. The ramp is one way there and cars were not supposed to go out. But there was an extra car in there and some lieutenant wanted to go out that way because the other one was blocked temporarily, so he drove out that way. An officer who was guarding the entrance to the ramp stepped out into the street to help the car out, which he shouldn't have done, and I'm sure that Ruby just went in and came down. He didn't have any help from another policeman as some have said. There wouldn't have been any way that anyone would have ever gone along with a deal like that. That's crazy!

It was absolutely coincidental that he got there because there wouldn't have been any way he could have timed it with a man up front and a man downstairs giving signals to get him down there at the exact moment. He just happened to be there at that particular time. What triggered him will always be a mystery to everybody. But something did at that exact moment, and he just decided that he would eliminate him.

Knowing Jack Ruby, that he was emotionally unstable, and knowing that he could be triggered instantaneously, plus the fact that he always carried that pistol with him and was distraught over the fact that the President had been shot and having compassion for Jackie Kennedy, I think getting down there at the exact time that he did, it wouldn't take but a second for him to make up his mind to do what he did.

If Ruby hadn't shot Oswald, I doubt seriously if much more would have been clarified. I don't think Oswald would have ever confessed to anything because I think he was the kind of guy who had no remorse. He was just that kind of bird. He was an atheist who didn't believe in God, and certainly not in Jesus Christ.

When we transferred Ruby, we hadn't learned a lesson from the previous transfer of Oswald. Captain Fritz was so distraught over the whole situation, I'm sure, that he didn't care to discuss it because they had stripped him of any authority so far as operating under procedures that we knew how to operate under for the sake of everything and everybody concerned. If anybody knew how to handle a situation, a bad situation or bad people, it was old man Fritz. And we knew how to do it, too! We knew that transferring Oswald under those conditions was not right, and we took the brunt over something that we didn't have any control over; that's what burned us up!

We had doubts about the transfer of Oswald, absolutely, especially when there had been threats made against him. Every man in there knew what was going on. We had transferred some bad people, and we knew how to handle the situation. Knowing the circumstances, we knew the possibilities because you never know what triggers people in a situation like that where animosity had already started building up in people's hearts and minds. As a result, they tend to do crazy things, so why take a chance?

The great mistake was in ever announcing the time of the transfer world-wide, and that's what it amounted to: a world-wide announcement of the transfer time that gave every kook in the world a chance to do something if they wanted. Unfortunately, in our case, it was one of our own citizens that took it upon himself to do it, and he had a better opportunity than most under the circumstances.

The proper procedure for transferring a prisoner from the city to the county after a case had been filed was that the sheriff would send his deputies with a paper and they would take the prisoner on to the county with them. But so many times through the years, we'd just done it ourselves for the sake of time. That was the actual proper procedure. Why they didn't elect to do that

that time, I don't know. I lay the blame I think where it belongs, and that was with Elgin Crull, the city manager. Had he taken the restrictions off, it wouldn't have happened.

The city manager had control of most of the functions of the city operation. The mayor was more or less a figurehead. The city manager had control over just about everything that happened in the city, including the police department. And Elgin Crull was an ex-newspaperman, so I think that accounted for his leniency towards the press and why he let them have the run of City Hall when the influx of newsmen flooded us. Also, in something of that magnitude, everybody wanted to get their two cents in. I suppose his being city manager and head of the police department per se, he wanted to show his authority. But it was under his orders and instructions, not those of Jesse Curry, that the situation developed as it did and was carried out as it was, yet I never heard him take any blame for it after it was done.

Because of the events of that weekend, the Dallas Police Department and the city of Dallas itself came under a great deal of unjust criticism. I think the tincture of time will take care of that because the facts are that we had, in 1963, and still do have, one of the best police departments in the United States. It's also a fact that we had, at that time, and still do have, one of the cleanest cities in the country, absolutely. I think statistics bear that out. Sure we have a lot of crime and we have a lot of murders, but the biggest portion of them are momma and pappa, boyfriend-girlfriend deals where the police have no control over anyway. Occasionally we have racial violence, but how are you going to control that? As a city grows, as this one has, you're going to have that sort of thing. But Dallas isn't like Los Angeles or San Francisco where you have wide spread vice. Certainly you can find a dice game or a card game or a good looking whore to bed down the night, but it's not out in the open as it is in so many of the other cities.

Along with the negative publicity about the city of Dallas came the conspiracy theories about the assassination. I don't work with theories, never did; I worked from facts. As an officer, you don't work on theory except when you're trying to solve a case. But once you solve the case and get the facts together, then you stick to the facts, and that's the way it is. The case against Oswald and Ruby is closed, absolutely, and I'll defy anybody to prove otherwise. They haven't yet and they never will! You know, if you knew the background of these people proposing all these theories, I think you'd find it's for monetary purposes. They're doing this to sell their books and to promote their cause as sure as I'm sitting in this chair.

I guess I could do the same thing. Just recently, I made the statement a time or two that I was going to write a book, and the title would sell the book regardless of what was in it. Of course they wanted to know what the title was, and I said in jest, "How I Held Oswald While Ruby Shot Him." But I've never believed in capitalizing on a bad situation, and this was a bad situation. A few years ago a guy wanted to put Leavelle and I in wax for a museum, but I turned it down. He became rather huffy about it claiming it was public domain. After I had my attorney write him a letter, he dropped it and I never heard from him again. But this was early in the game, and as the years have passed, I've thought that maybe I was kind of foolish. I knew that this person was doing it for monetary reasons and that vexed me at the time. Even so, I probably should have let it go on through since maybe the grandchildren would have gotten a kick out of it.

In any case, I retired from the police department in 1970 and was the chief polygraph examiner those last three years. My brother-in-law, Paul Bentley, taught me the polygraph in 1958, and we had a business together moonlighting on the side. I eventually sold that and went to work as a fraud investigator in the credit card division for the Republic National Bank for thirteen years and retired in 1983.

L.C. Graves and his wife, Myrt, moved to nearby Kaufman, Texas, to be near their sons, one of whom is a policeman. In his retirement, he would occasionally meet for breakfast with several of the former homicide detectives and twice a year for the gathering of the "Cracker Jacks," those homicide detectives who served under Captain Will Fritz. Graves died in February 1995.

JAMES R. LEAVELLE
Homicide Detective
Dallas Police Department

"When he stepped up and pulled the trigger, I reached over and grabbed Ruby by the shoulder and shoved back and down on him. At the same time, I could see that Graves had the hammer of that pistol locked with his thumb while Ruby was still flexing his fingers trying to pull the trigger..."

Born and raised in Red River County in Northeast Texas, James Leavelle joined the Navy in 1939 and served on board the USS Whitney in the Pacific Theater. After his discharge, Leavelle then joined the Dallas Police Department in 1950. Serving as a detective in the Homicide and Robbery Bureau under Captain Will Fritz, he is best known as the man who was handcuffed to Lee Harvey Oswald at the time when Oswald was murdered by Jack Ruby on November 24, 1963.

My assignment on November 22nd was to cover anything that came in to the office along with another officer, Charlie Brown. The rest of the officers in the bureau, including Captain Fritz, were going to cover the parade and the luncheon.

I was at City Hall when I received information that there was an armed robbery suspect in the North Dallas area. Charlie Brown and I went out and made the arrest, brought him in, and were listening to the progress of the parade as we drove into the basement of City Hall. The parade was approaching Houston Street at the time we turned the radio off and got out of the car. By the time I reached my office on the third floor, the assassination had already taken place.

Lieutenant Wells was in charge of the office up there, and when I walked in, he told me that the President had been shot. I said, "Oh, yeah, I'm sure they did." I thought he was just kidding me because earlier that morning, before we all went out, when we were sitting around talking about our different assignments, I said, "Well, I wish you good luck. But you can't put enough people around to keep him from getting shot if somebody really wants to shoot him." So I thought he was just making reference to that remark that I'd made that morning. But he was serious about it. Then he suggested, as soon as I got the prisoner upstairs, to go to the Book Depository and see how I could help with what they needed down there.

When I got to the Depository, I saw one of the police inspectors, Sawyer, on the front steps, and asked him if the building had been secured. He said, "Yes, we're taking all the witnesses over to the sheriff's office."

I said, "Well, I'd better go over there and check and see what's happening."

So when I got there, the chief deputy, Allen Sweatt, who was wringing his hands, came over to me and said, "Oh, I'm glad you're here! I've got all the witnesses here. What do you want me to do with them?" Right away, they became our witnesses.

So I said, "We've got to have statements from them, that's the main thing we've got to have." At the time, he had five or six people in there.

About that time Detectives Edwards, Maberry, and four or five others from the Burglary and Theft Division walked in and asked, "We were sent down here to give you a hand, so what can we do?"

I told them, "You're just what I need. Take one of those witnesses, scatter out on one of these desks here, and take down whatever they tell you. I don't care how insignificant it might be, just take down everything and I'll get to you later and we'll assimilate it altogether. But take down whatever they tell you." So it worked out just fine, and I started back to the Book Depository. At that time, I heard the radio mention that some officer had been shot in Oak Cliff.

As a result, I picked up the phone, called Lieutenant Wells and asked him who was covering the shooting of the officer. He said nobody. So I said, "I'll make it because, to me, that's part of the family. I'd rather cover that than the President's assassination." I went back and got Edwards' keys because my car was blocked in way the heck up at head of the street. He'd left his sitting in the middle of the street, so I went and got it and headed to Oak Cliff where the shooting of the officer had taken place. I never did get into the Book Depository because I got sidetracked each time I started there.

When I got to the scene of the shooting of the police officer, he'd already been carried away. His car and some of the witnesses were there, including two women, one of which eventually identified Oswald for us. I got their names and had the officers in the area get the names of anybody else that had seen anything and to turn them in to me. At that time, I took charge. Anytime there's a murder that takes place, a Homicide detective takes charge of it, and I was the only Homicide detective there.

I also talked to the Crime Lab man, Pete Barnes. He offered me the hulls on the ground there and I believe the officer's pistol. I said, "Pete, there's no point in me taking that and making a longer chain of command. You just take it and put it in your property yourself and tag it. That way we'll eliminate one more link in that chain later on." We tried to cut out as much as possible because when you get into a trial situation, which can be rather lengthy, you can be made to show from the time it's picked up, who saw it, who handled it here and who took it here, and you've got to put it all in chronological order.

I don't remember the exact time of this, but they had called and told me that the suspect in the officer's shooting was seen here and there. Finally I got a call telling me that the suspect in the shooting of the officer had been arrested in the Texas Theater. I said, "Well, meet me in my office with him and I'll take him from there."

I never got to the Texas Theater. You've got to realize that the traffic was so jammed up on most of those streets in

Oak Cliff that you had to take side streets to get wherever you wanted to go. The main thoroughfares were all clogged because of this and the fact that everybody was wanting to go downtown.

In any case, Captain Westbrook and Paul Bentley were over at the theater when I got the call from them. I don't know which one of them called on the radio when I was told to meet them at the front office with the prisoner, but they took him up there.

When I got back in the office, he was already there. I asked where he was, and they told me that the suspect on the Tippit shooting was in the interrogation room, so I walked in there and started talking to him. I was the first officer, other than Bentley and the others, I guess, to talk to him.

I was working on him strictly from the standpoint of the officer's shooting since I made no connection with the Kennedy deal at all. He seemed really quite calm, much calmer than I think I would have been under the circumstances had I done what he had done. I asked him about the shooting of the officer, and he said, "I didn't shoot nobody!"

I told him, "Well, you strike me as a relatively intelligent man. You know that we can take that pistol that you had on you and run a ballistics test and prove that your gun was the one used to shoot him."

And he said, "Well, you'll just have to do that." So he was very calm and collected. He wasn't upset or anything. In fact, I would say that he was too calm. If I had just shot at the President of the United States, I think I would have been a lot more concerned than he appeared to be.

He struck me as being just an average individual. I ran into them everyday. He didn't strike me as being unusually intelligent, and he certainly didn't strike me as unusually retarded either. I had but fifteen minutes or so with him, and in that length of time, you don't have time to really reach much rapport with an individual. I have gotten people to confess to murders and robberies after spending as much as two or three hours with them. But, in this case, in fifteen minutes, you just don't reach a rapport where you have give and take.

After about fifteen minutes, the Captain and some of the other men came back into the office. They were getting ready to fan out in different directions because, by process of elimination, they knew that Oswald was one man that didn't show up for work after lunch, and they were going to see if they could find him. While they were getting set to send people to different places where they might locate him, somebody remembered that the name of the suspect in the Tippit shooting was similar to what they were looking for. One of the officers stuck his head in the door and asked me what his name was. I told him and he shut the door. Then, about two minutes later Captain Fritz and the Secret Service piled in and took my prisoner away.

After that I just waited around till I knew there was some work to do. We were all sent out on different assignments, and I supervised some of the lineups that afternoon.

Contrary to what some have alleged, they were normal lineups. In our line of business, you can't afford to fake a lineup because you pay for it down the line if you do. So we got four other people that looked just as much like the individual as possible: the height, the skin coloring, the age bracket. You can't get all blacks and put them in there with one white because, if you do, the court's going to kick it out.

In our lineups, we usually had the jailers upstairs, who had seen the prisoner and knew what he looked like, go along through the cells and had the prisoners stand up to the bars to see if they were the right size, etc.

There was really no one in charge of a situation like that. I think Captain Fritz actually was sitting in on most of the lineups. Whoever was in charge with the witness, Helen Markham, we'd say, "Which man in that lineup do you think is the man that shot the officer?" They were numbered one, two, three, and four. And we had them face and then turn sideways, and back and sideways the other direction.

She then picked him out, and whoever the officer was near her would say, "She picked number four out of this lineup." Then we'd keep the names of those people that were in that lineup so if anything ever happened later on, we'd know who was in that lineup.

The following morning, Saturday, I was back in the office before 7:00 A.M., and we were given different assignments. I don't remember where I went or what I did, but we had different people we had to interview and re-interview to see if anything new had come into their minds.

During the course of that weekend, I sat in about three different times with Captain Fritz and Mr. Kelley from the Secret Service while they were doing their interrogations of Oswald. He never volunteered anything. Now you'll get some of the officers that will say that he was belligerent and all that. The only times he ever showed any belligerence at all while I was there was when they had to move him, and he would get in front of the cameras and give that iron fist salute. There was also the time when FBI agent Hosty came in, and he got a little upset at him for going out and talking with his wife. But one of our other officers, who was a rookie at the time, has made several statements to the public that he was arrogant. He couldn't be more wrong. He has made several statements that were completely untrue about how belligerent he was because I talked to him first. He's also made the statement that he talked to him. I don't think he ever talked to Oswald at the time by himself. But that's another one of those deals where the officer's trying to improve his part in this thing.

I remember on one occasion Kelley asked him about the Hidell identification which he had on him and if he knew anybody by that name. He answered, no. Kelley then asked him, "Did you ever use that name?" And he said, no. Kelley said, "Well, isn't it true that when you were arrested, you had an ID card with your picture and the name on it in your possession at the time of your arrest?"

Oswald responded, "I think that's right."

Kelley further asked, "Well, how do you explain that?"

Oswald replied, "I don't." Just like that! So what are you going to do with something like that?

I feel that we could have got it out of him if we'd had the opportunity to talk to him, if we'd have handled it in a routine manner. But you've got to realize that that hallway on the third floor at the police station's about six feet wide. When you cram 150 photographers and people in that hallway, which is about fifty feet long, with cameras and microphones and all that, you can't move one way or the other. Everybody was clambering for information. He knew this was going on out there, and he's the type of individual that liked publicity, too. I feel that that's the main reason he did it.

I think Chief Curry probably bent over backwards to try to help out the media. Of course, we stationed uniformed officers outside the office door to not permit anybody in, but that didn't keep down the clamor and everything outside. We had a glass door there, and it looked like people at the zoo looking in. I know how the animals in the zoo felt with so many people looking in trying to see or do something. Probably what happened was that somebody said, "Can we take our cameras up there?" And I'm sure that the chief and some assistant chiefs were thinking in terms of maybe two or three, but you've also got the beat reporters, too. I would have cleared them out and suggested that at the time. They even ran a cable up through the hallway to run their cameras up.

In fact, I made a suggestion to Curry on Sunday morning when we got ready to transfer Oswald. Captain Fritz and I went over to the White Plaza Hotel and drank coffee that morning, waiting for something to take place. I forget now what it was. Anyway, when we walked back to the police station across the street, we stopped and met Chief Curry on the first floor, which was completely deserted. There wasn't a soul on the first floor. We talked about it for a little while, and I told the chief then, and Captain Fritz agreed with me; I said, "Chief, we don't owe those people a damn thing! Why don't we take him out on this floor? See, there's not a soul here and you could stop the elevator on the first floor and still go into the basement. Why don't we stop the elevator here on this first floor, take him out, and put him in a car on Main Street? We can be in the county jail before these people down here have any idea we've even moved him?"

"Well, Leavelle," he said, "I made a promise to the news media that they could film the transfer. I'd like for them to see that we haven't abused him or mistreated him or anything, and I'd like to keep my promise on it." I can see the chief's reasoning on that. I didn't agree with it particularly, but that was what he wanted and he was the chief.

Anyway, Cap and I came back to the office, and Graves and I were sent upstairs to bring Oswald down for interrogation and the transfer. On the way down, we didn't talk to him. You really didn't have much time for conversation.

Meanwhile, the main thing was they were waiting to get one of those armored cars to move him. That wasn't our idea! I think it was the chief's or somebody who thought it might be a good idea. The transfer wasn't any secret by any means, so of course, we had several phone calls down there saying, "If you load the armored car, we're going to turn it over and set it afire" and this kind of stuff. These were all anonymous calls, and under the circumstances, was common. When they started getting the threats on him, that's one reason why it was decided to use the armored truck. Then they couldn't get it down into the basement, so they were stymied there. I didn't know when and neither did anybody else as to what exact hour or time he was going to be moved.

In that last interrogation, Kelley, the chief of the Secret Service was there, along with Holmes, the postal inspector, and some other officers; Captain Fritz did most of the questioning. Oswald just answered their questions and never volunteered any kind of information. Kelley asked him about one incident, "You were involved in that Fair Play for Cuba Committee in New Orleans?" And Oswald replied that he was. Kelley said, "Well, now that the President has been killed, do you think the U.S. government's policy toward Cuba will change in any manner?"

He responded, "Well, I don't think under the circumstances..." and he turned toward Captain Fritz, "I believe I'm charged with the President's murder, is that correct?" And the Captain said, yes. He said, "I don't think it would behoove me to make any statements about it because it might be construed in a different light than what I intended for it to. But I will say this," he said, "so far as I know, in any country, and this is no exception, that when the President or whoever dies or is killed or whatever, there's always a second in command that takes over, and in this case, I believe his name is Johnson. So far as I know, I think Johnson's ideas on Cuba are the same as Kennedy's, so I don't see any possibility of change."

That's a pretty good answer to me. I don't think I could be calm like that. I don't think he anticipated the questions, but I think he had enough intelligence that he was able to answer whatever questions they asked him. Of course, he had no way of knowing that they were going to question him in any kind of depth about that Fair Play for Cuba thing or any of that other business, so he couldn't very well anticipate what they were going to ask him.

The Cap made the decision on the time of the transfer. I don't know exactly what held it up. We could have transferred him an hour earlier, or it could have been an hour later. There wasn't any set time because I asked him when we were going to transfer, and he said he was waiting to talk to somebody. I don't remember what it was. It didn't have anything to do with Oswald, but it was something else. Curry, I think, just let it rest with the Cap. Whenever he got through and thought it was time to transfer him, he let him.

Curry wasn't in the picture much. One has to realize that the chief of police of a large metropolitan police department has got a lot of other things to do besides fool with one case. And even though it might be a case of some notoriety, he had other things to do. I'm sure that he was getting many calls and so forth from out of the city and out of state that he had to answer, so I'm sure that he was doing many of those things.

Meanwhile, as I mentioned, they couldn't get the armored truck backed down into the basement. That might have been what the holdup was; they were trying to make arrangements for the armored car. When they found out they couldn't get it in, then the Cap said, "Well, we'll just move him by car." The armored car was then moved and taken back to wherever they got it. I didn't agree with that idea anyway.

I've been asked many times why I was picked over somebody else regarding the transfer. I don't think there was any particular reason why Graves and I were picked over anybody else. We just happened to be available at the time. We had done some work together, but we weren't assigned as partners; Montgomery was Graves' partner. I've also been asked about the suit I was wearing that appeared in the pictures of the shooting of Oswald. I usually didn't wear that ice cream suit, as they called it later, but I only had two or three suits, so I didn't have too much change.*

As we were getting ready to leave the office, while I was handcuffing him, I just jokingly told him, "Lee, if anybody shoots at you, I hope they're as good a shot as you are."

He said, "Aw, there ain't nobody going to be shooting at me."

And I said, "Well, if they do, you know what to do, don't you?"

He replied, "Well, the Captain told me to follow you."

So I said, "Well, in that case, you'll be on the deck pretty quick then!" It was more in jest than anything else. I didn't realize how soon it was going to happen.

Nothing was said as we came down on the elevator, Graves holding his left arm and myself being handcuffed to his right hand. The Cap said, "I'll go down and stand in the doorway leading into the basement. When you come out on the elevator, when the car is in position, I'll give you the high sign and you come on out."

The jail office was in the basement at that time, so we came in through the jail office and started out the side door. The jail sergeant's desk was just across from the elevator, and you had to walk past that and then to the right around it, then you entered a hallway and through the doors leading to the garage. They had the door propped open, so I could see the Cap through the door. For some reason, I don't know why, I asked Graves, "Hold it for a second," and I said, "Cap, is that car in position?"

Evidently he didn't hear me because Cap did have a little trouble hearing sometimes, and he said, "Yeah, come on." But the car wasn't in position, and the news media was so thick that Dhority was pushing them back with the car. The car was supposed to be sitting directly across the entrance way so that the back door would be open and you could walk right in the

---

* Although the suit and hat appear to be white or cream-colored in the Bob Jackson photograph of the shooting, both are actually more of a tan or beige color.

back door with him while Cap was going to get into the front seat. When I walked out, all the camera lights came on, and it was blinding. I could see the car moving into position, but it was only about two feet past the wall in front of us.

I was surprised that there were that many people and surprised that the car wasn't in position. I expected to see the car right across the driveway when we got down there. I knew there was going to be a bunch of news media on the other side, but I certainly didn't expect them to be standing where they were. They were supposed to have been back on the other side of the railing across the driveway so that the car would have been between us and the news media. But when all this happened, you know how news media are; they just rush in there like flushing a commode; you get them all coming out. You've seen it happen many times in these Presidential news conferences; there'll be half a dozen shouting questions at one time. There's no way you can answer all of them. That's exactly what was happening down there. All of them were sticking microphones out and asking Oswald, "Did you do it? Why did you do it?" and shouting at the top of their voices, and none of them was going to get an answer. But there was a lot of noise because of the news media.

It was only ten to fifteen feet to the car. As I walked out, all those floodlights came on, blinding us momentarily. I could see this ring of people there. As we made two or three steps, I saw Ruby step out from the crowd. I say Ruby; I knew it was somebody I'd seen, but I didn't realize who it was at the time. Of the two photographs that were taken, one by the *Morning News* and the other by Bob Jackson of the *Times Herald*, the *Morning News* picture was taken a split second ahead of Jackson's, and you'll notice that I was looking to my right. It looked like Ruby was standing right in front of me. I saw Ruby when he stepped out of the crowd and still had the pistol by his side. I could see it out of the corner of my eye with my peripheral vision. But we're only talking about a second and a half. That's about how long it took him to take two short steps and bring that gun up and... Bang! We timed it later with the camera's film because we knew how many frames that goes per second, and we were able to go back and check that. That's one thing that Alexander and I did, and it was determined that it was about a second and a half from the time Ruby stepped out of the crowd till he pulled the trigger. So you don't have much time to react.

When he stepped up and pulled the trigger, I reached over and grabbed Ruby by the shoulder and shoved back and down on him. At the same time, I could see that Graves had the hammer of that pistol locked with his thumb while Ruby was still flexing his fingers trying to pull the trigger. Since I was handcuffed to Oswald, and quite naturally he was sinking to the floor, I had to turn my attention to him.

As soon as that hit, the officers in the basement shoved all the reporters back out of the way immediately. They'd been wanting to do that anyway, so that gave them the opportunity. Billy Combest, another detective who was standing behind us, picked up one arm and leg, and I got the other arm and leg on the right hand side, and we carried him back into the jail office and laid him down. I gave Billy my handcuff keys and told him to unlock the handcuffs. We laid him on the floor because we knew the officers weren't going to let anybody down that hallway, so we knew he was safe there. Meanwhile, the intern that was stationed was summoned and started artificial respiration on him.

While we were in the jail office, Ruby was hauled through and headed upstairs. He was ruffled up a bit because about six or seven officers piled on top of him and had him underneath them.

The ambulance arrived in just a matter of minutes. As it pulled in, we put him on the stretcher while Dhority and I crawled in the back and rode to Parkland with him.

At the time, I didn't know if the wound was fatal or not. He was shot through the stomach, but I've seen people shot through the stomach that lived. A few years later I was shot at by a man, and my partner shot him in the stomach with a shotgun and blew a hole in him that you could stick my fist in, and he lived. So you can't just assume that because somebody's gut shot that they're going to die.

But he didn't look too good; he was unconscious and out of it. About a mile before we got to Parkland, as I was holding his pulse on the way and the intern was still giving him chest massage trying to get him to breathe, he rolled and groaned and said, "Oooooh," and then went limp. I think that's when he died.

The first thing I told the doctors when they took him in the emergency room was, "I want that bullet." I could feel the bullet that went all the way through him just under the skin. So the doctor just took a scalpel and pushed it like a ripe grape, slit it, and it just popped out onto a little tray. I handed the nurse my pocket knife and told her, "Now before you give that to me put your initials or mark it some way in the butt of that so you can identify that as the one coming out of him." She did that and I wrapped it in gauze or Kleenex, put it in my pocket and later took it to the lab for testing.

I was at the hospital long enough for them to tell us that he was deceased. As soon as they gave us the official announcement, somebody else from the office had come out there and took Dhority and I back. When we arrived, Cap was interrogating Jack Ruby in that little office.

After that I don't remember what all I did other than make out some reports. I think I wrote up a little narrative of what took place from the time we got to the basement, to Parkland and back. In that kind of business, you've always got reports to write up.

I didn't have time for reflection and fault finding and all that. I never really gave it a thought at that particular time because I was too busy with other things. We were busy trying to tie up loose ends and get as much evidence as we could because we still had to prove the case on Oswald, which we pretty well did. The fact that he was dead didn't have anything to do with it, so we had to go on and pursue that. I didn't have time for speculation like these writers have done. We leave the speculation to the writers and somebody else.

But I didn't feel any guilt, no. There certainly wasn't any guilt there because I didn't feel like it was my fault that he got shot. I had done everything that I could think of, even to the point of making the suggestion to the chief that we take him out upstairs. So I felt like I had done everything that was in my power to prevent it.

When I saw Ruby coming with the pistol, when he pulled it up, I pulled back on Oswald. But we were right together, so I didn't have any leverage. As a result, when I jerked back on him, all I succeeded in doing was just to turn his body. If I hadn't done that, the bullet would have entered just above the navel area straight ahead. As it was, it entered about four or five inches off to his left side. Some of these conspiracy writers later indicated that I jerked him that way so that the bullet would hit all the vital organs. You get all kinds of things being said. You can't win for losing in something like that.

But as far as who was responsible for what happened, certainly somebody was, and I don't think it was anyone in particular. I've told the news media many times, "You're going to have to share that responsibility for this death because, if we hadn't been catering to you, it wouldn't have happened. Whoever else gets the blame for Oswald being shot, you, the news media, are going to have to share about 50 percent of it. If we had cleared the media out of there and kept them at arm's length so that we could have conducted business in a normal routine manner, things would have been different."

The following day, on Monday, the lieutenant told us not to leave the office, that the Cap wanted certain ones of us to be there. I got worried about him because he hadn't shown up. In fact, Buster Kearn, the sheriff from Houston, had called and said that he had been unable to reach him. I was afraid something might have happened to him because he was under a little pressure and he'd had some heart problems before, so finally I called him and he said he was on the way down. Graves and Montgomery were with him when he called back from the Greyhound Bus Station and asked the secretary if I was there. She said yes, and I took the call in the squad room. At that time, there were some FBI agents and Secret Service people in the squad room, so when I answered the phone, I was told to go into his office and close the door. He said that he was with Graves and others; they'd been down to the county jail; everything was clear down there, and he was wondering if we could sneak Ruby out past the news media and get him down there without anyone being the wiser. I told him, "Yeah, I think it will work. I think we could do it."

He said, "Well, don't tell anybody. Don't even tell the lieutenant. Just get some of whoever you want with you and do it." I thought it was a little odd. Even Cap said, "You think we'll get in trouble?"

I said, "Well, we might get our ass eat out, Cap, but I'd rather have that than lose another prisoner."

He replied, "I think you're right."

Normally, when I'd walk in the office, the officers would want to know what you wanted or, in jest, give you a hard time. In this case, when I walked in, I just touched on the shoulder Charlie Brown, E.R. Beck, and Charlie Dhority and just bent my head, and, for once, they didn't say a damn word; they just got up and followed me out as I told them to come on.

So when we went down to the basement, I said, "Here's the layout. The Cap's going to drive through the basement at exactly such time. Dhority and I will go up and get Ruby and bring him down. Beck, you get a car and get it started and ready to go in the basement. Charlie, you stand there at the window of the jail office, and when we come down off that elevator, if everything is all right, you just stand there like you had talked to the jail sergeant. When the Cap and them drive through and park right across this deal," same procedure as the Oswald transfer. "If everything is all right, you give us the high sign; if it's not, we won't go any further."

So Beck got his car ready; Charlie got there and was talking to the jail sergeant, and Dhority and I got Ruby started. When some of the officers saw us start out of there, they said, "Hot dog, y'all going to transfer Jack Ruby? I'm going to get out of here! I don't want to be around this place!" So they took off!

When we got down to the basement, Ruby wanted to wear my hat, and he wanted to put my coat on for a disguise. I told him, "Jack, there ain't nobody going to shoot you! Who in the hell wants to kill you?" But he was afraid somebody was going to shoot him.

When the Cap and them pulled through, Graves was sitting in the backseat and L.D. was driving; the Cap was sitting in the passenger side of the front. The car door was thrown open, Charlie nodded his head, and as we went out in a hurry, Jack tore loose from us and ran and jumped into the back of that car and laid down on the floorboard. I just crawled in on top of him, put my feet on him, and slammed the door. Dhority, Beck, and Charlie got in that other car, tore out and went right around the block and headed down to the county jail.

We were there in just a matter of minutes. Beck drove up in front of the sheriff's entrance and old Dhority and the others fell out with shotguns. One of the deputies, a man named Townsend, started out one of the side doors when Dhority hit him in the belly with that shotgun and shouted, "Hold it!" Townsend nearly dirtied his britches right there.

He said later, "God, I thought it was a jail break going on!"

So we brought him on in and Judge Brown said, "Sign him to my court." That's how Judge Brown got him assigned to his court.

We were all congratulating each other when we got back to the car about how that was the way the other one should have been done when we began to hear the radio popping, "305, call your office. 305, call your office. 305, call the lieutenant. Call the lieutenant."

My call number was 305, so I picked up the microphone and told them, "Call the lieutenant up there and tell him that everything's under control and we're on our way back." Somebody was in the office at the time and relayed the dispatcher's message to Lieutenant Wells. He apparently just slammed the phone down because he didn't know where we were. He could just see the Cap coming in there and jumping all over him because we were gone and his not having any idea where we were.

When I got back to the office, he said, "Well, I guess I'll forgive you this time. But don't let it happen again!"

The Dallas police came under criticism because some of the officers had known Ruby. I'd met him on several occasions. In fact, I'd met him back in 1950, shortly after I went to work for the department when he had a Longhorn Club down on South Ervay at that time. I'd been in his clubs. He'd often want me to come down and take in a show and eat a steak dinner on him. But I never did that. I know some of the officers did, but I never would because, at the beginning of my career, I made it a point not to accept any kind of gratuities from anybody because I always felt like there'd be a day when they'd say, "Well, I've done this for you, now you do this for me." Probably a cup of coffee is about the most I ever accepted from anybody.

Jack was a whole lot like Oswald in many respects. They were both losers in that they wanted to be somebody and they weren't. As an example, everybody has fantasies about wanting to be a hero. We all think we'd like to be the quarterback that flings the touchdown pass that wins the game or does any number of things. That's that Walter Mitty that everybody has, but we don't let it get the better of us. Jack was the type of individual that just let it get ahead of him. Ruby told me an interesting thing when I was a patrolman which didn't make any sense to me at the time, but it did after this incident, years later. He told me, "I'd like to see two police officers sometime in a death struggle about to lose their lives, and I could jump in there and save them and be a hero."

I guess there's a lot of people that would like to do something like that, but that's strictly Walter Mitty type thinking, and that's the kind of individual he was. When I transferred him, I told him when we were going down on the elevator, "Jack, in all the years I've known you, you've never done anything to hurt a police officer, but you didn't do us any favors this time."

He replied, "Well, all I wanted to do was be a hero, and it looks like I just fouled things up," except he used another word for it.

"You can say that again," I told him.

But I don't think he planned it; it just happened. There was no way he could have planned it because he didn't know when the transfer was going to happen, and he didn't know he could get into that basement. It was a thirty second break in security that let him get in the basement. Roy Vaughn, who was a patrolman, was assigned to the top of the Main Street ramp and was not to let anybody in, which he didn't. But just prior to the shooting, a lieutenant and a sergeant wanted to go somewhere, and they couldn't get out because they were still jacking with that armored car. So they went up the wrong way up the ramp going out onto Main Street. Roy walked out in the middle of the street and held up his hand to stop traffic so they could come out and make a left turn. According to what

Ruby told me, that's the precise time that he walked right on down the ramp.

We checked it, and it had to be right because we knew the exact time that the shooting occurred in the basement. I went down and got a copy of the telegram that he sent to a girl in Fort Worth, and the time stamped on that thing was four or five minutes from the time of the shooting, so it had to have been just like he said. It was just one of those unfortunate things that just worked out.

I didn't know that they had let anybody go out the wrong way. I checked on it and found out later that the sergeant and lieutenant did go out the wrong way to that basement. Then I checked the time element of the telegram when he paid the money to send to Fort Worth. I even stepped it off to see how long it would take me to walk from the Western Union. In fact we got out there and tape measured it, too. It was almost a block, and it took two or three minutes to walk.

He made a number of statements after the shooting about how he didn't want Jackie Kennedy to have to come back down here and testify, so he shot him for that reason. He didn't have any reason; it was just a spur of the moment type thing, and he couldn't have planned it. He always carried that pistol with him, or quite often did, so it wasn't unusual that he had that with him. In fact, he'd been arrested two or three times for carrying a pistol. He had very little interest in Kennedy. He didn't even bother to go down and watch the parade. Instead, he was at the *Dallas Morning News* writing out an ad for his club. Those stories about sparing Jackie Kennedy coming back to Dallas were a bunch of BS. That was just hot air spouting.

I've got my own theory about what his thinking was when he would shoot Oswald. I think that he felt that we'd probably arrest him, put him in jail, and he'd probably go before the grand jury, and the grand jury would say, "Jack, this is a bad thing you've done, but since Oswald needed killing anyway, well, we're going to turn you loose this time." Then he could stand there at the front door of the Carousel Club and people would come from afar to shake the hand of the man that killed the assassin of the President. He'd be in all the papers and all the television programs, and he'd be a celebrity. I think that's exactly what his thinking was.

People have speculated as to whether Oswald would have confessed and why Captain Fritz didn't use a tape recorder or take notes during the interrogations. Let me say a few things about Captain Fritz.

He was one of the old time police officers who had started back in the early days and had come up through the ranks. He had worked in his younger days as a cowboy on a ranch in New Mexico. When he got into police work, he devoted himself to it exclusively; in fact, he was married to it. There's no telling how much vacation time he had on the books because he never took a vacation. The only time he took off was a day or two when he might have a little spell with his heart. That's why his marriage didn't work out because I'm sure he spent more time with police work than he did at home. So he lived by himself.

He was a very fair individual who had his thumb on everything. When I went into that division, those detectives waited for him to speak before they moved. He had his likes and dislikes, and he had officers that he favored over others. I don't think that I was one of those, but I think he had a lot of respect for me. I was kind of like him; I came up through the ranks, and I kind of thought for myself. If I thought something needed to be done, I went ahead, not asking should we do this or should we not. But quite often he would ask who had done something, and if he learned that it was me, he'd never say anything about it. I'd seen him get on some of the other officers for doing something he hadn't told them to do, but he very seldom ever said anything to me about a situation. And if he wanted something done or a little extra put into it, he came to me several times to do certain things. There were several officers in there that had more seniority, but when we'd be in a group somewhere, he'd single me out, "Why don't you take these men, some of you go here and send some over there." He made me kind of a supervisor because I think he respected my judgment in a lot of things. But Cap was very particular about who worked for him and hand picked all of his men. In fact, somebody said that the reason he picked me was because I wore a hat like his, but I wore that before I ever got into the Homicide Bureau.

Cap seldom took notes. He might make some later, but you couldn't find them even though they'd be on his desk. It looked like a jumbled jungle, but he could reach and scratch through there and find what he wanted.

Looking back, in hindsight, we should have used a tape recorder or taken notes in the interrogations of Oswald. I'm sure that the department probably had tape recorders, and they could have been used, but we didn't have any in our office. Anyway, there's a lot of people that don't want to say anything on tape because they know they can't later deny it. If they say something that isn't taped, then later, if they decide it wasn't in their best interest and they want to deny it, then it's your word against theirs.' There's some that would just flat refuse to do it.

You've got to realize also that, at that particular time, that was just another killing. It wasn't a President of the United States; it was just another killing, and it was in our jurisdiction. There wasn't a federal law against shooting the President or a congressman. It was just like shooting a man on the street, and it was our jurisdiction from the word go.

Cap didn't want any of the men giving out statements to the press because he said it might come back to haunt us later. So he said, "Let's get together. I'll make any statements that need to be made." He wanted to carry it out in the same routine manner, but he was having the same problems that the rest of us were having with the media and everybody wanting information.

If we had cleared the media out of there, Oswald would not have been able to see the cameras running and would have realized that he wasn't getting on television and that he was just another prisoner. As a result, I think things would have been much different.

Some have emphasized the fact that Oswald denied everything. Why should he admit it? He was getting the publicity anyway! If he'd have admitted it, then it would have died down faster because they would have said, "Well, there isn't anything to it; it's a cut and dried situation." But as long as he denied it, then you've got a few of these speculators out there with all these theories that's going to say maybe he didn't do it and find a reason that he didn't. If I'd been in his place, I'd have said not guilty, too, just like he pleaded to the Tippit shooting.

The reason that they've got all those theories is that they're writing a book. Is anybody going to buy a book that says that the Dallas Police Department was 100 percent right and Oswald was guilty? Nobody! But if you say that you've got a theory and that he wasn't guilty, then the people will read it. Another thing, if you'll go back and look, most of the those that have written the books have never been to Dallas.

Another example was the pathologist from New York who came up with a completely different theory on the Kennedy shooting that he was shot from the front. He was flown all over the country and was paid big fees despite what all of the other doctors who had examined the same information had said, including Doctor Petty of Dallas. SMU brought him down here, and I was called by one of the local reporters for a comment. I said, "Let me tell you, if he had agreed with the pathologists in Washington and Doctor Petty, would you have given him $10,000 to come down here and address this group? No!"

A few years ago there was a courtroom drama on television which featured some of the actual people as witnesses. It was filmed in London, but I wouldn't have gone. They didn't want me because I'm sure they have heard enough of what I had to say about it.

One of those that was on the show was Tommy Tilson of the police department. He's a nut from the word go! Five or six years after the assassination he called me and said, "I was driving out Industrial, and I saw this man running over the ledge with a rifle in his hand." I asked him what he did.

"I didn't do anything. I had something else to do," he said.

I replied, "Tommy, I don't believe I'd go around telling that bad story because it ain't too late yet to charge you with dereliction of duty." Then he changed his story. I have no idea where Tommy was that day, but I can tell you one thing: not a bit of that happened as he said, not a bit! In fact, he's changed his story at least three times. It's all a bunch of lies, and I as much told him that. But it did gain him some notoriety, and it did get him that trip to London.

Here's another little story. Of course, there were so many of these going around. We had a black come up there one day and said, "I want to tell you something. I don't want no publicity, and I don't want my picture taken, and I don't want no television, nothing like that."

I said, "Well, all right, I can assure you that you won't get that in here."

So he said, "That morning that the President was shot I was going to work and (of course it had been determined by that time where Oswald had parked and walked to the Book Depository) I was standing out on the corner and this man walked up to me and said, 'What do you think about the President?' And I said, 'I think he's a pretty good man.' He said, 'Well, me and Jack don't think so.' "

So I said, "Well, who was that? Do you know who he was?"

He replied, "Yes, sir, that was Lee Harvey Oswald I was talking to. Now I don't want no publicity on it."

I said, All right, I'll promise you that. Why don't you go to the FBI office about two blocks down the street and tell them about it? They're handling that and they'll be glad to talk to you."

"I was just down there, and they sent me up here," he replied. He was just somebody who was trying to get on the bandwagon like so many others have done over the years.

Another question of the writers is where Oswald was going after he left the Book Depository? He denied everything, so we didn't have the opportunity to talk to him about it. My theory on that is that when he went into his boarding house and changed into that jacket he just wanted to get out and make himself inconspicuous. But I don't have anything concrete to base it on.

As to whether he had the time to get from his boarding house to where Tippit was killed, I don't know that that was ever a factor with us because there was no way of timing him exactly. The landlady said that he was there for about such a time, but when you're talking about whatever time she mentioned you could be off five, ten, or fifteen minutes. From her house to Tenth Street, where Tippit was killed, was about nine blocks. So when you say about, that's not going to make it. Timing was never a problem as far as I was concerned.

Where he was headed, I've thought about. The best theory that I can think of is that he knew that they knew about that room he rented and they were going to miss him at work, and that they'd probably start looking for him, so he got his stuff and got out of there. You can add two and two together and figure it out because the police had talked to his wife and Mrs. Paine, and they told them about the room over on Beckley. So that would be just a small matter to put it together. I'm also aware that he was headed in the general direction of where Ruby lived, but how many other people lived over there? I'll put it like this: besides the Dallas police, there was the sheriff's department, state department, the FBI, the Secret Service, and an untold number of other law enforcement agencies working on it, and there was not one iota of evidence ever to show that Oswald and Ruby had ever come together anywhere. And I think, with all of them working on it and all the informants that they had, that somebody would have talked. But, over the years, I've heard all the stories, and I haven't seen or read anything yet that has caused me to change my opinion that Oswald acted alone, as did Jack Ruby.

We had convicted many in Dallas on far less evidence than what we had on Oswald. A police officer deals with physical evidence, and that is what we generally use to convict a criminal. All the theories and speculations of the writers on the assassination are nothing more than that: theories and speculation, without any basis of concrete evidence or proof.

Leavelle retired from the Dallas Police Department in 1974 and ran a polygraph business for several years. Now retired, he and his wife, Taimi, currently reside east of Dallas along the shores of Lake Ray Hubbard. Unlike most former Dallas policemen, he has a continued interest in the assassination and the conspiracy theories, along with the personalities who still do research on the subject. Recognized by many from the Bob Jackson photo of the shooting of Oswald, he has been one the most accessible, cooperative, and popular people who were involved in the events of that tragic weekend. Leavelle is in constant demand for interviews and frequently lectures to schools and other civic groups in addition to having appeared on numerous television and radio programs. He served as a consultant for the scenes involving the Dallas police in Oliver Stone's film *JFK*.

L.D. MONTGOMERY
Homicide Detective
Dallas Police Department

"Ruby was very friendly, especially to the police, and I'm sure that some of policemen frequented his clubs either on or off duty. But I don't draw any inference from that because, as a police officer, you're supposed to know the business people in your district, especially the ones that operated bars and places where there was a potential for a problem. I've got all kinds of ideas as to why he killed Oswald, but the story about his being upset over the killing of the President is a bunch of hogwash!..."

Born in Lewisville, Texas, L.D. Montgomery graduated from Woodrow Wilson High School in Dallas and served in the Navy during the Korean War from 1951 to '53. After attending North Texas State University for a year, he joined the Dallas Police Department in 1954. Promoted in 1960, Montgomery was a detective in the Homicide and Robbery Bureau under Captain Will Fritz in 1963.

––––––––––––

Most of the guys in Homicide were at Market Hall, but there were two two-man squads also operating that day: Jim Leavelle and Charlie Brown made up one of the squads while Marvin Johnson and I made up the other. We had some leads on two or three hijackers out in North Dallas and were trying to track them down and arrest them, which we did.

Jim and Charlie were going to take them to City Hall to our office and prepare show-ups and have the complainants come in and look at them. After the arrest, they said, "Why don't you guys stop and eat lunch on the way in? That way when you get through, you can come on to the office, then y'all can take over and we can go to lunch." So Marvin and I stopped at a restaurant at Lemmon and McKinney. We were required to call in to our office to inform them where we were, but I'd neglected to do so.

After we'd sat down and ordered, I happened to think, "Oh, gosh, we forgot to call the lieutenant!" So I got on the phone, called the lieutenant, and told him about Jim and the hijackers and that we were going to grab a bite before we came in.

He said, "No, y'all don't have time to eat. Come on to the office!"

"Oh, lieutenant, come on, we want to eat! We've already ordered our food."

"No, he said, "I'm not kidding with you. Now come on to the office right now! The President's been shot!"

So I went back to Marvin and said, "We can't eat; the President's been shot!" Everybody looked around and it became real quiet; I didn't think I'd said it that loudly. We told the waitress we couldn't stay, so we walked outside where all you could hear were sirens screaming.

The lieutenant had ordered us to report to the School Book Depository to assist in the investigation. Apparently it had been determined that the shots came from that location. When we arrived around 1:00 P.M., there were a lot of officers outside surrounding the building. We went to the sixth floor where there was another bunch of officers conducting a search for a gun. Boxes were over by the window where the shells were found.

I don't remember exactly where I found the brown paper that Oswald had wrapped the rifle in. It was probably close to 36 inches long with tape on it and no writing. I recall that it was stuffed between the boxes, not lying out open on the floor as were the shell casings. Since we were looking for the rifle, we figured that it must have been used to wrap the rifle. None of the items had been touched at that time. Marvin and I also found the sack where he'd eaten, and I believe that he drank a Dr. Pepper. We later took the bottle back to the Crime Lab to dust it for prints.

While searching the floor, I heard somebody say, "Hey, this is the rifle!" Several of us responded and I got a good look at it, but I didn't know much about it other than it was an old bolt action military rifle.

After that we took the Dr Pepper bottle and the brown wrapping paper back to the Crime Lab to be fingerprinted. We then returned to our office on the third floor and were there when Oswald was brought into the Cap's office to be interrogated. In that small office, which was probably eight feet by ten feet, you couldn't get more than eight or ten people in, thus I wasn't involved to any great degree with the interrogations. Captain Fritz and normally one or two detectives would be there in addition to agents of the Secret Service and the FBI.

I only recall sitting in on one of them. On that occasion, Bill Senkel and I were there when the Cap and others were looking at Oswald's little address book which contained the license number of the FBI agent who had been following him. It was rather comical! Oswald looked up at Mr. Hosty, the FBI agent, and said, "You're the one that's been harassing me and following my family!" Overall though, I couldn't really tell much about him because at that time he was so quiet and arrogant.

Saturday was mostly a day of wrapping up interviews with those associated with Oswald. My partner and I were stuck in the office answering the phones and didn't participate in any of the interviews. The magnitude of the story was obvious. Additional telephones had been put in our office with extra manpower to handle the phones. We were receiving calls from all over the world! Also, we were getting long distance calls from drunks accusing us of killing the President. Since they were paying, we'd just sit and let them run off whatever phone bill they wanted. It was a job that had to be done, and the pay was all the same: very little!

From Friday afternoon on, the news media had set up at City Hall: our offices being on the third floor. At the end of the hallway, there was a small news room where two or three local reporters stayed. But since this room was so small, all these reporters from all over the world congested the hallway along with their television cables along the floor and bright lights. It was hard to get out of the office to the restrooms.

Logically, they should have been cleared out. Jesse Curry, the chief, was the only one responsible for the operation of the department, but I think he was told what to do by the city manager, Elgin Crull. Obviously, it would have been much more orderly if it had been possible to have kept the news media in the small detail room. But Crull and others were bending over backwards to accommodate the press, especially at a time like that when we didn't want to be made to look like we were hiding something, which we weren't.

On Saturday night, Curry told the news media that if they wanted to get live pictures of the transfer of Oswald to be there by 10:30 the following morning. I really didn't think that was a wise idea, but the chief ran the department.

On Sunday morning, the news media had already been relocated to the basement, so it was quiet on the third floor compared to what it had been on Friday night and Saturday. I don't recall any cables even being on the floor. They'd already moved all their televising capabilities down to the basement.

Early that morning we were all talking in the office about where we were going to get breakfast, a usual topic of conversation. We all knew that we were going to be involved in some way with the transfer. About 9:30 Oswald was brought down from the jail and was interrogated for at least an hour and a half. It wasn't constant, though. They would talk to him for a while, then somebody would stop and take him back to the interrogation room to get a cup of coffee or whatever. No tapes or stenographer's notes were taken during the interviews. At that time, we didn't have the capability to tape them nor did we have stenographers. I imagine those individuals who were questioning him took notes, which was standard procedure.

I was not in the room during the last interrogation. Several of us were outside answering calls and attending to other business. About 10:30 Chief Curry called and told us to move him. It had nothing to do with whether Fritz was finished with the interrogation or not.

At that time, it was customary to transfer a prisoner who had been filed on at City Hall to the sheriff's department at the county jail. Usually the transfer would be handled by the sheriff's department, but since they had less manpower than the Dallas Police Department and were concerned about maintaining security at the county jail, they asked us to go ahead and bring him down.

Captain Fritz called us in and was discussing the fact that he did not like the set up they had for transferring Oswald. The original idea was to use an armored car, but then it couldn't get into the basement anyway. Matter of fact, he said, "My God, we're going to be locked up in that armored car! We'll get wiped!"

He felt that what we ought to do was to have somebody already bring a car around the Harwood Street side at City Hall, take him down the regular elevator to the first floor, jump in the car, and have him down to the jail before anybody even realized what was going on. All of us there agreed with the Cap and said, "Hey, let's try it!" But the chief had already told the news media to be there at 10:30 to get their pictures; they were waiting downstairs, and the Cap would do whatever he wanted. But the Cap was the one they would hang if anything went wrong because he was the Captain.

So we were rather disgusted at that point when Curry called and said, "Get him down here now!"

After this call, some of us discussed this other method of transfer versus what the chief wanted. Back then, we worked three-man squads. Marvin Johnson and L.C. Graves were my partners, but Marvin was off that Sunday. So L.C. and I were there along with Jim Leavelle when Captain Fritz said we were going to transfer him. Oswald decided to put on a black sweater, which was part of his personal effects, and was handcuffed to Leavelle. The Cap said, "I'll walk in front and you follow us. Mr. Graves and Mr. Leavelle will be on each side." I was to go down on the elevator with them, get him in the car, then Graves and I were to follow up in another car.

After Oswald put on the sweater, Captain Fritz, Graves, Leavelle, Oswald, and myself went through the interrogation room to the inside elevator on the third floor. Once you walk around to the elevator you've got to press a button and wait. I don't know how long we waited, but it wouldn't take but just a matter of 45 seconds to a minute to get from the third floor to the basement even though those elevators were antiquated and decrepit.

As we got off the elevator, turned left and went around in front of the jail sergeant's desk, and as we approached the door to step outside, I recall that Captain Fritz was told to wait. There was a pause, I guess, for cameras or something, then they said, "Come on!"

I was right behind Oswald when we walked through the door of the jail office. As we turned to the left to go toward the car, we were immediately blinded by the lights from all the TV cameras. You couldn't see anything! This was not what we had expected! The press was supposed to have been behind the rail on the other side of the car which was still trying to back up but couldn't. With all the lights blinding us, I was literally scared to death! I pulled my pistol but then recognized the crowd and put it back in my holster. I was that scared! There were people lined up on both sides of the wall. News media were crowding in sticking those long shotgun mikes over our faces trying to get Oswald to answer questions.

We'd only walked a few steps when I heard, who was later identified as Detective Billy Combest, say, "Jack, you son of a bitch!" That was right about the time of the shooting. Then, as Oswald started going down, Blackie Harrison and I grabbed Ruby from the back, got him on the ground and were trying to find the pistol.

"Where's the pistol!" I hollered.

And L.C. replied, "I've got it!"

While we were on the floor with Ruby, Oswald was dragged back into the jail office while we followed with Ruby. As we walked by, it looked like Oswald's wound was fatal. I was just glad that it didn't come on through because I was right behind him. If it had, I figure that I'd have gotten at least a stomach ache!

Once Ruby was taken in and the ambulance with Oswald left, Captain Fritz, Detective Beck and I then rode in a squad car to Parkland. Captain Fritz and some others went up on the elevator since Oswald had been pulled off from the emergency room, put on the elevator, and taken to the O.R. The elevator was full, so one or two others and myself stood back as we weren't going to help them any in the operating room anyway. In a short time, Captain Fritz returned. We were there only long to learn that Oswald had died.

As soon as we got back to the office, the FBI was there. The local agents had called Washington, and Hoover wanted them to take statements from all of us that were involved with the transfer. The Cap said, "The agents are here. Y'all get with them and tell them what you did," which we did.

S.A. Bookhout asked me, "What did you do?"

I told him, "You were right there, Bookhout. We handcuffed Oswald; we walked around to the elevator, got on the elevator to go down. Where'd you go? You were right there with us?"

He got a little funny and said, "I walked back to the squad room and turned up the squawk box."

I said, "Why?"

I don't remember the exact wording of his response, but it was something to the effect—"to hear the shooting. Didn't you know that the chief had received a call during the night that Oswald was going to be shot?"

"Hell, no," I said, " I didn't!" I was pretty angry at the time. His whole response, I thought, was very odd.

I didn't feel any guilt about what had happened with the transfer; I just felt disappointment because we had lost a prisoner which was really uncalled for. Had we transferred Oswald as Captain Fritz had wanted, who's to say that we wouldn't have gotten him to the county jail without his being killed. Of course, somebody might have wiped him there, but it just didn't seem like a very good setup. This is all hindsight, but I didn't like it at the time. When we stepped out of the jail office, it was the biggest mess I'd ever seen, and it was due largely because we tried to be cooperative with the news media.

I didn't appreciate the chief or the city manager or anybody else jeopardizing my life in that basement like that because I had a wife and two kids I had to be concerned about. The chief and the city manager weren't concerned about me and my family, that's for sure! And the news media that was down there weren't concerned about any safety factor either. They were the ones that impeded the safety of that transfer.

It hurt me that our department had fallen down by letting Ruby in and by having that holy mess in the basement. But I wasn't concerned with how this would reflect on the Dallas Police Department. I knew that the Homicide Bureau, myself included, had done our job. We could only handle what we were supposed to; we didn't run the whole department.

The following day, Monday, we successfully transferred Ruby to the county jail the way the other should have been handled: unannounced. Captain Fritz made the decision.

Captain Fritz at that time was living in an apartment out on Gaston Avenue. That morning my partner and I had gone out to pick him up and bring him to the office. On the way, we stopped to have breakfast. During the conversation that ensued, he said, "You know, we ought to transfer Ruby. Let's go back to my apartment and we'll set it up."

The Cap called the lieutenant and asked who was in the office. When informed, he said, "Okay, don't let them out of the office because we're going to transfer Ruby in a little while. Let me work out the plans and I'll call you back." When he called back, the lieutenant didn't answer the phone, Jim Leavelle or one of the others did. The Cap told him, "Okay, we're going to pull through the basement at 11:30 sharp. Y'all have Ruby and walk out and get in that car, 11:30 sharp."

So we whipped down in the basement; Graves and Leavelle had Ruby, jumped in the backseat and we took off. Matter of fact, I was driving. Old Jack said something to Jim like, "Where do you want me to sit?"

Jim replied, "If I were you, I think I'd get on the floorboard; somebody might take a shot at you!"

As I drove out of the basement and down the streets, the Cap said, "Don't stop! Don't stop! Don't stop!"

I asked, "Cap, can we use the red light siren?"

"No! Don't stop! Don't stop!" We got red lights everywhere! I'd get to an intersection, look around, work my way through it and go on. We finally made it to the county jail and bailed out. The Cap had said, "As soon as we get there, Mr. Leavelle, you and (whoever) get him, and we'll run to that front door of the jail. Mr. Montgomery and Mr. Graves, I want y'all to get shotguns and cover us." So, as we bailed out, some with shotguns, they went running through the gate to the front door. The deputies at the sheriff's department didn't know what was going on. All they could see was a couple of guys out there with shotguns. Fortunately, it all worked out fine.

When we got back in the car, the lieutenant was on the radio hollering, "All Homicide units call your office immediately!"

The Cap said, "Don't acknowledge anything." After we got back to City Hall and to our office, the Cap told us, "Y'all stay out here a minute; I'll walk in." As he went in, he asked, "Lieutenant Wells, where's all the men?" The lieutenant didn't know. He'd been told by the Cap to not let anyone leave the office, but somehow Leavelle and the others just walked through the squad room, got on the elevator, went up and got Ruby, went back down, all without the lieutenant's knowledge.

So when the Cap came in and asked where the men were, I'm sure the lieutenant must have thought, "Oh, my gosh, the Captain told me not to let anybody leave and they're all gone!" The Cap pulled that on the lieutenant knowing that it would shake him up. I guess you've got to have a little humor in everything.

Looking back, Mr. Hoover and the FBI looked down their noses at the Dallas Police Department over the assassination. He spanked us really hard and wouldn't allow us to send anybody to the FBI Academy. But tough stuff! They concealed information that we should have been informed about. The assassination strained relations between the Dallas Police Department and the FBI, and I'm one of those that had some hard feelings over it. Certainly the press should share the blame for its actions that weekend, but they were just trying to get their pictures and stories. The FBI knew better!

L.D. Montgomery was promoted to sergeant of detectives in 1968, then became an administrative assistant to the Criminal Intelligence Division chief in 1971. Two years later he joined the Legal Liaison Division which coordinated legal efforts between the Dallas Police Department and the district attorney's office. In 1980, Montgomery retired to become the manager of security for Texas Electric. Now retired, he lives in Mesquite, Texas.

CHARLES O. ARNETT
Captain, Dallas Police Reserves

"After the handcuffs had been removed from Oswald as he was laying on the floor, I bent over him and asked if there was anybody that he wanted me to contact, but he didn't say a word. He was dead instantly..."

Born in 1911 near Coppell in Dallas County, Texas, and raised in Estell and Euless, Charles Arnett, upon high school graduation, drove buses for Continental Trailways and later an eighteen-wheeler for Certainty Products Company for 27 years, delivering in seven states. During that time, Arnett attended the police academy and became a member of the Dallas Police Reserves. By 1963, he had attained the rank of captain in the reserves.

On November 22nd, I was stationed at Harwood and Main on the route of the parade. Before its arrival a lady came up and told me that there were three boys there that had a gun. I checked it out and found that they were teenagers who had a starter gun used for races. So I carried them up to the second floor of the City Hall and left them with some officers that were working in the office. To the best of my knowledge, they weren't put in jail but were just detained until after the parade was over.

After I had released the boys to the officers and while still at City Hall, we heard on the radio that Kennedy had been shot. As I came downstairs, I met with a deputy chief with the Highway Patrol and told him, "President Kennedy's been shot!"

He responded, "What size camera was it?" thinking I was kidding.

Later that afternoon I went to a funeral in Grapevine for my aunt. While en route I heard about the Tippit shooting on the car radio. That night when I got back, I worked down at City Hall until 1:00 or 2:00 o'clock in the morning. People were there from everywhere! Our job was to have them identify themselves before we let them on the elevators. I was there again the following night when Curry made the announcement about the Oswald transfer at, I believe, 11:00 o'clock the next morning.

Pat Dean and I were assigned to the basement that Sunday morning to check every car there and to check any place that led into or out of the basement. The locations were checked, officers were then placed to secure those locations, then we'd move on to another section. We searched the basement thoroughly, that's a fact!

I'd say that we searched for an hour and a half or two hours looking for bombs, guns, or potential suspects. We found four hunting rifles in the squad cars of officers who were going deer hunting but nothing else. Everything was searched and all doors secured. There was no way for anyone else to come in.

There were two ramps that came down into the basement. The Main Street ramp was an entrance into the basement while the Commerce Street ramp was an exit. Early that morning when I arrived there was an armored truck backed in on the Commerce side, but it wasn't in all the way because it was taller than the ramp. Across from the ramp was the parking area for the police cars. That morning TV cameras were located around the railing where the ramp flattens out.

It was estimated that 63 officers were stationed in the basement and a bunch of news reporters at the time of the transfer of Oswald, probably the most I'd ever seen at one time jammed in down there.

Shortly before Oswald was brought out Rio Pierce drove up the Main Street ramp in a blue Ford. From where I was standing, I had to move to let his car go out. At the top of the ramp you could see a guard posted if you turned and looked up, but we were all looking where Oswald was to be brought out. Standing in front of me was Detective Blackie Harrison. He kept turning and looking back all the time, though I don't think it was for any purpose.

When Oswald was brought out, he was handcuffed to Leavelle while L.C. Graves had him by the arm on the other side. Jack Ruby then ran right by me on my right side and shot him. The bullet tore him up inside and he fell. If I'd been looking up that ramp, I'd have seen Ruby running down. But I didn't see him until he passed just a split second before the shot. At that moment, I was afraid that he was going to shoot again. Everybody was grabbing at him, so I grabbed him by the leg hoping that the gun wouldn't go off again. After the handcuffs had been removed from Oswald as he was laying on the floor, I bent over him and asked if there was anybody that he wanted me to contact, but he didn't say a word. He was dead instantly.

I went inside and stayed until around 5:30 or 6:00. When I came home, I was greeted by my little grandson who said, "Poppa, I saw you grab that old, mean man!"

Later the Dallas police investigated the shooting of Oswald and interviewed a number of those who were in the basement or who might have known Jack Ruby. I spent a lot of time with Jack Revill, who investigated me. Though I don't recall all that was said in that interview, he did tell me when it was completed, "You're as clear as the sky will ever be!"

I told him, "I knew I was clear when I came in here."

I think the police department did everything they could to get to the bottom of the story as to how Ruby got in to that basement. I think he came down the Main Street ramp just as the investigation revealed. When Rio Pierce's car pulled up and the officer stepped out to stop traffic, Ruby then ran in. Obviously I didn't see that, but that's the only way that he could have gotten in.

I was unaware of any other way that he could have gotten in, though I vaguely recall that one of the Warren Commission lawyers thought that Pat Dean was being untruthful with him. I wasn't buddy-buddy with Dean, but as far as I knew, he was all right. I'd always heard that he was a friend of Jack Ruby, but I didn't know anything about him otherwise. I just worked with him, but he seemed honest to me. I can't imagine that he would helped Ruby get in.

The day after the Oswald shooting I worked traffic at the Tippit funeral. The church was on one side of I-35 and Laurel Land Cemetery was on the other. Our job was to assist people going across the interstate to the cemetery. I didn't go to the grave, and as it turned out, it was to be the last time I was in uniform.

I had become acquainted with Tippit while I was driving a truck and would stop at a little store that stayed open all night on Illinois Avenue. We'd stop in to get something to eat at that cafe and sometimes he'd come in. He talked about his kids, but I didn't know him personally. I was just sorry that it happened.

Right after the assassination people would go down the street, and when they'd see an officer, they'd say, "Y'all let the best president we ever had get killed," and things like that. One day when I was working in plain clothes I was at the Skillern Drug Store on Jefferson in Oak Cliff at the magazine rack and heard some people saying that Oswald had stayed all night in Clarksville, Texas two or three nights before all this happened. That's the area where Tippit was from. I turned the information in to the Highway Patrol who, in turn, investigated it. From what I heard, the information was true. But you hear all kinds of stories.

Personally, I disagree with some of the conclusions of the Warren Report, but as far as somebody shooting from the grassy knoll, I don't believe that. As for Jack Ruby, I think that he thought that if he killed the man that killed the president, then it would make him a hero and possibly some money. That's just my opinion, but everybody has one.

Arnett continued his regular employment as a truck driver until 1976 then worked at a grocery store another nine years. He remained in plain clothes with the Dallas Police Reserves until 1981. Today, Arnett still lives in Oak Cliff in the general location frequented by Oswald and Ruby.

ORVILLE A. JONES
Captain, Forgery Bureau
Dallas Police Department

"There was a lot of criticism of the police department because many of the officers knew Ruby. But Jack Ruby had been in Dallas close to twenty years and ran nightclubs downtown. If a policeman didn't know him, he wasn't doing much of a police job..."

Raised in a family whose father worked in the oil fields, Orville Jones moved numerous times in his early years throughout Texas, Oklahoma, Mississippi, Louisiana, and Illinois before coming to Dallas after Pearl Harbor. Jones joined the Dallas Police Department in 1942 then served with the Seabees overseas for the next three years. Returning to the police department after the war, Jones was promoted to detective in 1947, lieutenant in 1952, and captain in 1957. He was in charge of the Forgery Bureau in 1963, and was later appointed by the Dallas Police Department to head the investigation into the shooting of Lee Harvey Oswald.

I had gone to the Trade Mart out on Industrial Boulevard and had charge of security of some of the floors there when the President was to arrive. At the time, I was up on the overhanging balcony of the fourth floor overlooking the main dining table down on the first floor. Also on the fourth floor were the media with the TV cameras. So I had more or less an overall view of the situation.

The setting didn't really pose a security problem although a potential problem is always there anytime you've got the President of the United States with multi-floors and all. But it was not insurmountable, and we had it pretty well covered. Of course, one never knows what would have happened had the President gotten there, but we felt that we had a good plan and had it well organized.

About the time we were expecting the President, the White House Press Corps filed in. They had just sat down around their positions when they got up and ran out the door. About the same time we heard the news on a portable radio that shots had been fired down around the courthouse and that the motorcade had broken up. That's all we had at that time.

After that, I suggested that Lieutenant Cunningham take the men he wanted and go to the scene of the shooting to assist in any we he could. This was prior to our knowledge of any sightings in the area of the Oak Cliff Library. No reports had been received at that time of anything but the fact that there had been a shooting. When Lieutenant Cunningham contacted me later, he informed me that on the way to the shooting scene at, or near, Commerce and Houston, he had heard over the police radio about reports regarding the Oak Cliff Library. Since the traffic situation was impassable near the scene of the shooting, he decided to answer the calls to the Oak Cliff area. I advised him that he had done just as he should have under the circumstances. Of course, before he got over there the situation, I believe, had changed; it was a mistake at the library, and he went down Jefferson and ended up at the Texas Theater.

I then returned to the police department, got to my desk, and from then on it was just a hullabaloo of answering phone calls from all over the country, the media gathering, and people coming in. It was around 26 hours before I got to go home, change clothes, shave, and rest a few minutes. That was the case with many of the others, as well.

The next day, Saturday, I was back at work doing whatever was necessary in carrying out routine business. Captain Fritz's office was located adjacent to mine. He was handling that particular murder case and was putting some of the witnesses in my office while we were assisting him in any way we could, which included interrogating and transporting of witnesses to and from their homes. During that time, I saw Oswald once or twice, but he wasn't saying anything, not to me at any rate.

We let Oswald's wife stay in my office while Fritz was holding her and getting translators and so forth. She could speak fairly good English, but some of her friends and one or two others were there to help her with some of the questions that she couldn't understand. I talked to her a little, and there seemed to be little doubt in her mind that her husband had killed the President. She also told me later that he had shot at General Walker.

It was hard to form an opinion about her other than I don't think that she was a member of the Soviet police or a spy or anything like that. I think she was just a stranger in a strange land who was doing the best she could, which has apparently been born out by her staying here and raising her daughters.

On Sunday morning when I went up to the office, I saw Chief Stevenson. He told me that they were going to transfer Oswald to the county, and he specifically asked me to go down to the basement and be in charge. What he actually said was, "Gather what detectives that are up here on this floor and take them to the basement and place them wherever you think they might do the most good." Those were actually all the instructions I got along that line.

Going down there was voluntary on my part. There was such a commotion and a stew and a stir going on around there while there was still routine police business to be carried out that I just felt that my help was needed. I was keeping in touch with Chief Steve, who was not only my boss, but the best friend I ever had.

The cars coming into the basement of City Hall turned down the ramp off of Main Street and, as you got even with the jail office, you could turn left into a parking area which contained between 50 and 100 spaces. At that point, you were actually under the new city hall which was built adjacent to the old city hall. If you continued straight ahead, you'd exit onto Commerce Street. The jail was to the right across the ramp. In fact, if you did more than a right-hand turn going down the ramp there was a little slope, and through it was a door leading into the jail office. There were also double doors leading into the basement of City Hall itself.

When we got down there, there were supervising officers and radio patrolmen milling around clearing out any people aside from the media that were in the basement that shouldn't be there. There were even some mechanics who were working on a squad car that were run out. I had no knowledge as to what time they were going to transfer the man, but the media was crowding around giving me the feeling that it was getting close.

As some of these officers, along with the radio patrolmen, started clearing out the basement, they kept other people from coming in. There were people in the incoming and outgoing entrances to the ramps of City Hall, and there were others around in the hallways in the basement. I'm not really sure how many officers were there or what their instructions were since that was not part of my job, but the people were checked fairly closely for identification, at least the ones we didn't know. Later our investigation did not disclose any unauthorized person in the entire crowd that didn't belong there besides Jack Ruby. In fact, I believe I was checked. Since we had officers from several different stations there, unless some of them had been into the office or had seen something on TV, they probably wouldn't have known me.

I looked around in the jail office itself, but you couldn't hardly get in there because of the reporters and TV men. There were so many of them. Some were inside the hallway, but they could not get into the jail office. Some of them were lined up I don't know how many deep blocking the ramp so that you couldn't get a car in. I just have no idea of the actual number of people that were there including around where the cars were parked to the left in the garage area. So I tried to look up Charlie Batchelor, who was the executive assistant chief, to see if I could get permission to move the media out of the way. Actually I had trouble talking to him, so I went ahead and moved everybody out of the jail office anyway. I didn't endear myself to those people at that time, but we got them all back and had a cordon of officers from the jail door to the car that was to be used for the transfer, with instructions to the officers not to allow any of them through, press or otherwise. The press who were standing in that immediate area were told as much as I could tell them: that there'd be no questions, and that they were to stay behind the line.

But there was a roar and a din going on, and there might have been one that heard it—I don't know. Certainly they weren't paying any attention to me. Even if one of them heard me, he didn't pay any attention.

I think they first decided to use an armored truck to transfer the man, but as they backed it down the Commerce Street ramp into the City Hall, the top of it hit one of the beams and lodged there, so it was going to have to be moved. Then they changed their minds and decided what they would do there was to take three cars, put Oswald in the middle car and have a car behind him go up the ramp onto Commerce Street and turn right, which would be going the wrong way, then go directly to the County Jail. In the process, they were going to have to move that armored truck out also and get one of the cars in position to put him in the middle car. But there was a tie up with some car being in the way or something. At that point, I walked up to a position which put me between those cars closer to Commerce Street than I was to the jail office. Just as I went up to see if we could help clear the way, I heard a shot, and that's when Jack Ruby shot him. When I turned around and looked back, they had Ruby in handcuffs.

Immediately I raced back and saw that he was handcuffed and being helped into the jail office away from that crowd. Shortly after, there was a call down to the jail office to release Ruby on a writ from a judge. They asked me about it and I said, "Hell, no!"

When I got on the phone to the judge, he said, "Well, I just thought we'd run a dry writ." Apparently he was going to issue the writ, but I told him that we weren't going to release the man. Don't ask why or anything about it, but trying to get them out on a writ of habeas corpus happens every day in every part of the country.

Years ago we had a bunch of safe burglar mobs that were around here headed by Cecil and Lois Green and others. Lois Green was the big shot who handled the girls, the safe burglaries, and a lot of dope, not here, but the circuit as far as Brooklyn, the Carolinas and all over the country. Anyway, he had one of the first mobile phones in Dallas. Whenever he would see the police coming and would be pulled over, he would get on that phone, call his lawyer, and the lawyer would be waiting with a writ in his hand by the time Green had gotten to the jail. I don't understand it, but I'm sure it's all for the rights of the citizens. Unfortunately it just happens that it does favors for the criminals as well as the citizens. But that's what the judge had in mind with Ruby.

The media was a real problem. There were hundreds, perhaps thousands there that weekend. Only if you've ever been in public service and tried to keep the media satisfied can you understand the problem. At this late date, and it seems like I told you so, but I've wondered why they weren't cleared out of there many times. I don't know if it was Chief Curry's or the city manager's idea, but somebody had to decide that they were going to allow them in there rather than to cordon off the place and keep them out on the streets, or at least have four or five of them act as a pool for the rest of them. So, whoever made that decision, I cannot say, but I don't blame anybody for it.

In about all instances, the media was responsive or cooperative, but not at the moment the shooting occurred. At that point, they were milling around, pressing through, pushing the officers to one side and going between them. Of course, we had quite a few officers to form that line, but it was nothing compared to the hundreds of people who were there. The situation was under control until they started out the door with Oswald, then those who were back behind the lines started pushing forward. The TV stations carried the melee with all the people breaking the lines and charging in between them acting like a mob of barbarians, each of them thinking they could get their question in so that he would talk to them and tell them something he wouldn't tell to somebody else. I don't know why they did it; I guess it was just human nature.

We were upset with the press individually, but not collectively. But again, I guess that's human nature. It's much like people driving down a highway and they see an accident with bodies lying around; everyone will slow down, gawk and look. Few will go out and try to help; most of them will just delay traffic and emergency vehicles. That's the same way they were in the basement. They lost all semblance of civilization and manners, each of them wanting to get a scoop from the others. They were naturally interested, and I could see their interest. But as far as my opinion of them individually, many of them were, and still are, my very good friends. I had no difficulties with any of them outside of the fact that it was just an uncontrollable mob after the melee started.

At the time, the chief of police was Jesse Curry. Jay was an all-state football player at Crozier Tech High School in Dallas. As a young man, he went into the police department and climbed through the ranks. As a motorcycle officer in his younger days, he decided that he wanted to settle down and go somewhere with the department. On some of the exams, his wife told me that he would fall asleep studying at night, but he made his advancements. As far as good intentions, there was never a better man than Jay Curry. He wanted to do right for everybody and held no ill will toward anyone. But if he did get upset, it took him a while to forget.

On the other hand, Will Fritz, the Homicide captain, never forgot, or at least that's what was said about him. He was very jealous of his position and everybody was picking and wanting because that was the prize position of the police department, and Fritz held it for many, many years. I never knew of him doing anything wrong to people, trying to hurt anybody, or lying. But he didn't take many into his confidence. If he had held any ill will, it would have been toward me because of some earlier instances involving both of us, not justified, but a few cases come to mind.

In 1946, we had two Negro brothers who were killing a series of liquor store operators in robberies which went as far away as Plano where a station agent was killed. Rewards were being placed on them everywhere. A rookie, who was working with me while my regular partner was working the Fair in October that year, and I arrested the two brothers at separate times. Fritz was out of town, and since his men were afraid of him, they wouldn't even interview them till he got back. In those days, we didn't worry near as much about writs of habeas corpus as we do now. So they held them in jail till Fritz came. When he started interviewing, one of the brothers said, "You turn all those other niggers loose. We're the ones you're looking for." That was one instance where we got quite a bit of publicity.

Later, in 1949, we had what we called the Love Burglar Case where a guy was burglarizing houses in the early morning hours, stealing money, and raping the women. I don't know how many cases we finally really proved, probably as many as fifteen, but I'm sure there were many, many more. Another partner and I broke that case which one of the biggest around here at the time.

In September 1945, there was a drug store that was hijacked out on McKinney Avenue and the druggist was killed. After I helped break the Love Burglar Case, we received some information as to who killed that Fairmount druggist four years earlier while I was still overseas. So we furnished Fritz the information. He had a couple of men act on our information that he pick up a certain lady that lived out in Irving, who was the wife of one of the hijackers. He had died since, but she had almost come in several times to tell about it. As it turned out, she eventually named Jack Price, who had done some time in the Missouri Pen and who was still alive, as the trigger man. Fritz arrested him, and all those people were electrocuted: the two colored brothers, the rapist, and Jack Price. So if Fritz was going to hold a grudge, he might have thought that I was interfering with his business through the years. But Fritz and I were good friends.

Assistant Chief Stevenson, or Steve as I called him, was called a policeman's policeman. He had been a street car operator prior to joining the police department and had apparently been busted a time or two for some kind of trouble. But he was one of the best policemen that I knew. As I've mentioned, he was one of the best friends I ever had, so I'm not really one to give an unbiased opinion about him.

Steve was the one that appointed me to investigate the shooting of Oswald. I had taken a few days off that Thanksgiving to visit my father in Shreveport. But just two or three hours after I got there, Steve called and said, "You told me to call if I needed anything. I need you back over here."

What's the problem?" I asked.

He responded, "I want you to look into the killing of Oswald in the basement of City Hall." So I returned to Dallas that night.

When I arrived, he gave me my choice of anybody in the department to work with, so I chose Captain Westbrook and Inspector Sawyer, and as investigators, paired off Jack Revill and Frank Cornwall, Paul McCaghren and Cecil Wallace, Detective H.M. Hart was involved as well. So I had some pretty good men. As it turned out, Sawyer had little to do with it as he went into the hospital and had his rear end operated on about the second day we convened. When he got back, I asked him to sign the report. Westbrook, on the other hand, worked on the investigation and had been appointed to the committee because he was in charge of the Personnel Office. In my report, I gave credit to Curry for assigning the committee, but as far as I know, it was Steve's idea. Now Steve may have talked it over with Curry, and Curry may have told him to do it, but I have no knowledge of that.

Steve wanted to find out if there was talk of collusion and to discover just what had happened. A lot of policemen did know Ruby, and he wanted me to see if anybody had helped or assisted him or let him stay down there all the time because he had been seen bringing food to some of the officers the night before when Oswald was there. In fact, he'd brought food not only to the police, but to the press, as well.

The shooting of Oswald screwed up the prosecution on one of the best murder cases that ever involved prominent people. I don't know anybody anywhere in the department that wanted Oswald killed like that and not go to trial. I think they had a perfect case and didn't see any way out for him. In all these mock trials which they've had through the years, nothing has indicated any fact of innocence. But, of course, you can put a lot of rocks on the roadway of anything when you start to ask "What if? What if?"

The defense came up with psychomotor epilepsy in trying to explain Ruby's innocence of killing Oswald. You had to go far out to find a defense. You put somebody on TV and shoot someone, how are you going to find him innocent except by the use of chicanery or legal tricks? Hell, millions of people saw it!

The investigation lasted from just after Thanksgiving until December 16th. I figured at that time that three weeks ought to cover it, then I could make a report and was sure that if any leads came up we could check them and follow them up. Everybody was interviewed that we could possibly find.

My report stated that Jack Ruby got up that morning at his apartment here in Oak Cliff and received a phone call from a stripper in Fort Worth. She needed money, so he got in his car, drove down and parked in a parking lot across from the Western Union and went in to send this telegram.

There were stories about Ruby receiving a signal. When he went in and sent the telegram, it was stamped 11:17, and when the shot was fired and the melee occurred, the TV cameras showed 11:21 on the clock in the basement. That's four minutes! If there was some type of conspiracy, he had four minutes and would have had to have known what time the man was coming down, which we didn't know, Fritz didn't know, nor did any of the policemen. The only reference to it was made by Curry when he told the press that if they'd get there by 10:00 or 11:00 o'clock, or whatever he said, that it would be early enough. He didn't know exactly what time it was going to be. So if there was a signal or something, somebody had to have some rather Divine Knowledge of what was going happen.

So from 11:17 till 11:21, he had to complete his transaction at the telegraph office; he had to walk out the door and either walk down Main Street, as we thought, or go around to the alley and come in there, get into position, be standing there when they walked out with Oswald, charge through and shoot the man. Now that's a lot of coincidence!

Now, as to what actually happened, some of this comes from my own knowledge because I was there. Roy Vaughn was a patrolman who was assigned on Main Street to control the traffic coming down into the basement of City Hall making sure that no unauthorized person came in. Who assigned him there, I had no idea. But he was out there clearing the way for these cars and armored cars, and then later the three squad cars to come out. Roy stood up there keeping everybody out when one or maybe two police cars came up the ramp. Now Roy had been in the police department just a few years, and in those years, he'd never seen a police car come up the ramp the wrong way onto Main Street. So here they came. I don't know how much of a crowd was outside then, but I do know that he stepped out, held his hands up to hold traffic back since Main was a two-way street, while these squad cars got out. Then he turned and stepped back to his position to keep everybody out.

Our theory, as stated in the report, was that in the time that he turned and stuck his hands up, Jack Ruby had walked from the Western Union office, went down the ramp, and was standing there whenever they brought him out, charged through the people and shot Oswald.

A headline several years later in the newspaper said that Jack Revill, one of our investigators, changed his mind. Revill was a good friend of mine who worked for me off and on for a long time and who was smart enough to later become assistant executive chief. I haven't talked to him about it, but according to what I've read, he figured that Ruby must have come down the alley at the back. Even so, that changes nothing.

There could have been other ways for him to get in. As Revill has apparently come to believe, he could have come down an alley that ran behind the Western Union office and come in through a freight elevator into the new City Hall and then down to the basement through some doors that should have been, and usually were, locked, and in my opinion, were locked.

One of the officers, P.T. Dean, became involved in some type of confrontation about that. He was a sergeant in Radio Patrol then and later became a detective. I think that he may have been the one who assigned Vaughn out there on the street. I'm not sure whether anybody put Dean in charge of security in the basement or not. If they did, I wasn't told about it.

There was a lot of criticism of the police department because many of the officers knew Ruby. But Jack Ruby had been in Dallas close to twenty years and ran nightclubs downtown. If a policeman didn't know him, he wasn't doing much of a police job. As it was, I knew very little about Ruby. As I found out later, some of my men had filed on him for assault just a few months before the assassination. He'd been put in jail for carrying a pistol a time or two and, as far as I know, no one had tried to get him off without filing. At least I know our cases were filed on him. Now, if the charges were dropped, that would have to be done through the district attorney's office after they were filed.

I had known him when I was a detective back in the '40's. I was in Burglary and Theft for many years as lieutenant and acting captain, and Jack was a good source of information. He liked to get along with the police, but all those people liked to get along with the police. They liked to have you around, but you might create a problem with them by showing up at their place too frequently because it might scare off some of their legitimate business.

While we were conducting our investigation, the FBI was looking into the Oswald shooting, as well. Up until the assassination, we had had a good relationship with the FBI for many, many years. In fact, Dallas was one of the few cities in the country that graduated a representative at every one of the FBI Academy classes. In fact, I was at the 61st session.

I didn't know Hoover personally, but I approved of what he was doing. The actions he took were more or less necessary to have a cohesive unit since it was spread all over the world and had so many responsibilities, as well as some of the unofficial responsibilities that some of the chief executives put on him.

Despite that, there was always a tendency that working with the FBI was a one-way street, which I could understand, though I didn't agree with. I had a half-way agreement with the FBI during our investigation. It was obvious to me, with all the news media that were in the basement at that time, that I could not send people all over the world to interview them. So we made the results of our investigations available to the FBI, and they would give us what information was important. They interviewed every one of the media on that no matter where they were in the world. Their report to me, which was unofficial, was that none of them came up with anything that could be pertinent to our case that we didn't already know.

After the assassination, relations between the police department and the FBI were strained to the point where we did not have a representative in the FBI Academy classes. I'm not really sure about all that I'm told, but Jack Revill was apparently talking with FBI Agent Hosty shortly after the assassination, and Revill allegedly mentioned that Hosty told him that they had some information on Oswald and knew that he was capable of committing an assassination. But this gets back to some of the criticisms of the conspiracy angle on the assassination.

Oswald worked at the Book Depository for some time. The President decided to come to Dallas and went right in front of where Oswald worked. So that's why Oswald got his job there; so that he could kill the President. The only thing wrong with that is that there was much talk about holding the Presidential speech at Fair Park, which meant that he certainly would not have come by the Book Depository. The decision for the final route was made just a few hours before the shooting. The Secret Service and a lot of other departments thought it would have been a much safer route for them to leave Love Field, go down Inwood Road to Industrial, down Industrial to the Trade Mart and never come downtown. But the President decided that he wanted to see the people, a political move, and it was good politics to be seen by the people. So he ultimately was the reason that they came downtown and eventually by the Book Depository. Neither Oswald or anyone else could have known that that was going to happen, so that's all out the window.

But the conspiracy books have a price on their corner, and the writer's are trying to sell the books. They're going to influence a lot of people, as well as a few that they wouldn't have influenced otherwise. But most who are influenced are those who have just gotten a traffic ticket, been burglarized, or been put in jail. It used to bother me to a certain extent, but now I more or less have learned to sit in my house by the side of the road and watch the world go by.

It's hard to say how the Dallas Police Department has been portrayed in all this. Each individual gets some information and makes up their mind about it, and so many of us seldom ever change our minds once they've been made that we'll look for something that will prove that we're right rather than prove what really happened. I know that in the annals of the police associations, the Dallas Police Department has always ranked rather high, even at the lowest ebb at that time. In fact, one of our deputy chiefs, Glen King, was a director of the International Association of Chiefs of Police since then.

But it is true that after the assassination, morale in the police department was rather low due to the opinion expressed and implied by people outside of Dallas on the radio, TV, and in newspapers. One comical incident occurred the day after the Oswald killing. A lieutenant on the Boston Police Department called me on the phone, and after we had exchanged greetings, I asked him how I could help him. He said, "You can't help me at all. I just wanted to tell you that you fellows did a fine job down there! That's the way to settle that: get that son of a bitch shot! He was giving us credit for something we didn't do, intentionally, at any rate.

Orville Jones retired from the Dallas Police Department in 1966 after almost 25 years service. Following his retirement, he became the security director for American Express Company for the Southwestern part of the United States. After ten years on the job, he retired and five years later became the chief of security for the Harris Corporation in Dallas for another three years. Orville Jones died in 1989.

RIO SAM PIERCE
Lieutenant, Patrol Division
Dallas Police Department

"I didn't see Jack Ruby at the top of the ramp. I believe that if he had been standing there that I would have recognized him because I knew him. In fact, I'd probably known Jack Ruby eight or ten years at that time..."

Born in Turkey, Texas, and raised in Littlefield, Rio Pierce entered the United States Marine Corps during the Second World War and served with distinction in the South Pacific. He joined the Dallas Police Department in 1946 and gained the reputation of his colleagues as being a tough but fair policeman.

Most of my career was spent in the Patrol Division with some of it being in Special Operations, Tactical Section. I was off duty the day of the assassination and spent the day here at the farm in Ennis.

That Sunday, the 24th, since I was working days, I came in at about 7:00 A.M. My orders were to secure the basement for the transfer of Oswald which meant to put men at all entrances and exits and not to allow anybody except authorized personnel in there. By authorized personnel, to me that meant anybody with a press card because the basement was full of people. I would estimate there were as many as a hundred people down there. It was the most I'd ever seen in the basement at one time.

The layout of the basement was such that you had a ramp leading down into the basement coming off Main Street and an exit ramp leading out onto Commerce. The ramps were fairly steep and narrow with just enough room for a car and maybe a person to walk beside a car. You could drive straight through by going down the ramp from Main and driving up the ramp onto Commerce. Then there was an entrance in to the basement of City Hall that went to the jail office. There was a hallway, then the jail office was just off that wall.

When I arrived that morning, of course, we made our detail first. In other words, we made our assignments. I'm rather fuzzy on what time we went to the basement, but there were people down there at the time. There weren't that many at first, but eventually, they began coming from inside City Hall out into the basement because City Hall was full of reporters from all over the nation.

In my opinion, there should have been more control. I'm not for suppressing news, but I think it needs to be done in an orderly manner so that business can be carried on without being interrupted by reporters. They were all over the building! I was aware that they posed a potential problem! We could have cleared them out, but if they had the sanction of the chief, which they did, then they're going to be there. And I'm sure the chief had orders from the city council or whoever as to how to handle the situation.

These people in the basement all had press cards or were authorized to be there. They were either officers or the press, or at least they were supposed to be. I didn't talk to any of the press.

It was my understanding that they had all been told what time that Oswald would be transferred. I believe ten o'clock in the morning was the time mentioned by Chief Curry. Then they began congregating in the basement. The ramp was full of people with as many as you could cram in there, all of them having their cameras and all of their equipment. They were just outside the entrance into City Hall.

I thought the basement itself was secure, but I was a little uneasy about the people that were coming out from City Hall because I did not have control of what was in City Hall. It was just that basement area that I had control of. When I looked at the people out on Commerce Street, apparently everybody knew which way the prisoner was going to go. There were lots of people out there! There were a lot on Main Street, too, but most of them seemed to know that the exit was going to be on Commerce Street because that was the normal exit from City Hall.

I didn't know until just a few minutes before what the plan was. When I arrived in the basement, there was an armored van backed in as far as it could get. Nobody had told me anything, but I supposed that they probably were going to transfer him in that armored van, at least that was my thinking at the time. I was either summoned to Captain Fritz's office or went up on another matter, but that's when I was told that I was to escort the armored van. That was my first knowledge of it. Chief Stevenson actually gave me the order. Stevenson, Chief Curry, and Captain Fritz were all in Fritz's office at the time. So it was my understanding that it was to be a decoy mission. A plain police car with, I suppose, Captain Fritz and some of his men would escort the prisoner to the county jail.

My car was in the basement and was unmarked, as lieutenants had plain cars. Since the armored van was on the Commerce Street ramp, I had to exit the entrance ramp on Main Street. It was always an entrance ramp, so it was unusual to go out that way. Sergeant Putnam rode in the passenger seat and Sergeant Maxey was in the back.

There were several of the press out there then. At the top of the ramp, there was a sidewalk. When we drove up, there were two or three people on the sidewalk on each side of the ramp. Traffic wasn't all that heavy, but there were several automobiles up and down Main Street because it was a two-way street. I didn't recognize anybody up there except the officer guarding the ramp, Roy Vaughn. As far as I know, the other officers in the car didn't recognize anybody either, at least there wasn't anything said about it.

When I got to the top of the ramp, I stopped because of the traffic out on the street. Pedestrians weren't the problem; it was the cars out on the street and getting out safely that were the problem. Vaughn stepped to the street to stop the traffic to let me out. As I recall, he stepped to the edge of the street just enough to be seen by the passing cars. I looked at him just long enough to see that the traffic was clear so that I could get out. I don't think that he was surprised by the car coming out because he knew whose car it was, at least I think he was aware of that.

In any case, after making the turn onto Main, and by the time I had circled the block and arrived on Commerce Street to get in front of the armored van, I knew that something had happened. I couldn't hear the shot. Somebody met me out there, and I just parked on the street and went down to see what was going on. That's when I learned what had happened!

When I ran down the Commerce Street ramp, what I found was chaos, absolute chaos! By that time, they had already taken Ruby inside the jail office. I didn't know that it was Ruby at that time. Oswald was still there. They had to get an ambulance for him and take him to the hospital. From there, I went to Parkland Hospital to try to gather information.

I didn't see Jack Ruby at the top of the ramp. I believe that if he had been standing there that I would have recognized him because I had known him for eight or ten years at that time. When I first met him, he was running the Silver Spur at 1717 South Ervay which was on my patrol district at the time. It was just normal routine on our part to check all those taverns and places of that nature, so I had known him long enough so that I would have recognized him at the top of the ramp if I had seen him.

Back then he was existing on sardines and crackers. As far as I knew, he had no morals and was suspected of being homosexual. Ruby, who had probably been run out of Chicago, would give out passes to his club for future favors. He was nothing more than a small time operator who wanted to be a big shot and have his name in lights at his club.

One of those who was involved in the security of the basement was Sergeant P.T. Dean. Dean evidently ran into problems with some of the Warren Commission investigators because of statements that he made regarding Ruby after his arrest. Whatever the case, Dean was a publicity seeker who could always be seen around a microphone if one was around. He had no business going upstairs with Ruby anyway. That was CID's business.

The question has always been: How did Ruby get into the basement? There's several ways he could have gotten into the basement. He may have gotten in like he said: down the Main Street ramp. I suppose he could have. But he could have also been inside City Hall and come out with the reporters. He'd been around there ever since the assassination. There's also a number of other ways he could have gotten in.

You had the steps off of Main Street that go into the first floor of City Hall, and you had the steps off of Commerce Street that go into the first floor. There were also steps going down into the basement off of Harwood Street.

The FBI investigated the Dallas Police Department on that matter as did Captain Westbrook of Internal Affairs. If there were any allegations, I'm sure that they investigated it.

I wouldn't say that he didn't come down the Main street ramp as he said. That's a very good possibility because I know that Vaughn stepped to the street. Ruby could have been a few yards up the street when I came out and then slipped down the ramp before Vaughn got back in place. I think it's very possible that he could have gotten in that way. But I also say there are other ways he could have gotten in.

I don't think that we had problems with security. Because of the freedom granted to the press, with the number of people and no more planning than there was that went into it, most anything was possible to happen. Again, I didn't know what my assignment was until a very few minutes before.

As a result, the Dallas police took it on the chin from the news media and from the public all over the nation. Up until the time Oswald was shot, there was absolutely no criticism of the way things were handled. I blame the city government for what happened. I just don't believe that Chief Curry took it upon himself to tell the nation when Oswald would be transferred; I believe that he was following orders.

That was not a natural transfer. The city never transferred any prisoners from the city to the county jail; the sheriff's department did that. I think that if they had gone ahead and handled it that way that Oswald would have lived to see his day in court. But I think that somebody was too anxious, since we had all the criticism, and they wanted to make sure that there was no more criticism on the interrogation and whatever statements that Oswald made. I think they were determined to show the world that he survived the city jail and came out of it in good shape. But in city government, you never know where to lay the blame.

Curry came in at a new time in the early 1960's. Everybody is aware of the mood of the country at that time. Curry was working under a different set of circumstances than our previous chief, Carl Hansson, so I guess it would be unfair for me to judge him. Personally, I liked Curry. All my duties with him were pleasant; I had no adverse problems with him. But this event was a very demoralizing thing to him. It probably had something to do with his leaving the department when he did. I think he just faced all the heat he wanted to face and then left.

In regard to the assassination, I think the Dallas Police Department was given an unfair rap, but in regard to the Oswald shooting, they just messed up and they're going to have to take the criticism.

I'm convinced that if Sheriff Decker would have handled it that it would have been a joint effort. But I doubt very seriously if there would have been any need for security because Decker would have sent some deputies down there when nobody knew they were going to transfer, and the next thing anybody knew Oswald would have been at the county jail.

Of course, I'm second guessing, but I don't think that Decker would have been under the pressure to yield to someone else's decision since he was elected by the people and not appointed like Chief Curry. Decker was very well respected and very, very strong politically.

This may come as a surprise to many, but some of the people least interested in the case are the Dallas police. Basically, the police are tired of all the talk, and much of what has been written has been nothing more than speculation. If the press couldn't get an interview that weekend, then they made things up. But whatever they chose to write about us, I can say this: The Dallas Police Department was one of the cleanest in the country at that time.

The department also lost one of its officers, J.D. Tippit, that weekend, which seemed to get lost in all the other events. Since I was his supervisor, I knew him fairly well. Tippit was just a plain home boy who shuffled as he walked and seldom made eye contact. After many years as a patrolman, he was never promoted because of that inability to make eye contact and because he couldn't do well on tests. Promotion required a written exam and an interview. In both cases, he would have failed.

I retired from the Dallas Police Department in January 1974, then for a couple of years worked on the farm and worked on a

442   NO MORE SILENCE

part-time basis for the Soil Conservation Service for about five years. In December, 1981, I joined the Dallas County Sheriff's Department, working in one of the jails.

Rio Pierce has since retired after ten years service with the Dallas County Sheriff's Department. He and his wife continue to live on a farm outside Ennis, Texas.

ROY VAUGHN
Patrol Officer
Dallas Police Department

"I've never been in a sense bashful about defending myself about this thing. I don't believe that Ruby went down that ramp, and I'll go to my grave believing that until somebody proves otherwise..."

Roy Vaughn joined the Navy in 1954 and served in air squadrons and on several aircraft carriers. Upon discharge in May 1958, he worked for a freight line until passing a civil service exam in September of that year. The following month Vaughn joined the Dallas Police Department. Working mostly out of the Central Station, the majority of his experience until 1963 had been spent in the Patrol Division.

I was working days and was assigned to the South Dallas area with another officer named G.F. Temple. I was driving on the far side of Dallas just after lunch, and we were flipping the toggle switch on the radio back and forth from the primary channel to the secondary channel: the secondary channel being largely for special events such as the Presidential parade. As we arrived at Hatcher and Colonial, we heard all the confusion on that second channel; we didn't know what was going on. You could tell there was a lot of confusion and that the escort was going to the hospital. Then the dispatcher came over the primary channel, which was the normal operations channel, and said, "All squads in the immediate downtown area report to Elm and Houston! Code 3!" I can't remember who asked, but somebody asked what the deal was. The dispatcher said, "Signal 19," which was a shooting involving the President.

So we rolled up down there, and I parked over on Houston Street right beside the east side of the School Book Depository. We got out and Temple disappeared. Some supervisor assigned me directly across the street from the* School Book Depository on the west side in front of what I believe was a sewing factory, which later became a museum.* Nobody really knew what was going on or what had happened, totally. This was all prior to anyone knowing that the President was dead.

Anyway, I was standing there on the sidewalk amidst all this mass confusion when a security guard from that building brought a man down who he had found up in the building. I don't know what floor he was found on, but he had no reason to be there. I talked to the man, got his ID, and noticed that he was well dressed, nice expensive suit, and had on a hat. The one thing that caught my eye that I'll never forget was when he opened his billfold and showed me some identification. Of course, I don't remember his name, but he had a bunch of credit cards. Back in those days, not many people had credit cards. I talked to him briefly and then carried him across the street to the sheriff's office, told them what I'd found and what the circumstances were, and they took custody of him. What happened to him then, I don't know.#

Somewhere in that period of time, there was a car that was parked right beside the School Book Depository that became quite interesting. In other words, somebody wanted to get into that car or didn't know whose car it belonged to or this type of thing. Again, it was mass confusion! Nobody really knew what was going on! Events were happening so fast! Sometime after that I heard over the radio that the President was dead, and then shortly after that that there was an officer who had been shot. This, of course,

---

* Commonly referred to as the Dal-Tex Building. It was the location of Abraham Zapruder's dress shop.

The man in question is believed by many to be Eugene Hale Brading, also known as Jim Braden, a suspected organized crime figure from southern California.

was Tippit in Oak Cliff, and I was going to that scene since they were looking for squads. Upon hearing the confusion over there, I tried to get to Oak Cliff, which was across the river, but my car was blocked in; I couldn't get out! So I remained on my assignment. Sometime later, I can't say how long, there was a man who identified himself as working for the railroad in the yard tower, and he told me that somebody had reported to him that three or four individuals had gotten into a boxcar down on Houston Street. This was, as the crow flies, probably a quarter of a mile or better away. So I reported this to a supervisor at the scene and was told, "Get two or three men and go down there!" I located Marvin Wise, Bill Mitchell, and Billy Bass, and we ran down the railroad tracks toward that location which was near the Houston Street Viaduct and the Union Terminal Train Station.

When we arrived, there was somebody waiting there who pointed out the car they were in; who he was, I don't know, but the car was connected to a train which was fixing to pull out. It was a half car, open, like a coal car; you couldn't see up inside so you had to climb up the ladder and look over into the car. I climbed up the south end of the car while Marvin Wise climbed up the other which was where they were located. They didn't have the appearance of really rugged, dirty type bums. We didn't know what they were, but we arrested them and took them out of the car. Wise and Bass walked them back to the sheriff's office while Mitchell and I rode back on the caboose with another guy and got off at the railroad yard.

I've been asked many times about those individuals in the railroad car. They were what you would classify as general wino-bums, unkempt in a sense, didn't have beards, but they didn't have the appearance of that really rugged, dirty type bum.

Anyway, from there I then returned to the scene and got involved in helping search the building. The building was pretty well blocked off by that time. I ended up on the sixth floor, though searches were also going on on the other floors. Captain Fritz was up there along with most of his Homicide people. I hadn't been there but just a short time when the rifle was found. I remember the boxes that were stacked around and somebody picking the rifle up and holding it up after it had been found by the window. At the time, I was standing back toward the center of that floor about fifty feet away. This was all prior to anyone knowing anything about Oswald, so the investigation continued and we stayed past our normal schedule time until we were relieved.

Saturday was a blur. I'm sure that I was in and out of our Patrol office on the second floor of City Hall, but nothing I did really rings a bell as far as unusual that day. That night, prior to the transfer, Dallas was under a big magnifying glass with a spotlight on it, and the city was trying to appease the press to get them off the city's back. I don't think that Jess Curry, the chief of police, would have ever taken it on himself to make a transfer and publicize it as he did. I think it was done probably by some political factions such as the city manager, Elgin Crull, or the mayor, Earle Cabell.

Anyway, that Saturday night we'd gone up to my wife's parents who lived at Lake Dallas, twenty-five to thirty miles north, for supper. They had a fish place up there, and we spent quite a bit of our time up there with the kids. While we were there, they advertised the transfer on the goddamn radio, and I told them then that it was a mistake publicizing the time. I couldn't believe that they'd say that on the radio! The crime of the century and they're going to say something like that on the radio!

Sunday morning, again I came in, probably around 7:00 o'clock. I was working relief in the downtown district right around City Hall. We changed uniforms in the basement in those days, so I noticed people setting up cameras in front of the parking area adjacent to the bottom of the ramp with high intensity lights strung over the rafters. Sometime early that morning we got a call to report to the Patrol office. There, Lieutenant Rio Sam Pierce met with me along with some others and told me, "Go down to the basement and tell Sergeant Dean..." He had some specific instructions, something to the effect, "Don't let anybody in! Secure the basement!" The sergeant that he told me to see, P.T. Dean, wasn't the one that I actually saw. Instead, I talked to Blackie Putnam who then assigned me to the Main Street ramp. I don't know what other assignments he gave to anybody else, but my instructions were to not let anybody in unless I knew them and could identify them.

When I came out into the basement and as I started up the ramp, I encountered a man coming down that I didn't know. I stopped him, required identification, and discovered that he was from DPS, Department of Public Safety, Highway Patrol Driver's License Division. They had free access since they had an office in the building. This was very early.

So I reached the top of the ramp, and I'm up there by myself. There were half a dozen, maybe ten people standing around spread on both sides of the driveway including a black guy named N.J. Daniels, who had shown up and was standing near the pillar on the east side, or the left side of the driveway leading down into the basement. I knew N.J. He had been a policeman at one time and had been either terminated or resigned.

A short while later Tommy Chabot, who was a mechanic at the police garage, drove in in a police car. He told me, "They sent for me to come over here and do some re-parking and stuff in the basement." I'd known Tommy for years, so I said, "Fine, go on in. Change squad cars." So he went down.

Sometime later Sergeant Dean came up and told me that they were going to bring in an armored car. Nobody really knew what they were going to do with it, but they were apparently going to bring the armored car in the Commerce Street side and back it down the ramp. I assumed that's what they were going to transfer Oswald in. I remember the armored car backing down the Commerce Street ramp, but they couldn't get it all the way to the bottom because of some lights. Amidst the crowd at the bottom of the ramp I heard somebody holler, "Watch the car!" The next thing I knew I saw a car start up the ramp toward me, which was unusual because it was one way coming in. As the car approached with its red lights on, I noticed in the car Rio Sam Pierce, Sergeant Maxey and Sergeant Putnam. Nobody said anything to me. Of course, as narrow as the ramp was, I stepped aside and let the car go on out, still not knowing what the hell was going on. After the car went on out, I stepped back to my position.

Just a few minutes later I heard somebody in the crowd in the basement holler, "Here he comes!"

I couldn't see this, but as Oswald came out, I heard what didn't sound like a pistol shot; it was muffled. Then all hell broke loose, all mass confusion! I didn't know what was going on, so I backed up in a corner of the ramp and pulled my pistol. I could see at the edge of the crowd some people fighting. I could see a head come out of the crowd, then a pistol. They were fighting over the pistol! Then a man broke away from the crowd and started up the ramp toward me, but he was tackled immediately and brought down by who I learned later was a reserve officer in plain clothes inside the perimeter of that crowd at the bottom of the ramp. I was unaware that there were any reserves down there. When he broke loose and got close enough, I recognized that it was a Vice detective, D.L. Burgess; I asked him, "What happened?"

"A reporter shot him," he said. I stayed on my post.

If I'm not mistaken, at some point in time after this, some man who knew, was connected with, or worked for Jack Ruby came to me and wanted to talk to somebody up in Homicide. I sent somebody to tell them, and they came down, got him, and carried him off. I still remained at my post.

A little while later C.E. Talbert, my captain, who had been at Parkland when Oswald was there, called me to the phone. Talbert asked me, "Do you know Jack Ruby?"

I said, "Yes, I know Jack Ruby."

"Have you seen him today?"

"No," I replied, "I haven't." I suspicioned there was something, but at that time I still didn't know that it was Jack Ruby that had shot Oswald. I didn't find that out for another hour or two. He was the furthest thing from my mind. Not being around the station, shit, I had no idea. Anyway, that was all that was said. Later in the day I was relieved from my assignment.

I had met Ruby two or three years prior out in the Oak Lawn area where he owned the Vegas Club. I had been working relief and might be out there a night or two a week working late nights and had met him on a couple occasions at the cafe next door after he had closed the club. I'd see him there drinking a cup of coffee; that was all. I'd never been in his club other than strictly in the performance of my duty. But I did know him on sight, and he usually wore the same type clothes: business suit and hat, and nine times out of ten he would wear an overcoat, especially in the fall of the year.

On Monday, I came in and worked my regular shift. Nothing was said. By that evening, I assume that I heard that Ruby was supposed to have gone down the ramp, so I called N.J. Daniels at home. I didn't know N.J. other than on sight, but I asked him about the rumor going around that when I stepped out as the car came up, that Ruby then went down that ramp. I did not believe that he did, still don't, and I'll go to my grave saying that he did not go down that ramp. But I called N.J. at home, in a sense, to be sure in my own mind. "Could it have happened?" I told him who I was and asked him, "Did anybody go down that ramp?"

"No, nobody went down that ramp," he said, which reaffirmed what I already knew.

Also that night I received a telephone call from Lieutenant Pierce who said, "I want you to come down and write a special report. And while you're down here, if you want a part-time job, I've got you a job driving for an NBC news team out of California." We didn't make much money back then, probably around $400 a month, plus I had five kids.

So I went down on Tuesday morning, wrote my special report, and included that I had talked to Daniels. Meanwhile the NBC crew never left City Hall all night long. I never went anywhere and still got paid. Wasn't bad! They told me that they would need a driver the next day, so being off, I drove them around wherever they wanted to go in the downtown area.

Thursday, being Thanksgiving, Pierce called me and said, "The chief wants to talk to you. I want you to come on in." I had my suspicions what it was. So at seven o'clock that morning I came in and was assigned regular patrol duty. I don't remember who I rode with that day, but later in the morning I was told to report to 511, which was the Patrol office. While I was sitting there waiting, N.T. Fisher, who was a deputy chief, came in and told me to go into his office. I kind of felt like they escorted me up there like I was a criminal. That still sticks in my mind.

I was not overly concerned because I knew that I hadn't done anything. I knew I hadn't done a shitten thing! So we went into Fisher's office and sat there and talked. He, of course, had read my special report and wanted me to verbally tell him what had occurred, which I did. I brought up the phone conversation I had had with Daniels; the inference I got was that he had apparently also talked to Daniels. During the course of the conversation, he asked me, "Not that we doubt your integrity, but would you take a polygraph?"

I told him, "Well, you know, that's bullshit! Not that you doubt my integrity, but I know somebody's putting it on me!"

Paul Bentley ran the polygraph while they were all back there watching through a one-way mirror. I knew that. Bentley ran the polygraph on me so long that he had to let me off to rest awhile.

I still wasn't overly concerned because, in my own mind, I hadn't done a thing. When I got off and walked out of the room, C.E. Talbert, who was a grand old man, was standing outside the door of the polygraph room said, "Roy, I want you to know that I believe you're all right! That's one of the straightest tests I believe I've ever seen run!" And I believed him because I'd worked under the man a long time, and he was a good old man. N.T. Fisher, who was standing in the hall, looked like he'd eaten sour grapes because I had just passed that test.

One of the last things Fisher told me was, "Don't tell anybody about this." I got on the elevator immediately, went to the basement and got off. There, apparently going upstairs, was Red Edwards, a detective.

He asked me, "Why in the world did you take that polygraph?"

"Red," I told him, "I didn't really have any choice. I knew I hadn't done it, and I've got five children. This is my bread and butter. My feeling is that I had everything to lose and nothing to gain." I knew the heat was on, but again, I knew I hadn't done anything. So I went home later in the morning. It wasn't long until the FBI came out a couple of times to interview me.

I've always maintained that Jack Ruby didn't come down that ramp. He was there at City Hall on Friday night, on Saturday, and again on Sunday morning, and yet claimed that he didn't know about the transfer. That's bullshit! Hell, he probably knew more about what was going on than I did. But I don't think he was part of a conspiracy. I really don't.

It wasn't until the reinvestigation several years later* that I learned that Don Flusche was there. I'd been interviewed two or three times by investigators and had another scheduled later that morning. I happened to be down in the Inspector's Division and ran into him. I had known Don a long time and in the conversation, he told me, and was very adamant, that Jack Ruby didn't go down that ramp. I asked him, "How do you know that?"

And he said, "Because I was sitting across the street." He said that he had told his lieutenant, Earl Knox, and some others about it, but they weren't interested in talking to him. All those years and I didn't know that!

---

* The House Select Committee on Assassinations, 1976-79.

I said, "Don, let me tell you something. I've got an interview here within the next two hours, and I'm going to tell them what you told me."

"Fine," he responded.

So I went in and talked to one of their investigators from the committee and carried him down and showed him the door that I seemed to remember was there. There was a stairway that went from the first floor down to the basement out of the Municipal Building, not the police station, which adjoined the City Hall where the police station was located. Very easily somebody could have gone to the back door, which is still there today, opened the door, let the man in, walked straight and come right into the basement. It wouldn't have been a problem.

Next to the Western Union Building, where Ruby sent the telegram, there used to be Rutherford's Business College and a cafe. Those are torn down now, but there was an alleyway behind those buildings which led to a double door at the Municipal Building. You could go through that double door, through an elevator into the Municipal Building and on into the police department at City Hall. Now, whether that door was locked that day, I don't know. I find it highly improbable that it was unlocked, which means that somebody would have had to let him in. In addition, it being Sunday, the elevator probably wouldn't have been activated.

The other possibility was that there was another alley running off Main Street toward the same double doors. As you went in those double doors, if they were open, there was a hallway around the elevator which led to a door that opened into the main corridor of the Municipal Building. You could walk through that corridor, open another door, and that would take you right to the basement.

Somewhere in my mind, and I can't positively say that it's true, but from where I was standing, at one point I saw a man go down that alley off Main Street, but I can't say that it was Jack Ruby, and I told them that.

Getting back to the ramp. Basically, it was just barely wide enough for one car, maybe a maximum of ten feet in width. On each side of the entrance were big pillar type things. The ramp itself entered off the south side of Main Street. That was the entry into City Hall. And when you came out, you went out on the Commerce Street ramp. If you worked in the downtown area, you made numerous trips in and out of there. That's where the Patrol office was; that's where the locker rooms were; that's where the jail was.

When Pierce drove the car up the ramp, there is a slight possibility that my vision could have momentarily been impaired. I was stationed in the middle of the ramp and had to move aside, I believe toward the Western Union side of the ramp. I then stepped to about the curb to check for traffic, then returned to my post. I don't recall ever stepping out in the street. In addition, height was to my advantage since I'm 6'4" and could see readily anybody coming up and down that ramp.

I also looked at a bunch of pictures which, to me, showed that Ruby came from inside the basement. In other words, the pictures seem to indicate that he came up the driveway ramp where the cars were parked inside the basement, not down the Main Street ramp from the outside. Had he gone down that ramp as he supposedly said he did, he'd have had quite a crowd to get through in a very limited time.

Maybe a year after this happened, I ran across N.J. Daniels in a restaurant in South Dallas where I was assigned to work. My partner and I were two white officers eating in a black cafe in a totally black area, which was the only place we had to eat. In any case, N.J. Daniels was there. By this time, he had changed his story. He then claimed that I had allowed Ruby to go down that ramp. My understanding was that he was run on a polygraph, and it showed him to be untrue.

Knowing he was there, I certainly wasn't going to bring up the subject with him. Instead, Daniels came up to me in that restaurant and said, "I just want you to know that I did not say that the man came down that ramp." Well, I knew goddamn well that he had because he appeared on some TV shows and said it. Why in the world he'd do that, I don't know. Maybe he had an ax to grind; maybe he had a guilty conscience; I don't know. But he damn sure said it, and I'd be lying to say that it didn't piss me off!

Several years later I became involved in a law suit involving the movie *Executive Action*. I sued the film company because they handed out a fact sheet which alleged that Roy Vaughn knowingly permitted Ruby to enter the basement to kill Oswald. I found out about it when one of my older kids went to the movie and brought that sheet home to me, so I ended up suing them.

In those days, you had to have permission from the city attorney to sue if it was related to your duty. So I retained an attorney, and we looked at the whole situation. I wasn't interested in money; that wasn't the point. I wanted them to leave me alone and get off my ass! I had my kids to think about. I'm sure they were aware to some degree, but it wasn't a subject that we would normally sit and talk about. I just wanted to clear my name; that's what it amounted to.

My attorney had had some communications with the city attorney, and he told me that at some point in the conversation the city attorney had told him that the possibility existed that another individual had let Ruby in. After that I met with my attorney, the city attorney, and Chief Don Byrd in the city attorney's office. The city attorney didn't want me to file the law suit. I said, "Well, I've got an attorney who's already put in his time. Who's going to pay for that?" I was told, in a sense, that they'd make it all right. I then stated to the city attorney, "You know, I understand that you made the statement that there was another person who may have let the man in."

He sat back and answered it something to the effect, "Yes, there was someone else," but he would never tell me who. It was weird! I don't think he said that that's the way they ever determined he got in, but they had looked at someone else.

I think Ruby was let in, and deep in my heart I think I know who let him in. But it was from the standpoint of friendship, not any type of conspiracy. P.T. Dean had been the supervisor on my shift and had been in the basement that morning. I hate to say this, but whenever there was a camera running, he was going to be there talking to it. That's the way P.T. was. He was a character! Though I was never a social friend of his, I knew him fairly well, and he knew Jack Ruby very well. His name has been mentioned as the one who may have let Ruby in. It wouldn't surprise me, wouldn't surprise me!

Another character that was in the basement that morning was Jimmie Putnam, "Blackie" Putnam. I worked partners with him before he made sergeant. He was something else! He was very difficult to work with and got extremely crossways with troops and people. He had a lot of problems and was later sent to the penitentiary for killing his wife.

Several years after the assassination I came to Midlothian. Roger Craig was probably the reason I'm here today. We first met back in high school when he was going with a girlfriend I knew, and eventually they were married. Later he became a deputy sheriff about the same time that I joined the police department. Roger was a pretty good fellow.

I did not know that Roger played any part whatsoever in this Kennedy thing for several years. I knew that I hadn't seen him in quite some period of time, and I knew that he had left the sheriff's department, but I didn't know what he was doing. Around 1967 I was living in Dallas and was off for a couple of weeks with appendicitis when Roger suddenly appeared at my house for a visit. At that time, I learned that he was the justice of the peace here in Midlothian and worked for an oil company outside the town. He told me all these stories about going to New Orleans and Jim Garrison and all that bullshit. He also mentioned having been shot at. I didn't know any of this because I never kept up with it.

After I was able to get back on my feet so that I could travel, I came down with my family to Midlothian to visit Roger. Since we had five kids and needed a bigger house, we eventually purchased a two story, thirteen room house on four and a half acres for $29,000 right across the street from where Roger lived. So we moved here and lived across the street from Roger.

I don't know why Roger got involved in it, but in my opinion, his involvement in this Kennedy assassination destroyed the boy's life, totally destroyed his life. He began seeing conspiracies everywhere and went all over the country with Penn Jones giving talks. After I saw *Executive Action* two or three times, I noticed that the man at the ramp who portrayed me, I think, was Roger Craig. He never would admit to it, but he never denied it either. I would have never held it against him anyway if he'd tried to make a buck, but if you look closely, I believe it's Roger.

I saw Roger go from what I'd classify as an intelligent individual to one who couldn't provide for his own family. In fact, when we could afford it, we were feeding his family. He claimed it was health problems and he couldn't work. I don't know if that was true. Personally, I think this subject just damn near drove him crazy. He and his wife separated; he lost his family, the whole route. I don't know all the circumstances which led up to it, but eventually he moved back to Dallas to live with his mother and finally ended up killing himself. But I have Roger to thank for my being in Midlothian today where I eventually became the chief of police.

In looking back as to how Ruby got into the basement, I don't believe that I was made a scapegoat, though there was probably an effort to do so, and I don't think that I was the only one. I think that it would have been a lot easier if the department could have pinpointed it and said, "Yes, he got in this way, and we've taken care of that problem." I think that if they could have absolutely put it on somebody, they would have suspended him and probably fired him, and probably justifiably so if it would have been a case of criminal negligence. I think they made a sincere effort to do that, but they were unable to do so.

The only official black mark against me was that my efficiency rating was cut. That's all. But since my efficiency ratings had always been very high, I requested an audience with the chief to find out why mine was cut. His explanation was that I had let Tommy Chabot, the man from the garage with the squad car, in. I couldn't argue with that because I had let him in.

I spent half my adult life in the Dallas Police Department, and I can truthfully say that it was one of the finest police agencies in the country at that time. There was very little, if any, corruption. I put in twenty-two years and hold fond memories of that department.

Roy Vaughn retired from the Dallas Police Department in 1980 to run a glass and mirror business which started as a part-time job two years earlier. When a vacancy opened for the chief of police in Midlothian, Vaughn applied and won the position out of 42 applicants in 1986. He still holds that position.

DONALD FLUSCHE
Patrol Division
Dallas Police Department

"If Roy Vaughn tells you it's Christmas, go on and hang the stocking because he won't lie to you!"

Born in Cooke County, eighty miles north of Dallas, Don Flusche was educated at St. Mary's Parish Parochial School, then moved to Dallas and graduated from Jesuit High School in 1945. After a short stint at Western-Electric Company, a subsidiary of the Bell System, he served in the Army from 1946 through 1949 as a drill instructor and as a telephone repairman, with military police work as a collateral duty. Upon his discharge, Flusche worked for Chance-Vought as an aircraft electrician, attended SMU, and was married in 1950. He joined the Dallas Police Department in 1954 working Patrol, went into plain clothes assignments in 1959 and was promoted to sergeant in 1961. Two years later, in 1963, he was decorated with the Dallas Police Department's Medal of Honor, the highest award granted by the police department. On November 22, 1963, Flusche was serving as a sergeant at the Northeast Substation on Goforth Road near White Rock Lake and Loop 12.

I was patrol sergeant in charge of one and two man units working seven or eight beats. There wasn't much going on out that way and knowing what time the motorcade was going by, I drove down to Lemmon Avenue and parked about half a block off of Lemmon hoping to catch a glimpse of the President, which I did. After seeing him there, I thought, "Well, I'll drift on downtown and go by the Patrol office to pick up some paperwork that was pending down there."

As I was entering the downtown area, I heard the dispatcher on Channel 1, Bubba Hulse, issue a Signal 19, which involved the shooting of the President. The dispatcher gave the location where it had occurred, so I went down to the School Book Depository. Since I had been near the downtown area when I heard the dispatch, I was on the scene probably within two or three minutes of the time it was dispatched.

When I arrived, there was a large crowd and a lot of confusion. They were still in a state of shock since the motorcade had apparently just passed. As I got out of the car, dressed in full uniform with the white supervisor hat, I remember seeing Roy Vaughn, who was assigned to Central Division at that time, and I asked him, "What the hell's going on?"

He said, "As near as we can determine, the shots came from up there," referring to the School Book Depository.

I further asked, "Has anybody secured the building?" and he responded that it had been. So I went on into the building, meeting Inspector Herb Sawyer in the process. He told me to go to the sixth floor and assist with whatever search that was needed up there and to try to secure that floor.

When I got up to the sixth floor, there were several other people there, mostly in plain clothes. I can't recall the names of those I saw, but I found out later that most of them were federal officers, either from ATF and even Federal Game Enforcement people. I thought this was rather unusual because why were they so involved in all this, especially since murder, even a president, at that time was a state crime, thus it was our crime and our investigation that would have to be conducted? There was some confusion on the part of the people there as to what their roles should be in this thing.

There were some deputy sheriffs there as well as a number of Dallas policemen. I recall in particular W.C. Flowers, Paul Wilkins, and Roy Westphal. Upon arrival on the floor, I saw the shells on the floor which were being watched at that time by someone. This was before Carl Day had arrived. I also noticed the boxes had been stacked up to what reminded me of what one would use if you were going to bench rest a rifle to do some precise shooting in a shooting match.

When I saw the shells were being covered, I told the man, "Now stay with this. Don't let this be the start of anything!" Later, Paul Wilkins came up and told me that the rifle had been found. "Where is it?" I asked, and he showed me that it was between two stacks of boxes in an inverted position. I saw this myself and asked, "Who else knows about this?" No one seemed to know, so I said, "Captain Fritz is on a lower floor. Go find him and get him and his crew back up here!" In just a matter of a few moments, they were back up and they then took charge of the scene. Lieutenant Day then arrived to do crime scene work along with some of his folks. The boxes were set aside and Day picked up the rifle.

I don't know how some of these stories get started about the rifle being a Mauser or whatever. I'm no expert on firearms, although I am interested and somewhat familiar with them because of the nature of the business I've been in, and it was a 6.5 mm. Italian Carcano. There was no question about that. I saw the rifle later and looked at it after it had been processed. It was a junk military thing. Like most military rifles, it was serviceable, rugged, and durable. It wasn't anything like the deer rifle I have back in my gun case.

We conducted a pretty thorough search of the sixth floor and then went up into the attic of that building, which was also the seventh floor. There was some thought that the scuttle hole was open up there, and for some reason the manager or somebody in that building thought that was strange, so Westphal, Flowers and I conducted that search. There was nothing there at all, but it was real strange that, with all these federal people and other folks that were standing around, we were the only three that would go up there. After about two hours at the Book Depository, I was released and went back to the substation. It was changeover time when I arrived, and I was instructed to hold my people there and get them together.

The following day, Saturday, I went down to the central office where Captain Fritz's office was located to pick up some papers. It was unbelievable! The reporters were so desperate for interviews that they would ask anybody in uniform questions that might be able to tell them something. I don't know how the international press got here so quickly!

I was also on duty on Sunday. Early that morning when we first went to work there was some talk about moving Oswald. I had heard the previous day that they were going to move him at nine o'clock in the morning and then later, ten. But on Sunday morning, I was hearing the updated information around five-thirty or quarter till six. At the substation, I was hearing some of these things from phone calls from people downtown. I was told to hold back three or four people in case we needed them down there on the street. It was pretty well confused. It didn't seem to me that there had been any real plan worked out at that point. Eventually we sent down, I believe, four people to provide for security on street corners on Main Street from Harwood down to the county jail.

I went there myself, though I had no assignment. Like everybody else, I was curious, so when I turned these people over, I decided to stay around. I knew that the car carrying Oswald was supposed to come out of the basement onto the Commerce Street side, go that half block against traffic, then come back north on Harwood, and then come back west on Main Street to the county jail. Realizing this, rather than trying to get in position over on Commerce Street where I could see, I just stopped on Main Street across from the east end of the Municipal Building where there wasn't anybody.

At that time, going back further east on that block, the Western Union Building was where it is now, but what is now a parking lot between the Western Union Building and the Municipal Building was a row of commercial buildings including the Rutherford Business School. I was just above that point.

In any case, I was standing out by the driver's side of the car between ten to fifteen minutes; the car was headed west on the north side of the street. I was just standing out there leaning on the top of the car door just watching. I saw Roy Vaughn there guarding the ramp into the basement. The story was, of course, that Jack Ruby had stopped at the Western Union to wire some money to this stripper over in Fort Worth and that he decided to walk down Main Street toward the ramp to see what was going on. As Rio Sam Pierce and Billy Maxey drove out of the basement the wrong way, and Vaughn stepped out in the street to cut traffic for them, that gave Ruby the opportunity to step in behind the car and go down the ramp.

That's a damn lie; it didn't happen! I knew Jack Ruby on sight, and he did not go down that sidewalk and into the ramp. I saw Pierce and Maxey come out of the basement, and I saw Vaughn barely step off the curb. He really never got into the street; he just stepped to the curb to check the traffic to see if they needed any help. They did not! The traffic was very light and they pulled on out. Vaughn then stepped back over into position there by the ramp.

There was hardly anybody on my side of the street. That's why I was there. I had a clear view all the way from the Western Union Building to the ramp and there was nothing! Vaughn didn't turn his back enough to allow anybody to go down that ramp. I don't think anyone could have gone down that ramp unobserved by Vaughn or me. I just don't think that was possible; I'll stay with that!

There was a plain clothes policeman there named Napoleon Daniels who said that Vaughn allowed Ruby to go down the ramp. He later failed a polygraph. Vaughn said he didn't go down the ramp and passed the polygraph. If Roy Vaughn tells you it's Christmas, go on and hang the stocking because he won't lie to you! In my estimation, he's a totally honest person.

Roy worked in Patrol and later went to Vice. After this I had some contact with him but generally just to say hello. I'd never been able to sit down and talk to him about this because I didn't know the significance of what I had to say.

I didn't hear about the shooting until I heard the radio and it was talking about the ambulance coming. I then followed the ambulance out to Parkland because I knew they would need to set up a security net around the hospital since there were no provisions for that. So I helped in that regard and cut traffic off to keep people from coming in.

The following morning on Monday I gave my lieutenant, Earl Knox, a verbal report about everything I'd seen. I also wrote a handwritten account on one of those legal-sized tablets that we used so darned much over the years and gave it to him. It was a rough draft and I said to him, "Now we can make a better report on it in what we call a 'Dear Chief' if you need it, but this is basically what happened."

"Well, fine," he said, "I'll talk to Captain Talbert." To be very candid, I never heard another word about it. Knox and

Talbert are both dead, so hell, I don't know what the story is. Knox wasn't the only one who knew about this. I had also told Billy Joe Maxey, the acting watch commander that weekend, so I figured that I had discharged any obligations I had. I just didn't feel like pushing it. Later I was told that the police department investigated how Ruby got into the basement, but I never saw any paperwork on it. I knew that they were doing some things but nobody contacted me. I figured that if they wanted to talk to me they'd come to me; I didn't need to be bothering them. Really I think there was an attempt to make a scapegoat out of Roy Vaughn. It wasn't until 1978 in casual conversation with Jack Revill that this subject came up again.

Frankly, I don't know how Ruby got into the basement, although there are two other ways he could have gotten in. Pat Dean and "Black" Jimmy Putnam had security in the basement that day, but I don't know what arrangements they had or what they did. But there are two other ways to get in, one of them very simple. There was an alley that ran north and south alongside the Rutherford Building, and there was also a T-alley which came into that from Central Expressway behind the Western Union Building. They met at a T at what we call the back door of the Municipal Building, which was the service dock. That door was generally left unlocked on weekends during the day so its maintenance people and building engineers could come and go. All other doors in that building were normally locked. That was the condition at that time.

Ruby could have also come on Main Street, turned and gone down that alley and into the loading dock door. Down that hallway past the elevators, then to the right there was another door leading to a single flight of stairs which came out in the basement right behind where all the newspeople were gathered. In each case, it would have taken less than a minute for Ruby to have entered the basement. I don't know if this was investigated, but I'm aware of those doors and I'm no different from anybody else. If Ruby did come in one of those alley doors, and if a Dallas policeman let him in, it was not because of any conspiracy; it was because Jack Ruby had some friends, some associates, down there who might have wanted to let Jack get down there to see something.

I was surprised and still don't understand why it happened. Perhaps he just wanted to be a hero. In a murder case, if you've got a bad person that is the victim, it's pretty easy to defend your client by prosecuting the deceased, and it would have made sense to me. I believe it would have happened had it not been for all the Melvin Belli hoopla which accompanied the trial. I think Jack Ruby would have walked out of that courtroom if Tom Howard, his original attorney and a past master of doing just what I described, had been allowed to prosecute the deceased. Tom was no slouch as an attorney and was a good courtroom lawyer, but they fired his ass and ran him off.

My father sat on a jury one time in Cooke County and they walked a man up there for a killing. I asked him why it happened, and he told me, "That man needed killing!" Maybe Oswald needed killing; I don't know. If you had a jury here in Dallas made up of people of lower middle class background and pretty simple values, as in Cooke County, it could have happened again.

Jack Ruby ran the Vegas Club out on Oak Lawn, the beat that I worked when I was on patrol. I knew him on sight because of my answering calls out there and in dealing with him as a proprietor of that beer joint. I had dealt with him many, many times arresting drunks in there and answering disturbance calls. Sometimes he would be very businesslike and calm, as what you would expect from one in that kind of business. At other times, he could be very irrational, which I think was an act. I think he was performing for someone or something. Thinking back, that's the only way I can explain it because it seemed like he would overreact to various situations. We would handle disturbance calls to his club maybe a day or two before or after this incident and he would act totally different. What made this one different than the other disturbance? So I think he was sometimes performing. I never thought that he was mentally unbalanced. I just think that he was a good performer and entertainer, but that goes with the nature of the business.

Let me dismiss very quickly some of the charges made against the Dallas Police Department. Stories have circulated that the Dallas police allowed Ruby to kill Oswald for the sake of instant justice, assuming Oswald would go for years through a series of appeals and there would be no justice in the killing of Tippit. I don't know what it's like to be a policeman anywhere else because this is the only place I've ever been a policeman, but Dallas officers are much more professional than that, and I don't think they would do that. Don't misunderstand, but if they're going to kill somebody, they'd do it themselves; they wouldn't get some beer joint operator out there to walk in off the street and do it for them. That's ridiculous! Again, I think that if someone permitted him to be in that basement, it was just to let him be an eyewitness to history.

It's true that Ruby had lots of acquaintances among the policemen and was generally well liked, but they saw him as kind of a clown. He'd pass out a bottle of whiskey here and there, and he'd let some people come into his clubs: the Silver Spur, the Vegas Club, and the strip joint downtown. I understand policemen would go in those clubs and he'd pick up the tab for them and that sort of thing. I'm sure that he made acquaintances or contacts that way. All totalled, I'd say that Ruby knew forty or fifty policemen like I knew him, who were in Vice or answering calls in his clubs, and there might have been another twenty or thirty that went around to his clubs socially. The figures of fifty percent of the police force knowing him are horseshit! That's not right at all!

Of particular concern to us that weekend was the shooting of Officer J.D. Tippit. John and I worked together in West Dallas. He was really a good and decent man. I recall a story about him which I think would explain why he wouldn't be capable of being involved in anything as complicated as a conspiracy because he was just not that type of individual. He was from up in the country around Greenville and was pretty much a country boy, as we all are sometimes. One day his mother or his sister had sent a swath of cloth to him and had asked that he go by a sewing store to match that color with some thread and then send them the spool of thread. They were making a dress or something and they couldn't find that color of thread that they needed up there. And he did that. Now don't tell me that a man who would do something like that could be so complex or involved in something like an assassination! It just doesn't make sense to me because he was just a common ordinary old boy. He was a paratrooper in World War Two, was kind of bashful, thought a little slow, moved a little slow, but there was nothing dishonest about him. As far as I know, he had no vices. He was a good policeman who knew his business.

There's no doubt in my mind that when he made that contact over in Oak Cliff he knew what he had. But I think he had gotten to the point, like a lot of policemen, that he thought that nothing would happen to him. We had a rookie officer named Johnny Sides who was killed in 1951. It was another eleven years almost to the day before we had another officer killed, Leonard Mullenax; we called him "Slip." So we had a history of time in which some attitudes were built up among officers that nothing was going to happen to them. After Mullenax's death in 1962, the following year John was killed, of course, and since then it's been pretty bad. But I think John had that attitude—"Nothing bad will happen to me. I'm a policeman; nobody's going to hurt me." As a result, he may have gotten careless.

When he encountered the suspect, it was not necessarily customary to call in to the dispatcher. They had broadcast the description, as I understand, and it was a fairly accurate description of Oswald. The clothing was a little off because he had changed his jacket for a sweater, or a sweater for a jacket, but the general physical description was pretty good. They had moved John in from way south in Oak Cliff. When he cleared from eating lunch with the dispatcher, he was out of service during the assassination. Shortly after that the dispatcher, Murray Jackson, told him to go into the business district of Oak Cliff because all of the people had been pulled to Parkland Hospital or to the School Book Depository because of the shooting. When you have an emergency, you bring them in from the outlying areas and just hope that nothing bad happens out there. That's why he was up there off Jefferson Avenue; that's why he was so far off his beat.

Speculation and rumor has swirled around this for years. Governor Connally said something that I think may have been overlooked. He had been Secretary of the Navy at the time Oswald tried to get his discharge reinstated and was turned down, and that was ultimately Connally's responsibility. Connally said that he thought that Oswald did exactly what he intended to do, and that was to shoot both of them. When you think of it from that standpoint, it makes sense. I don't know what Oswald did anymore than anyone else. There's so many loose ends about his going to Mexico City and Jack Ruby meeting him there; Jack

Ruby had Cuban contacts; the CIA was involved, and any number of other stories. I don't have any solid information that would lead me to suggest anything. But I do know about the Dallas Police Department and its role that weekend.

I spent over thirty-two years with the department, and I've seen some things that were gut-wrenching. Hell, it wasn't too long before I went to work there that we had a lieutenant on the late night crew that was committing burglaries. This department sent those people to the penitentiary; it wasn't some outside agency. Nobody else had to come in here and clean house for us—not some other agency, not the Texas Rangers, not the FBI. We did it! And that's been the case every time we've had serious misconduct on the part of an officer—it resulted in firing or penitentiary time. This department cleans its own house, kills its own snakes!

Paul McCaghren was one of the investigators for the Dallas Police Department in its investigation of how Ruby got into the basement. He's one of the best investigators anywhere. My God, you had some of the best detectives since Sherlock Holmes on this.

When the assassination occurred, I think it was probably true that more Dallas officers were more concerned about Tippit than they were Kennedy, and I think that's understandable. Believe this or not, but the police department here, from my observations, was generally apolitical. They didn't have much politics one way or the other, and still don't. "Whoever sits in the White House, what does that do for me?" I think that was their attitude at the time.

But we were raked over the coals that weekend, and ever since. President Theodore Roosevelt once said something about criticizing people: "The man that goes in and does his job, that's the man that knows what's going on." I think those people who have been so critical of us don't know what's going on. This was, is, and will be a good department because of the people here. The conspiracy theories are bullshit to me! I don't know any other way to put it! How many books could you sell if you said the Dallas police did a good job?

You have to remember that we had a President of the United States and a police officer killed, and within forty-five minutes of the officer's death members of this department had a suspect in custody. Now that speaks pretty well for the efficiency of this department, how well the citizens of this town depend on us, and what kind of confidence they have in this department.

The tragedy that happened that Sunday morning was in an effort to be open with the press. We could have moved Oswald at three o'clock in the morning, leaving the press to speculate on what we had done to him. But we paraded him before the press to show them that we hadn't whipped, beaten, or otherwise abused him. Of course, Curry was the chief, and everything that happened in that department was his responsibility. But he answered to Elgin Crull, the city manager, so where do you want to stop the buck? Crull, being a former newsman, I'm sure was sensitive to the situation with the press, not that it makes a whole hell of a lot of difference; Jack Ruby's still the man that pulled the trigger. There's no question about that!

In looking back at the events of that weekend, with me particularly, it brought home again how vulnerable the police officer is as we saw when John was killed. Then, too, I think this whole area, the people on my level, just your ordinary lower middle class people in this town realized that suddenly this city where we lived and worked was international, and because of that, things could happen. Dallas was described one time as the world's largest little town, and we all had a little town mentality with little town values. There's nothing wrong with that, but I think it made us realize that this world is a bigger place than we thought. We began to realize that we were part of a bigger world, and bad things can happen to us.

Flusche remained at the Northeast Substation until 1974 as a patrol sergeant and later served in the Inspections Division and the Traffic Division. Throughout much of his career he also was an instructor at the police academy teaching a course on street survival the last ten years of his career until his retirement from the Dallas Police Department in 1986.

JOE R. CODY
Detective, Burglary and Theft
Dallas Police Department

"After I watched it forty times, shooting him and shooting him, and after hearing the captain announce that it was Jack Ruby, it all hit me that Jack Ruby was a friend of mine and that I had bought that pistol for him, and the pistol was in my name..."

Born in Dallas, Joe Cody joined the military in January 1944 and later attended North Texas State University. After playing professional sports, Cody then joined the Dallas Police Department in 1950 serving as a patrol officer until 1954, then as a detective in Narcotics and Vice. Later, he and Red Souter helped create the Criminal Intelligence Section. Cody was a detective in Burglary and Theft in 1963.

I was going to work about 2:30 that day but was in the office a couple of hours early when the call came in. My partner and I had planned to go to a movie until 2:30 but we never made it. They were grabbing everybody, so we jumped in our car and arrived at the scene where Kennedy was shot and killed in just three or four minutes. By that time, it was probably ten minutes after the shooting.

While we were there, I searched the plaza and found a bone lying in the gutter that apparently came out of the back of the President's head. It was mass confusion! People were spread around everywhere! Meanwhile, we were trying to find out what was happening inside the building. My partner, Charlie Dellinger, went inside the School Book Depository and helped find the rifle.

Part of the confusion at the time stemmed from the fact that there were tall buildings there. He shot the rifle from the sixth floor and there was another floor or two above that. In addition, the county jail and the post office were located there. You shoot a rifle from any of those places and you're going to get a ricochet noise or an echo.

I was back at the office by 1:30 and was there when Oswald was brought in by Hill, Bentley, and McDonald from the case in Oak Cliff where he had shot the officer. I don't know how long the fight lasted over at the Texas Theater, but I understand they tried to clear everybody out of the theater. When McDonald approached Oswald, that's when he pulled the pistol and McDonald grabbed it. At that point, Oswald snapped it but McDonald had his finger on the hammer with so much pressure that it apparently just barely fell against the cap and didn't go off. McDonald got a scar on his face where he was scratched or hit by Oswald and Oswald received one from McDonald. McDonald was very strong. It was apparently a hell of a battle over there.

At that time, we already had a tremendous amount of people in City Hall. Hill, Bentley, and McDonald asked, "What are we going to do with him?"

And I said, "Bring him over and we'll put him in Burglary and Theft." So I talked to him and said, "Now, what is your name?"

He said, "My name is Lee Harvey Oswald."

"Where do you work?"

He said, "Texas School Book Depository." Then it began to dawn on me what had happened when he told me where he worked.

Initially, I was alone in the little interrogation room with Oswald. When he told me his name, it kind of rang a bell. The only things that he told me were his name, that he had been in the Marine Corps, his serial number, and where he lived and worked. He wasn't arrogant. In fact, he reminded me of a captured war prisoner: Just give your name, rank, and serial number. I was sure that he had shot the officer and was pretty sure that he was the one who had shot the President, and still am. I figured that we finally had closed the case. It was relatively simple then, but in the years since, it's gotten rather complicated.

It was unusual. They had tried to get him into the homicide office and they were told to go away: "We're busy! We're working! Just get the prisoner out of here!" I had three officers guarding Oswald and eventually went over and tried to tell Fritz and was run off.*

Finally, I said, "No, hell no! Here it is!"

Fritz told me, "I'm hunting a suspect."

I asked him, "Who are you hunting?"

He responded, "Lee Harvey Oswald."

So I said, "I've had him over in my office for fifteen minutes!" Then they all ran over and got the prisoner and took him to Homicide. From that point, we were pretty well through with it.

Later we brought him down for a show-up. I was sent down to try to keep some order and stood right behind him. He kept his head down and all he'd say was "My name is Lee Harvey Oswald" and so on.

There was criticism for having that conference, but I don't think it hurt anything. After all, I don't think there had ever been a prisoner that important in any police department in the United States in my lifetime. Furthermore, let me say this: From the facts that occurred and the President being shot, the fact that Oswald was married to this girl, and that he had been to Russia and spoke Russian, and had been in the Marines; there was no question in my mind that he was a murderer, but he wasn't an ordinary murderer. Ordinary murderers don't shoot the President of the United States.

When the show-up was over, I took the prisoner back up to the jail on the fifth floor along with a couple of Homicide guys. We didn't ask him any questions on the way back up and he didn't say anything. I think Nick McDonald had taken that arrogance out of him at the theater.

About 9:30 on Saturday, the next morning, I flew to Lake Bisteneau, Louisiana to a gar rodeo. At the time, I owned Aqualand, a dive shop, in Dallas and an airplane, and each year we went to this rodeo. When you landed there, they had green metal posts with white signs, so that if you started down you saw the

---

* For a different version of this, refer to the narratives of Bentley (pp. 285-291), Hill (pp. 292-305) and Leavelle (pp. 384-407).

white signs. The Air Coupe I was flying didn't have rudders flared out so that when you turned the wheel to the right, the plane went to the right and banked around to the left and so forth. As we started down, we saw that sign, and I tried to pull it back to raise the wing because, with its fiber wing, the air would rip it out. When I did, it started off, so I had to come back. As a result, it ripped the back of the wing and pulled it back three or four inches. We were doing about 85 M.P.H. and went right on down near a filling station.

We had a party that night and put on our wetsuits the next morning. When you start that tournament at 7:00 in the morning, if you haven't got a bunch of gar by 9:30, then you're out of luck. I had a few little ones but never could find a big school. The gar that won the rodeo weighed 170 pounds and was eleven feet long including the needle.

Anyway, the next morning, Sunday, we were out there on the side of the highway trying to dope up that wing which was ripped (The wings were fiber while the body of the plane was metal) when George Yeoman, who was a friend of mine from Galveston, pulled up in his convertible and parked next to the wing of the plane. As we were sitting there talking and listening to the radio, I could just hear the news that Oswald was being brought out. Suddenly I heard a "pop" and the announcer screamed, "And he's been shot! He's been shot!"

We ran to the small filling station to watch it on TV. All I could see was this guy stepping out wearing a snap brim hat, suit, tie, shoes, with a snub nosed Colt pistol. I must have seen it forty times and thought it might have been Detective Buddy Munster. But I thought, "That can't be Buddy because he wears a cowboy hat." Then I thought, "Well, maybe it's Combest. No, Combest is taller than that."

I kept trying to think of these different detectives then a captain there said, "For your information, we just ran down the man that did the shooting: His name is Jack Ruby."

And I thought, "Oh, my God!"

They were just trying to get the prisoner down to the county and somebody shot him. That concerned me. You can't just be taking prisoners out and letting people shoot them. After I watched it forty times, shooting him and shooting him, and after hearing the captain announce that it was Jack Ruby, it all hit me that Jack Ruby was a friend of mine and that I had bought that pistol for him, and the pistol was in my name.

About a year or so before, Jack Ruby was having problems at his Carousel Club. He'd walk out of there with $1,500 to $2,000 in his pocket which, back in the '50's and early '60's, was a bunch of money. So he called me down there and said, "Look, I've got to build a safe. How much is it going to cost?"

I said, "Jack, if you're going to put a safe in here, you've got to put in a money box which is going to cost you about $2,000. Then it's going to have to be wired to the wall before you can put it in. Two people with a dolly can come in and carry it out. They'd have all kinds of time to work on it."

He said, "I can't afford $3,000 or $4,000."

So I asked, "Why don't you just get a pistol?"

"Can I carry it?" he asked.

I told him, "Jack, as long as you're carrying this money to and from wherever, you can have that pistol."

In those days, the Dallas Police Department allowed that if you had a laundry or a business and you went home with the day's receipts, you could carry a pistol. Now if you stopped by a nightclub and drank till midnight and you were caught with a pistol, then they were going to put you in jail, but if you were going to and from, no.

So, he said, "I believe I'll buy a pistol."

"You got $62.50? That's what they cost, $62.50."

He said, "Yeah, I'll be out." So we went out to Ray Brantley's Hardware on Singleton Boulevard in West Dallas and paid the $62.50, plus there was eight or nine dollars sales tax.

Since Jack didn't have a bunch of money, I said, "Let me put it in my name," since police officers weren't required to pay the sales tax for guns. So I put it in my name, Joe R. Cody, gave Ray the $62.50, took the pistol, handed it to Ruby, and he walked off with it.

All he wanted it for was self-defense. It was a .38 Colt Cobra, which had an aluminum frame, a metal barrel, and a steel cylinder. Since it was extremely light, you could easily put it in your pocket. It was also single or double action.

As I took Ruby around, I said, "You look at all the pistols and whichever one you like best, let me know and we'll get it."

He looked them over and asked, "Which one do you like?"

I said, "Now, Ruby, I carry a Colt Cobra." I had one just like the one he purchased except mine had a three-inch barrel while his was either 1 3/4 inch or two inch. That's the way they were made. His pistol, with the shorter barrel, was made only to shoot people that you're holding by the tie with one hand and shooting them with the other, or till somebody got on you. After 25 yards, I doubt if you could hit an elephant with it with the bullets taking off in different ways.

What I did for Ruby, by saving him the sales tax, was probably a common occurrence among policemen. After the shooting, I knew that this would come back on me. It had to. They were going to check to see who owned the gun, and it was going to be by Joe Cody. So I went to the chief, knocked on his door and said, "Yes, sir, I need to talk to you. The gun's in my name."

Well, he kind of dropped his mouth and said, "Tell me about it." So I told him the story and said that I'd met Ruby at Ray's to purchase the pistol. Ray is a pistol himself!

He's still got that big hardware store.* He's crazy! When you go into Brantley's and look at all the pistols, if you see one that is brand new, and it is brand new, buy it. He then writes your name down on a list. But if the pistol is not brand new, and you frequently cannot tell by looking since he oils all of them, then he wouldn't put your name in the book. But I'm pretty sure that Joe Cody's name is in that book, but I wouldn't swear to it. Ray Brantley is a crook!

Jack Ruby moved to Dallas from Chicago and bought the Roundup Club on South Ervay Street while I worked that beat. My partner and I met him and would stop in every night. He was a likable guy.

I used to play ice hockey, had skated all my life, and I had an interest in the local ice rink. I'd run the rink lots of times, then during the State Fair would work the Ice Capades all night long. One day I was out there skating and here came Jack Ruby on a pair of racing blades, and he could skate. He and I decided that we would skate together once or twice a week on Wednesday and Thursday afternoons. The sessions would begin at 1:00, so I had an hour or two since I had to be at work by 3:00. As a result, I got to know him quite well.

---

* Ray Brantley is now deceased.

I don't believe that he had much of an education, but he wore nice clothes and always had one of those strippers with him. He was in the nightclub business and that was it. Lots of people said that he must have been wealthy since he had $1,500 or so on him when he killed Oswald. But he owed $2,700 or so and was down to a few hundred dollars.

Jack could be rough. He'd throw people down the stairs of the Carousel. But he would try to talk to them, and if they started getting smart with him, he'd say, "Look, I don't want none of your smartness! I'll throw you out of this club!" Jack was about 5'6" or 5'7," weighed maybe 190 pounds and was extremely strong. People underestimated him. We'd get a call about a disturbance at the Carousel and would just wait at the bottom of the stairs for them to come bouncing down end over end. Then we'd catch them and put them in jail.

But generally everybody that I knew kind of liked Jack Ruby, and that included policemen. There'd be ten or twelve of us up there having a few beers every night. I imagine as many as 200 knew him by having been in his place and meeting him. He had strippers and so forth. When people from out of town would come in, he'd charge them a $1.50 for a beer when he'd only pay 9 1/2 cents. When the police would come in, he'd charge them 35 cents.

These clubs had nice furniture and carpet and always had probably three strippers doing their numbers to the music along with a combo which included a drummer, a saxophone player, and maybe a trumpeteer.

The Vegas Club out in Oak Lawn was owned by his sister Eva. I had heard that he was going to advance her out there, but he couldn't come up with the $5,000 to $10,000. He couldn't come up with that kind of money but might have signed some papers somehow. Anyway, Eva ran that club, though I'd seen Jack out there a time or two.

Jack liked to exhibit class, and I thought he was a fairly classy fellow. He dressed nicely with initials on his clothes.

I knew some of the strippers who worked in the clubs. They were about the same as prostitutes, at least their intelligence was about the same. They had the same ideological thinking except they were in a different profession. In fact, some of the strippers were prostitutes. But if a girl started hustling in his club, he'd fire them in a minute. Jack was constantly going down to the Western Union sending money to one of them who would call and tell him that she was knocked down on dope and that her husband had beaten her up and taken all her money. So he'd wire money to get her home on the train or plane.

I didn't think that Jack was as impulsive as some have said. Now when he got in a fight, he became rather emotional. In Chicago he was a strongman for labor bosses in strikes.

I don't know why some of these stories get started—for instance, that Jack was homosexual. No way! No way! I base that on his physical body and his going out with girls. I'd call him before and he'd say, "Just a minute," and I'd hear him talking to a girl. He just wasn't homosexual as has been claimed. Here in Texas, if you don't like somebody, you call them queer and that puts them down.

I was originally scheduled to testify at Jack's trial after he shot Oswald but was never called. I was to be a character witness along with Detective Blankenship and a news reporter, Wes Wise, who later became mayor. I have no idea why we weren't called. We were subpoenaed to testify when Tom Howard and Phil Burleson were his attorneys. Somewhere in there Tom Howard was kicked out and Melvin Belli came in.

I followed the trial but didn't agree with Belli's defense that Ruby had a mental blackout, and neither did Jack. After the trial, I visited him in jail once or twice. He was still in good shape when I saw him. He told me, "Well, the trial, I'm the only thing they've got their hands on now. We'll have an appeal."

He was a firm believer in appeals, and I told him, "You bet, you'll have an appeal."

It's my opinion that he should have kept Tom Howard and Phil Burleson and let them plead him guilty to murder assault because Jack Ruby didn't enter the basement to kill that boy. He parked his car with his dogs in it, had $1,500 on him, and saw all this crowd coming out of the basement of City Hall. Sergeant P.T. Dean ran them out and they left all their cameras down there. Then Assistant Chief Charlie Batchelor, who was in uniform, tailored the night before, since he hadn't worn a uniform in years and wanted to be before the cameras said, "Sergeant, what are those men doing out there?"

Dean said, "I ran them out."

"Ya'll come on back," Batchelor replied, and here came Ruby and everybody else. Nobody checked them.

In fact, I didn't find it unusual that Ruby was in the basement. He had gone to the Western Union down the block and saw all these people coming out of the basement when he left. Now we're talking 80-90 people, so he went walking in that direction. When they were told to come on back, he just went right in with them.

Some people have mentioned that he was stalking Oswald. Hell, he shot Oswald in front of about 150 people. There's not much question as to who did the shooting, is there? He just stepped out and shot him. He could have done that on Friday or Saturday night when he was there. He could have done it anytime.

I think that he had convinced himself that, with all that had happened that weekend, he just wasn't going to put up with the piece of crap that had killed, to Jack Ruby, the most important man in the world: the President, John F. Kennedy. Besides, he felt that they were going to put him in jail and let him out on three year's suspended sentence.

When Jack Kennedy was elected President of the United States, Jack Ruby probably didn't even vote. I'm sure that he was knowledgeable as to who the President was as he had seen him on television, and the Age of Camelot, and that Kennedy was especially a very popular man in the United States. Now if Jack Kennedy had walked into Ruby's club at 1:00 o'clock in the morning, I'll guarantee that he'd cut the lights on and introduce him to everybody there.

I wasn't surprised that he received the death penalty. There's a hell of a lot more death penalties given around here than there are executions.

Somehow my name has become linked to some of these conspiracy theories. I think some of them came from that district attorney in New Orleans. One of those was that I had a plane at Redbird Airport and that I was to supposedly fly the assassin to, I guess, Mexico. Let me say this—the airplane wasn't at Redbird Airport; it was at Grand Prairie Airport. Redbird wanted too much to store my airplane, which was a little two-seater which had a range of 450-500 miles and cruised at about 150 miles an hour. Now I had flown to Mexico a bunch of times out of Redbird in a DC-3 on diving trips when I had the dive shop.

In those days, we'd fly to the Isle of Cozumel which, at that time, had only about 300 people and one hotel. It's not like that now. I was one of the first skin divers ever on the Isle of Cozumel. Now, I don't mean just a mask, fins, and snorkel; I'm talking about mass tank regulators where you could get down and get the fish. Back then we'd sell twenty tickets which would cost $350 each, which would include three meals a day, most of your booze, everything on the boat, the diving, tanks, the whole bit, including the flight to Cozumel. There we'd be picked up and taken to the hotel. Now I understand that package costs $1,200-$1,500 for three days; whereas, we did it for seven. The point is that my plane wasn't at Redbird, and I wasn't waiting around for an assassin. Right after the press conference with Oswald I flew to Lake Bisteneau for the gar rodeo and was there when we heard that Oswald was shot.

My uncle's name was listed in Oswald's notebook which also led to all kinds of speculation. Kenneth Cody lived in Oak Cliff behind the Redline Apartments, not a block and a half from Methodist Hospital, and drove a bus for Continental Trailways for probably 35 years, the last twenty between Dallas and Shreveport. He was a senior driver by that time and would take the bus out at 8:00 A.M. and drive the passengers to Shreveport, set them off, eat lunch, take on more passengers, then drive home. He did that five days a week.

He was also quite a good carpenter and bought old homes in Oak Cliff, some within a couple of blocks where Oswald lived, would fix them up, then rent them out. In front of his homes, he would have signs with his name and phone number. The only thing I can figure is that Oswald, in looking for a room, wrote his name and number down. Now whether he called the number, I don't know, and Kenneth Cody is dead now.

A few have even questioned my background in counterintelligence in the Army. At the end of the war, I joined the inactive reserves, came home, started college, threw my uniforms in my mother's attic, played sports, and joined the police department. Then came the Korean War. I did Advanced Infantry Training at Camp Roberts, California and was then shipped up to San Francisco where I applied for CIC. I was only one of nine who were taken out of 70,000 and was scheduled to go to Korea for an amphibious landing north of Seoul. Fortunately, my orders came through, and I went to Fort Haliburton where I became a CIC agent and was stationed all over the United States. I worked in plain clothes as a warrant officer in the Counterintelligence Agency which dealt with treason, sabotage, subversion, disaffection, etc.

When I came to work in the police department, Jesse Curry was just made captain and was assigned to the police school along with Inspector Batchelor where both of them taught. Curry was an ex-Crozier Tech [High School] football player who had returned from the service and had married. He made promotion through the ranks: sergeant, lieutenant, and captain. Then he was sent to a police school at Northwestern in Chicago where he met and fell in love with another woman. He then divorced his wife, married the other and brought her down here.

Years ago I had a friend named Jackie Blair who was a lightweight prize fighter. He had 120 fights and had fought Sandy Sadler for the lightweight championship, as well as Willie Pep. He knocked out Pep in the second round.

Anyway, one night in '49, Blair was in a car at a drive-in and Jackie began cursing. Curry, who was there with this other woman, suddenly got out of his car and said, "Now I've had enough!"

Jackie apologized saying, "I'm sorry, I didn't see you all sitting in that car." Curry, who had been drinking, apparently just decided that he'd whip Jackie's butt. Jackie apologized again five or six times.

Curry told him, "I'll just whip your ass!"

Jackie said, "No, I apologize, but you're not going to whip my ass!" And he didn't! Curry spent about six days in the hospital. You jump on one of the top three contenders, you've erred, you've erred!

Then in 1951 or '52, we had a bunch of robberies in the police department. We had a lieutenant who was the night chief of detectives who had gone up to a gun shop on Pacific Avenue. My partner, Bob Pettis, and I were working that district when an alarm went off. We made a U-turn and went two blocks back. It couldn't have been more than a minute to a minute and a half from the time the alarm went off till the time the dispatcher broadcast it to us. As we slid down there, we noticed a front window broken and four detectives and the night detective standing there. He said, "Boy, they sure must have got away fast.

You all go on and check service; we'll take care of it." The next day it was in the papers that $45,000 worth of guns had been taken out of that damn place. They sent the lieutenant and a bunch of others to the penitentiary.

Curry was a big strong man who was about 6'2," weighed about 240, and was solid muscle. For Chief Hansson, who was getting old and white-haired, it was nice to have a big inspector around in case somebody jumped on him. Because of Curry's loyalty, I think that's why he was named chief after Hansson died.

Jesse Curry never worked anything in his life but traffic, blew that whistle and flagged those fingers. Unfortunately, Curry wasn't very capable. It seems like in the police department that if you're going to be chief, you can't do police work. You haven't got time because you've got to politic to be chief.

Charlie Batchelor, who followed Curry as chief, was a corner man, later made captain of the Traffic Division, then became an inspector, and the police department put him in a school. When Curry became chief, he pulled Batchelor out of the school and made him assistant chief. When Curry left, Batchelor, who knew absolutely nothing, replaced him.

Will Fritz came to work for the police department around 1916 or '17 when there were only eighty or ninety people in the department. In those early days, I hate to say this, but Dallas was awfully loose on gambling. You'd walk into a gambling hall and there'd be six blackjack tables, four roulettes, and maybe two dice tables with professional gamblers. Carl Hansson was made chief to stop this gambling. When he did, he told J. Will Fritz, "Now I'm demoting you to the rank of captain."

Fritz told him, "Well, that's okay with me, chief, but I want to take over the Homicide Bureau. You need to make me a senior captain because I've adjusted my life to this salary I'm making and I can't take a cut." Hansson looked at him like he was crazy. But what he didn't know was that the mayor, the richest man in Dallas, was a personal friend of Fritz. As a result, Fritz was made senior captain without a cut in pay.

J. Will Fritz was captain in Homicide. He had about 28-30 detectives down there and not one of them except Holloway did a damn thing unless they were told to. He'd say, "Now you run down and get the record on him and run over here and talk to her and bring back a report," and they'd just stand around with those boob hats on until he told them to go.

Fritz carried in the back of his squad car a saddle, a .30.30 rifle, bridle, and so forth. He apparently told others, "In case somebody rides off into the mountains and I have to get a horse and go after them, I'll have my own saddle."

I always thought, "If I had a horse, where in hell do I go to the mountains around here!"

You have a problem when you go from a small piece of pumpkin to a larger one. For instance, if there were four people in the Homicide Bureau you could handle all the important cases yourself. Fritz had a secretary named Mary Rattan who made details and did all the paper work. All he had to do was sign the forms. He really wasn't a captain of police; Fritz was a super cop. If you had a bad case, he'd do the interrogating, and it was all the same. When he got Oswald up there and said, "Now, Mr. Oswald, you've got to confess to this or you're going to get the electric chair."

Oswald looked at him like, "Well, you crazy son of a bitch. You know I killed the President of the United States, and you're going to keep me from going to the electric chair?"

Things weren't normal in the police department at that time. Burglary and Theft detectives would be running here or there, then somebody would get them and say, "Hey, come here, you! Go over and find this or that." They would have people from Forgery working on a case, then I might walk out to get a drink of water and I'd be grabbed and sent somewhere else.

You've got to remember that this was the most important crime to ever occur in this nation in our lifetime, including the lifetimes of all the policemen who worked down there, and it occurred in Dallas, Texas. As a result, some of the policemen sought publicity from this. Tommy Tilson was one of those.

He claimed that he heard a shot above the overpass, sped there in his car and saw this guy jump in another car and drive off. I've heard the story different from everybody, though I've never heard Tommy tell it to my face, but I'll tell him that he's a goddamn liar if he does.

By 1965, Cody left the Burglary and Theft Division to become a motorcycle sergeant for the next eight years. The remainder of his career was spent with assignments in the Tactical Section, Homicide and Robbery, General Assignments, and Intelligence. Since his retirement from the Dallas Police Department in 1980, he has served as a private investigator.

BILL COURSON
Detective, Criminal Investigation,
Dallas County Sheriff's Department

"After Ruby shot Oswald, and when the city was preparing to transfer Ruby to the county jail, Decker commented to me and several other officers sitting in his office. 'Hell, no, let them transfer the son of a bitch! I don't care nothing about it. They'll screw it up again...' "

Born in Hopkins County, Texas in 1930, Bill Courson joined the Marine Corps, became a drill instructor, and served in the Korean War. After leaving the Corps in 1958, he drove a Continental Trailways bus out of San Antonio and joined the Dallas County Sheriff's Department in January 1961. Courson was a deputy sheriff under Bill Decker at the time of Kennedy's visit to Dallas.

I started out in uniform patrol, and after a year or a year and a half, I went into plain clothes as a night criminal investigator. My job was to keep track of known criminals with a record, personnel files for Mr. Decker of known criminals, who they were associated with, what cars they were driving, and where they were living, just so he'd have some ready information.

I'd never heard of Mr. Decker before I joined the sheriff's office. A friend of my father's suggested that I go down and talk to Mr. Decker because he knew him well. He had apparently become sheriff the year that I went into the Marine Corps.

I was surprised that I was promoted to plain clothes as rapidly as I was, but I guess Mr. Decker apparently noticed that I was conscientious about my work when I was in uniform and was impressed with my appearance and the way that I handled people, the public out there, which was a big campaign thing with him. He started his campaign for reelection for the next term the day that he took office by being the type of politician who knew that you could catch more flies with honey than you could with vinegar. So your job was to get out there and take care of the public. The only time that he had an opponent was when one of the reserve deputies, a Republican, kept running against him, which became something of a tradition. Like any young officer, I got a little eager once in a while but I kept my nose clean, and I guess Mr. Decker liked my work.

My wife phoned me from downtown Dallas on the afternoon of November 22nd and told me that the President had been shot. Since I usually went to work at 3:00 or 4:00 o'clock in the afternoon, though there was no set time, I was in bed at my house in DeSoto at the time, just a couple of blocks from where I live now.

In any case, she convinced me during that call that she wasn't kidding about the President, which I didn't think she would about something like that. It was a shock! At first, I just couldn't believe it and that it had happened in Dallas. So I dressed, put on the old rumpled clothes that I had worn the night before, and within five minutes, since the squad car was at the house, I was on the way to downtown Dallas and checked into service about halfway between DeSoto and Oak Cliff.

There was quite a bit of radio traffic along with confusion. A lot of squads were checking in trying to find out what had happened while probably a lot of others who had been called at home like I had been were also just getting into service. I just listened to the radio until I was about halfway into Oak Cliff. I didn't try to break in and check in sooner because of the traffic since I ascertained that there had been a shooting in the motorcade. Then it came on that the President had been shot, but they didn't know how serious that it was. Other traffic followed on the radio that there were some suspects in cars, etc. It was kind of like Keystone Cops; everybody was running in different directions till they were finally coordinated.

In fact, I had a suspect in mind out in Grand Prairie when I learned of the shooting. I think this man now lives in Mississippi. But he had made a statement, which had gotten to me, that "He hoped Kennedy got his damn head blown off while he was in Dallas." This had been just a week or two prior to the time Kennedy came to Dallas.

So I thought that if there's that many officers downtown there's no use in my going there, so I thought I'd go out Jefferson Boulevard to Grand Prairie and bring in the suspect. I didn't know that he was the one who had shot the President, but everyone that had made a statement like that was a suspect at that time. Of course, in those days there was no federal law against threatening a president like there is now.

At that time, I was on radio frequency 37-300. I also had a 37-180 frequency which I could flip over to and hear the state traffic, but I couldn't monitor the two frequencies of the city of Dallas. I think the city police probably knew more about what was going on since they had more squads and more radio contact. Our dispatcher had to monitor their frequency and pass it on to us.

The assassination occurred near the sheriff's department where many of the deputies who weren't providing security watched the motorcade as it went by. It was not all that unusual for us not to provide security for any of the officials unless they were going outside the city limits into the county or into a small town or suburb around Dallas which didn't have a police department at that time. There's a stadium north of Dallas that we used to have to provide security for football games. If the motorcade had gone out there, then we would have probably provided security because that was outside the city limits of Dallas. But it was the policy of the sheriff's department not to interfere in the business of the city of Dallas as long as the city had enough officers to handle it and they didn't request us. Anything that involved the investigation of a murder or anything that happened outside the incorporated city limits that didn't have a police department, we handled, since our authority went countywide. The Dallas County Sheriff's Department was the highest law enforcement agency in the county, including the city of Dallas, thus Decker had ultimate authority. If he wanted to take a case, he did. But it was just a matter of policy with him not to interfere into something that the city had working unless they asked for our help. Mr. Decker was in the motorcade, but it was strictly protocol.

There was some professional jealousy between the departments and more between the FBI and the police department than the sheriff's department. Still, though, there was quite a bit of professional jealousy between the sheriff's department and the police department. I'm not sure whose fault it was, but it was more in the lower echelons than in the high.

In any case, I hadn't gotten up to Jefferson and Zang around Twelfth Street when I received a call that a suspect had been seen running into the library at Marsalis and Jefferson. In the meantime, I had also gotten a call that a Dallas police officer had been shot near that location. As I was coming up Jefferson, running fast with red lights and siren, there was an island in the center of Jefferson; at some point, I made a right turn at between 50 and 65 M.P.H. I don't know how I did it, but I bounced off quite a bit of concrete and went down to the library.

As I stepped out of the car, a uniformed officer who had seen the red lights and realized that it was an official car, even though I was in the rumpled plain clothes that I had worn the night before, hollered at me and said that it was a false alarm. He said that it was just a young man who had run in to tell his mother that the President had been shot. So I left there and went to the location where the officer, Tippit, had been shot.

Tippit's car was on the right hand side of the street facing east while I was on the right side facing west. As I pulled up alongside the car, there was another uniformed officer at the location who was evidently waiting for the wrecker to come and get Tippit's car. I don't recall whether I had heard that he was dead, but I believe I did. As I stepped out of the car, the call came in on Tippit's radio, which was still on, that "The suspect, wearing a white or light colored jacket, has been seen running into the balcony of the Texas Theater."

We were only a few blocks from the theater, but I had to back up and turn to get back onto Jefferson. Another officer was headed the same way, so he and I ran a race, my going backwards and his going forward to see who could make that turn to get onto Jefferson first. He was in front of me and went on around to the back of the theater. I'm inclined to believe this was McDonald, the one who eventually captured Oswald, but I'm not sure.

Anyway, he went on in his squad car around the theater and probably went down the alley.

I pulled up and bumped the bicycle rack in front of the theater, left the car and went in and identified myself as an officer to the ticket taker. I didn't know whether she even saw me or not, but I flashed my badge, then walked from there onto the stairs.

I started up the stairs of the balcony because that is where the call said that he was hiding. I'm reasonably satisfied in my own mind that I met Oswald coming down. I was looking for a man in a white or light colored jacket because at that time I hadn't been told that he had discarded the jacket and that it had been found. So there were two reasons why I didn't stop him: I'm looking for a man in the balcony, not coming down walking casually, and the description didn't fit because he was wearing a kind of plaid or checkered patterned shirt, not the light colored jacket. But I'm reasonably sure that it was Oswald.

I think what he had done was to run into the balcony and sat down, then saw that there wasn't enough people there for him to blend in since there was only five to seven people there. So he decided to go to the lower part because, at that time, he didn't realize that anybody had called in about his going into the theater. That's the reason that he didn't shoot me coming down the stairs—that, and the fact that I had on some old wrinkled clothes and really didn't look like a police officer and didn't have my revolver out. I had stuck my wallet back in my coat pocket after I had identified myself to the ticket taker and was walking at the time. If I had been running and had had my pistol out, he would have probably tried to shoot me. Or maybe I'd have gotten lucky and changed history!

Anyway, I went into the balcony and had the projectionist flip on the lights. I didn't see anybody that fit the description, so I got to checking the balcony area and found a room that was dark, but I couldn't find a light switch. There was a ladder going down, no stairway, just a ladder, so I went down the ladder with a cigarette lighter in one hand and my pistol in the other. Strange things began to go off my backbone like big bumps. I was afraid that I was crawling down into a tiger's nest. I didn't know what I was getting into, so I came out and ran downstairs to grab a flashlight out of my squad car. As I started back in, I saw my partner, Buddy Walthers, who was working days at the time. We had been working a murder case at the time; Buddy was working the day leads, and I was following the night leads.

As Buddy drove up, I threw him a flashlight, and as I started back in, the doors opened and several Dallas police officers came out with Oswald after they had captured him downstairs. I remember one officer putting his cap over Oswald's face as they had him with his arms pinned behind him. When they got him to the squad car, one pushed his head down inside. The scar that Oswald had on his forehead I'd always thought came when he bumped his head getting into the car, but after they described the scuffle in the theater between the seats, I assume that he got it there. I don't believe that Oswald was saying anything when he came out. I was thirty feet or so feet away standing to the right of the door facing the theater.

There was quite a crowd milling around. I don't know how all these people had gotten word so fast that this was the assassin of the President because I didn't even fully realize that at the time. But there were people hollering, "Kill him! Kill him!" I assume that it was in reference to his having killed the President since policemen weren't that popular. In fact, I don't think the people in that particular location would have even known that there was a policeman who had been shot. Word had spread quickly, but that was several blocks away and these were apparently just people in the neighborhood.

Jefferson Boulevard was an old neighborhood. Most of the shops and businesses were open in that area at the time. There was a Sears up the street, a major grocery store, Safeway, L.B. Mercantile was down the street, and various other sporting goods and jewelry stores. It was a decent lower middle class neighborhood where a lot of old timers had built homes in Oak Cliff years earlier. But it was still a fairly good neighborhood to live in at that time. Now it's run down with a lot of narcotics.

At that time, I knew that there had been a shooting in the motorcade due to the radio traffic on the way to the location of the theater, and knew that the President had either been wounded or shot in some way. But I don't think that anybody, anybody, unless they were right there with the President in the car, realized the magnitude of the thing. There were a lot of hopes that this was just a wounding, but during the capture of Oswald, and in that time frame, you just didn't have time to even speculate on the scope or the magnitude of it all.

When I realized that they had the suspect, there was no reason for me to go back into the theater since they had sufficient help. So I stood and watched till they got him in the car and had left.

After I returned to my squad car, I got on the radio and told them that the suspect had been apprehended in the Texas Theater and that I'd be in service. I then went on to the Dallas Police Department to see if I could be of any assistance there in any investigation.

I went to Will Fritz's office but didn't talk to him, though I knew him well. Instead, I asked one of his officers there, "Can I be of any assistance? You know, I was at the location when he was captured, but I didn't actually see the scuffle or anything. Is there anything else you guys need me to do? If not, I'll go back to the sheriff's department."

They told me, "No, we've got everything under control. Thank you." So I left after being at the police department around ten or twelve minutes.

The following day Decker talked to several of the officers about transferring Oswald: these included, I believe, H.A. Bockemehl, a criminal investigator, Bill McCoy, a Station 4 desk sergeant, and myself. There might have been another couple of officers involved because we were going to have two cars: one decoy car and one car with these officers to take Oswald out. The decoy car was to go out the up ramp onto Commerce like normal traffic to the county jail and was supposed to have three officers: one driving, one decoy Oswald, and another officer who was supposedly handcuffed to Oswald. The followup car was to have one driving, with another in the front seat, while McCoy was supposed to sit on Oswald on the floor in the back of the car.

Meanwhile, we were going to get Oswald out of the jail, take him downstairs, and throw him in the car where McCoy was going to sit on him and keep him on the floor board. We would be going against one-way traffic, so we were supposedly going to have a uniformed squad outside to stop traffic in case there was any problem. Since this was to take place in the wee hours, we didn't anticipate any problems. At 3:00 o'clock in the morning in those days in Dallas, there was nothing; it was dead. And it probably would have been dead except for some straggling of news media around City Hall.

We were aware, though, of potential problems. In fact, I have a written transcript of conversations on the telephone between Decker and McCoy about threats against Oswald that came in to the sheriff's department, and really that transcript shows a need for more security than what they had there at the Dallas Police Department. I think it's a fact that Jess Curry yielded to political pressure from Mayor Earle Cabell for the city to transfer Oswald. Normally that was a sheriff's department function. After a person had been convicted of a felony or been indicted or charged, then they were transferred to the county jail by deputy sheriffs.

As I've said, Mr. Decker was the kind of person who didn't interfere with the city unless they wanted him to. And in this particular case, I think that I heard somewhere, maybe in the transcript, that Decker said, "Do you want us to transfer him?"

And Curry said, "Yeah, that's what we usually do, isn't it?" But he yielded to political pressure plus the news media was allowed to be just about anywhere they wanted to be in the building.

If Decker had handled it, there wouldn't have been any reporters that would have known that Oswald was even out of the city jail until we had him removed unless there was someone hiding that might have spotted him. But by the time they could have gotten to a telephone and alerted anyone and gotten to their cars to follow us, we would have been to the county jail and had him inside the bars. There's no doubt in my mind that if we would have transferred the man that history would have totally been changed because Ruby wouldn't have gotten to him and neither would anyone else.

Very seldom did the Dallas Police Department transfer any prisoner to the county jail. We had a paddy wagon that made routine trips to the city jail just to get prisoners who had been charged with felonies that were going back to the county jail for trial. Now there wasn't a written law that said that we had to transfer prisoners, and I'm sure that the city of Dallas probably transferred some prisoners at times. For instance, there might be an urgency where a prisoner was indicted or charged and had to be in the county jail for some reason, or he might have been an escapee from Alabama or Georgia or some other area, then they'd just bring him on down to the county jail. But it was more common for us to do the transfer when I was with the sheriff's department.

In this particular instance, Mr. Decker wasn't really relishing the idea. He didn't care whether we transferred him or not. After Ruby shot Oswald, and when the city was preparing to transfer Ruby to the county jail, Decker commented to me and several other officers sitting in his office, "Hell, no, let them transfer the son of a bitch! I don't care nothing about it! They'll screw it up again!"

That was typical Decker! All through the day there were officers coming and going, and he'd call some of his favorite officers in that he depended on and would have informal conferences with them to let them know how he felt about certain matters. Decker was a congenial person, and if he didn't have something serious on his mind, he'd sometimes express his opinion in rather spicey language. But he never revealed that side of him to the public.

In any case, Mr. Decker told us, "We're not going to transfer him; the city's going to transfer Oswald, so you guys might as well go on home." Of course, I was glad to go home because I'd worked some long hours.

The next morning I decided to watch the transfer on television. When Jack Ruby shot Oswald, I said, "Oh, shit!" I had just arrested the man a short time before that, and I recognized him after the shooting.

I had just arrested Ruby on a threats warrant. I can't remember the exact date, but it was a threats warrant that Jada, one of his strippers, had filed against him. I think the Warren Commission called it a civil dispute. But I did make a return on the warrant, though I can't find it anymore.

Let me start at the beginning. I was in the office one morning when Judge Bill Richburg called. Richburg was a unique kind of justice of the peace. We called him the "Law West of the Trinity." He was a large man who was congenial, smoked a cigar, and had a way of settling disputes that was effective without hurting people or putting them in jail. Anyway, he called the office around 7:00 o'clock in the evening and asked me if I knew Jack Ruby. I said, "Yeah, I know him. I've been up to his club several times."

And he said, "Well, I'm sending a young lady over there with a warrant for his arrest." Apparently Jack had threatened her in some way, and she had filed a threats warrant. So he said, "When she gets over there with the warrant, go to the club, bring him down to the jail, book him, mug shot him, fingerprint him, and release him on a personal recognizance bond."

So when Jada came in, I read the warrant and asked her what time Ruby would be in the club; I think she said right at 8:00 o'clock. So she left and went on to the club. At 8:00 o'clock I went to the club with another deputy, Bill Walters, I believe. As we started up the stairs, Jada met us coming down and said, "Officers, I don't want you to arrest him. All I want you to do is scare him."

So I told her, "Young lady, we're not in the scaring business. Now you've filed a warrant here for his arrest. This warrant says bring his warm little body down to the county jail, and the judge said to book him, fingerprint him, mug shot him, and release him on a personal recognizance bond. Now if you don't want him arrested, you call Judge Bill Richburg and have him call me at the sheriff's office and tell me what to do; I'm going back down there."

So I left and had just gotten back when the judge called. Richburg, who at times used rather spicey language, said, "Bill, go back down to the damn club and get every son of a bitch that gives you any trouble and bring them to the sheriff's office. Call me when you get them there and I'll be down. I'm going to hold court there."

So I went back to the club, Ruby wasn't there; nobody knew where he was. I told them to have Ruby call me. I finally called the club and got hold of Jack and told him that I had a warrant for his arrest and asked him if he wanted to come down on his own or if he wanted me to come and get him. He said, "Give me thirty minutes and I'll be down there." In about an hour, he arrived along with Lynn Burk, who was with the Liquor Control Board at that time, a talent scout for Warner Brothers, so he said, and a couple of other witnesses that he had brought with him. Jada then came in with two or three other people with her; I don't remember exactly how many. But this was no big thing at the time; there was no sensationalism to it.

Anyway, the judge held court and listened to both sides. Apparently Jack was supposed to pay Jada a couple of grand if she fulfilled her contract which was due to expire in a short time, a week or so. Jack was probably wanting to get out of paying that $2,000, so he had threatened Jada. She said that he had threatened to cut up her wardrobe which she said was worth about $40,000. I asked Jada, "Young lady, how in the world could you have $40,000 worth of G-strings because that's all I've ever seen you in?"

Ruby claimed that Jada was taking off too much and that the Liquor Control Board would control that type of thing. That's the reason that he had brought Lynn Burk down there that night as a witness. Jada probably was taking off too much, and probably some of the other girls were, too. I'd been in the club several times and would sit down for a few minutes and would naturally watch the show while I was there because my job was to keep track of known criminals for Mr. Decker, and that was the type place that they would hang out.

In any case, the judge held court till 3:00 o'clock that morning. Finally he got tired of playing cat and mouse with them and said, "I want to tell you people something. Neither one of you are Sunday school teachers, and I'm going to give you ten minutes together back in that interrogation room to settle this thing. If you haven't settled it in ten minutes, I'm going to put both of you in jail!" So they went into that room and in a few minutes came out with some kind of agreement. I don't know what it was, but Jack was going to pay her something, though I don't think that she got all of it.

I asked the judge, "You want me to go ahead and book Ruby?"

He said, "Yeah, go ahead and book him."

So when we were three or four doors through to the book-in gate ready to turn the key gate, I told Ruby, "Come on, we'll book you right quick and get you on out of here."

As we started through the hallway, he said, "Oh, hell, I've got a pistol in my pocket." I hadn't thought to shake anybody down because this was an informal arrest at the time. He had come down on his own, so I had never even thought about his bringing a pistol with him.

He then pulled out a little derringer, a real antique, and said, "I just bought this antique a couple of days ago and there's not any shells in it. It's just a single shot, but I don't want to lose it. I'm afraid they'll take it away from me in booking in there."

So I said, "Well, now here, let me have it. I'll put it in my coat pocket and we won't even declare it."

We did that, then while we were standing there talking, Richburg said, "Just let him go and just make a return on the warrant. We don't need to book him," which was fine with both of them.

Meanwhile, since I had my pockets full of everything else: notes, papers, cigarette lighter, cigarettes, I didn't realize that I still had the pistol in my pocket until I got home. Apparently Jack had also forgotten about it since he was really tickled that he didn't have to be booked.

The next day I took it back to the sheriff's department. I called Jack and said, "Jack, I've still got that little pistol that you handed me the other night. I'll bring it by the club."

He said, "I just bought that thing."

So I asked him, "What did you give for that little gun anyway?" He told me $25, so I asked, "What would you take for it?"

He said, "I'll take fifty." We agreed and I said that I would bring the money by the club. That doubled his money. I didn't ask him whether it was hot or not, but it didn't look like a gun that had been stolen and he was a businessman, even though sometimes a little shady. Now I didn't know Jack to be shady; I just knew that anybody that ran a club like that in Dallas at that time had been shady since this is where Benny Binion began his career. Back in those days Binion and Abe Cessna and people like that were known to be gamblers and a little shady. But I didn't think the pistol would be hot, so I didn't bother to check the serial number. Later I found a three digit number.

Though I never got a bill of sale, I legally bought it from Jack. Later, I did some research on the gun and learned that it was a Hopkins and Allen, single-shot, .32 rimfire with no rifling in the barrel. It was made sometime before 1896 because the factory burned that year and no more were made. Apparently Jack had been looking for ammunition for it which I later found at Smitty's Gun Shop.

The main reason that nobody ever knew about this was when the assassination occurred I brought this pistol into the office and tagged it as found property because I wanted nothing to do with anything that Jack Ruby had at that time. I was scared for my job. Mr. Decker, being the type of person that he was, I was afraid that if I got caught with something, even though I had bought it legally, I'd lose my job with the sheriff's department, and at that time it wasn't worth it to me. So I tagged it as found property and put it in the property room. Just a few months after that, during the Ruby trial, I left the sheriff's office and was gone for three years. When I came back, I found this gun in the desk of another deputy, Charlie Player, with my tag still on it.

Player worked in the office. One night I brought a prisoner down to the jail and was looking for a form or something through his desk and found this gun in his desk drawer. It was supposed to have been in the property room because it was found property. As far as they knew, it was just an old antique. Apparently Charlie was trying to confiscate it, or liberate it, whatever you want to call it, for himself. So I took the gun and put it in my uniform pocket, since I was back in uniform then, and took it back to the substation.

We were having a domino game after everybody got off the next morning when I told another deputy, Charlie McComb, about the gun. I didn't tell him where it originated, but I did tell him about my finding it in Charlie Player's desk. So I called Mr. Decker on the phone and explained the situation. I said, "I'd like to have that gun, sheriff. I found it, no one else has claimed it, and I'd like to have it." Mr. Decker didn't tell me that I could have it. He just said to come by and see him by and by and hung up. Well, I didn't hang up; I kept talking and said, "Thank you, sheriff. I appreciate that." The sergeant and everybody else heard the conversation.

When I hung up, the sergeant asked, "Did he give you that gun?"

I told him, "Sure did!" So I took it out of my pocket, took off the tag, and I've had it ever since.

Ruby wasn't into antique guns that I know of. I think that he just bought it because it was a cute little gun. It's small enough to cram in your mouth. But when I was in uniform patrol, I carried it in my shirt pocket with a bullet in it after I finally found some bullets and used it as a hideout gun even though it's a little dangerous to carry since it's a single-action with no safety, and the trigger lays on the firing pin almost all the time.

I'd been in Ruby's club, the Carousel, on several occasions. The other clubs he ran I'd probably been in but didn't know that he owned them—at least I never saw him in them. From my experiences with him, Ruby was always very pleasant with me. But I learned during that hearing with Judge Richburg that he was a very impulsive type. He would be talking calmly one minute then become very excited and hyper as he went on. I've heard that he would put on an act when he was trying to scare someone into making them think that he was getting higher and higher losing his temper. But Jack was a very impulsive person, and it's my opinion that just on an impulse he pulled the pistol and shot Oswald.

Ruby also catered to officers. If we'd have out of town officers come in to pick up a prisoner, they'd have to spend the night, and Decker would tell us to show them the town. He didn't mean to take them out and get them drunk or anything like that. He really meant for us to show them the town so that they wouldn't be bored to death. So I'd take them up to the Carousel Club and I'd say, "Jack, here's these two hustlers from New York City," or wherever they were from, "and I'm going to have them here for a while." Whether they paid or not, I don't know; that was between Jack and them. If he wanted to entertain them for free, I didn't care.

Jack was just like any other businessman in Dallas. Any restaurant owner, any cafe or eating establishment in Dallas where the police would come in, the coffee's free. Eat half-price because they wanted the police there. They didn't want a show of force coming in and looking around like, "Hey, we're fixing to raid the joint," but they wanted the police to be seen there. They kept down robberies and let the undesirables know that the police were around.

Now Jack seemed like he might have been partial with the police officers, but I don't think that it was because he had any on the string. I think that it was just because he liked police officers. I had some wealthy men here in Dallas like Sy Guthrie, Tom Lively, and W.O. Bankston who would call me and say, "Hey, Bill, could I ride with you tonight? I need some excitement." So there were a lot of people who catered to the police officers, especially the criminal investigators and the plain clothes officers, not because they could do something for them, but just because they liked to be around them. They were just frustrated would-be policemen. In fact, I think that Jack Ruby would have probably been a police officer if he had wanted to be.

The Carousel Club I wouldn't say was a really high class club, but it wasn't low class either. It was a place where the average businessman and some wealthy people would go. I don't think that it was a meeting place for criminals or anything like that. It was just a night spot, and there weren't that many in Dallas then, though there were a lot of "honky-tonks" and dives.

As long as I was a night criminal investigator, I never dealt with or knew any type of Mafia or organized crime figures in Dallas. Later, when I rejoined the sheriff's department, there was a "Dixie Mafia" which sprang up here, and I was very familiar with its leader, Kirksey Nix, and some of his associates. But it didn't amount to much and didn't last long. At that time, there was only one person in Dallas that even bragged about being Mafia. And you knew that if he was Mafia, he wouldn't have been bragging about it. That was Joe Civello who owned the Egyptian Lounge in North Dallas. If Jack knew Joe Civello, so did everybody else. Joe was a very well known man. I don't think that Ruby was the type of personality that the Mafia would have had a hell of a lot to do with. Jack was flamboyant in his dressing ways, impulsive, and kind of a horn blower, a bragger. From what I've heard about the Mafia, they just don't deal with people like that. Now it's possible that he could have been used in some way, but I never had any indication of that as a criminal investigator. In fact, I've never heard of any police officer since the assassination say that they knew of Jack having any Mafia connections.

Some of the girls who worked at the Carousel were well-known strippers. In fact, at one time Walter Winchell had raved about Jada's exotic dancing. I didn't know any of the girls personally and wasn't intimate with any of them for sure, but I heard that some of them ran around with burglars, and yet some of them were probably just good housewives who were just doing that to make a living. Whether any of them worked on the side, I don't know. But I imagine that they did.

I have never known a stripper that couldn't be bought, so I'm sure that there was some prostitution involved. I never knew which ones, but I would see the girls leave the club with various men. However, I don't think that they made the dates right there on the job. I think they were later dates. But I want to say this: I never respected Jack Ruby for anything, and I didn't know him that well to know his deep, intimate, personal life, but I just couldn't see him as a pimp. I just couldn't see him taking a prostitute's money.

So, in a sense, he was moral in a lot of ways. He was in a business that wasn't exactly moral, but the way that Jack was raised in Chicago it was probably moral in a way to him, even though it might not have been to his relatives who were Jewish.

With what I knew about him, it really surprised me that he had shot Oswald mainly because I had just dealt with the man not long before that in the Judge Richburg incident. I had probably been in the club two or three times maybe a week or two prior to the assassination because I was liable to make ten to fifteen clubs a night from the time those businesses opened in the evening till closing time, especially if I was working an investigation like the murder case I was on at the time. In fact, that investigation led me in and out of several clubs because the victim had frequented any place that he could get a drink.

I wasn't surprised that he was found guilty at the trial, but the death sentence did surprise me. I wouldn't have been surprised at life in prison without parole, which was common in the state of Texas. Usually you get life and do it in twenty years.

After the sentencing, Jack was incarcerated at the county jail. Bill McCarthy was one of Jack's babysitters or guards there. One day he said, "Bill, I've got to go down to the sheriff's office. Come and go with me and we'll see Jack. Jack's asked about you a couple of times, you know." So I agreed and we went in and upstairs. A guard was out in the hall; Jack was lying asleep on his bunk with his feet sticking out. Bill walked up, kicked him, and said, "Hey, son of a bitch, get up! You've got company!" Bill didn't do that to belittle Jack; they had become friends as guards sometimes do. Jack was an amiable fellow and friendly anyway.

When Bill kicked him, Jack sat up and Bill said, "You remember Bill Courson?"

Jack said, "Oh, yeah. Hi, Bill." The very next words he said were, "Bill, they're killing me!" I just took that with a grain of salt because who was killing him? I knew damn well that Decker or those jailers weren't killing him, so I didn't know what he was talking about. I just figured that he had awakened from a deep sleep and was dreaming something. But I talked to him for about three or four minutes about one thing and then another. The subject of the little pistol wasn't mentioned. In fact, I don't recall much about what was said. Then Bill and I left. Of course, at that time, it was no big thing; Jack was a prisoner up there, and I could get in the jail about anytime I wanted.

I later heard a story about Jack. One of the guards told me that Jack would smuggle peeled boiled eggs under his armpit back to another prisoner who had killed a couple of people. As Jack would come up to his cell, he'd drop his hand down and let the egg fall into his hand, then he'd shake hands with the guy. This guy would then be eating those peeled eggs that came from under Jack's armpit.

Ruby wasn't in solitary confinement. His cell door was open most of the time with a guard posted. There was a hallway outside which had bars on each side that separated into cells. In fact, there may have been two cells up there. I can't remember exactly since I wasn't real familiar with the upstairs part of the jail because I usually booked people in and then went back out. I had no reason to go upstairs unless they had a riot or a disturbance up there. In which case, whoever was in the office would go with Mr. Decker. Decker would lead the parade, and by the time he got there, he would have it settled.

I don't know why, but he wouldn't let the regular jailers guard Ruby. Instead, he called in his uniform patrolmen like Bill McCarthy and Beddingfield and about a dozen others. Apparently he had more confidence in his uniform patrolmen than he did the jailers, even though there had never been that many escapes out of that jail. But their attitude was, "Man, I don't like this. I'd rather be back out on the street." It was really boring and there was quite a bit of griping about that.

Ruby stayed at the jail until they took him out to the hospital where he died. I didn't keep track of that since I had left the department and had gone into business and was gone until my partner was killed in a gunfight.

My partner, Buddy Walthers, was raised in a good family with a fine mother and father. But Buddy was just a little immoral in some ways. In fact, he would have made a better thief than a cop.

The only thing that made Buddy a good cop was his sources of information, and that's the reason that Decker relied on him so much. He was the best source of information that I've ever seen in my life. He could get more through some of his prostitutes in Dallas than I could in a dictionary, I guarantee you. But Buddy was disliked as a police officer.

Most of the people down there were afraid of him because of his ties to Decker. Now Decker was a fair man, but he had to have his sources of information both inside and outside the sheriff's department. My job was to go out and find who was hanging out with who so that Decker would know first hand in case some other agency asked him. That way he could give them that information by just going to the files which Buddy and I had made up for him. Actually the files were started by Morgan and Deshazo when they were 35 Squad. Buddy and I merely continued them.

Buddy and I would go out and target practice, and he would always shoot up every round he had. Then he would either borrow enough to fill his pistol or one round if he could bum one off somebody just to have a bullet in his gun when he went home till he could buy some more since we had to buy our own ammunition back then.

In a way, I liked Buddy, but I didn't like some of his ways either. We fished and ran around together back in the early days. But I asked to be taken off the squad with him because of some of the remarks that he made to some of the women, and I was scared I'd get fired over it. I didn't like it either.

Anyway, when Decker called me in and asked me if I thought that I could work with Buddy and if I wanted that 35 Squad job, I took it. He said, "I need somebody to keep Buddy from getting killed. You think that you can work with him?"

"Sure I can, sheriff," I said, and that's how I got my promotion.

I don't know what he meant about the remark about "keeping him from getting killed." It may have been just a joke with Decker, or he could have been serious. You never knew what was on his mind by looking him in the eye. In fact, you didn't look Decker in the eye because he had one eye that went one way and the other that looked straight through you.

Buddy and I never really talked much about the assassination and the role that he played in the investigation because we didn't start back to work together for quite awhile. Then, not long after the assassination, I went into the hospital for an injury that I had at home, and I remember Buddy coming out to see me then.

But when I got out of the hospital, Buddy and I went back to work together, and it wasn't but a few days later that we got into an altercation. We were mouthing at each other about a friend of mine who had gotten in some trouble. He was an old friend of the family, and I had done him a favor by getting him out of jail on a personal recognizance bond and had taken him out to my house. Being the son of an old friend of my father's back during the Depression days, this man had done my father a great service, so I figured that I owed it to the family. I was trying to get this boy straightened out, and Buddy had made some smart remarks about him. So I told him that I had heard enough.

This occurred about 2:00 or 3:00 o'clock in the morning in the sheriff's office, which was small, only about 1,200 to 1,500 square feet. Buddy and I had both just finished working on that murder case, and we were getting on each other's nerves. First one thing led to another, and Buddy made like he was going to swing at me, and I popped him on the ear, or somewhere near there. I don't remember exactly where I hit him, but he was hurt pretty badly. Buddy tried to pull his gun on me, then I became frantic and had my hand on his hand which held the gun while I was trying to beat him down with the other. Buddy may have been hurt badly, but it hurt his pride more than anything else.

As a result, Mr. Decker and I got crossways, though he didn't fire me. In a way, I issued Decker an ultimatum: Either he goes or I go! You didn't issue Decker ultimatums. He didn't fire me; he just told me, "Well, go ahead and resign."

Buddy was killed a few years later in a gunfight out on Samuell Boulevard in a motel by James Walter Cherry. I'd handled Cherry before. At that time, he was wanted on an escape; he was always wanted on something. On this occasion, Decker had gotten wind that Cherry was shacked up with some gal named Twyna Blankenship, who was from an old police character family here in Dallas.

Anyway, Buddy and another deputy, Al Maddox, went in. Buddy was a very careless person when he went in somewhere like that unless he knew definitely that somebody was behind him. Then he'd send me to the back door, to the bad spot.

In this case, they went in and James Walter Cherry got the drop on them in some way and supposedly shot Buddy. It's been said that Al shot Buddy accidently. In the frantic struggle, falling on his back and shooting around, Al claimed that Cherry shot him through the bottom of the foot. The man who did the ballistics and had Al's shoes said, "No, the bullet went in the top of the foot and came out the sole. Al shot himself in the foot!" But anyway, Al was a frustrated cop who definitely didn't belong in that particular job. He was a follower—that's all that he was.

Roger Craig was another deputy who I always thought was a stable officer, though I really had never worked with him that much. I was never around him that much nor had I worked a district next to him in patrol, but I did know him fairly well.

Later I heard things about what Roger had done and read the manuscript *When They Kill the President* that he wrote, but it just didn't sound like Roger. I think that he was easy to lead, and I think that manuscript was probably more of Penn Jones, the newspaper editor from Midlothian, than it was Roger.

Roger got himself in trouble at the sheriff's department with Bill Decker by getting involved with Garrison in New Orleans and that mess, which was a big joke at that time with every police agency except the New Orleans District Attorney's office. And I'm not real sure that a lot of the New Orleans Police Department and people down there weren't embarrassed about it. But it was a big joke here in Dallas. Roger was told by Decker to get off that mess, and Roger was the type who would have said, "Well, I'm going to go ahead and testify whether you like it or not!" So Decker fired him because, again, you didn't issue ultimatums to Decker. But I don't think that it was like Roger said in his manuscript. I don't believe that Decker ruined him and drove him to suicide. That's not the way it was at all! Decker wasn't that kind of man.

The last time I remember talking to Roger was when I saw him at the sheriff's department. At the time, I believe he was working for a bail bondsman as a private investigator. He was wearing a trenchcoat and trying to look like a Scotland Yard detective.

At one time, when he was in patrol, he was a very conscientious officer. But something seemed to happen after he was fired. Apparently he went off the deep end and got led into this conspiracy thing. I think the more that people laughed at him, or the more that he was picked on about it, the worse he got, especially when he got involved with Garrison.

Roger sounded really convincing in the manuscript about certain things. I know that Lummie Lewis, one of the deputies, was the type of guy that he said he was. He would have walked up and said in a very scratchy voice, Lummie had a voice that sounded like he always had a real bad cold, "Yeah, let me have this lady. I'll take care of it," and probably got sidetracked on his way back to the sheriff's office. This was in reference to some of those who were taken into custody after the assassination. Those people that Roger depicted as being arrested were merely taken into custody for taking statements more than anything else.

He commented that many in the sheriff's department were anti-Kennedy, and I'm sure that there were probably some smart remarks that were made from all the officers. Police officers have opinions that they spread amongst their own ranks which in many cases may be a joke, just like some of the motor jockeys in the escort back-firing those old Harley-Davidsons. They had no idea that there was going to be a killing. They were laid back, everything was fine, it was a sunny day. The motorcade was nearly over, so they back-fired them a couple of times and made noise behind them to make Kennedy jump a bit. I don't think that Kennedy even had an idea that such a thing could happen, even though it had nearly happened to General Edwin A. Walker. Of course, the evidence bears out that Oswald had taken a shot at Walker, too, but he was such a controversial character that you couldn't connect him with Kennedy.

There were a lot of officers down there that had their own ideas, just like myself. Before I came up to Jefferson, after I'd heard about the assassination, I was going to make a left turn instead of a right to go out to Grand Prairie and pick up the suspect that I'd heard say, "I hope the President gets his damn head blown off!" But he wasn't the only one that said that. I think there were a lot of people who said similar things because he wasn't a very popular president here or in a lot of other places.

There was also a sign about that time which stayed up for years over the Trinity River in a tree around the Cedar Crest Viaduct that said: "Impeach Earl Warren." But Dallas really wasn't that hostile an atmosphere anymore than any other place. It was a very vocal minority which most people heard about.

Most people were like me. At that time, I was a Democrat. Nearly everybody in the sheriff's office and in the courthouse were also Democrats. My father was a Democratic county commissioner, but I could have cared less whether Kennedy came to Dallas or not. In fact, I could have had a front row seat there at the sheriff's department to see him pass in the parade, but instead, I went home and went to bed because I didn't care about it.

Some criticized Kennedy because he was Catholic, which didn't bother me at all. I didn't care what he was as long as he was a good president. I liked what he did in Cuba when he told Khrushchev to either shit or get off the pot and get the missiles out. I think that he used good judgment there, but I just don't believe that he was a sincere president especially as far as the black people were concerned. I think that he was just as much a racist as anybody else, and being an opportunist, saw that issue as a way to make a big name for himself. Personally, I think John F. Kennedy, and all the Kennedys, had the morals of an alley cat.

Law enforcement agencies in Dallas were much like they were in other cities. They would coordinate on something that was really big, but there were a lot of glory hunters and glory happy people along with some professional jealousy between departments. I remember one case in particular, a bank robbery in Rice, Texas, right around the time of the assassination. Mr. Decker went out to a location somewhere here in Dallas County where the getaway car had been found. While he was there he had to use the telephone and found in the booth a waitress's bill with a telephone number on the back. So he picked it up and put it in his pocket; Decker didn't miss much. It didn't seem important, but it turned out that it helped catch the robber.

When he came back, two officers were interrogating the car lot owner who had sold the suspect the car. Decker then handed me this telephone number. The first thing that I did was to criss-cross the telephone book by checking the phone number against an address. Sure enough, there was an address with a name on it. Next I headed for book-in and ran a record check on that particular man. I didn't know his age, but I pulled everybody in the files that had a name that checked out to this phone number.

When I pulled the mug shot from the files and threw it on the table, I said, "Check this one!"

The car lot owner looked at it and said, "That's him! That's it!" There was an FBI agent in the interrogation room at the time, and he picked it up, looked at it, and, of course, all he had to do was get the number off of it, and off he went. Mr. Decker nearly shot me because I had let the FBI have the damn thing. They later arrested the guy and grabbed all the headlines. I didn't like to operate that way and didn't like that type of professional jealousy because I didn't think that it was good law enforcement. It wasn't effective law enforcement because there were too many stumbling blocks. I thought that everybody in law enforcement, everybody that carried a badge, and everybody that swore to uphold the law should cooperate.

Bill Decker was a well respected man in law enforcement. He was a fair, firm, and a fatherly figure who had a heavy hand over the politics of Dallas County. If Decker said that someone would get elected, they would. And I'm not talking about crooked politics; I'm talking about good, honest politics with a man who had a lot of pull and who knew a lot of people.

Even though we had our words on occasion, I never had a low opinion of him. He would go to bat for you as long as you told him the truth, even if you were wrong, unless it was going to hurt the voters or the public. Then he would have a problem and would say, "Well, now you're on your own, son. This I can't handle because it hurts my people."

On one occasion when I was on the carpet about something, I said, "Sheriff, I'm not lying to you. You know that I'm not lying,"

And he would say, "You'd better never lie to me. Tell me the truth no matter how much it hurts. The first bite on the bullet's not as hard as the second. Me and you both may have to lie to stay out of the penitentiary, but you had better never lie to me."

He wouldn't have backed one of his deputies for just beating the fire out of somebody on the street unless that somebody took a swing at the deputy first. Then Decker expected you to knock the man loose from his damn glasses. He would probably chastise you for it, but he wouldn't say, "Hey, it could have been done a different way," and he wouldn't fire you for it.

I've mentioned that you didn't issue ultimatums to him. I remember one in particular, I won't name him, but Decker called him into the office to see him. Decker happened to be at a funeral while the man sat in his office waiting for two hours. Finally, he said, "Tell Decker that if he wants to see me to come to my house." Needless to say the man didn't have a job when he came back to work the next day.

Buddy and I used to carry Mr. and Mrs. Decker out to eat because he got to where he didn't like to drive in the evenings. So he would always call and ask Squad 35 to come over to his house at 6302 Palo Pinto and he'd buy our dinner at some nice place.

I remember one time I was riding in the back seat with Mrs. Decker, Buddy was driving with Mr. Decker alongside and Buddy said, "Sheriff, when you decide to retire, who are you going to endorse for sheriff?"

Decker looked over at him and said, "I'm not going to endorse no son of a bitch to get out here and screw up what I've built up all these years! I'm not going to endorse anybody!" Buddy had ambitions of being sheriff, and might have if Decker had died, but I doubt it. I don't think that he would have had many deputies down there campaigning for him.

I called Buddy "White Rat." He was known not only as a source of information from the criminal element, but also as a source of information to Decker about his own deputies if they got into something controversial, though few ever got into anything. I do remember one deputy who was fired for not paying big debts he had run up at a liquor store; another was fired for going in and tearing up a bar and whipping everybody when he was off duty. Mostly, though, they were married deputies who were fired for women troubles.

Buddy sometimes looked more like Bill Decker than Bill Decker. In fact, at a distance Buddy had acquired a dress and stance that looked just like Decker, and he did it on purpose. Some resented it, others thought it was funny, including myself. Decker dressed nicely but wasn't vain. Buddy was vain and had just begun dressing classy. One day he came into the office, and while he was standing there looking at these expensive shoes he'd bought, said, "You know, I got to looking at myself when I was dressing for work today. You know, I've got over $300 worth of clothes on?" Of course, back then, a $150 or $200 suit was a high dollar suit, especially when you consider that I was then making about $550 a month as a criminal investigator. The rest of the deputies laughed their heads off. Buddy was a vain bastard!

In recent years, I have become reinterested in the events surrounding the assassination. My brother Jim was a motorcycle police officer who was escorting the motorcade. After the President was shot, he was one of the officers that got beside the limousine and escorted them to the hospital. Jim has told me that one of the Secret Service men told him to stand by and hold an open phone to the White House. He was told, "Keep everybody out of here! Don't let anyone in, and that means anyone!" They didn't want anyone in there.

In my opinion, and in the opinion of several others around here, the Secret Service made a bunch of fools of themselves in the whole assassination, especially when they confiscated evidence and tainted it by breaking the chain of evidence. I think that if Oswald had lived that they would never have convicted him of killing President Kennedy. However, he would have been convicted of killing J.D. Tippit, and the punishment would have been the same: the electric chair. But I don't believe that under the state law at that time that a jury could have found Oswald guilty because the evidence was so screwed up, and actually it was only circumstantial since they had no eyewitnesses. They did have some fingerprints, but they had been tainted because the rifle had been confiscated, and the ballistics were done in Washington. That is just not done under state law. That is supposed to be done in the state of Texas by a ballistics' expert, and the autopsy is supposed to be done by a state certified pathologist. The ballistics can be done by the FBI here, but you don't take evidence out of the state and bring it back because a defense attorney could really tear it apart.

The interference from Washington has led to numerous conspiracy books being written about the assassination. I wouldn't close the door on conspiracy, but at this time I don't think there was any. The conspiracy writers, I think, are just money grabbers. If I were ever to write a book, the glory that I would receive would be that it was truthful.

In my opinion, the Warren Commission probably made a lot of mistakes, but the biggest mistake was made by Lyndon Baines Johnson when he closed the files. I don't think there was any conspiracy in that, although I'll say that Johnson was capable of wanting to have it done. But I don't think that anyone was capable of coordinating such a "Mission Impossible" conspiracy without somebody spilling the beans.

Bill Courson left the sheriff's department after the altercation with Buddy Walthers in 1964. In the years following, he opened a business, which failed, and worked as a truck driver, but still remained in touch with law enforcement by working for the Duncanville Police Department and for the well-known private investigator, Bill Dear, as an investigator and bodyguard for his clients in Dallas and in Europe. He returned to the Dallas County Sheriff's Department in 1969, shortly before the death of Bill Decker, and later ran for Sheriff of Dallas County but lost by a margin of 229 votes out of 76,000 cast. At the time of his death in 1990, Bill Courson was working on a manuscript which he believed would shed further light on the assassination.

AL MADDOX
Deputy Sheriff
Dallas County Sheriff's Department

"I suppose my reasons for getting into law enforcement were rather selfish. My father was murdered in Mohall, North Dakota, when I was sixteen. We were on a wheat harvest when two guys robbed, murdered, and decapitated him. As a result, I always wanted to be a lawman 'cause I felt that I could change the world, but apparently the world didn't want to be changed..."'

Al Maddox was born in Limestone County, Texas, in 1930. Following graduation from high school, Maddox attended college, then joined the Navy where he remained eleven years. Upon discharge, he then finished college at Sam Houston University in Huntsville, Texas, and later became an auditor for the Texas State Liquor Board. Maddox joined the Dallas County Sheriff's Department in 1963 prior to the assassination.

———————

The night before the assassination I had talked to and had coffee with someone and was getting out to my car which was a '57 or '58 Edsel. About midnight, as I came off my regular shift across the street on Elm where my car was parked, there was a man standing across from the School Book Depository in front of a clothing manufacturer's store where the Oak Cliff bus stop was located. He was most certainly a law enforcement officer as he had on a light brown coat that we called a 007 coat. The only people that could afford them were high ranking officers and FBI agents who were wearing them then. They were popular at that time, though I could I could never afford one. He also had on extra-soled shoes and had a good sized bulge under his coat. Knowing that he was a lawman, I stopped and asked if he wanted a ride to Oak Cliff, but he looked into my car and said, no. I didn't know who he was, but he didn't want a ride and he didn't want to talk. He was just standing there in the middle of the night looking around.

Twenty-five years later Malcolm Summers* and I were talking. My daughter and his son were married twenty years after all that happened. As a result, I got to know him as the one who ran up the grassy knoll and was told by a man, "Get back down or I will blow your head off," or something to that effect. The man showed him a badge of some kind and had what Malcolm thought was an Uzi type gun under his coat. When I asked him what the man looked like, he described the man that I saw the night before at the bus stop almost identically.

I worked at the Book-In Department at the sheriff's office. I also did some accounting for the executive assistant which included statistics on the jail and what it cost to keep a prisoner per day. Much of it had to do with the budget. But my main job was the Book-In Department.

That Friday, November 22nd, my wife was going to drop me off at work. We were coming up Houston Street just as the parade passed without either of us realizing that the President had been assassinated. I had seen the motorcade from a distance and noticed that everyone was running in every direction, but I thought they were just running to get a look at the President.

I had heard three shots, but let me preface that. Years ago, when you came out of the jail on the Houston Street side, you'd hear jets coming over sometimes in the afternoon. You'd be looking in one direction to see the jets, and they would come over from a different direction. You couldn't tell which way because of the reverberation of the sounds. So I knew where the problems were when eyewitnesses said the shots came from one direction and others said they came from another. Those shots came from the School Book Depository in my opinion, even though a bunch of people were running in the direction of the grassy knoll.

---

* Malcolm Summers' narrative is on pages 102-108.

I didn't talk to any of those people. I stayed back and observed because I was not a detective and felt that I would be in the way. However, I did talk to Forrest Sorrels, who was the local head of the Secret Service at the time, but I was doing the talking. Forrest wasn't saying much. He realized the impact of this thing and maybe I didn't. We were right in the middle of an historical event which is becoming more so every year.

Eventually I went up in the School Book Depository, but by the time I got there the gun had already been found and Carl Day was on his way down with it. In fact, a photographer snapped a picture of me alongside Day outside the building.

In addition to the rifle, I also saw human tissue lying in the street which was being wiped and cleaned up at the time. That was right about where the President was said to have been hit. I also saw one of the motorcycle officers who was splattered with blood.

Buddy Walthers, who later became my partner, later told me about a bullet that had hit a manhole skirt on the southside of Elm Street. We were good friends long before I became his full-time, plain clothes partner. But he'd always come down in Book-In every night or two and talk. He also told me about some guy who was hit by a chip in the face and blood trickled down his face. Buddy told me that, so I knew it had happened.

There were so many people that had similar good information that was ignored. It's the little bits and particles that brings an investigation together and gets a conviction. But they were looking for big things, and they weren't very prevalent. I believe that a lot of the little information was ignored, though I don't think that it was overlooked deliberately.

I stayed in Dealey Plaza about two hours then went back to the sheriff's office. As I walked in, whoever was on the desk, it may have been Tom Allen, wanted to keep it a little longer in hopes that the murderer would be brought in. Anyway, he asked, "Let me work a little longer, Maddie. They'll have that guy in here in a little while and I want to book him."

I worked the 3:00 to 11:00 shift with nothing big happening that evening as far as I was concerned. A lot of people were brought in for investigation and "Hold for Decker" which was legal. Once that was on you, they were held until Decker talked to them. That was before Judge Sarah T. Hughes screwed things up. There was also a bunch of talk about the upcoming transfer of

Oswald. They knew when he was coming, and I would have been on duty then.

This was to be a special transfer. Decker didn't want to handle it until they got him to his jail. In fact, I don't think he wanted to make the transfer at all. I think he wanted him delivered because the people that were transferring for us were men just like me who weren't trained to handle assassins like Lee Harvey Oswald. Apparently Will Fritz and Decker had agreed that Fritz's men would bring him to the county jail because when word came over the speaker that Ruby had shot Oswald, Decker made the statement, "He belongs to y'all."

The City of Dallas detectives outnumbered us two to one and were trained professionals. They weren't politically appointed as in some cases in the sheriff's department where a commissioner would ask Decker to put a certain guy on, and he would wind up on the force. I could name a few who were political appointees who didn't know snuff from wild honey.

But in reality, I think Decker would have handled the transfer the same way. Whoever would have thought that some fool would run down there and shoot the most valuable witness in the United States that we've ever had in our lifetime? He robbed the people of finding out what really happened. But if Oswald would have ever gotten to the Dallas County Jail, Decker could charm a bird out of a tree, and I feel that he could have gotten him to talk.

At that time, I had known Jack Ruby a little over a year and had been in his Carousel Club a number of times. He was hyper and went out of his way to drop names and impress people. He liked to please people and would go out of his way to make you like him. He also wanted to know everybody and especially liked police officers. He tried to please police officers by trying to give them a drink or buy them a steak, anything to gain favors.

When I was with the State Liquor Control Board, if he could get you in his place just for a few minutes, it would tickle him to death. He didn't want you sticking around too long, but he'd introduce you to everyone. "This is Al Maddox, State Liquor Board," or "This is Johnny Crank," who was the head liquor man out of Austin. Then when I became an officer with Bill Decker, every time you'd see Jack or Milton Joseph on the street they'd always want to buy you something or do something for you. I don't think they were trying to bribe you because it was never that much, but Ruby was the kind of guy who most any mother would have loved, regardless. But I also agree that he had his own interests to protect.

Ruby was interested in keeping his liquor license, so the Liquor Control Board was important to him. But I wasn't in any position to help anyone with getting their license. I had probably caused some people to not lose their license, but they'd have to have a three-day close-up. Usually that would be on a Sunday, Monday, and a Tuesday when there wasn't much business anyway, and they would then talk with Coke Stevenson, Jr. I never heard of him closing a club down other than for a three day suspension for a violation. But Jack was always asking us if we knew certain people in the hierarchy in the Liquor Control Board such as Coke Stevenson, Jr., who was influential in the liquor business.

The day after Oswald was shot, Jim Leavelle brought Ruby to the jail, though I didn't see him. I recently learned that he was taken up to the third floor and brought down from inside the jail so that there wouldn't be any chance of his being assassinated. He came in with a little fat detective that we had who was another political appointee who sat in Decker's office all the time. Ruby had his shoes off and was wearing his clothes and a pair of socks. I don't know whether someone had said something to him coming down the elevator or what, but he was very hyper and was crying. He already knew what the charge was, but he asked me again, and when I told him, he just really boo-hooed. Then I booked him for murder.

Personally, I liked Jack. The other officers that had contact with him were always asking me, "Well, did he get smart with you? Did he talk down to you?"

I would tell them, "No, Jack has never talked smart to me. He's never been abrasive in any way. But then, too, he knows that I'm the one that handles the money." I controlled his money as well as every other prisoner's since I was the book-in officer that delivered the money to them whether it was five dollars or two dollars, whatever they got. But he had special privileges. Instead of every other day, as it was with most, I'd take him his money anytime he wanted it.

As the trial progressed, I noticed that Jack became more relaxed. He thought he was going to get out, and if he hadn't contracted cancer, he would have gotten out. He could have made the $200,000 bond if his attorneys had been on the ball. This was a regular murder case. At that time, there was nothing federal about shooting a president. He could have made bond; everybody makes bond right after they shoot somebody. He became agitated only when his people didn't come for him like he thought they were going to. But some way he knew that someone was going to make bond for him as soon as the trial was over whether he was vindicated or whether he was found guilty.

Each day at the trial Ruby was guarded by the heavyweights in the department: Bill Wiseman, Jack Faulkner, Buckalew, Charlie Deshazo, Harry Weatherford, Lummie Lewis, Ralph Weaver and others. Decker put me up there one day searching people before they went into the courtroom—the day that Karen Carlin was found with a pistol in her purse and a jail break occurred.

Some of the prisoners had made a pistol out of soap which looked real and bluffed a guy by the name of Hunt. Hunt was no coward, but one of the prisoners pulled this soap gun and made Hunt think it was real, and they came right down the stairway where I had been standing a few minutes earlier. No telling what might have happened on that stairway since I was a relatively new officer if I hadn't just left with a man named Henry Campbell. Thank God they pulled me away because there'd have been some people hurt otherwise. Fortunately one of the deputies, Charlie Player, managed to bluff the prisoners and it was all over.

The ones who usually guarded Ruby in his jail cell were patrolmen. Occasionally we would have officers that didn't show up or were called away, so Decker would send me up to stay with Ruby. He was always wanting you to bring him something. Most of the time you couldn't do it, although I did take him a few things which was strictly against Decker's orders. My thinking was that one day he'd make bond, and I didn't want the man mad at me. We were taught the political game in that jail, and Decker was the grandfather of them all.

On his way to Parkland when he was dying of cancer, Jack gave me a letter. He was sweating badly as he put this letter in the palm of his hand. The part of the letter that was next to his palm today is very dim; you can hardly read it. But if you fold it just right, you can see that he was sweating. At that time, he didn't know that he was sick; otherwise, he couldn't have handled it.

The letter in part said: "You've known Lynn Burk and Johnny Crank. You've known me for a long time, and you've all been out to lunch with me, and this all adds up to what I'm going to tell you—that I'm being framed for the assassination, period, that I shot Oswald to silence him." He wasn't referring to the assassination of Lee Harvey Oswald. What he meant was Kennedy's assassination and that he was being framed for it because whoever was supposed to make bond for him didn't show up. In his mind, he believed that.

When these people didn't show up, he wrote this letter, and he told me to keep my eyes open. "Keep this letter for a later date and you'll learn something," he said, and I've learned a lot. But at that time, I didn't know what he was talking about.

A handwriting expert was paid $500 to authenticate that it was his handwriting. I'm the only one that has anything written from Jack Ruby telling it like it was as far as people who were supposed to come and get him. I didn't believe what he was saying for years, but I do now based on conversations with people like Victor Marchetti, formerly of the CIA, who explained what the letter meant. Some have asked why I didn't come forward a long time ago. I did. I showed the letter around, but it was too insignificant at the time, so I just hung on to it.

There has been some question about how he was treated in jail. I saw him get penicillin shots, at least we thought they were penicillin. There was a doctor who came in and spent a lot of time with him. He was a small guy from Chicago with a pockmarked face and light complexion who sometimes wore a white straw hat and was very nice. He was hired by Judge Lew Sterrett. What he gave Ruby, if he did, I don't know. Our regular county doctor, MarDock,* may have seen him at one time, but he was taken off the case.

But to my knowledge, he was treated very well. He had a large double cell with a bed and a large walking place and received extra privileges. If he wanted something, he'd tell one of the jailers that was passing through.

Roger Craig was one of the deputies in the sheriff's department. Everybody knew Roger, and I liked him. But he had a serious operation, and he then went from just a ho-hum type

---

* Dr. Julian MarDock.

person to a schizophrenic or something. Roger kept getting these phone calls from all over the country and was saying that he saw Oswald leaving the scene in a gray station wagon. Even though he wasn't a detective, he wouldn't stay out of the investigation. The rest of us stayed out of it because Decker didn't want you messing in his business in any way, form, or fashion. Leave him alone! He had a chosen few that were allowed to discuss the assassination, and he didn't want Roger Craig in on it, but Roger kept butting in.

Decker controlled us with his right finger. By that I mean when you walked into his office and somebody was talking and he did not want you to say anything, if he ever raised that right finger, you'd better shut your mouth. Roger never learned that!

Roger wrote a manuscript called "When They Kill A President" which contained a lot of meat. It had some truth in it, but most people disregarded it. In the manuscript, Roger made reference a number of times to my old partner, Buddy Walthers.

Buddy was a fine officer who dressed professionally, had a nice family, and received a lot of special favors from the sheriff which aggravated the tar out of many of the other officers. Buddy and I worked special investigations off of Decker's desk and took care of what he wanted taken care of. We didn't go through anybody.

Buddy even looked like Decker. We all wore black hats and dark suits, but Buddy also had the frame and stature to look like Decker. Even the curves in his ears were the same as Decker's. I noticed it many times.

Roger Craig alleged that Buddy built a swimming pool at his home and even grew marijuana in his back yard. Let me set the record straight. The swimming pool was built in Buddy's sister's back yard by his sister; it wasn't in Buddy's yard in Oak Cliff at all. The marijuana allegation was untrue because they were weeds. Buddy and I went out and looked at the weeds which looked like marijuana, but they didn't have the five leaves on them. If somebody just looked over the fence, they might have thought that that little patch was marijuana, but it wasn't. Buddy wouldn't jeopardize his job for anything so simple. It was also alleged that he wore expensive rings, but I never saw an expensive ring on him, ever.

One of his major assets at the sheriff's department was his ability to talk to informants. He could talk their language. Buddy had been a cab driver in his earlier years and was very likable. He had very little education, which was no secret, and he came from one of the roughest sections of Dallas. But he came from a good family and had to fight for everything he got, which was quite a bit. I never saw him steal anything, but people were mostly after him because Bill Decker thought he was great and so did I.

Buddy had been known to pull your leg, but at one time he did show me a bullet that he claimed he found in Dealey Plaza which he may have eventually given to his son. When he first told me about it, I was a little apprehensive and didn't pay much attention to it. But he'd never lied to me before. He also told me about an FBI man, or someone on the scene of the assassination, who was hit by a piece of cement which flew up and hit him in the face and blood was running down his face. Later I saw that man, so there was some credence to his testimony.

Several years later on January 10th, 1969, I was with Buddy when he was killed, though a television show falsely depicted the scenario. They had Buddy looking like a goofy person with long hair. I was shown with white hair, which in reality didn't turn white until the last few years, and being handcuffed to a sink which my four-year-old grandson could have broken away from. I talked to the man who made the movie when I was in Hollywood not long ago and was told, "Well, we had the wrong information."

I said, "You sure did," and that was the last that was ever said about it.

What really happened was that it was just a routine disturbance call that Buddy and I went into and were both careless, were caught off guard and shot. We knocked on the door of a motel on Samuell Boulevard and were met by a guy who was 6'4" with dyed hair. He gave us a fake driver's license, so we walked in and noticed his girlfriend, Twyna Blankenship, lying nude on the bed. The suspect, we learned, was James Walter Cherry, a well known local criminal. Since Buddy was looking in another direction, I had to work around him to get hold of Cherry, who was fixing to disarm or shoot both of us.

I had been shot three times: once in the hand when I grabbed for the gun so that he couldn't pull the trigger, and two more through the ankle by this fool and was numb when Twyna Blankenship hit me in the head with the butt of a steel lamp. I felt like they were hitting someone else, but I could not afford to pass out. He kicked me in the stomach as we were shooting at each other, and I went backwards over a bed and sat up behind this bed to get back my senses since I'd already been hit. I thought at the time that there was no word in the vocabulary that could express how I felt, but I didn't know what had happened to me.

I crawled back around the bed because I couldn't walk. At that point, Cherry came up and snapped the bullet in my face which sounded like thunder going past my head. Buddy carried him back to the bed and reached for the gun thinking it was empty. Cherry then pulled back and shot him at point blank range in the heart. Decker later told me that Buddy was shot with a .38 Ruger, a rather cheap gun, and as it went into his chest cavity, the bullet stood up and went parallel instead of straight through. As a result, it practically ripped out his heart.

I lay up against the door so they couldn't get out, but they beat me in the head badly and dragged me away from the door. Now, mind you, I weighed around 220 pounds. As they then ran out to get their car, I reached into Buddy's pocket, got a cigarette lighter that wouldn't stay lit, and crawled up behind the car as Blankenship was trying to get it started. I managed to get the gas cap off and the lighter going and dropped it into the tank but the lighter went out. They then backed over me. Fortunately they didn't hit any of my limbs, but I was so messed up that I wouldn't have known anyway.

That was January 10th, 1969. I'm the only one still living that was in that room that day, but everybody in the police department and the sheriff's office claims to know more about the gunfight than I. In fact, a little insignificant fellow named Jimmy Kitchens, who was reconstructing the crime scene, never found the bullet till I got well. I told him, "He shot at my head. I'm going back to Room 13 and show y'all where the bullet is." It was found under a window sill where the hole is still there today.

Sheriff Decker took Buddy's death very hard. As much as he thought of Buddy, I think that is probably what literally killed Bill Decker.

After the shooting, the doctor that originally operated on me told me that It was a very dirty wound and they just sewed it back up until they could operate and get the copper jackets out of my ankle. Six months later I told Decker, "Well, they're ready to do the operation and get this metal out of my ankle."

He said, "What the hell are you talking about? I just got through paying $3,000 for that room you tore up at the motel!" That was his answer which was typical Decker. It didn't bother me at all because I knew how he thought, and I thought it was rather funny. One of the copper slugs is still in my ankle today.

But Decker was a great man. He was the grandfather of all politicians. I never heard him tell anyone that was looking for a job that he didn't have one. Instead, he'd say, "Well, you come back later." He'd absolutely wear them out, and finally they'd give up. They'd be down there every day to get a job, but he'd probably still wind up getting their vote.

He was very particular. He wanted you to enforce the law as long as it was a political enforcement. But if it was going to cause a stink, or if somebody was going to raise a question, he wanted you to go on and forget it. But I liked Decker. I thought sometimes that he was unfair, but he had a reason for everything he did, and it usually worked out right. He was a living legend. He was one-eyed, and the people that were afraid of him would tell you that the only eye that had any humor in it was the glass eye.

The assassination seemed to have little effect on Decker, but it did have on the city of Dallas, though. One of the deputies, Charles Deshazo, was in some Northern state not long after the assassination, and when they saw his Dallas County Sheriff's credit card they told him to get his ass out of town just because he was from Dallas.

I haven't followed the conspiracy stories closely because I don't believe them. I do have some questions about the guy on the corner who Malcolm Summers thought he saw the next day. Who was he? I was never asked a damn thing about him one way or the other. But after all these years, my mind is still open, and I haven't come to any conclusions about the assassination.

Al Maddox left the sheriff's department in 1978 and lost a bid for sheriff in the election of 1980. Eventually he was employed with Beverly Enterprises in long-term care and helped run a nursing home in Weatherford, Texas. Maddox, though semi-retired, currenty works part-time at a Tom Thumb grocery store in Duncanville, Texas.

W.W. "BO" MABRA
Deputy Sheriff
Dallas County Sheriff's Department

"I turned to the lady bailiff sitting at her desk and said, 'I'll bet you five dollars that Bill calls him "Mr. Belly" in less than five minutes.' She just grinned as the judge called on the prosecution first. Bill got up and said, 'You Honor, "Mr. Belly" over here,' and I became strangled and had to leave the courtroom to keep from laughing..."

Born and raised on a farm in Dallas County, Bo Mabra spent ten years working in a machine shop before joining the Dallas County Sheriff's Department in March 1950. Mabra was present in Dealey Plaza on November 22, 1963, and later was one of the two bailiffs in the Jack Ruby trial.

Another deputy, Orville Smith, and I were standing on the sidewalk on the Main Street side of the Old Criminal Courts Building with the sheriff's office right behind us. My normal job during the day was to take care of the jury if court was in trial, but we weren't busy that day so we had come down and joined a lot of other people waiting for the caravan to come by. When they passed, I could have reached out and touched President Kennedy as they drove slowly around the corner onto Houston Street. I was impressed by the whole affair, especially with the President coming by, and the governor, with the chief of police and Sheriff Decker in the preceding car.

After the procession passed, we continued standing there talking when, in just a short time, we heard the first shot which sounded like a backfire from an automobile or truck well down in the Triple Underpass. That had happened a lot of times in the past and had sounded like a rifle shot. But when that first shot went off, of course, it startled both of us. We looked at each other, kind of caught our breath, wondering, since they had just gone around the corner. Then the second shot went off. Smith said to me, "That was a deer rifle!"

"It sure was," I responded. Then in a very few seconds a third went off. We then went around the corner as hard as we could run and could see people over on the grassy knoll. As we were crossing Houston running in the direction of the grassy knoll, I could see what looked like a whirl of smoke.

So we thought, "That's where it's at!"

Somebody then said, "The President just got shot and they headed for Parkland." By the time I got there, the smoke had disappeared; evidently it was from a cigarette.

We didn't know whether the assassin had left the building, where he had been, or where he was. But I knew that there was a parking area behind the knoll behind a wooden fence because I parked my car there, so we went over and searched that. A uniformed Dallas police officer, whom I didn't know, was standing there and said, "I don't know what's going on, but there hasn't been a thing move back here in a hour or more because I've been here all that time." When he said that, I took it for granted that nobody had been there, so I didn't search any further.

A lot of people that worked in the courts and in the jail parked in that parking area. It wasn't a large lot, maybe holding 25 to 30 cars near the railroad tracks toward the street which was an ideal place for a few cars to park.

Later I heard stories about tramps who were arrested that might have been involved, but we always found them out there. In fact, I'd run into them when I'd go to get my car. I ran into one of them one time asking for a dollar or a dollar and a half for something to eat. On the day of the assassination, they just happened to be there. I don't believe there was anybody out there that had anything at all to do with it or had the slightest inkling that something was going on up there.

In any case, I was there just a couple of minutes then we went up to the door of the book store building then we found out what happened. All the officers had been up in the building, and as they were coming downstairs, one of them said, "Bo, you'll have to climb all the way up the stairs!"

I said, "I don't believe I can make it!"

A Dallas officer was right inside the door while his motorcycle was parked out front with the radio on. I was standing beside it when the call came in that Tippit had just been killed. Of course, that provoked a lot of excitement and pandemonium. Several of the officers then headed over to Oak Cliff with the idea that the more who got there, the better the chance of capturing him.

Smith and I then went to the sheriff's office where the sheriff told me, "Well, you better go home. You look like you're sick."

I told him, "Well, I am," and I was sick. The whole affair made me ill, so I went home.

After that evening, I had no part whatsoever in the investigation until the Warren Commission called me in and talked to me just a very few minutes. They wanted to argue with me about the timing of the shots, telling me that you couldn't work a bolt action rifle that fast. I think more than anything else they were trying to shake my story that a bolt action rifle could be worked with three shots being fired in six seconds. That was because my recollection of the timing was that the three shots were spaced within two to four seconds apart. It seemed like they were spaced longer between the second and third than the first and second.

It was my opinion that it could be done. A right-handed man firing a rifle with his hands on the stock and on the trigger pulls the trigger—the bolt's right in front of his right hand and he just raises that. It just takes a fraction of a second to operate it, not several seconds. I'm left-handed and I can work a bolt action faster than that. Evidently, Oswald had a rest to lay the gun barrel on which would have given him ample time to aim because the car was moving so slowly. When they had passed in front of us, you could walk along beside it. So from up there, the aiming wouldn't have been any problem as slowly as they were moving.

Personally I don't think there was any more than one gunman. Now there very well might have been somebody else in the conspiracy in the background, but as far as I can remember in reading and keeping up with it, it was never proven that Oswald had anybody helping him. Nor do I think there was any effort to frame Oswald. As far as I know, he wasn't that well known. It was known that he had previously been to Russia and that he was a radical thinker, but the town was full of those.

Why people don't accept the results of the investigation, I can't understand because nothing was ever dug up that would indicate, with any proof at all, that he had help or that there was somebody with him or that somebody knew that he was going to do that. People who write books don't always stick to the plain truth in the matter because a lot of times it doesn't make for good reading, so they add a little here and a little there.

Early the following year, 1964, the grand jury was reporting to Judge Joe Brown's court during that particular term. Everything came to Judge Brown's court and then was divided among the other courts. As a result, he got first pick of any choice of trials that he wanted, so he said, "Bo, we're going to try this one," meaning Jack Ruby.

I told him, "Judge, I don't want to try this one."

"Oh, yeah, look at all the publicity we'll get," he said.

I told him, "I don't want any publicity. I want to go fishing."

But anyhow, the Ruby trial was held in his court, though it was actually held in Judge Wilson's courtroom due to the difference in size. But Judge Brown was the presiding judge, and a lady* and I were the two bailiffs.

Originally, I was a patrol sergeant, and when I became a bailiff it was a demotion because I took a pay cut in salary. But I had asked for it because I was tired of driving a patrol car and my knees and legs bothered me a lot. All told, I was a bailiff for twenty years: ten in the Criminal District Court and another ten in the grand jury.

The job of bailiff was to see that the jury was sequestered. Back then, before the law was changed, the jury wasn't allowed to talk to anybody, including calling home at night. We did all the telephone calling to get their supplies brought to them, and when

---

* Nell Tyler

we took them to eat, we saw to it that nobody approached and tried to talk to them. Nobody was allowed to approach them while they were dining. All this was under close supervision by the two bailiffs because of the law being as it was. The law was so old and had been written way back when juries had a lot of trouble with people trying to influence or threaten them.

Jack Ruby was well known to the Dallas police, but I had never heard of him prior to his shooting Oswald. Though I was never around him, in talking to those who did know him, I concluded that his morals were lower than a snake. What little I did know of him was that he was a name-dropper. He loved to hang around with police officers, especially the detectives and upper crust, and call them by their first names.

Sheriff Decker wasn't taking any chances on anything happening. Ruby was strictly under the personal supervision of three or four deputies who brought him from the jail to the courtroom and from the courtroom back to the jail on account of the terrific crowd of reporters which created crowded conditions in the hallway there. They had to be careful in case somebody wanted to kill him.

Sheriff Decker was not going to have another shooting such as what happened at the police department. What little I know that took place there was that they were supposed to move Oswald from the city jail to the county jail at night around 2:00 o'clock when everything was quiet. This is only hearsay on my part, but the press talked to the chief of police and begged him to hold it in daylight so that they could take their pictures. They had no idea that anything like this was going to happen, and that's when they changed their plan.

I was told that Decker wanted to go up and take three sheriff's cars and two Dallas police cars and put him in one and a whole bunch of people in the others and go on down to the county jail. If anybody would look in or was looking for a chance, they wouldn't know which car he was in.

I'm sure that Decker would have handled that situation differently compared to the police. Decker was always honest with the press and everyone trusted him. There's no telling how many have told me, "Now if Decker says that's the way it is, that's the way it is" because he never lied to the press and was friends with every one of them. Now what went on up there at the police department, I don't know. But Sheriff Decker was a living legend. I made several transfer trips going somewhere to pick up a prisoner and bring them back, and as soon as I mentioned the name Decker, they knew him or knew of him.

Everybody had a good time who worked for him. I remember one time while I was still in uniform patrol I went to McKinney to pick up a prisoner. When I got there, they didn't have him ready, so I just walked across the street to the drug store to get a cup of coffee. Several older men sitting at the back said, "Hey, tell Decker we'll be down and vote for him as usual." Of course, they were just kidding since it was out of the county, but that's the way they felt about him nearly everywhere.

On another occasion, I went to Tacoma, Washington, after a prisoner and talked to the sheriff. He said, "Yeah, I know Decker and I think he's fine. When we're in Dallas after a prisoner, he treats us real nice. He feeds the prisoners, and so when we get one of his we don't charge him anything for the food or anything. There's an understanding between he and us, and I think he's as understanding with nearly everybody." If he was holding a prisoner for some other county and they came to get him, they didn't owe the sheriff any food bill for that prisoner.

Once an officer who had retired from the Dallas Police Department and had gone to work for Decker as a plain clothes investigator was fooling with an old shotgun laying on a table that somebody had brought in. It was called "Long Tom" because it was a 12-gauge with a long barrel. I don't remember the officer's name, but his nickname was "Onion" because his head looked like one. Anyway, he picked up the shotgun, examined it, pointed it at the wall, pulled the trigger, and nearly tore down the wall by blowing a hole in it. He knew that Decker would fuss at him about it, so he saw a calendar and hung it over the hole. This was in a little room behind the sheriff's office where anybody could bring in items picked up at burglaries and would stack them back there till they went to the property room. Soon after, Decker was back there looking around and saw this calendar which he remembered was supposed to be on one wall but was on another. So he went over and raised the calendar and there was the hole. "Now who did this?" he said. Somebody told him and he started fussing.

Then one of the old men who had known Decker for a long time said, "Now, Decker, ain't no use about you getting riled about that! I've seen you do worse than that yourself." The sheriff grinned and showed a sense of humor about it because he had let one or two guns go off in his hand like that himself.

The trial featured a host of characters. Judge Brown was a good natured, fun-loving guy who loved to go somewhere to eat, pancakes or whatever. He was like me; he'd eat anything. But he was even tempered and was always kidding with somebody. I never saw him when he really looked like he'd lost his temper.

As I understand, Judge Brown didn't get a law degree from one of the major colleges, but he had a law degree, nevertheless, because he was judge of the county court for years. Whether he knew the law really well, I don't know, but there weren't any reversals in his court. There was some talk of wanting Judge Henry King of Criminal District Court One or Judge Wilson of Criminal District Court Two to try the case, but again, Judge Brown said, "It's in my court and I'm going to try it!"

Now he had prosecutors in his court that were as sharp as anybody, so I wasn't worried about his not knowing the law all that well because he had people there that knew the law as well as anyone.

He wasn't stiff-lipped or anything like that. In fact, he'd be apt to say something rather comical now and then. We would have a panel picking the jury, and he might say something funny and they'd laugh about it. But they understood that nothing being said would influence their minds one way or the other. It was just something to relieve the monotony more than anything else. After they'd sit there day after day and listen to the lawyers examine the jury, you could shut your eyes and do it yourself because you'd heard it so much.

Henry Wade I'd known ever since he became the district attorney. Evidently, he was about the sharpest lawyer who was ever district attorney in Dallas. He became district attorney shortly after I went to work for the sheriff's department. I knew some of them who were the D.A. before, but of course, I associated with Wade a whole lot longer and was closer to him than any of the rest. My associations with him came when I worked with the grand jury which was just across the hall from him. He didn't control the grand jury; it was controlled by the district judges, but the D.A. furnished a lawyer to be with the grand jury to help them, though they didn't have to have one.

Wade didn't try too many cases himself. He had several top notch lawyers with the first assistant usually being assigned the hot cases. Over a period of time there were several first assistants there because after a few years they would go with some big oil firm and get out of it. Either that or they would get appointed to one of the courts. But Wade wasn't afraid to try cases himself. If there was something really hot, then he'd get in there and try it, and he never lost one.

Jim Bowie was a gentleman, a smart lawyer, and a dedicated prosecutor. He believed that if you did wrong, you should get whatever it called for. What or who you were didn't make any difference to him. If it was a criminal, it was a criminal. If it was so and so's brother, son, or lover, it didn't make any difference. If he had the evidence on a criminal in front of him, he was going to prosecute him, and that's what he did.

James J. Allen was another top notch lawyer who was one of the best prosecutors that I'd ever heard. He later became a judge in one of the courts and eventually went to the Court of Appeals. I thought a lot of him.

Bill Alexander was, you might say, just a bit mean when it came to prosecuting because if he was convinced that the person did what he was charged with, then he was going to do everything in his power to see that he got the proper punishment. Whatever the law said, that's what he asked for. Now he didn't use any method that was unethical; I don't think Henry would have allowed that. But his personality, too, was such that made him controversial to a point. He was just a plain old Texas boy who thought, "Now I'm not going to get run over, and I'm not going to let anybody run over me. And I'm going to prosecute that dude with everything that I can to see that he gets the punishment that is due to him." He had a country style about him, and being country myself, I liked him a lot.

All the criminals knew Alexander. Whenever I'd bring one in and mention Alexander, they'd say, "Oh, yeah, I know him. He's tough!" Saying what was on his mind was a trait of Bill's. Whether you liked it or not, it didn't bother him, and he would fight you at the drop of a hat if you wanted to fight.

When I was on patrol, he would ride with me on occasion and would carry a gun. It really wasn't that unusual for them to ride with us, though Bill rode more with the Dallas police than he did the sheriff's department. Personally, I loved to have one of them ride with me. If I ran into something I wasn't sure of, I had the law with me; he was sitting right there and I could ask him.

Ruby's first lawyer was Tom Howard. I didn't know a whole lot about him other than he eventually fell off a horse and was killed. But Howard was replaced by the Ruby family with Melvin Belli, whom I took an instant dislike to because of his arrogant attitude toward the people of Dallas. He damned the whole city for what had happened to the President. According to him, the whole city was to blame. He was so egotistical and thought that he was so superior, and his attitude clashed with mine. I just about didn't like him. He was interested in anything of a sensational nature. The more sensational the better he liked it.

He was a flamboyant guy and a fancy dresser. His briefcase was covered with velvet which drew a lot of comments from the other lawyers. The first day in court there were a lot of motions to be taken up. When everybody arrived, Judge Brown called the court to order, which was an ordinary procedure. I turned to the lady bailiff sitting at her desk and said, "I'll bet you five dollars that Bill calls him 'Mr. Belly' in less than five minutes." She just grinned as the judge called on the prosecution first.

Bill got up and said, "Your Honor, 'Mr. Belly' over here," and I became strangled and had to leave the courtroom to keep from laughing. I knew that Bill was going to say that.

The judge apologized to Belli and Belli said, "Don't worry about it. I've been called a lot worse than that." It didn't seem to bother him as he took it in stride good naturedly.

Belli wanted a change of venue, but the court denied it. As a result, he was working for a mistrial because he didn't think he could win in Dallas. But in some other city he might, with a different jury, win the case.

This was a trial which included complicated testimony regarding psychology and psychiatry. But I don't think that that jury was fooled a bit about all that, and they took it for what it was worth. In court cases, when you get a well known psychiatrist up there testifying, it depends on who he's testifying for. I've seen the same psychiatrist testify for the state in one trial, then maybe three or four months later something else would come up, and the defense would hire him to testify for them. So the jury in the Ruby trial wasn't the least bit fooled by the high sounding phrases from some of the psychiatrists.

Those people on that jury were quite sensible and they would be hard to fool on most anything. I think most of them felt like I did. The guy knew right from wrong; therefore, he was guilty. All this about how he was temporarily insane to the point where he didn't know what he was doing, I don't believe that.

Few of the jurors were college graduates, though one was a teacher, but there were no dummies on it either. They were all pretty sharp about common ordinary living and operating according to the law of the land. I don't think there was much chance of Ruby getting a mistrial or an innocent verdict. Later he was granted a retrial, though I could never understand why.

I don't believe that any jury would have found him innocent because so many people were there when he walked out and shot him, in addition to the pictures which were taken, if they were allowed into evidence. You just couldn't refute that kind of evidence.

During the trial I had been told that Belli was doing everything he could to influence the jury by getting them to see or hear anything that he could use. I was being extra careful and told the sheriff. He said, "Well, I've got plenty of men and will send them with you when you take the jury to eat, but it's all unhandy to get them somewhere to eat." So anytime we took them down the street to a restaurant, there was the lady bailiff and myself plus two to four extra deputies with us.

On one particular occasion, I was tipped off by some reporters that Belli was up to something. We were in a little restaurant not far from the court house which had a small room set back so that if you came in the front door you wouldn't be able to see that room until you were well into the restaurant. That's where we fed the jury. The room was fixed up especially for juries so that if we called and told them we were coming, they would clear it out for us. The lady bailiff and I were with the jury in that room and four deputies were sitting at the first table eating their lunch as you came in the front door. I jumped up as one of them called me and there was Mr. Belli wanting to come in and have lunch. He had all this tribe with him carrying placards along with an old preacher from some kind of church. I can't remember what he said he was, but the placards were worded so that if the jury were to see them then he could ask for a mistrial. So I told him, "Now you're not going to come in here and bring that tribe. The jury's in here eating their lunch."

He said, "I want to come in here and eat my lunch and I'm coming in."

I told him, "Now if you do, I'm going to put you in jail because I know that you're trying to influence the jury. You come in here with that tribe behind you and I'm going to put your fanny in jail if it's the last thing I ever do, and I mean that!"

Burleson was with him and Belli said, "Well, I've got to eat somewhere."

I said, "Cafe right down the street there." So he and Burleson left, but the old preacher had discovered that the jury was there and he wouldn't leave until they saw what he wanted them to see.

One of the deputies came in and told me, "The old preacher's still out there, and he's standing there facing the door so we can see him.

I said, "Okay, I'll go talk to him." So I went out and punched the old man in the chest with my finger and told him, "Now, preacher, I'm going to start counting to ten. When I get to ten and you're still standing there with this stuff, I'm going to put you in jail." As I started counting, he left just like that.

That night after we fed the jury and got them upstairs, I went down to get some baggage for some of them and was approached by a man. "Now I'm a reporter," he said, "I'm not from this state, I'm from another, and was sent down here. What happened over there at noon was planned because I heard them planning it. I'm not going to tell you my name."

I said, "I'm not going to ask you." But I already knew as soon as I saw them that it was planned because I had already been told what he was doing.

He said, "I heard when they planned it, and they found out where you were."

In any case, Belli didn't win any friends in Dallas, and I don't think the verdict would have been any different whoever was representing him. The evidence was too damning. Ruby didn't have a chance because he just walked out and shot the man. Who the man was that he shot was beside the point. Since he was well known by the police officers because they'd seen him around all the time, they didn't pay any attention to him. They trusted him.

But when he just walked out and shot him, you just can't hardly get by that kind of evidence.

Bo Mabra left the Criminal District Court in 1965 and went to work with the grand jury until his retirement in 1975. Mabra now lives in Hutchins, Texas.

WILLIAM F. "BILL" ALEXANDER
Assistant District Attorney
Dallas County, Texas

"We were very naive. We didn't realize what the writers then and now would do and that our motive of just trying to do a good job in handling a bad situation would be criticized... I don't have any apologies to make to anybody!... I begin to burn when I think about it. I did a goddamn good job, gave 150 percent, and accomplished my purpose. I just feel real bad when some ignorant son of a bitch from the Northeast criticizes what we did down here..."

Born and raised in Wichita Falls, Texas, Bill Alexander attended New Mexico Military Institute, the University of Arkansas, and Southern Methodist University. After serving in the infantry in Italy during the Second World War, he joined the district attorney's office in Dallas in 1952, eventually becoming the top trial lawyer in the Trial Division by 1963. Alexander was personally involved in more aspects of the events of that weekend than any other person and was the key figure for the prosecution in the Jack Ruby murder trial in 1964.

I had intended to go deer hunting since deer season was about to open, so I went to lunch early and had gone over to Oak Cliff to a hardware store to pick up some things. I came back across the viaduct and was about a block east of *The Dallas Morning News* heading toward the courthouse complex when I heard sirens, and then more sirens. My first impression was that there had been an industrial accident somewhere; otherwise, there wouldn't have been ambulances and the number of official vehicles moving with sirens. As I got closer to the courthouse, I saw two pairs of detectives that I knew, running, and I knew that something bad had happened. So I drove on down just past Elm Street on Market Street about a block east of the School Book Depository and parked my car and could then see the crowd. Of course, I knew there had been a big crowd because of the Kennedy parade, but then I saw a lawyer running up the sidewalk who said, "The President's been shot!" So I went on up to the district attorney's office and made a call to the sheriff's office.

Henry Wade had told the employees that since he was going to be gone because the President was in town, everything was shut down and for everyone to just go ahead and take off. We had an old fashioned plug in switchboard, and I asked the switchboard operator to stay because I knew that we'd be getting a lot of calls and there'd be a lot of activity, so she did. I went down to the sheriff's office, which was in the same building, to see what was happening, but nobody seemed to know anything. But I did find out that the city police were over at the School Book Depository, so I walked over to that location at Elm and Houston.

There I found a deputy chief, Herbert Sawyer, who had set up a command post using a motorcycle radio and was coordinating things there. There was no traffic moving at all; it was just absolutely gridlocked down in that area. I saw a couple of Homicide detectives and a Crime Scene Search man come out of the School Book Depository; one of them held Oswald's rifle above his head.

In the meantime, there were many, many things happening. Different officials were calling in to find out what was going on, and a roll call was being held to find out if all the employees of the School Book Depository were present and accounted for.

Amidst all this, a call came in that an officer had been shot over in Oak Cliff. There were no squads in Oak Cliff to cover that, so Sawyer looked around to see who was available. Sergeant Bud Owens had his car parked right there at the intersection and said, "I'll take the call!"

"Well, you better take somebody with you," Sawyer replied.

When Owens said that there wasn't anybody, another officer, Jerry Hill, remarked, ""I can go if you can spare me!"

Sawyer consented, and I said, "Well, I'll go, so let's go!"

I figured at that time they needed a warm body, and I was carrying a pistol and was just as competent as those police officers. With the nature of the business, as long as I'm breathing and off my property I always carried a gun because I didn't want to have to go home and get one. If something happened, it's a lot easier to explain to twelve jurors than it is to six pallbearers. Early on, when I went out with the police, I was told that they weren't my baby-sitters. They didn't want to be worried about me and that I needed to be able to take care of myself. If you knew that someone might kick your ass, you're going to carry a gun. They had always treated me just as I was one of them because, at that time, the assistant district attorneys felt that we should go to crime scenes. It helped cement relations between the departments to have somebody along that they could work with and letting them know that we were interested and would take care of their cases. I always thought it helped you prepare your cases better, and also they liked being told what the rules of evidence were and how to handle evidence. Frequently, they would ask us questions about what to do or if they needed a search warrant, things like that. They felt more comfortable with a knowledgeable assistant district attorney along, and besides, they liked me and I liked them. I worked with Captain Fritz's people very closely handling murder, robbery, and rape cases and had worked with the same officers on case after case. Besides, hunting men in Dallas was about as much fun as hunting deer!

So, anyway, we got into Bud Owens' car. We didn't try to go across the Houston Street Viaduct because the traffic was so jammed up, so we went through the Triple Underpass down to Beckley Street and worked our way over. We hadn't gone far till a description of the person that shot the officer started coming over the radio, then we learned that there was a School Book Depository employee missing. The description of the shooter of the officer was repeated several times and we began to think, or contemplate, that the man who shot the officer might be the same one who was missing from the School Book Depository and might very well be the person who had shot the President.

We arrived at Tenth and Patton and found the officer's squad car, J.D. Tippit's, just as the ambulance was pulling away with Tippit's body. Apparently we were the first police to get to Tippit's squad car. I spoke to a few witnesses, got a fragmentary summary of what had happened but didn't write anything down. There wasn't time for that since there was a killer on the loose, and we could always come back later and talk to witnesses. What a couple of witnesses said at the scene was that the officer had pulled up to the side of the street and that a man walking on the sidewalk walked up to the car. When the officer got out of the car, the man just started shooting. So we knew that there was no real confrontation. It wasn't a matter of the officer putting pressure on the man; it was the man trying to get away, which makes a lot of difference. I figured that somebody must have been pretty desperate to shoot a policeman under those circumstances.

In the meantime someone said, "He ran toward Jefferson Street," so we went in between some houses. At that time, there was a Texaco Station and a used car lot that occupied a large part of the Jefferson Street side of that block. As we went past the first row of used cars that were lined up there, there was a gabardine gray jacket, which turned out to be Oswald's, that was folded up and laying on the fender of a car. I don't remember who picked up the jacket, but I was there.

There were a bunch of old houses, mostly two-story old white frame houses that were vacant there on Jefferson Street, so we spread out and started searching them looking for the suspect. We didn't know it was Oswald, but we were looking for the person that fit the description that shot Tippit. We searched two or three of the houses then some squad cars began to arrive. Jim Ewell, a newspaper reporter, was in one of them.

Within a few minutes, someone said, "He's across the street at the public library," so the attention was focused there. I didn't go there, though. Instead, I went with three or four officers a block or two away to search a church with negative results. After searching the church, which would have been a likely place to hide, a call came over the radio that the suspect was in the Texas Theater. So we went over there and were in the alley where around half a dozen officers were watching the back door and providing backup in case something bad were to happen. Shortly after, the word came that Oswald had been apprehended inside the theater and that he was en route to City Hall. I never saw him at that point.

I rode back with a captain, whose name I don't recall, to the Tippit scene where he took possession of the empty hulls that were found there. What brought the captain originally into that part of Oak Cliff was a traffic accident about four miles away on Loop 12. Since he had photo equipment, we went to the scene, snapped some pictures, went back to town, and he dropped me off at the district attorney's office.

I knew that there was a possibility that we might need search warrants; we might need to file a complaint that day, and that I was available. Henry Wade and the first assistant had tickets to sit at the head table at Kennedy's speech at Market Hall and had told me that he was sorry that he couldn't get a ticket for me but would I please run the office while he was gone. The food's usually bad and the speeches are boring, so I could have cared less about going. With Henry gone, there was no question that I was the man.

I was aware that the federals had no jurisdiction in the case. I was also aware that Captain Fritz needed all the help he could get and that whatever he needed from us we wanted to be available and do it immediately.

The phone was busy at the district attorney's office. I hadn't been back at the office too long when Fritz called and said that he needed a search warrant, that he had information that Lee Harvey Oswald, their suspect, had an apartment over in Oak Cliff. He gave me the description and the probable cause on the thing, so I told him that it would take me a few minutes to get the search warrant affidavit and suggested that we take a justice of the peace along with us because, at that time, and even now in Texas, the justice of the peace has considerable power. He can issue a verbal order for a lot of things, or if you write it out on a piece of paper, he can sign it. You can write a motion, an order, on a piece of toilet paper, and if he signs it, it's just as legal as if were on bond stationary. So I packed a little kit to take along and called David Johnston, a justice of the peace. I called back and didn't talk to Fritz but let them know that David Johnston was en route to our building and that if they would have a couple of squads down there to pick us up in front of the sheriff's office at Main and Houston, that we'd all go together. So we went out to the house where Oswald had his room and searched it.

When we arrived, there were five or six old people there, and the old lady that had the house made coffee and we had a cup of coffee with them. She said that they didn't know how he got back to the apartment but that he came running in, went into his room, and a very short time later came out wearing a gray jacket. There was nothing of any importance other than he was in a hurry.

In his small room, we found a couple of cameras, his diary, a bunch of correspondence between him and the Communist Party, as well as a lot of Communist literature. Frankly, it came as a shock to us to realize that this was a true, genuine, card-carrying Communist. We did a deluxe search of that apartment and brought everything in. Everything was very carefully packaged and marked for identification. At least two or three people marked each item so that there'd be no doubt about identification. I think on some of those items everybody marked their initials for identification. When we got through, it was after six o'clock when we left.

At that time, the idea of a Communist conspiracy went through our minds. Of course, relations between us and Russia were not too good and there were all kinds of spy rumors and that sort of thing, so we didn't know what we had. But we knew that whatever we had, we would do our best to handle it locally.

The others dropped me off at the district attorney's office and took the evidence on to Captain Fritz's office at the City Hall. The reason I dropped off there was to pick up what I thought might be necessary in case we had to file cases; specifically, I got the affidavits for some warrants. I was not in touch with Henry at all during this time since I was told that he had left Market Hall earlier and would be at home.

I got to Captain Fritz's office, and I'm guessing now, sometime around seven or a little after. Oswald had a little black book that we had found at his apartment. We looked at it and it was so scary to us because it contained a diagram of Red Square in Moscow; it had a diagram of several government squares; it had a bunch of addresses, and we noticed that there was a name of an FBI agent named Hosty along with a phone number. Hosty was up there at the office, so I got him and wanted to know what the hell his name was doing in this man's little black book. He explained that he had been assigned a folder as part of their anti-Communist, counterintelligence efforts and that he had been out to Mrs. Paine's house where he thought Oswald lived but that Oswald wasn't there and that he supposed that he had left his card, and he supposed that that's how Oswald got his name.

As I understand, Oswald had arrived at the City Hall around two o'clock in the afternoon. Early that evening Captain Fritz asked me to come in and talk with Oswald. I don't know, but if all the people who have claimed to have interviewed Oswald were put in one group, I doubt if the city auditorium would accommodate them. Every son of a bitch wants to claim he interviewed Oswald, but I know this: I know that Captain Fritz and I were alone with Oswald in Captain Fritz's office the first time that I saw him and Fritz tried to question him.

At that time, Fritz tried to get some information from him and Oswald was not responsive. He would answer a question with a question. Fritz asked him if he had a lawyer or wanted a lawyer, and he said yes, that he wanted John Abt. Well, I'd never heard of John Abt, but I found out after I left the office, through a discreet inquiry, that Abt was a Communist lawyer in New York. Captain Fritz said, "We'll pay for the phone call if you want to call him." Oswald didn't pursue that. So the Captain said, "Well, do you want us to get you a local lawyer?" But he didn't want a local lawyer. Fritz tried to talk to him about Tippit.

"Who's Tippit?" As I've said, he responded to almost every question with a question.

I had some phone calls to make to find out this and that. When I returned, a couple of FBI agents were there. At that time, FBI agents wouldn't write notes down in front of a suspect. They'd listen until they thought they'd gotten all they could remember, then they'd go outside to write up whatever they heard, then others would come in and out.

Throughout these two sessions, Oswald was in command of himself and aware of his surroundings. He seemed intelligent, used good English and expressed himself well. In fact, he almost seemed rehearsed for the questions. He wasn't giving any meaningful answers. Personally, I don't think that he would have ever talked. As time wore on, there was always the question of conspiracy and what next?

The third time that I saw Oswald I needed to get him filed on and have a warrant to hold him under and a judge to set some sort of a bond, so I got hold of David Johnston. I filled out the paperwork to file on Oswald for the Tippit murder. By this time, it was getting on towards nine o'clock and I was hungry and so was Fritz, so we decided that we'd just stop what we were doing since we needed a chance to talk.

In the meantime, the goddamn media people were arriving in droves. You could hardly force your way through the halls. If I had had my way about it, I'd have run them all out, locked the doors, and let just a few people in! But the chief of police said, "Oh, no, they're reporters. We've got to treat them decent," so he let them in like a bunch of cattle.

Anyway, Captain Fritz wanted a chance to talk about what evidence we had, so we went over to the Majestic Cafe along with Forrest Sorrels, the local head of the Secret Service, an FBI guy, a couple of Dallas police, and I don't remember who else. We went and got a big table, ordered, and then began to talk about the evidence we had and whether we had enough to file. In working closely with Fritz, I had the benefit of whatever information he had, and the case looked solid to me. Fritz and I had the opinion that we had enough to file seriously for both the Tippit killing and the murder of the President, so I drew up both complaints. I signed the complaint against Oswald for killing Tippit, and then I got a phone call from Wade. Wade told me not to sign the complaint for the killing of the President because he wanted his signature on that. I worked for the man, so that suited me fine.

It must have been sometime after ten o'clock and Henry hadn't come down to City Hall yet. Fritz and I were on our own, so we brought the justice of the peace, David Johnston, and Oswald in to Captain Fritz's office. Johnston then arraigned him there, which is to say that he read the complaint to him, told him that he was being charged with murder and that there would be no bond.

Oswald's demeanor was that of one of the most arrogant people that I have ever run into in a situation like that. He just disclaimed any knowledge of anything. All in all, he was a very unpleasant person. Of course, I've run into unpleasant people all my life, but if you're sitting in a Homicide captain's office being charged with murder, you really ought to be at least semi-courteous.

Late that night a so-called news conference was held in the basement of City Hall. It was an unfortunate news conference because Henry Wade didn't know what the hell he was talking about and neither did the chief. They hadn't had time to get a full rundown on who the witnesses were or what the evidence was, and they even garbled that. I have no idea what the purpose of it was other than I guess they thought that with that many media people around and since you had the "Lord High District Attorney" and the chief of police, along with the man in custody, the press and the public was entitled to some kind of statement. I wasn't happy about the way they were accommodating the press. They were in the way! When they displayed Oswald to the media, I could have killed him myself. But you really shouldn't shoot a man in handcuffs. That takes the sporting element out of it.

I didn't attend that news conference. I was busy getting another search warrant. At that time, there was another employee of the School Book Depository, Joe Molina, who worked with Oswald who was a card-carrying member of the Communist Party. So, being careful, we got a search warrant.

It was about midnight when I got the search warrant and went out to his house with Captain Gannaway and a group of his Vice Squad officers. We had no idea what we would find. Joe was in bed, so we told he and his wife to just stay in bed and keep the kids quiet and that we would try not to tear anything up, that we just wanted to do a search job. He was very cooperative in that he lay there and spoke only when spoken to. Really there wasn't anything for him to say. It was about three o'clock in the morning when we finished the search. Not finding anything that would connect him to the assassination, we thanked him and told him that we hoped we hadn't disturbed him too much. Later he sued Channel 4 but didn't get anything out of it. After all, we had a valid search warrant based on probable cause, and card-carrying Communists were very few and just really didn't have too much standing in Dallas at that time. So I went on home and got to bed at 4:15 that morning.

The next morning, Saturday, I was down at the district attorney's office at eight o'clock and the phone was running over. Wade was there. I was back at the switchboard screening his calls. A lot of kooks were calling in then, but Oswald's brother called to disclaim any responsibility and to offer any help that he could. Meanwhile, Captain Fritz had his people bringing in the witnesses to both killings, so I went up to City Hall and took statements from a number of them.

We learned that when Oswald left the School Book Depository, he walked east on Elm Street and boarded a bus, in fact, right in front of the building where my office is located now. He did a couple of things that attracted attention to himself. Traffic was not moving, so he got a transfer, got off the bus and walked approximately a block and a half, could call it two blocks, to the Lamar Street side of the Greyhound Bus Station. A woman was going to take a cab, but he had gotten in ahead of her and had the cab take him over to his rooming house on Beckley.

When Oswald was arrested, he had the transfer that had been punched by the bus driver, and the bus driver identified him. That transfer on him when he was arrested with the right time and right route corroborated the bus driver's identification of him. The same applied to the cab driver, Whaley. I don't remember who all I talked to, but most of these interviews were taken from the standpoint that they would be complete under the facts as we knew them so that they would not have to be re-interviewed. If you look at all those statements, you'll see that they were in more detail and more specific than the average statement taken in the average case.

On Sunday morning, I pulled up on the Main Street side of City Hall intending to drive down the ramp and park in the basement. I was there to pick up copies of evidence and statements coordinated with Captain Fritz in preparation to send evidence to the grand jury on Monday or Tuesday. Just as I pulled up the ambulance that was carrying Lee Harvey Oswald's body came out the down ramp onto Main Street. I had no idea what was going on. I knew that the transfer would be that morning, but I didn't know what time or what the arrangements were. So I walked down the ramp and found that Jack Ruby had shot Lee Harvey Oswald.

I'd known him for about ten years. The first time that I ever met him he had had a partner named Joseph Locurto, alias Joe Bonds. They had been partners at some time and Bonds had a case against him. We were looking for Bonds, so I went with the captain of the Vice Squad down to Ruby's. We understood that Ruby was operating a joint called the Silver Spur on South Ervay. We went down there about noon; an employee was in there cleaning up and told us where Ruby roomed close by.

It was a pitiful, cold water, second-story, two-room flat. Jack was asleep. We beat on the door, got him up, went in, talked to him, and he agreed to go down to the police station and talk to us. We looked around his apartment, if you could call it an apartment. Pitiful! You could have put everything he owned in a pillowcase and walked off with it. He was down to just one suit, a couple pairs of pants and about two pairs of shoes. He just didn't have any personal belongings. Anyway, he cooperated with us and we took him back.

Let me explain that back in those days you had to reapply for your beer license every year, and that beer license had to be approved by the county judge. When the beer license renewal time came, there were five agencies that were asked to submit reports on how the licensee had conducted his business, which is to say, that if the city had made arrests there, if they were what they called "on site arrests," that is, the police just stumble in and find a drunk or a fight and haul them off, that's a mark against the license. On the other hand, if the licensee calls the police, then that does not count against the licensee, but on the contrary, was a mark for the licensee.

Part of my duty in the early part of my tenure at the district attorney's office was to go over to wherever the county judge had those liquor license hearings. I'd go representing the district attorney's office and make a recommendation as to whether it should be approved or disapproved. Yearly, I'd see Ruby over a period of time, and he had a good record for calling the police if he thought trouble was going to happen or if there was somebody in his place that looked like a police character or was wanted. For example, he would call the Vice Squad or one of the other divisions and say, "Hey, there are a couple of guys in my place that don't look right. Maybe you ought to send somebody by to take a look at them."

Now I've heard stories that he was an FBI snitch; I have no idea whether he was or not. If he was, I didn't know about it. But I do know that he did try to stay in the good graces of the police so that he could keep his beer license. He wasn't all heart! All this business about his being a "cop buff" is just fantasy! He didn't give a damn about the police any more than he did about anybody else. He had a very valuable asset in his beer license and he was going to protect that.

As soon as I found out that Ruby had shot Oswald and was in custody, I wanted a psychiatric examination. So before I went in to talk with Jack, just after the shooting, I called Dr. Holbrook, our premier forensic psychiatrist, and had him there in about forty-five minutes. I then went right up to where Ruby was, I believe, on the fourth floor. They were in the process of putting the white coveralls on him when I got up there and talked to him.

At that time, he was excited. He didn't say anything about how he'd gotten into the basement, but I asked him, "Goddamn, Jack, what'd you do that for?"

"Well, you guys couldn't do it," he responded. "That son of a bitch killed my President."

Keep in mind that any contact I had with him was pretty much official. He tried to ingratiate himself with everybody. I don't think I ever had what would be called a personal conversation with him about him or me, and I had never known of him to have any political interests of any nature. Later he began talking about sparing Jackie the ordeal of coming here for the trial. I talked to him at a later time and to paraphrase it: "He was going to open a Jack Ruby's on Broadway, write a book, make a movie, make a million dollars, and prove that Jews have guts." Now that's what Jack said. He was fairly proud of himself at that time.

I know of no believable evidence, as of this moment, to connect Jack Ruby with Lee Harvey Oswald in any manner, in any way, period! But at that time, I didn't know. We had a president killed; we had a policeman killed; we had the suspect of the man we had filed on for killing the President being shot in the police station. The first thing that flashed through my mind and that of Captain Fritz was, "Hey, this is a double cutout!"

But I guess I just couldn't believe that he would have any ulterior motive in being a part of anything, but then what do I know? In personal affairs, I may jump to an opinion very quickly; when it comes to criminal prosecution or cases, I don't make an opinion fast, but I may have ideas. You've got to look at the facts. You can kid yourself if you decide what something was or why somebody else did something. You kid yourself if you form an opinion before you have all the facts, which is one of the reasons why I was fairly successful in prosecuting trial cases.

Within a short time, Tom Howard, Ruby's first lawyer, got a writ from Judge Joe Brown. I called him and told him to cancel that goddamn writ, that this man was not going to be writted out. Hell, we didn't know what we had.

In the meantime, we were aware of the national media attention the upcoming trial would bring. But we were just naive enough to treat the media people like they were a bunch of ignorant liberal shit and ignored it. Let me qualify that.

All the media people down here were our friends. They didn't come and go every six weeks; they were stable people. They had a job to do, and we respected them. They would not expect us to do anything unethical or illegal for them as far as bootlegging stories; that wasn't necessary. We could tell them things, say, "Hey, look, here's what the deal is on this. Don't break the story yet because we're still in the process of investigation," and they would honor a request like that.

The Northern and Eastern press was a different matter. They were more of a nuisance, just mooching clowns! All those bastards wanted was a free sandwich or a free drink; they'd suck up anything! They just wanted to get a fast headline or a sound bite and then get to a bar or mooch anything they could! You couldn't do anything without their looking over your shoulder asking stupid questions, and whatever you said to them you'd hear it on national radio or see it on TV in the next fifteen minutes. In most cases, they were writing fantasy!

The trial was held in March 1964 in the Old Criminal Courts Building. I took the lead as chief prosecutor since I was the only one that did any preparation on it. I put the prosecution's case together. Henry Wade, of course, being the district attorney, sat in on it. He insisted on having two more lawyers,* although they didn't know anything about the witnesses or what was coming off. They just sat there to make objections and maybe to look up some law if we needed it.

For the defense, there was "marvelous" Melvin Belli, the "King of Torts" from San Francisco, assisted by Joe Tonahill, a

---

* Assistant District Attorneys A.D. "Jim" Bowie and Frank Watts.

big fellow from down in East Texas close to Beaumont, and a young fellow named Phil Burleson that they hired locally.

Judge Joe B. Brown was to preside over the trial. I didn't want him to be the judge. He just didn't have the legal education or the experience to handle a case like this. I liked Joe, you couldn't keep from liking him, and actually he didn't do a bad job of trying the case. Anyway, how can you beat a guy named Joe Brown? But we were very apprehensive about him because he had no background in constitutional law, and he wasn't that smart in evidence.

We had to prove murder with malice to obtain a guilty verdict. Malice is the intentional doing of a wrongful act which cannot be excused in law and demonstrates a heart regardless of social duty and fatally bent on mischief. We did not have to prove premeditation.

From the start, we just planned to put the facts before the jury. But there was also a strategy. In any case, murder, robbery, or rape, you have to decide the order of the witnesses. One way is to begin chronologically with the very first act, utterance, or declaration that has any relevance to the crime. That's what I decided to do. The other way is to begin with the crime itself, the shooting or rape, and then flash back to the beginning and connect it up later. Henry did not consult with me on that at all. So, my idea was to pick up Ruby's activities. Since we knew that the defense would be insanity, I wanted to demonstrate by all witnesses that he was in contact with reality: that he was oriented as to time, place and person, and that he wasn't off in la-la land exhibiting weird, bizarre conduct.

He had arrived at the *Dallas News* very early and talked to the business section about his account and planned his ads for the weekend. My method of demonstrating his mental condition was to begin with the first person that he contacted at the *Dallas News* and let them detail what their conversation with him was to show that his questions were appropriate to the situation and that his answers to questions were responsive and appropriate. So I put on the first morning three *Dallas News* employees and traced his whereabouts and activities from early that morning to past the time that the President was shot. I wanted to show what Ruby's attitude was toward the President. One thing which I thought was rather subtle was to show that this guy who "loved the President so much" didn't even bother to walk two blocks to see him in the parade and that could best be demonstrated by showing where he was and what he was doing at the *Dallas News* at the time.

Wade hadn't consulted with me about this. He didn't have time for me to even tell him what I had planned. All he did was say, "Well, goddamn, when are we going to get to the murder case? I want some blood! Sounds like you're probating a will!"

I went ahead with it anyway. Hell, if he had told me that he wanted to start with the shooting of Oswald then flash back, we could have done that. But I felt that my way was the best, though others might have disagreed.

The point is that we knew that the fight would not be whether he killed Oswald or not, but what his mental condition was at the time. What better way could you show his mental condition than by showing that the day of the President's visit that he was transacting business in a businesslike way and that he exhibited no strange or bizarre conduct, and that's by the people who actually saw and talked to him. Another thing to show that he was not interested in politics was that he did not mooch a ticket to Market Hall for the President's speech. He didn't go out there to take part in anything. So I felt that if I could just show the physical facts, beginning with the morning of the President's arrival here and take him right on through, that the jury could see that this man was mentally competent.

Belli's strategy was to try to prove that Ruby was mentally incompetent, but Ruby didn't want anyone to think that he was mentally incompetent. He resented the idea that he was being presented as "crazy." Belli brought in two doctors, Guttmacher and Gibbs, who talked the language. They didn't impress me! They'd testify for whoever would pay them. From their standpoint, if they testified for the winning side of a murder case, that would enhance their reputation. I didn't realize at the time how many people had so many things to gain by advancing their own publicity.

During the course of the trial, we teased Melvin a lot, or at least I did, and it was deliberate. The man could not take a needling. He was really burned when somebody told him that I said that he was like a goddamn Arab standing by a camel that had not heard of radio with transmissions running past his ears and he didn't know it. Let's face it, Melvin was out of his element! This was not his ballpark. He never understood us at all. Here's this flashy, flamboyant, on the jet set Hollywood circuit prima donna who said that if he wanted to hide anything from Alexander and Wade to put it in a law book and we'd never find it. Well, we showed that smart son of a bitch two or three things, too, because he thought that we had never heard of psychiatric defenses. I had had nineteen hours of psychology in college, so I was conversant with the language of psychiatry.

When I first went to the district attorney's office you had to have a jury trial to commit anybody, even a civil commitment. That was one of the dirty details. The first year that I was down there I went over on a Wednesday and put on the evidence to show that people needed to be committed. A year later, when I advanced to the felony section, if there was an insanity defense, they always put me on the case to handle the psychiatric end of it. I had worked with the better forensic psychiatrists, so I was perfectly at home.

Belli gave his case away when he was trying to show off at the writ hearings. He mentioned the psychomotor epilepsy, and I snapped on that real fast because I didn't know whether the fight would be in the area of a functional mental psychosis or whether it would be over on the neurology side. He didn't think we caught on when he mentioned the psychomotor epilepsy, but it put me to work. I got a fast education in neurology, in EEG, and this so-called psychomotor epilepsy. I'll say this about Melvin Belli, when you got off into medical and psychiatric aspects, he was good. He's made a jillion dollars and has proven himself in tort cases, but he wasn't in his element in a criminal case. He just misjudged the situation completely.

I learned that psychomotor epilepsy was a one doctor disease that was invented and named by the Menninger Clinic in Kansas, and it was based principally on abnormal EEG readings. In the writ hearing, Belli wanted Ruby examined by a neurologist and wanted EEG readings, so we selected Dr. Sheff Olinger, who was a highly competent man. He ran readings on Ruby twice. In both those readings, there was only five seconds of unexplained electrical activity in the brain, and that could have been because an airplane went over and the pilot transmitted, and the machine wasn't properly shielded from that frequency. I asked Olinger who the five best neurologists in the United States were, and he named them for me. I asked, "Do you know any of them?"

He said, "Yes, I know Frank Forster up in Wisconsin." He was in charge of neurology at Johns Hopkins when Eisenhower had his stroke and had treated him at the time.

I said, "That's my man! Call him!" That was about ten o'clock in the morning. By two o'clock in the afternoon, I was on my way to Wisconsin with the EEG tapes. This was after the writ hearing but before the trial.

Forster had me bring EEG's of other people that were made on a comparable ten-pin machine. He looked at three EEG's and gave me an opinion on each before he knew which one was Jack Ruby's. That was to eliminate the possibility that he was predetermined to some opinion. He said that Ruby was fine—only five seconds of unexplained discharges.

I asked Forster who he thought was the best EEG man in the country and he said MacKay. I had never heard of him and asked, "Do you know him?" He said that he did. "Well, where is he? I asked.

"He's in Chicago."

"Call him!"

So the next day I was in Chicago in MacKay's office. He looked it over and gave me an opinion. Then we got another doctor involved who was the head of neurology at Harvard Medical School, as well as another at a children's hospital in Houston. They all determined that Ruby's EEG's were essentially normal.

In layman's terms, psychomotor epilepsy, or a state of fugue, is where you would have a temporary blackout but you would continue to function on learned reflexes. For example, if you're dead drunk, you could still get home.

Oddly enough, one of the engineers at Atlantic Richfield used the EEG technique in oil field exploration, so I spent a morning at Atlantic Richfield's offices with them explaining the theory and operation of EEG machines. So Melvin didn't exactly catch us unaware. He didn't realize that I'd talked to the world's greatest neurologists.

At one time, I thought that the real fight in court would be over functional mental psychosis, so I had Dr. Holbrook call Dr. Silvano Arieti, one of the world's greatest psychiatrists in the area of functional mental psychosis, and we paid his way to come down here.

The first time Arieti came he arrived in a snow storm. I took him down to the jail and sent him up to talk to Ruby. Ruby spent an hour or more telling Arieti why he wasn't going to be examined by a psychiatrist, but throughout the session Ruby couldn't remember Arieti's name, and I wouldn't tell him who he was. The man introduced himself to Ruby, so if Ruby was too stupid to remember his name, so be it. If you guess who it is, I'll tell you.

Over an hour's conversation with Ruby gave Arieti all the examination that he needed. But in an abundance of precaution, I had him come down a second time and Jack was glad to see him. It was someone he had talked to before, so they talked for an hour or an hour and a half. Arieti did not testify in the case because the point of contention in the trial was not Arieti's specialty; it was in the field of neurology. But Belli almost had a stroke when he learned that Arieti had seen Ruby without his knowing it. He thought that was dirty pool and unethical and all that. We didn't hide it.

I wasn't surprised at all by the guilty verdict and the death penalty sentence. It had to be. You had to be in that trial. Belli dared that jury to give him the death penalty. It was all or nothing with his gambling with someone else's life. That jury wasn't sentencing Jack Ruby, they were sentencing Melvin Belli. If there had been a different defense, more of a factual defense and not so much foolishness, I think that Ruby would have gotten a lesser penalty.

One of our local lawyers would have probably gotten Jack found guilty of murder without malice and maybe a suspended sentence. Let's take Tom Howard, who was Ruby's initial lawyer. After the state put on it's case, Howard, or one like him, I could think of fifty that would have done the same thing, would say, "Your honor, we don't need a recess. We're just going to put on a couple of witnesses, and we'll call the defendant first."

So the questioning goes something like this; I'll short form it: "Your name Jack Ruby?"

"Yes."

"Are you the defendant in this case?"

"Yes."

"You've heard the testimony that the state's officers put on?"

"Yes."

"Is that substantially true and correct?"

"Yes, sir, it happened just like that."

"And this gun here, State Exhibit One, is that your gun?"

"Yes, sir."

"Is that the gun you used to shoot Oswald with?"

"Yes, sir."

"What'd you shoot him for?"

"The son of a bitch killed my President."

"Well, Jack, what do you think the jury ought to do to you?"

"Well, sir, I just really don't care but please don't give me the death penalty."

"Thank you, pass the witness." Now, how do you cross examine a guy like that? That was my one concern that the defense would be just that.

As it turned out, Belli hustled the case and the family accepted it. I've heard that there was a contract where he was to get paid out of any book or movie rights, but he didn't get any money out of it. However, he recognized what we did not: that the trial would be the focal point of world attention. He didn't care anything about Ruby; all he was trying to do was to enhance his own reputation and to show off. I just didn't realize that you could make money out of a flamboyant appearance on TV. Then again, if he had been successful in the defense of Ruby, I'm sure that he would have gotten a lot more personal injury cases, plane crashes, and things like that.

Some weeks after the trial, while they were seeking an appeal, Jack wanted a lie detector test because he wanted to prove that he was not part of a conspiracy and that he had no connection with Oswald. But there were too many people at the test and it probably ran too long. They say that the person reacts to only a certain number of questions, and his questions went well beyond that. Jack looked to me to help phrase the questions, and I did help. Joe Tonahill was trying, in my opinion, to skew that lie detector test. By that, I mean that he was attempting to slant or cause it not to show up truly and accurately. It was rather interesting because after the test one of the agents asked him,

"Why did you want Alexander in there when he's the one that asked the death penalty for you and took the lead?"

And Jack said, "Well, when all this foolishness is over, either he or Wade will call Governor Connally and tell Connally to commute my death penalty to something less." And I probably would have. By that time, Ruby was just a pitiful object.

You could see Jack go down day by day during the trial. Belli was doing exactly opposite of what he wanted. Jack knew that he was going to be found guilty of something. He didn't mind being found guilty of killing Oswald because Oswald killed the President, but he didn't want anybody to think that he was retarded, or mentally handicapped, or an insane person. Whatever else you can say about him, Jack had a lot of pride.

I hate to put myself in a position of defending Ruby, but we had several hundred interviews with people about his lifestyle, and out of all the things that have been said about him: he was not a thief; he was not a pimp; he was not a law breaker. Nor was he a criminal who was involved with organized crime.

If you knew the guy, or knew anything about him, you'd know that no organized crime group would let him come near their organization because he was a blabber mouth. He'd tell anything he knew to anybody that he saw.

Anyway, back at that time we had no organized crime in Dallas. Our local criminals were too tough for them. I would be the one to have known because I screened all the cases that came through the district attorney's office. Carlos Marcello had no influence here, and as far as two of our locals, Joe Civello and Joe Campisi, they never did anything here. Campisi owned the Egyptian Lounge, an Italian restaurant, which still has the best spaghetti and meatballs. Joe thought it would add a little flavor, a little romance, to his place if he let on like he was Mafia connected.

But in his own way, Ruby was a publicity seeker. He excused that on the point of trying to get people to go to his club. He always had passes to his club to give away. In fact, he came in to the district attorney's office the day before the assassination to check on his beer license and to pay a ticket on a hot check for one of his strippers, which he did. He saw me there and gave me one of those passes to the Carousel Club. To illustrate this type of behavior, when they had boxing matches at the city auditorium, he would come in after the preliminary, just before the main event, and while the house lights were on, he'd walk down the aisles greeting everybody and inviting them to the club that night. He made sure that everybody saw that he was seated ringside. My having one of those passes meant nothing; I knew him like I knew ten thousand other people.

I wasn't surprised that a retrial was scheduled, although I don't think it would have served any useful purpose. Ruby's lawyers pitched it on change of venue and *res geste*. *Res geste*, short form explanation, is any act or utterance or declaration that's made under the stress of the situation. But once the excitement and stress of the situation is over and the utterance becomes a response to a question, it's not *res geste* and not admissible. In this case, I felt that Jack's *res geste* statements that he made to the police while they were wrestling him down to the floor were admissible. But I also felt that once the elevator door closed, with him going upstairs, it then became an interrogation and that was the end of *res geste*, and the court agreed. As it turned out, it was all of no consequence since Jack died before it went any further.

A funny thing happened that weekend which wasn't funny at the time. Joe Goulden, who had been a reporter for the *Dallas News* and was then on the city desk of the *Philadelphia Inquirer*, remembered the phone number of Captain Fritz's office. So about ten o'clock that Friday night he called and said, "What is going on down there?"

And I said, "This Communist son of a bitch killed the President!"

"Well, I can't run with that," he replied.

I said, "Well, I'm getting ready to write the complaint, How about if I wrote it up 'Did then and there, voluntarily, and with malice aforethought, take the life of John F. Kennedy in furtherance of a Communist conspiracy'? Could you run with that?"

"You got it!" They got several thousand copies on the street before they killed that. Had it not been for Joe Goulden and me, I doubt if that Communist connection would have come out like it did. But I did that deliberately and with malice aforethought because we had already gotten some accusations about right-wing extremists being involved. I wanted to expose Oswald for what he was, a Communist. While the press played down his Communist involvement, I thought someone should emphasize it. I knew that it wouldn't hold up, but it needed to be said.

After that came out, Clark Clifford called Henry from the White House and told him, "Stop that talk about Communist conspiracy. What are you trying to do start World War Three?"

We had a reporter here at the time, Lonnie Hudkins, from Houston who was trying to find out if Oswald was an FBI informant. Lonnie made up some numbers that were supposed to be confidential informant numbers where they paid him and passed those around to the reporters and got them to call up the FBI and ask, "Isn't it true that this number was Lee Harvey Oswald's informant number?" It was pure fairy tale, but since the FBI wasn't telling anybody anything, the purpose was to smoke them out and see if they would respond.

The FBI denied the existence of a very small pocket Minox camera found among Oswald's belongings. We picked up a Minox camera which had some film in it and turned it over to the FBI. Despite their denials, claiming that it was a light meter, I examined it, and I know a camera when I see one. We had the Minox camera and that was all there was to it! In those days, a Minox camera probably cost around $200. What inference can be drawn from it? Who knows, unless he was an intelligence buff and had bought it through a PX. Obviously, it leads to speculation about his being involved in some kind of intelligence.

All I know is that when he went to Russia he renounced his citizenship, they accepted him, sent him to Minsk, and he married the niece of the head of the OGPU Spy School in Minsk. From his diary and what Marina has said, he wandered around the Russian countryside shooting rabbits with a shotgun at that time. And then when he got ready to come back to the USA, he made his movement into Moscow, went to the American Embassy and said, "Hey, guys, I'm ready to go back to the States." And according to his diary and from what we know from other people, he wandered around Moscow without any restraint, which is something that no Russian citizen could do at that time. So the reasonable deduction, the logical inference, would be that the Russians knew what they had and they let him do it. And when he got ready to come back to the States, we footed the bill. Was he declassified when he came back from Russia? We don't know. Oswald was around intelligence since he was in the Marines. He could have been involved in any or all intelligence agencies. This is just my guess, but it could have been that he was a double agent or a pickup agent who burned whoever took him under their wing.

Back in those days the FBI had their own little game going which bore no relationship to anything the locals did. We had pretty good relations with them before the assassination, then after that they just froze. For example, I wanted to know what the addresses belonged to that were in Oswald's personal notebook. One of the addresses was in Washington. I queried the FBI repeatedly, and they just wouldn't give me an answer. So when Waggoner Carr and I were in Washington, we were early risers, up at six o'clock, we called a cab and took a 75-cent cab ride out to this address. It turned out to be an annex of the Russian Embassy. Now why in the hell couldn't the FBI have made one phone call and let us know that that was the Russian Embassy?

Dealing with the FBI was a one-way street. They would suck up anything they could from the locals, but if they gave you anything back, it was surreptitiously. But I can't fault them. They were all nice men who were all 100 percent patriotic Americans.

One of the unanswered questions of that weekend was where Oswald was headed after he left his rooming house and shot Tippit. Based on what other people said and what his history was, he very seldom did anything that did not have a purpose. I don't think that he was just running wild. One guess is that somebody was supposed to pick him up and he missed the connection. Was someone to pick him up on I-35? We checked the airports and their flights, especially Red Bird Airport, but found nothing. The thing that has bugged me more than anything about all his activities was how did he get to Tenth and Patton without anybody seeing him?

I went down to the cab company and personally checked the logs for that period of time, and there's no log on the cab records that anybody picked him up. He did not ride a bus because, number one: the buses weren't running, and number two: each driver on that run was thoroughly interrogated. So the bus didn't take him out there. Captain Fritz had his men going door to door to see if anybody had seen him. At that time, that was a very stable neighborhood and somebody should have seen him on the street. The timing: He would have had to have run to get where he was on foot. A running person at that time of day in Oak Cliff would have excited somebody's attention, especially at that time. My perception, which is based on the totality of what I know, is that he was headed west instead of east. Why, I don't know. Captain Fritz had timed at different speeds the ways that Oswald could have gotten out to Tenth and Patton. There were about three streets that he could have taken. We walked it, we ran it, we drove at different speeds, followed different bus routes, followed non-bus routes. I just have no idea how he got out there with nobody seeing him, and that's an intelligent I don't know.

Captain Fritz and I worked closely on numerous cases for years as well as on this particular case. The Dallas police and Fritz in particular were chastised by many for not recording the interrogations of Oswald. What most people don't realize is that we had *Miranda* in Texas before the *Miranda* decision. Nothing that he said to us would have been admissible. Under Texas law at that time, the only [admissible] statements of a man made under arrest would be in writing after he'd been warned that he did not have to make any statement which could be used in evidence against him. He therefore voluntarily made his statement reduced to writing and signed it in the presence of a witness. In that first interrogation that I attended, Captain Fritz wanted information and Oswald wouldn't give him a statement.

The assassination is something I don't dwell on. I don't read the books or usually talk to people about it. I can't match these assassination buffs who can call names and titles. All I know is what I know. But the assassination has created a whole new industry. There are many people who have made a living by writing, going on talk shows, and appearing in public professing to have inside information which, for a fee, they will disseminate to an audience. Much of it is fantasy, pure fantasy! I can only imagine that their motive is money, unless some of these left-wing liberals are trying to tear down the government by trying to debunk the Warren Commission and attacking the Establishment.

As stated, we were naive. We didn't realize what the writers then and now would do and that our motives of just trying to do a good job in handling a bad situation would be criticized. All the Dallas police officers exerted every effort to be true and faithful to their oath and to do the best job that they could in handling this thing. I don't have any apologies to make to anybody! Very little evidence was developed after that weekend. Practically all of it was gathered and cataloged that weekend. I begin to burn when I think about it. I did a goddamn good job, gave 150 percent, and accomplished my purpose. I just feel real bad when some ignorant son of a bitch from the Northeast criticizes what we did down here!

Let me put it in the proper frame of reference. People down here are probably more patriotic than your Eastern liberal types, and they've demonstrated that. There are a lot of people that strictly do not like Yankees. And as far as anybody giving a particular rat's ass about John Kennedy getting his ass wiped in Dallas, who cares? A goddamn Yankee comes off down here and gets killed, for whatever reason, big deal! On the other hand, if the President of the United States gets killed, that's our problem! We respect whoever is the President of the United States, and many of the people down here, many of the police officers, would have laid down their lives to protect Kennedy no matter what they may have thought about him personally.

Dallas got blamed, but the city of Dallas is what? Shit, most people don't know their next door neighbor. You can't say the city did anything. Certainly everybody was sorry that the President got killed, but hell, they didn't pull the trigger; they didn't invite Oswald down here.

There's one thing that they've got to admit: We had the killer of the President in custody before two o'clock in the afternoon and had him filed on before midnight, which ain't bad!

By 1968 Wade and I came to a parting of the ways despite the fact that I had no political ambitions. He was scared to death that I was going to run against him, which I wasn't. But I had also criticized Chief Justice Earl Warren on national television over the Supreme Court's decision to revoke the death penalty. I had tried five death penalty cases around that time and had gotten the death penalty on all five, and this decision had the effect of reversing each one. The Supreme Court held that just because a prospective juror did not believe in the death penalty that that was not a challenge for cause. All I said was that Earl Warren ought not be impeached; he ought to be hung! My personal opinion is that we can blame Earl Warren for about 90 percent of our crime problem in the United States right now, at least in the court system! Anyway, Wade thought it was funny until the letters started pouring in. Then he said, "Hey, I'm a politician. I'd rather do without my right arm than do without you, but it's time for you to seek fame and fortune somewhere else." So I left the district attorney's office with a lot of job offers, a box full of laudatory mail and have done rather well since.

———————————

Since leaving the district attorney's office, Bill Alexander served as a United States assistant district attorney in Dallas, three years on the Texas State Bar Board, and as President of the Dallas Criminal Bar. Currently in private practice, Alexander's law office was, for several years, located on Elm Street just a few blocks from the Texas School Book Depository.

EPILOGUE

In the aftermath of the tragic events of that weekend, the majority of those featured in this book, for the most part, returned to their everyday lives and sought the anonymity of ordinary people who had been placed in extraordinary circumstances. Few sought the limelight of television talk shows or the authorship of books, nor did they seek monetary gain. In fact, most seldom talked about the events outside their small circles of friends and family. This was especially true of the policemen. The consensus of the policemen in this book is that they were only doing their jobs that weekend and should not merit whatever praise or criticism they have received over the years. Most have difficulty in understanding why the subject of the assassination remains an obsession with writers and the public and feel that it is time to move on. Many believe that the majority of the books on the subject have been created by those with vivid imaginations, and have classified them as fantasy writers.

It is the sincere hope of the author that *No More Silence* has recorded faithfully for these people their actions and responses to those tragic events. Whatever the views of the general public, their stories deserve to be heard.

Regrettably, the recollections of several in this book will be their last. Since the inception of *No More Silence*, the following are no longer with us: James Altgens, Charles Brehm, Clemon Earl Johnson, T.E. Moore, Otis Williams, Joe Murphy, Jack Faulkner, W.R. Westbrook, Roy Westphal, Harry D. Holmes, L.C. Graves, Orville A. Jones, and Bill Courson. Posterity will owe them a debt of gratitude, as well as to the others featured in this book, for their efforts in attempting to clarify many of the aspects of the assassination.

GLOSSARY

American GI Forum: One of the Dallas liberal organizations considered "subversive" by the Dallas Police Department. The group briefly became a focus of attention of the police when it was learned that GI Forum member Joe Molina worked at the Texas School Book Depository, resulting in a search of his residence the night of the assassination.

Barrett, Bob: FBI special agent. Barrett accompanied police officers to the Texas Theater at the time of Oswald's arrest.

Batchelor, Charles: Assistant chief of police, Dallas Police Department, and later chief of police following the resignation of Jesse Curry.

Beers, Jack: Photographer for the *Dallas Morning News*. It was Beers' photograph in the basement of City Hall which clearly showed Ruby stepping in front of Detective Graves a split second before the fatal shot fired at Oswald.

Belin, David: Assistant counsel to the Warren Commission and one of its most vocal defenders. Belin is the author of two books on the assassination: *November 22, 1963: You Are the Jury*, and *Final Disclosure*.

Belli, Melvin: Hired by the Ruby family as chief counsel to Jack Ruby. Belli argued the point that Ruby was in a "state of fugue" when he shot Oswald and was thus temporarily insane. Belli lost the case and Ruby was given the death penalty. Later, Belli wrote of his experiences in Dallas in his book, *Dallas Justice: The Real Story of Jack Ruby and His Trial.*

Blankenship, Twyna: Police character and intimate friend of James Walter Cherry. She was in the motel room when Cherry killed Deputy Sheriff Buddy Walthers.

Bookhout, James: FBI special agent involved in some of the interrogations with Oswald.

Brantley, Ray: Owner of Brantley's Hardware on Singleton Avenue where Jack Ruby apparently purchased his Colt Cobra revolver.

Brennan, Howard: Key eyewitness for the Warren Commission. Brennan claimed to have seen a gunman in the sixth-floor window of the Texas School Book Depository but failed to identify Oswald, claiming initially that he was afraid. Brennan later identified Oswald as the gunman. Brennan's account was recorded in the book, *Eyewitness to History*, as told to his minister.

Brian, Jack: Dallas police officer in the Intelligence Division. Brian was present with Jack Revill when FBI Special Agent Hosty allegedly stated that the FBI knew of Oswald's presence in Dallas and that he was capable of the assassination.

Brown, Joe: Judge in the Jack Ruby trial.

Burleson, Phil: Dallas lawyer who was a member of the Ruby defense team.

Cabell, Earle: Mayor of Dallas who was in the motorcade with President Kennedy. Cabell was on the telephone with Chief Curry at the moment Oswald was killed by Ruby.

Callaway, Ted: Used-car salesman and eyewitness near the Tippit murder scene. Callaway testified that he saw a man running from the scene carrying a pistol in a raised position. Later, in a police line-up, Callaway identified the man as Lee Harvey Oswald.

Campbell, Ochus V.: Vice President of the Texas School Book Depository who was an eyewitness to the assassination.

Campisi, Joe: Owner of the Egyptian Lounge Restaurant in Dallas who reputedly had ties to the Mafia.

Carlin, Karen "Little Lynn": Stripper who worked at Jack Ruby's Carousel Club. On the morning of November 24th, Ruby sent her $25 from the Western Union office near Dallas City Hall.

Carr, Waggoner: Attorney general of Texas who planned a Texas investigation of the assassination before it was stifled by the Warren Commission.

Chabot, Tommy: Garage mechanic who was allowed into the Dallas police basement via the Main Street ramp by Roy Vaughn before the shooting of Oswald.

Chaney, Jim: Dallas Police Department motorcycle officer who rode to the right rear of the Kennedy limousine.

Cherry, James Walter: Habitual Dallas police character who shot and killed Deputy Sheriff Buddy Walthers in a motel room on Samuell Boulevard in Dallas in January 1969.

Civello, Joseph: Reputed Mafia character from Dallas. Civello attended the Appalachian meeting in New York along with other mob figures in 1957.

Cody, Kennedy: Uncle of Joe Cody. Kenneth Cody's phone number was found in Oswald's address book.

Conforto, Jada: Striptease dancer who worked for Jack Ruby.

Connally, John B.: Governor of Texas, seriously wounded during the assassination of President Kennedy. Connally testified before the Warren Commission and later the House Select Committee on Assassinations that he was wounded by a shot other than that which struck the President; thus, he believed the single-bullet theory to be invalid. Despite his belief, Connally contended that the Warren Commission was correct in its findings that there was no conspiracy in the assassination.

Craig, Roger: Dallas deputy sheriff who claimed to have witnessed a person he thought was Oswald getting into a Nash Rambler station wagon ten minutes after the assassination. Shortly thereafter, Craig claimed to have spotted three shell casings neatly aligned in the sixth floor near the "sniper's nest," and later wrote a manuscript, "When They Kill a President," which described his activities in the sheriff's department and his claims of conspiracy. Craig committed suicide in 1975.

Criminal Courts Building: Located at Main and Houston streets, the Criminal Courts Building was the headquarters of the Dallas County Sheriff's office and the site of the Jack Ruby trial. The jail upstairs was where Ruby was incarcerated from November 24, 1963, until December, 1966, when it was discovered that Ruby was suffering from terminal cancer.

Crull, Elgin: City manager of Dallas. Many Dallas police officers blamed Crull for requiring Chief Curry to permit the news media into the basement to witness the transfer, thus creating a chaotic atmosphere conducive for allowing someone such as Jack Ruby to enter unobtrusively.

Curry, Jesse: Dallas chief of police, 1960-1966. Curry later wrote a book, *The Assassination File*.

Dallas City Hall: Building in which the Dallas Police Department was located. It was in the basement that Jack Ruby murdered Oswald on Sunday morning, November 24.

Dallas Morning News: The morning newspaper in Dallas, referred to sometimes as the *Dallas News* or the *News*.

Dallas Times Herald: The afternoon newspaper in Dallas.

Dallas Police Tapes: The record of all Dallas police radio traffic recorded on Gray audio disks. On November 22, 1963, two channels were in operation: Channel 1, being for normal police business, and Channel 2, designated for affairs related to the motorcade. Controversy arose over the tapes when a police microphone allegedly became stuck in the "on" position approximately two minutes prior to the assassination and remained there for five minutes after the assassination. The House Select Committee on Assassinations concluded that four shots were picked up by the open microphone, a contention which has been strongly rebutted by J.C.Bowles and other Dallas police officers.

Daniels, Napoleon: Former Dallas police officer who claimed to have seen Roy Vaughn allow Ruby to enter the Main Street ramp leading into the basement of City Hall. Daniels later failed a DPD polygraph exam.

Davis, Barbara and Virginia: Eyewitnesses at the Tippit shooting scene. Sisters-in-law, the Davises identified Oswald in a police lineup as the man they saw emptying shell casings while cutting through their yard at the southeast corner of Tenth and Patton streets immediately after the shooting of Officer Tippit.

Dealey Plaza: Site of the assassination. Dealey Plaza was built during the New Deal period of the 1930s and named for George B. Dealey, Dallas civic leader and long-time publisher of *The Dallas Morning News*. The plaza, located on the west end of downtown Dallas, is symmetrical with Main Street dividing the plaza, Elm Street on the north and Commerce Street to the south. On the north side of Elm is the Texas School Book Depository with the grassy knoll being located further to the west. All three streets, Commerce, Main, and Elm, converge under the Triple Underpass.

Dean, P.T.: Dallas police patrol officer and friend of Jack Ruby. Dean was one of those who headed the search of the basement at City Hall prior to the Oswald transfer and is suspected by some as being responsible for allowing Ruby into the basement.

DeBrueys, Warren: FBI special agent involved with the investigation of Oswald in New Orleans.

Decker, Bill: Sheriff of Dallas County, 1949-1970. Decker had worked in the sheriff's office for twenty years prior to being elected sheriff. He was one of the deputies who helped track down the infamous Dallas outlaws, Bonnie Parker and Clyde Barrow in 1934.

Dhority, Charlie: Dallas police homicide detective. Dhority was the driver of the car in the ill-fated transfer which was to take Oswald to the county jail.

Dodd, Richard: While standing at the Triple Underpass, Dodd stated that there was smoke coming from behind the fence on the grassy knoll immediately after the assassination.

Doughty, George M.: Captain in charge of the Identification Bureau of the Dallas Police Department.

DPD: Dallas Police Department.

Dulles, Allen: Head of the CIA until fired by Kennedy in 1961 as a result of the failed Bay of Pigs invasion. Dulles served as one of seven members of the Warren Commission.

Euins, Amos: Fifteen-year-old eyewitness who told Dallas police officer D.V. Harkness that he saw an object resembling a pipe being pulled back into the window of the sixth floor of the Texas School Book Depository just after the last shot was fired.

Fair Play for Cuba Committee: Pro-Castro organization with headquarters in New York City. Oswald started a chapter in New Orleans in the summer of 1963 with a mailing address at 544 Camp Street in the same building in which was located the office of Guy Banister, former FBI agent and right-wing operative. The Camp Street address was one of the focal points of Jim Garrison's investigation and the trial of Clay Shaw.

Ferrie, David: The key suspect in the trial of Clay Shaw. Ferrie was initially called into Jim Garrison's office to answer questions about a strange trip to Galveston to an "ice-skating rink" on the day of the assassination. Eventually, Garrison linked Ferrie to

Clay Shaw and Lee Harvey Oswald in a plot to assassinate the President. Despite the murky waters of the New Orleans aspect of the assassination, a recently discovered photograph does show Oswald at a meeting of a local Civil Air Patrol attended by David Ferrie. Several individuals claimed to have seen Oswald, Ruby, and Ferrie in meetings at Ruby's Carousel Club. Ferrie allegedly committed suicide in February 1967.

Frazier, Wesley Buell: Employee at the Texas School Book Depository. Oswald rode to Irving with Frazier on Thursday night, November 21st, and returned to work with him the next morning, allegedly carrying with him a package which he claimed contained curtain rods.

Fritz, J. Will: Long-time captain of the Homicide and Robbery Bureau, Dallas Police Department. Fritz was in charge of the investigation of the assassination and the interrogations of Oswald. Fritz served with the police department from 1921 to 1970.

Gannaway, Pat: Dallas police captain in charge of the Special Service Bureau who led the search of Joe Molina's residence the night of the assassination. Gannaway instructed Lieutenant Revill to write a memo to Chief Curry regarding the controversial meeting between Revill and FBI Agent Hosty in which Revill claimed that Hosty was supposed to have stated that the FBI was aware of Oswald and that Hosty knew that he was capable of an assassination.

Garrison, Jim: New Orleans district attorney who conducted an investigation of the assassination from 1967 to 1969 which resulted in the arrest of Clay Shaw and his ultimate acquittal. Garrison later wrote three books about the assassination: *Heritage of Stone, Star Spangled Contract*, and *On the Trail of the Assassins*. Garrison and his investigation was the subject of Oliver Stone's movie, *JFK*.

Givens, Charles: Employee of the Texas School Book Depository who told the Warren Commission that he had last seen Oswald at 11:55 A.M. on the morning of November 22nd on the sixth floor.

Golz, Earl: Reporter for the *Dallas Morning News* who explored the possibilities of a conspiracy for a number of years after the assassination.

Goulden, Joe: Reporter for the *Philadelphia Inquirer*. Goulden wrote of the possibility of a Communist conspiracy in the assassination of the President.

Guinyard, Sam: Eyewitness near the Tippit shooting scene. Guinyard, who worked at a used car lot at Patton and Jefferson, saw a man running down Patton towards Jefferson while tucking a pistol into his pants. He later identified the man in a police line-up as Lee Harvey Oswald.

Gurley, Bob: Dallas police lieutenant who in 1952 was found guilty of a series of "inside job" robberies.

Hansson, Carl: Dallas police chief, 1945-1960.

"Hidell, A.J.": Alias purportedly used by Oswald in Dallas and New Orleans. "Hidell" was the name Oswald allegedly used to order the pistol which killed Officer Tippit and the Mannlicher-Carcano rifle which killed President Kennedy.

Hill, Clint. Secret Service agent. Hill climbed onto the presidential limousine to shield Mrs. Kennedy and the President after the shooting.

Holland, Sam "Skinny": Foreman for the Union Terminal Railroad. Holland was an eyewitness to the assassination while standing on the Triple Underpass. He claimed to have seen smoke from behind the picket fence at the time of the shooting.

Hoover, J. Edgar: Director of the FBI. Hoover stated within hours that Lee Harvey Oswald acted alone in the assassination and therefore there was no conspiracy.

Hosty, James: FBI special agent. Hosty was Oswald's case agent and was at the center of controversy following statements by Dallas Police Lieutenant Jack Revill that the FBI knew about Oswald and that he was capable of the assassination. Hosty was ordered by SAC Gordon Shanklin to destroy a note left at FBI headquarters by Oswald, information which was not revealed until 1975. Hosty was censured by Hoover for his actions regarding the handling of Oswald and was transferred to Kansas City. He is the author of *Assignment: Oswald.*

House Select Committee on Assassinations: Convened in 1976, the HSCA was the second major effort on the part of the federal government to investigate the assassination of President Kennedy. Also included in its agenda was an investigation into the assassination of Martin Luther King, Jr. Its first chief counsel, Richard A. Sprague, was soon replaced due to political infighting by former Justice Department official and professor at Notre Dame, G. Robert Blakey. Due to Blakey's expertise, Blakey steered the HSCA toward possible Mafia involvement in the Kennedy assassination, largely through scientific evidence. Toward the conclusion of the hearings, the Dallas Police Tapes were scrutinized and the Committee ruled that four shots could be heard on the tapes, thus pointing to a conspiracy. The HSCA concluded its findings by publishing its Report in January 1979.

Houston Street Viaduct. One of the main connector thoroughfares running south from Dealey Plaza into Oak Cliff. It was across this viaduct that Oswald traveled by cab to his boarding house at 1026 N. Beckley.

Howard, Tom: Commonly described as a "jailhouse lawyer," Howard was Jack Ruby's initial lawyer. He was replaced by Melvin Belli at the insistence of the Ruby family.

Hudkins, Lonnie: Reporter for the *Houston Post*. Hudkins was, in part, responsible for the rumor which spread that Oswald was a paid informant for the FBI.

Hughes, Judge Sarah T.: Federal judge from Texas who gave the presidential oath of office to Lyndon Johnson on Air Force

One at Love Field approximately two hours after the assassination.

Jackson, Bob: Photographer for the *Dallas Times Herald*. Jackson was in the presidential motorcade on November 22nd, and two days later in the police basement. The photograph he took at the instant Ruby shot Oswald won for him the Pulitzer Prize.

Jarman, Junior: One of three employees of the Texas School Book Depository who were watching the motorcade from the fifth floor immediately below the "sniper's nest."

Johnston, David: Justice of the peace in Dallas. Johnston accompanied police officers in their search of Oswald's room on North Beckley Avenue and later arraigned Oswald in the murders of Officer Tippit and the President.

Jones Jr., Penn: Critic of the Warren Commission and editor of a small-town newspaper, the *Midlothian Mirror*. From 1976 to 1984 Jones edited the assassination newsletter, *The Continuing Inquiry*, and he wrote *Forgive My Grief*, volumes 1 through 4.

Katzenbach, Nicholas: Deputy attorney general under Robert Kennedy.

Kelley, Clarence: Hoover's successor as director of the FBI.

Kelley, Thomas J: Secret Service inspector from Washington. Kelley was present at the last interrogation of Oswald just before the ill-fated transfer on Sunday, November 24.

Kennedy, Robert F.: Attorney general of the United States.

Klein's Sporting Goods: Store from which Oswald allegedly purchased the Mannlicher-Carcano rifle under the name of "Hidell."

Knox, Earl C.: Dallas police lieutenant in charge of the Northeast Substation who received Don Flusche's written report that Jack Ruby did not enter the police basement via the Main Street ramp.

Lane, Mark: Warren Commission critic and lawyer who was retained by Marguerite Oswald to defend her son before the Commission. Lane is the author of *Rush To Judgment, A Citizen's Dissent,* and *Plausible Denial.*

Lehrer, Jim: Reporter for the *Dallas Times Herald* and later anchor of the Public Broadcasting Service evening program on current events, "NewsHour."

Love Field: Before the completion of DFW International Airport in 1974 Love Field was the primary airport for Dallas. It was the site of Kennedy's landing at 11:38 A.M., November 22, 1963, and the site three hours later of the swearing in of Lyndon B. Johnson as President.

Lovelady, Billy Nolan: Employee at the Texas School Book Depository. From a distance Lovelady bore a resemblance to Oswald and was confused by some from a photograph taken by James Altgens as being Oswald while standing on the steps of the Depository.

Lumpkin, George: Deputy chief of police, Service Division, Dallas Police Department.

MacNeil, Robert: White House news reporter and later co-host of the "MacNeil-Lehrer NewsHour." MacNeill charged up the grassy knoll and onto the Triple Underpass after the assassination. It has also been claimed that as he entered the School Book Depository looking for a telephone he was told where to find one by the departing Oswald.

Marcello, Carlos: Crime boss of New Orleans and the Southeast. Marcello is believed by some critics to have ordered the assassination of President Kennedy .

Market Hall: Located across Industrial Boulevard from the Trade Mart. Market Hall is sometimes referred to as the site of

President Kennedy's noon luncheon rather than the actual site, the Trade Mart.

Markham, Helen: Standing at the corner of Tenth and Patton, Markham witnessed the murder of Officer Tippit.

McCaghren, Paul: Dallas police lieutenant. McCaghren had possession of the Dallas Police Tapes in the years following the assassination.

McDonald, M.N. "Nick": Dallas police officer given primary credit for the arrest of Oswald in the Texas Theater.

Minox camera: Small camera frequently used by spies and intelligence agents. The Dallas police claimed to have discovered a Minox camera among Oswald's effects. The FBI claimed, however, that it was a light meter, a claim still disputed by Dallas police officers and Assistant District Attorney Bill Alexander.

Molina, Joe: Employee at the Texas School Book Depository and member of the American GI Forum. Since the GI Forum was considered a subversive organization by the Dallas police, officers searched Molina's residence on the night of the assassination. When Molina's name was mentioned by Chief Curry to the news media, Molina sued Curry.

Mullenax, Leonard "Slip": Dallas police officer killed while working undercover in 1962.

Norman, Harold: One of three employees at the Texas School Book Depository who were watching the motorcade from the fifth floor immediately below the "sniper's nest." Norman said he heard three shots which were accompanied by the sound of a bolt being cycled on the rifle and three shell casings hitting the floor above him.

Oak Cliff: Section of Dallas located across the Trinity River from downtown. Oswald's boarding house at 1026 N. Beckley and Ruby's apartment on Ewing both were located in Oak Cliff. So, too, was the site of Officer Tippit's slaying at the corner of Tenth and Patton.

"Lee, O.H.": Alias used by Oswald at the boarding house at 1026 N. Beckley Avenue.

Oswald, Lee Harvey: After serving nearly three years in the Marine Corps, Oswald was granted early release in 1959 due to a hardship on behalf of his mother. Oswald then left the United States, emigrated to the Soviet Union, and lived there until mid-1962 when he returned to the Dallas-Fort Worth area with his new Soviet-born wife, Marina Prusakova, and baby daughter, June. Unable to find any work other than menial labor, Oswald moved to New Orleans after allegedly shooting at General Edwin A. Walker in April, 1963. While in New Orleans he established a one-man chapter of the Fair Play for Cuba Committee and became involved in a scuffle with well-known anti-Castro activist Carlos Bringuier. With this notoriety, Oswald participated in two radio programs on WDSU Radio in New Orleans. After leaving New Orleans in September, Oswald is reported to have visited the Soviet embassy and Cuban consulate in Mexico City in an effort to secure a transit visa to the Soviet Union. Failing at both locations, he returned to Dallas, ultimately renting a room in Oak Cliff while Marina stayed with Ruth Paine in Irving. It was through the efforts of Ruth Paine and her neighbor, Linnie Mae Randle, that Oswald secured employment at the Texas School Book Depository five weeks before Kennedy's trip to Dallas. On Thursday, November 21st, Oswald visited Marina in Irving and is alleged to have retrieved his rifle from the Paine garage, took it to work the next morning, and assassinated the President at 12:30 P.M., November 22nd. After being arrested in the Texas Theater after his apparent shooting of Officer J.D. Tippit, Oswald was arraigned for the murders of the President and Officer Tippit. During the approximately twelve hours of interrogation, he denied his guilt in both cases. On Sunday morning, November 24th, Oswald was shot and killed by Jack Ruby in the basement of City Hall while being transferred from the Dallas city jail to the Dallas County jail.

Oswald, Marina Prusakova: Married Lee Harvey Oswald in the Soviet Union in 1961 and emigrated with her husband to the United States the following year. Marina gave damaging testimony to the Warren Commission regarding her husband's effort to kill General Walker and the likelihood that he assassinated the President. The Oswalds had two children, June and Rachel. Today, Marina questions the findings of the Warren Commission and believes that Lee was innocent of involvement in the assassination.

Oswald, Marguerite: Mother of Lee Harvey Oswald and steadfast defender of his innocence until her death in 1981.

Owens, Bud: Sergeant with the Dallas Police Department. Owens was one of the first to respond to the call regarding the shooting of Officer Tippit.

Paine, Michael: Husband of Ruth Paine, though separated at the time of the assassination. Paine, employed by Bell Helicopter in Fort Worth, entered the home of Ruth Paine as it was being searched by police detectives and sheriff's deputies. Paine, along with his estranged wife Ruth, Marina, and her two children, were all escorted to police headquarters late in the afternoon of November 22nd.

Paine, Ruth: Quaker housewife in whose Irving home Marina Oswald stayed. According to Mrs. Paine, she felt sorry for Marina and allowed her to stay in return for instructing her in the Russian language. It was in her garage that Oswald supposedly kept the rifle used to assassinate the President.

Parkland Hospital: Site to which President Kennedy and Governor Connally were brought after being shot in Dealey Plaza. Two days later, on November 24th, Oswald, too, was taken to Parkland and was pronounced dead at 1:08 P.M.

Randle, Linnie Mae: Sister of Wesley Buell Frazier. Randle informed Ruth Paine of a job opening at the Texas School Book Depository which led to Oswald being hired on October 16th. Randle witnessed Oswald placing a package which allegedly contained curtain rods in her brother Wesley's car on the morning of November 22nd in Irving.

Redbird Airport: Located south of downtown Dallas on U.S. Highway 67, Redbird Airport has been alleged by some critics as the place where a pilot was to pick up an assassin and transport him out of Dallas after the assassination.

Revill, Jack: Lieutenant in charge of the DPD Intelligence Division. Revill became embroiled in controversy when he informed Captain Gannaway that he had met FBI agent Hosty in the basement of City Hall at 2:50 P.M. and had been told by Hosty that he had known of Oswald, that he was a Communist, and that he was capable of the assassination. As a result, J. Edgar Hoover pressured Chief Curry to fire Revill, which led to strained relations between the Dallas Police Department and the FBI. Later, Revill was one of the investigators for the Dallas police in the investigation of the shooting of Oswald.

Richburg, Bill: Justice of the peace in Dallas, known by some as the "Law West of the Trinity."

Ruby, Jack: Shot and killed Lee Harvey Oswald in the basement of Dallas City Hall on Sunday, November 24, 1963. Ruby had come to Dallas in the late 1940s from Chicago. With help from his sister Eva he operated the Silver Spur Club on South Ervay Street. At the time of the assassination, Ruby operated the Vegas Club on Oak Lawn Avenue and the Carousel Club on Commerce Street. Ruby claimed to have no recollection of events from the time he entered the basement until after he had shot Oswald. Ruby was found guilty of murder, sentenced to be executed, and was awaiting a retrial scheduled for Wichita Falls, Texas, when it was discovered that he was suffering from terminal cancer. Ruby died at Parkland Hospital on January 3, 1967.

Russo, Perry Raymond: Jim Garrison's star witness at the Clay Shaw trial. Russo claimed to have attended a party at which Shaw, David Ferrie, and Oswald discussed the assassination.

Sawyer, J. Herbert: Inspector of police, Dallas Police Department. Sawyer set up a command post in front of the Texas School Book Depository shortly after the assassination. Later, with Captains Jones and Westbrook, he headed the Dallas police investigation of Oswald's death.

Shanklin, Gordon: FBI special agent in charge in Dallas. Shanklin ordered Agent Hosty to destroy a note which Oswald had left for Hosty at FBI headquarters. When called to testify before the House Select Committee on Assassinations, Shanklin claimed to have no recollection of the affair.

Shaw, Clay: New Orleans businessman accused by Jim Garrison of conspiring to kill the President. Shaw was found innocent in March 1969 after the jury deliberated just one hour.

Sides, Johnny: Until J.D. Tippit was slain, Sides was the last uniformed Dallas police officer to be shot and killed in the line of duty. This occurred in 1951.

Sorrels, Forrest: Dallas head of the Secret Service. Sorrels, along with Secret Service Agent Winston Lawson were ultimately responsible for the planning of the motorcade through Dallas. In the motorcade, Sorrels was in the lead car which was driven by Chief Curry.

Specter, Arlen: Warren Commission counsel and author of the so-called "single-bullet theory."

Stafford, Jean: Author of *A Mother in History*, a book which recounted her experiences with Oswald's mother, Marguerite.

Stevenson, Adlai: U.S. Ambassador to the United Nations. Stevenson was heckled and hit over the head with a placard during his visit to Dallas in October 1963 on United Nations Day. Recognizing the potential for hostility from right-wing groups in Dallas, Stevenson cautioned Kennedy about his upcoming trip to Dallas.

Stevenson, M.W.: Deputy chief of police, Criminal Investigation Division, Dallas Police Department.

Stone, Oliver: Controversial director of the movie *JFK*.

Studebaker, Robert Lee: Working with Carl Day as the two members of the Dallas Police Crime lab, Studebaker took most of the photos for the police department on the sixth floor of the Texas School Book Depository on November 22nd.

Terminal Annex Building: Site of the U.S. Post Office and the office of Postal Inspector Harry Holmes, immediately south of Dealey Plaza. It was also the location of postal boxes rented by Oswald and Ruby.

Texas School Book Depository Building: Located at the northwest corner of Elm and Houston streets, the seven-story building was determined by law enforcement officials to have been the location from which three shots were fired at the President by Lee Harvey Oswald. Existing for several years in ignominy, it is now the site of the Sixth Floor Museum.

Texas Theater: Located in Oak Cliff approximately a mile from Oswald's boarding house on North Beckley, the theater was the site of the arrest of Oswald by Dallas police.

Tilson, Tommy: Dallas police patrolman who claimed to have chased a possible assassin in his car after the assassination.

Tippit, J.D.: Dallas police officer killed at Tenth and Patton in Oak Cliff at approximately 1:15 p.m., 45 minutes after the President's assassination. David Belin, Warren Commission counsel, described Tippit's murder as the Rosetta Stone of the assassination.

Tonahill, Joe: Lawyer from Jasper, Texas, who aided Melvin Belli in the defense of Jack Ruby.

Trade Mart: Located on Stemmons Freeway, it was the site of Kennedy's planned luncheon speech.

Triple Underpass: Located at the west end of Dealey Plaza over Elm, Main and Commerce streets, the Triple Underpass provided an excellent vantage point for the assassination for at least a dozen railroad workers and two Dallas police officers.

Truly, Roy: Texas School Book Depository superintendent and eyewitness to the assassination. Truly accompanied Officer Baker to the second floor lunchroom where Oswald was encountered 90 seconds after the shooting.

Walthers, Buddy: Deputy Sheriff Walthers is a alleged by some to have told the story that he had found a .45 caliber slug in Dealey Plaza, thus evidence of a conspiracy. Walthers was killed in a motel room in Dallas in 1969.

Warren, Earl: Chief Justice of the United States. Under pressure from Lyndon B. Johnson, Warren reluctantly headed the commission to investigate the assassination of the President.

Warren Commission: Created by Executive Order No. 11130 on November 29, 1963, by President Lyndon B. Johnson and headed by Chief Justice Earl Warren, the Warren Commission was assigned the task of determining the facts of the assassination. The Commission heard or obtained depositions from 552 individuals and published its findings in what became known as the Warren Report in September 1964. Based on 26 volumes of testimony and evidence published by the Government Printing Office, the Commission ruled that Lee Harvey Oswald acted alone in the assassination, that Jack Ruby also acted alone in shooting Oswald, and that there was no evidence of a conspiracy.

Wade, Henry: District Attorney of Dallas, 1950-1987. Wade headed the prosecution in the Jack Ruby trial.

Walker, General Edwin A.: Right-wing spokesman who resigned his commission in the Army following efforts to expose his troops to John Birch materials in Europe. Following his involvement in opposing integration at the University of Mississippi in 1962 and after a failed campaign for governor of

Texas in the same year, a shot was fired at him on the night of April 10, 1963. No suspects were arrested. Marina Oswald later revealed that her husband had admitted to her the attempt on Walker's life.

Watson, Jay: News reporter at WFAA-TV. Watson, who was an eyewitness at Dealey Plaza, conducted the first television interviews of key eyewitnesses at the television station shortly after the assassination.

Western Union Building. Located at the opposite end of the block on Main Street from the Dallas City Hall and Police Station, it was at this location that Jack Ruby purchased a $25 money order for Karen Carlin in Fort Worth with the time stamp indicating 11:17 A.M. Four minutes later, at 11:21 A.M., Ruby shot Oswald in the city hall basement.

Williams, Bonnie Ray: One of three workers who viewed the motorcade from the fifth floor of the Texas School Book Depository just below the "sniper's nest."

Wilson, Stephen F.: Employee for Allyn and Bacon Publishers, Wilson witnessed the assassination from his office on the third floor of the Texas School Book Depository.

Zapruder, Abraham: Eyewitness to the assassination. While standing on a pedestal on the western end of the pergola on the grassy knoll, Zapruder used his 8 mm. Bell and Howell home movie camera to record the clearest and most graphic film of the assassination. The film showed the limousine from its turn onto Elm Street until its disappearance under the Triple Underpass. The Zapruder film provides a time frame for the assassination with the camera running at 18.3 frames per second. Zapruder sold the film shortly after the assassination to *Life* magazine for $150,000.

Zoppi, Tony: *Dallas Morning News* entertainment columnist and acquaintance of Jack Ruby.

INDEX